"It's Your Misfortune and None of My Own"

As I was a-walking one morning for pleasure,
I spied a cow-puncher a-riding along;
His hat was throwed back and his spurs were a-jinglin',
As he approached me a-singin' this song:

Whoopee ti yi yo, git along, little dogies,
It's your misfortune and none of my own;
Whoopee ti yi yo, git along, little dogies,
For you know Wyoming will be your new home.

—From "Whoopee Ti Yi Yo, Git Along, Little Dogies," in John A. Lomax
 and Alan Lomax, comps., *Cowboy Songs and Other Frontier Ballads* (New
 York: Macmillan, 1948)

"It's Your Misfortune and None of My Own"

A New History of the American West

by Richard White

UNIVERSITY OF OKLAHOMA PRESS

NORMAN AND LONDON

By Richard White

Land Use, Environment, and Social Change: The Shaping of Island County, Washington (Seattle, 1980)

The Roots of Dependency: Subsistence, Environment, and Social Change among the Choctaws, Pawnees, and Navajos (Lincoln, Nebr., 1983)

"It's Your Misfortune and None of My Own": A History of the American West (Norman, 1991)

The Middle Ground: Indians, Empires, and Republics in the Great Lakes Region, 1650–1815 (New York, 1991)

Published with the assistance of the National Endowment for the Humanities, a federal agency which supports the study of such fields as history, philosophy, literature, and language.

White, Richard, 1947–
    "It's your misfortune and none of my own" : a history of the
American West / by Richard White. —1st ed.
        p.   cm.
    Includes index.
    1. West (U.S.)—History.   I. Title.
F591.W69   1991
978—dc20   91-50309
ISBN: 0–8061–2366–4 (cloth)   CIP
ISBN: 0–8061–2567–5 (paper)

The paper in this book meets the guidelines for permanence and durability of the Committee on Production Guidelines for Book Longevity of the Council on Library Resources, Inc. ∞

4   5   6   7   8   9   10   11

To Vernon Carstensen

Who taught me to think deeply about the West while
always distrusting deep thinkers

Contents

Figures

Maps

Tables

Acknowledgments

WITHOUT John Drayton, my editor at the University of Oklahoma Press, this book would not exist. It was John who suggested that the new literature on the American West, particularly the new minority histories and the literature on gender and the environment, was full enough to deserve treatment as part of a larger synthesis that included the older literature as well. The effort necessary to make such a synthesis turned out to be far greater than I originally expected, and it is due largely to John's patience and encouragement that this book was finished.

Patty Limerick, too, has to bear part of the responsibility for this book. In winning our original arguments about western regionalism, she greatly influenced the ideas that inform this book. Patty forced me to rethink my own position on the West and the relation of the West to the rest of the United States and the world. Her victory, however, produced the kind of situation that Bob and Ray used to refer to as a fine kettle of fish. She had to read this entire manuscript with the kind of meticulous care that her friends have come to appreciate and dread.

Bill Cronon read an early draft of this book with such close attention that he wrote what amounted to a small manuscript in response. Discussions with Bill about the West over the past few years have convinced me that history, despite the solitude its writing demands, is at its most satisfying a collaborative effort. Readers only enter during the pauses in the argument, when positions are summarized and everyone regroups. Bill will recognize where our compromises have been made and where our differences remain.

Beverly Purrington is not a historian, but she, too, has read this manuscript with the care and insight that has made her the best naive reader that I know. Beverly does not have to read academic history regularly to recognize when I don't make any sense. And if our discussions about what was wrong with these chapters once alarmed our children, they no longer raise an eyebrow.

John, Patty, Bill, and Beverly have had to endure this manuscript the longest, but Elliott West, Peter Iverson, and Floyd O'Neil also read virtually all of it. Elliott's criticisms led me to rewrite several chapters, and Peter's suggestions helped in telling me where my own enthusiasms had run away with me. Floyd, too, helped to tame what was becoming a monster, but even better, he gave a real sense of life in the mountain West during the mid-twentieth century. Ed Marston, the editor of the *High Country News,* also deserves thanks for his criticisms of the later chapters of this manuscript. As anyone who reads the *High Country News* knows, the paper itself is a critical source on the late-twentieth-century rural West and a far better place to go to learn about that West than the large western metropolitan dailies.

Two other colleagues in the history department at the University of Utah also helped me immensely in the writing of this book. David Gutierrez, now at the University of California at San Diego, shared with me his own then unpublished work on Mexican immigration, immigration policy, and Mexican American communities, critiqued several early chapter drafts, and forced me to rethink my own too facile formulations. I value my disagreements with David as highly as I do those with Bill and Patty, and they will, I am sure, profitably endure for many years.

Peggy Pascoe also critiqued several of these chapters and gave me what was then her dissertation and is now an excellent book, *Relations of Rescue*, which was critical to the formulation of my own thinking about gender in the West. Like any of the others named above, Peggy will not agree with all my interpretations, but she was an incisive and helpful critic who always forced me to sharpen my own thinking. I was fortunate to have her and David as colleagues, and I was fortunate to be at Utah during a time when Larry Gerlach, against considerable institutional odds, made the history department a vital and interesting place to work.

Clyde Milner read large sections of this manuscript and his suggestions helped me avoid embarrassing mistakes. As editor of the *Western Historical Quarterly*, he helped me, by his own knowledge of current work, to locate my arguments within newer developments in the field. Carol O'Connor read my chapters on the urban West, and both she and Clyde assured me that my arguments were fruitful and helped me with the strong and sometimes daunting literature on western urban development. The presence of Floyd, David, Peggy, and Robert Goldberg, at the University of Utah and Clyde and Carol at Utah State made Utah a particularly stimulating place to think about the West in the late 1980s.

In selecting the photographs for the book, my son Jesse's teenage eyes often proved more perceptive than mine. He saw the images of the nineteenth-century West more freshly than I did, and he did much of the work of combing through photograph collections. I would also like to thank Carlos Schwantes, who, besides writing books that I found extremely useful, generously shared with me his own knowledge of western photographs and where to find them. Many of the maps in this volume came from Warren Beck's and Ynez Haase's *Historical Atlas of the American West*, which has proved invaluable. They have my hearty thanks.

My greatest thanks for this book should go to my colleagues in western history, including those who have considerable ambivalence about considering themselves historians of the American West. Any synthetic work such as this depends on the plundering, and in some cases reinterpreting, of thousands of scholarly books and articles, not all of which, given the nature of the bibliographical listings, are mentioned. Recognition of the uses to which I have put their work may appall many of these scholars, but I hope that it pleases at least a few. I largely confined my research to published work, but since I did borrow considerably from Betsy Jameson's as yet unpublished dissertation on Cripple Creek, I want to give her particular thanks.

Finally, I'd like to thank all of those who have over the last twenty-five years revealed to me aspects of the West I otherwise would have missed. Certainly my reading of the West's past and my own sense of the West's diversity has been decisively shaped by experiences outside university libraries and classrooms. Those who have shared my own travels, encounters, conversations, and confrontations in the West have contributed, without knowing it, to this book.

With so much credit already given out for whatever is credible and useful in this book, I'll happily retain credit for whatever might be misguided and stubbornly contrary, for these are probably the most western parts of all.

RICHARD WHITE

PART ONE

The Origins of the West

THE boundaries of the American West are a series of doors pretending to be walls. On the north and south the West ends in arbitrary lines drawn on the map. On the east and west real physical entities—the Missouri River and the Pacific Ocean—do mark its limits, but these bodies of water have historically more often been avenues of entry than barriers. The West does not clearly stand apart from the lands bordering it. Physical barriers aplenty abound in the West, but western mountains, deserts, and canyons hinder movement within the region itself; they do not shut it off from the outside. If simple geography determined regions, the West, open to the outside and divided within, would not exist.

Geography did not determine the boundaries of the West; rather, history created them. The West that Americans recognize in the twentieth century is their own work. It is not something that has always existed in some neat geographical package awaiting discovery. Pick a geographical criterion to make sense of western boundaries, and vast sections of the region fail to fit and drop away while neighboring regions demand entrance. Historians and geographers often use aridity to distinguish the West from other sections, and over most areas of the West there is insufficient rain to grow crops without irrigation. But what about western Oregon, western Washington, and northern California, let alone the eastern parts of Nebraska, Oklahoma, Kansas, Texas, and the Dakotas: Are they to be excluded? Aridity certainly separates vast sections of the West from the East and South, but it also divides the West itself.

Selecting some geographical criterion to define the West not only does not work, but also distorts the nature of the western environment itself by making static what was dynamic. The land and the plants and animals that live on it are not just "natural"; they are also a result of past actions by human beings. The environment, to be sure, is not infinitely malleable. It limits as well as creates human possibilities, but it simultaneously reflects the actions of human beings upon it.

Long before the first Europeans reached what is now the western United States, Indian peoples shaped this land. In California, Indians burned the foothills and valleys, increasing the spread of grasslands and the number of deer. California's mountain forests had larger and more widely spaced trees, and people traveled more easily within them than they would have if Indians had not burned. Similarly, part of the forests of the Pacific Northwest bore the mark of Indian fires, as did those of the Rocky Mountains. The types of trees that grew in these forests, whether Douglas fir in the Northwest or ponderosa pine in the interior mountain forests, were not simply the results of natural processes; they thrived because of Indian burning practices. Even the vegetation of the deserts of the Southwest and the grasslands of the prairies and plains reflected Indian use. Paiutes diverted streams to water wild plants in the Great Basin. Indian farmers formed a great arc from the Pueblos of the desert Southwest east to the prairies bordering the Great Plains and up through the Missouri Valley where the Mandans, Arikaras, and Hidatsas farmed. If by "wilderness" we mean environments uninfluenced by human actions, then the lands that would become the West had ceased to be wilderness long before the first whites ever arrived.

The geographical boundaries of the American West were not naturally determined; they were politically determined. The American West is that contiguous section of the continent west of the Missouri River acquired by the United States, beginning with the Louisiana Purchase of 1803; continuing through the acquisition of Texas, the Oregon Territory, and the Mexican Cession in the 1840s; and ending with the 1853 Gadsden Purchase of the lands between the Gila River and the present Mexican boundary.

Accepting this political definition gives us a way to approach a question as perplexing as asking, "Where is the West?" This second question is, "When did the West begin?" We could date the West's beginnings from the moment particular sections of it became part of the United States. For all its logical consistency, however, this definition ignores everybody who was living in the places that would become the West until the moment that the territory actually became American. This would be fine if the continent were empty or if the historical processes that shaped the area had not yet begun. But the continent was, after all, not empty, and events clearly related to the eventual emergence of the West as a particular section of the United States had been underway for some time.

When, then, do we date the beginning of Western history? One possibility would be to begin with the migration of the first Indian peoples into the area that would become, thousands of years later, the American West. This would certainly be an odd way to write the history of Indian peoples who lived here for thousands of years. Until the last century and a half, the American West was extraneous to their history. They were not some opening act to Western history. Their history has its own logic and its own physical boundaries that historians are bound to respect. Although Native American history begins with the movement of Indian peoples onto this continent, the history of the American West begins much later. We cannot ignore the role of Indians in creating the West, but we must seek that role in later events that more clearly pertain to the eventual creation of the region.

I will use relatively simple criteria in deciding which events are pertinent to the creation of the West and thus deciding when Western history begins. The American West is a product of conquest and of the mixing of diverse groups of peoples. The West began when Europeans sought to conquer various areas of the continent and when people of Indian, European, Asian, and African ancestry began to meet within the territories west of the Missouri that would later be part of the United States. The West did not suddenly emerge; rather, it was gradually created.

CHAPTER I

The Seeds of the West

THE first Europeans to penetrate the West arrived neither as conquerors nor as explorers. Like so many others whom history has treated as discoverers, they were merely lost. Alvar Núñez Cabeza de Vaca and three companions entered the West on as unlikely a journey as any that followed. These men had left Cuba as part of the disastrous Florida expedition of Pánfilo de Narváez in the hopes of pillaging and enslaving the Indians of the Gulf Coast. Instead they were shipwrecked and themselves temporarily enslaved on the Texas coast. In 1536, eight years after their shipwreck, they began a journey back to Mexico that took them across Texas, up the Rio Grande, and into southern New Mexico. From there they crossed into Arizona and traveled south to the Spanish outpost of Culiacán. As these Spaniards moved from village to village, Indians greeted them as supernatural emissaries and healers. This odd and unlikely little party of would-be *conquistadores* had gradually changed into agents of the Almighty who were as convinced as the Indians that they had the power to cure the sick.

Such experiences can change people, and Cabeza de Vaca and his companions were, at least for the duration of the journey, no longer typical sixteenth-century Spaniards. The little party met more typical Christians when they reached the borders of Mexico proper. Turning south, they found "a fertile and beautiful land, now abandoned and burned and the people thin and weak, scattering or hiding in fright." Christians had been there "razing the towns and carrying off half the men and all the women and boys." In the valley of the Río Sinaloa, Cabeza de Vaca and his companions encountered the prowling slavers. These slavers were, it appears, happy enough to see their wandering countrymen, but they were overjoyed at encountering Cabeza de Vaca's Indian escort, whom they could envision profitably transformed into human chattels. Cabeza de Vaca barely saved his Indian companions from enslavement.

If Cabeza de Vaca, in his guise as a peaceful healer, had unintentionally misled Indians about the nature of Spaniards, he equally, if unwittingly, misled the Spaniards about the condition of the Indians whose country he had skirted. He had heard stories, he told officials, of large and rich Indian towns to the north of his route in what would become Nuevo México.

It was one of Cabeza de Vaca's companions, the black former slave Estevánico, who led the Franciscan friar Marcos de Niza back toward the future New Mexico to find these towns. A black man leading a white man among the Indians: this is a fitting beginning for the diverse, complex West. Estevánico's and Fray Marcos's task was to prepare the way peacefully for a larger expedition under Francisco

Vásquez de Coronado. Estevánico only increased the confusion about the nature of New Mexico. Traveling ahead of Fray Marcos, he proceeded from village to village demanding turquoise and women. Among the Zuñis he overplayed his hand. Suspecting he was a spy for approaching strangers and resenting his demands, they killed him. Fray Marcos, who only glimpsed from afar the pueblo where Estevánico died, returned with a tale of the seven cities of Cíbola, the smallest of which was supposedly larger than Mexico City. The tallest houses there, Fray Marcos reported, were ten stories high, and the most magnificent of them had their doors and facades inlaid with turquoise. What he had actually seen was the small Zuñi pueblo of Háwikuh. It was one of approximately 130 independent villages, each populated by from 400 to 2,000 people. With their supplies of corn, textiles, and pottery and their construction of stone and adobe, these villages might have been wealthy compared to others of northern Mexico. They were hardly, however, duplicates of the Aztec or Inca cities. There was no gold and silver in their towns, and, except for turquoise, no precious stones. The total Pueblo population numbered in the tens of thousands, not in the millions. With his wonderfully inaccurate report, Fray Marcos inaugurated a long and persistent tradition of western travelers whose West was more strongly imagined than accurately perceived.

Coronado came north in 1540. He arrived as a conqueror, but he thought of himself as a beneficent conqueror who sought to avoid the cruelties of the earlier Spanish conquest of Mexico. He told the Indians, who had heard neither of kings nor of the Pope, that the king of Spain claimed the area on the basis of the Pope's donation of most of the hemisphere to Spain. He sought a peaceful conquest, but he made forced levies of supplies and evicted some Indians from their homes. When he met with resistance, he responded with what he considered restraint. Tired of the levies, some men from a Tiguex pueblo killed Spanish horses. In retaliation Coronado in March 1541 attacked and burned the pueblo. Then, as an example to other Indians, the Spanish burned those men who had survived the siege.

Coronado exercised his cruelty to exploit a Cíbola that had never existed, and mercifully for the Pueblos his improbable dreams sent him off during the summer of 1541 to search for an equally imaginary kingdom of Quivira on the Great Plains. He found only Apaches and other nomads on the plains and then, later, the Wichitas, whose villages of grass lodges sat in the midst of small fields of maize, beans, and squash in the Arkansas River valley. Disappointed, Coronado turned back and wintered among the Pueblos before he yielded to his men's entreaties to abandon the whole enterprise.

Over the intervening half-century Spaniards would return only sporadically to the Pueblos along the Rio Grande. The Spanish remained dangerous and violent men. They counted on terror to overcome Indians who resisted their demands for supplies. Sometimes officially sanctioned, sometimes only unauthorized military adventurers, these occasional Spaniards warned the Pueblos of storms brewing on the horizon.

The storm broke in 1598 when Don Juan de Oñate, the son of a wealthy silver miner, set out to fulfill his contract for the colonization of New Mexico. He announced to the Pueblos that they were now vassals of a king who would protect them if they submitted and punish them severely if they resisted. The Franciscan

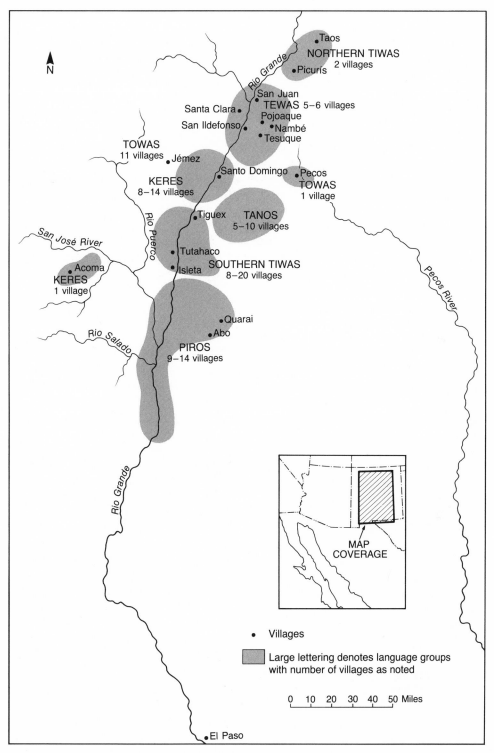

Eastern pueblos about 1600. From Edward Spicer, *Cycles of Conquest* (Tucson: University of Arizona Press, 1981), p. 12.

friars offered them Christianity with its equally stark choice between heaven and hell. In Spanish America the church and the state colonized together. The protection of the king and the salvation of their souls meant less to the Pueblos than the loss of their corn, their blankets, and occasionally their homes. The Spanish, who arrived too late to plant their own fields, took the supplies they needed from the Pueblos. Some supplies they took as tribute; others they paid for. But they bought even when Indians did not wish to sell. This was a harsh land, and stored corn, firewood for a winter, and blankets of turkey feathers were not to be disposed of lightly.

On one of these Spanish forays to requisition supplies from the reluctant inhabitants of Acoma, a melee broke out and thirteen Spaniards died. In retaliation the Spanish in January of 1599 took, sacked, and burned Acoma, the Sky City. Most of its population died in its ruins; the Spanish put the 70 to 80 men and 500 women and children who survived on trial for complicity in the death of those Spanish who had died in the earlier melee. They sentenced all the males over 25 to have one foot cut off, and all the survivors over 12—men and women— to serve as slaves for 20 years. The Spanish took all children under 12 under their direct supervision, which meant that they, too, became servants. The Spanish were not being unusually cruel; this was the common cruelty of Christendom. There would not be another major pueblo revolt for 80 years.

The Spanish parceled out many smaller pueblos to *encomenderos*, or proprietors—men who had distinguished themselves in the conquest. The holder of an

Joseph de Payba Basconzelos memorialized his passing at Inscription Rock (El Morro) near Zuñi Pueblo in 1724. For centuries Indian and white travelers have left inscriptions on El Morro.

The Pueblo of Acoma, the "Sky City."

encomienda had no rights to Pueblo lands; instead he received tribute and the right to Pueblo labor. In return, he promised protection, which he often did not deliver, and spiritual care to his charges. The *encomendero* was supposed to compensate the Pueblos for their labor, but abuses were the norm, not the exception. Pueblo lives and Spanish lives were interlocking, and the first component of what would be, in our terms, the West had begun to coalesce in New Mexico.

Spanish in New Mexico

In the shedding of blood, the buying of food, and, eventually, the begetting and raising of children, the once separate lives of Spaniards and Pueblos had overlapped. The Spaniards arrived in New Mexico as conquerors, as agents of a global Spanish empire, but they survived in New Mexico only partially because of their superior weapons, wealth, and mobility. They survived also because there were always some Indians who wanted them to remain. At the heart of Spanish settlement were the ties that bound the Spaniards and the Pueblos.

In the larger Pueblos, the most obvious of these ties was the mission. Spanish missionaries, both the Franciscans and the Jesuits, did not desire to destroy Indian communities; rather, they wanted to reorient them into church-centered agricultural villages with a native leadership that bowed to missionary instructions. In the missions later established in California, Texas, and Arizona, the missionaries, aided by soldiers from the garrisons located near the missions—the *presidios*—

often forcibly relocated Indians into mission villages. This was unnecessary among the Pueblos, who already lived in tightly knit agricultural villages. At each pueblo the Spanish had only to add the church, a priest, and a few soldiers.

The arrival of a priest and soldiers began the contemplated reorganization of Indian communities along Spanish and Catholic lines. This organization was not simply religious; it was also economic and political, since the Spanish tended to see certain economic and political beliefs as an intrinsic part of Christianity. Ideally, each mission should have a choir; an *alcalde*, or chief judge; and a governor, who would not only cooperate with Spanish officials but also enforce church attendance and Christian observances. The missionary would also appoint a head herdsman and an official to oversee general work and would obtain training for blacksmiths, leather workers, carpenters, and other craftspeople. The men learned to weave with wool as well as cotton. Women also undertook skilled work for the mission. Women built and plastered houses; the surviving mission churches are the product of their labor. Women served as servants for the priests and, less regularly, through both persuasion and force, as their sexual partners.

The Pueblos were ambivalent about the changes the Spanish brought to their towns. The Spaniards were a dangerous people, but they were also a people who offered certain opportunities. The horses and sheep that grazed around the towns and the technical skills practiced by the new craftsmen were all tangible benefits of the new order. So too were new crops: peaches, wheat, oats, plums, and apricots. Similarly, the missionary was a ritual specialist. Given Spanish military success, their spiritual power had to be taken seriously.

Such Spanish power was a potentially valuable addition to an individual pueblo. The Pueblos were not, after all, a single people, but instead independent towns eager for allies against rivals. They had often fought bitterly against each other before the Spanish arrived. And even if local rivalries faded, the Spanish offered the Pueblos protection against all the less settled peoples—Navajos, Apaches, and Utes—who lived in the surrounding lands and whom the Spanish initially lumped together as "Apaches."

Such protection was increasingly necessary because raiding by "Apaches" increased dramatically following the Spanish conquest. The Spanish themselves were largely responsible for this. Spanish levies on Pueblo supplies disrupted the older trade relations of the region. As long as the Spaniards commandeered their surplus goods, the Pueblos had few commodities left to exchange with surrounding Indians. Shut off from their old exchange, the Indians who neighbored the Pueblos simultaneously discovered new and valuable goods brought by the Spanish. Mission livestock and metal tools created new incentives for raiding while making the raiders more formidable. Once mounted and armed with metal weapons, the Apache, Navajo, and Ute raiders became far more dangerous opponents than they had ever been before the Spanish arrived.

Conversions are the best evidence for the strength of the appeal of the Spanish to the Pueblos under these conditions. By 1607, after nearly a decade of Spanish settlement, there had been only 400 converts. Then, despite resistance to the Spanish at Taos and Zuñi, at Picurís and Pecos conversions reached 7,000 the next year, with many more clamoring for baptism. By 1626 total conversions numbered over 20,000. Given later Pueblo resistance to the Catholic church, there is a certain irony to these conversions: without them, the Spanish probably would have abandoned New Mexico. Oñate had failed to find the mineral wealth he sought, and the colony teetered on the edge of ruin. New Mexico survived only because in 1609 the crown declared it a royal colony to be maintained at government expense. The announced Spanish rationale was to defend the baptized Indians and to protect the friars who ministered to them from surrounding Indian enemies.

Despite growing conversions, the missionaries never succeeded in achieving their goals as fully as they did, for example, among the Pimas in neighboring Sonora. Precisely because the Pueblos were already a tightly organized village society, the church and the priest remained more an appendage to an existing social organization than the center of a new one. The Franciscans and their soldier escorts did not transform the villages. Pueblo people practiced Catholic rituals, but they did not abandon their own religious rituals. Instead, the Pueblos made Catholicism into a village religion which supplemented and partially merged with existing rites.

In the pueblo of Santa Ana, for example, the ceremonial calendar came to include the celebration of Christmas and observances at Holy Week. On All Souls' Day inhabitants of the pueblo made gifts of food to their ancestral dead. And annually, the pueblo celebrated the saint's day of their patron saint, Santiago (Saint James). Individual residents of the pueblo learned prayers in Spanish and displayed Christian pictures and images in their houses. But even as members of the pueblo adopted these Catholic elements, they modified them. Saint James became much more central to the religious life of the pueblo than was Christ. His saint's day became a fiesta celebrated by dances of indigenous ceremonial organizations. Saint James joined the pueblo's religious pantheon just as Christian feasts joined pueblo feasts on the annual religious calendar. Dios, the Christian God, also joined the pantheon, but he was a minor deity whom the Indians later referred to as "the Mexican God." Sin, heaven, purgatory and hell, confessions— all these basic tenets of Catholicism remained foreign to the Pueblos.

As the persistence of native beliefs dawned on the priests, they became more determined to prohibit Pueblo ceremonies and to destroy masks and other sacred objects. Pueblos who had been attracted to the Spanish by a desire to tap their spiritual power now found that Catholicism imposed a larger burden than they had anticipated. In addition to observing their own native ritual obligations, converts had to attend mass and other Catholic services. Lapses often brought the lash. Pueblo peoples not only had to perform their usual work in their fields and at the loom, but they also had to work for the missionaries, building churches and cultivating fields.

In addition, the *encomenderos* placed sizable burdens on the Indians. Governors drafted Indian laborers for public projects such as the construction of buildings in Santa Fe. Private *encomenderos* illegally forced Indians into their own households as servants and laborers. Spanish demands consumed the very wealth that Spanish livestock and technology helped increase, and the Spaniards often proved disappointingly ineffective against raiders. Under the Spanish system, the Pueblos worked harder and produced more wealth, but the Pueblos declined in numbers and grew poorer.

Spanish religious and economic oppression gradually eroded the tacit Pueblo consent that enabled Spain to govern New Mexico. When in the face of epidemics, Spanish exploitation, and continued raiding the Pueblos turned publicly to their own religious ceremonies for a solution, the clergy and government united to suppress them. In 1675 they imprisoned 47 religious leaders for idolatry and witchcraft. In doing so, they pushed the Pueblos toward revolt. Even a relaxation of tribute and a lull in Apache raids could not dissipate the hatred accumulated from years of grievances.

In 1680, rejecting the imposition of Catholicism and Spanish rule, the Pueblos rose in revolt. In cooperation with some of the surrounding "Apaches" (either Navajos or actual Apaches), they destroyed the missions and killed 21 of the 33 priests. Of the 2,350 colonists, 375 died in the fighting, and the rest fled the province.

Common Pueblo resentments could not, however, achieve Pueblo unity. Before the revolt some Pueblo leaders had warned the Spanish that Popé, a religious leader of San Juan Pueblo who had fled to Taos, was planning a rebellion. The Spanish, overconfident after generations in New Mexico, heeded such warnings too late, but the very existence of these warnings demonstrated the divisions still extant among the Pueblos. Such divisions became even more pronounced following the expulsion of the Spanish. Popé, who desired to restore the Pueblos to their pre-Spanish state, unsuccessfully attempted to get his followers to renounce not just Christianity but also all the artifacts of the Spanish: their plows, tools, horses, sheep, and weapons. Many Pueblos not only refused to give up these tools and animals but also deserted Popé. This was only one division among many; during their decade of freedom from the Spanish, the Pueblos resumed their old internecine rivalries.

In the absence of the Spaniards it was not so much the Pueblos as the Athapaskan-speaking peoples—the Navajos and Apaches—who prospered. Apache raiders pursued the retreating Spaniards, raiding Spanish towns and ranches around what is now El Paso and in northern Mexico, but most Navajos and Apaches thrived at the expense of the Pueblos. The Navajos, for example, absorbed Pueblo refugees uprooted by the quarrels among the villagers of the Rio Grande even as they continued to raid other Pueblos. The Navajos added new clans to encompass the children of intermarried Pueblo women. They adopted Pueblo horticultural techniques, built up their sheep herds under Pueblo instruction, and began to weave. With their new skills and new herds, the Navajos grew prosperous.

Spanish reconquest began in 1692. The new Spanish governor, Diego de Vargas, intended to pardon and not to punish, or so he said. But when the Tanos at Santa Fe resisted, Vargas acted as his predecessors had before him. Vargas executed 70 of the captives he took; he distributed four hundred more to serve ten years as slaves. Slowly the Spaniards, and those Pueblos who joined them as allies, defeated those who continued to resist.

Initially it seemed that eviction and reconquest had taught the Spanish little. By 1695 they had resumed commandeering Pueblo lands, and the priests were forcibly suppressing native ceremonies. And once more in 1696 all but five of the Pueblo towns rose in revolt. When the Spanish crushed this last revolt, not all of the defeated rebels returned home. Some joined the Navajos and Apaches; others retreated to the Hopis, who, isolated on their western mesas, still refused to accept Spanish domination.

After the revolt of 1696 came stability of a sort. The Pueblos and Spanish compromised. The Rio Grande Pueblos were Catholic: baptized at birth, attending mass on Sundays and feast days, married in the churches. But the old ceremonial life continued from the kivas, the large, often partially underground chambers that were the religious centers of the pueblos. The Pueblos were also subjects of the Spanish king. He, in turn, acknowledged their title to their lands. Each pueblo had a governor responsible to the Spanish governor in Santa Fe, but clan and spiritual leaders continued to govern the internal life of the villages. The crown abolished the *encomienda* and replaced it with the *repartimiento*, a less demanding labor levy.

The Spanish and the Pueblos came to need each other, for surrounding them were other Indians who increasingly preyed upon Spaniard and Pueblo alike and were preyed upon in turn. The Spanish labeled these other Indians as *bárbaros*. Always the hostile *bárbaros* included the Faraone Apaches; initially they also included the Navajos, and for much of the late seventeenth century the Comanches were the most feared of the *bárbaros*. Against these *bárbaros* the Spaniards, the Pueblos, and usually the Utes stood together. It was the most successful Indian alliance the Spanish would forge in their northern provinces, and it meant that the history of the region became more complicated than a simple chronicle of Indian resistance to attempted Spanish conquests.

A Fragment of Empire

Eighteenth-century New Mexico—based on a Spanish-Pueblo alliance— became a fragment of empire. Set far to the north of the major centers of Spanish power and wealth in Mexico, it sat weak and isolated at the end of a tenuous supply line that Apache raiders closed to all but strong parties. It became, from necessity, largely self-sufficient, relying on its agriculture, its herds, and its crafts to survive. For most of the century, the colony remained the stranded flotsam of an imperialism whose force had ebbed to the south.

Because weak and isolated Spanish settlers could not risk alienating the Pueblos, they gradually ceased to commandeer their labor. To replace Pueblo laborers, the government allowed the New Mexicans to consider their wars against the *bárbaros* to be holy wars. Defined as Satan's minions, the Athapaskan peoples who surrounded the Spanish became legitimate targets for the "just war" that New Mexicans proceeded to wage. War created captives, most often women and children. Such captives, along with others sold by the Plains Apaches and other Indians who came in to the Taos and Pecos trade fairs, became slaves.

Many of these slaves were Apaches or Navajos, but some slaves came from greater distances. They were captives taken in eastern Nebraska by Apaches who raided the Pawnees and other peoples. Such slaves were valuable both for their labor in New Mexico and as commodities to be sold farther south in Mexico proper. Slavery was, however, temporary—an indenture rather than a lifetime sentence. At the end of ten years, slaves entered New Mexican society as *genízaros*, or freed slaves. Indians without tribes, *genízaros* were at the very bottom of an elaborate and distinctive caste system that distinguished Spanish society in the West.

There is no understanding the social order of the villages and small towns of eighteenth-century New Mexico, nor for that matter the later colonies of Texas and California, without examining the seemingly obsessive concern with racial ancestry. Every person in New Mexico belonged to one in a series of hierarchical castes based on race. These castes ranged from the freed Indian captives or Indians who had left their tribal communities—the *genízaros*—at the very bottom to *españoles*, or Spaniards, who were at the top. In between were people of African and Spanish descent (mulattos); people of Mexican Indian and Spanish descent (mestizos); people of mixed African, Indian, and European descent (*pardos* or *color quebrados*); and those of New Mexican Indian and Spanish descent (*coyotes*). Indios, or Indians such as the Pueblos who retained their tribal affiliation, were not so much within as on the borders of the system. Unlike Indios, *genízaros* had adopted large elements of Spanish culture and thus entered the Spanish world more fully. The names of these castes varied from place to place, but each province had similar elaborate rankings.

These racial castes supposedly corresponded with class divisions. Ideally the elite or nobility of dons and doñas were all *españoles*, and the peasants were mestizos, *coyotes*, or mulattos. The elite had private grants of land; the peasants either had much smaller grants or, more often, had a share in communal land grants or *mercedes*. If the lowest class, the *genízaros*, obtained land at all, it was along the raiding routes of the Apaches or Comanches. Seemingly in this society your race determined your place.

In fact, however, race and class did not always coincide, and the various castes themselves did not always accurately reflect the actual descent of their members. Indeed, race did not so much determine caste as caste came to determine race. If a man was a don, then he was Spanish no matter what his actual racial derivation. Similarly, if a person accepted Catholicism and Spanish culture and had access to land, then that person gradually acquired at least some Spanish ancestry no matter who the person's parents and grandparents actually were.

How did this situation come about? In all the borderland provinces settled by Spain, Spaniards (that is, people of pure Spanish ancestry) were a tiny minority. The settlers and soldiers who accompanied Vargas back to New Mexico included substantial numbers of black, mulatto, and mestizo families, and even the old, exiled New Mexico families who returned with him often traced their original ancestry to Mexican Indians who had come north with Oñate. Similarly, when Juan Bautista de Anza led the settlers and garrison of San Francisco to California from Sonora, he was leading a largely mestizo and mulatto group. Only one-third of the men and about one-quarter of the women who came to San Francisco and San Jose in California between 1776 and 1778 were *español* or *española*, and many of the "Spanish" settlers were probably of mixed ancestry. In Texas the situation was similar.

Race increasingly became a social fiction. The obsessive concern with racial categories remained, but they so little reflected actual racial derivation that children of the same parents were sometimes classified in different racial castes. In practice, mestizos or mulattos who succeeded in acquiring land became "whitened." Extraordinary service in Vargas's reconquest, for example, might bring honor, land, and status. Since land, honor, and social status were, however, equated with being *español*, people tended to acquire the necessary Spanish ancestry as they rose in status. The converse, however, was not true. One's children apparently did not lose Spanish status if they failed to prosper. Thus, as increasing numbers of people became "Spanish" during the eighteenth century, what was actually a mestizo peasantry contained more "Spaniards" than did the

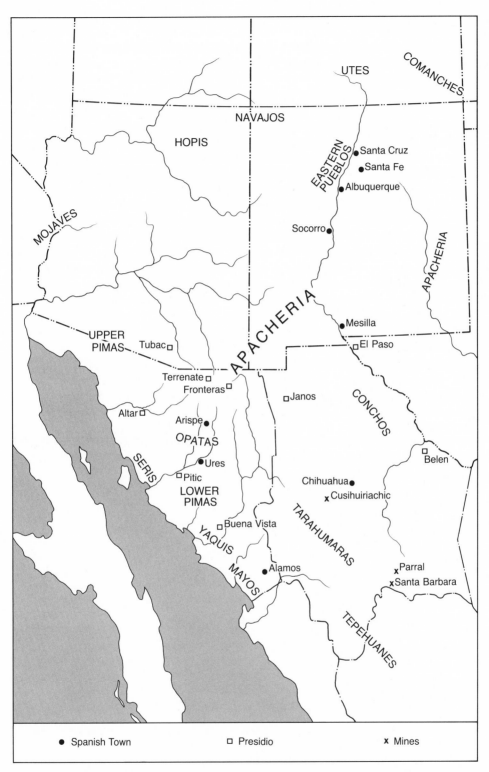

Legend		
● Spanish Town	□ Presidio	✕ Mines

The northwestern Spanish military frontier about 1760. Copyright © 1991 by the University of Oklahoma Press

very small "Spanish" elite. By 1790 most of those designated *españoles* in a town like Albuquerque were probably actually mestizos. Hispanic New Mexicans to this day often insist on their pure Spanish ancestry, but there is little in the historical record to justify it.

If racial classifications did not reflect actual racial descent, they did measure a quite real hierarchical system based on the concept of honor. Like other societies, the Spanish justified their hierarchial rankings by cultural criteria which were not always either apparent or persuasive to outsiders. If asked to explain why one person was better than another and so deserved higher social ranking, a New Mexican would have done so in terms of "honor." The particular meanings attached to honor had originated several hundred years before when the Spanish had reconquered Spain from the Moors. Some people had more money, had to work less, and got more respect because they possessed more honor than others. What was honor? In the Spanish empire, honor derived from an individual's inherent personal worth and referred to both a person's status by birth and a person's acquired virtue. In practice, it consisted not only of the measures of descent and ethnicity embodied in the racial classifications, but also of an individual's religion, profession, and possession of land. Elite families in New Mexico claimed old Christian ancestry and pure Spanish descent; they disdained physical labor and possessed elegant manners. They dressed as ostentatiously as they could manage, flaunted such wealth as they had, and expected respect. They bore the titles *don* and *doña*. Honor explained why certain people had precedence, why some were necessarily superior and others inferior no matter what they accomplished. By definition, each class had limits on the amount of honor that its members could possess. There were ceilings as well as floors. No matter how poor the reputation of an aristocrat, that person always had more honor than the most virtuous peasant. The *genízaros* had no honor at all; they were poor, Indian, and doomed to a life of physical labor.

Honor, too, differed for men and for women. In this society while men worked to gain more honor, women could only hope not to lose whatever honor they had at birth. Since unsuitable marriages or the sexual conquest of a wife or daughter by an outsider were perhaps the most obvious sources of dishonor, families isolated and sheltered their daughters and wives as much as possible to save them from sexual temptation. A prime measure of a man's honor was the extent to which he dominated and protected his wife and daughters and sexually conquered the wives and daughters of other men. Honor, not love, determined marriage. Elite families arranged marriages to consolidate a family's honor and prestige; parents often arranged such marriages when their children were quite young.

Preserving social status and obtaining status for one's own family through marriage became an obsessive concern of the elite. If a father allowed unsuitable people to marry his children and to act disrespectfully toward his relatives, then the family honor was sullied. A family whose honor diminished would lose access to the proper marriages, privileges, offices, land grants, and connections, which in fact gave them such wealth and power as they possessed. They could thus decline in standing. In this situation women became at least theoretically prisoners of honor. Their virtue was the prime guarantee of the standing of their male kinsmen.

As with the system of racial classification, the rigidity of this system of honor relaxed considerably in practice. The class lines indicated by the system of honor, while real, did not during the eighteenth century harden into a system of class domination in New Mexico. The province was too poor; the elite lacked the wealth and resources to dominate. Women, too, partially escaped the restrictions that the code of honor sought to impose. Capitalizing on both Spanish law and local customs, and indeed on the familial emphasis of the code of honor itself, they managed to carve out a surprising amount of autonomy. Under Spanish law, married women in New Mexico retained title to the property that they possessed before their marriage. New Mexican women owned, loaned, pawned, and conveyed property and often managed their own estates.

The actual lives of women thus often did not conform to the model of seclusion and subordination that the ideology dictated. If women of property used their wealth to attain some autonomy, peasant women capitalized on work to escape the strictest demands of honor. Young women meeting young men in the course of a day's labor found sexual dalliances more appealing than the requirements of familial honor. Nor were married women as subordinated to their husbands as the code of honor assumed. Both elite and peasant women brought suit and appeared in court to maintain their rights within a marriage. Similarly, women whose husbands were soldiers, muleteers, or shepherds necessarily lived in a world where cultural ideals had to bend to economic realities. Their husbands were often absent, and they had to perform "masculine" duties. Finally, among the *genízaros* the demands of honor were, of course, hardly practical, and other groups interpreted this both as a sign of their dishonor and as an excuse for the sexual exploitation of *genízaro* women.

Landholding

New Mexicans sincerely saw the status of the territorial elite as a manifestation of their greater degree of honor, but, looked at from outside, theirs was a class system based largely on descent and differential rights to land. Land buttressed the elite's status in this isolated colony, but it also, at least initially, prevented large differentials in wealth from emerging in New Mexican society.

There were, basically, three ways to obtain land in New Mexico. The first, and most important, was the community grant. The crown granted each family private title to a residential grant and to a plot of irrigated land. In addition, each family had the right to graze livestock on and to cut timber from the common lands of the village. Such lands were far greater in extent than the private plots. The second way to obtain land was through a proprietary grant, by which a proprietor secured settlers, distributed land, and provided for irrigation works. He became the *patrón* of the village, and villagers had certain economic and military obligations to him. Under the third type of grant, the *sitio*, the crown rewarded military, economic, and political services and expected the grantee to secure settlers for the lands that the king provided.

Proprietary grants and *sitios* clearly buttressed the status of an elite, but the existence of separate communal grants and the rights to the commons that came with settlement on a proprietary grant or a *sitio* simultaneously ensured a measure of economic equality. As long as communal grants remained available, *patrónes* and holders of *sitios* had to offer roughly equivalent terms to secure settlers for their grants. And while the elite might accumulate far larger herds of livestock than other New Mexicans, they were unable to monopolize grazing lands or accumulate much wealth outside of livestock. Settled hundreds of miles north of Mexico proper and connected to it only by an annual mule train, the elite of this isolated, rural, and noncommercial economy could really acquire no great wealth.

For all its elaborate caste gradations and class divisions, eighteenth-century New Mexico remained a small, relatively homogeneous society. New Mexico had a "Spanish"—or, more accurately, nontribal—population of about 3,800 in 1750. The elite might have been rich in lands and herds, but during much of the eighteenth century the actual economic distance between them and their peasant neighbors remained small.

Ecological Invasion

The irony of New Mexico was that the Spanish who had entered New Mexico as the vanguard of what was then the most successful of the European imperial powers remained in New Mexico only as an isolated fragment of empire. Conquistadores and soldiers became ranchers and peasants; the conquerors went on the defensive. But despite this weakness, the invasion of North America launched by the Spanish continued in another guise. Human agents did not lead the second stage of the invasion of North America; instead, cattle, horses, and sheep, and even more significantly, germs, headed a phalanx of invaders. The Spanish and other Europeans were at once the beneficiaries and the victims of this invasion. They introduced to the continent, both intentionally and accidentally, the exotic plants and animals that spread far ahead of them and permanently altered the natural systems of the American West. Europeans served, too, as carriers of exotic diseases that killed millions among the Indian peoples of the West. Because this ecological invasion was never fully under European control, because diseases and horses (to cite only two examples) passed beyond the early European settlements and appeared in places where Europeans were but vague rumors, the alteration of the American West became a tangled mixture of purpose and accident. This ecological invasion only partially conformed to European design.

In its initial stages this invasion and the changes that came in its wake were most apparent at the extreme ends of the biological spectrum. At one end of the spectrum was the horse, the large animal whose population exploded in the grasslands; at the other end of the spectrum were the epidemic diseases, invisible killers that ravaged Native American populations. Both horses and disease had a far-reaching effect on peoples who might never have seen the Europeans who brought them to the continent.

As far as we know now, no epidemic diseases were present on the North or South American continents when Columbus landed. Apparently, the long, slow passage through the subarctic regions of Asia, across the land bridge, and into North America by the small Asiatic groups from whom the Indians descended had acted as a disease filter. When descendants of the original migrants gradually moved into the rest of the continent, no viral or bacterial diseases capable of taking epidemic form accompanied them.

The long freedom of Indians from epidemics that ravaged Europe, Asia, and Africa, it turned out, had come at a price. Over the centuries Europeans, Asians, and Africans gained some immunity to epidemic diseases; Indians did not. Not only had smallpox, measles, whooping cough, and other diseases culled the populations of the Old World, leaving only the most resistant members, but they also had created antibodies in exposed survivors. When infected by foreign antigens, the body produces antibodies to repel them. Mothers can pass such antibodies on to a fetus or to a nursing child, thus granting some resistance. Indians lacked both the genetic resistance that comes from selection and historic resistance that comes from antibodies. Indians thus constituted a virgin population: they lacked immunity to the epidemics prevalent in other areas of the world. When epidemics did arrive, Indian peoples expired in numbers that are hard to imagine today. Any number from 15 to 90 percent of an exposed population might die. And very often several diseases arrived simultaneously, escalating the death rates.

Disease is a biological phenomenon, and once exotic germs reached North America, Native Americans were bound to die in large numbers no matter what Europeans did or did not do, but we must be careful not to dismiss the deaths of so many Indians as a sad but unavoidable biological catastrophe. Death rates varied. They fluctuated according to the disease, or combination of diseases, and previous exposures of the population to the disease. But death rates also varied according to the material conditions of the exposed population. Those people living in relatively densely populated horticultural villages, for example, proved to be better hosts to the disease and communicated it more quickly than did the members of small bands of nomads scattered across the Great Plains or the deserts.

The uneven effect of disease portended great changes for Indian society. People who practiced ways of life that had once promised security now found that security stripped away. Horticultural peoples whose fortified villages and stored crops had given them security now had their advantages partially turned against them. The people of the Pueblos or the horticultural village peoples of the prairies of Kansas, Nebraska, Texas, or the Dakotas were more likely to suffer heavy casualties than the nomads whose life might have seemed, by other measures, far riskier.

But settlement patterns were not the only social factor that influenced the mortality rates from disease. Where war, slavery or forced labor, and famine prevailed, Indian vulnerability to disease seems to have increased. People who are well fed, well sheltered, and have means for keeping the sick nourished and warm will not suffer losses on the same scale as people who are hungry, cold, homeless, and without means to care for the sick.

The most precise early measure we have of the depopulation of western Indian peoples caused by disease, war, and famine comes from among those closest to the Spanish. The Pueblo population of 60,000 fell to 40,000 in 1638. In 1640, 10,000 more died as an epidemic struck a hungry people who had just suffered a devastating series of raids in which "Apaches" had burned an estimated 50,000 bushels of corn. By 1644 disease, raids, and drought had reduced the number of Rio Grande pueblos to 43. For another century and a half the decline proceeded inexorably. There were 12,000 people living in the pueblos in 1750 and a little over 9,000 in 1790. By the end of the eighteenth century only 19 Rio Grande pueblos remained. The same pattern held outside New Mexico. In eastern Texas, epidemics drastically reduced the Tejas and neighboring horticultural peoples.

The flip side of environmental change, however, brought not horror but opportunity. Horses reached New Mexico with the Spaniards and spread from there.

Table 1

Probable Epidemics on the Middle Missouri River and in the Southwest,
Southeast, and Northeast

Middle Missouri	Southwest	Southeast	Northeast
		1513	
	1520–24	1519–24	
		1528	
	1531–33		
		1535–38	1535
		1545–48	
		1549	
		1550	
		1559	
		1564–70	1568*
			1574*
		1585–86	
		1586	1586*
			1592*
		1596	
		1613–17	1613–17
	1635–38		1633–41
			1647
		1649	1649
		1653	
			1654
		1659	
			1662
			1666
			1668–70
	1671	1672	
		1675	
			1679
		1686	
			1690
		1698	
		1716	
		1718–34	
1780	1780		
1837			

Source: Ann F. Ramenofsky, *Vectors of Death: The Archaeology of European Contact* (Albuquerque:
University of New Mexico Press, 1987).
    *Not supported archaeologically.

By the 1690s all the plains tribes of Texas had, either by trading or raiding,
acquired horses, and the animals had reached the Caddoan peoples on the Red
River. From there they spread gradually northward. There were apparently very
few horses north or east of the Missouri River in the 1730s, but once horses
crossed that river they spread rapidly. They had reached the northern limits of

their range by the 1770s. A second route for the diffusion of the horse lay west of the continental divide. Horses there passed from the Navajos to the Utes and then north to reach the Shoshones and Flatheads by the turn of the eighteenth century. From there, horses spread both east to the Blackfeet and west to the tribes of the Columbia Plateau: the Cayuses, Yakimas, Nez Percés, and others.

The meeting of horses, buffalo, and grass made mounted nomadism possible, but it did not make it inevitable. Not all peoples who obtained the horse and hunted buffalo became nomads. The Pawnees, Caddos, Arikaras, Wichitas, and Mandans and numerous other groups from Texas to the Dakotas who hunted the buffalo remained horticulturists. They lived in villages, often made up of large semisubterranean earth lodges, and farmed the river valleys on the margins of the plains. There was a basic gender division of labor in these villages: the women farmed and the men hunted. And there was also a pronounced hierarchal division. There were leader households and commoner households. The power of the leader households was spiritual power derived from religious ceremonies. As representatives of leader households, an elite of priests and chiefs (there was no consistent division between the two) dominated the horticultural villages. They were the keepers of the bundles (hide containers enclosing various ritual paraphernalia), and they alone knew the ceremonies appropriate to the bundles. It was these ceremonies, the horticulturists believed, that made life possible.

The acquisition of the horse changed but did not transform the horticultural villages. The horse allowed tribes like the Pawnees to migrate west onto the plains proper in what became semiannual buffalo hunts. To see a Pawnee encampment with its buffalo-hide tepees, its meat drying in the sun, and its herds of horses, a casual observer might easily confuse it with a camp of nomads, but the Pawnees never became nomads. Their excursions onto the plains remained seasonal; they never gave up their crops, their villages, their hierarchy, or their ceremonies. The few horticulturists such as the Cheyennes and the Crows who did abandon horticulture for nomadism remained anomalies.

Who then did become nomads, and why? The most powerful of the buffalo nomads were people who originated outside of the plains and moved onto it. The Comanches were a Shoshonean people originally located in the area where today southwestern Wyoming, northern Colorado, and eastern Utah meet; the Sioux were from Minnesota; and the Blackfeet were Algonquians from the east who had come to the plains on foot, acquiring the horse before they reached their historic homeland in Montana and Alberta. All these groups were hunters and gatherers for whom the horse offered access to the buffalo herds and, with that access, a more abundant future.

Buffalo hunting had existed before the horse, but horses made hunting buffalo more secure and profitable. The introduction of the horse increased the efficiency of the hunters and their ability to transport stored food. With horses to carry meat, tepees, and hides, the buffalo could now provide most of the nomads' food, clothing, and shelter. Looking at the possibilities that the horse and buffalo offered, those who came in from the west and north saw escape from a harsh land. Those who came from the east saw an alternative to a dwindling fur trade.

The buffalo and the horse provided the essential, but not entirely reliable, supports of nomadic life. One could die as well as live by the buffalo and the horse. Bad weather or failure to locate the herds in their often erratic wanderings

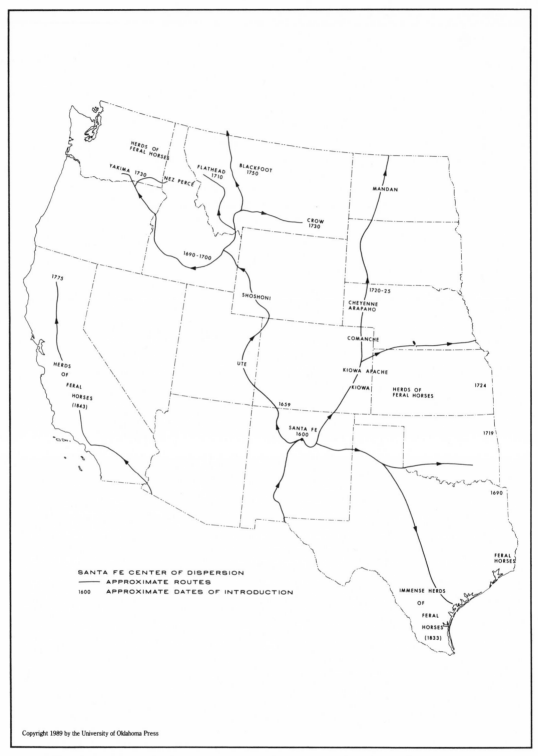

Dispersion routes of the horse in North America. From Warren A. Beck and Ynez D. Haase, *Historical Atlas of the American West* (Norman: University of Oklahoma Press, 1989), map 9.

could ruin a hunt. A harsh winter or raiders could reduce the horse herds upon which a hunt depended. Warfare could prevent hunting, and rival warriors could destroy the meat and robes villagers had gained from the hunt. The horse may have lessened the risks of nomadism, but it did not eliminate them.

The nomads built their society upon the opportunities that the buffalo and horse provided, but there was never a single nomadic culture on the plains. What peoples had done before they mounted horses and hunted buffalo shaped what they did as nomads. The cultures of hunters and gatherers such as the Blackfeet who migrated onto the plains from the east differed from those of former horticulturists such as the Crows or from those of hunters and gatherers who entered the plains from the west, such as the Comanches. Still, the general outlines of a common core of nomadic society, distinct from surrounding horticultural societies, are apparent.

Among the Sioux, as among the horticulturists, there were strictly defined gender divisions of labor, but the tasks of women, who did not farm, differed. Men hunted, fought, and scouted, and they were shamans and doctors; women did virtually everything else. Each sex had its proper sphere, and both spheres were honored, but the activities of men clearly enjoyed higher symbolic status. In a society that increasingly depended on warfare and raiding to secure horses and gain access to the buffalo herds, the Sioux expected men to be aggressive and women to be passive.

Nomadic societies such as the Sioux tended to be less rigid than those of the horticulturists. The Sioux themselves were but a loose collection of family groups which often changed band and, indeed, tribal allegiance. Power in such a situation tended to lodge less in a hereditary elite than in a shifting leadership which gained status by success in war, hunting, or curing. For the Sioux such success, however, was not necessarily as much a mark of individual skill as a sign of access to spiritual power and spiritual help. Access to such power tended to be more democratic among the nomads than among the horticulturists. Any Sioux man could seek a vision that granted power; only a small portion of horticulturists could conduct the ceremonies that brought power. Among the Sioux, women did not directly seek such visions, but they often obtained them anyway. A woman's spiritual power, however, pertained only to the woman's sphere.

The horse allowed buffalo nomadism to spread and prosper, and maintaining the horse herds, in turn, committed the nomads to trading and raiding, usually toward the south. Keeping horses alive over the winter was more likely on southern instead of northern pastures. It is no surprise then that the general drift of the most successful nomads was southwest toward the southern plains. Both raiding and southerly migrations increased the scale of conflict on the plains.

Nomads valued the horse because the animal, by both improving the efficiency of the hunt and increasing the range hunters could travel, seemed to limit the risks of hunting buffalo, but the advantages the animal provided were not always equally distributed within the society. The horse opened new avenues of influence within their societies; men of wealth appeared in what had once been egalitarian societies, and their wealth was based on horses. Those who had the most and the best horses became those who controlled participation in the hunt. Those without horses had to borrow animals from the wealthy or beg for meat. The sharing of food was widespread, and the poor did not starve, but a person who gave food away put the recipients under obligation, and such obligations paved the way to creation of new hierarchies in these societies. Only the wealthy could be generous to many, and generosity, in turn, yielded power. Among the Blackfeet, for example, chiefs had to be wealthy because their followers expected them to be generous. When a chief could no longer be generous, his influence ceased.

Among both the horticulturists and the nomads, the benefits of the horse accrued disproportionately to men. Horses did reduce some burdens women had to bear, but they also increased the difficulty of other work women performed and introduced whole new tasks for women. Among the horticultural peoples, for example, horses often ate crops planted by women. And it was women who often had to find corn nubbins and other crop refuse to feed the horses during the late fall. Much later among the Pawnees, missionaries reported that the major cause of conflict between men and women and the separation of husband and wife was arguments over the work involved in feeding and caring for horses. Similarly, among the nomads women had to labor more because of the horse. In the winter they often had to strip the cottonwoods of bark and young growth to feed the horses.

Indian women on the plains also had to worker harder to treat and tan the increased number of buffalo hides that men obtained by hunting on horseback. Hunting buffalo was dangerous, exciting, and over quickly. A well-mounted hunter could kill four or five buffalo in a single run at a herd. Tanning the hides and drying the meat, on the other hand, was long and arduous labor, and this was women's work. If freed of all other labor, a woman could tan a hide in three days. Later, with the rise in the hide trade in the mid-nineteenth century, women found the time they spent tanning hides increased dramatically. One result was an increase in polygamy as successful hunters took more than one wife in order to increase the number of women to tan their robes. Men also apparently became more eager to raid and secure women captives whose labor would add to the wealth of their household.

Nomads and Villagers

The distinctions between nomads and horticulturists grew more and more significant as horses, diseases, and trade goods radiated northward out of New Mexico and westward from French settlements to the east. Just as in the Southwest, old accommodations between nomadic hunters and sedentary villagers gradually broke down under the pressure of changes introduced by the Europeans.

The shifting native balance of power on the plains came gradually. Between 1700 and 1750 cooperation between villagers and surrounding nomads was as apparent as conflict. In the first years after the acquisition of the horse, nomads did not so much replace the sedentary peoples who lived on the margins of the plains and the river valleys as become dependent on them. From Taos in New Mexico to the Wichita villages on the Arkansas and Red rivers to the Mandan villages on the Missouri, nomads came to horticultural villages to trade as well as to raid. Sometimes the nomads existed in a symbiotic relationship with these villagers, exchanging horses or buffalo hides for agricultural products; sometimes they lived as parasites upon them. Nomadic life without the villagers was, however, unimaginable.

As the century wore on, the original relations between horticultural villagers and nomads changed. The original combination of trading and raiding with the villagers became increasingly a system of raiding. These raids, in combination with losses from disease, forced the abandonment of villages from Mandan towns on the Missouri to Pecos in New Mexico.

The Comanches were the first of these nomads to dominate the plains. Their initial victims were the Pueblos, the Plains Apaches, and the Navajos. Although the Plains Apaches and the Navajos had often been at odds with the Spanish and Pueblos, they shared with them a common reliance on farming and, in the Navajo case, sheep raising. They thus possessed small settlements— rancherias— vulnerable to Ute and Comanche raiders. At the same time that the Plains Apaches faced growing and effective resistance to their slave raids against villagers to the east, they themselves came under attack from Utes and Comanches. The once-feared raiders of the plains increasingly found their access to the buffalo herds curtailed, their ability to raid for slaves weakened, and the road to the markets of Taos, Picurís, and Pecos blocked by the Utes and Comanches. Because these nomads lacked fields and permanent habitations of their own, the Apaches found retaliation to be difficult. By the 1750s the Comanches had largely replaced the eastern Apaches on the southern Great Plains.

The Navajos in New Mexico came under the same kind of pressure, and they sought peace with the Spanish in order to resist more effectively. Although from 1720 until the end of the eighteenth century, the Navajos remained largely at peace with the Spanish in New Mexico, they still could not resist the raiders from the north. Gradually the Navajos shifted westward until by 1750 they had entirely abandoned their older homeland north of Santa Fe and had moved into what is now northwestern New Mexico and northern Arizona.

The expansion of the nomads on the northern plains came later in the century. The villagers there survived a probable first wave of European epidemics in the seventeenth century and actually regained population in the early eighteenth century. With direct European contact, however, came increased exposure to disease. In the 1780s epidemics struck repeatedly along the upper Missouri. In 1795 the trader Jean Baptiste Trudeau reported that the Arikaras had been reduced from "32 populous villages" to two, and from 4,000 warriors to 500. (Europeans usually measured Indian populations only in terms of adult male warriors.) The Mandans and Hidatsas suffered proportionate losses.

The nomads, too, suffered, but not to the same degree. In 1781, Piegans of the Blackfeet confederation attacked a Shoshone village on the Red Deer River. When they entered the village and ripped open the lodges, they found their enemies already dead and dying, their bodies a mass of sores. Along with the horses and camp equipment, the Piegans carried away the smallpox, and they, too, soon sickened and died. The relatively compact villages of the horticulturists, however, suffered greater losses than the scattered camps of the nomads. As the horticulturists declined, the Sioux, the northern equivalents of the Comanches, advanced past them and moved out onto the Great Plains.

The late eighteenth century on the northern plains repeated the same story of horticultural decline enacted on the southern plains earlier in the century. The once formidable horticulturists of the upper Missouri suffered devastating defeats at the hands of the Sioux, and during the 1790s retreated upriver. Below them on the lower Missouri yet another powerful horticultural group, the Omahas, lost more than half their warriors and their famous and powerful leader Blackbird in an epidemic at about the turn of the century.

By the beginning of the nineteenth century, the Sioux had emerged as the most powerful people on the Missouri River. They had embarked on a career of expansion that would carry them west to the Rocky Mountains and south across the Platte. In the course of this expansion they forged an alliance with the Arapahos and Cheyennes, and these three tribes by the mid-nineteenth century had become the leading military power on the northern and central plains.

The Spanish had unleashed changes of a depth and magnitude that they neither fully comprehended nor controlled. The horse can serve as both an example and a symbol of these changes. An ecological invader, introduced by the Spanish, the horse became the most valued possession and the identifying mark of the plains nomads who raided Spanish settlements. In the centuries following the conquest of New Mexico, people far from its boundaries had felt the effects of the European presence. Disease drastically reduced Indian populations; trade goods and horses helped transform the lives of those who survived. Within a century of the Spanish reconquest of New Mexico, there was no untouched "West" existing beyond the borders of New Mexico, for the changes rippling out from that fragile Spanish colony, and from other European colonies to the east, had already transformed the region before the first whites ever arrived. The Spanish who ventured north of the Sangre de Cristo Mountains and other Europeans who moved west across the Missouri found a world already in the midst of tumult and change.

Readings

Anderson, H. Allen. "The Encomienda in New Mexico, 1598–1680. *New Mexico Historical Review* 60 (October 1985): 353–79.

Gutiérrez, Ramón A. "Honor Ideology, Marriage Negotiation, and Class Gender Domination in New Mexico, 1690–1846." *Latin American Perspectives* 44 (Winter 1985):81–104.

Hall, Thomas D. *Social Change in the Southwest, 1350–1880.* Lawrence: University Press of Kansas, 1989.

John, Elizabeth A. H. *Storms Brewed in Other Men's Worlds: The Confrontation of Indians, Spanish, and French in the Southwest, 1540–1795.* College Station: Texas A&M University Press, 1975.

Jones, Oakah L. *Los Paisanos: Spanish Settlers on the Northern Frontier of New Spain.* Norman: University of Oklahoma Press, 1979.

Knowlton, Clark S. "Causes of Land Loss Among the Spanish Americans in Northern New Mexico." *Rocky Mountain Social Science Journal* 1 (April 1964): 201–11.

Ramenofsky, Ann F. *Vectors of Death: The Archaeology of European Contact.* Albuquerque: University of New Mexico Press, 1987.

Spicer, Edward H. *Cycles of Conquest: The Impact of Spain, Mexico, and the United States on the Indians of the Southwest, 1533–1960.* Tucson: University of Arizona Press, 1962; reprint, 1981.

CHAPTER 2

Empires and Indians

Eighteenth-century imperialism—whether in Africa, Asia, South America, or North America—sought wealth and advantage for the mother country. Economically, the rationale for imperialism was mercantilism. The purpose of colonies, mercantilists believed, was to provide wealth to the mother country. Wealth, above all, consisted of precious metals, and a country should by all means stop bullion from flowing beyond its borders. Colonies existed to supply the mother country with goods that it could not provide itself. And if the mother country could sell such exotic goods to other countries for gold, that was all the better. But if a colony cost more than it yielded, or if the produce of a colony flowed directly to another country, then the colony's purpose had been subverted.

For mercantilists, therefore, a large empire was not necessarily a powerful empire. Indeed, throughout North America, European empires grew weak and ragged on their edges. Their continued growth, like the growth of a tumor, often sprang from political sickness instead of health. An empire's rapid expansion could contain the seeds of its own demise. Expanding, empires created native enemies who preyed on them, and they came into competition with rival imperial powers. Instead of contributing to the mother country, they drained it.

Yet a combination of fear and greed impelled each empire toward further growth. Early in the eighteenth century the French advanced west from Louisiana and Illinois, lured by the fur trade and dreams of tapping the wealth of Mexican mines. The possibility that these Frenchmen would succeed in attracting Indian allies and eventually capturing the trade of Mexico created a perennial Spanish nightmare. The appearance of a few Frenchmen on the margins of Mexico at the opening of the eighteenth century thus sparked incredible alarm. And to an empire in which New Mexico already existed as a weak and isolated fragment, the Spanish, to protect Mexico, added yet another set of weak, isolated settlements: Texas. Oddly enough, the original agent of the French threat and later a leader of the resistance to it was the same man: Louis Juchereau de St. Denis.

That the founding of a French post by St. Denis and a few French companions along the Red River in 1713 seemed to threaten the Spanish empire shows how precarious the imperial structures were. St. Denis was but one of the many Frenchmen to dream of fortunes to be made in trade with the Spanish empire. His new post was a means to that end. He hoped to use it as a base for the Indian trade and eventually for trade with Mexico as well. When St. Denis traveled to the Rio Grande to initiate trade with the Spanish, however, the Spanish commander there seized him and his goods because the Spanish would not suffer

28

outsiders to tap the trade of their empire. And here the clash of empires took an odd turn, for during his captivity St. Denis fell in love with and eventually married Doña Emanuela Ramón, the niece of his captor. St. Denis was prepared to link his own future with that of New Spain.

St. Denis offered to help the Spanish establish missions in eastern Texas, missions which would help to hold Texas against the French. There were signs that at least some of the Texas Indians would welcome such missions. Indeed, the Coahuiltecans and Jumanos actively sought missions as a means to obtain Spanish protection from Apache raiders. The missionaries desired souls, Spanish imperialists desired posts and settlements to restrict the advance of the French, and the Coahuiltecans and Jumanos sought protection. St. Denis presented an opportunity to attain all these ends. In 1716, Spain, with the aid of St. Denis, began the first four of a string of Texas missions. Missionaries hoped to convert the settled Indians of eastern Texas—the Tejas, Nacogdoches, Nasonis, Nadacos, Adaes, Ais, and others—as well as those refugee Coahuiltecans who had gathered farther west at San Antonio for protection from the Apaches.

As a servant of the Spanish crown, St. Denis did not abandon his original ambition of a trade between French Louisiana and Spanish Mexico; he simply pursued it from the other side of the boundary. The Spanish imagined the Texas missions and forts, or presidios, would quarantine the region from French contact. St. Denis intended to use them as bases for trade. He returned to Louisiana to convert his assets there into trade goods, but when he returned to Texas, his own in-laws seized his goods as contraband. He thereupon returned to Louisiana and took up the command at the French post at Natchitoches, where he, and after him his son, supervised French efforts to trade in Texas and on the southern plains.

The arrival of the French in the West, and the Spanish response to their presence, threw the two empires into direct competition and entangled the fates of Indians and Europeans more deeply than ever. With each move the rivals sought new Indian allies and dependents. And with each move they acquired new Indian enemies. The numerous French traders who began pushing up the river valleys toward the Great Plains during these early decades of the eighteenth century, for example, threatened the Apaches as deeply as they threatened Spain. The traders provided village Indians on the eastern margins of the Great Plains—the Pawnees, Wichitas, Taovayas, Otos, and others—with guns that made them dangerous targets for Apache slave raiders. The Apaches and Spanish made common cause against the French in some areas even while the Spanish fought Apaches elsewhere. Apache reports of Frenchmen among the Pawnees and neighboring peoples prompted Lieutenant Governor Pedro de Villasur to set out in 1720 with a force of New Mexicans and Pueblo Indians to banish the French from the region. Near present-day North Platte, Nebraska, French traders and Indians—probably Pawnees, Otos, or Missouris—virtually wiped out his expedition.

Competing empires confronted a native world of competing villages and tribes. In the eighteenth century a world balance of power that was shifting against Spain and its empire and toward France and England paralleled a Native American balance of power that was shifting against settled horticultural villagers and toward nomadic hunters. It was these intersecting changes that shaped the eighteenth-century West.

The pivot of these struggles was the villages of the horticulturists. Europeans found that these villages, where nomadic and settled Indian life intersected, were ideal sites for connecting Indian exchange systems to imperial exchange systems. The Spanish goal was to divert these exchange systems so that goods flowed south; the French goal was to divert them so that goods flowed east. The Spanish trading centers of Taos (both the Indian pueblo and the neighboring Mexican village), Picurís, and Pecos drew southern Plains Indians toward New Mexico. French traders at the Wichita or Pawnee villages funneled goods east and west. There was also a northern flow of goods. In the 1730s and 1740s Pierre Gaultier de Varennes, Sieur de La Vérendrye, his sons, and his nephews established a French presence in the Mandan villages of the upper Missouri. La Vérendrye discovered that English trade goods, carried south from Hudson's Bay by Indian intermediaries, had reached the Mandans before he had. La Vérendrye and those who followed him diverted this exchange to eastern Canada.

The kinds of goods that flowed into the Indian villages, the means by which they were exchanged, the peoples involved in these exchanges, and the ultimate origins and destinations of the goods exchanged all make clear the dynamism and complexity of the society evolving in the West. At a trade fair in Taos, slaves, silver, metal tools, corn, buffalo robes, horses, and dried meat all changed hands. At the Mandan or Wichita villages, Indians gained access to guns while Europeans gained access to beaver. At all these places goods moved from one party to another through combinations of ritual gift exchanges, direct trade, and theft. The parties involved were Pueblos, Apaches, Navajos, Comanches, Sioux, Wichitas, and innumerable other Native American peoples; they were French traders and voyageurs; they were New Mexicans and Tejanos. Beaver furs taken by French traders found their way to Europe; cloth manufactured in France ended up in Indian villages deep in the interior of North America.

Lurking within all these exchanges was the threat of violence, and in a sense, trade between Indians and Europeans was born in violence, for the French initially and the Spanish virtually always sought more than furs, food, and horses: they wanted slaves. In the early eighteenth century, war parties of Plains Apaches, partially in response to Spanish demands for slaves, regularly struck east into the Great Plains. The Apaches sold the captives they took in this fighting to the Spanish in New Mexico, who shipped some of them south to work in the Mexican silver mines. In the east, Frenchmen armed warriors of the Illinois confederation, who raided west across the Missouri for slaves. The French derived their name for one of the largest groups of western horticulturists, the Pawnees, from the word for Indian slaves: *panis*.

Slave raiding long remained important in New Mexico, but the French found that it limited their larger imperial and economic aims. Slave raiding created enemies in areas where French traders sought furs and, by promoting war, undercut the ability of Indian hunters to take furs. The French wanted furs and allies more than they wanted slaves. And so the Frenchmen who appeared among the horticultural peoples of the eastern margins of the Great Plains and the Missouri Valley came largely as traders rather than slave buyers.

Europeans and Nomads

The rise of the nomads greatly complicated the imperial clash in the West, because, particularly on the southern plains, the nomadic assault obstructed the

imperial strategies of both France and Spain. The Spanish suffered direct raids
from Comanches, who obstructed the trade fairs at Taos, Picurís, and Pecos. The
Spanish saw their own Indian allies dispersed and defeated. Comanche expansion
forced the Plains Apaches south and east, where they in turn increased pressure
on the Texas missions. The French established trading connections with the
horticultural villagers only to find those people coming under increasing nomadic
pressure as the century wore on. Changes in Native American society and changes
in the ambitions of empires intersected. Europeans had unleashed forces they
could not control.

By the mid-eighteenth century the Spanish, who had entered the region as
conquerors, held, in alliance with the Pueblos, a small, isolated island of villages
along the Rio Grande besieged by increasingly powerful and confident nomadic
enemies. Their only other foothold in the West was a string of equally beleaguered
missions and presidios in Texas. Everywhere the Spanish looked in the mid-
eighteenth century, they saw enemies. To the south the Apaches cut off New
Mexico from Mexico proper and raided deep into New Spain. In Texas the Lipan
Apaches and Plains Apaches raided the missions. The Comanches themselves
fell upon New Mexico, stripping it of horses. The French compounded the pressure
by arming the Wichitas and other tribes that the Spanish lumped together
as *norteños*, "northerners"; these tribes raided Texas missions that the Spanish
established to try to settle the Apaches. To these actual threats the Spanish
added potential threats: England and Russia might seize California, claimed but
unoccupied by Spain, thus placing new imperial rivals on the border of New
Spain.

The weak missions and settlements of Texas and New Mexico seemed incapable
of resisting this pressure. In 1758 a united Comanche-*norteño* expedition destroyed
the San Sabá mission on the San Gabriel River in Texas. In the 1760s the
Comanches, first under a formidable leader named Cuerno Verde and then under
his son, who took his name, scourged New Mexico. They fell on both the Pueblos
and the Spanish villages and, aided by a prolonged drought, virtually stripped
New Mexico of horses. Their attacks spelled the doom of the once prosperous
pueblos of Pecos and Galisteo. The decline of Pecos proved particularly long and
painful. When its few remaining Indian inhabitants finally abandoned it in the
early nineteenth century, Spanish settlers seized the lands.

Worse still was a new round of attacks by the Apaches. The Apaches had always
been a problem to Spain. The numerous Apache bands acted independently, and
at any given time some would be friendly with the Spanish and some at war. The
Jicarilla Apaches of northern New Mexico were usually friendly. The Plains
Apaches, too, were usually friendly, but only with the New Mexicans; they raided
the Spanish missions and settlements in Texas. Some Apache groups such as the
Faraones and the southern bands (the Gilas, Mimbreños, Chiricahuas, Arivaipas,
San Carloses, and others) were more consistently hostile. They threatened not
just New Mexico and Texas but also the "silver provinces" of Nuevo Léon, Nueva
Vizcaya, and Nueva Galicia. When Apache raids on these provinces increased,
Spanish administrators began to panic, for the mines of these provinces were far
more vital to imperial solvency than were the limited resources of the borderlands.
In Nueva Vizcaya alone between 1771 and 1776, Apache raiders killed 1,674
people, captured 154, forced the abandonment of 116 haciendas and ranches,

and stole 68,256 head of livestock. These figures do not include casualties and losses at the presidios or losses to people traveling through the province.

To protect what they had already, Spanish officials decided that they must gain even more. They undertook a policy of defensive expansion which, by the late eighteenth century, seemed to succeed. International politics and good fortune removed the threat from the east. Although Spain feared France in North America, European politics made France and Spain allies against England in the Seven Years War. When peace came in 1763, it cost France her North American empire. Canada went to England, and the French, to keep the province out of English hands, gave Louisiana to the Spanish in compensation for their losses. Spanish Louisiana removed the French threat to Spanish Texas and gradually allowed the Spanish to cut the norteños off from French trade.

The Spanish success in keeping French guns from the norteños had the further effect of opening up the Caddos, Taovayas, and Wichitas to attacks from the Osages, who were advancing from the northeast. The Osages, who retained contacts with English and French Canadian traders operating across the Mississippi, had access to the guns that gave them a great advantage over their more westerly enemies. They launched devastating attacks for slaves and livestock at a time when the Wichitas' alliance with the Comanches was breaking down. As a result, the Wichita confederation had to retreat from the Arkansas River valley to the Red River valley. Short of goods and seeking help against the Osages, the norteños were ready for peace with the Spanish. The Osages themselves became a problem for New Spain, but they were a less formidable threat than the norteño-Comanche alliance had been. By the 1770s the acquisition of Louisiana had brought the Spanish a huge, if ill-defined, chunk of territory and a partial respite in the east.

Securing their northern and western borders demanded more effort. Spanish attempts to consolidate and protect the borderlands began with an extended northern tour of inspection by the Marqués de Rubí in 1766–67. To secure a better defense, Rubí suggested a line of presidios extending from the mouth of the Río Concepción in Sonora to the Río Guadalupe in Texas, with a distance of about 40 leagues between each fort. Rubí's primary objective was to protect the silver mining provinces, for virtually all of New Mexico and Texas, including both Santa Fe and San Antonio, lay unprotected beyond his line of presidios. The Spanish, however, never seriously entertained the possibility of abandoning these northern provinces. Even Rubí's expedition looked toward their economic development. Rubí charted water and mineral resources, laid out lines of communication, and made suggestions for increasing agricultural productivity. In the end, the government decided to retain these areas as enclaves of settlement with strengthened garrisons.

Making these northern settlements effective buffers for Mexico itself involved both increasing their size and freeing them from Indian attack. Gradually, the New Mexicans managed to reestablish peace with the Comanches and, less successfully, with the Apaches. The death of the younger Cuerno Verde in battle and deteriorating Comanche trade in Wichita villages led Comanche leaders to press for a peace with New Mexico. Although Comanche raids on Texas persisted, New Mexico's Governor Juan Bautista de Anza eagerly concluded a peace with the Comanches. By 1786, Spain, by transforming the Comanches into allies against the Apaches and reopening the Taos trade fairs, had begun to relieve pressure on New Mexico. With *norteño*, Navajo, and Comanche alliances, Spain could put increasing pressure on the Apaches during the 1770s and 1780s, but the Spanish never succeeded in completely subduing them. Apache raids continued to take a toll because the Apaches by now treated Sonora as a convenient supply depot to be raided for livestock and trade goods. They had no desire to depopulate the region. Who then would raise the horses and livestock and bring in the goods they desired? The best the Spanish could do was achieve temporary periods of friendship with some Apache bands. The Spanish encouraged Apaches to settle near the presidios in special villages—the *establecimientos de paz*—where the Spanish promised protection, fed them, encouraged them to drink liquor, and generally tried to make them dependent and pliable. It was cheaper than fighting them. Some Apaches around Tucson had by 1800 become dependent enough to be known as the Mansos, or tame Apaches. They were regarded as enemies by those Apache bands on the north. Despite longer and more frequent interludes of peace, however, most Apache bands maintained a mutually predatory relationship with the Spanish. They raided the Spanish for food; the Spanish raided them for slaves.

The elimination of the French threat from the east and the gradual if partial reestablishment of peace with the *norteños*, Comanches, and Apaches still left open the threat from California. The Russians and British replaced the French as imperial rivals in Spanish nightmares. Although it would be 1778 before Captain James Cook began a series of British expeditions along the west coast of North America and 1812 before the Russians actually established a settlement at Fort Ross on the California coast, Spanish fears of their rivals long preceded the actual threat.

California

The Spanish had known of California well before they moved to secure the area from imperial rivals. Spanish sailors had visited Alta California, as the area north of present Baja California was known, as early as 1542, when Juan Rodríguez Cabrillo died while looking for the Northwest Passage. More than two centuries later, in 1769, the Spanish set out to establish a string of missions, presidios, and towns along the coast that Cabrillo had only glimpsed through the ocean fog. By 1770 they had two presidios: one at Monterey and the other at San Diego. In 1769, Fray Junipero Serra began establishing the 21 missions which would eventually stretch from San Diego to San Francisco Bay. In 1774, Juan Bautista de Anza succeeded in traveling overland to California from Sonora, thus providing the new province with a land link as well as a sea link with older settlements. Anza duplicated the trip in 1775–76, bringing west the settlers who founded San Francisco in the fall of 1776. A nearly simultaneous attempt by Fray Silvestre Vélez de Escalante and Fray Francisco Atanásio Domínguez to reach Monterey from Santa Fe in 1776 failed. The Franciscans and their party spent most of their time wandering around Utah. Anza's success led the Spanish in 1779 to attempt to secure the Gila-Colorado route from Sonora to California by erecting a presidio and two missions among the Yuma Indians who lived along the Colorado.

Although largely successful, the attempt to secure California did gain the Spanish some new Indian enemies. The Yumas, who had first been visited by the

Jesuit Father Kino in 1698, initially welcomed Franciscan missionaries. They expected trade goods and spiritual power, but they were unprepared for the Franciscan zeal for reorganizing their lives. Nor had they anticipated the lust for property of the soldiers who accompanied the Franciscans. When the friars set about rearranging Yuma landholdings, and settlers and soldiers allowed their cattle to ruin both Yuma crops and the mesquite trees from which Yumas gathered food, the Yumas rebelled. They destroyed the missions, the settlements, and the presidio and cut California off from Mexico. The Spanish retaliated with punitive expeditions to kill Yumas, but they never did reoccupy the lower Colorado. The Yumas had blocked Spanish attempts to reorder Indian lives on the Colorado, but in California a massive reconstruction of Indian society was underway.

In California the Spanish created a way of life quite distinct from that of Texas or New Mexico. At a time when missions were crumbling elsewhere in the northern territories, missions formed the heart of the social order in California. Missionaries, aided by soldiers, gathered virtually the entire coastal population of California Indians south of San Francisco Bay into their missions. The missionaries worked not only to convert them, baptizing nearly 54,000 Indians in all, but also to "reduce" them from their "free and undisciplined" state to a regulated and disciplined condition. In the eyes of the Franciscans who supervised them, the California missions were humanitarian endeavors.

The missions controlled land, livestock, and labor. As in New Mexico, the missionaries instructed the neophytes (as baptized Indians were called) in a wide variety of new skills. Indian weavers, brick makers, blacksmiths, farmers, shepherds, and vaqueros—cattle drovers—created the California economy, and the missions prospered on their labor. At their height, the mission herds numbered more than 400,000 cattle, 60,000 horses, and 300,000 sheep and goats. The Indians did not, however, freely bestow the labor that maintained the missions. It was forced labor. Neophytes could not leave the missions, where the priests attempted to exercise absolute authority over them. If Indians persistently refused to work or resisted orders, they faced the lash, stocks, or irons. If neophytes fled the missions, soldiers were sent to retrieve them and whip them publicly. The results of Indian labor did not personally enrich the missionaries. The proceeds became part of the communal wealth of the mission, but the missionaries decided how these proceeds would be allocated. Under the mission system, Indians controlled neither their own labor nor its proceeds.

The cost of this wholesale transformation of Indian life was horrifying. During the mission period the Indian population between San Diego and San Francisco declined from 72,000 to 18,000, most of it from introduced diseases aggravated by the poor sanitation, the lack of medical care, the change in diet, and the often harsh social discipline of the missions. As the anthropologist Alfred Kroeber summarized the results, "The Fathers . . . were saving souls only at the inevitable cost of lives." If dying because of the actions of saintly men had advantages over dying at the hands of sinners, the mission Indians were lucky people indeed.

Pacific Northwest

The fear of rival empires that brought the Spanish to California and introduced wrenching changes in the life of California Indians carried Spanish sailors even farther north. In 1774, Juan Pérez sailed up the coast as far as Nootka Sound in

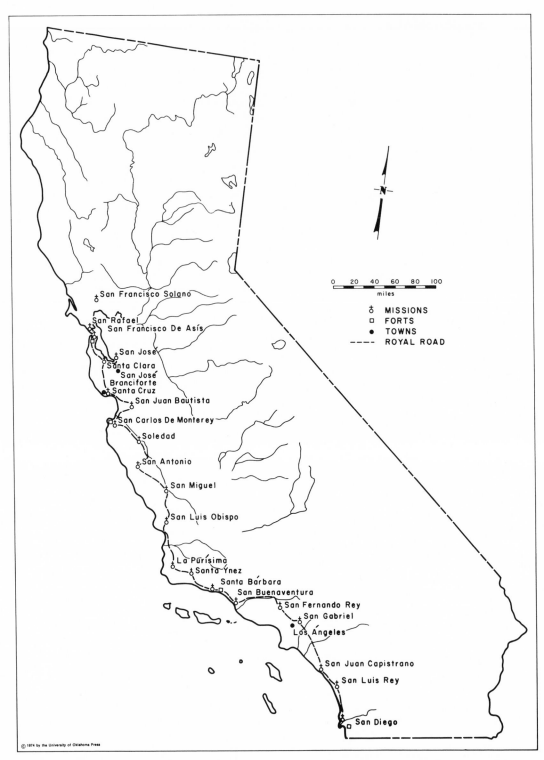

Missions, forts, and towns of California during the Spanish period, 1769–1822. From Warren A. Beck and Ynez D. Haase, *Historical Atlas of California* (Norman: University of Oklahoma Press, 1974), map 19.

Table 2
Birth and Death Rates in the California Missions

Period*	Mean birth rate per 1,000	Mean death rate per 1,000	Ratio: birth rate/death rate
1771–80	49.0	75.0	0.654
1781–90	36.9	69.6	0.530
1791–1800	43.4	80.9	0.525
1801–10	35.9	90.0	0.399
1811–20	37.5	76.3	0.492
1821–30	33.1	77.4	0.428
1771–1830	39.3	78.2	0.503

Source: Sherburne Cook, *The Population of California Indians, 1769–1970*. (Berkeley, University of California Press, 1976), p. 107.
*Each value is the mean rate for all the missions during the ten-year period indicated.

present-day British Columbia, and in 1775 two Spanish ships under Bruno de Hezeta made a landfall off the Quinault River in Washington. The Spanish erected a cross and claimed the land, but their stay did not go smoothly. The Indians attacked a small landing party, and the Spanish counterattacked an Indian canoe. The Spanish, who arrived with orders to avoid conflict with the Indians, sailed away having sealed the contact with blood.

These first Spanish expeditions had sailed to deter the southern advance of the Russians from Alaska, but it was the English who proved the more immediate threat to Spain. In 1778, Captain James Cook with his two ships, the *Resolution* and the *Discovery*, touched land at Nootka Sound on Vancouver Island. Sailors purchased 1,500 otter skins from local Indians, thinking to use them for clothing on their northern voyage. Instead they discovered that "skins which did not cost the purchaser six-pence sterling sold in China for 100 dollars." The promise of fortunes to be made in the sea otter trade brought English merchantmen sailing to the coast in Cook's wake. Behind them would come even more numerous American traders.

This trade alarmed the Spanish. In 1789 a Spanish expedition under Estéban Martínez occupied Nootka, seized three ships trading there, and arrested all foreigners trespassing on what Martínez regarded as Spanish territory. The seizures brought Spain and England to the brink of war, but in 1790 Spain backed down, granting England trade rights along the coast.

With English trading rights guaranteed and American incursions growing more frequent, the Spanish gradually retreated in the Pacific Northwest. The trade in sea otters quickly passed from English to American hands and spread south from Nootka. The British government had dispatched George Vancouver to implement the Nootka Convention, as the Spanish concession of trading rights to the English was called, and on his voyage up the coast in 1792, Vancouver became the first European to explore Puget Sound. That same year, the American Robert Gray entered the Columbia River, whose existence the Spanish had already noted. By the late 1790s the Columbia had become a center of trade; American ships manned and captained by "Bostons," as the Indians called New Englanders, dominated the coast. These seaborne traders brought syphilis and smallpox as well as trade goods, and together disease and traders wrought the same destruction on the Northwest Coast that disease and missionaries had wrought in California.

In California itself the Russians, skipping over the Pacific Northwest entirely, established a post of their own at Fort Ross just north of San Francisco Bay in 1812 to supply their Alaskan possessions. They remained there until 1841, when they sold their herds and buildings to John Sutter, a Swiss adventurer who had his own establishment on the Sacramento River.

Change in the Borderlands

The changes that the Spanish brought to California were a direct result of their efforts to secure and reorganize their empire, and this same search for security brought sweeping change to New Mexico and Texas. Making these colonies defensible involved integrating them more thoroughly with Mexico proper. In New Mexico mule trains between the province and the regional market in Chihuahua grew more numerous and more regular, money began to circulate, and new immigrants arrived. Relative peace with the Indians between 1786 and 1810 aided this increase in commerce and growth in population. Life in the villages began to alter. The way people earned their livings changed; marriage patterns changed, and so, too, did relations within families. Not all these changes were intentional, and not all were welcome.

The growth of Spanish population in New Mexico from 3,800 in 1750 to 16,000 in 1790 to 19,000 in 1800 put great stress on the village economies. The supply of irrigable land did not keep pace with the population. As long as the province remained at peace with surrounding Indians, villagers could relieve this population pressure by moving to new lands. Individual families took what came to be called smallholding claims, informal grants of agricultural plots and use rights on surrounding communal lands. Others, both native New Mexicans and newcomers, gained access to *mercedes*, or royal grants of land.

But smallholding claims and new village grants could not wholly remedy the land shortage. Because the amount of irrigable land was limited and the Spanish were unable to seize sufficient additional lands from surrounding Indians without provoking war, the plots of peasants necessarily became smaller as the population of the villages grew. By 1796 there were 1,500 people in New Mexico without any land to till.

The combined result of an increasing number of landless people and of the growth of commerce was a substantial increase in the number of people who earned their living outside of farming. In Albuquerque, for example, roughly one-third of the working population were either craftspeople or day laborers in both 1790 and 1827, but within this group independent craft production was declining while wage labor was increasing. Only 10 percent of the workers were day laborers in 1790, but 19 percent were in 1827.

These economic changes brought other changes in their wake. The code of familial honor had been enforceable because fathers could control their children's access to land and social privilege. Children had consented to arranged marriages in order to obtain land and establish a place for themselves within the village world. Economic change undercut this system and lessened the authority of parents. Children who from necessity became wage laborers lost the security of land, but in the process their parents lost control over them. Because such people could no longer count on a significant inheritance of property, they had less reason to follow parental dictates. Arranged marriages persisted among the elite, but among others love, not property or familial honor, became the rationale for marriage. This was a significant crack in the ideology of honor.

In Texas, the situation was somewhat different, for Texas more than other regions continued to suffer under Comanche and Apache attacks. In order to consolidate settlement, the Spanish in 1772 ordered the missions, presidios, and villages of eastern Texas abandoned. The settlers complied, but by 1779, disgusted with their new homes around San Antonio de Béxar and seeking to escape Comanche raids there, many returned to Nacogdoches. Enough Spanish settlers remained at San Antonio, however, to make it less and less a cluster of missions and more and more a Spanish settlement. In 1793 the Spanish secularized the mission of San Antonio de Valero (later known as the Alamo), distributed its lands, and turned the buildings over to the military. Only 43 settled Indian converts remained, and none of the other surrounding missions held many more. The rest had died or fled. This Spanish dominance in the old mission areas should not, however, be overstated. There were by then only about 3,000 Spaniards—including soldiers and converted Indians—in all of Texas.

Still, among these small groups of Spaniards, scattered from the forests of eastern Texas to the settlements and ranches around San Antonio and to the large ranches growing along the Rio Grande, a distinctive way of life was emerging. Unlike California, dominated by missions and missionaries, and unlike New Mexico, with its small agricultural villages and sheep herds, all of Texas but the eastern forestland was dominated by cattle and ranches. Along the Rio Grande, Spanish *rancheros* acquired huge grants—*mercedes*—from the king, stocked them with cattle, and manned them with vaqueros who were themselves Indians and mestizos. Anglo Americans would not introduce a ranching culture into Texas. They would find a fully developed culture in place.

Mexican Independence

Although Spanish efforts to revitalize the northern provinces during the late eighteenth century focused on the need to repel external threats, the real threat to New Spain turned out to be internal. By the early nineteenth century Mexico and its northern provinces stood on the edge of revolutionary transformations. For Texas, New Mexico, and California the political result of nineteenth-century upheavals would be independence from Spain and territorial status within an independent Mexico. Socially, the result would be the secularization of missions and the declining influence of the church. Economically, the result would be the increasing privatization of property and a foreign trade dominated by Americans.

Mexico gained independence from Spain in 1821, but far-reaching political change had begun more than a decade earlier in Spain itself. Following Napoleon's invasion of Spain in 1808, Spanish liberals in the Cortés, a parliament that previously possessed little power, had led resistance against the French while simultaneously undertaking reforms within the empire. The liberal Spanish constitution of 1812 provided for representative institutions, and bodies ranging from provincial *deputaciones*, or legislatures, to town councils appeared in Mexico. When the restoration of the monarchy led to the suspension of these representative bodies, a revolt by the liberals and military in Spain forced their reinstitution.

The movement for representative government that began in Spain took firm root in the colonies themselves and, combining with mestizo discontent with the Mexican social order, led, ultimately, to revolts against Spain itself. Beginning in 1810 and lasting until independence, a cycle of revolt and repression shook Mexico. In 1811, Texas became directly involved in the most famous of these early revolts. Acting in support of Padre Miguel Hidalgo's call for independence, a militia officer, Juan Bautista de las Casas, led a successful coup against the royalist government at San Antonio. His uprising drew upon the discontent of poor soldiers and civilians who resented the Tejano elite's growing monopolization of wealth in the province. A countercoup led by clergy and army officers soon led to Bautista's capture and subsequent execution, but in 1812 one of his supporters, Bernardo Gutiérrez de Lara, invaded the province from the United States. With an army composed of Americans, Indians, Mexican rebels, and Louisiana French, he captured San Antonio in 1813, declared independence, and executed the Texas governor, a Spanish general, and fifteen others. Gutiérrez's triumph was brief. He and the American Volunteers, as his American supporters called themselves, quarreled over the future of Texas and the execution of the royalists. Many of the American Volunteers returned home as the royalist general José Joaquín Arredondo invaded and reconquered the province. Arredondo took bloody revenge on those Tejanos suspected of republican tendencies. He executed 327 people in San Antonio alone and virtually destroyed the Nacogdoches settlements of eastern Texas. From 1813 until 1821 royalist troops and armies of liberation, which included American mercenaries who coveted Texas for themselves, took turns pillaging the province. Violence and flight cost Texas perhaps two-thirds of its population between 1809 and 1821.

None of the other borderland provinces suffered this kind of destruction. Everywhere, however, revolts caused supplies to fail to reach the presidios and missions. Officials did not receive their salaries, and trade declined. Effective administration of the empire had ended. When Mexico finally achieved independence on February 24, 1821, the basis for governance was the Plan of Iguala issued by the revolutionary general Augustín de Iturbide. The plan temporarily united Mexicans under the "Three Guarantees": independence from Spain, recognition of Catholicism as Mexico's only religion, and equality for all Mexicans. With the collapse of the Spanish regime in July, even the governors and military officers of California, New Mexico, and Texas who had remained loyal to Spain joined the revolutionaries in giving allegiance to the new government. In less than a dozen years the inhabitants had gone from subjects to citizens. The people began to elect representatives to replace outside appointees within the provinces, and they now sent delegates to the Mexican congress.

Just as demands for representative government in Spain had helped spawn demands for representative government and autonomy in Mexico, so Mexican independence led to demands for greater local autonomy in the north, where none of the borderland provinces had become states in the Mexican republic. Texas became part of the state of Coahuila, while New Mexico and California were territories under the direct supervision of the Mexican congress. Liberal regimes, devoted in theory to a federalist system, governed Mexico during the 1820s and 1830s. They granted the northern territories far more self-rule than Spain had given them, but representative institutions took hold unevenly. New Mexico, for example, had a *deputación*, and most towns there and in Texas had functioning municipal governments, *ayuntamientos*, which combined the duties of both an American town council and county commissioners. But in California the *deputación* and *ayuntamientos* failed to thrive.

Independence from Spain and the beginnings of representative institutions did not quell discontent in the north; indeed, in many ways they exacerbated it. Most Tejanos desired separate statehood, and many people in New Mexico and California chafed under a congress that drew up no overall plan for their government. And when centralists took control of the Mexican government in the mid-1830s, they eliminated many of the political gains the northerners had made by abolishing states and territories. New Mexico, California, and Texas became separate departments to be governed under a system resembling the old Spanish bureaucracy. The result was revolt not only in Texas (which was already in rebellion for other reasons) but also in New Mexico and California. New Mexicans and Californians only grudgingly yielded to the centralists, acceding to greater control from Mexico City in the 1840s.

Politically, the Mexican Revolution had thrust the village and mission world of the borderlands into revolutionary upheavals in the late eighteenth and early nineteenth centuries. Mexican liberalism represented an attack on hereditary privilege and established institutions, but this attack did not necessarily lead to benefits for the poor and impoverished. In Mexico the great target of liberals was the Roman Catholic church, for the church, above all, was a bastion of wealth and privilege in Mexican society. Liberal attacks on the church would have profound consequences for the borderlands.

Secularization and Social Change

During most of the Spanish era the church had rivaled the state as an agency of colonization, but by the time Mexico won independence, the Catholic church, while wealthy and important, was already in political decline. Spanish liberals had begun the attack on the church, and in 1717 they had struck a significant blow by expelling the Jesuits from the Spanish empire. Jesuit activities had extended up into what is now Arizona; their expulsion exacerbated the grave problems the missions faced. In Texas the missions had never really prospered. Indian neophytes died or ran away, and constant warfare with the nomadic tribes decimated the mission herds. Similarly, in what is now the Santa Cruz Valley of southern Arizona, the two missions located between present-day Tucson and Nogales had dwindled as disease ravaged Pima neophytes. The missions had remained open only by recruiting neighboring Papagos to replace the Pimas. In New Mexico, too, the number of Franciscans serving the Pueblos had dwindled in the last decades of Spanish rule. The weakening of the missions sparked a struggle within the church between Mexican bishops and the religious orders. The bishops used the diminishing number of friars and falling mission Indian populations to "secularize" some missions. In Texas, and later in New Mexico, missions had been partially "secularized"— that is, transformed into regular parishes with part of their land opened to non-Indians. In secularized missions priests were directly under the control of the bishops instead of being members of independent religious orders.

The revolution further fragmented the church. By forcing most Spanish priests out of the country, the revolution indirectly damaged the remaining missions, many of whose friars were Spanish. Mexican liberals, who ardently desired to end the mission system itself, mounted a more direct attack. They wanted to secularize all the missions, to distribute their holdings, and to make them parishes. This policy sprang, in part, from a sincere desire to liberate the Indians from the often onerous control of the priests. But it also sprang from a desire of non-Indians in the borderlands—who revealingly called themselves the *gente de razón*, or "people of reason"—to gain access to the large mission holdings and to make use of Indian labor.

Not only the church but also Mexican conservatives, who saw the missions as the primary agency for controlling Indians, resisted the campaign for secularization, but theirs was a doomed cause. In Texas secularization amounted to the dismembering of a corpse. Local pressure for mission lands and a shortage of neophytes led to the system's complete demise with a secularization order in 1823. In Pimería Alta, which would eventually become part of Arizona, the expulsion first of the Jesuits and then Spanish priests deprived the missions of missionaries. These missions, too, collapsed. In New Mexico the missions declined rapidly during the 1820s from the simple inability of the Franciscans to staff them. By 1832 only five missions had resident priests, and by 1840 there were no Franciscans left in New Mexico at all. The Pueblos, because the Mexican republic recognized their title under royal grants, did not, however, lose their lands.

The only place where the liberal attack on the missions met significant resistance was in California, for that was the only place where the mission system remained strong. There the missions were wealthy and powerful, and this made the Mexican government reluctant to proceed too quickly against them. Levies on the wealth of the missions, after all, supported both Mexican garrisons and public officials in California. Officials feared that the wealth that supported them would disappear if they dismantled the mission system. But the wealth of the missions made their opponents all the more eager to dismember them. The missions' near monopoly on land and Indian labor frustrated *californio* economic ambitions. The Mexican government compromised. It attempted during the 1820s to institute a gradual program of secularization. Instead of decapitating the missions, officials dismembered them limb by limb. They permitted some Indians to leave the missions and take up part of the mission holdings as their own land.

Gradualism ended in 1833, however, when a liberal government in Mexico City ordered the immediate secularization of all the California missions. Although Mexican liberals intended secularization to benefit the Indians, secularization delivered the wealth of the missions into the hands of a *californio* elite. Mission Indians did receive land, but most showed no interest in farming it or in remaining near the missions. Even if the Indians had sought to assimilate into Californian society as small landholders, the *californios* had no intention of granting them, in the words of Governor Figueroa, "a legal equality [that] would unhinge society." Some mission Indians quickly moved inland to live with still independent Indian communities; others became laborers in Mexican communities or on the ranches established on mission lands. The bulk of the mission lands and herds came under the supervision of *mayordomos*, whom officials chose from among the *californio* elite. These *mayordomos* sold off the herds and lands to their cronies enabling them to establish the huge *ranchos* that came to dominate the coastal landscape.

Secularization not only eliminated the missions, but it also nearly removed the institutional church from the borderlands. The Roman Catholic church lost title to its vast mission estates, and the Mexican government eliminated compulsory annual tithes—a 10 percent levy by the church on crops and increases in livestock. This loss of revenues contributed to the failure of secularization to achieve its announced goal: the transformation of missions into parishes. Few Mexican priests found the poor parishes in the northern provinces attractive. They did not replace the Spanish priests who left Mexico for Spain. Vast areas contained few priests. There were eight secular priests in New Mexico in 1829, two in Texas in 1830, five in California in 1846, and none in what is now Arizona.

The paucity of clergy (and the corruption of the few who were present) helped in turn to fuel the rise of a lay brotherhood—the Brothers of Our Father Jesus, popularly known as the Penitentes—in New Mexico. In the absence of regular clergy, the brothers worshiped together, developed their own liturgy and ceremonies, helped the sick and poor, and buried the dead. They were a mutual aid society upholding communal ideals of fraternity and community, but they were a mutual aid society obsessed with the precariousness of life and the ubiquity of suffering. They engaged in extreme forms of penance during Lent, whipping themselves in order to achieve a mystical oneness with the suffering Christ. In some years they tied one of their members to a cross on Good Friday and left him hanging there until he lost consciousness.

Economic Change

When Mexican liberals began their campaign of secularization, they never imagined that it would encourage groups such as the Penitentes, nor did they envision the outcome of their program for economic change. Economically, liberals believed in eliminating economic privileges while protecting private property rights, ending state monopolies and regulations, and freeing trade. They were classical liberals not to be confused with the modern definition of the word *liberal*, with its connotations of economic regulation. Liberal attacks on the missions were, in this sense, as much an economic as a social measure, since they forced the church to surrender its economic privileges. Mission lands passed into private hands. But the result of these policies was not economic equality; it was greater inequality. Nor was the result a stronger Mexican economy; although economic growth occurred in the borderlands, it did not benefit the larger Mexican economy.

In the borderland provinces, the privatization of church property deepened the gulf between the rich and the poor. In California, for example, some settlers, often the descendants of Spanish soldiers of modest military rank, were fortunate enough to secure large land grants after the breakup of the mission estates. As they acquired cattle and lands, and as they gained access to Indian labor, they grew rich. The Indians simultaneously grew poorer. By advancing former mission Indians a few goods, a little money, or some liquor, ranchers forced them into debt peonage. Once Indians sank into debt and were unable to pay, the law required them to work for their creditors for a year to pay back their debts. Any new debts that the Indians incurred brought further service. The division of

A rare picture of a nineteenth-century Penitente ceremony in New Mexico.

California mission lands thus created an elite of wealthy ranchers and an underclass of impoverished Indian *peones*, whose numbers continued to dwindle through disease and flight to the interior.

In New Mexico, too, the concentration of wealth in the hands of a few increased, but there the distribution of royal lands and not church lands accelerated the process. Mexican officials made land grants on a much more lavish scale than the Spanish had. For example, during the relatively brief period of Mexican rule, Mexico granted more lands in New Mexico than the Spanish had during the previous century. Recognized grants during the Mexican period totaled nearly 22 million acres of land, and most of them were large private grants. These grants contributed to the creation of a class called *ricos*—men of wealth as well as honor—in New Mexico.

As *ricos* gained new access to land, peasants saw their holdings dwindle. In New Mexico the Rio Grande valley was divided into two regions: the Río Abajo south of Santa Fe and the Río Arriba north of Santa Fe. It was in the Río Abajo that the dons of New Mexico became *ricos* and villagers became *peones*. In the Río Arriba, where the land was mountainous and arable soil scarce, villagers maintained a subsistence economy on their communal lands.

In the Río Abajo, *ricos* managed to gain control of the best grazing lands on the plains adjacent to the Rio Grande and used the *partido* system to create a system of debt peonage. Under the *partido* system, sheep essentially became capital lent at interest. The owner (banker) of the sheep turned over a certain number of ewes (capital) to the *partidario* (borrower), who agreed to make set annual payments of wool and lambs, usually 20 percent of the original head count (interest). If the *partidario* could realize a return greater than the interest that he paid the owner, he profited and could establish his own flock. If he failed, he sank into debt and lost his collateral: land, if he had any, or if not, his own labor. *Partidarios* hoped the arrangement would lead to wealth and freedom, but it often led to poverty and peonage. Sheep owners, on the other hand, succeeded in transferring part of the risks to the *partidarios*, solved their own labor problems in a cash-short economy, and freed themselves from active management of the herds. Large landholders gradually became *patrónes* to the surrounding villages of dependent laborers.

Economic reform in the borderlands thus widened the social divisions between classes. These growing divisions, in turn, helped to breed violence. In 1837 the villagers of the Río Arriba revolted against the New Mexican government. The revolt itself began in the divisions between New Mexicans and the central government of the Mexican republic, but it was fed by social divisions within New Mexico itself. The conservative centralist government in Mexico City provoked the revolt with a plan to increase taxes to support new administrators. The peasants of Río Arriba denounced the taxes and also denounced the fees that the few remaining local priests charged for burials, weddings, and other religious services. Their discontent soon encompassed all that they regarded as the ostentation, wealth, and arrogance of New Mexican officials. The rebels of Río Arriba, after defeating and killing the governor, briefly seized Santa Fe and at least flirted with the idea of joining the United States. Up to this point many *ricos* of New Mexico, who were themselves federalists and liberals, supported the rebels, for they, too, opposed the centralist government. But peasant discontent went beyond fees and taxes; militia service under the command of the *ricos* themselves also aroused their anger. Peasants saw themselves suffering and dying to protect rich men's sheep, receiving in return only the scorn of the *ricos*. Once in power, the rebels began a short but harsh reign of terror. They turned against the *ricos*, and the rebellion became a small civil war within New Mexico. The rebels' own disorganization and the union of the *ricos* with government troops doomed the rebellion.

In California, too, there was a social war of sorts, but there it took place under the guise of an Indian war. American adventurers led by Jim Beckwourth, a free black, and Pegleg Smith, a trapper who had amputated his own injured leg, cooperated with Ute Indians under Walkara to steal vast amounts of livestock from California ranches. More significantly, these American mountain men and New Mexican traders both encouraged Yokuts and other Indians of the California interior to steal horses from the ranchos for resale in New Mexico. The Yokuts, who had already begun stealing horses for food, now stole them for trade. They were tremendously successful in large part because former neophytes guided them on the raids and betrayed the ranchos from within. These raids, which pitted tribal Indians and Indian *peones* against wealthy rancheros, reached such a scale by the 1840s that they had badly weakened the Mexican ranchos by depleting the herds.

Economic reform had sparked social turmoil. The distribution of wealth grew more unbalanced, and the borderlands grew more divided. Amidst all this, economic growth did take place, but by the 1840s many Mexicans were wondering if the growth was worth the price. Not only did they have to face the bitter social divisions spawned by economic change, but also many of the benefits of increased commerce seemed to be flowing to the United States instead of to Mexico proper.

Trade with the United States

American trade with the borderlands began when the newly independent Mexican government decided to reverse previous Spanish policy and allow foreigners to enter the country on business. Mexican officials believed that the foreigners would invigorate a national economy severely damaged by the revolution. As Spaniards and Spanish capital left Mexico, the economy had begun a downward spiral that would last for half a century. Per capita income declined, and with the loss of customary Spanish markets, foreign trade dwindled. Not until 1870 would Mexico's postrevolutionary economy reach its 1805 peak.

Even as they solicited foreigners to do business in Mexico, Mexicans themselves disagreed on the extent of foreign involvement that they should allow and on the conditions that they should impose on foreign merchants. Mexican liberals, who hoped foreigners would provide both the capital and the goods Mexico lacked, tended to favor policies of relatively free trade. More conservative centralists, however, sought a policy of high tariffs and close regulation. Policies changed with each change in government, but in a larger sense, such laws mattered only as statements of intent. Mexico lacked the customs officials, naval vessels, and bureaucracy necessary to enforce the laws the government enacted. Smuggling and bribery were rampant. Mexican officials discovered that they could attract foreigners, but they could not control them. Foreign imports and merchants moved freely in the borderlands. They came across the Texas border from Louisiana, down the Santa Fe Trail to New Mexico, and from American ships engaged in the coastal trade of California.

In all three provinces, trade represented a very real net transfer of wealth to the United States. The consequences of the new trade were most apparent in New Mexico. Chihuahua merchants whose pack trains had once plied the route to the Rio Grande settlements had dominated the trade of New Mexico before the opening of the Santa Fe Trail. In the 1820s they lost the New Mexican trade to the Americans. Wagon trains from the east replaced mule trains from the south on the roads to Santa Fe.

In 1821, barely two months after Mexican independence, William Becknell, a Missouri merchant seeking to stave off his own impending bankruptcy, arrived in Santa Fe. The United States was suffering through one of its recurrent depressions, and Missouri was short of cash and full of merchandise for which there was no market. Becknell brought a wide array of this merchandise to New Mexico and sold it at two-thirds the price of lesser-quality goods brought up from Chihuahua. In exchange, Becknell and the Americans who followed him obtained mules and silver coins—so many silver coins that New Mexico itself was starved for currency by the mid-1820s. Possessing more goods than New Mexicans had the wealth to buy, the Americans looked for fresh markets and turned south to the silver mining states of Chihuahua, Durango, Zacatecas, and Sonora. New Mexican middlemen, too, prospered as they joined in this transfer of American goods into Mexico proper.

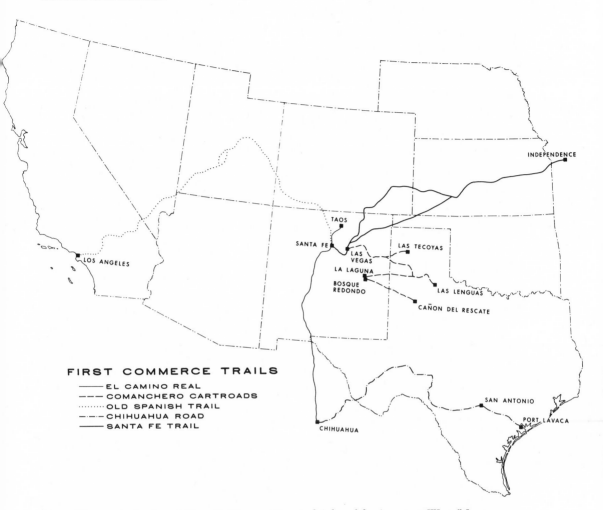

FIRST COMMERCE TRAILS
——— EL CAMINO REAL
——— COMANCHERO CARTROADS
········· OLD SPANISH TRAIL
—·—·— CHIHUAHUA ROAD
——— SANTA FE TRAIL

From Warren A. Beck and Ynez D. Haase, *Historical Atlas of the American West* (Norman: University of Oklahoma Press, 1989), map 29.

By 1831, when Josiah Gregg departed with a caravan along the Santa Fe Trail, the American trade with New Mexico was a decade old—old enough to have developed its own customs and business procedures but still new enough to be exotic and exciting. Gregg's *Commerce of the Prairies* (1844) captures the romance of the caravans of wagons approaching Santa Fe; the citizens yelling, announcing the arrival of "*los Americanos*"—"*los carros*"—"*la entrada de caravana*"; the wagoners, dressed in their best suits, cracking their whips on the way to the customhouse; and the round of *fandangos* that followed the arrival of the caravan. It is easy to forget that this was not just an adventure, but also a serious business.

Becknell and his successors captured an existing north-south commerce and reoriented it into an east-west commerce. Other Americans meanwhile entered the region not to capture an existing trade but to create one where none had

This Karl Bodmer sketch captures the artist's first impressions of Fort Union on the Yellowstone in the summer of 1833.

existed before. As the fur trade spread west along the Missouri and Platte rivers and into the Rocky Mountains, it changed its form. Until the early nineteenth century in the Great Lakes country, along the Missouri, and in Canada, Indians had been the primary trappers. But in the early decades of the century white trappers—Anglo Americans and French Canadians—along with Canadian Iroquois began to take beaver.

These shaggy adventurers who hunted beaver in the mountains formed an odd wedge for American commercial expansion. The mountain men, as they came to be called, first moved up the Missouri River, creating a complex series of links with the Indian peoples they encountered. They entered the West as harbingers of an American imperialism that would deliver the West to the United States, but most of them probably never thought of themselves as either imperialists or capitalists. They recognized a more personal reality: they were single men living among peoples of another culture whose values, traditions, and abilities they usually scorned. But scorn or no scorn, they were men who needed women. And their relationships with first Indian and later Mexican women added a significant element to the multiracial and multicultural society arising in the West.

Despite the romantic vision of mountain men and traders as supreme individualists who depended only on themselves, most would certainly not have prospered and probably not have survived without the liaisons they formed with Indian and Mexican women. The relationship between these white men and the women of the West was sexual, but it was also much more. Indian and Mexican women did not just sleep with the Americans; Indian women also provided much of the necessary labor of preparing furs and skins that made the fur trade possible, and Mexican women provided the Americans with the familial connections necessary to survive in that strongly familial society. Both groups of women served as cultural mediators between their lovers and husbands and their kinspeople. Without this mediating role, the fur trade would have been a far more precarious enterprise than it was—and it was precarious enough. Indian women secured aid and protection for the trappers and traders; Mexican women would provide them with access to land grants and trade connections.

Social necessity and human affection combined to make the sexual relationships among whites, Hispanics, and Indians relatively long-lasting. According to one study of mountain men (Americans, French Canadians, and Anglo Canadians), almost 40 percent of them married Indian women in their first marriages, and almost 20 percent more married Mexican or Mexican American women. Anglo American men were the least likely to take Indian wives, but even among them, one out of three initially married an Indian. Although as many of 20 percent of all the marriages ended in desertion or separation, most of the rest proved stable. Altogether such marriages averaged 15 years in duration and produced three children. Those trappers who married a second time were even more likely to take an Indian wife.

The American trappers who reached the front ranges of the Rockies and either turned south or continued west thus were not an isolated white nucleus penetrating but never connecting with the peoples around them. Their relations were far more complicated, their loyalties far more ambiguous. It is no wonder that they emerged both as agents of American expansion and as men not fully trusted by those Americans who followed.

Most of these trappers entered Mexican territory at its northern border, crossing into modern Utah, but almost simultaneously others advanced into New Mexico itself on the heels of William Becknell. By 1823, Etienne Provost and other American trappers were trapping north from Taos. Trappers made Taos the headquarters for an assault on the southern Rockies that virtually exterminated beaver over a wide area. Trappers who had entered Mexican territory in northern Utah meanwhile spread west and south.

These mountain men of the central Rockies were part of a major innovation in the fur trade engineered by William Ashley. Driven off the Missouri by Arikara attacks, and unable to get Indians in the central plains to trap on the scale he desired, Ashley persuaded his white trappers to stay permanently in the mountains. He sent a supply train to annual rendezvous, where trappers and Indians exchanged furs for supplies and engaged in an extended bacchanal. The Rocky Mountain trappers who gathered at the annual rendezvous fell into three broad categories. There were *engagés*, men supplied and salaried by a fur-trading company; skin trappers, the sharecroppers of the fur trade who operated on credit advanced by a company; and finally free trappers, the small entrepreneurs of the trade who sold their furs to the highest bidder. For all of them, trapping was hard and extraordinarily dangerous work. Trappers may have had the common entrepreneurial ambitions of Jacksonian America, but unlike other Jacksonians, they risked their lives as well as their capital. The lucky ones lived, but they often ended up, in the words of Nathaniel Wyeth, who organized an unsuccessful fur company, "mere slaves to catch beavers for others." The real profits went to the large companies who organized production or brought goods west. These companies would maintain the so-called Rocky Mountain trapping system, in one form or another, until 1840.

The career of Jedediah Strong Smith illustrates the peculiar blend of adventure and business that gave the western fur trade an appeal far greater than its limited economic importance. Smith provided much of the leadership for the more northerly American entrance into Mexican territory. He had first gone up the Missouri as a greenhorn trapper in 1822. He survived Indian attacks and an assault by a grizzly bear that left an ear "torn from his head out to the outer rim." ("O you must try to stitch [it] up some way or another," he told James Clyman, who dutifully reattached the ear as best he could.) By 1825, Smith was a partner with William Ashley, and in 1826 he formed Smith, Jackson and Sublette, one of the most famous of the fur trade companies. Smith came to know northern Utah and the northern borders of Mexico well, and in 1826 and again in 1827 he launched a much deeper probe of Mexican territory in search of the mythical Buenaventura River that supposedly flowed from the Rockies to the Pacific.

Smith's 1827 expedition was a disaster. The Mojaves attacked him along the Colorado, killing ten of his 18 men. He and the surviving members of his party found the men he had left the year before, sold their furs, and began traveling north up through California into Oregon with a large herd of horses that Smith hoped to dispose of at the next year's rendezvous. On the Umpqua River in Oregon, Indians attacked his party, 20 men at that time, after the Americans had sexually molested an Indian woman and had beaten a man who had stolen an axe. Only Smith and three men escaped.

Smith made a final venture into the Mexican provinces in 1831. On this last expedition Smith came not as a trapper but as a trader—a trader whose goods, however, contained supplies for trappers operating out of Taos. He never reached New Mexico. On the Santa Fe Trail his luck finally ran out. Searching for water along a notoriously dry section of the trail, he found a deep buffalo wallow that had become a small pond. Around the water, waiting for buffalo, were Comanche warriors. They killed Smith and later sold his weapons to *comancheros*—New Mexican villagers who traveled to the plains to trade with the Comanches. Smith's guns and the stories the *comancheros* brought back of his death were the only memorials of his fate.

Smith's ten-year career is evidence enough of what a bloody and dangerous business the fur trade could be, but romance, death, and adventure should not obscure the extent to which the fur trade remained primarily a business in which Americans took resources from Mexican territory in ways that benefited the Mexicans little if at all. Gaining nothing from a trade that stripped the mountains of beaver, the Mexicans eventually attempted to halt the American trappers. In 1826 the governor of New Mexico banned foreigners from trapping, but he had only ten soldiers to patrol the entire Taos frontier. Americans either easily avoided the edict or became Mexican citizens. In 1838 the Mexicans declared a six-year moratorium on trapping beaver and otter in the depleted Rio Grande drainage, but this law, too, proved unenforceable. Only changing styles (and thus lessening demand), declining prices, and depleted beaver populations brought the fur trade to an end.

In many ways the failure of the beaver trade to provide any benefit to Mexico mirrored the earlier history of the otter trade along the Pacific Coast. Americans had been hunting sea otter off the Pacific Coast since the late eighteenth century and trading the pelts in China for tea and silk. As the traders depleted sea otter populations in the Pacific Northwest, ship captains began hiring Aleuts and Indians from the North Pacific and transporting them to California to hunt the otter. They hunted well. The number of sea otters was already dwindling in the 1820s; by the 1840s, the Americans had hunted the sea otter nearly to extinction.

A cargo of sea-otter furs was extremely valuable, but it did not take up much room. To fill the holds of their vessels, the ship captains who journeyed to the California coast began to complete their cargoes with tallow—a waxlike substance made from the fat of cattle and used mainly to make candles—and cattle hides to carry back to New England. As the trade developed, *californios* annually slaughtered cattle, dried the hides, rendered the fat, and left the rest of the animal to rot. Hides and tallow replaced the dwindling sea otter as California's largest export. American ships trading along the coast, usually in violation of Mexican regulations, became floating country stores that bartered American manufactures for cattle hides and tallow. As a British resident of Monterey in the 1840s reported: "There is not a yard of tape, a pin, or a piece of domestic cotton or even thread that does not come from the United States."

Just as Josiah Gregg transformed commerce into literature in *The Commerce of the Prairies*, so Richard Henry Dana preserved this California trade in his *Two Years Before the Mast*. Dana, a Harvard student who shipped out to California to recover his health, captured the combination of fascination and disdain that Americans brought to their encounter with the inhabitants of Mexico's northern provinces. The *californios* were, he thought "an idle thriftless people, and can make nothing for themselves." Indians did "all the hard work." Yet the people had fine figures and courteous manners, and there were, Dana concluded, "probably no better riders in the world." Dana, as an American, attributed the ability of Americans to capture the wealth of California to the idleness of Mexicans, but many Mexicans saw something else. Without capital, without a merchant marine of their own, and without a government powerful enough to enforce its own regulations, they saw no way of preventing the Americans from siphoning off a valuable trade. Until Mexico could provide an internal market for cattle hides, the ships to move the hides to market, and the manufactures to trade for the hides, the *californios* would trade them to a people who disdained the *californios* themselves.

The conditions that pulled California into an American economic orbit were even more pronounced in Texas. There, in an attempt to attract settlers, Mexico had promised American and European settlers partial exemption from tariffs and other economic regulations until 1830. During the 1820s, foreign settlers and Tejanos, native-born Mexican Texans, used this exemption to smuggle goods into both Texas and the interior provinces of Mexico. When after 1830 the Mexican government attempted to enforce tariff regulations, it met widespread resistance which culminated in the attack on the customhouse and garrison at Anáhuac on Galveston Bay in 1835 by angry Americans.

By the 1830s the Mexicans were clearly losing control over the economy of their northern provinces. They had failed to integrate California, New Mexico, and Texas into the national economy, and Americans, capitalizing on Mexico's weakness, were steering the economy of the border provinces into an American orbit. What made this process even more dangerous to Mexico was that this integration into the American economy was taking place with the complicity of the elites of New Mexico, Texas, and California. In California, rancheros who sold cattle hides and tallow to the Americans prospered. In Texas, too, many large landholders benefited from their economic connections with both American smugglers and American settlers. In New Mexico the elite *ricos* of the Río Abajo had come to rely more on mercantile activity and speculation than livestock raising for their prosperity. They were the Mexican partners in the Santa Fe trade.

In each of these provinces, too, expatriate Americans settled and married into the existing elite. Many became Mexican citizens, but they had only an expedient and tenuous loyalty to their adopted country. Such immigrants, as we shall see, posed the most serious threat in Texas, but they also existed in California and New Mexico. In California, resident American merchants converted to Catholicism for the sake of trade—"A man must leave his conscience at Cape Horn," was how they put it—and some rose to be alcaldes at Santa Barbara and Monterey.

The appearance of so many Americans in Mexico's northern provinces pro-voked dread of the territorial ambitions of the Yankees. Mexican governors, as did Spanish governors before them, feared for their borders, and such anxieties provided the rationale for granting immense tracts of land to members of the elite during the 1820s and 1830s. Those who received the lands agreed, as condition of title, to put settlers upon them. These settlers would then, in theory, act as a barrier to the Americans. In fact, the governors gave a significant number of the land grants to Americans who had become "Mexicanized" by marrying into Hispanic families and by becoming naturalized Mexican citizens. Americans and the New Mexican elite, already connected through trade, buttressed their economic connections by jointly seeking land grants. Former wolves were being asked to guard the flocks.

Mexico's attempts to regain economic control proved self-defeating. Without the infrastructure of roads, ports, and ships necessary to link the borderlands to the larger Mexican economy, the prohibition of American trade—such as Mexican president Antonio López de Santa Anna attempted in New Mexico in 1843—only alienated the most powerful of the northerners by lowering their living standards and angered the United States. Long before Americans achieved politi-cal domination, they were thus pushing the borderlands out of the Mexican orbit. In many respects by the 1830s Mexico's northern territories had become an American economic dependency, a region whose wealth gravitated toward the United States. Internally divided by growing class divisions, New Mexico, Texas, and California were ill prepared to meet the threat of powerful outsiders.

Repercussions Among the Indians

Compounding these difficulties was Mexico's inability to maintain Spain's pain-fully constructed Indian alliances. Mexico's failure, partially a result of internal weaknesses, also arose from the changing political circumstances in the region. These changes had begun in the last chaotic years of Spanish rule. In 1800, in a secret treaty, Napoleon reclaimed Louisiana for France, only to sell it to the Americans in 1803. These complicated transactions more properly belong in the story of American expansion, but first for Spain and then for Mexico the results were disastrous. American traders established posts on the upper Arkansas, Platte, and Red rivers. Operating from Bent's Fort (1828) on the Arkansas River and Fort St. Vrain on the South Platte, they supplied the Indians of the southern plains with trade goods and firearms. They also accepted in trade, and indeed solicited, livestock obtained from raids on Mexican settlements. These trading

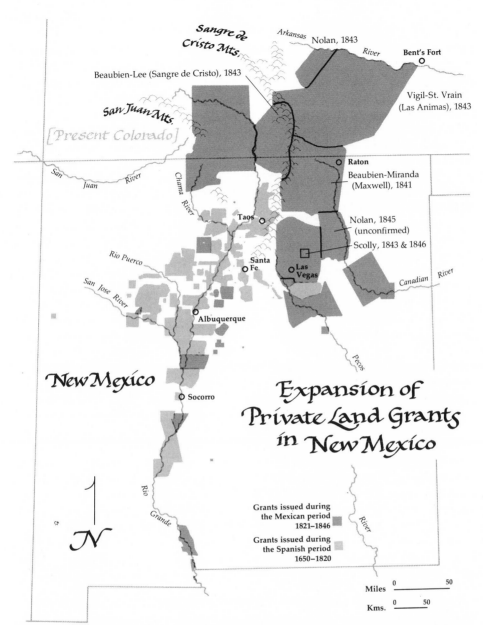

Nearly 150 Spanish and Mexican land grants, as confirmed by the United States government, are represented on this map. Among the largest were those granted late in the Mexican era, especially to foreign-born residents. During litigation in American courts, grants such as the Maxwell grew, the Scolly grant shrank, and Nolan's grant on the Canadian River disappeared. From David J. Weber, *The Mexican Frontier* (Albuquerque: University of New Mexico Press, 1982), p. 192.

posts extended as far west as the Gunnison River in Colorado and the Uintah River in Utah, where Antoine Robidoux, a French-American who had obtained Mexican citizenship, opened posts among the Utes.

The possibility of trading the booty taken in raids on Mexican settlements for trade goods brought by American traders induced Pawnees, Arapahos, Kiowas, and others to raid New Mexico. The Comanches ended their peace in the 1820s. They not only raided Texas and, for a period, New Mexico, but they also struck deep into Coahuila, Nuevo León, Tamaulipas, Chihuahua, and Durango. These new raids added to the terror of continuing Apache attacks in northern Mexico. Indeed, Indian control in these provinces seemed so great that the Chihuahua legislature in 1846 lamented that "we travel the roads . . . at their whim; we cultivate the land where they wish and in the amount that they wish; we use sparingly things they have left to us until the moment that it strikes their appetite to take them for themselves."

In New Mexico itself, the Navajo alliance broke down, and in 1818 Navajo raiders launched a devastating series of attacks. New Mexicans and Pueblos retaliated by conducting slave raids on Navajo encampments. Even the Utes— longtime allies of the New Mexicans—went to war in the 1840s when their attempt to gain reparations for warriors killed by New Mexicans (who had mistaken them for Navajos) ended in a bloody brawl. In California the wide-ranging Utes, the Yokuts of the Central Valley, and other Indians struck the ranchos. Apaches and Navajos in New Mexico and the Utes who raided California boasted they could have stripped the entire country of livestock if they wished, but they preferred to leave the Mexicans a few to breed new herds for the Indians to steal.

As serious as these attacks were, they were not unrelenting. Tribes did not exist as centralized political units; not all bands of a tribe were necessarily at war simultaneously. Warfare was, as before, punctuated by periods of peace and trade. The periods of peace came, however, at Indian discretion. Poorly equipped, often unpaid, and sometimes destitute, the Mexican soldiers could not stop Indian raiding. Desperate for recruits, the government sent convicts to man the border posts; criminals proved an unfortunate choice for protecting the property of the border. Increasingly defense depended on the militia, and militia burdens fell unevenly on the poor, who resented risking their life to protect the property of the rich. Beset by renewed Indian attacks, each region tended to act on its own. New Mexicans secured peace with the Comanches in the 1830s and 1840s by allowing the Indians to pass unmolested on raids farther to the south. By the middle of the nineteenth century, the northern territories were thus not only alienated from Mexico and socially split by deep class divisions, but also divided among themselves in the face of Indian pressure on a scale unknown since the previous century. They were in many ways utterly unprepared to meet an assault from a new expansionist power that had grown up to the east.

Readings

Cook, Warren L. *Flood Tide of Empire: Spain and the Pacific Northwest, 1543–1819.* New Haven: Yale University Press, 1973.

DeBuys, William. *Enchantment and Exploitation: The Life and Hard Times of a New Mexico Mountain Range.* Albuquerque: University of New Mexico Press, 1985.

Gibson, James R. *Imperial Russia in Frontier America: The Changing Geography of Supply of Russian America, 1784–1867*. New York: Oxford University Press, 1976.

Hall, Thomas D. *Social Change in the Southwest, 1350–1880*. Lawrence: University Press of Kansas, 1989.

LeCompte, Janet. *Rebellion in Río Arriba, 1837*. Albuquerque: University of New Mexico Press, 1985.

Morgan, Dale. *Jedediah Smith and the Opening of the West*. Lincoln: University of Nebraska Press, 1964.

Weber, David J. *The Mexican Frontier, 1821–26: The American Southwest Under Mexico*. Albuquerque: University of New Mexico Press, 1982.

Wishart, David. *The Fur Trade of the American West, 1807–1840: A Geographic Synthesis*. Lincoln: University of Nebraska Press, 1979.

Worcester, Donald E. *The Apaches: Eagles of the Southwest*. Norman: University of Oklahoma Press, 1979.

PART TWO

The Federal Government and the Nineteenth-Century West

IN the imagination of modern America, the West has come to stand for independence, self-reliance, and individualism. Rhetorically, at least, modern westerners see themselves as part of a lineage that conquered a wilderness and transformed the land; they spring from a people who carved out their own destiny and remained beholden to no one. This is an odd and interesting image for two reasons.

First of all, as we have seen, the setting is wrong. The West was a wilderness to Anglo Americans only because they defined it as such. Since humans had not shaped the West into a landscape familiar to expectations conditioned by western Europe and eastern North America, they concluded that humans had not shaped the land at all. In fact, Indians had been altering the land for millennia.

If the setting is wrong, so too is the cast. The American West, more than any other section of the United States, is a creation not so much of individual or local efforts, but of federal efforts. More than any other region, the West has been historically a dependency of the federal government. What makes this so striking is that for the nation as a whole, it is the absence of a sense of state—a centrally organized coercive power capable of intruding into individuals' lives—that marked American political culture in the nineteenth century.

Except during the Civil War, most nineteenth-century Americans had little direct experience with federal influence over their daily lives. Westerners were the great exception. Westerners usually regarded the federal government much as they would regard a particularly scratchy wool shirt in winter. It was all that was keeping them warm, but it still irritated them. Westerners, unlike southerners, never actually tried to remove the source of irritation; they were content with complaining. Thomas Hart Benton, the leading advocate of western expansion, set forth the basic rationale for the western dismissal of federal control before the modern American West even existed. American expansion, Benton wrote, "was not an act of government leading the people and protecting them, but like all the other great emigrations and settlements of that race [that is, Anglo-Saxon] on our continent, it was the act of the people going forward without government aid or countenance, establishing their possession and compelling the Government to follow with its shield and spread it over them." Westerners, in other words, took the West and developed it. They owed the government nothing, but under the guise of protecting and aiding them, the federal government has been irritating them ever since.

Benton's racial mysticism reveals much about nineteenth-century American attitudes, but his theory of western expansion does not inform us about the actual role of the federal government in developing the American West. Indeed, in most cases the more mundane political history of the West contradicts Benton on point after point. The government did not pursue pioneers west; it more often led them there. Anglo Americans did not compel the government to follow; instead, the government guided and molded their settlement. The armies of the federal government conquered the region, agents of the federal government explored it, federal officials administered it, and federal bureaucrats supervised (or at least tried to supervise) the division and development of its resources. All of the American West, outside of Texas and California, whose early statehood place them in a different category, was at some stage of its history a colony of the United States. The federal government controlled the governments of the territories and withheld from their citizens rights and privileges held by American citizens elsewhere.

While the federal government shaped the West, however, the West itself served as the kindergarten of the American state. In governing and developing the American West, the state itself grew in power and influence. A state, as one political scientist has observed, "can be readily identified by its civil service, its army, and its regulation of the economy." Although often only in fledgling forms, all of these accouterments of a powerful state began to develop in the American West, and they set the West off from other regions.

In the West federal power took on modern forms. Institutions which in the East were locally based and locally controlled became in the West reflections of the federal government. Except during the Civil War, for example, the American army was a western army. In the East, state militias represented the armed power of the American people. In the West, federal troops represented that power. Similarly, bureaucracies such as the Post Office and the Customs Service existed in the East, but the basic bureaucracies of the nineteenth-century American state—the Bureau of Indian Affairs, the Land Office, the U.S. Geological Survey, and other Interior Department agencies—were primarily western bureaucracies. Initially, these bureaucracies were only loosely controlled. The president and Congress made administrative positions with the federal government patronage positions; they were the rewards that victorious political parties bestowed on their loyalists. In these western bureaucracies, however, professionalization and administrative centralization gradually restricted the domain of patronage. The Bureau of Indian Affairs, the U.S. Geological Survey, and the Forest Service had by the twentieth century taken on modern form. Professionally staffed and centrally controlled, they were often more powerful than local political interests in the West. The expanding administrative power of the federal government and its bureaucracies would become apparent across the country in the early twentieth century, but that power took shape earliest and extended farthest in the West.

Federal power could expand so rapidly in the West because rival sources of political power in the states, local communities, and political parties were so weak. Local communities and local politics inhibited the growth of administrative power in the East. But in the West existing local communities were Indian and Hispanic, and they were conquered peoples. Anglo Americans thought of the federal government as a necessary agency of order in the West that did not seem necessary in the East. The government had to control and administer the land and Indian affairs. It had to supervise the creation of governments. And because not all land passed into private hands, the government began to supervise the use of remaining public lands.

This federal supervision and maintenance of order was, of course, supposed to be temporary; the central state was supposed to wither, but instead it expanded. In response to conditions generated by industrialization and the growth of a national economy, the federal government took on new administrative functions all over the country in the early twentieth century. It became, historians assert, "a qualitatively different kind of state." But in the West, this process had begun earlier. This head start gave added momentum to the larger national trend of bureaucratization and made the impact of the federal government on the West in the twentieth century even greater than it had been in the nineteenth.

In some basic ways the federal government created itself in the West. The West provided an arena for the expansion of federal powers that was initially available nowhere else in the country. By exercising power, the government increased its power. The western expansion of the United States thus is not so much the story of a powerful state expanding at the expense of weaker states as much as the story of a state growing stronger as it expands.

CHAPTER 3

The Conquest of the West

AMERICAN expansion involved more than a gain in territory, although the growth of the American nation at the expense of Mexico, France, Great Britain, and the independent Indian tribes of the West was its most obvious attribute. Expansion also involved the growth of federal power and the gradual creation of a bureaucratic state in the West. Each of these aspects of expansion reinforced the other. The American nation that began to expand westward was neither militarily formidable nor a centralized state. How relatively weak and disorganized the United States was in the first years of the nineteenth century became apparent in the almost comic-opera maneuvers of the Louisiana Purchase.

Louisiana Purchase

For all its eventual voraciousness, the American appetite for land west of the Mississippi was originally meager. Western expansion was an unexpected dessert that came as Americans swallowed the last of the lands east of the river. From the time that they had occupied the Ohio and Mississippi valleys, Americans had worried about Spanish possession of New Orleans. That city controlled the mouth of the Mississippi, and the Mississippi was then the only practical route by which Americans living along the lands it drained could market their crops. The Spanish cession of Louisiana to France threatened this American outlet to the sea. By regaining the vast territory of Louisiana, the world's most powerful nation, France, had replaced the decrepit Spanish empire not only in New Orleans but also all along the western borders of the United States.

To President Thomas Jefferson the French presence threatened to change the foreign policy of the United States. With France on the Mississippi, Americans would have to abandon neutrality and, in Jefferson's words, "marry ourselves to the British fleet," because only English naval power could offset French strength. Jefferson's fears were not unreasonable. Napoleon and his foreign minister, Talleyrand, did envision a new French empire in North America. For the moment, however, Louisiana remained under Spanish control. The French planned to reconquer their old Caribbean colony of Santo Domingo, lost in an earlier slave rebellion, before occupying Louisiana. And then in 1802, with Louisiana still under Spanish control, the event that the Americans had long dreaded finally happened: Spanish officials shut New Orleans to American commerce. President Jefferson, who had already instructed his envoy to France, Robert Livingston, to see if he could purchase New Orleans, assumed that the Spanish closure was the work of Napoleon. The president quickly sent James Monroe to hasten Living-

The Louisiana Purchase and Oregon country around 1818. Based on Warren A. Beck and Ynez D. Haase, *Historical Atlas of the American West* (Norman: University of Oklahoma Press, 1989), map 40. Copyright © 1989, 1991 by the University of Oklahoma Press

ston's negotiations. Jefferson authorized Monroe to spend up to $2 million to acquire New Orleans and as much of West Florida as he could get.

Two days after Monroe's arrival in France, Napoleon made a surprising offer. Discouraged by the loss of his army in Santo Domingo to fever and black guerrilla fighters, and certain that Louisiana would be lost in the impending war with England, Napoleon offered the whole of the colony in what amounted to an imperial fire sale. For $15 million and the American government's assumption of outstanding claims by her citizens against France, the United States could have Louisiana.

What the United States was buying for its $15 million was not entirely clear. The eastern boundaries of Louisiana were in dispute. And to the west, no one agreed on exactly where Texas and New Mexico stopped and Louisiana began. The matter would not be settled until the Adams-Onís Treaty between the United States and Spain in 1819. Jefferson, moreover, had doubts whether he had the authority to buy Louisiana at all. He believed in a strict construction (that is, interpretation) of the Constitution, and nowhere in that document could he find authorization to acquire foreign territory. He would have liked a constitutional amendment to cover such situations, but there was obviously not time to have one approved. He swallowed his scruples and made the purchase in 1803. The federal government had settled one question about the extent of its powers simply by exercising them.

The acquisition of Louisiana was not the cause of unrelieved rejoicing in the United States. Sectional identity and interests often clashed with national interests in the new republic. Many Federalists, the dominant political party in New England, thought the purchase had secured only "a vast wilderness world which will . . . prove worse than useless to us." Louisiana, they thought, endangered the republic by threatening to disperse its population over a huge area in which it would prove to be ungovernable. And if the republic did survive, the West and South would dominate the government to the detriment of New England and the Northeast.

Jeffersonians countered such arguments with what would become a recurring American justification for expansionism. The American republic, they believed, would survive only so long as it remained both agricultural and commercial. Agriculture and landownership insured independence and virtue. Commerce insured prosperity and progress. But the maintenance of a society based on commercial agriculture depended on access to land for a rapidly growing population. Without land, the United States would face a Malthusian crisis and sink back into European conditions of overpopulation, inequality, decadence, and dependence. According to the Jeffersonians, Louisiana—providing as it did millions of unsettled acres—insured that the United States would remain youthful and republican. It postponed, perhaps indefinitely, the decay that republicans feared was otherwise inevitable. Jeffersonians proclaimed an American "empire of liberty" in the West; they severed imperialism from older associations of luxury, corruption, and despotism.

Jefferson's "empire of liberty" presumed a relatively weak federal government, but the political maneuvering that came in the aftermath of the Louisiana Purchase revealed that weak central governments had difficulties controlling empires of any kind. The Burr Conspiracy, for all its buffoonery, underlined the dangerous weakness of the federal government and demonstrated how the government had to grow in strength if it were to hold control of the West.

Following the Louisiana Purchase, some New England Federalists, along with some of the Federalists in New York, conspired with Aaron Burr in a plan to detach New York and New England from the Union. Burr was to run for governor of New York and then join that state to New England to form a new country. Burr, however, was not a Federalist. He was a member of the Democratic-Republicans, the party then in power, and he was the vice-president of the United States.

When the secessionist plot to detach New England went awry, Aaron Burr blamed Alexander Hamilton, the leading Federalist of the period, an ardent nationalist, and a man who had long despised Burr. Although dueling was outlawed in New York, Burr challenged Hamilton to cross the Hudson and meet him in a duel. On a July day in 1804 at Weehawken, New Jersey, the vice-president of the United States, Aaron Burr, shot and killed the leader of the opposing political party, Alexander Hamilton. Burr fled to escape arrest.

Burr was nothing if not resilient. With time on his hands and his political career seemingly in ruins, he turned his attention to the trans-Appalachian West, where he saw opportunities on the border. Burr decided to try his hand at nation making one more time. He helped to hatch a conspiracy that involved raising a private army, fomenting rebellion among the French and Spanish of New Orleans, and invading Mexico. He envisioned a new country that would be composed of Mexico, the western territories of the United States, and the new Louisiana Purchase. The logistics of all this were dismaying. Burr planned to combine discontent among the French of Louisiana, secessionist sentiment in the interior, and British support for anything that would weaken the United States. In all of this he had the knowing cooperation of James Wilkinson, commander of the western American army and governor of all the Louisiana Purchase outside of New Orleans. He also had the cooperation of Andrew Jackson, who apparently thought Burr's only aim was to seize Texas and perhaps some additional parts of Mexico from Spain.

In Wilkinson, Burr had obtained a dubious ally. Like Burr himself, Wilkinson demonstrated how weak the American government's hold was on even its highest officials. Wilkinson had become commander of the western army despite having betrayed his country in prior attempts by Spain to detach the western territories from the United States. Wilkinson capitalized on this surprising display of faith by renewing his earlier arrangements with Spain: the Spanish provided him with a pension in exchange for the military and political information that he funneled them. Put more bluntly, the leading American army officer in the West was a spy and a traitor. When Jefferson dispatched Meriwether Lewis and William Clark to find out what the United States had bought in Louisiana, it was Wilkinson who informed the Spanish and suggested that they intercept and arrest the explorers.

By joining with Burr, Wilkinson reached a professional pinnacle of sorts. He was not only betraying his own country, but he was simultaneously betraying his Spanish employers. When it became apparent the scheme was not going to work, he crowned his efforts by betraying Burr. His soldiers arrested Burr in Mississippi Territory in 1806 and shipped him back to Washington to be tried for treason. Burr was acquitted on the grounds that, for all his conspiring, he had committed no overt act of treason. All of this conspiring, posturing, and confusion indicates that territorial expansion had begun before the federal government was powerful enough to control its new territories. But Louisiana's very acquisition and the task of exploring it and dealing with the Indians who inhabited it had in and of themselves begun a process that would eventually strengthen the state.

Texas

In acquiring Louisiana the federal government had increased its potential power even as it had demonstrated its own weakness and the strong pull of sectional loyalties. A similar situation developed when federal officials attempted to acquire Texas. Texas forms a link between American expansion east and west of the Mississippi. American filibusters—armed private American citizens intervening in the affairs of another country—played the crucial role. Federal officials cheered them on from the sidelines. Such filibustering by Americans, either invaders from the outside or people who were actually living in the region being subverted, had been common in Florida and had helped convince Spain that holding onto that province was impossible.

The response of first Spain and then Mexico to American filibustering seems in hindsight an odd one. The Spanish and the Mexicans tried to use American immigrants both as a barrier to Indian raiders and to block the annexation of their territory by the United States. They believed that they could make American immigrants loyal citizens of their adopted country. Following this logic, Spanish officials in 1821 had negotiated an agreement with Moses Austin to bring 300 Catholic families to settle in Texas in exchange for a grant on the Brazos River.

The revolution against Spain voided this contract, but the colonization policy of the new Mexican government closely followed the Spanish precedent. The Mexican Colonization Law of 1824 guaranteed land, security, and exemption from taxes for four years to foreign settlers. The law, indicating a lingering doubt over the loyalty of immigrants, prohibited foreign settlement along international borders and the seacoast and indicated a preference to granting land to Mexican citizens, but otherwise the Mexican government placed few restrictions on the immigrants.

In promoting immigration Mexico was simply following the same policy of attracting foreigners that brought growth to the United States. There was, however, a major difference. The U.S. government did not depend on the immigrants it attracted to repel attacks from their home country on American territory. Mexican officials did need immigrant assistance to defend Texas. Mexican officials hoped eventually to recruit other foreigners to dilute the percentage of Americans in Texas, but until then they had little choice but to rely on the Americans. Their options were, after all, limited. Mexican officials could not, in any case, keep Americans out. By 1823 there were approximately 3,000 illegal aliens from the United States settled in Texas, and Mexico hoped to win their loyalty by making them landowners with a stake in the country.

Certainly the Mexicans were generous. The state of Coahuila y Texas offered any foreign colonists able to prove their "Christianity, morality, and good habits" 4,428 acres of grazing land and 170 acres of farmland for a modest fee payable over six years. Such lands were far cheaper and the terms far more generous than those for equivalent land in the United States. These cheap lands, suitable for growing cotton, attracted a steady stream of immigrants from the American South. In practice, however, most of these migrants did not obtain land directly from the government. Instead they came under the sponsorship of *empresarios*, immigration agents like Austin who procured large grants in exchange for the promise of settling a certain number of families on the land.

Stephen F. Austin, son of Moses Austin, was the most successful of the *empresarios*. After his father's death, he persuaded the Mexican government to recognize his father's grant. He subsequently got three more contracts to settle an additional 900 families. Virtually all of these families were American, and Austin theoretically had authority over them and responsibility for them. Commissioned a lieutenant colonel in the Mexican army, Austin was political and military commander of his colony, but in practice he delegated local authority to officials elected by the settlers. He confined most of his efforts to collecting a small fee for land—a fee the settlers resented—and to mediating difficulties between the American settlers whom he recruited and the Mexican government.

Although no other *empresario* was even remotely as successful as Austin, there were still roughly 7,000 American immigrants in Texas by 1830, outnumbering the Mexicans living in Texas by better than two to one. Mexico, it turned out, could attract immigrants, but it could not assimilate them. The Americans, who clustered in eastern and central Texas, remained isolated from the Mexican settlements of Goliad and San Antonio farther to the southwest.

The dangers inherent in the situation became apparent when another *empresario*, Haden Edwards, attempted to separate Texas from Mexico and create the independent nation of Fredonia in 1826. Edwards's difficulties in getting clear

Empresario grants in Texas and the Southwest, 1833. From Warren A. Beck and Ynez D. Haase, *Historical Atlas of the American West* (Norman: University of Oklahoma Press, 1989), map 21.

title to his land grant provoked his rebellion. Few of the American immigrants supported him, and Edwards's revolt collapsed, but conservative centralists in the Mexican government grew increasingly fearful of the danger Americans presented and undertook measures to curtail American immigration. Under the law of April 6, 1830, Mexico prohibited further American immigration, canceled outstanding *empresario* contracts, and prohibited the introduction of slaves, since slavery had been abolished in Mexico a year earlier. Mexican officials realized it would take more than laws to keep Americans out, but they hoped that a combination of increased military occupation and countercolonization by Mexicans and Europeans would save the region.

These measures were not effective. Stronger garrisons did move in, but countercolonization largely failed. Illegal immigration from the United States actually increased. By 1835, Anglo American immigrants along with their approximately 3,000 slaves numbered slightly over 30,000 people. The garrisons alone could not keep out the Americans when the Mexican government itself was in the midst of revolution, turmoil, and upheaval, and many Tejanos, or Spanish-speaking inhabitants of Texas, themselves welcomed the immigrants. The Tejano elite in particular saw immigration and the economic growth it brought as crucial to their own prosperity, and they shared with the Americans a desire to maintain slavery in the province. In November 1833 the Mexican government abandoned the attempt to restrict immigration and rescinded the ban on American immigration.

As American immigrants grew more numerous, they also grew more restive. The causes of their discontent were varied, but they hardly sprang from persecution. Many of their complaints differed little from those made by inhabitants of other border provinces. They resented Texas' lack of autonomy and had numerous, justifiable grievances against a slow, cumbersome, and often arbitrary legal system. Other complaints arose from the desire of American immigrants to form what essentially would be an American republic within Mexico. The American migrants wanted a freer trade with the United States. They also wanted a legal recognition of slavery in Texas. In this a familiar pattern reappeared: Anglo Americans demanded greater political liberty for themselves even as they demanded the right to enslave others.

One supposed cause of discontent among American immigrants that popular histories frequently cite today as a cause of the Texas revolt had, however, little to do with the rebellion. Texans did not fight for freedom of religion. This simply was not an issue. Catholicism was the established church in Mexico, and a nominal condition of immigration into Texas, but Mexican officials never forced it on the Texans. As in the other border provinces, the Catholic church lacked the means to minister to its own communicants, let alone the means to force others into its nonexistent churches. Indeed, the state of Coahuila y Texas, in its zeal to encourage immigration, guaranteed in 1834 that "no person shall be molested for religious or political opinions provided the public order is not disturbed."

Political and economic discontent united the Americans in Texas, but in seeking solutions to their problems, they divided into the so-called war and peace parties. The peace party, led by Stephen Austin, saw the chance for obtaining redress for their grievances by attaining greater autonomy within the Mexican republic. Their tactics aligned them with those Mexican liberals struggling for decentralization in a federalist Mexico. The war party, led by William Travis, demanded independence from Mexico itself. Travis was an Alabama lawyer who, after killing a man in his home state, abandoned his wife and fled to Texas. For most of the early 1830s the peace party not only had the most support but also was relatively successful in achieving its ends. By 1834, Austin had secured judicial reforms, greater self-government, and increased representation for Texans. He had not, however, won statehood for Texas within the Mexican republic, and before he could, Mexican politics overtook him.

Mexico in 1834 was drifting toward civil war. When General Antonio López de Santa Anna abandoned liberalism and became a dictator in a conservative, centralized government, revolts broke out in the provinces. Austin, in Mexico City at the time, had written an inflammatory letter that seemed to encourage such revolts, and he was arrested. In Texas, meanwhile, the war party saw its opportunity. In June 1835, 30 members of the war party forced the surrender of the tiny garrison and the customhouse at Anáhuac. Although communities throughout Texas disavowed the revolt, Texas authorities failed to apprehend the rebels. The Mexican government concluded that only force could resolve the situation, and by the end of 1835 it had decided to send additional troops northward. Rumors that these troops would free slaves, enslave Texans, and loot the province alarmed and united the Anglo Americans. By 1835 even Austin's position had shifted. Freed from prison, he now supported what he saw as inevitable separation from Mexico and annexation by the United States. He wished, unrealistically, only that it be peaceful.

Anglo Americans in Texas took up arms, but they did not initially declare independence. Instead they resisted in the name of liberal federalist principles. Such a stance gained them some Tejano support. Most Tejanos and Mexican liberals as a whole, however, distrusted the intentions of the Texans. Their distrust was well founded, for the Texans had already sent a delegation, including Austin, to Washington to feel out the American reaction to annexation. In early March of 1836, the Texans of both parties abandoned any pretense of seeking greater autonomy within Mexico and declared their independence. The Texans accomplished all this amidst revolutionary maneuverings more appropriate to Groucho than to Karl Marx. Texas initially boasted armies with officers and no soldiers and a separate volunteer army that refused to acknowledge the officers of the new republican government. It had for a time two competing governors and four supreme commanders. Some of the new arrivals from the United States, such as former Congressman Davy Crockett, late of Tennessee, hoped that their political careers, moribund in the United States, might be revived in Texas.

While Texans attempted to organize resistance, Santa Anna personally led forces to suppress the revolt and to eradicate Anglo American control of Texas. At a terrible cost to his own army, he won early victories at the Alamo in San Antonio, where Travis and Crockett died along with all the other defenders, and at Goliad. At Goliad, Santa Anna ordered the execution of 371 rebel prisoners. He considered those who were shot to be mercenaries and pirates, since most of them were not Texans but recent arrivals from the United States. By the end of March 1836, Santa Anna believed that he had broken Texan resistance. Texans panicked, and in what became known as the Runaway Scrape thousands fled east before the Mexican army, which Santa Anna had divided into columns to destroy the farms and ranches of Texas.

In April the Texans, under Sam Houston, who had outlasted his rivals to command the Texan army, finally halted their retreat at the San Jacinto River. Santa Anna, having split his army, had only 1,100 or 1,200 troops with him. He disdained the 900 Texans he faced, his disdain led to carelessness, and his carelessness allowed the Texans to surprise the Mexican camp. The battle took only a few minutes; the ensuing slaughter took longer. As Mexicans had slaughtered Texan prisoners, so the Texans slaughtered the Mexicans. Santa Anna survived, and the treaty he signed under obvious duress gave Texas its independence. A new Mexican government disavowed both Santa Anna and his treaty, but as Mexico was unable to reconquer Texas, merely withholding recognition did not change the fact that Texas was independent.

This was an independence that would serve the interests of the Anglo Americans who had fought for it more than those Tejanos who had joined them. The most prominent of the Tejanos who had fought alongside the rebels in the Texas revolt, Juan Nepomuceno Seguín, later fled independent Texas, fearful for the safety of his family amidst Texans who doubted his loyalty. He said that the Texans had made him and other Tejanos foreigners in their native land.

Most Texans assumed that the outcome of their revolt would be the rapid annexation of their republic by the United States. The United States had, after all, already unsuccessfully attempted to purchase Texas. The American ambassador, Joel R. Poinsett, who later brought back from Mexico the colorful plants that now bear his name, had interfered egregiously but futilely in Mexican internal affairs in trying to acquire Texas in 1825. Poinsett's replacement, Anthony Butler, advocated more straightforward tactics. When bribery failed, he advised President Andrew Jackson to seize Texas by force.

The American desire for Texas, however, proved to be less than universal. Growing sectional divisions in the United States undercut support for annexation. The United States recognized the independence of Texas, and American citizens continued to migrate into the new country, but Congress refused to annex it. Many northerners believed that the United States had violated its own pledge of neutrality and had aided the Texas rebels by allowing men and supplies to flow across the border. Many more northerners feared adding so large a slave territory to the Union. As a result, between 1836 and 1843 in the Jackson, Van Buren, and Harrison administrations, the United States rebuffed Texan overtures for annexation. Texas became an independent republic.

The federal government remained as yet too weak to assert control over adjoining territories even when the majority of the people in those territories desired annexation. Americans had seized Texas, but the United States in the 1830s could not absorb Texas. The United States was not yet a centralized state; it had instead evolved into a union of two often antagonistic sections, one slaveholding and one free. Only when political representatives of those sections reached a consensus could the federal government act with confidence. To do otherwise threatened to upset the delicate balance that held the republic together. Because of this need for balance, expansionist pressures within the American republic took on an odd form before 1845. U.S. citizens and private organizations agitated and even seized foreign territory with the implicit approval of some federal officials, but these same federal officials could not forge the sectional consensus necessary to annex the territory. This had happened in Texas, and in a different manner it happened in Oregon.

Oregon

As a region, Oregon was far more ambiguously a part of a foreign state than was Texas. The Americans and British had jointly occupied much of the Pacific Northwest for a considerable time. In the spring of 1792 two ship captains, one American and one British, met in the waters off the Northwest Coast. The American, Robert Gray, was a private fur trader and commander of the ship *Columbia*. The Englishman, George Vancouver, was a British naval officer in charge of a squadron sent both to find a Northwest Passage across the continent and to reclaim a British fur trading outpost on Nootka Sound seized earlier by the Spanish. After their brief meeting, Gray traveled south, where he became the first person of European descent to sail into the mouth of the Columbia. His stay was brief, barely recorded, and for years largely ignored. Vancouver continued north, where, in the course of the extended labor of creating the first reliable maps of the Pacific Coast from Alaska to California, he became the first European to sail into Puget Sound. Vancouver was a self-conscious imperialist bent on expanding the English empire. Gray merely wanted some furs. And yet Gray, not Vancouver, laid the basis for a successful imperial claim in the region.

The American government did not make a serious claim to the Pacific North-west until it purchased Louisiana, the western boundaries of which were the crest of the Rocky Mountains. Then, relying on the principle of contiguity (a doctrine which held that the claims of a country bordering on a disputed region were, all other things being equal, better than those of a more distant nation), it laid claim to the lands drained by the Columbia. Beyond contiguity, the American claim relied on Gray's "discovery" and a hodgepodge of other American intrusions into the region. Meriwether Lewis and William Clark had partially explored and mapped the Columbia River region in 1803–1804. And John Jacob Astor's Pacific Fur Company had established Astoria as a fur trade outpost at the mouth of the Columbia in 1811–12.

Meanwhile, the British used Vancouver's explorations as the basis of claims of their own. They buttressed these claims with the explorations of David Thompson, the geographer of the North West Company who explored and mapped the Columbia south from its headwaters to its mouth, and with trading posts the company opened in what is now British Columbia and Washington.

In part, too, the question of who had the best claim to Oregon revolved around a rather silly incident that occurred in 1813. In 1812 the North West Company bought Astoria from the Americans. The English government did not know about the purchase, and when the War of 1812 broke out, they sent out a ship to seize the post. The ship arrived in 1813. Undeterred by the lack of Americans to fight, the British navy "conquered" Astoria during the War of 1812. And so matters rested until the Americans and the British negotiated peace in 1814. The peace treaty that ended the war, however, specified that each belligerent was to return all the territory that it had conquered with the exception of a few islands.

Astoria itself was not mentioned in the treaty, but that small post had became central to the American claim to the region. Since Astoria had been "conquered," the Americans insisted that it should be returned according to the treaty. They went on to assert that all of the territory south of the 49th parallel, the present boundary, belonged to the United States. The British refused to restore Astoria. They claimed that they had bought it before they conquered it. The Americans threatened to reoccupy Astoria without delay.

The United States was, however, a weak country with a small navy; there were not any ships immediately available to send to the Pacific. It was 1818, four years after the treaty, before the sloop *Ontario* departed to make a peaceful demonstration of the American claim to the Columbia. Captain Biddle of the *Ontario* landed near the mouth of the Columbia in August that year. Before a bewildered group of Chinook Indians, he turned up a piece of sod, flew the flag, had his crew give three cheers, and nailed an inscribed leaden plate to a tree to claim possession. When he sailed away, the Chinooks took the lead plate down and put it to more practical use.

The arrival of the *Ontario* triggered a compromise. Britain agreed to restore Astoria to the United States, but negotiations broke down over the boundary issue. The Americans demanded the 49th parallel, and the British insisted on the Columbia River. For the time being both nations agreed to a joint occupation of Oregon Territory. During the next twenty years negotiations proceeded fitfully. Although the two sides did not reach an agreement, American diplomats proved more than a match for their British counterparts. They used British procedural errors and their own acquisition of Spanish claims to the region to strengthen an originally weak claim.

American diplomatic skill was particularly important, given what threatened to become a de facto British occupation of the region. In 1821 the British crown gave the Hudson's Bay Company an exclusive charter to trade in the Oregon country. Under Dr. John McLoughlin, the company established a series of posts north of the Columbia. At those posts, which relied heavily on Indian labor, the British not only traded for furs but also grew crops and raised sheep and cattle. To deter American penetration of the region, the company attempted to trap out the Snake River valley and the lands surrounding it. They hoped American trappers and traders, faced with a fur desert, would go elsewhere. Such efforts, however, involved the open violation of American law by incursions into American territory that had been acquired by the Louisiana Purchase. Americans, of course, were simultaneously trapping out beaver in Mexican territory in open violation of Mexican law. Americans ignored Mexican laws, but Britain ordered the Hudson's Bay Company to desist.

Although American agitation to occupy the Oregon country began much earlier, Americans had no counter to the Hudson's Bay Company posts of the Oregon country until the early 1840s. In the 1820s a New England schoolteacher, Hall Jackson Kelley, became interested in propagating "Christianity in the dark and cruel places along the shores of the Pacific." His preferred mode of spreading Christianity was colonization, and he formed a society devoted to promoting settlement and wresting the region from England. Despite his attractive descriptions of a country he had never seen, Kelley secured few settlers. His writings did, however, encourage Nathaniel J. Wyeth to attempt to form his own domestic version of the Hudson's Bay Company—the Pacific Trading Company—designed to win the Oregon country for Wyeth and the United States. Wyeth's initial effort to weld together personal and national ambition failed, but he soon formed a successor to the Pacific Trading Company, the Columbia River Company, which proved no more successful. Wyeth did establish Fort Hall on the Snake River and a farm and fishing station on the Willamette River, but in 1836, Wyeth, plagued by misfortune, abandoned the entire enterprise, selling Fort Hall to the Hudson's Bay Company.

Wyeth's original inspiration, Hall Jackson Kelley himself, arrived in Oregon in 1834. Sick and distraught, Kelley came up from California in the company of suspected horse thieves. McLoughlin of the Hudson's Bay Company, who had received advance news of the party from the Mexican governor of California, received Kelley coolly and eventually shipped him off to Hawaii. From there, Kelley, convinced he was a victim of persecution by the Hudson's Bay Company, returned to Boston to continue as a propagandist for an American occupation of Oregon.

Unintentionally helping Kelley's plan to encourage American settlement were four Flathead and Nez Percé Indians who arrived in Saint Louis in 1831. The purpose of the Nez Percé–Flathead delegation has remained unclear. They lacked a decent interpreter. Advocates of missionary efforts, however, were eager to turn the Indians to their own purposes. For the Indians the trip was a disaster. Two members of the party sickened and died while in Saint Louis. A third died of disease on the way home. The final member of the party died in battle before reaching his home village. But to Christian evangelists whose missionary zeal had already been stimulated by the Second Great Awakening then sweeping the Northeast, the visit became a miraculous summons from the wilderness.

William Walker, a Christian Wyandot Indian who may never have even seen the Nez Percé or Flathead delegates, spread the story of a western tribe so desperate for conversion that they had sent emissaries across more than a thousand miles of mountains and plains. Walker's letter about the visit was published in the *Christian Advocate and Journal and Zion's Herald* in March 1833.

The Methodists and the American Board of Commissioners for Foreign Missions responded enthusiastically but in the long run ineffectually. The Methodists sent Jason Lee west in 1834. Lee chose to interpret his mission rather broadly. He bypassed the Nez Percés and the Flatheads in the arid plateau country and went on to the Willamette Valley, where epidemics had largely eliminated the local Indian population but where the land was good and the winters mild. Around him a so-called Methodist Colony grew. An employee of the Hudson's Bay Company thought that "though the missionaries were not of the best class, yet they were better than none at all." Visitors to Oregon were not even this generous. They, somewhat unfairly, described the Methodists as fanatics with no real interest in the Indians. The missionaries made no converts and dismissed the peoples of the Willamette as "a stupid, melancholy, and . . . doomed race of men."

The missionaries of the American Board had more interest in Indians, but little more success. In 1836, Marcus and Narcissa Whitman opened a mission among the Cayuses that was later to become an important way station on the Oregon Trail, while Henry and Eliza Spalding went to the Nez Percés. The Spaldings and Whitmans redoubled their efforts when the Catholic missionaries Fathers Blanchet and Demers arrived on the Columbia River in 1838. For the American missionaries, the Catholic missionaries represented a threat not only to Indian souls but also to American possession of Oregon. Great Britain and Rome, Henry Spalding thought, were conspiring to prevent Oregon from becoming part of the United States. American expansionism and Indian salvation thus began to become synonymous, because only an American Oregon could produce Protestant Indians.

The instruments of an American and Protestant Oregon began to arrive in increasing numbers after the "Great Emigration" of 1842. By 1845 about 5,000 Americans citizens had occupied the Willamette Valley south of the Columbia. The numbers may not have been large, but by the mid-1840s they were sufficient to pose a threat to the Indians and to the 750 British subjects who lived in or around the string of Hudson's Bay Company posts and farms north of the Columbia. Many American migrants, encouraged by Marcus Whitman, stopped at his mission on their way to western Oregon. Whitman was unbothered by the threat this influx posed to the Indians. For Whitman, the Indians by refusing conversion had lost their rights to the land. "When a people refuse or neglect to fill the designs of Providence," he asserted, "they ought not to complain at the results."

Although the immigrants largely passed through the lands east of the Cascades, they left disease in their wake. A measles epidemic killed large numbers of Cayuse children, and the Cayuses blamed the deaths on the missionaries. Fearing more deaths and resenting white intrusions on their lands, the Cayuses attacked the

Whitman mission and killed Marcus, Narcissa, and eleven other whites in 1847. By then Oregon was, as we shall see, American, and the plateau world was breaking into pieces.

Manifest Destiny

As late as 1844, the federal government, despite diplomatic successes in Oregon, continued to play a largely reactive role in expansion. American filibusters, settlers, missionaries, and merchants were actively subverting the attempts of Mexican and British officials to maintain their sovereignty over large sections of the continent, but for all the sympathy it extended to its citizens, the government proved both unwilling and unable to acquire this territory. The march toward an "empire of liberty" faltered before increasingly volatile sectional divisions. The imperial republic proved unable to forge a consensus for nationalist expansion.

There was, however, a resurgence of republican imperialism in the mid-1840s. To counter the obvious reluctance of many Americans to expand beyond existing boundaries, new expansionists enlarged the older rationale for expansion. Not only was such expansion a triumph for liberty, they contended, but it was also foreordained and inevitable. Not just Texas and Oregon, they insisted, but Canada, Mexico, Cuba, and all the other lands of North America belonged to the United States by the right of "manifest destiny." The phrase *manifest destiny* was the product of a New York newspaperman named John O'Sullivan. O'Sullivan's exuberant and long-winded prose captured the aims and arguments of the extreme expansionists who sought to revive and enlarge Jefferson's "empire of liberty":

> Away, away with all these cobweb tissues of rights of discovery, exploration, settlement, contiguity, etc. . . . The American claim is by the right of our manifest destiny to overspread and to possess the whole of the continent which Providence has given us for the development of the great experiment of liberty and federative self-government entrusted to us. It is a right such as that of the tree to the space of air and earth suitable for the full expansion of its principle and destiny of growth. . . . It is in our future far more than in our past or in the past history of Spanish exploration or French colonial rights, that our True Title is to be found.

The basic ideas here were not ones open to rational argument. They relied not on past experience, but on a future destiny. Providence, O'Sullivan asserted, had given the United States the right to occupy the continent. The intention of providence cannot be easily demonstrated, and O'Sullivan did not really make an effort to do so. He simply asserted it as a natural law that he had apparently discovered by observing what must have been an unusual forest devoted to producing one great big tree. Providence made the United States the big tree for this continent because of Providence's fondness for favoring liberty and self-government (a tendency of providence rarely discerned by most observers of human history.) Before the claims of Providence, legal claims of other nations, let alone the unmentioned claims of Indians who actually lived on these lands, were mere "cobweb tissues."

O'Sullivan contributed the phrase *manifest destiny* to American politics, but contributing a phrase is not the same thing as convincing people. Historians would have an easy time of it if everything written in newspapers or delivered in political speeches could be presumed to have met with the approval of its audience. People who read papers or listen to speeches, however, do not always agree with them. O'Sullivan clearly believed in manifest destiny, and so did other propagandists for expansion, but did most Americans?

The burst of American expansion that began in the mid-1840s tempts historians to believe that faith in manifest destiny did dominate the nation, but if it did, we have some difficult things to explain. Why, if Americans were so eager to have the entire continent, did the U.S. government refuse for so long to annex the large and valuable territory of Texas, whose people repeatedly sought admittance between 1836 and 1844? And why was the Mexican War, which was fought to acquire even more territory, the source of bitter divisions in the country and the seedbed of future quarrels that would culminate in the Civil War? And, finally, why would O'Sullivan himself, the prophet of a glorious *national* destiny, side during the Civil War with the South and try to split the Union? Had providence changed its mind and decided not to give all of North America to the United States but instead to split up existing American territory?

An explanation based on manifest destiny cannot answer such questions because it ignores sectionalism and racism. Manifest destiny was a nationalist doctrine that proclaimed a national destiny for a united citizenry. But the United States was, in fact, a country whose citizens were not fully united but were instead divided into two distinct and antagonistic sections: the North and the South. Manifest destiny also assumed that Americans wanted the continent no matter who was already living on it. Yet most of the people living in territory the expansionists coveted did not have white skins. In a country that was loudly and proudly racist, the absorption of large numbers of nonwhites was a proposal unlikely to draw wide support.

Looked at this way, American expansion was not as much the outcome of a widely shared belief in manifest destiny as it was the compromised achievement of an incipient nationalism. In expanding west, the U.S. government, like the Spanish and French empires before it, acted more from fear and anxiety than from confidence. Expansionism partially succeeded because for a relatively few years expansionists managed to forge a sectional alliance that convinced Americans that expansion could solve problems that, if untreated, would destroy the republic. The irony would be that expansionism itself would very nearly destroy the republic.

Expansionists retained Jefferson's old vision of an "empire of liberty," for the imperial republic would remain a republic of white freemen who made their living farming the land and trading in agricultural products, but they added to it new rationales aimed at changing conditions. Operating in a sectionally divided America only recently recovered from a deep economic depression, expansionists argued that expansion provided a cure for both America's political and economic ailments. Expansion, they claimed, would provide the key to economic stability and prosperity while simultaneously cooling sectional conflict by solving the dispute over slavery.

Expansionists formed an influential political coterie that gained influence within the Tyler and Polk administrations during the early and middle 1840s. Pennsylvania-born Senator Robert Walker of Mississippi was their most successful strategist and propagandist; President James K. Polk of Tennessee became their most successful leader. Their first great triumph was the annexation of Texas.

The Expansionist Presidents: Tyler and Polk

The successful push to annex Texas began in 1843 with secret negotiations between representatives of the United States and the Texas republic. American expansionists offered a dual set of arguments to make annexation attractive. In the South they had no trouble persuading southerners that an independent Texas would inevitably come under British influence and abolish slavery. It would then become a mecca for runaway slaves and undermine slavery in the South.

The major obstacle to annexation, however, was the reluctance of the North to accept another slave state into the Union. Expansionists such as Walker overcame this obstacle by appealing to northerners through a second set of arguments. Walker courted the North by playing on northern racism. Northerners disliked slavery in principle and feared increased political power for the South, but they also feared the consequences of emancipating slaves who might migrate north. Texas, the expansionists argued, would prevent such a migration. Blacks, slave and free, would shun the "uncongenial" north and move south. Texas would rapidly drain blacks out of the border states of the upper South and thus lead gradually to the end of slavery there. Eventually, all blacks lured by the warm climate and the "kindred" races of Central America would move first into Texas and then into Latin America, emptying the United States of black people. Texas would be a safety valve protecting the United States from racial turmoil. Walker did not succeed in converting all or even most northerners to this argument for containing slavery by expanding it, but he did win over most northern Democratic congressmen, and he thus managed by 1844 to turn Texas into a partisan rather than a purely sectional issue.

Expansionists linked their Texas safety valve argument with a commercial argument for expansion, the logic of which could be extended beyond Texas. During the Jacksonian era, most Americans continued to subscribe to a Jeffersonian version of the republic that was both agrarian and commercial. Northerners and southerners agreed that American access to foreign markets was necessary to absorb the large agricultural surpluses that American farmers, north and south, could generate. Without such markets the American economy would stultify. Fearing a recurrence of the depression of the late 1830s, many politicians, including James Polk, saw the struggle for markets in apocalyptic terms. They spoke of a domination of world markets that American control of raw materials would give, but this bravado masked a fear that other countries, particularly England, would either develop alternate sources of supply or close off necessary markets to American merchants. Thus expansionists argued that England wanted Texas in order to develop an alternate source of cotton and ruin the American South.

This economic argument also took deep root among the agricultural states of the Midwest, which in the 1840s sent pugnacious expansionists of their own, usually Democrats, to Congress. These agrarian expansionists stressed the importance of Oregon as the key to the entire trade of the Far East. As then Congressman Stephen A. Douglas said of the Oregon dispute with England, "The great point at issue . . . [was] the freedom of the Pacific Ocean, . . . the trade of China and of Japan, of the East Indies, and . . . maritime ascendancy."

By 1844 northern and southern expansionists controlled the Democratic party, and they nominated an ardent southern expansionist, James K. Polk, for president. Polk made the immediate annexation of Texas and the acquisition of Oregon central issues of the campaign. Whigs, on the other hand, remained far less enthusiastic about expansion. Henry Clay of Kentucky, the Whig presidential nominee, and other party leaders such as Daniel Webster of Massachusetts did not demand annexation of Texas and Oregon. They only desired that friendly republics surround the United States. The vote in the 1844 election provided no clear mandate for expansion. Three candidates—Polk, Clay, and James Birney, an abolitionist running on the Liberty party ticket—split the popular vote, with the result that Polk won with only a plurality. Had Birney's votes gone to Clay, the Whigs would have won the election. In politics, however, mandates are what you make them, and Polk declared that he had one to pursue expansion.

Polk partially achieved his expansionist ends even before he was inaugurated. In the last days of the Tyler administration, Congress passed a joint resolution calling for the annexation of Texas with the consent of the Texans and with the final arrangements to be made by the president. Northern Democrats accepted the bill because it left open the possibility that the United States might later carve free states (that is, states in which slavery was forbidden) out of Texas. Annexation carried on what amounted to a partisan split in Congress. Democrats, northern and southern, favored annexation; it was a consensus northern Democrats would eventually come to regret. Most Whigs opposed annexation, for even southern Whigs could not forgive the renegade Whig Tyler, who had deserted his own party and gone over to the Democrats. To antislavery northerners the annexation seemed a catastrophe. Former president John Quincy Adams of Massachusetts thought it was "the heaviest calamity that ever befell myself and my country." In the summer of 1845 a Texas convention accepted the American offer, in October the people of Texas ratified it, and in February of 1846 Texas joined the Union.

The Annexation of Oregon

Texas was only the first step in the expansionist agenda. In his campaign for the presidency Polk had coupled Texas with Oregon, and he also wanted to purchase California from Mexico. Polk wanted to annex all of Oregon; he demanded a northern boundary at 54°40' north latitude, the southern boundary of Russian Alaska. The successful annexation of Texas fed the belligerence of expansionists who believed that Britain would not dare resist the United States for fear of losing access to southern cotton necessary for English textile mills. But in the confrontation with Britain the weakness of the expansionist coalition became apparent. Many southern Democrats had no desire to risk their British markets to gain Oregon, the acquisition of which would only strengthen the North.

Expansionism foundered on the shoals of sectionalism. In 1845, Polk, abandoning latitude 54°40' north, offered the British a division of Oregon at the 49th parallel. Without consulting his government, the British ambassador refused the settlement. When the English government learned of their ambassador's action, they asked Polk to reopen negotiations. He refused, not only demanding the boundary at 54°40' but also asking Congress to abrogate, or nullify, the joint occupation of Oregon. In the Senate southern Democrats and most Whigs proved reluctant to force a confrontation with England. An alliance of northern expansionist Democrats—the last in a line of "war hawks"—and some northern congressional Whigs who had opposed the annexation of Texas insisted on acquiring all of Oregon. John Quincy Adams and Joshua Giddings, an abolitionist congressman from Ohio, asserted that such an acquisition would redress the imbalance caused by the annexation of Texas. But most members of Congress were ready to compromise, and so, it turned out, were the British.

By 1845, American settlers south of the Columbia were threatening to cross the river, seize the Hudson's Bay Company lands, and plunder its forts. The Hudson's Bay Company, conscious of the danger, relocated its headquarters from Fort Vancouver on the Columbia to Fort Victoria on Vancouver Island. Britain, fearing strife and seeking to rid itself of a burdensome issue, sought to have the boundary arbitrated by an independent party. The Polk administration rejected arbitration and continued to insist on abrogation of joint occupation. Congress, however, while endorsing abrogation, invited England to reopen negotiations. When England once more offered to accept the boundary at the 49th parallel, Polk submitted the offer to the Senate, where he knew it would be welcomed. Polk had reason to change his stance; he was in no position to push a war with England, for the United States had already begun a war with Mexico. On June 10, 1846, the Senate ratified a treaty annexing that portion of Oregon Territory below the 49th parallel to the United States. Although considerable diplomatic skill had laid the basis for the American claim, the government had once again largely followed in the footsteps of its own citizens in acquiring new territory. The next acquisition, however, was to be the product of a consciously imperialist federalist government and would mark a new stage in western expansion.

Outbreak of the Mexican War

Predictably, the annexation of Texas had triggered a crisis with Mexico. Since the Mexicans had never formally recognized the independence of their lost province, the joint resolution to annex Texas prompted Mexico to break diplomatic relations with the United States in March of 1845. Polk aggravated an already sensitive situation by insisting on the Rio Grande as the Texas boundary. Previously both the United States and Mexico had recognized the Nueces River, 150 miles north of the Rio Grande, as the Texas border. Mexican citizens inhabited the sparsely populated land between the two "borders." To support the new American claim, Polk sent American troops into the town of Corpus Christi, just beyond the Nueces, even before the United States had formally annexed Texas. By February 1846, American troops were advancing toward the Rio Grande. In March, American soldiers encamped opposite the Mexican town of Matamoros, near the mouth of the river, while U.S. naval vessels blockaded the port.

Polk applied force believing that a weak and internally divided Mexico would have no choice but to accept a boundary settlement imposed by the Americans. The president's ambitions, however, went well beyond gaining Mexican acceptance of a Rio Grande boundary for Texas. He also attempted to use Mexican debts to U.S. citizens as a lever to force the sale of New Mexico and California to the United States. And he coupled this attempt with the kind of innovative diplomacy well suited to the great age of empire building.

In 1845, Captain John C. Frémont set forth on an expedition with the modest goal of mapping the Red and Arkansas rivers within American boundaries. For reasons that remain a matter of controversy, however, Frémont continued west, pushing on across the continental divide to the Great Salt Lake and then on into California. There his conduct, according to John Sutter, who had established his own small fiefdom where Sacramento now stands, was "extremely mysterious." Flitting about the country with an armed body of men, he was regarded with suspicion by everybody. Ordered out of California by the Mexican governor, Pío Pico, he went north towards Oregon, only to be overtaken by a special messenger from President Polk. What message Polk sent Frémont has never been ascertained; the Pathfinder, as Frémont was called, claimed to have eaten it. But Frémont, either on Polk's orders or on his own authority, turned south and helped organize the Bear Flag Rebellion. In this last of the old filibustering expeditions within the present continental United States, the filibusters no longer had to incite a reluctant government to act; instead, the government itself incited the filibusters. The fighting was quickly absorbed into the Mexican War, but not before Frémont's men murdered Mexican civilians in retaliation for the earlier death of Americans.

Polk designed his deliberately provocative actions to force Mexico to do what the United States would itself never consider doing: yield to the threat of force and exchange territory and national honor for cash. Mexican officials, for their part, publicly threatened war and denounced the United States, but privately most had few illusions about the outcome of such a war and feared its outbreak. They were willing to receive a commissioner to discuss the question of Texas, but they were unwilling to reopen full diplomatic relations, let alone sell territory to the United States. When Polk in April 1846 received news that the Mexicans had refused to receive the American minister, John Slidell, he decided on war. Slidell himself advised Polk that "we can never get along well with them [that is, the Mexicans] until we have given them a good drubbing." Polk had come to agree. On May 9 he held a cabinet meeting at which he gained approval for a war message to be sent to Congress. The *casus belli*, for lack of anything better, would be Mexico's failure to pay her debts to U.S. citizens.

That particular war message proved to be unnecessary. Later that same afternoon Polk received word of a skirmish between Mexican and American troops north of the Rio Grande in which eleven Americans had been killed and the remainder wounded or taken captive. He immediately seized the incident as a pretext for the war he was already prepared to declare.

In his message to Congress, Polk proclaimed that Mexico had "invaded our territory and shed American blood on the American soil": war, "not withstanding all our efforts to avoid it, exists by act of Mexico herself." Congress approved the declaration of war, but as the facts of the clash—a skirmish between U.S. and Mexican troops on the disputed north bank of the Rio Grande— became known, the Whigs denounced the message as "an artful perversion of truth—a disingenuous statement of facts to make people believe a lie." In most of the country, the initial popular reaction to the war was overwhelmingly favorable; northern and southern expansionists backed the president. Only in New England and New York was there immediate strong opposition. New Englanders tended to regard the war as an attempt by a slaveholding president to add slave territory to the Union. Political opposition centered on the Whigs, but although the Whigs

Santa Fe, New Mexico, about 1850. From a lithograph based on a drawing by Richard H. Kern, circa 1850 (James H. Simpson, *Report of Exploration . . . Fort Smith, Arkansas, to Santa Fe* [Washington, D.C., 1850]).

regularly denounced the administration's war, they just as regularly voted funds for it. Talking peace while voting war characterized congressional opponents of the war for the duration.

War in the West

Federal officials had provoked a war, and through the war the federal government grew stronger. In wartime, governments usually gain powers otherwise denied them, and it is significant that the first strong federal presence in the West arrived in the form of conquering armies. It became apparent very quickly that the United States was not engaged in a defensive struggle but instead in a war of conquest against a badly overmatched Mexico. The northern territories of Mexico, long neglected and alienated from the central government, and themselves the sites of numerous rebellions, did not resist the army that the Americans sent against them. The Army of the West—fewer than 2,000 men, mostly Missourians, led by Stephen W. Kearny—took Santa Fe on August 18, 1846, without losing a man. Governor Armijo, either because he had been bribed or because he thought resistance futile, never ordered the New Mexican militia, ready to fight and occupying superb positions near Pecos Canyon, into action. Kearny promptly announced that the United States would retain the freshly conquered province and began appointing officials.

The *californios*—descendants of the original Spanish colonists in California— mounted more effective resistance. At the outbreak of the Mexican War the *californios* were involved in their own conflict with the Mexican government. Their internal disputes preoccupied them when Frémont and the American settlers organized the short-lived Bear Flag Rebellion in northern California. To

The Mexican War, 1846–48. From Warren A. Beck and Ynez D. Haase, *Historical Atlas of the American West* (Norman: University of Oklahoma Press, 1989), map 41.

the *californios* the war waged by the *osos*, or "bears," seemed little more than organized murder and rapine. The arrival of the U.S. Navy's Pacific squadron, under Commodore John D. Sloat, ended the Bear Flag Rebellion, and Sloat took over supervision of the conquest from Frémont. *Californio* guerrillas, preparing to resist the Americans, instead largely accepted Sloat's guarantees of life and property. Sloat occupied southern California without firing a shot.

Commodore Robert Field Stockton, who relieved Sloat in the summer of 1846, and Frémont managed to undo everything Sloat had achieved. Stockton turned the Bear Flag rebels into the California Battalion and ordered them, under Frémont, to march south to "pacify" an already pacific California. Frémont managed to provoke guerrilla warfare in parts of California that, by and large, had already surrendered. Wherever Stockton's men or the California Battalion appeared, trouble erupted.

In southern California the guerrilla fighting became a full-scale revolt. The *californios* captured the small American garrison holding Los Angeles and then in November, at San Pascual, defeated American troops under Stephen Kearny, who had entered California from New Mexico. It was, for the *californios*, the high point of the revolt. After a series of skirmishes with American troops advancing north from San Diego to retake Los Angeles, the *californios* capitulated. In January

1847 they signed the Treaty of Cahuenga, the terms of which were similar to the ones Sloat had originally accorded the *californios*.

The fighting in California was, however, but a sideshow to the main campaign against Mexico. Despite the nearly constant string of victories over Mexican troops that punctuated the American drive toward central Mexico, the war dragged on, and its support eroded. Once Whigs revealed Polk's claim of Mexican attacks on U.S. troops on U.S. soil to be false and the initial patriotic enthusiasm dissipated, northerners again began to view expansionism in sectional terms.

The Mexican War, despite Polk's pretensions, was a war of conquest, and the major practical issue confronting the government became the acquisition of Mexican territory. By the fall of 1847 American armies had conquered Mexico City, but the Mexican government, itself in collapse from the pressures of war, was unable to come to terms. As the war dragged on, ardent expansionists began to assert that the United States should simply forego negotiations and take all of Mexico. The demand for all of Mexico was consistent with manifest destiny, but it revealed all the contradictions of expansionism for a country that was at once republican, racist, and divided into antagonistic sections.

Jefferson's "empire of liberty" had sought to reconcile imperialism with republicanism, and later expansionists made the same attempt. They argued that American imperialism differed from European imperialism because, as Thomas Ritchie, a leading journalist subsidized by the Polk administration, put it: "Our government is not extended by the sword. By its own merits it extends itself." To make such claims expansionists had to ignore wars against the Indians, two attempts to take Canada by force, and many filibustering expeditions, but they often made them nonetheless. The Mexican War, however, presented the most formidable problems for such claims of the pacific spread of the "empire of liberty." Opponents of the Mexican War seized on the contradictions; they contended that Americans, not Mexicans, had provoked the war and that it was a war of conquest foreign to American ideals and a perversion of republican principles. Congressman Joshua Giddings of Ohio accused Polk of "planting the standard of the United States on foreign soil, and using the military forces of the United States to violate every principle of international law and moral justice." Such wars of conquest, the Whigs believed, endangered the republic by dangerously enhancing the power of the president, feeding the rise of militarism, and causing corruption to sap a virtuous citizenry. These principled arguments were rhetorically effective in putting the Polk administration on the defensive, but they were hardly sufficient to prevent a victorious nation from reaping the spoils of war.

More effective was a second objection. Northerners, including prowar northerners, worried that the Mexican War would dramatically increase the amount of territory open to slavery. The expansionists had painstakingly created a coalition between northern Democrats and southerners to extend the nation's boundaries, but now the northerners began to feel that they had been cheated and deceived. Northerners seemed to be paying the cost of a war waged for the benefit of their sectional rivals in the South. To counter northern Whig accusations that the North was expending its blood and treasure only to expand slavery, David Wilmot, a prowar Democrat from Pennsylvania, attached an amendment—the Wilmot

Proviso—to a war appropriations bill in 1846. The proviso declared that no territory acquired from Mexico as a result of the war would be open to slavery. Although defeated in Congress, Wilmot's proposal became a symbolic political watershed. It proclaimed what was to be one of the great issues that led to the Civil War: the question of slavery in the territories. The slavery issue, sidestepped in Texas, reemerged to slow down the drive to annex densely populated areas of Mexico.

In his proviso, Wilmot also capitalized on a third obstacle to expansionism: racism. Expansionists had achieved support in the North by arguing that Texas would provide an outlet for blacks to migrate south and, eventually, merge with Mexicans. But if the United States acquired Mexico, not only would the rationale for having acquired Texas collapse, but the country also would add large numbers of nonwhites to its population. Wilmot called the expansionists on the contradictions between their arguments of 1844 and 1845 for the annexation of Texas and their desire for Mexican territory in 1846. It was a move of political genius, for although many Americans did not object to the acquisition of new lands from Mexico, they did have grave doubts about adding the Mexicans who lived in that territory. Such people, they contended, would form a racially inferior and unassimilable population unsuited to republican institutions. What would the United States do, the editor of the *Cincinnati Herald* asked, with eight million Mexicans "with their idol worship, heathen superstition, and degraded mongrel races?"

By linking these racist fears with republican and antislavery appeals, northern Democrats and Whigs blunted the extreme expansionist demands. Even some southern Democrats, John C. Calhoun among them, eventually joined the opposition to the "all Mexico" movement for fear of allowing "impure races" into the Union. As the war came to a close, the brief political dominance of the expansionists foundered on the shoals of sectionalism and racism. Those who wanted all or most of Mexico were a small minority in Congress and the press.

James K. Polk, whose wish list of Mexican territory had increased beyond California and New Mexico (which included present-day Arizona, most of Utah, and a large part of Colorado), thus found that sectional splits prevented him from gaining all the territory that he desired. Polk's opponents often accused him of duplicity, but at the end of the war he found himself the victim of independent scheming and maneuvering by his own generals and his peace negotiator, Nicolas Trist. In the spring of 1847, Polk had dispatched Trist to work out a peace with the Mexicans, but the Mexicans had rejected the peace terms Trist proposed. Polk ordered his emissary to return home. General Scott, however, persuaded Trist to offer a new and more malleable Mexican government one more chance to sign a treaty. The result was the Treaty of Guadalupe Hidalgo, signed on February 2, 1848. For 15 million dollars and the assumption of all claims by American citizens against Mexico, the United States took Texas above the Rio Grande, New Mexico, and California. Polk was furious. He wanted a larger cession and regarded the treaty as the work of an unauthorized agent. He was also a realist, however. Persuaded that antiwar sentiment would not permit the rejection of a treaty ending the war, he submitted it to the Senate, which ratified it early in 1848.

Territorial expansion after 1846. Adapted from Warren A. Beck and Ynez D. Haase, *Historical Atlas of the American West* (Norman: University of Oklahoma Press, 1989), map 41. Copyright © 1989, 1991 by the University of Oklahoma Press

Gadsden Purchase

The last piece of territory acquired in the contiguous United States came in 1853. Seeking a southerly railroad route, the government named James Gadsden to negotiate a new boundary with Mexico. The United States purchased the land lying between the Gila River and the present international boundary in Arizona, a strip of about 29,000 square miles. Antonio López de Santa Anna, whose career involved the transfer of so much of his country to the United States, was now back in power, and he agreed to the sale. Because the purchase was largely sparsely populated desert, it touched none of the raw sectional nerves bared by the Mexican War. With the Gadsden Purchase the boundaries of the modern American West were complete.

These boundaries hardly matched the dreams of the most extreme expansionists, those who had believed in manifest destiny. Canada, Mexico, Central America, and the Caribbean remained outside the United States. Expansionism was an expression of nationalism in what was an increasingly sectionalist country. Expansionists were a powerful group, and they forged a real if temporary political majority, but after the Mexican War, their very success did them in. As Ralph

Waldo Emerson remarked: the nation would swallow the territory, but the territory would inevitably consume the nation.

The new western territory Emerson spoke of consumed the nation because expansion had left unsettled whether the lands taken from Mexico would be slave or free. Polk had made the federal government strong enough to conquer Mexico and seize a large section of Mexican territory, but he had not made the federal government strong enough to govern the new lands. Hampered by sectional divisions and a deep ambivalence about federal power, Congress between 1846 and 1850 floundered in its attempts to provide governments for the new territories. As one historian of expansion has noted, the United States had acquired a 100-horsepower empire, but had only a 10-horsepower government to manage it. The West itself would force the government to grow, but the effort would be a long and difficult one.

Readings

Fehrenbach, T. R. *Lone Star: A History of Texas and the Texans*. New York: Colliers Books, 1968.

Graebner, Norman. "The Mexican War: A Study in Causation." *Pacific Historical Review* 49 (August 1980): 405–26.

Hietala, Thomas R. *Manifest Design: Anxious Aggrandizement in Late Jacksonian America*. Ithaca, N.Y.: Cornell University Press, 1985.

Hine, Robert V. *Bartlett's West: Drawing the Mexican Boundary*. New Haven: Yale University Press, 1968.

Horsman, Reginald. *Race and Manifest Destiny*. Cambridge: Harvard University Press, 1981.

Merk, Frederick. *Manifest Destiny and Mission in American History: A Reinterpretation*. New York: Alfred A. Knopf, 1963.

Merk, Frederick. *The Monroe Doctrine and American Expansionism*. New York: Vintage Books, 1972.

Pletcher, David. *The Diplomacy of Annexation: Texas, Oregon, and the Mexican War*. Columbia: University of Missouri Press, 1973.

Singletary, Otis. *The Mexican War*. Chicago: University of Chicago, 1960.

Weinberg, Albert K. *Manifest Destiny: A Study of Nationalist Expansionism in American History*. Baltimore: Johns Hopkins University Press, 1935.

CHAPTER 4

The Federal Government
and the Indians

NINETEENTH-CENTURY expansionists believed that the United States was an empire of liberty peacefully extending itself into an untamed wilderness and populating the empty land with settlers thankful for the empire's blessings. But the incorporation of Indians into the United States was not peaceful, and Indians were not thankful. Indians were the inhabitants of the "unpeopled continent," and they surrendered their lands to the empire of liberty only under duress.

Americans inherited a legacy of several centuries of previous Indian-white contact in the West. With relatively few exceptions, they met peoples who already knew Europeans and who had built, to varying degrees, a common world with them. There is no need to romanticize this common world. It was often violent and full of betrayals. But from the villages of Texas and New Mexico to the missions of California to the Hudson's Bay Company posts in the Pacific Northwest, and through the villages of the Missouri, it was impossible to find a social world in which Indians did not play intimate and essential roles. Indians might often be abused and oppressed, but Indians mattered.

It was precisely this common world that Americans were to reject as they advanced into the West. They did not do so immediately, for when Meriwether Lewis and William Clark led the first American-sponsored expedition across the continent to the Pacific in 1804–1806, their multiracial party lived intimately with Indians. This intimacy with the Arikaras, Hidatsas, and Mandans on the Missouri and the Chinooks on the Columbia gave the expedition's members a working knowledge of Indian cultures and politics. This same intimacy also gave many of them a "dose" of venereal disease that was as much in the tradition of contact as were exchanges of gifts and food and the acquisition of allies against common enemies. On the Missouri and in the Pacific Northwest this dual transmission of culture and sexual disease completed a cycle of sorts, for the knowledge that Indians had obtained of European cultures through fur traders had also come only at the price of syphilis. Lewis and Clark traveled through a world where Indians maintained their political, military, and economic significance. They came, as Europeans had usually come, seeking Indian allies against rival European powers and attempting to open trade relations.

Indian Sovereignty and Wardship: Eastern Precedents

Politically, Americans treated Indian tribes as miniature nations existing within the boundaries of the United States. These tribes were often themselves artifacts of European contact, for most Indian peoples did not have political loyalties that extended much beyond their immediate village or band. Just as much as white Americans, Indians were in the process of creating new political structures. The United States negotiated treaties with Indian nations and acknowledged tribal title to land. The United States thus accepted the notion of Indian sovereignty and embedded it in the most basic documents of the republic. Indian tribes became nations within a nation.

Since Indian nations were sovereign, the federal government logically had exclusive control over Indian affairs and thus sole authority to purchase Indian lands. Foreign relations were clearly the domain of the national government. In the East, this federal control over Indian affairs encountered a significant challenge in the 1830s and 1840s that did much to shape subsequent American Indian policy in the West. President Andrew Jackson refused to honor federal treaty commitments to southern Indians and illegally surrendered control over Indian relations to the states.

The issue that triggered federal abdication of its responsibility was the removal of those tribes living east of the Mississippi to new lands west of the river. Virtually all the early-nineteenth-century American presidents had advocated such a removal policy, but the vast majority of eastern Indians had refused to migrate. In order to end the resistance of the Cherokees and other southern tribes, Jackson allowed Georgia and neighboring states unilaterally to extend their laws over Indian nations living on unceded lands within their boundaries.

This unilateral extension of state authority inspired a series of crises among the so-called Five Civilized Tribes of the South—the Choctaws, Chickasaws, Creeks, Seminoles, and Cherokees. Cherokee resistance to Georgia's assault on their sovereignty led to what was probably the most significant series of Supreme Court decision regarding Indians in American history. In *Cherokee Nation* v. *Georgia* (1831) Chief Justice John Marshall, writing for the court, ruled that Indian tribes were "domestic dependent nations," and in *Worcester* v. *Georgia* (1832) he held they were exempt from state laws. Marshall ruled that Indian tribes were domestic dependent nations who had alienated their external powers (their ability to establish independent dealings with foreign nations) when they came under the "protection" of the United States. They retained their internal powers, however, and Georgia's laws had no effect among them.

Marshall's ruling was a ringing endorsement of Indian sovereignty against Georgia's claims of authority, but one which did the Cherokees little good. Andrew Jackson refused to enforce it, and the missionaries among the Cherokees decided against provoking a constitutional crisis by getting a court order that would force him to do so. That the decision vindicated Indian sovereignty— making the tribes in effect a third level of government along with the federal government and the states—was important, but what was equally significant, and less noticed, was Marshall's emphasis on the weakness of Indian nations and their dependence on the United States. The tribes were sovereign, but they depended on the U.S. government to protect their rights; they could not do so themselves. Thus, while acknowledging Indian sovereignty, Marshall also stressed a second and opposite doctrine: Indian nations existed as wards of the federal government. That is, the United States acted in relation to them and their property as guardians did toward minors under their care.

Logically, sovereignty and wardship are contradictory conditions. Sovereignty usually denotes independence and a freedom of people to manage their own affairs. Wardship makes a stronger party responsible for the actions of a weaker dependent. Politically, however, the contradiction between sovereignty and wardship is not so absolute. As articulated by Marshall, wardship and sovereignty paralleled in some ways Indian conceptions of a patriarchal alliance in which a "father" owed his "children" protection. Wardship acknowledged American duties to protect Indian nations. Marshall certainly eroded sovereignty while asserting it, but it must be emphasized that Marshall still thought of federal power over Indians in terms of relations between strong and weak nations. He rejected Georgia's contention that they had authority over individual Indians. The federal government, according to Marshall, had granted the Indians a "measured separatism" which promised tribes homelands largely free from interference by non-Indians or future state governments.

The tenuousness of this combination of wardship and sovereignty became immediately apparent in the aftermath of *Worcester* v. *Georgia*. When the United States under Presidents Jackson and Van Buren proved unwilling to uphold the treaty guarantees to the Cherokees and other tribes, southern Indians faced a difficult choice: they could remain in the South, retaining, at least temporarily, their individual ownership of land but surrendering their political identity, or they could remove across the Mississippi, protecting their political identity but surrendering their homeland. Sovereignty proved impossible to maintain once their "guardian" refused to protect them. Under duress, most Indians left the South.

Removal

The removal controversy, by at once reaffirming and narrowing Indian sovereignty, laid the foundation for Indian policy in the West. Even under Marshall's comparatively generous formulation, Indian nations were *domestic dependent* nations that had surrendered aspects of their sovereignty in order to gain the "protection" of the United States. The United States embedded this reduced sovereignty in the removal treaties themselves. The Treaty of Dancing Rabbit Creek with the Choctaws, for example, not only removed most of the Choctaw people from their homeland in Mississippi and placed them in Indian Territory (now part of Oklahoma), but it also forbade the Choctaw government to pass laws not consistent with the U.S. Constitution and American laws. Beyond that, the treaties allowed the American government to interfere in Choctaw internal affairs when necessary to implement congressional supervision over Indian affairs or to protect the Choctaws from domestic strife and from foreign enemies.

The actual removal of Indians to the West exhibited the vast potential for injustice and tragedy in the new American policy. Removal held out the ideal of continued Indian independence and sovereignty across the Mississippi, but its immediate actuality was the "Trail of Tears," on which one out of eight emigrant Cherokees died on the way to, or soon after their arrival in, Indian Territory. Jackson contended that through removal the "remnant of that ill-fated race" had "been at length placed beyond the reach of injury or oppression." He refused to recognize either the brutal cost of his policy or the fragility of his guarantees.

Removal made it clear that there was no room for a common world that included independent Indians living with whites. The world that existed in the

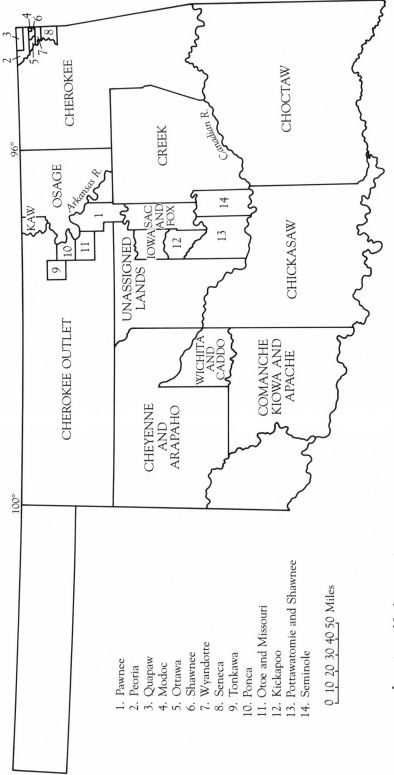

Location of Indians in the Indian Territory, 1866–1889. Based on a map in Martha Blaine, *Pawnee Passage, 1870–1875* (Norman: University of Oklahoma Press, 1990), p. 267.

1. Pawnee
2. Peoria
3. Quapaw
4. Modoc
5. Ottawa
6. Shawnee
7. Wyandotte
8. Seneca
9. Tonkawa
10. Ponca
11. Otoe and Missouri
12. Kickapoo
13. Pottawatomie and Shawnee
14. Seminole

0 10 20 30 40 50 Miles

CHEROKEE OUTLET

CHEROKEE

OSAGE

KAW

100°

96°

9 10 11

1

Arkansas R.

UNASSIGNED LANDS

IOWA

SAC AND FOX

12

13

14

CREEK

Canadian R.

CHOCTAW

CHICKASAW

CHEYENNE AND ARAPAHO

WICHITA AND CADDO

COMANCHE KIOWA AND APACHE

2 3 4 5 6 7 8

Pueblos or in Texas, the world that had existed among the Five Civilized Tribes, was not to be tolerated. Thomas Jefferson's promise that "we shall all be Americans" had yielded to Andrew Jackson's assertion that Indians had "neither the intelligence, the industry, the moral habits, nor the desire of improvement" to live among whites. The message that removal contained for western tribes as well as the Cherokees was that Americans believed that even when a common world of Indians and whites developed, it could not and should not be allowed to continue.

Jackson's refusal to acknowledge a common world only deepened the irony of removal, for in exiling southern Indians to the West, he turned the southern Indian victims of American expansionism into carriers of American political culture. The Cherokees brought west many aspects of their old common world: representative government, the Christian religion of many Indians, and the slave-based agriculture of the mixed-blood elite. The Five Civilized Tribes established governments and laws in the West modeled on those of the United States. Institutions Americans proudly identified as their own came West in the hands of the very people whom those institutions had betrayed and victimized.

In phrasing removal as the alternative to disappearance for a wild and fragile people, Jackson implicitly argued that Indians could exercise sovereignty only on the borders of American society. In the 1830s American officials were briefly willing to believe that land given the removed from the South and the Old Northwest could be guaranteed them, if not forever, then for the indefinite future. Congress set about building up a new bureaucratic and legal order based on the idea of a permanent Indian occupation of vast sections of the West.

In 1832, Congress authorized the creation of the office of commissioner of Indian affairs, and Jackson named Thomas McKenney—a supporter of removal— as commissioner. In 1834, Congress passed new legislation to reorganize the Indian Department, which would become, in time, the Bureau of Indian Affairs. The Trade and Intercourse Act of 1834, a successor to legislation first passed in 1790, regularized a confusing, and legally tenuous, system that had grown up over the previous half-century and provided federal supervision for trade within the unceded lands of the West—the Indian country. The government would, for example, provide trade licenses and restrict whiskey traffic. Before the West even really existed as an American region, it was being differentiated from the East in terms of the American obligations to, the status of, and the federal relationship with Native Americans.

The Collapse of a Permanent Indian Territory

Although not stillborn, the idea of a permanent Indian country died early in its childhood. The architects of removal had imagined an Indian country where whites entered only with federal permission and under federal supervision and where the federal government mediated and kept the peace between Indian nations, each of which had its own clearly bounded territory. This Indian country fell victim to American expansionism. The assumption of federal policy makers that most of the land west of the Missouri River, not just Indian Territory proper in what is now Oklahoma, would remain Indian country began to collapse when Americans acquired Texas, California, and Oregon. Congress had no intention of leaving these new territories to the Indians. Their occupation, in turn, called into question the status of the lands acquired earlier under the Louisiana Purchase.

The weakness of the policy of permanent Indian country was everywhere apparent in the 1840s and 1850s. Migrants encroached on Indian lands along the Missouri and crisscrossed them on their way to Oregon and California. The Trade and Intercourse Act proved incapable of maintaining the boundaries between Indians and whites or of controlling white access into Indian country. Whites crossing the plains inevitably caused resentment among the Indians. Travelers killed and drove away game, particularly along the Oregon and Mormon trails. The immigrants' livestock sometimes ruined the crops of horticultural peoples, such as the Pawnees, who lived near the trails. White emigrants, too, occasionally blundered into conflicts with Indian war parties that were engaged in battle over access to the buffalo plains. The Indians, for their part, raided the trains for livestock and demanded payment for passage across their hunting lands.

The United States attempted to reduce these tensions and create a new order on the Great Plains in a pair of treaties negotiated in the early 1850s. In 1851 the United States signed the Treaty of Fort Laramie with the Sioux, Cheyennes, Arapahos, Crows, Assinboines, Gros Ventres, Mandans, and Arikaras. The treaty attempted to regulate the Indian country by giving the United States the right to establish posts and roads across the northern and central plains. Since the treaty also established boundaries for the territory of each tribe, the United States would hold every tribe responsible for any attacks on whites that took place within its territory. In return, the Indians would receive annuities (annual payments) for ten years in compensation for the loss of game and other damages that resulted from white travel. The second treaty, negotiated in 1853 between the United States and the southern plains tribes at Fort Atkinson, secured safe passage on the Santa Fe Trail. These treaties introduced the idea of northern and southern "Indian colonies" divided from each other by an American corridor across the plains. They compromised the idea of Indian country while securing neither intertribal peace nor the confinement of the nomads to bounded territories.

The United States proved no more successful in controlling its own citizens. On the Missouri border white traders evaded the prohibitions on the sale of liquor to Indians, and whiskey traders demoralized and impoverished border tribes like the Otos, Missouris, and Omahas. White settlers, meanwhile, exerted pressure on Indian lands. The greatest pressure came in Texas, where the state already claimed title to all land within its boundaries. Texas had adopted a policy of exterminating or removing all Indians within the state. Despite treaties of friendship with the Texas tribes that the United States signed at Council Springs in 1845, the federal government could control neither the Texans nor the Comanches and other Texas tribes. In 1848 continuing incursions of Texans onto Indian lands and atrocities committed by the Texas Rangers sparked renewed Indian war in Texas.

Treaties proved no more binding farther north. In 1853, Congress sought to remedy its hastiness in promising the Indians possession of Kansas and Nebraska in perpetuity. Anglo American settlers were already encroaching on these Missouri borderlands, but the government had a second motive in seeking new treaties: it sought a route for a transcontinental railroad. When many Indians proved reluctant to cede lands that only a few years before the Americans had promised were theirs forever, the United States allowed its citizens to persuade the Indians to change their minds. A horde of speculators, settlers, and timber thieves flocked onto the Indians' lands with little federal interference. When Indians tried to protect their property themselves, intruding whites murdered them. Most Indians in eastern Kansas and Nebraska reluctantly decided that they had no choice but once again to cede their lands. In the 1850s there began a new round of cessions among tribes only recently removed from the East; these cessions continued into the 1860s and early 1870s. Only Indian Territory—the lands allocated to the Five Civilized Tribes—remained an island of relative serenity.

The chaos east of the Rocky Mountains also erupted elsewhere in the West. In California, Americans who flooded into the region with the Gold Rush ignored Indian land titles. And through the Oregon Donation Act of 1850 the United States, in violation of its own laws, allowed its citizens to claim lands in Oregon and Washington territories before the government had acquired title to them from the Indian owners. In Utah, too, the Mormons established residence on Indian lands without any federal acquisition of title. By 1850 the idea of a permanent Indian country with the separation of Indians and whites along an east-west axis was in shambles.

The Evolution of the Reservation System

To a remarkable degree, the policy that followed the demise of a permanent Indian country was an improvisation. American officials, in attempting to halt conflict between Indians and whites, prevent expensive wars, and open up lands to white settlement, created reservations the way survivors of a shipwreck might fashion a raft from the debris of the sunken vessel. Reservations evolved on an ad hoc basis as a way to prevent conflict and enforce a separation of the races.

Proposals for reservations appeared in several places during the late 1840s and early 1850s. In 1849 special agent Robert Neighbors, an unusual Texan in that he knew and liked Indians, proposed placing all of Texas' Indians on reservations directly under federal supervision. In California the federal government attempted in 1851 and 1852 to negotiate treaties and establish reservations for California Indians. Californians, however, complained that the proposed treaties reserved too much good land for the Indians. Like Texans, but with much less legal authority, Californians objected to any recognition of Indian rights to land. To protect the Indians from gold seekers after the failure of the treaties, Superintendent Edward Fitzgerald Beale suggested in September 1852 that the government unilaterally create a system of military posts to which the Americans could remove the Indians. The posts would, in effect, be small concentration camps, supervised by troops, where Indians would be subject to a system of "discipline and instruction." Their nearest equivalent was the Spanish missions.

Beale and Neighbors envisioned their reservations as alternatives to extermination in situations in which whites refused to acknowledge any Indian rights to the land, but the goals of reservations soon extended beyond simple protection and racial separation. In 1850, Luke Lea, the commissioner of Indian affairs, forcefully advocated the idea of reservations as a tool for assimilation:

There should be assigned to each tribe, for a permanent home, a country adapted to agriculture, of limited extent and well-defined boundaries; within which all, with occasional exceptions, should be compelled constantly to remain until such time as their general improvement and good conduct may supercede the necessity of such restrictions. In the mean time the government should cause them to be supplied with stock, agricultural implements, and useful materials for clothing; encourage and assist them in the erection of comfortable dwellings, and secure to them the means and facilities of education, intellectual, moral and religious.

Reservations that would segregate in order to integrate were contradictory from their outset. Reservations were sovereign remnants of Indian lands on which the federal government treated Indians as virtually powerless wards. Reservations were paradoxical places where Indians were to be temporarily segregated in order to prepare them for ultimate integration into the larger society. Riddled with contradictions, reservations were to become the hallmark of American Indian policy in the West.

Indian Reservations and Changing American Policy

The reservation system grew like Frankenstein's monster, bolted together from the corpse of the older hope for a permanent Indian territory west of the Missouri. The new policy involved locating tribes on tracts of lands literally reserved either on lands cut out of their previous domains or on lands ceded by other tribes. Proponents of the reservation system argued that reservations would speed acculturation. By acculturation they meant making Indians Christian farmers; they meant organizing them in nuclear families with "proper," that is, Anglo American, gender roles. But this was only a beginning. Many Cherokees were, after all, already Christian farmers living in nuclear families, but they still belonged to a sovereign entity with some control over its own destiny. The reservation was not supposed to be just a place where Indians adopted elements of white belief systems and technology; the reservation was, above all, supposed to be a place where Indians were to be individualized and detribalized. That is, Indians would break their communal bonds, give up their tribal identity, and then as individuals enter into white society. In the words of Commissioner Lea in 1851, the goal of the reservations was the Indians' "ultimate incorporation into the great body of our citizen population."

American policy makers intended reservations to be the means to destroy the tribes as political entities, but ironically, in order to obtain land cessions and reservations, those policy makers had to make treaties that explicitly recognized the legal standing of the tribes as nations. In yet another paradox of Indian policy, negotiated treaties were the means by which the United States forced a unilateral Indian policy onto Indian peoples.

The new reservation policy went into effect gradually and incrementally as Congress and the Office of Indian Affairs sought to find a way to contain the chaos unleashed by the collapse of the idea of a permanent Indian territory. All the early attempts ended in failure. The fate of reservations in Texas and on the West Coast was typical. Despite treaties of friendship with the Texas tribes that the United States signed at Council Springs in 1845, it was not until 1854 that the federal government persuaded Texas to provide land for two reservations. One reservation was for the Comanches and the other was for the various horticultural tribes of eastern Texas.

The Texans themselves agreed to reservations for the Indians in the hope that they would end armed Indian resistance to Texas settlement. Both the reservations and Texas' hopes failed. Few Comanches came onto the reservation; most continued to attack those Texas settlers who encroached on their lands. Other Indians did settle on the reservations, but the Texans, making no distinction between warring and peaceful Indians, retaliated for losses to the Comanches by attacking the reservations.

In California the federal government confronted similar problems. Superintendent Edward Fitzgerald Beale's system of military posts to which the Americans removed Indians was not, strictly speaking, a reservation system. The posts differed from reservations proper. First of all, the government did not acknowledge any Indian ownership of land. The posts were located on small tracts of federal land, and the government could evict the Indians at any time. Second, the government did not create these posts by treaty. The government simply invited the Indians to assemble there.

In the 1850s Beale's system of California Indian reservations eventually included perhaps 10,000 of California's remaining 50,000 Indians. The system faltered and then largely failed during the 1860s. Whites attacked Indians on the reservations, and agents defrauded and cheated their charges. Of seven California Indian reservations and farms, only three survived in 1869.

The inability of the government to control its own citizens and the inability of Indians to make a living on the reservations also doomed early reservations in the Pacific Northwest. The Indians of Oregon had agreed in a series of treaties during the early 1850s to cede title to much of western Oregon, land which the government had already opened to white settlement, in return for reservations in their homelands. The Senate, however, voted the treaties down because Oregonians thought the reservations were too near white communities.

In 1854 and 1855 the Americans negotiated a second set of treaties in both Oregon and Washington territories. These treaties established an extensive system of reservations in both territories, but they eliminated the objections of Oregonians by placing the new reservations farther away from areas settled by whites. The Senate approved these treaties, but they did so in ignorance of real Indian discontent created by the tactics of white negotiators.

The treaties were troublesome documents. In many cases both the "tribes" and the "chiefs" who had signed the treaties were creations of the American negotiators. In the Puget Sound region, for example, where Indians lived in a series of independent villages, there were no "tribes" for the United States to negotiate with. To expedite negotiations, the United States had simply created tribes and then arbitrarily appointed chiefs to do the negotiating. Washington Governor Isaac Stevens proved particularly eager to rush through the treaties; he was more interested in getting land cessions than in obtaining real Indian consent. His treaties brought war in their wake while the reservations the treaties established remained virtually uninhabited for years as Indians attempted to remain in their old villages.

By the outbreak of the Civil War the government's reservation policy had yielded few functioning reservations. Existing Indian reservations, when Indians lived on them at all, were notorious for their fraud and mismanagement. The reservations were political plums available to the party in power. National administrations doled out the offices of agent, teacher, and reservation farmer as political rewards to minor party functionaries.

Reformers and Federal Power

As late as 1865, despite the beginnings of the reservation system, Indian relations in the West seemed an unlikely arena for the expansion of federal power. Widespread corruption on the reservations underlined the inability of the government either to administer the affairs of the Indians or to control its own agents. Federal policy clearly sought to limit Indian sovereignty and to assert the government's own authority, but the result was most often a demonstration of federal impotence.

Widespread violence marked relations between Indians and whites during the 1850s and 1860s, and this violence, too, was a mark of federal weakness. Wars against many of the more powerful tribes were both expensive and inconclusive. Wars against the smaller tribes usually arose from the central government's inability to control its own territorial officials or its own citizens. Wars yielded atrocities that embarrassed the government and raised an uproar in the East. And the very fact that Indians could resist demonstrated the continued practical independence of western Indian tribes.

What made these wars particularly disturbing was that by the 1850s, with the exception of the Seminole and Creek wars in Florida and the Sauk and Fox War in Illinois and Wisconsin, the United States had enjoyed nearly 40 years of peace with Indian peoples. A series of western wars that would last for the next 30 years marked a breakdown in Indian relations that seemed both unnecessary and stupid. The reaction against this period of conflict and near chaos would yield a peace policy during the late 1860s and early 1870s. The policy provided precious little peace during its early years, but it did increase the power of the federal government while diminishing Indian sovereignty.

The wars that began in the 1850s and 1860s fall into three overlapping categories. The first, and most bitterly fought, pitted the expanding Americans against formidable Indian groups engaged in expansion of their own. These conflicts raged most fiercely on the Great Plains. On the northern plains the Americans confronted the Teton Sioux or Lakotas and their allies. On the southern plains they faced the Comanches and their allies.

The second group of wars centered less on American attempts to control Indian territory than on attempts to suppress Indian raiding. These wars occurred most commonly in the Southwest, where raids for livestock had become a basic part of Indian subsistence patterns. American attempts to halt Navajo and Apache thefts of horses, cattle, and sheep led to the Navajo wars of the 1850s and of 1862 and wars against the Apaches that would stretch into the 1880s.

The final group of wars also involved Indian attempts to maintain their independence from American interference, but in these wars the Americans faced much smaller and less powerful Indian groups who were engaged in a defensive struggle to try to maintain their homelands, economies, and ways of life against American aggression. The fighting in western Washington in the 1850s can serve as an example of this kind of struggle.

Wars on the Great Plains

On the Great Plains in the nineteenth century American expansionists confronted groups of mounted nomads who were themselves expanding. The nomads were at the height of their own power and prosperity. Various groups of Lakotas, together with their Arapaho and Cheyenne allies, had gained control of much of the northern plains, while the Comanches had established their own hegemony over the southern plains.

Initial American diplomatic relations with the Sioux were largely cordial. The United States and the Sioux, each for its own reasons, had even cooperated in an attack on one group of horticulturists—the Arikaras—in 1823. By 1850, however, American-Sioux relations had soured considerably. The Lakotas had driven the Skidi Pawnees from the forks of the Platte River and were hunting lands on both sides of that river. They watched with increasing resentment as American migrants along the Platte gradually drove off the buffalo herds, thus ruining lands the Sioux had fought for. In 1849–50 the Americans had struck an even more deadly blow by unintentionally carrying cholera among the Lakotas.

American attempts to reduce tensions instead exacerbated them. In the Fort Laramie treaty conference of 1851 the Americans attempted to confine the Sioux to lands north of the Platte, thus halting their inroads into the buffalo grounds south of the river. But Black Hawk, an Oglala Sioux spokesman, had protested that they held lands south of the Platte by the same right by which the Americans claimed the lands they took from Mexico: the right of conquest. "These lands once belonged to the Kiowas and the Crows," Black Hawk said, "but we whipped those nations out of them and in this we did what the white men do when they want the lands of Indians." The Americans backed down and conceded the Lakotas hunting rights south of the river, an act which, for the Lakotas, confirmed their own title.

Like other nomads of the plains, the Sioux were not a group united under a central authority. They were a loose confederation of bands connected by intermarriage, common culture, and common interest. They did not seek conflict with the Americans, but they expected free rein in their wars with their own Indian enemies. They regarded these wars as the necessary means to expand their access to the buffalo plains and as a source of horses to replenish the herds that diminished with each harsh northern winter. In turn, the Pawnees and the Crows, who had suffered substantial losses to the Sioux, eagerly welcomed American aid against them.

A relatively trivial incident initiated conflict between the Sioux and the Americans, but the confrontation that it sparked had long been building between two expanding peoples. In 1854 a young American officer, Lieutenant John L. Grattan, set out to punish the Brulé Sioux for butchering a stray cow. Despite Sioux offers of restitution, Grattan's soldiers shot and killed the Brulé Sioux chief seeking to mediate the quarrel. The Sioux, in turn, wiped out the lieutenant and his command. This brought on war with the Lakotas in 1855, followed by war with the allies of the Sioux, the Cheyennes, in 1857. These wars demonstrated to the Lakotas and their allies that the United States was now a powerful and determined rival on the western plains, but the fighting settled nothing. Conflict continued to simmer with small-scale raids and occasional murders on each side.

Full-scale war erupted again in 1864. In 1862 the eastern Sioux had risen against the Americans in Minnesota, and many of the defeated warriors and their families had fled west to the Yankton and Yanktonai Sioux. The U.S. Army had rather ineffectually pursued them, prompting hostilities with yet another branch of the western Sioux. While this distant war flared, the governor of the territory of Colorado, John Evans, was seeking to eliminate Indian title to eastern Colorado. By doing so, he hoped to increase his popularity and gain election as a U.S. senator when Colorado entered the Union. He and the commander of the Colorado militia, Colonel John M. Chivington, who had abandoned the Methodist ministry for a military career and now was running as a delegate for Congress, welcomed the possibility of a wider war. War would, they believed, remove both themselves and the Indians from Colorado. Evans and Chivington would go to Washington. The Indians, as far as they were concerned, could go to hell. When the spring of 1864 produced only a few scattered raids instead of general war, Evans and Chivington appear to have been disappointed. Chivington set out to secure the war he and Evans wanted.

The orders given by one of Chivington's officers, "Burn villages and kill Cheyennes whenever and wherever found," suited Chivington's tactics. In May when a Cheyenne chief, Lean Bear, rode toward Chivington's soldiers to demonstrate his peaceful intent by showing them the papers given him by President Lincoln during a visit to Washington, they shot him from his horse and opened fire on his people with howitzers. Lean Bear's murder, and the American desire to punish the Cheyennes for their raids on ranches and stagecoaches, secured the war Chivington and Evans had desired.

The Cheyenne chief Black Kettle, who had been present when the Americans murdered Lean Bear, still sought to avoid the war, however. Together with Major Edward Wynkoop, a federal officer in command of Fort Lyon, he traveled to Denver to make peace. Evans did not want peace, but he could hardly reject Black Kettle's overtures. Black Kettle concluded from the Denver meeting that he could have peace by bringing his people in to Fort Lyon.

When Black Kettle brought his band to the fort, Wynkoop ordered him to camp at Sand Creek to hunt. The Cheyenne chief believed he was safe. But at daybreak on November 29, 1864, with the American flag flying above them, Chivington's command of 700 men, many of them drunk, rode down on the Sand Creek village. Most of the Cheyenne men were absent hunting. In the slaughter that followed, 105 Cheyenne women and children and 28 men died. Chivington's soldiers scalped and mutilated the Indian corpses, gathering trophies to take back to Denver. Soldiers stretched the genitals of dead women over their saddlebows and wore them as decorations on their hats. Cheyenne runners carried war pipes to the Lakota, Arapaho, and Cheyenne camps. The entire central plains exploded into war.

By early 1865, Sioux, Cheyenne, and Arapaho bands had retaliated for Chivington's attack by burning virtually all the ranches and stage stations along the South Platte. They, too, killed men, women, and children. The Indians threatened to sever communications across the plains, but in the face of an American offensive, they pulled north of the Platte. In pursuing them, the American troops once more displayed their limitations in plains warfare. Many of these soldiers were Civil War veterans who had expected to be sent home at the end of the war. Instead, they were fruitlessly chasing Indians across a sea of grass. The troops were sullen and mutinous. Whole units deserted. The long, slow federal columns under the command of General Patrick Connor, dragging their lengthy supply trains, could neither find nor fight Indians. Supplies failed, horses and mules died, and the soldiers nearly starved. Only the help of Pawnee warriors, who had enlisted to fight their enemies, the Sioux, saved them. The plains campaign of 1865 was a fiasco. Coming on the heels of the atrocities of Sand Creek, it discredited the whole idea of a military solution to the conflict.

The military solution lost further credibility in Congress the next year. Despite peace talks, the United States began building a string of forts north of the Platte to protect goldseekers on their way to Montana along the Bozeman Trail. Now the influential Lakota "shirt wearer," or head warrior, Red Cloud, began organizing resistance among the Teton Sioux and their Arapaho and Cheyenne allies to white encroachments north of the Platte. They harassed the soldiers who were building the forts and attacked those parties they could lure away from the outposts. In December of 1866 the Sioux and their allies under High-Back-Bone wiped out a detachment from Fort Philip Kearny led by Captain William Fetterman in a fight that the Lakotas called the Battle of One Hundred Slain.

The Battle of One Hundred Slain humiliated the American military, and the generals promptly prepared to expand the war. They not only planned to retaliate against the Sioux, but they also prepared to attack Cheyenne warriors who had refused to accept their chiefs' cession of buffalo lands along the Smoky Hill River. American troops proved as incapable of imposing a military solution on these Cheyenne warriors south of the Platte as they had been of subduing the Sioux, Cheyennes, and Arapahos north of the river.

By 1867 the expense of these wars, their lack of results, and their well-publicized atrocities had turned Congress against them. In 1868 a peace commission concluded the Medicine Lodge Treaty with the Southern Cheyennes and began negotiations with the Sioux at Fort Laramie. When the peace commissioners promised that the Americans would abandon the Bozeman Trail, the Brulé Sioux under Spotted Tail, who lived south of the Bozeman Trail, agreed to peace. Those Teton Sioux north of the Platte—the Oglalas who followed Red Cloud as well as the Hunkpapas and Blackfeet Sioux—refused, however, to participate in negotiations until the Americans actually surrendered the Bozeman Trail and its forts. The Americans gave in and abandoned the forts, which the Lakotas then burned to the ground. The next year Red Cloud signed the treaty.

With peace seemingly secured on the central plains, however, war flared again. After the Cheyennes had raided the Kaw, or Kansas, Indians, the Americans refused to issue the Cheyennes arms promised earlier. Although Indian agents eventually relented and issued guns and ammunition, it was too late to prevent trouble. A Cheyenne raiding party on its way to attack the Pawnees turned aside and swept through settlements in Kansas instead. They killed fifteen men, raped five women, and reignited the war. The Cheyennes scourged the Kansas frontier that summer as American soldiers organized for a winter campaign. The Americans, in turn, made the southern plains a free fire zone where they would shoot at any band they encountered. Ordering all friendly Indians to gather at the Washita River, American troops under General Philip Sheridan prepared to attack any Indians who refused to come in.

Black Kettle, the survivor of Sand Creek, journeyed to the Washita, seeking to include his band among the friendlies. But since many of his young men were raiding, the Americans rebuffed him. He made camp at the Washita anyway, and there on November 27, 1868, he once more woke to the clamor of soldiers charging at dawn. This time they were federal troops under George Armstrong

In a scene similar to numerous others enacted over the course of the nineteenth century, an 1868 Lakota (Sioux) delegation poses with government negotiators.

Custer, who had followed the trail of a party of raiders to Black Kettle's camp. Once more American soldiers attacked, and once more they slaughtered a camp that consisted largely of women and children. This time Black Kettle, too, died.

After the slaughter on the Washita, fighting largely ceased between the Americans and the Lakotas and their allies. Both Red Cloud and Spotted Tail advocated peace with the Americans, but both continued to pursue their wars against their Indian enemies. The Pawnees suffered terribly. The climax came in 1873 when the Sioux defeated a Pawnee hunting party at Massacre Canyon, killing over one hundred men, women, and children. The defeat prompted the Pawnees, who were looking for a refuge, to abandon their homeland in Nebraska entirely and retreat to Oklahoma. Sioux attacks on the Pawnees were part of Red Cloud's policy of delay. He yielded to the Americans when necessary while continuing to make gains at the expense of Indian enemies on the plains. After twenty years of fighting, the Americans had not yet broken the Sioux.

As the Sioux were to the northern and central plains, so the Comanches were to the southern plains. Americans advancing up the Arkansas found the Comanches a confident, expanding people, the terror of the Mexicans whom they raided and soon the terror of Texans as well. Less numerous than the Sioux but probably richer in horses, the Comanches were buffalo nomads who could call on allied tribes such as the Kiowas and Kiowa-Apaches for support.

The main source of discord in American-Comanche relations was Texas. Texans continued to advance into Comanche lands, and the Comanches continued to regard Texans as enemies even as they made peace with the Americans who traveled along the Arkansas River. The Texans took Comanche lands; the Americans merely traveled through them. American insistence that the

Comanches recognize Texans as Americans led in the late 1850s to war with all Americans—Texans and non-Texans alike—as the Comanches and Kiowas began to strike the Santa Fe Trail. Then, following southern secession, the Comanches discovered that they had apparently been right all along: Texans were not Americans. During the Civil War, the Comanches reverted to their older pattern of maintaining good relations with the whites along the Arkansas while raiding south into Texas and Mexico.

The end of the Civil War made the Texans into Americans again, and the Comanches once more faced federal insistence that the Indians maintain peace in Texas despite the continuing expansion of Texan settlement on their lands. The federal government thought it had secured such a peace in the Treaty of Medicine Lodge in 1867. In the treaty, the Comanches and other southern plains tribes accepted a reservation policy. They accepted programs in acculturation, and they surrendered their claim to immense tracts of land, but they retained hunting rights on those lands as long as the buffalo remained. The government located the new reservations in Indian Territory on lands that the Five Civilized Tribes had been forced to surrender as a punishment for siding with the Confederacy during the Civil War.

The Treaty of Medicine Lodge brought great changes, but they were gradual ones. The Comanches and allied Kiowas now had regular annuities to supplement a subsistence system rendered more precarious than before by the decline of the buffalo. During General Sheridan's campaign against the Cheyennes in 1869, the Comanches and their allies remained on the reservations to escape attacks by soldiers who regarded any Indians found roaming the plains as hostile. Even on the reservation, however, the Comanches still continued to pursue a modified version of their annual cycle on the plains. They hunted the buffalo, and they raided Texas. As one chief informed the agent, if the Americans did not want the young Comanche men to raid in Texas, then they should move Texas far away where they could not find it. The Comanches, like the Sioux, remained a potent and largely unsubdued group in 1870, but other tribes who resisted the Americans were not as fortunate.

Suppressing Raiding: The Wars in the Southwest

In the Southwest the Americans also confronted Indian peoples of formidable military ability, but the primary issue in these wars was livestock and not land. Like the Sioux and Comanches, the Navajos and Apaches sought to continue a pattern of native warfare that they regarded as necessary to their security and wellbeing. There, too, as on the Great Plains, Americans intervened in a military and political conflict which long preceded their arrival.

In 1846 when General Stephen Kearny had conquered New Mexico, he had promised both the Mexicans and the Pueblo Indians that he would end Navajo, Ute, and Apache raiding. This the United States proved unable to do. In 1855 the Americans signed treaties with some Navajos, Utes, and Apaches that would have established reservations, but the Navajos, Utes, and Apaches ignored the treaties, and the U.S. Senate rejected them as too expensive. The United States did establish a series of military posts to curtail the raids, but the raids continued much as they always had. The only new development was that the Navajos, Utes, and Apaches added Anglo American livestock to their list of targets.

Unable and unwilling to distinguish between various bands, Anglo Americans in pursuit of raiders often retaliated against the first Indians they could find, and this created additional difficulties. When the Mimbreño Apache leader Mangas Coloradas made a friendly visit to a mining camp in 1850, Americans bound and whipped him. Later, in 1861, the American military seized the Chiricahua Apache leader Cochise and his relatives for a raid committed by Coyotero Apaches. Cochise escaped; his relatives remained as hostages. Cochise then seized hostages of his own to secure their return. When the soldiers refused to exchange prisoners, Cochise killed his hostages, and the army hanged Cochise's relatives in retaliation. Both incidents prompted wars with previously friendly groups. In the fighting that followed, Mangas Coloradas was captured by American soldiers while under a flag of truce, tortured, and murdered. Soldiers cut off his head and boiled away the flesh in order to sell his skull in the East. Americans sowed treachery and reaped a crop of murder and revenge. For the next ten years, soldiers, miners, ranchers, and travelers fell victim to Mimbreño and Chiricahua raiders.

To the north, American military pressure proved more immediately successful. In 1863 the New Mexican Volunteers commanded by General James Carleton but led in the field by Kit Carson, the former mountain man, defeated the Mescalero Apaches, forcing them to accept a reservation at Bosque Redondo in the Pecos River valley. The militia then turned against the Navajos, whose own raids had increased with the withdrawal of American troops at the beginning of the Civil War. Substantial numbers of Navajos wanted peace, but the price Carson demanded was exile from their homeland and life with their enemies, the Mescaleros, at Bosque Redondo. When they refused these terms, Carson invaded their strongholds. Carson's soldiers did little fighting in the campaign against the Navajos. They confined themselves to burning crops, cutting down orchards, and waiting. They waited while warriors from the Rio Grande Pueblos and Utes, Hopis, and Zuñis—all longstanding enemies of the Navajos—ranged through Navajo country, driving off stock and attacking the Navajos where they found them. Hungry and demoralized, the Navajos streamed in to surrender.

Carson fed them, gathered them in camps, and then marched them south to Bosque Redondo. Three-quarters of the Navajos made the journey; the rest remained hidden in their homeland. The "Long Walk" became an event seared into the Navajo memory, a lasting reminder of the power and ruthlessness of the federal government. It would be four years before the Diné, as the Navajos call themselves, returned to their own country—four years in which the government tried to make them settled villagers farming irrigated tracts. These were four years of humiliation, suffering, death, and near starvation. On their return to their own country, the Navajos received a reservation a fraction the size of their earlier homeland, but despite numerous provocations they would never again risk war with the U.S. government. The defeat of the Navajos and the Mescaleros left only the more southerly bands of Apaches at war with the Americans in the Southwest.

Subduing the Small Tribes

In both the Southwest and the Great Plains the Americans confronted confident peoples who were either expanding themselves or who had a long history of successful resistance to Europeans. In fighting these wars the Americans had little trouble in soliciting allies from among those peoples victimized by plains nomads or southwestern raiders. Despite abundant American provocations, the Crows, Pawnees, and Arikaras all viewed the Americans as allies against the Sioux, who seemed at the time a far more immediate danger. The Pueblos fought alongside Americans against the Navajos just as they had earlier fought alongside Mexicans and Spaniards when faced with Comanche, Apache, or Navajo enemies. Such peoples were not collaborators against their own people, for they defined their loyalty according to community, not race. Larger pan-Indian loyalties would come only after conquest.

For other small groups, however, it was the Americans who represented the greatest danger to their survival and independence. The Americans provoked wars and then harshly repressed those who resisted them. The wars of the Pacific Northwest can serve as an example of such small but brutal conflicts.

Wars of resistance in the Pacific Northwest began with the Cayuse attack on the Whitman mission in 1847; it was a relatively minor incident, but it established the pattern of attack and harsh retribution. The wars that followed in the wake of Governor Isaac Stevens's heavy-handed and deceitful tactics in negotiating the treaties of 1854–55 were both more extensive and more deadly. The treaties created an anger that grew even greater as white settlers west of the Cascades and miners east of the mountains beat and robbed local Indians. In 1855 miners allegedly raped the daughter of one of the leading men of the Yakimas, a tribe of the Columbia Plateau; the Yakimas pursued and killed the rapists. When their agent, A. J. Bolon, came to investigate and threatened them with punishment, the Yakimas killed him, too. The result was war.

West of the Cascades whites feared that the Puget Sound Indians who lived near the mountains and who had intermarried with the Yakimas would join their kinspeople in attacking the Americans. In seeking to prevent such a union, the whites extended the war they sought to contain. Acting Governor Charles Mason of Washington Territory ordered the arrest of Leschi, a leading man on the Nisqually River. Forewarned, Leschi fled, leaving his plow standing in his field, to organize the very resistance Mason had sought to prevent. Surveying the whole sorry history of the events leading up to the war, General John E. Wool, who commanded the federal troops who fought the Indians, laid the blame for the fighting on the settlers and government officials. But it would be the Indians who suffered.

East of the mountains the Oregon Volunteers set the tone for the war when they marched against the neutral Walla Wallas in November of 1855. When Peupeu-mox-mox, the dignified and much respected leader of the Walla Wallas, came to them under a flag of truce, they seized him. They later murdered him, and in the words of a witness, "They skinned him from head to foot, and made razor-straps of his skin." The officers, reportedly, drank toasts from glasses containing his ears.

The war that ensued followed what became the usual pattern in such conflicts. All Indians not on the reservations were presumed hostile and open to attack. Fighting consisted largely of small-scale raids. Both sides burned cabins and villages and destroyed livestock and food. In many ways the Indians who sought to remain neutral fared worse than those who were at war. Confined to small reserves, poorly fed and sheltered, and denied access to their usual seasonal foods, they sickened and died in large numbers. Those who fled the death traps became, by definition, hostile, and soldiers shot them down when they found them.

Like so many others, this war did not end with a decisive action but simply dwindled to a halt. The whites in the Puget Sound region declared in the end that they had not fought a war at all. The hostile Indians, they persuaded themselves, were simply murderers. They hanged Leschi. A supposedly unknown killer murdered his brother, Quiemuth, in the governor's office in Olympia. Quiemuth's killer was never brought to trial. East of the mountains, when initial truces failed, federal military force finally subdued the Indians in 1858. Colonel George Wright's howitzers and long-range rifles made the Indians reluctant to engage him as he destroyed their horse herds and systematically set about punishing the leaders that he held responsible for the war. Wright dispatched Qualchin, whom he suspected of being the killer of Agent Bolon, with an easy disregard for the conventions of war. When Owhi, a leading Yakima chief, surrendered, Wright sent word to Qualchin, the chief's son, that if he did not come in, his father would be hanged. "Qualchin came to me at 9 o'clock," Wright reported, "and at 9¼ A.M. he was hung."

Reform

Wool's revulsion at the war he himself commanded found echoes throughout the United States during the 1850s and 1860s. The voices crying most loudly for reform came from eastern Protestant churches. These Christian philanthropists shared a common American perception of the vanishing Indian. Henry Clay, one of the most powerful figures in antebellum America, had phrased this view to John Adams in 1825. He said that "they were destined to extinction, and, although he would never use or countenance inhumanity towards them, he did not think them, as a race, worth preserving. He considered them as essentially inferior to the Anglo-Saxon race which were now taking their place on this continent. They were not an improvable breed, and their disappearance from the human family would be no great loss to the world." Instead of applauding the demise of the Indians, however, the reformers lamented it. Believing that the final crisis in Indian-white relations was at hand, they thought that the actual survival of American Indians depended on their efforts.

Bishop Henry Whipple of the Episcopal church was one of the first and most vocal of the reformers who came to dominate American Indian policy after the Civil War. Whipple, who began his efforts in the 1850s, was convinced that the only hope of survival for the Indians was their rapid adoption of Christianity and Anglo American culture. In this he differed little from the architects of the emerging reservation policy. But Whipple also believed that the corruption of the Indian agents and injustices perpetrated on the Indians made changes in their way of life impossible. The Minnesota Sioux uprising of 1862 seemed to vindicate his prediction that "a nation which sowed robbery would reap a harvest of blood."

Whipple wanted a thorough reform of Indian administration, but to accomplish this the United States would have to recognize that the Indians' "rude patriarchal government" had been "destroyed or cannot be exercised," leaving the Indian without "a vestige of government or law." Whipple told Congress that it faced "the absolute necessity of providing a government for your Indian wards."

In Whipple's call for Christianization and "civilization," in his attack on corruption and inefficiency, in his belief that war could be avoided through the decent administration of a decent policy, and in his demand that Congress provide for that administration lay the basic outlines of the reformers' program. His program, too, contained the seeds for a sizable expansion of federal power and a clear diminishment of Indian sovereignty. In Whipple's proposals were the seeds of a professional bureaucracy to administer the affairs of the tribes and the withdrawal of recognition for the "rude patriarchal governments of the tribes."

The reformers who came in Whipple's wake anointed themselves the "Friends of the Indian." They considered Indians human beings equal to themselves. They did not share the pervasive racism of the period that thought Indians inherently inferior to whites. Instead, they supported another strain of Indian policy visible as early as 1822 in Reverend Jedediah Morse's well-known report on Indian policy. Indians, Morse asserted, were "an intelligent and noble part of our race, and capable of high moral and intellectual improvement." Politicians, scientists, and a majority of the American public often doubted such sentiments, but the reformers held majority opinion at bay. Racism did not dominate Indian policy until the twentieth century. Until then, reformers effectively argued that Indians were inferior to whites not because their innate capacities were different, but because they, like children, were still advancing up "the ladder of civilization."

This belief in Indian equality perversely made the reformers all the greater enemies of Indian cultures, for they believed that for Indians to survive they had to shed all that made them obviously Indian. If Indians would not do so willingly, then the reformers would have to force them to do so for the Indians' own good. This determination to destroy Indian cultures in order to save Indian peoples gave the peace policy of the reformers a ferocious edge.

The peace policy took its inspiration and its name in reaction to the predominantly military policy of the 1850s and 1860s. In essence, the peace policy argued for a new emphasis on kindness, honesty, and justice in dealing with the Indians. Such a policy would, reformers thought, end Indian wars and turn Indians into American citizens. In the sincere pursuit of this policy of kindness, honesty, and justice reformers would over the next 30 years become involved in the wholesale repression of Indian cultures and the conscious violation of numerous treaties.

The conviction that Indians must be coerced into changing opened up a whole new realm for the exercise of federal power, for the government would become the agent of coercion. This increase in federal powers did not, however, come immediately. In the first and most famous phase of the peace policy under President Ulysses S. Grant, the government actually diminished its power by turning over to the churches the management of most Indian reservations and Indian agencies.

Beginning in 1869 and 1870, President Grant invited the churches to nominate people to staff the reservations. Congress also created the Board of Indian Commissioners to oversee the administration of Indian affairs and prevent corruption. Wealthy Protestant philanthropists controlled the board from its outset. Churches that welcomed the chance for captive audiences for conversion found, however, that they could not find the necessary people to staff the Indian agencies. The missionary boards lost interest in Indians when more exotic converts awaited them overseas.

The new regime secured neither peace nor consensus over how to administer the reservations. Being unable to manage an agency did not stop the churches from engaging in bitter interdenominational battles among themselves as well as fighting with the remaining political appointees. Indian wars continued into the 1870s, and this necessarily interjected the army into the actual management of Indian policy. Many who questioned both the premises of reform policy and the actual ability of the churches to administer the reservations wanted to see the army do more than fight Indians. They, in support of an older idea, sought to give the army total control of Indian affairs. Several times Congress seemed on the verge of delivering the Indians over to the army, an act known as "transfer," but always the proposal failed.

Completing the Conquest

Reformers staved off army control, but they could not prevent the army from fighting Indians. The peace policy proclaimed a peace that the reformers had not in fact secured. There would be a final round of Indian warfare as Indians fought desperately to retain at least a semblance of autonomy. The fiercest fighting would be on the Great Plains.

In 1874 the policy of Red Cloud, the leading figure among the Teton Sioux, began to collapse. He had hoped to conciliate the Americans while continuing to expand at the expense of other Indian peoples, but the Americans proved hard to satisfy. In 1874 an American expedition under Colonel George Armstrong Custer penetrated the heart of the Sioux country, the Black Hills, and announced the discovery of gold. The Americans demanded either the cession or the lease of the Black Hills. When the Lakotas refused, the federal government sent troops to protect American miners who had flooded into the region. Red Cloud, apparently considering war against the Americans hopeless, advocated peace, but the younger warriors, including his own son, flocked to the camps of Sitting Bull, a Hunkpapa holy man, and Crazy Horse, the most prominent Oglala war leader. American troops converged on these camps along the river for which the Lakota name translated as the Greasy Grass and which the whites called the Little Big Horn. The Sioux turned back one American column at the Battle of the Rosebud in June, but a second column launched a strike force of 600 cavalry under Custer. About 2,000 warriors awaited him. Custer divided his troops and attacked. The colonel and those soldiers in his immediate detachment died to a man.

By 1876, however, the Sioux could win battles but not wars. They and other plains Indians repeatedly proved themselves more than a match for the blue-coated federal soldiers in battle, but what happens between battles more often determines the outcome of wars. Lakota warriors had to hunt to provide for their families, and the women needed time to dry meat, prepare hides, and gather wild foods. The soldiers gave them little chance to do so. The army pursued the Sioux through the winter and the Pawnees and the Crows, bitter enemies of the Sioux, now guided the long, slow columns that had previously been so ineffective. These Pawnees and Crows could find the Sioux when whites could not. The war ended in the winter of 1876–77, not through any spectacular American victories but through attrition. The warriors and their families came in to the agencies and surrendered.

Sitting Bull and Crazy Horse took the remnant of their followers to Canada, but even they eventually returned. Crazy Horse would die at an American post

This photograph of Red Cloud's bedroom captures the cultural complexities of white-Indian contact in the nineteenth-century West. Agents often denounced Red Cloud as an unreconstructed traditionalist.

with a soldier's bayonet in his back. The Americans regarded the incident as unfortunate; most Sioux looked on it as murder. Sitting Bull would die years later, shot down by Indian police sent out to arrest him during the Ghost Dance movement.

The murder of Crazy Horse initiated a long Sioux ordeal that culminated in 1890 with the slaughter of Lakota Ghost Dancers at Wounded Knee. In 1877 the Sioux had no way of knowing what lay ahead. But as they surrendered their arms and their horses, they knew that military resistance and the free-roaming life were over. In the Sioux winter counts, the annual chronicles painted on buffalo hides, the Lakotas recorded 1876–77 as the year the Americans took their horses.

On the southern plains, the Comanches, too, resisted and lost. The incident that triggered their downfall was a raid into Texas in May 1871 led by the Kiowa chief Satanta, a close ally of the Comanches. Satanta's warriors destroyed and looted a train of freight wagons, slaughtered most of the teamsters, and mutilated their corpses. General William Tecumseh Sherman, who commanded the American armies, happened to be on a tour of inspection nearby. Sherman, although named after an Indian, had limited sympathy for Indians. They constituted a problem to be solved, and he was willing to solve it by peaceful means if he could and by harsh means if he must. He had supported General Sheridan when Sheridan had ordered Custer's attack on Black Kettle at the Washita. Sherman did not, as Sheridan did, think "the only good Indians I ever saw were dead," but he was not likely to tolerate live Indians who resisted and attacked whites. He had Satanta and other Kiowa leaders, who freely confessed their participation, arrested upon their return to the reservation. They were sent to Texas to be tried

Dead Lakota women and children lie where Hotchkiss guns cut them down as they fled
the soldiers at Wounded Knee.

for murder. Convicted and sentenced to be hanged, all but one had their sentences
commuted. They were eventually pardoned in 1874 except for one Kiowa who
had died trying to escape.

Raiding declined only briefly after Satanta's capture. In 1874, Comanche,
Kiowa, and Southern Cheyenne warriors, angry over attacks on the camps of
Comanche bands who refused to come into the reservations and the slaughter of
buffalo by hide hunters, escalated their raids once more. They ambushed Texas
Rangers and attacked hide hunters on the buffalo range. The government, over
Indian Office protests, retaliated by giving troops permission to pursue raiders
onto the reservations. In 1874, Cheyennes, Comanches, and Kiowas moved their
camps from the reservations and outlying areas into the breaks surrounding the
Red and Washita rivers in the Texas Panhandle, an action which gave the ensuing
war its name: the Red River War. As with the war against the Sioux, the
Americans won by their persistence and by their ability to prevent the Indians
from securing food for themselves and their families, not by battlefield victories.
When Satanta surrendered along with the other Kiowas and Comanches, the
Americans sent him back to prison, where, three years later, according to the
whites, he committed suicide. The Indians said he was pushed out a hospital
window. The military shipped other prominent Cheyenne, Kiowa, and Comanche

leaders to Florida and imprisoned them in an old Spanish fortress. The United States government no longer treated Indian warriors and leaders as defeated soldiers; it treated them as common criminals.

The Sioux, the Comanches, and the Apaches had been the great obstacles to complete American control of the West, and by 1876 only the Apaches remained unsubdued. In the late 1860s and early 1870s, most Apache bands, tired and weakened by constant conflict, had made their peace and settled on reservations. Conditions on the reservations, however, were harsh, and many groups and individuals left to resume their old life. They were tracked down and pursued not only by American soldiers but also by Apache scouts recruited from among the reservation Indians. Defeat here, too, usually came not through pitched battles but instead through the Americans' ability to deny the Indians food and shelter. The key to victory, an American officer concluded, was "permitting the Indians no rest and rendering any and every hiding place insecure."

The last Apache attempts at resistance confronted precisely this kind of strategy of relentless pursuit. Victorio of the Mimbres and Geronimo of the Chiricahuas had resisted attempts to resettle them and their followers on the hot and malarial San Carlos reservation. Instead they resumed raiding. In 1879 and 1880, Victorio raided on both sides of the international border before being cornered and killed with most of his followers by Mexican soldiers. In 1881, Geronimo, disgusted by conditions at San Carlos, went to war. American soldiers and Apache scouts pursued him, allowing him neither rest nor sanctuary, and brought him back. But Geronimo again escaped the reservation in 1885, to repeat the old pattern of raid, pursuit, and ultimate surrender in September of 1886. The United States, as it had so often before with other Indians, exiled these Apaches from their homeland in the hopes of breaking their resistance.

In defeating the Comanches, Sioux, and Apaches, the Americans subjugated peoples who had long contested their advance into the West, but the Americans also provoked wars with peoples who had tried to accommodate themselves to American settlement in the West. The most famous of these peoples were the Nez Percés. Some Nez Percé bands had signed Isaac Stevens's treaty of 1855 and others had not, but all the Nez Percé bands had remained aloof from the Indian war of 1855. The treaty bands had accepted a reservation, and in 1863 they accepted a second treaty that narrowed the reservation after miners discovered gold on it. The nontreaty bands had refused to sign either treaty.

The nontreaty bands had no history of armed conflict with the United States, and they managed to live relatively quietly into the 1870s. The most important of these bands lived in Oregon's Wallowa Valley. In the 1870s their leader was Hin-mah-too-yah-lat-kekht, called by the whites Young Joseph to distinguish him from the previous leader of the band, his father Tuekakas, or Old Joseph. The U.S. government had accepted Nez Percé title to this land, but in the mid-1870s, under pressure from Oregon settlers, it reneged on its previous agreement and demanded the band's removal to the Nez Percé reservation. With resistance hopeless, the chiefs agreed to move. On their way to the reservation in June 1877, however, four young Nez Percé men got drunk and, in anger and resentment over their eviction, killed four white settlers. Fearing retribution, Joseph's band fled, and when pursuing militia and federal cavalry ignored a flag of truce and attacked, the Nez Percés defeated them at White Bird Canyon.

From White Bird Canyon the Nez Percés set out on a tragic and astonishing flight. Pursued by converging columns of thousands of federal troops and militia, the Nez Percés fled, fought, and fled again. Accompanied by their families, two hundred warriors led by Looking Glass and Ollokot (for Joseph was a civil or peace chief and did not lead warriors) crossed the Bitterroot Mountains and moved toward Yellowstone, hoping for refuge with the Crows, their old allies against the Sioux. But the Crows, the Nez Percés discovered, were serving as American scouts, and so the pursued turned north, hoping to cross over into Canada and find refuge among their old enemies, Sitting Bull's Sioux. Behind them in this incredible flight they left a string of defeated and humiliated American soldiers. Most of the pursuing soldiers never found them; those who did, the Nez Percés defeated. The generals looked like fools, and partly to hide their own incompetence they praised Joseph, who in fact was not even the Nez Percé war leader, as a "red Napoleon."

Forty miles short of the border, General Nelson Miles finally cornered the exhausted Nez Percés. A few hundred managed to slip through his lines and flee into Canada, but Joseph met with Miles. "I am tired of fighting," he said. "Our chiefs are killed. Looking Glass is dead. Toohoolhoolzote is dead. The old men are all dead. It is the young men who say yes or no. He who led the young men [Ollokot] is dead. It is cold and we have no blankets. The little children are freezing to death. . . . Hear me, my chiefs! I am tired. My heart is sick and sad. From where the sun now stands, I will fight no more forever."

Joseph surrendered on Miles's promise that he and his people would be returned to the Nez Percé reservation in Idaho. General Sherman overruled Miles. Sherman, who had earlier summarized his own views on Indians by saying that he was convinced that "they all have to be killed or maintained as a species of paupers," ordered the prisoners transported to Fort Leavenworth, Kansas. Shifted from place to place over the next several years, the Wallowa Nez Percés sickened and died. In 1885 the government allowed remnants of Joseph's band to return home. During the intervening seven years the 418 people who had surrendered with Joseph had dwindled to 268. As was typical of many tribes, more Nez Percés had died after surrendering to the Americans than had died fighting them.

From Sovereignty to Wardship

Whether they were allies of the Americans, whether they remained neutral, or whether they opposed the American advance, all Indian peoples in the years after the Civil War saw their sovereignty erode. The national wardship implied in Chief Justice Marshall's formulation of "domestic dependent nations" became instead an individual wardship. The United States would administer the affairs of its Indian wards as if they were incompetent children.

Reformers regarded Indian nations as legal fictions which the federal government should no longer recognize. As bitterly as advocates of civilian control over Indian affairs quarreled with proponents of military control, their disagreements masked a deeper consensus. Both groups disdained Indian sovereignty; both agreed that the treaty system was dead. Each camp regarded Indians as powerless savages and the treaties as a farce, as Indians had no means of compelling the United States to honor them. As early as 1868, the Indian Peace Commission had asserted that the time had come to cease regarding the Indians as domestic dependent nations; Indians instead should be "individually subject to the laws of the United States." It would be better, reformers said, to treat the Indians as wards, to stop negotiating treaties, and to find a "just" way to abrogate those that existed.

In 1871 the United States did abandon the treaty system, but it did so for reasons that had little to do with the reformers' objectives. The House of Representatives had long wanted a voice in agreements with Indians, since the terms of Indian treaties often affected their constituents' access to land. The constitution, however, gave only the president and the Senate a role in treaty making. Denied an equal voice, the House moved to abolish the treaty system altogether. The Senate agreed as long as existing treaties, which governed potentially lucrative transfers of land to individuals and corporations, remained in force.

The end of treaty making, however, neither ended negotiations with Indian nations nor abrogated Indian sovereignty. Congress continued to negotiate "agreements" to obtain land cessions from Indians. These differed from treaties largely in that both houses of Congress and not just the Senate had to ratify them. With the old treaties in force and with sovereignty ignored instead of being legally terminated, the United States proceeded to reform Indian policy by deepening its contradictions. Reformers pushed the federal government toward direct supervision of the lives of individual Indians whom the law now defined as wards of the state. A partial and reduced sovereignty and a new doctrine of wardship stood uncomfortably side by side.

Programs of Assimilation

During the 1870s, the churches lost control of administering the agencies, but Protestant reformers nonetheless continued to steer American Indian policy. The friends of the Indians exerted tremendous influence on Indian policy through the Indian Rights Association, the Womens National Indian Association, and the annual conferences that brought government officials and reformers together at Lake Mohonk, New York. Effective publicists with strong connections in the eastern Protestant churches, Indian reformers capitalized on the outrage bestsellers such as Helen Hunt Jackson's *Century of Dishonor* provoked among the public at large when these books exposed past and present American duplicity and corruption in dealings with the Indians.

Well into the twentieth century, reformers continued to see themselves as a heroic and dedicated minority working for the good of the Indians. Given the context in which they worked, this was not an unreasonable view. Reformers challenged prevailing racist assumptions by proclaiming Indian capabilities and their equality with whites. Reformers demanded efficient and honest administration at a time when Indian land and property was the focus of considerable white greed. Reformers struggled to preserve Indian peoples in a society in which many Americans were convinced that Indians must disappear and were not sorry to see them go. That Indians themselves resisted the reformers' efforts seemed to the reformers only more evidence of the ignorant and benighted state from which the Indians had to be rescued.

The reform policy had three basic components. The first was the suppression of Indian norms of family life, community organization, and religion. Reformers sought to accomplish this suppression by persuasion when possible and by force when necessary. Simultaneously, reformers tried to educate Indian children in

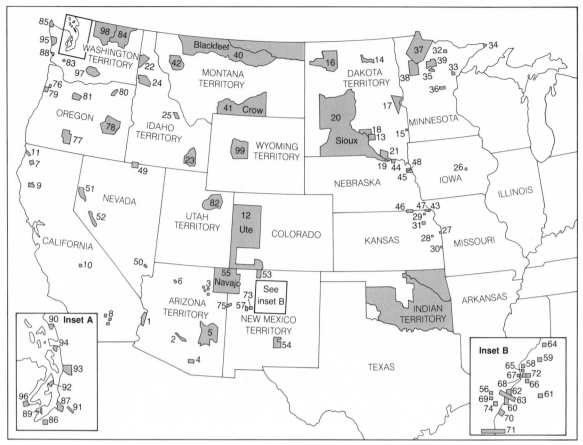

ARIZONA TERRITORY	25. Lemhi	NEVADA	OREGON
1. Colorado River	IOWA	49. Duck Valley	76. Grande Ronde
2. Gila River	26. Sac and Fox	50. Moapa Valley	77. Klamath
3. Moqui Pueblo	KANSAS	51. Pyramid Lake	78. Malheur
4. Papago	27. Black Bob	52. Walker River	79. Siletz
5. White Mountain	28. Chippewa and	NEW MEXICO	80. Umatilla
6. Suppai	Munsee	TERRITORY	81. Warm Springs
CALIFORNIA	29. Kickapoo	53. Jicarilla Apache	UTAH TERRITORY
7. Hoopa Valley	30. Miami	54. Mescalero Apache	82. Uinta Valley
8. Mission	31. Potawatomi	55. Navajo	WASHINGTON
9. Round Valley	MINNESOTA	*Pueblos*	TERRITORY
10. Tule River	32. Bois Forte	56. Jémez	83. Chehalis
11. Klamath River	33. Fond du Lac	57. Acoma	84. Colville
COLORADO	34. Grand Portage	58. San Juan	85. Makah
12. Ute	35. Leech Lake	59. Picurís	86. Nisqually
DAKOTA	36. Mille Lac	60. San Felipe	87. Puyallup
TERRITORY	37. Red Lake	61. Pecos	88. Shoalwater
13. Crow Creek	38. White Earth	62. Cochiti	89. Squaxin Island
14. Devils Lake	39. Winnebagoshish	63. Santo Domingo	90. Lummi
15. Flandreau	MONTANA	64. Taos	91. Muckleshoot
16. Ft. Berthold	TERRITORY	65. Santa Clara	92. Port Madison
17. Lake Traverse	40. Blackfeet	66. Tesuque	93. Snohomish or Tulalip
18. Old Winnebago	41. Crow	67. San Ildefonso	94. Swinomish
19. Ponca	42. Jocko	68. Pojoaque	95. Quinaielt
20. Sioux	NEBRASKA	69. Zia	96. Skokomish
21. Yankton	43. Iowa	70. Sandia	97. Yakima
IDAHO TERRITORY	44. Niobrara	71. Isleta	98. Columbia
22. Coeur d'Alene	45. Omaha	72. Nambé	WYOMING
23. Ft. Hall	46. Oto	73. Laguna	TERRITORY
24. Lapwai	47. Sac and Fox	74. Santa Ana	99. Wind River
	48. Winnebago	75. Zuñi	

Indian reservations in the West, outside of Indian Territory, 1880. From the Annual Report of the Commissioner of Indian Affairs, 1880.

The mark of dependency: reservation Utes, once self-sufficient, gather at the agency to receive rations.

order to instill mainstream American Protestant values in place of tribal values. Finally, reformers sought a policy of land allotment that would break up communal landholding patterns and create private ownership. In the end, Indians would be Christian farmers living in nuclear families on their own land. The remaining lands could then be opened to white farmers. In the end, all supposedly would be reconciled.

In imposing these policies on the Indians, the reformers operated at a considerable advantage. Not only had the military made effective resistance by Indians impossible, but conquest itself also had proceeded to destroy existing Indian subsistence systems. With the exception of some tribes in the Southwest and the Pacific Northwest and the Five Civilized Tribes of Oklahoma, most Indian peoples could no longer feed or clothe themselves without federal aid. Most reservation Indians depended for survival on payments due them from the government for their lands and on rations issued by the government. This condition of dependency gave government officials significant control over the social and cultural life of Indian peoples. Agents could use annuities to reward friends and punish enemies; they could use the distribution of supplies to alter the usual political arrangements of a community.

The strength of Indian communities during this period declined while the power of the federal bureaucracy that supervised them increased. The Bureau of Indian Affairs had made its first moves toward centralization before the Civil War, when the government began removing the supervision of Indian affairs from the duties of the territorial governors and transferring them to special officers, the superintendents. The failure of the churches to supervise Indian affairs adequately—and subsequent scandals under Columbus Delano, President Grant's particularly corrupt secretary of the interior— increased pressure for a strengthened bureaucracy. The need to assimilate Indians and protect federal wards thus spurred the growth of the Bureau of Indian Affairs from a corrupt patronage system into a not as corrupt group of professional bureaucrats. Between 1881 and 1897 the bureau nearly doubled in size, and although its 4,000 employees would be a small staff by twentieth-century standards, it was a significant one by those of the nineteenth century.

The struggle to turn the Bureau of Indian Affairs into a centralized organization with standardized procedures was a long one. Perhaps the secretary of the interior most responsible for eventual bureaucratic centralization success was Carl Schurz, an exiled German revolutionary who helped organize the Republican party in Wisconsin. General, ambassador, senator, newspaperman and editor, historian, and later renegade from Grant's Republican party: his tenure as secretary of the interior under President Rutherford B. Hayes from 1877 to 1881 was but one stop in a tumultuous career. A fervent supporter of civil service reform, Schurz took the office of Indian inspector and made it a tool for centralizing the bureau. He appointed former superintendents and agents to the post, used the inspectors to investigate irregularities in the agencies, and had those men report directly to him. They were officials whose loyalties were to Washington and not to the agents or locally controlled Indian rings—that is, coalitions of government officials and businessmen designed to divert Indian funds into white hands. As reform proceeded, the bureau increasingly controlled its employees by an elaborate set of rules and procedures. Complete bureaucratization occurred in the early twentieth century when all important field employees of the Indian Bureau came under the Civil Service System. Now administrators rose within the Bureau of Indian Affairs, were familiar with its procedures, and had more loyalty to the organization. Political appointees finally lost out to professional bureaucrats.

Weakened tribes, an increasingly assertive and professional bureaucracy, and a conviction among reformers that change must come quickly allowed the Bureau of Indian Affairs to launch what amounted to a wholesale assault on Indian culture and community organization in the 1880s. In 1883 the Indian Bureau banned "medicine making," polygamy, and bride payments and set up a system of courts of Indian offenses—staffed by Indians—to enforce their directives. When a few whites protested such actions, claiming that these were the natural conditions of an Indian's life, the commissioner of Indian affairs replied that "So are superstition and sin but that is no reason against trying to improve his condition."

By withholding rations, imprisoning recalcitrants, forcibly cutting adult men's hair, seizing children for schools, physically breaking up religious ceremonies, and seizing religious objects, the Indian Bureau mounted direct assaults on Indian cultural and religious practices that would continue well into the twentieth century. The government successfully banned the Sun Dance among the Lakotas for the first time in 1884. That tribe thus lost not only its central religious ceremony but also associated social and religious rituals. The Sun Dance had been a time of courting and fun, and other rituals had flourished in the shadow of the sacred tree of the Sun Dance. In the encampments visionaries had acted out their experiences, healers had demonstrated their power, and babies' ears had been pierced in a ceremony as central to identification as a Lakota as circumcision was to the identity of a Jewish man.

In 1888 the government enforced a further prohibition by banning bundles. When a person died among the Lakotas, the family had cut a lock of his or her hair and saved it in a ritual bundle for a year, thus causing that person's spirit to remain with the people. At the end of the year the spirit was released, and goods amassed over the course of the year were given away in honor of the deceased. The government, it seemed, would not even let the dead escape its power. As Short Bull, a Lakota religious leader, saw it: "The white people made war on the Lakotas to keep them from practicing their religion. . . . The white people wish to make us cause the spirits of our dead to be ashamed."

Most reformers backed repression in prohibiting cultural and religious practices among adults, but they had real hopes of getting Indian children to change their ways voluntarily once they were properly educated. Indian schools would both refute those who believed that the Indians were racially inferior, and thus ineducable, and would also break the resistance of those Indians who tried to preserve old ways. With proper education, reformers contended, Indian religions and practices would disappear within a generation.

The most famous of the Indian educators was Richard Henry Pratt, an army officer who was in charge of those Kiowa and Comanche prisoners sent to Florida after the Red River War. Pratt's success in working with those prisoners convinced him that education was the key to the "Indian problem," and in 1879 he convinced the government to help fund the Carlisle Indian School in Pennsylvania. At Carlisle, Pratt adopted a policy of isolating children from their tribe, forcing them to speak English, and compelling them to follow Anglo American customs. With its mixture of academic training and manual labor, Carlisle resembled Booker T. Washington's Tuskegee Institute for blacks. It set the pattern for the Indian boarding schools that followed it.

Reformers like Pratt were quite determined to destroy existing Indian cultures. Reformers believed that until they eliminated existing Indian beliefs and social forms, they could not assimilate Indians into American life. And if Indians were not assimilated into American life, then they would disappear. As Pratt put it, the goal was to "kill the Indian and save the man." The deculturization Pratt demanded was virtually total: "the sooner all tribal relations are broken up; the sooner the Indian loses all his Indian ways, even his language, the better it will be for him and for the government and the greater will be the economy for both."

The reformers were unwilling to brook any opposition to their goals from Indian parents. Commissioner of Indian Affairs Thomas Morgan told parents that they did not "have any right to forcibly keep their children out of school to grow up like themselves, a race of barbarians and semi-savages." Yet many Indian parents did resist. Not only was the avowed goal of these schools to make the children strangers to their own people, but they were also often cruel, dangerous, and sickly places where disease claimed the lives of many students. Indian reform policies placed Indian parents in a difficult position. Their children obviously needed new skills, but the price exacted for those skills was cultural destruction and loss of identity. And for many children the culmination of schooling was not graduation but death on a sickbed hundreds of miles from their home.

This picture of a South Dakota school (named after Sitting Bull), showing the children, the Indian policeman, and the white school teachers, captures the attempt to force cultural transformation of Indian peoples.

In the end, however, the resistance of Indian peoples was probably less important in halting the expansion of boarding schools than the cost of the schools themselves and their failure to achieve the results they had promised. Some students returned to the reservations without skills. Others came with skills that had no application in the stunted reservation economy. Often, too, these returned students found themselves out of place in communities whose values they no longer fully understood or shared. The attempt to eradicate tribal values and practices through education would continue into the twentieth century, but increasingly the main educational tool would be local schools, not boarding schools.

If the suppression of Indian cultural practices and education were two supports of the reform program, land allotment formed the third. The middle-class reformers who controlled Indian policy believed that private property and individual autonomy formed the heart of civilization. As long as Indians held their land in common, that heart could not beat, and the entire "civilizing" process could not take place. Reformers were determined to divide tribal lands among tribal members. Because with dwindling populations many tribes held what the reformers regarded as too much land for the members to use efficiently, reformers proposed selling the excess to white settlers. Proposals to allot land in severalty, as this division was called, were not new. They had already been written into some of the first treaties establishing reservations in the years before the Civil War, and Congress had passed several partial measures following the war.

The main severalty measure, however, came in 1887 when Senator Henry Dawes of Massachusetts sponsored the Dawes Act. The law provided varying amounts of land for all tribal members with the maximum amount, 160 acres, being allotted to a head of a family. This land was to be held in trust by the government—it could neither be sold nor taxed—for twenty-five years. The decision to allot a reservation was not up to the Indians. It rested with the president. If he decided that a reservation should be allotted, there was nothing Indians could do to stop him.

The law pleased both eastern reformers, who saw it as vital to the civilization program, and western settlers and developers, who were less interested in assimilating Indians than in gaining access to Indian lands. With the passage of the Dawes Act, reformers believed that the end to the "Indian problem" was in sight. Reservations, the commissioner of Indian affairs wrote in 1889, belonged to the vanishing order of things. He declared that "tribal relations should be broken up, socialism destroyed and the family and autonomy of the individual substituted. The allotment of land in severalty, the establishment of local courts and police, the development of a personal sense of independence and the universal adoption the English language are means to this end."

As with education, the reformers failed to achieve their goals, but they once more exacted a heavy price from those they wished to help. In the late nineteenth and early twentieth centuries, the Bureau of Indian Affairs applied the Dawes Act with a speed and a lack of safeguards that appalled even its sponsor. In 1881, Indians held 155,632,312 acres of land. By 1890 this figure had dwindled to 104,314,349, and by 1900 it had declined to 77,865,373 acres. Most Indians did not become independent farmers, and the federal government did not fulfill its trust responsibilities. Particularly during the early twentieth century, fraud and relaxation of trust provisions allowed allotted lands to pass to whites. Between 1887 and 1934, Indians lost 60 percent of their remaining land and 66 percent of their allotted lands.

As the sovereignty of native western tribes buckled before the reformers' zeal, the Five Civilized Tribes of Oklahoma initially held out as a bastion of the older order of domestic dependent nations. They managed to obtain exemption from the Dawes Act, but the sovereignty they had been promised in the West was about to be undermined once more. The same combination of reformist zeal and white desire for Indian land that had contributed to the Dawes Act strengthened the desire of corporations for access to Indian resources and created pressure for the dissolution of the governments of the old Indian Territory. With reformers ideologically committed to severalty, even the success of Indian governments became an argument for disbanding them. As one reformer explained after interviewing a chief of one of the Five Civilized Tribes, there was not a family in the nation without a home of its own. Nor was there a pauper in the nation. Nor did the nation owe a dollar. It had built its own capitol, schools, and hospitals. Yet he argued that their system was defective: "They have got as far as they can go, because they own their land in common. . . . There is no enterprise to make your home any better than that of your neighbors. There is no selfishness, which is at the bottom of civilization. . . . Till this people will consent to give up their lands, and divide them among their citizens so that each can own the land he cultivates, they will not make much more progress."

Indians had no recourse against this kind of stubborn ideology that used even the Indians' success against them. The reformers rarely made their case for individualization so revealingly; at bottom, they believed, civilization was based on selfishness. Progress came only through the uninhibited pursuit of self-interest. Indians were not innately inferior. They simply lived in a society whose communal values inhibited the greed and selfishness necessary for progress. The reformer's program, in essence, was to give selfishness its head.

Such ideology, powerfully buttressed by federal power and by the self-interest of railroad companies that would by law get large grants of land if Indian Territory was dissolved, created an unstoppable momentum for dissolving the governments of the Five Civilized Tribes. What the federal government had failed to get at once, however, it worked at obtaining piecemeal. From the 1870s onward there was intense pressure from surrounding whites to organize Indian Territory as a federally governed western territory, to allot lands to the Indians, and to open up the remainder for white settlement. While representatives of the Five Civilized Tribes fought off proposals to make the Indian Territory a federally governed western territory, they lost other battles. As corporations built the railroads and opened coal mines, the federal government limited the ability of the Indian nations to regulate these corporations or their workers. In 1889 the government extended the federal judicial system into the region, establishing a court at Muskogee for whites living in Indian Territory.

The assault on the sovereignty of the Five Civilized Tribes culminated in the efforts of the Dawes Commission of 1893. Assigned the task of negotiating with the Five Civilized Tribes for an end to national or tribal title to their lands, the Dawes Commission finally brought allotment of lands in severalty to the Indian Territory. With allotment secured, Congress then demanded the end to the tribal governments themselves. When some of the Five Civilized Tribes resisted, the Curtis Act of 1898 unilaterally terminated the governments of those tribes that had not already agreed to disband "voluntarily."

Trajectories of Power

By the early twentieth century all available choices seemed bad for American Indian peoples. They had reached their population nadir, and in many respects their cultural and social nadir as well. The reformers and federal policy makers, whose own programs had accelerated this descent, began to lose faith in their own solutions. The reformers did not admit their own fault. Instead, they blamed Indian capacities. Indians, they said, might not be the equal of whites after all. The reformers did not abandon their goal of assimilation, but relying on the resurgent racism of the early twentieth century, they slowed their timetable. Accepting Indian abilities as limited, they no longer thought assimilation would be rapid. This did not, however, stop the alienation of Indian land and resources at a rate even faster than that of the late nineteenth century.

Together the decline of the tribes and the rise of the Bureau of Indian Affairs traced the trajectories of power in the nineteenth-century West. Americans had fought and conquered Indians, but this was only part of the change, for the

Indians who never fought the United States as well as those who had allied themselves with the Americans declined in power. American officials gradually perverted the promises of one sovereign nation to protect other far weaker, but still sovereign, nations into a mandate for bureaucrats appointed by one government to oversee the personal lives of individual members of those weaker nations.

Federal officials succeeded in imposing this altered definition of wardship on Indians for several reasons. First, Indian power had declined to a point at which Indians themselves could not prevent the government from acting unilaterally. Second, government officials following the Civil War recognized a real need to protect at least some of the remaining Indian property against rapacious whites. Finally, as the courts accepted assimilation as the ultimate goal of Indian policy and wardship, they granted the government extraordinary coercive powers in order to force assimilation on the Indians. In 1903 the Supreme Court ruled in Lone Wolf v. Hitchcock that Congress had a plenary (or absolute) power to regulate Indian affairs even when congressional actions violated existing treaty provisions. "It is to be presumed," the Court said, "that in this matter the United States would be governed by such considerations of justice as would control a Christian people in their treatment of an ignorant and dependent race." Such plenary power mocked Indian sovereignty as fully as the reasoning mocked actual history.

In reducing the Indians to wardship, the federal government had enhanced its own power. Congress could, according to the courts, dictate the fates of hundreds of thousands of people in the American West and control tens of millions of acres of Indian land. In gaining such powers, the federal government had also built up the means to exercise them. The military had subdued the Indians, and a modern bureaucracy, the Bureau of Indian Affairs, had arisen to administer the reservations and steer the government's wards toward citizenship.

It is true that reformers believed both the reservations and the bureaucracy would be temporary, that they would disappear as the Indians assimilated and joined with the larger populations. Indians and bureaucrats would supposedly vanish together. But it would not turn out to be that way. The significance of Indians in the West did not end when they were herded onto reservations. The plenary power that the courts granted Congress would in practice only limit instead of destroy Indian sovereignty. The history of nineteenth-century Indian policy clearly marks the decline of sovereignty and the rise of wardship, but the process was never complete. Indian sovereignty would have its own resurgence. Both bureaucrats and Indians would turn out to have a much larger role to play in the West than nineteenth-century reformers imagined.

Readings

Hagan, William T. *United States-Comanche Relations: The Reservation Years.* New Haven: Yale University Press, 1976.

Hurtado, Albert. *Indian Survival on the California Frontier.* New Haven: Yale University Press, 1988.

Hutton, Paul. *Phil Sheridan and His Army.* Lincoln: University of Nebraska Press, 1985.

Josephy, Alvin. *The Nez Percé and the Opening of the Northwest.* New Haven: Yale University Press, 1965.

Milner, Clyde. *With Good Intentions: Quaker Work Among the Pawnees, Otos, and Omahas in the 1870s*. Lincoln: University of Nebraska Press, 1982.

Miner, H. Craig, and William E. Unrau. *The End of Indian Kansas*. Lawrence: University Press of Kansas, 1978.

Phillips, George. *Chiefs and Challengers*. Berkeley: University of California Press, 1975.

Prucha, Francis Paul. *The Great Father: The United States Government and the American Indians*. Lincoln: University of Nebraska Press, 1984.

————. *The Indians in American Society from the Revolutionary War to the Present*. Berkeley: University of California Press, 1985.

Rawls, James. *Indians of California: The Changing Image*. Norman: University of Oklahoma Press, 1984.

Ronda, James P. *Lewis and Clark Among the Indians*. Lincoln: University of Nebraska Press, 1984.

Smith, Sherry. *The View from Officers' Row: Army Perceptions of Western Indians*. Tucson; University of Arizona Press, 1990.

Stuart, Paul. *The Indian Office: Growth and Development of an American Institution, 1865–1900*. Ann Arbor: UMI Research Press, 1979.

Trennert, Robert A. *Alternative to Extinction: Federal Indian Policy and the Beginnings of the Reservation System, 1846–51*. Philadelphia: Temple University Press, 1975.

Utley, Robert. *The Indian Frontier of the American West*. Albuquerque: University of New Mexico Press, 1984.

White, Richard. "The Winning of the West: The Expansion of the Western Sioux in the Eighteenth and Nineteenth Centuries." *Journal of American History* 65 (September 1978): 319–43.

Wilkinson, Charles F. *American Indians, Time, and the Law: Native Societies in a Modern Constitutional Democracy*. New Haven: Yale University Press, 1987.

CHAPTER 5

Exploring the Land

AMERICAN Indian peoples have long
been bemused at the idea that Europeans not only discovered their land but
also somehow discovered them. And Indian peoples are right to find European
pretensions somewhat silly. The exploration of the West has meaning only in
terms of European ignorance, not in terms of any contribution to universal
knowledge. And if discovery means finding what was previously unknown to any
humans, then there was certainly precious little left to discover in the nineteenth
century when American explorers finally reached the West. Indeed, by then not
only Indians but also many peoples of European descent had already traveled
widely over the region.

And yet we cannot simply assert that the various American expeditions into
the West added nothing to a larger body of knowledge. American explorers rarely
found unknown places, but they did distill, codify, and make available a great
deal of knowledge about places which were previously known only to those with
first-hand experience in them. Explorers took merely personal knowledge and
made it social and purposeful. By recording what they found, they made knowledge
available in some systematic way to others. By the nineteenth century, explorers
had become, among other things, agents of science who thought themselves the
tools of progress.

Lewis and Clark and John Colter

To make the nature of exploration clearer, we can look at the differences between
the first major federal exploration of the West, the Lewis and Clark expedition
of 1804–1806, and the independent travels of a member of that expedition, John
Colter, who left Lewis and Clark during their return journey. Between May
14, 1804, and September 23, 1806, Captain Meriwether Lewis and Lieutenant
William Clark traveled up the Missouri River, across the Rocky Mountains, and
down the Columbia River to the Pacific Ocean and back. They inaugurated a
whole new age of exploration. Their expedition marked the culmination of three
centuries of failed European attempts to find something that did not exist—a
Northwest Passage, a water route across the continent. In eliminating the Northwest Passage, Lewis and Clark replaced the search for what the West did not
contain with a search for accurate and detailed knowledge of what the West did
contain.

The Lewis and Clark expedition was a federal undertaking planned down to
the smallest details by leading America scientists of the day and Thomas Jefferson
(an American president who was himself a man of considerable learning) before

the Louisiana Territory was even part of the United States. Lewis was Jefferson's private secretary. Clark was the brother of George Rogers Clark, a hero of the Revolutionary War. Jefferson instructed them to map the region, to gather information on water routes for future trade, and to collect detailed data on Indian societies and Indian languages as well as the region's geology and climate. Jefferson made sure that the explorers received the training necessary to record their information in precise scientific detail. Once published and studied, their journals made accessible to any literate American a full account of the knowledge available on a large section of the West.

The journals of Lewis and Clark recorded an impressive achievement and a great adventure. Starting with 43 men, they poled and pulled their keelboat and two pirogues 1,600 miles up the treacherous Missouri that first summer, halting at the Mandan villages for the winter. This first stage of the journey was through land already well known to French traders, but in the summer of 1805 the expedition, now reduced to 32 people, including Sacajawea, the Shoshone wife of a French trader, pushed west across the Rockies into lands where Euro-Americans had not traveled. They wintered at the Columbia's mouth. The next spring they set out on their return journey, and they reached Saint Louis at the end of September, 1806. They had been gone two years, four months, and a few days. Although Alexander Mackenzie of the North West Company was the first Euro-American to cross the entire continent, Lewis and Clark—the "Great Captains," as they were later called—were the first to cross the present United States. Their route was precisely recorded and described in detail.

John Colter, a hunter from the Shenandoah Valley of Virginia, accompanied Lewis and Clark on their expedition, but he did not return to Saint Louis with them. He received permission to leave the expedition at the Mandan villages on the Upper Missouri and join two traders on a trapping expedition to the Yellowstone country. The next year he entered the service of Manuel Lisa, who had established a trading fort on the Big Horn River in central Montana. From that fort over the next four years Colter went out, either alone or as the leader of a company, to look for prime trapping grounds and to induce Indians to come to trade with Lisa.

Where Colter went and how exactly he got there will probably always be partially a mystery precisely because his personal knowledge remained personal. What Lewis and Clark saw and learned became, in time, available to all who wished to know of it. John Colter's West remained largely in John Colter's head. Historians have only guessed at the route Colter followed in 1807–1808 when he became the first white man to glimpse the Grand Tetons, Jackson Hole, and much of the area that is today Yellowstone National Park. Information on his route survives only in second-hand accounts that reached William Clark and by guesses made from finding his name and the date carved into trees and stones at strategic points. The larger ignorance of the West that existed before Colter set out remained after he returned.

Whereas the Lewis and Clark expedition bequeathed detailed knowledge, Colter left only stories. The stories were, to be sure, incredible. Colter had in his travels joined the Flatheads in a battle with the Blackfeet. His rifle had a deadly effect on the Blackfeet, and his actions, coupled with the sale of guns to the enemies of the Blackfeet by American traders, cemented Blackfeet animosity toward the Americans. The Blackfeet were not prepared to show mercy when they eventually captured Colter. They stripped him naked, gave him a head start, and forced him to run for his life across a rocky plain full of prickly pear cactus. One pursuing warrior gained on him, but Colter killed him with his own weapon and then, after a run of five miles, plunged into the ice-cold Madison River, where he hid under a tangle of logs and beaver lodges. When the remainder of his pursuers gave up, he walked under the cover of night until he reached Lisa's fort. In a sense, Colter proved as elusive to other Americans as he did to the Blackfeet. There were more stories available about him than information provided by him. He probably preferred it that way. But as a result, the country as a whole never remembered Colter and his journeys, whereas Lewis and Clark's journey survived as a basic source on the West.

Despite their association, Colter and Lewis and Clark stood at the extremes of American travel in the West. Most of the travelers and explorers of the American West during the first four decades of the nineteenth century fell somewhere in between them. Fur traders, mountain men, and later leaders of emigrant trains all accumulated knowledge about the West, but they gathered this knowledge for private profit and released it only when profitable. Some later systematically recorded and publicized their travels, adding to an accessible body of data about the American West. But many retained their special knowledge, hoarding it against a day when it might pay them well.

Mid-Century Explorations

Government expeditions continued in the years between Lewis and Clark and the Civil War, but neither their ambitions nor their accomplishments were as significant as those of the Great Captains. These expeditions continued to combine American imperial ambitions with scientific interests. Not surprisingly, General James Wilkinson saw no good reason why geographical exploration could not serve both imperial interests and his own Machiavellian enterprises. Wilkinson ordered Lieutenant Zebulon Pike to lead an expedition across the southern plains in 1806. Ostensibly Pike was attempting to find the sources of the Red River, but actually Wilkinson had ordered him to spy on the approaches to Santa Fe in case of a later American military attempt on the region. Pike was therefore setting off, as would Frémont after him, to explore someone else's country without permission. This was complicated enough, but Wilkinson, who was in the pay of the Spanish, then informed the Spanish of Pike's plans. This ensured Pike's capture. Wilkinson thus managed at a single stroke to endear himself to his Spanish employers and also to guarantee that Pike, who was taken first to Santa Fe and then to Mexico proper, got a guided tour of the very Spanish territory that he had been sent to spy out.

The scientific results of Pike's expedition were more meager than the yields of his espionage. By portraying the southern Great Plains from Oklahoma to New Mexico as sandy deserts similar to the Sahara, Pike assisted at the birth of the image of the area as the Great American Desert. It was a picture of the plains later strengthened by Stephen Long's less than successful government expedition of 1820. To be fair to Pike and Long, the plains, given the agricultural technology of the period, might as well have been a desert. There seemed then little possibility of permanent American settlement.

Whatever their shortcomings, the Pike and Long expeditions focused on broad issues of public policy, and this distinguished them from the contemporary travels of traders and mountain men. Partially out of curiosity, but mostly from a desire for furs, the mountain men fanned out over the West. When taken together, the travels of James Bridger, William Ashley, Jedediah Smith, and Captain Benjamin Bonneville covered the Rockies, the Great Basin, and even California and the Oregon country during a period when federal expeditions remained confined to the Great Plains and the Rocky Mountains. By the 1830s such men had established the route that would become the Oregon Trail. And in the late 1830s and 1840s the mountain men turned their knowledge into profit by guiding emigrants to Oregon and California.

"The Great Reconnaissance"

The metamorphosis of mountain men into guides proved short-lived. They were, in effect, using up their intellectual capital—their knowledge of the West— because that knowledge no longer had value in terms of the failing fur trade. As guides communicated their knowledge, the guides themselves became extraneous. They yielded to a new group of government explorers.

The quickened pace of federal exploration in the 1840s arose in part from the renewed imperial ambitions of the rulers of the republic, in part from the desire to find suitable railroad routes across the continent, in part from a need to enumerate the resources that could serve American development, and in part from a search for knowledge. The government's renewed commitment to exploration manifested itself in the reorganization of the army's Corps of Topographical Engineers in 1838. The corps was a separate arm of the military attached to the executive branch of the government to perform duties assigned by the president and Congress. A group of military officers trained for scientific exploration, the corps embodied the amalgam of science, exploration, and expansionism that increased American knowledge of the West.

As exploration entered this new phase, it became considerably more ambitious and sophisticated. The explorers and scientists who took to the field under army and navy sponsorship in the 1840s were not satisfied with noting landmarks and blazing trails. They sought to establish American hegemony and dominance in the West, to give reliable descriptions of Indian cultures, to assess resources with scientific exactness, and generally to record an account of the West that would enable Anglo American settlers to make it the site of a complex industrial civilization. They very often pursued these imperial, scientific, and economic goals under conditions of romance and adventure, but their adventures cannot obscure the practical aims of the government.

The first of these expeditions, the Wilkes expedition of 1838–42, set sail in 1838 before either America's imperialist or scientific agenda had been fully worked out. The results were hardly auspicious. Wilkes's expedition ranged from Antarctica to the Canadian Pacific, with much of the expedition's attention focused on the Pacific Coast from San Francisco Bay to Puget Sound. The expedition returned in the midst of the Oregon crisis to find that the government sought to keep its discoveries quiet in order to find an accommodation with England. For years Congress refused to print or distribute the expedition's reports. The largest American expedition of the time thus left only the haziest political and scientific mark.

John C. Frémont, a member of the Corps of Topographical Engineers, proved far more fortunate than Wilkes. Frémont put exploration at the service of expansionism. Known as the "Great Pathfinder" in the popular press of the period, Frémont was a controversial and at times ridiculous figure, but he successfully joined adventure to the larger goals of public policy. Frémont's success and his rise to prominence were aided by his advantageous marriage to Jessie Benton, the daughter of Senator Thomas Hart Benton of Missouri. In the 1840s Senator Benton helped Frémont gain a virtual carte blanche in the West to serve science and American expansion while engaging in endless self-promotion. Frémont's explorations enabled him to achieve a prominence that eventually brought him the 1856 Republican nomination for the presidency.

Frémont's expeditions during the 1840s covered a variety of objectives. In 1842 and 1843–44 he sought to provide a map of the best route to Oregon. He succeeded admirably in the second expedition, and his map served thousands who traveled across the continent. Frémont also sought to serve science. He made the usual scientific collections of plants, insects, and animals, but lost most of them in the series of accidents, minor and major, that plagued his expeditions. Mapmaking and collecting scientific specimens were conventional activities; they were the established goals of the Topographical Engineers. But Frémont's real significance lay beyond them. He was a publicist for expansion. In 1843–44 he visited and described the Salt Lake valley, and he "explored" California under mysterious circumstances while it was still a part of Mexico. His description of Utah later attracted Brigham Young and the Mormons to the area. His description of California helped turn American migration in that direction.

His reports served as popular literature. Americans could read them both as adventures and as political tracts urging western settlement. Frémont dictated the reports to his wife, Jessie, who then turned his stories into romantic prose and transformed Frémont into a romantic hero. Jessie Benton Frémont created a public fascination with both the West and her husband. As a scientist, Frémont was prone to lose his specimens, and as an explorer he tended to favor dangerous winter mountain crossings that repeatedly cost the lives of his men, but as a romantic hero he rarely faltered. He climbed Mount Frémont (he was never a humble man) and planted an American flag while claiming to see from the height the sources of the rivers that drained the entire West. Frémont was wrong about his geography and wrong in claiming the first ascent, but he was perfectly correct in calculating the romantic image that his climb up a mountain which he named after himself would convey.

Frémont envisaged himself as more than an explorer, however. He also aspired to be a military conqueror and a commercial developer of the West. In those aims he did less well. His California adventures had yielded the Bear Flag Rebellion, but those same escapades marked the onset of his decline as an explorer. His quarrels with General Stephen Kearny over his attempt to claim the title of military governor of California led to his court-martial, and he would never again lead an official government expedition. Frémont would retain influence as both a large California landholder and as a U.S. senator from California, but his last two expeditions ended in tragedy. Promoted by his father-in-law, Senator Benton, and privately financed by Saint Louis businessmen, Frémont's expedition of 1848–49 sought a southern route across the Rockies. Attempting a December crossing

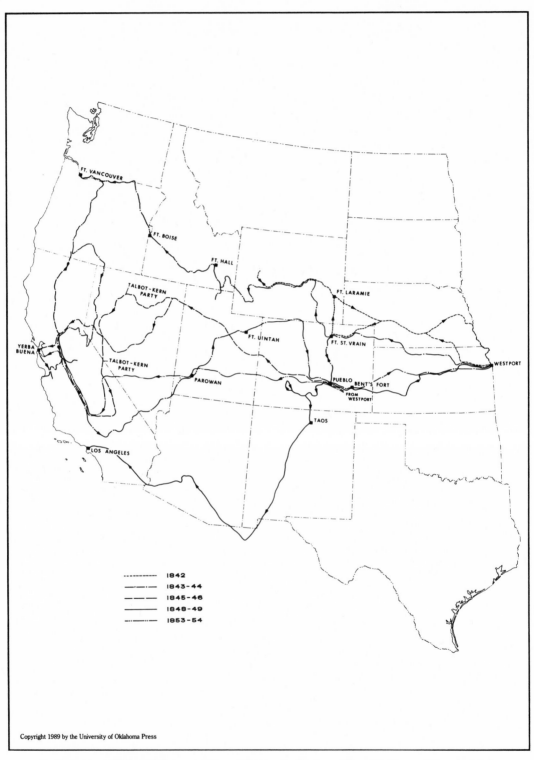

Explorations of John C. Frémont. From Warren A. Beck and Ynez D. Haase, *Historical Atlas of the American West* (Norman: University of Oklahoma Press, 1989), map 36.

of the San Juan Mountains in Colorado, Frémont's mountain man scout, Old Bill Williams, mistook his way and led the party up onto Pool Table Mesa, 12,327 feet above sea level. There, caught in blinding blizzards, their mules died. The expedition floundered and disintegrated. The Utes helped Frémont reach Taos, but in the end ten members of his party died of cold, starvation, and exhaustion. Two more men were killed by other Utes when they attempted to recover Frémont's supplies. In 1853 the San Juans again brought Frémont to grief, destroying a second expedition and claiming one of his men.

Railroad Expeditions

Frémont's disasters were only unfortunate sideshows to the much larger and better organized federal expeditions of the 1850s that sought the "best" route for a railroad to the Pacific Coast. The government had already made piecemeal attempts, such as Captain Howard Stansbury's expedition into the Great Basin in 1849–50 to survey such a route, but the railroad surveys authorized by Congress in 1853 were on a far grander scale. Since Congress considered more than one railroad to the West to be financially impossible, there was a great rivalry between sections and cities over the route and its eastern terminus. Much more than appropriate geography would go into the decision.

Congress tried to make the railroad surveys a scientific solution to what was essentially a political problem. The real issue was whether the North or the South would be the terminus of a transcontinental railroad. Congress deadlocked, and so public officials looked to scientists to consult nature for the best route. In charge of the organization of the expeditions was Jefferson Davis, then U.S. secretary of war and within a decade to be president of the Confederacy. Davis, like most southerners, had already decided upon the best route—the 32nd parallel route to San Diego—before the railroad expeditions even departed. He was willing to allow other routes to be surveyed, but he had decided in advance that none of them was likely to be feasible. Nature, Davis believed, favored the South. He thought that the other expeditions would find snowy mountain passes barring the way. Northern hopes would die in those passes; there would be no choice but to select the southern route.

Congress authorized four expeditions. A northern expedition led by Isaac I. Stevens, who had resigned his army commission to become the new territorial governor of Washington, was to explore the area between the 47th and 49th parallels. Captain John Williams Gunnison was to lead an expedition that would examine a central route along the 38th parallel. Lieutenant Amiel Weeks Whipple led an expedition along the 35th parallel. The final expedition would follow the extreme southern route, along the 32nd parallel, that Davis favored. No expedition explored what would eventually be the route taken by the first transcontinental railroad, the Union Pacific.

When these parties took the field, they included civilian scientists as well as soldiers from the Corps of Topographical Engineers. Their reports provided not only detailed accounts of the routes, but also a scientific examination of the geology, fauna, and flora of the West. Such reports conformed to the highest scientific standards of the time.

For all the information these surveys provided on the American West, they failed in their immediate goal. Politics had dictated the routes that the expeditions explored. The expeditions contained no experienced railroad engineers, so the surveys produced only crude gauges of the practicability of the routes. Their reports offered only rough estimates of grades, curves, ascents, altitudes, and other data engineers would need to build a railroad. Most congressmen assumed that one route would emerge as clearly superior, but instead the surveys discovered several possible routes, making the decision once more a political one. The surveys partially undermined Davis's favorite route because no satisfactory passes through the Sierra Nevada into San Diego existed along the 32nd parallel. Davis selected the 32nd parallel route anyway despite its lack of clear superiority over the alternates. His decision was so clearly partisan that Congress refused to approve it. Only when the Civil War broke the sectional deadlock could Congress decide on a route.

Scientists could not solve political controversies, but science could nonetheless serve political needs. The golden age of scientific exploration in the nineteenth century overlapped nicely with the heyday of American expansionism and European imperialism. Scientists saw themselves conducting an inventory of the planet and using that inventory to uncover nature's grand design. Such scientific goals fit well with the need for expanding nations to catalog resources and to chart the routes necessary to extract those resources.

This fit between science and expansion did not automatically yield a similar fit between science and development. Many scientists held a vision of themselves as people in pursuit of knowledge, not profit. They were unwilling to serve as so many waiters in a restaurant of development—taking orders and trotting into nature's kitchen to find the resources for settlers and business people to consume.

But as the century wore on, science and development reached their own accommodation. Scientists did not, as they liked to believe, serve only pure knowledge. In the United States after 1840, scientists inhabited an increasingly professionalized world of graduate schools, laboratories, and professional societies. This world needed patrons. Scientists found patrons both in the state and federal governments and, later in the century, in new industrial corporations. Those who provided support had much to say about the kind of knowledge scientists sought.

As the kind of knowledge patrons needed changed, the kind of research they funded changed. They could not dictate to scientists, but they could choose from a menu of innumerable research proposals. Initially, the government funded expeditions that cataloged resources. Later, government and industry were more interested in research that solved problems.

Increasingly in the West, developmental interests determined the problems that were to be solved. How could minerals be found? Where could dams be built? What were the best routes for railroads? What crops might be grown? Science and development, linked in the railroad expeditions, became paired for the rest of the century. The scientific exploration of the West remained inextricably joined to political, bureaucratic, and economic struggles for power. Economic interest largely determined the course of later western scientific exploration, even though scientists struggled to maintain a modicum of independence from commercial interests.

Wagon Road Surveys

Sectional divisions produced political deadlocks that blocked the building of transcontinental railroads, but they did not lessen the need of western settlers for a transportation network. The settlers looked to the federal government to build one for them. The immediate practical needs of the West and the professional orientation of government scientists and the Topographical Engineers met and clashed in the surveys for wagon roads.

The wagon road surveys reflected larger ideological, economic, and political struggles. In 1856 when Senator John B. Weller of California asked for federal appropriations for wagon roads to California, he included in his speech a denunciation of the Topographical Engineers and a plea that the contracts go to "practical men." Weller's request reflected a disgust with the careful scientific methods of the engineers, but it was more than that. He and other advocates of the roads wished to get road building away from the army. Strict constructionists of the Constitution argued that the federal government only had the authority to construct roads for military purposes. Weller hoped that by allowing a civilian agency to build roads, a precedent would be set that would allow an expansion of the federal role in western transportation.

Delegates from all the western territories and states clamored for federal roads. Transferring control of road building from the Topographical Engineers to the Department of the Interior promised to increase the influence of territorial politicians upon the selection of routes and the granting of contracts. There were fortunes to be made by those who could secure the road contracts, but western politicians found to their dismay that the Interior Department was no more ready than the engineers to surrender control of the program to westerners. The result was a constant and bitter struggle over routes and contracts.

The roads program did, however, ease another sectional struggle. Unlike railroads, wagon roads were relatively cheap. Northern and southern politicians could allocate funds for several routes and thus ease the conflict between the sections. In the 1850s the Interior Department controlled the largest roads program: the Pacific Wagon Road Office. Even with Interior Department control, however, the Topographical Engineers shared in the burst of road building. Westerners, despite their denunciations of the engineers, wanted roads so badly that they would accept them from anyone able to build them, even the engineers. Between 1850 and 1860 the engineers constructed 34 separate roads in western territories.

Although these roads were crude by later standards, they greatly reduced the rigors of western travel. The builders concentrated on finding the most feasible routes, leveling steep grades, clearing the ground by removing trees and boulders, building ditches alongside the dirt paths to prevent erosion, and bridging the largest streams and rivers. But even these limited efforts provided a major federal subsidy for the settlement of the West. Building roads brought money and jobs into the territories, and the roads themselves also helped to extend settlement. Settlers in many regions followed the road builders as they bridged rivers and connected outlying districts with existing settlements. In the future states of Utah, Kansas, Nebraska, Washington, Oregon, New Mexico, the Dakotas, Colorado, and Wyoming these wagon roads were the first steps in creating the infrastructure for development. Private capitalists and the state governments would later play a major role in the development of a western communication system, but initially the federal government nurtured the transportation system and guided the course of settlement through the roads it built.

Stagecoach and Pony Express

The federal role in western transportation did not stop with road building. Private entrepreneurs created stagecoach lines to carry passengers and freight in the West, but these lines came to life and survived because of federal subsidies. Major stage routes followed federal wagon roads. Stage and freight companies depended on federal mail contracts for their survival; their drivers and passengers sought the protection of federal troops when Indians attacked. The government let its first mail contract between the Missouri River and Salt Lake City in 1851, but not until 1857 did Congress award contracts to the first real transcontinental stage service: the Overland Mail Company.

Probably the most famous and the most ephemeral of the western companies created to carry the mails was the Pony Express Company. It, too, was in a sense a federal creation. Senator William Gwinn of California persuaded William Russell of the western freighting company Russell, Majors and Waddell of the practicality of a profitable express mail route from the Missouri River to Sacramento. Russell secured a federal contract, and his company laid out a 1,966-mile route and began operations in April 1860. Horsemen riding in relays covered from 35 to 70 miles each before handing the mail to the next rider. They moved the mail across country in an average time of ten days. The Pony Express, however, never proved profitable, and when the Pacific Telegraph Company and the California State Telegraph Company joined their lines on October 24, 1861, to form the first transcontinental telegraph, the Pony Express became obsolete. Its failure helped bring bankruptcy to the firm of Russell, Majors and Waddell.

Benjamin Holladay was the major creditor of Russell, Majors and Waddell, and he inherited most of the company's assets. More significantly, he managed to secure regular postal contracts from the Missouri to Salt Lake City. Through his Holladay Overland Mail and Express Company he expanded mail service across the Mountain West and the Pacific Northwest. The mail contracts netted Holladay nearly $2 million between 1862 and 1868 and proved to be the financial backbone of his operations. Holladay, realizing that the completion of the transcontinental railroads would doom long-distance stagecoach transportation, sold out to the Wells Fargo Express Company in 1866. With the completion of the railroads, the realm of the freight companies at once broadened and narrowed. It broadened because the railroads created an enormous demand for local freight and passenger traffic. It narrowed because on longer routes the railroads themselves replaced stagecoaches and freight wagons, leaving to long-haul companies only the dwindling area that railroads had yet to reach.

Postwar Exploration

The Civil War curtailed federal sponsorship of western exploration and returned many scientists to the East, but by forcing western science to rely on local resources, the war also helped bring into being a distinctive western science. Under Josiah Dwight Whitney, the California State Geological Survey began a

detailed survey of the state. The motive of the legislature in funding the survey
was to provide an inventory of California's unexplored assets, but state legislators
and mine owners were often frustrated by Whitney's methods. He aimed at
precise geological knowledge and sought to provide a blueprint for the rational
development of California; they wanted to know where to sink a mine shaft or
a well. "What respect can we have," the *Pacific Mining Journal* asked, "for a
fellow who spends his time in collecting sticks and stones and old bones like a
Chinaman?" When Whitney refused to endorse a wave of oil speculation in the
mid-1860s, the legislature (or "the jackasses at Sacramento," as Whitney referred
to them) retaliated by eliminating virtually all of the survey's funding after
1868.

Whitney and other California scientists insisted, in the words of one scholar,
on seeing the state as "a laboratory rather than a warehouse of salable goods."
Cut off temporarily both from eastern sponsors and funding and from eastern
professional organizations, they began to use their California experience to con-
ceptualize the natural environment in a new way. California's diversity, its
profusion of endemic species, and the dramatic changes that could be found over
short distances there led them to stress environmental adaptation and ecological
interdependence. That point of view made California scientists, as a group,
remarkably receptive to Darwin and his theories of natural selection and evolution.

The scientists who emerged as veterans of the California State Survey, who
served in the federal coastal survey of the state, or who, like John Muir, concentrated on private and amateur exploring, forged a distinctive view of the West.
In the winter of 1863, the paleontologist William Gabb observed of Clarence
King that he would "rather sit on a peak all day, and stare at those snow-
mountains, than find a fossil in the metamorphic Sierra." Gabb was half right.
King wanted both to sit on peaks and to find fossils. He also wanted both to enjoy
mountain scenery and to promote development. King became a famous geologist,
a failed mine promoter, and the author of *Mountaineering in the Sierra Nevada.* All
those activities were critical to his style; he was happy doing none of them alone.
For him the mountains were at once sublime, scientifically interesting, and a
source of adventure. They were also potentially profitable.

These California scientists applied a prism to nature, and where others saw
only the white light of resources, they saw sublimity, ecological interdependence,
and adventure. They helped shape the nation's view of the West and the western
environment. The Whitney survey became a model for later detailed government
surveys. John Muir and Clarence King became national figures. But the immediate
effect of the Californians on the goals of exploration and on scientific views of
the western environment were far less pronounced. The cataloging of resources
remained the primary goal of exploration even when veterans of the Whitney
survey like Clarence King moved over to the federal surveys organized after the
Civil War.

Clarence King and other civilian scientific explorers entered into federal service
during the late 1860s and early 1870s as the government undertook its last major
military campaigns against the Indians. Their exploration was inextricably linked
with these campaigns in both obvious and subtle ways. To kill and conquer
Indians, for example, military commanders needed topographical engineers who

could provide the maps and wagon-road surveys necessary for the army to travel. But the engineers and civilian scientists also aided the army in less obvious ways. By mapping exploitable resources and possible railroad and wagon routes, explorers created the means and the knowledge by which settlers could survive in an unfamiliar land. Exploration encouraged settlement, and white settlers took resources that Indians needed to survive. Anything that weakened Indians served the army's ends, for resistance would then become impossible. Civilian science thus promoted military goals.

Army expeditions, in turn, served science while pursuing short-term tactical ends and larger strategic goals. Different expeditions during this period combined the three purposes in varying proportions. Custer's exploring expedition of 1874 into the Black Hills was, for example, largely a military reconnaissance, but scientific experts accompanied him. By virtually inviting in miners and settlers with his announcement of gold and prime agricultural land, Custer also served the strategic goal of undermining the Sioux economy and loosening their grip on their land.

As the army defeated the Indians, the military emphasis of western expeditions declined. Where once army expeditions had been military reconnaissances accompanied by civilian scientists, they evolved into civilian expeditions conducted under military sponsorship. Clarence King's geological and geographical exploration of the 40th parallel typified this transformation. Having correctly perceived that the kind of intensive scientific exploration pioneered by Whitney's California surveys was the wave of the future, the army moved to sponsor expeditions of its own. Beginning in 1867, the Yale-educated King organized and operated his survey under army sponsorship.

King's expeditions were a compromise between civilian and military needs, and they were a compromise too between his own complex reactions to the West. Although King the adventurer and King the nature lover occasionally appeared, King the scientist and promoter dominated the surveys. King wrote his own orders and picked his own men, all of whom were civilian scientists. King used methods pioneered in California to map the basin and range country of Nevada and Utah and the mountains of Utah and Wyoming with a new degree of accuracy. He conducted geological, botanical, and zoological examinations and studied the possibilities for development along the railroad routes. Military considerations still, however, lingered. King's devotion to aiding the railroad and promoting settlement along it played into the army's strategy of creating wedges of settlement which would deny Indians the ability to maintain their ways of life.

King's expeditions were a huge success. They triumphed as resource surveys, as scientific contributions to geological theory, and as high adventure. King and his collaborators even won acclaim for their clever unmasking of one of the great nineteenth-century swindles. Two "prospectors" had successfully managed to sell San Francisco bankers their claim to an "American Golconda" where diamonds and rubies lay on the ground for the taking. Following clues to the secret claim, King proved that the diamonds and rubies had been planted. Popular acclaim came from the Golconda exploit, but the survey's scientific culmination came in an impressive series of scientific tomes with King's *Systematic Geology* as its centerpiece.

The 1874 Custer Exploring Expedition into the Black Hills mixed science, conquest, and boosterism. It helped prompt a gold rush that started the war that cost Custer his life and the Sioux their effective independence.

In one sense, the King surveys were a triumph for the army, but in another they signaled that the torch of exploration was passing to academic scientists in the West. The army would try to continue its domination of scientific exploration in the American West through the surveys of Lieutenant George Wheeler in the Great Basin, the Colorado River and Plateau country, and the southern Rockies, but Wheeler eventually lost out to civilian expeditions sponsored by the Interior Department. In the summer of 1873, when surveyors from both army and civilian expeditions met on the same remote mountain peaks of southern Colorado and proceeded to duplicate each other's work, exploration had reached a new stage. The West had shrunk. In the interest of avoiding expensive duplications of effort, Congress forced itself to decide between civilian and military explorers. The civilians would prove to be the winners.

Interior Department Expeditions

Congress decided in favor of civilian exploration in the name of consolidation and economy, but only gradually and in a piecemeal way. By the 1870s not only were the Wheeler and King surveys in the field, but they also competed for funds with two other large federal surveys. One was the U.S. Geological Survey of Territories under Ferdinand V. Hayden. The other, led by John Wesley Powell, was initially sponsored by the Smithsonian Institution. These men would eventually battle over control of the surveys that Congress consolidated in 1879 as the U.S. Geological Survey.

Ferdinand V. Hayden and John Wesley Powell were united in their common desire to open the West to rapid economic development and settlement, their lack of formal training in science, and their intense ambition. But Hayden and Powell also symbolized the two competing approaches to western development of the late nineteenth and early twentieth centuries. Ferdinand V. Hayden was the businessman's explorer. He saw himself as a promoter of western opportunity, and he would deliver up that opportunity to whoever wanted to grasp it. Although just as devoted to development, John Wesley Powell came to believe that the nature of the arid West demanded a degree of planning unprecedented in American history and that only the federal government could provide it.

Ferdinand V. Hayden

Ferdinand Hayden came to the U.S. Geological Survey as a largely self-trained geologist who had traveled in the West and had participated in the army explorations before the Civil War. Hayden was a practical geologist. He remained relatively unconcerned with geological theory, but he was not the ignoramus that his archrival, John Wesley Powell, portrayed him to be. Hayden's focus was always on practical possibilities, geological discoveries that could result in economic development. Practical people often dismiss scientists interested in theory and pure knowledge as intelligent fools whose work has no relevance to daily life. A preoccupation with the practical and a constant focus on the opportunities for gain can, however, also make humans foolish and gullible. Hayden was sometimes such a practical dreamer. He sought so eagerly to develop the West that he tended to dismiss all the obstacles that blocked development. Where John Wesley Powell saw problems, all Hayden saw were possibilities. Hayden often mistook what he wanted to be true for the literal truth.

Hayden's belief in the endless possibilities of the West occasionally made a fool of him, but it also won him wide support from western boosters and businessmen. If the Great Plains seemed too arid for normal farming, then Hayden was prepared to adopt and promote the theory that "rain follows the plow." According to the theory, as Anglo American settlers pushed west and planted crops and trees, rainfall would naturally increase. If the country was too mountainous for agricultural settlement, then Hayden stressed minerals or timber or scenic possibilities. He saw the possibility of development everywhere. Hayden could promote Yellowstone National Park and the rain-follows-the-plow theory with equal enthusiasm because each, in its own place, seemed the best route for the rapid development of an area he had explored.

Hayden explored a vast section of the West. He first led a federal survey in

Nebraska in 1867. The next year he extended the survey out to the Rocky Mountains. By 1869 his survey had become the U.S. Geological Survey of the Territories, and in the early 1870s Hayden explored Colorado, eastern Utah, and Wyoming. His reports included the most detailed examination to date of the wonders of the Yellowstone country.

A genius at publicity, and aided by the captivating photographs of William H. Jackson, Hayden endlessly promoted himself and his survey. His duty, as he saw it, was to promote the West before the largest audience possible. He advertised his findings and himself to scientists, Congress, and the public. As a scientist promoting the West, he endeared himself to western promoters who were as optimistic and uncritical as he. A man who believed all was possible, he left it to a generation of farmers to prove by their failures that optimism has its own dangers.

John Wesley Powell

Hayden's great rival was John Wesley Powell. Powell matched Hayden in his skill at self-promotion. Like Hayden, Powell was not an academic scientist. His early fame came more from his daring than from his scientific achievements. In 1869, Powell, who had lost an arm in the Civil War, led the first expedition to float the entire length of the deep canyons of the Green and Colorado rivers. He and his companions survived the river's terrific rapids and discovered the canyons' awesome beauty and isolation. Others had preceded Powell to portions of this region. Indians had lived in these canyons, and Powell found painted on a rock in Red Canyon of the Green River the inscription "Ashley 1825," a memento of an earlier partial descent by mountain men under William Ashley. But Ashley's exploits had so vanished from memory that not half a century after his descent, Powell did not even recognize who Ashley was or what he had been doing there. Powell filled in the last large blank spaces on the map of the United States, adding the last new river, the Escalante, and the last mountain range, the Henrys.

This expedition, achieved with virtually no government support, made Powell a hero to the public at large and won him first Smithsonian sponsorship and then federal funding of his later work. His survey over the next years explored and mapped the beautiful and seemingly desolate Colorado Plateau country. Gradually scientists replaced the collection of adventurers who had staffed Powell's first expedition. Powell's own interest increasingly turned from geology to ethnology. His studies of Indian peoples of the Southwest were far better than anything else previously written about Indians by federal explorers in the West. But as Powell's shifting interests indicated, Indians had gone from being sources of knowledge as well as objects of knowledge to being purely objects of knowledge. Lewis and Clark had learned from as well as about Indians. Powell only learned about them.

In addition to being an adventurer, a scientist, and an ethnologist, John Wesley Powell was also an accomplished bureaucrat. Faced with retrenchments in Congress and duplication of efforts in the West, Powell had joined the push for the unification of the surveys. A committee of experts from the National Academy of Sciences, convened to examine this and other matters, recommended the consolidation of the western surveys. Congress accepted the recommendation and created the U.S. Geological Survey.

The consolidation of the surveys institutionalized a significant change in west-

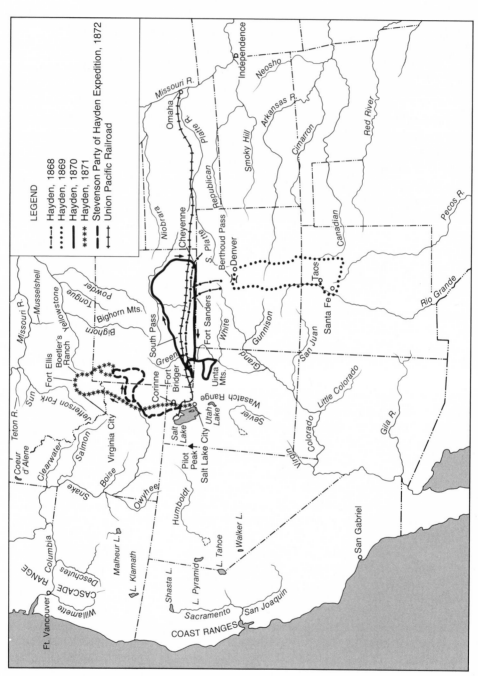

Ferdinand Hayden's geological surveys. From William Goetzmann, *Exploration and Empire* (New York: W. W. Norton, 1978), p. 472.

ern exploration. What had begun as a loose mixture of science and adventure had become a bureaucracy. And in a piece of political and bureaucratic infighting, Clarence King and Powell allied to destroy their common rival, Hayden. King became the first head of the U.S. Geological Survey. Under him the Geological Survey joined the other bureaus of the Interior Department that were coming to have such great power in the West.

The Clarence King who headed the Geological Survey was a simpler figure than the younger man who had gazed from the California mountain peaks. He had learned to compartmentalize himself. In Washington he was a bureaucrat and a developer. He managed a centralized government operation while maintaining his own private interests in western mining and ranching. The role of government and government scientists, as King saw it, was to aid those businesses which could most quickly and efficiently create wealth in the West. Federal science and development had achieved a community of interests just as certainly as federal science and expansion had found common interests. King worked to insure that bureaucracy and large businesses would complement and not oppose each other.

After King's resignation in 1881 to pursue his private business interests, Powell became head of the U.S. Geological Survey. He also maintained his leadership of the Bureau of American Ethnology, which conducted government-sponsored research on American Indians. As head of both these bureaus, he became perhaps the most powerful bureaucrat in Washington, D.C. A closer look at his career must remain for another chapter.

Exploration, Bureaucracy, and Public Policy

Powell, King, and Hayden became scientists whose job it was to reveal to settlers the conditions that they would encounter and the resources they could develop. Any such endeavor created a vision of the West, and creating that vision involved political and economic choices. When King chose to use the U.S. Geological Survey primarily to survey mineral deposits (rather than dam sites and water sources for irrigation), he chose to emphasize resources whose ultimate development would benefit mining corporations and not western farmers. He thus quite consciously contributed to corporate penetration of the West. When Powell emphasized large grazing units, as his opponents proclaimed, he favored "large" ranchers over "small" farmers. When Hayden adopted theories such as the idea that rain follows the plow, he offered a vision of the West in which small farmers could farm just as they had in the humid East. Such people were not simply offering information; they were trying to shape the way that people would use that information and the kind of society—however hazily envisioned—that these people would create.

Readings

Allen, John Logan. *Passage Through the Garden: Lewis and Clark and the Image of the American Northwest.* Urbana: University of Illinois Press, 1975.

Goetzmann, William H. *Army Exploration in the American West, 1803–1863.* New Haven: Yale University Press, 1959.

————. *Exploration and Empire: The Explorer and the Scientist in the Winning of the American West.* New York: Alfred A. Knopf, 1966.

————. *New Lands, New Men: America and the Second Great Age of Discovery.* New York: Viking, 1986.

Jackson, W. Turrentine. *Wagon Roads West: A Study of Federal Roads and Surveys and Construction in the Trans-Mississippi West.* Lincoln: University of Nebraska Press, 1980.

Ronda, James. *Lewis and Clark Among the Indians.* Lincoln: University of Nebraska Press, 1984.

Smith, Michael. *Pacific Visions: California Scientists and the Environment, 1850–1915.* New Haven: Yale University Press, 1987.

Stegner, Wallace. *Beyond the Hundredth Meridian.* Boston: Houghton Mifflin, 1954.

Winther, Oscar O. *The Transportation Frontier: Trans-Mississippi West, 1865–1890.* New York: Holt, Rinehart, and Winston, 1964.

CHAPTER 6

Distributing the Land

THE government expeditions that explored the West were, in effect, sophisticated scouting parties. Advancing relentlessly, if somewhat erratically and ineptly, behind them was a phalanx of government surveyors whose duty it was to divide up the land into the giant checkerboard pattern of townships, sections, and quarter-sections that remains so apparent over the prairies and plains today. This division and distribution formed one of the central activities of government in the nineteenth-century West: transforming public lands into private lands.

The federal government's role in distributing lands meant that American citizens in the West felt the presence of the federal government far more directly than did citizens elsewhere. That presence was supposed to be temporary, because the public domain, it was thought, would in time become entirely private property. But that did not turn out to be true. The federal government did not distribute all the public lands in the West. The government retained so much land that western states would stand in a different relationship to the central government than would those of the East.

In the West the same basic land system created earlier in the East yielded different results. The differences were not intentional. Congress wanted to replicate existing landholding patterns, agricultural systems, and republican institutions in the West. The federal bureaucracies of the land office and the territorial system were only to be a giant administrative scaffolding from which officials and citizens together would build models of the older states. When they were finished, the scaffolding would come down and the new states would stand as duplicates of the old.

Much of the scaffolding did eventually come down, but other sections of this administrative framework remained, and in fact the government began elaborating and adding to the framework until the scaffolding, in altered form, became a permanent fixture in the West. The portion of the scaffolding that remained and grew surrounded the public lands, which became a permanent responsibility of the federal government.

American Land Policy

As originally conceived, there was an impressive coherence to American land policy. The Land Ordinance of 1785 created simple procedures for the acquisition and distribution of public lands. After Indians ceded title to their lands to the federal government, surveyors would mark the land off into giant squares six miles on a side and then subdivide them into sections of one square mile. Each section,

W   Base Line   E

36	30	24	18	12	6
35	29	23	17	11	5
34	28	22	16	10	4
33	27	21	15	9	3
32	26	20	14	8	2
31	25	19	13	7	1

Range Line

Six Miles

The township numbering system set up under the Ordinance of 1785.

in turn, would contain four quarter-sections of 160 acres each. The government would then sell this land, a tier of townships at a time, at public auction. Any land left unsold after the auction could be purchased at the land office at a minimum price originally set at $2.00 an acre but reduced to $1.25 an acre in 1820.

The basic premise of this system, one not questioned until the end of the nineteenth century, was that the land system could best serve the country's interests by putting public land into private hands. The federal government would, in effect, serve as a real estate agent instead of a landlord. The orderly sale of public lands and their transformation into small farms would ensure a prosperous republican future for the United States. With public lands readily available, the United States would not imitate Europe and become a country of wealthy landlords and poor tenants. Small freeholders, eager to develop their own land, would "improve" the land and thus create the wealth that would spur the economic development of the country as a whole.

Not only would the land system promote the creation of a prosperous republican society, but it would also endow that society with a basic public infrastructure of schools, roads, and canals. Under the Ordinance of 1785, the government reserved one section (number 16) in each township to provide income for the public schools. After 1848, Congress added a second section (number 36) for the support of schools. Territories and states sometimes leased these lands and used the income for schools, but more often they sold them with congressional permission. In 1875, Congress decided that the states must charge a minimum price, originally set at $2.50 an acre, for school lands. They were then to invest the proceeds in a permanent interest-bearing school fund. Congress later applied this technique of granting lands to other social purposes. Congress granted lands to the states to fund the building of canals, the dredging and clearing of rivers, and the building of wagon roads.

On paper this was an elegant system. As Americans imposed it on the lands across the Appalachians, they created the checkerboard landscape so visible from the air today. But the system took on a Rube Goldberg quality as Congress repeatedly tinkered with it. Between 1789 and 1834, Congress passed 375 different land laws. It changed the minimum purchase, offered credit, and then decided against credit sales.

Even as modified, however, the land system never fully conformed to the actual way that Americans took up the lands in the trans-Appalachian region. Settlers moved faster than surveyors, and so when surveyors arrived in a region, they often found settlers already in place. These settlers were squatters, and what they were doing was illegal, for they lived on land to which they had no title. The existence of large numbers of squatters—people who openly defied the laws governing land distribution—created a political problem not easily evaded.

Early-nineteenth-century politicians took sharply contrasting views of these illegal settlers. Some portrayed them as a group of lawless vagabonds. In the view of many eastern and southern Whigs before the Civil War, squatters not only used property to which they had no title, but they also subverted the civilized communities that the law intended the land system to create. Antisquatter congressmen feared that if squatting continued, the West would become a region of thinly scattered barbarians who took their livings off the richest lands but who were unable to support the basic institutions of the republic. To oppose squatting was, in this view, to halt the descent of the West into anarchy.

Other politicians, particularly westerners and most Democrats, saw squatters differently. To them, squatters were not criminals or barbarians; they were noble pioneers. They were securing the rapid growth and development of the country. If they broke the letter of the law, they fulfilled its intent. The law intended to create a nation of small commercial farmers. And in the eyes of their supporters, squatters were simply capital-poor farmers who used the land to produce the very revenue necessary to buy the land. A squatter who settled, raised crops, and sold them was only "borrowing" the land in order to produce the income necessary to purchase it. This cost the government nothing, allowed people to acquire property, and prevented the growth of a landholding elite. How could anyone monopolize the land or force people into tenancy when the people always had unrestricted access to the public domain? Squatters, their supporters argued, were actually maintaining the social equality of the country.

In the battle over squatting, the prosquatter faction won. To protect squatters, Democrats in Congress, led by Senator Thomas Hart Benton of Missouri, succeeded in passing temporary preemption acts in the 1830s and then a permanent preemption act in 1841. Preemption was simply legalized squatting. Under these acts, squatters had first right to buy up to 160 acres of land on which they had made improvements. When the government was ready to offer the land for sale, a squatter had to appear at the land office and pay the minimum price before the auction.

As the debate over squatting shows, fights over land law were often arguments about the very nature of American society and how it should replicate itself in new territories. To forge a workable land policy, therefore, Congress on some level had to agree on a common vision of American society. Land served as a sort of seal of approval for social consensus. When Americans agreed that soldiers were needed for war, they gave them land grants to encourage enlistment. When they agreed that veterans should be rewarded, they gave them land grants. When Congress agreed that the government should make rivers navigable or aid the states in building the canals in order to facilitate commerce, it gave the states grants of lands that could be sold to pay for the improvement.

In what was a capital-short and land-rich country, Congress used land instead of money to secure agreed-upon public goals. It did so by issuing land scrip. Land scrip was the nineteenth-century equivalent of food stamps. Issued by the government, it could be redeemed in exchange for a specific commodity: land. Unlike food stamps, however, scrip could legally be traded and sold. When Congress distributed scrip to veterans, few of them actually took up land on the public domain. Most sold it to others. A regular market in land scrip developed, and speculators interested in western lands purchased scrip and then used it to buy lands. Speculators preferred scrip because it sold at less than the $1.25 an acre the law mandated as the minimum price for federal land.

Because Americans believed that how they distributed the public domain determined the kind of society they were creating, fundamental differences over the nature of American society and America's future deadlocked land policies. When the North and South struggled for dominance in the Union, they clashed over the distribution of land in the West. Southern congressmen in the 1850s opposed any attempts at homestead legislation that would give free land to small farmers. "Better for us," declared a Mississippian, "that these territories should remain a waste, a howling wilderness, trod only by red hunters than be so settled." A homestead policy would, southerners believed, only increase the number of "free farms with Yankees and foreigners pre-committed to resist the participancy of slaveholders in the public domain." In the 1850s proposals for homestead acts, land grants for a Pacific railroad, and grants to establish agricultural and mechanical colleges all fell victim to sectional divisions. All three measures promised to benefit the North at the expense of the South.

Land Policy in Operation

For all their differences, northerners and southerners usually agreed that land could go to actual settlers; speculation in land was an evil that ought to be prevented. Land speculators were people who bought land at auction from the government, using cash or land scrip, and then held the land until they could sell it to others at a profit. Such people were popularly perceived as economic parasites who added to the burden borne by the honest farmer.

This rhetorical agreement on the evils of speculation found, however, little reflection in the operation of the law. Speculators could buy virtually unlimited amounts of land at any U.S. land office, usually at the minimum price. Congress did little to prevent speculation, in part because without it the land system might not have worked at all. Once the federal government stopped offering credit, speculation in one form or another offered the easiest access to the cash necessary for purchase.

Iowa in the 1850s and 1860s can serve as an example of how the land system had come to depend on speculation. In 1862 speculators owned two-thirds of the privately held land in Iowa. Between 1850 and 1860 from 50 percent to 75 percent of those buying farms in Iowa obtained their entire holding either from speculators or from lands that the federal government had granted to the state. In all, 80 percent to 90 percent of Iowa farmers had bought at least part of their holdings from parties other than the federal government.

When looked at more closely, such figures do not present a picture of farmers being fleeced by speculators. The two were not always adversaries. Farmers and speculators not only cooperated, but on many occasions they were also the same person. Probably the most common form of cooperation between the speculator and the farmer occurred in the so-called time entry system. "Time entry" evolved because preemption could only work if squatters actually had the cash to pay for their land when it came up for sale. Very often settlers who had preempted land still lacked the funds to pay for it. To get the money, farmers went to a land agent, who advanced them the purchase price at 40 percent interest. As security for the loan the farmer put the title to the land in the land agent's name. At such high interest rates, the speculator obtained a handsome profit, but the farmer still acquired the land relatively cheaply. The total cost of the land to the settler (the purchase price plus interest) came to only $2 to $3 per acre, usually far less than the real market value of the land at the time of sale. The time-entry system probably accounted for about 70 percent of the speculation that took place not only in Iowa but also later on the prairies and plains west of the Missouri River.

The remaining speculative transactions did involve direct purchase and subsequent resale of tracts of land by speculators. Despite charges to the contrary, however, speculators could not afford to sit on lands until the price rose. Instead, they sought to resell the land quickly and thus avoid the burden of taxes. In the early years of settlement, rapid resale was not difficult, and profits were large. Speculators in central Iowa who used scrip to buy land beneath the minimum price could reap returns of from 30 percent to 120 percent annually on their investment at a time when other investments usually brought returns of only 5 percent to 10 percent.

With these kinds of profits possible, farmers themselves also speculated in lands. They formed claims clubs, which ostensibly existed to protect the rights of settlers against speculators or claim jumpers. Members of the clubs, usually the squatters who first took up land in an area, agreed not to bid against each other at land auctions and to prevent others from bidding against club members. If nonmembers ignored a club's warnings against competitive bidding, members of the club evicted them from the auction. Members of these claims clubs denounced large speculators, but they themselves were small-scale speculators. Actual settlers interested only in 160 acres of land did not need claims clubs. The Preemption Act already protected a 160-acre claim. The major reason people had for joining a claims club was to secure more than the 160-acre maximum guaranteed by the Preemption Act. They could then sell the land and use the proceeds to pay off or develop their home farm.

Claims clubs, the time-entry system, and the market in land scrip were all extralegal modifications of the system that made it more flexible and more suited to local conditions. Such extralegal modifications changed the system more effectively than legal changes could have done. Before the land system began to distribute lands in the West, there was thus a long tradition of extralegal and illegal modifications of the law.

Legal Changes to the Land System

Extralegal changes in the system were, in effect, all that could take place as long as the sectional crisis between the North and the South persisted. Only when the secession of the South left Congress in the hands of northern Republicans did changes in the land system proceed. Socially and economically, the Republican party of the 1860s aspired to be the voice of a united homogeneous North. The party embodied a utopian capitalist vision of a world wherein labor was rewarded, individual opportunity prevented class distinctions from arising, and progress and growth were the national destiny. Although this vision would yield to a much harsher reality after the war, it shaped Republican land policy. Republican congressmen, who spoke for northern farmers and artisans as much as for northern capitalists, modified the land system to insure the replication of a society of modern commercial farmers in the West.

During the Civil War the Republican land program revolved around three bills: the Homestead Act, the Pacific Railroad Grant, and the Morrill Act. These three laws, all passed by Congress in 1862, were supposed to complement each other. The centerpiece was the Homestead Act, which granted 160 acres of the public domain to citizens and noncitizens alike who would live upon the land and farm it. Northern farmers and those labor reformers who followed the theories of George Henry Evans had long urged such a proposal for free grants of land to actual settlers. Ideally, the law would allow unemployed northern workers and the children of northern farmers to begin lives as independent landowners in the West. By draining off unemployed laborers, the law would simultaneously increase the wages of eastern workingmen.

Accompanying the Homestead Act was an act providing a land grant for a Pacific railroad. The immediate goal of the railroad act was to tie the Pacific Coast to the Union, but Congress also recognized that railroads were necessary to give the farms provided by the Homestead Act access to markets. Congress approved land grants and loans to the first transcontinental railroad in 1862 and made similar grants to other railroads in the ensuing years.

The final part of the Republican triumvirate was the Morrill Act, which provided land grants to the states to create a public system of higher education designed to serve farmers and skilled workingmen. The lands granted by Congress lay almost exclusively in the West, and the states could sell them to fund state universities that would give their citizens access to the education necessary for progress and advancement. A common vision of a prosperous, progressive, economically expansive, and harmonious West inspired all three acts. There was little anticipation of the conflicts and contradictions their application would involve.

In the Homestead Act, Congress above all expected the American future to duplicate the American past. Congress embedded the ideal of a 160-acre farm in the Homestead Act. It was an ideal more suited to the East than to the West and more appropriate for the American past than the American future. Without irrigation, a quarter-section farm in the middle of the Great Plains or the Utah desert was not a ticket to independence but to starvation. Congress presumed, too, that all that land would be farmed. It made no special provisions for acquiring land for mining or logging or grazing. As in the East, actual settlers introduced extralegal improvisations to reconcile the various contradictions between the conditions they confronted and the conditions the law envisioned, but these improvisations did not solve the basic problems of what became an increasingly contradictory land system.

The Homestead Act and Distribution of the Public Domain

No laws revealed more about the difficulties of implementing in the West the Republican vision of a capitalist agricultural society based on smallholdings than the Homestead Act and the railroad land grants. In many ways these laws were tremendously successful, but they also involved conflicts and failures that Congress had not envisioned.

The terms of the Homestead Act were generous and straightforward. The law provided 160 acres of free land to any settler who paid a small filing fee and resided on and improved the land for five years. If after six months of residency the settler wished to buy the land for $1.25 an acre, he or she could do so. Purchasing the land was appealing to those settlers interested in rapid development, because once a settler obtained title, the farm could be mortgaged and the money then used either to improve the homestead or to buy more land. Originally, settlers could only homestead surveyed land, but in 1880, Congress extended the act to the unsurveyed public domain.

Advocates of the Homestead Act had grandiose hopes for the reform. Horace Greeley, the leading Republican editor of the period, wrote in the *New York Tribune* that the act embodied "one of the most beneficent and vital reforms ever attempted in any age or clime—a reform calculated to diminish sensibly the number of paupers and idlers and increase the proportion of working, independent, self-subsisting farmers in the land evermore."

According to its supporters, the Homestead Act ensured the final realization of the old paired goals that had inspired the land system: a class of prosperous small farmers whose own prosperity fed the economic development of the nation. But the Homestead Act never came remotely close to achieving the grandiose expectations of its advocates. In certain areas of the West, such as the eastern Dakotas and Nebraska, the law did work fairly well. In those places the federal government distributed 56.5 percent of the public domain through the Homestead Act, and numerous farmers established prosperous farms. But elsewhere the law was a disappointment. Certainly it did not drain excess population west and thus relocate the poor on the land. Between 1862 and 1890 the American population grew by 32 million people, but only approximately 2 million people settled on the 372,659 farms claimed through the Homestead Act.

The creation of nearly 400,000 farms and the distribution of millions of acres of land to farming families represented by any standard a formidable success, but it was nonetheless only a limited success in terms of the promises made for the act. Much of the reason for such partial success lies in the arid land that many farmers settled. They could not succeed in farming it with techniques suited to humid lands. That the homestead grant of 160 acres of land simply was not an appropriate unit for agriculture in much of the West was only one aspect of the

Original Land Entries, 1800–1934

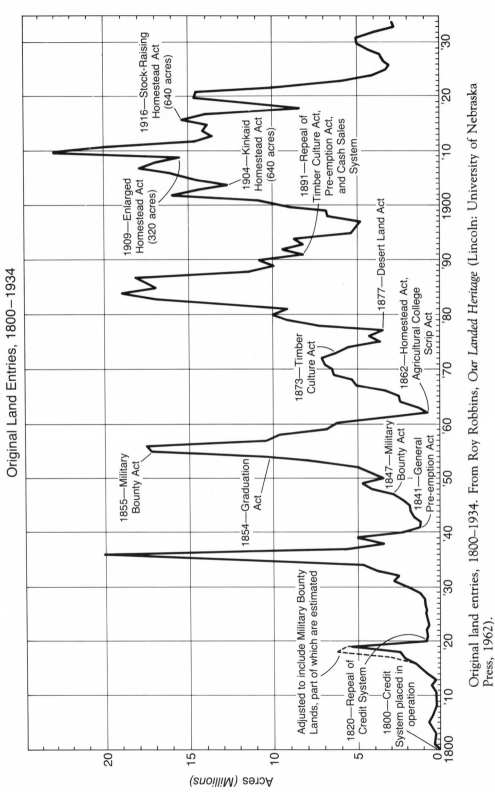

Original land entries, 1800–1934. From Roy Robbins, *Our Landed Heritage* (Lincoln: University of Nebraska Press, 1962).

problem. The limited success of the Homestead Act in distributing land also arose because there existed so many other ways of obtaining title to the public domain.

If we think of the American land system as a warehouse containing the nation's resources, then it was coming by the 1860s to be a warehouse that consisted almost entirely of doors. If the Homestead Act had been the only doorway to the public domain, then it probably would have distributed far more land than it did. But the Homestead Act was not the only doorway, and when farmers filed through it and reached the public domain, they found much of the land already gone. Those who took it had entered through other doors.

Congress did not have complete control over western lands. Texas, which had come into the Union with title to its public lands, operated its own state system. Nor, originally, did the federal system extend into Indian Territory, where the immigrant Indians maintained their own communal landholding patterns. Nor did federal laws apply to areas in the Southwest and California that Spain and Mexico had previously granted to private owners.

Over the rest of the West the federal system did hold sway, but laws that predated the Homestead Act continued to grant access to land. The public land offices continued to sell land, and a thriving market in scrip allowed speculators to buy it at less than the minimum price of $1.25 an acre. Congress continued to grant lands to the states which the states then sold to finance public improvements. Such grants, located largely on public lands west of the Mississippi, totaled roughly 100 million acres after the passage of the Homestead Act. In addition, Congress granted land to western states on their admission to the Union, and the Morrill Act gave each state 30,000 acres of land for each senator and congressman. Congress gave those eastern states that no longer had public lands within their boundaries land scrip, which they then sold. The purchasers used the scrip to claim public lands in the West.

Congress meanwhile continued enthusiastically to hammer away at the few remaining walls holding in the public lands. They created yet more doorways. The Senate ratified Indian treaties that specifically designated land to be sold to the railroads or to be sold by the government in the Indians' behalf instead of being opened up for homesteading. In time, the sales of Indian lands that were closed to homesteading would mount to well over 100 million acres. This figure alone is nearly half as great as that of all the lands granted under the Homestead Act.

Railroad Land Grants

The biggest new gateway to the public lands was, however, large enough to drive a train through. Congress had long made land grants for the development of transportation systems, and even before the Civil War it had made grants to aid railroads east of the Mississippi. Between 1862 and 1872, Congress extended this system of land grants to the West by giving more than 125 million acres of land to aid in the construction of the railroads. In toto, the railroads eventually received from the states and federal government more than 223 million acres of land, 35 million acres of which they later forfeited.

The greatest grants went to the transcontinental railroads. The Union Pacific and Central Pacific—the two companies that shared the first transcontinental route—received 20 odd-numbered sections of land for each mile of track they constructed. In addition, Congress loaned the railroads from $16,000 to $48,000 per mile, depending on the nature of the terrain through which the railroad passed. These loans were in the form of 30-year first-mortgage bonds that paid 6 percent interest. After various mergers, the Union Pacific received a little over 19.1 million acres from the federal government; the Central Pacific about 7.3 million. The largest grant, however, went to the Northern Pacific Railroad. In 1864 the Northern Pacific received 20 sections per mile when building through states and 40 sections per mile when building through the territories. The grant to the Northern Pacific gave that railroad about 40 million acres, or an area roughly the size of New England.

In theory this massive distribution of land was to cost the federal government nothing. Railroads received only every other section of land along their routes, thus creating a checkerboard pattern of alternating railroad and government sections. Congress correctly assumed that the nearer land was to the railroad, the more valuable it would be, and so the laws limited homesteaders to 80 instead of 160 acres within the alternating sections of the railroad grant. By the same logic, purchasers of land within those sections had to pay twice the price of land elsewhere on the public domain. Thus, in theory the United States would earn just as much revenue from railroad lands as if the grants had never been given. In fact, the government seems only to have derived a fraction of the revenue this plan promised, as many of the government sections had already been claimed and others were entered in ways that brought the government less than $2.50 an acre.

Congress obviously realized that in giving lands to the railroads it was closing these lands to free entry under the Homestead Act, but it believed that railroads would sell their own lands quickly and cheaply and thus facilitate settlement. In terms of total agricultural settlement, the railroads did accelerate the rate of settlement. Because railroads provided the cheapest corridor to market, farmers either settled along railroad routes or sought to attract railroads to areas where they had already settled. Western farmers desired railroads and offered incentives to get railroads to come to areas the roads had not yet reached.

Railroads, in turn, desired farmers. Congress gave land grants because not enough people lived in the trans-Missouri West to support a railroad, and so other incentives for building a railroad had to be made available. It was theoretically in the railroads' interest to sell the land they obtained from the government as quickly as possible. They obtained money from the sales to pay the construction costs of the railroad, and by building up population, the railroads insured their own future profits. The settlers would develop farms and ship goods on the completed line. Congress tried not to take chances on rapid sales. Although precise terms varied under individual land grants, the railroads had from three to five years after the completion of their tracks to sell or mortgage the land. At the end of that time the unsold lands would be open for purchase at $1.25 to $2.50 an acre. Thus, although the granting of huge areas of the public domain to the railroads might appear to enrich large private corporations, the Republicans thought that, in fact, the grants would quickly open up new and valuable land to small farmers.

In many places the railroad grants did promote rapid settlement, but in other places things did not work out as Congress had anticipated. The railroad land grants sometimes actually delayed the migration of Anglo American farmers into large areas of the West. Congress had not anticipated how slow some railroad companies would be in selecting their routes and laying their tracks. And until the railroads decided on their actual routes, the government closed all the land along the potential routes to settlement. By various estimates the railroads received from 7 percent to 10 percent of all the land in the United States, but they restricted settlement, for varying amounts of time, on nearly 30 percent of the land. Even when they knew their ultimate routes, the railroad operators often sought to delay making their land selections because land given to the railroads could not be taxed until the companies received their title.

Many western farmers who had initially applauded both the Homestead Act and the railroad grants quickly became frustrated with the new land policy. The railroad grants certainly had fueled national growth, but they had also delayed settlement on millions of acres of the best lands and had closed them to acquisition under the Homestead Act. Western opposition to the railroads, coupled with the consequences of financial irregularities in their management, led Congress to end grants to western railroads after 1871.

Thus, although in theory the Homestead Act opened a vast public domain to western settlers, in fact the act applied on only a fraction of the land. A settler entering Kansas in the late 1860s and early 1870s, for example, would find one-third of that state closed to homesteading. Railroad grants alone tied up 20 percent of the state. And much of the land open to acquisition under the Homestead Act was arid or distant from the railroads. As a result, settlers during every year between 1862 and 1873 purchased more western land than they obtained through the Homestead Act. Only a minority of those who attempted to use the act ever acquired free land under it. Even in a prime agricultural state like Kansas, only 41 percent of the settlers filing between 1862 and 1873 proved up their claims. Another 10 percent of those who filed commuted their entries to cash purchase and bought the land, but 49 percent failed to last five years on their land and thus never secured title. For the Homestead Act as a whole, only one-third of those who filed a claim finally proved it up and obtained title.

The end of railroad land grants still left other contradictions in western land policy. The numerous failed homesteaders who abandoned unworkable claims on the arid lands of western Kansas were one sign of the poor fit between a land policy designed to create small farms and a western landscape not particularly hospitable to small, unirrigated farms. Congress legally and westerners extralegally began to struggle with ways to make the land laws more congruent with western environmental and economic realities. Neither Congress nor western settlers fully succeeded.

The Extralegal Land System

In the West the improvisation of local changes in the federal land system began with the California Gold Rush of 1849. Gold seekers flooding into California discovered that the United States had no law to provide for the sale or lease of lands containing precious minerals. The laws covering claims for lands containing base minerals were clearly inappropriate. Congress was unable to agree on how to solve the problem, and so between 1851 and 1866 the federal government followed a policy of "noninterference." It left the regulation of mining claims to the miners themselves. In the camps miners developed a system of recording claims that had nothing to do with the official land system's provisions for the leasing and sale of mineral lands. Although Congress did pass a law to cover the sale of coal lands in 1864, not until 1866 did Congress finally pass a mining act for precious metals. The act essentially confirmed local practices developed in western mining regions. Only with the Mining Act of 1872 did Congress provide for the sale of mineral lands in the West.

Loggers and livestock raisers confronted a problem similar to that of miners: there was no practical way for them to pursue their occupations on the western public domain. They, too, began to develop a set of extralegal practices to appropriate necessary resources from the public lands. As it did with the miners, the federal government initially tolerated the illegal practices of western loggers, cattlemen, and sheep raisers.

At the root of these land problems was the supposition that agriculture was the highest use for all lands. The law treated other activities as inferior; they must in time yield to farming. The architects of the federal land system had presumed, for example, that lumbering was but an initial stage in the preparation of the land for agriculture. This idea of lumbering as a natural prelude to farming ran into difficulty before lumbermen ever turned to western forests. In Michigan, Wisconsin, and Minnesota awesome pine forests grew on lands that, once put under the plow, only yielded crops of misery. There, lumbering was not a preparation for farming; it was the major use Americans made of the land. Yet the land system contained no provisions for permanently timbered land.

The realization that timber was also the major resource of lands along the northern California, Oregon, and Washington coasts dawned slowly. Farmers proved unwilling to settle those lands, and although lumbermen sought to log them, no legal provision existed for the sale of timber alone. The temptation for loggers to steal timber or to acquire land by fraud and then abandon it became nearly irresistible. For most loggers, obeying the law meant going out of business.

Initially, loggers simply stole logs off the public domain, but in Washington the federal attorney for the territory moved to control the practice. He, and the officials who followed, however, were not unreasonable men. They were overworked and overextended, and they had no desire to spend their days in damp woods searching for timber thieves. They were willing to work out a modus vivendi with the lumbermen. If the timbermen agreed to report how much lumber they had stolen, the agents agreed to fine them at a prearranged rate. In effect, the government treated lumbermen the way most western cities treated prostitutes. They tolerated crimes they could not prevent in order to fine the criminals and gain public revenues.

This compromise with corruption proved unacceptable to Carl Schurz, the secretary of the interior from 1877 to 1881, but most of all it proved unacceptable to the Northern Pacific Railroad, whose officials hoped eventually to gain the land and timber. Federal officials and railroad attorneys began to force lumbermen to acquire the land. One way was to use their employees, or people recruited for the purpose, to claim land under the Homestead Act. The employees never intended to prove up their claims. After filing the claims, these so-called dummy entrymen simply accepted payment from the timbermen and allowed the loggers to cut the timber. The fraud became so open and widespread that lumber companies advertised for dummy entrymen in Seattle newspapers.

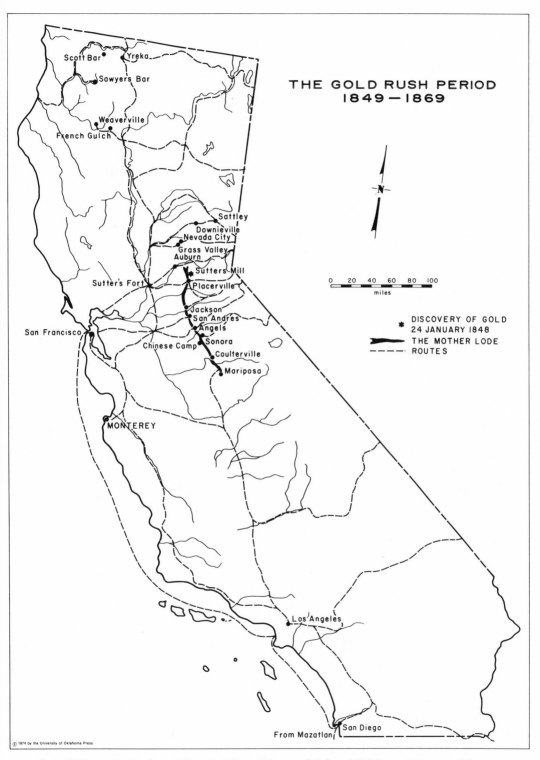

THE GOLD RUSH PERIOD
1849—1869

N

0 20 40 60 80 100
miles

DISCOVERY OF GOLD
24 JANUARY 1848
THE MOTHER LODE
ROUTES

Scott Bar
Yreka
Sawyers Bar
Weaverville
French Gulch
Sattley
Downieville
Nevada City
Grass Valley
Auburn
Sutters Mill
Sutter's Fort
Placerville
Jackson
San Andres
Angels
Sonora
Chinese Camp
Coulterville
San Francisco
Mariposa
MONTEREY
Los Angeles
From Mazatlan
San Diego

From Warren A. Beck and Ynez D. Haase, *Historical Atlas of California* (Norman: University of Oklahoma Press, 1974), map 50.

The passage of the Timber and Stone Act of 1878 allowed these fraudulent entrymen to double their take. The Timber and Stone Act permitted actual settlers to purchase 160 acres of nonagricultural land for $2.50 an acre, but settlers could only use the timber and stone they obtained from the land for their own fuel or construction needs. They could not sell it. Lumbermen, seeing their opportunity, had proxies file claims under the act. They then stripped the claims of timber in defiance of the law's intent. Not until the creation of the national forest system by the federal government and the wholesale purchase of timberlands from the railroads by the timber companies would the federal government be able to develop a realistic way to reconcile logging and the federal land system. By then the nineteenth century had ended.

Ranching proved no more amenable to the requirements of the federal land system than did logging. Cattle and sheep raisers, like loggers and miners, depended on harvesting the existing products of the land rather than cultivating crops. Instead of trees or minerals, livestock raisers sought grass for their livestock. Most could not afford to purchase the huge amounts of land necessary to sustain cattle under a free-grazing system and saw no reason to do so. Nor were there provisions in the law for leasing the public domain. So, like miners and loggers, livestock raisers appropriated the land they needed. They did so by using their employees to file homestead claims on lands bordering water sources. By claiming water sources, they made the surrounding public lands worthless to anyone else. On other occasions cattle ranchers simply fenced in public lands. In any given area the stockmen tried to work out extralegal means to regulate land use among themselves. The failure of such agreements would, as we shall see, lead to violence and range wars.

In a fundamental way, however, livestock raisers differed from loggers and miners; ranchers were often in direct competition with farmers. The extralegal appropriation of the public domain by ranchers—particularly on the plains— seemed a direct threat to the effort to turn the land into farms. Although ranchers contended that the lands they used were unsuitable for farming, the federal government would in the 1880s begin to move against many large ranchers who had fenced public lands for their own use. Given the presumption that farming was the highest use to which land could be put, nothing was to be allowed to bar its progress. The government encouraged the farmers' advance, and by the 1880s farmers had moved out of the prairies and into the arid plains country. There they and the land system faced the challenge presented by the arid environment of so much of the West.

Adapting Land Policy to the West

In the late nineteenth century Congress attempted to face up to the problems that the West presented to farmers. Congressmen introduced and Congress passed a series of land measures designed to allow farmers to produce crops successfully on the Great Plains, on western deserts, and on the heavily timbered lands of the Far West. All of these acts proved to be instructive failures, each revealing western environmental realities.

Congress passed the first of these laws, the Timber Culture Act, in 1873. The act was intended "to encourage the growth of timber on the western prairies." It provided a single quarter-section of land to any head of a family who planted and

Claim shacks such as this one fulfilled the letter, if not the spirit, of the Homestead Act's requirements for improvements on the land.

maintained 40 acres of trees for ten years. This attempt to forest the prairies recognized a practical problem—the lack of timber on the prairies and plains— but it attempted to solve that problem by accepting the dubious scientific theory that rain follows the plow. Rain-follows-the-plow theorists recognized that ade-quate rainfall was necessary for the growth of trees, but they also believed that trees also encouraged increased rainfall. By planting trees under the Timber Culture Act, farmers could, in effect, alter the climate and make it more humid.

The law, however, did not transform the climate; instead, the climate trans-formed the law. Drought, the destruction of young seedlings by grasshoppers, and the inability of settlers to care for 40 acres of saplings in a region unsuited to their growth convinced Congress to reduce the required planting to 10 acres in 1878. By 1882 the commissioner of the General Land Office was urging the repeal of the act. A law designed to promote the growth of trees had been put to more lucrative purposes. Claimants used the act to hold likely land from settlement until someone agreed to pay them to relinquish their claim. In Nebraska, Kansas, and Colorado, ranchers had their cowboys file false timber culture claims on regions near rivers and streams to prevent them from being settled by farmers. Not until 1891 did Congress give in and repeal the act.

Failing to change arid climates, Congress more realistically passed laws intended to enable settlers to adapt their farming to the land. In 1877, Congress passed legislation designed to encourage the irrigation of arid land. Under this first Desert Land Act a person could obtain 640 acres of land, a full section, in any of eleven western states and territories for $1.25 an acre if he or she agreed to irrigate it within three years of filing. The law reflected the general American ignorance of irrigation. No settler could bring 640 acres into irrigation within three years. Instead of helping settlers, the law was a boon to speculators. A speculator now had only to pay $0.25 an acre to hold potentially valuable land off the market for three years, when the remainder of the price was due.

At the end of three years, speculators easily avoided the intent of the law and completed their claim. The original Desert Land Act of 1876 called for adequate irrigation, but it did not specify how officials of the land office could determine what was adequate. This omission created vast opportunities for fraud. Speculators paid people to make claims and plow a few furrows. The speculators then claimed the furrows were irrigation ditches. To counter such fraud, Congress in 1890 detailed the necessary improvements and the amount of irrigation, but because the act continued to underestimate the costs of irrigation and did not close off all the avenues for fraud, opposition to the Desert Land Act continued.

The Desert Land Act at least indicated a willingness to recognize the need for irrigation on much western land, but Congress continued to think of farm development as largely an individual effort. Proponents of the legislation remained confident that once given a larger grant by the government, settlers would find some way to irrigate the land. They believed western farmers, aided by government land grants, would subdue the West as earlier farmers had subdued the East.

By the 1880s, however, it began to appear that individual settlement may have reached its limits. Congressional reforms seemed only to worsen the problems of a land system already ill-adapted to the West. To many late-nineteenth-century reformers, particularly to John Wesley Powell, the public domain had become a circus of inefficiency and corruption. In one ring ranchers illegally fenced off huge areas of the public domain; in another, loggers flagrantly stole timber from the public lands. In the third ring, speculators used the Desert Land Act and other legislation to derive profits that the framers of the law had never intended to make available. And through it all, or so it seemed, wandered the small farmers, transformed from hearty yeomen into perennial suckers, trying to establish 160-acre farms on a land that could not sustain them.

Powell's criticism of the land system emerged in an 1878 document entitled *A Report on the Lands of the Arid Regions of the United States*. Settlers could not occupy most of the western United States, Powell asserted, by following the methods developed in the more humid regions of the country. Instead, what Powell proposed amounted to zoning on a massive scale. The government surveys would map the region, discover its resources, and classify the lands according to their best use: mining, logging, grazing, agriculture, and so on. To exploit the land effectively, Powell proposed organizing settlers into irrigation and pasturage districts. In the irrigation districts the farms would be 80 acres, not the 160 acres granted under the Homestead Act. In the grazing districts, settlers could obtain 2,560 acres. In both districts the law would attach water rights to the land. Without rights to water, Powell wrote, western lands were commercially worthless. In both kinds of districts the government would require farmers and ranchers to form cooperatives to manage irrigation systems and to govern grazing on unfenced lands.

Water, Powell recognized, was the key to western development, and western water would have to be developed and controlled by the federal government, the state governments, or large corporations. No one else had the resources to do it. Powell's preference was clear. Water, he proclaimed, must be federally developed through dams, canals, and ditches, but control of its use must rest at the local level in democratically organized irrigation and grazing districts consisting only of small landholders. Powell blended an idealized view of communal control of water in the small Mormon villages of Utah with his memories of his own midwestern youth to foresee a rural, democratic, decentralized West. There, people would develop resources with federal aid and then cooperatively manage them. Federal development would supposedly yield a rural West of small farmers.

Powell's report was a challenge to the normal procedures of Anglo American settlement. Recognizing its implications, opponents united to kill it. Settlers rejected the notion that government experts would tell them the best use for land and restrict the size of their farms. The report, they thought, served the interests of large cattlemen. The big cattlemen, who knew that the control of water sources meant de facto control of huge areas of surrounding land, feared that Powell's irrigation districts would threaten their monopoly on water. Speculators feared that the report would deny them the opportunity to grow rich from buying and selling lands. Boomers thought it would restrict western growth, because a 2,500-acre ranch would support only one family, whereas 160-acre farms on the same tract would support 15. Boosters preferred to put their faith in the theory that rain would follow the plow. Knowing little of the wet and dry cycles of the plains, they cited contemporary statistics that seemed to show that the West was growing more moist.

Powell's report was not an argument against development. Instead, Powell was arguing for planning instead of chance, for conducting settlement according to the realities of the West instead of people's hopes about what the West would be. Cooperative, not individualistic, settlement, Powell contended, was best suited to the West. Although they often reached a pitch of hysteria, Powell's opponents did, in a sense, go to the heart of the matter. Basically they were asking, Whose interests would such reforms serve? What, when settlement began with 2,500-acre purchases, was to prevent the proposal from becoming not a democratic reform but a tool of large landowners or of big cattlemen? Would local people or large capitalists with access to Washington and Congress have the most influence with the distant federal bureaucracy that planned the use of the land? Westerners asked these questions repeatedly over the next 100 years as other federal plans to govern land use took shape. Development per se was not the issue. Americans would not question western development until the late twentieth century. The quarrel over development evolved over how it would proceed and whose interests it would serve. This was a question of politics and power.

Politics killed Powell's larger aims. Powell's vision of the West alienated too many powerful constituencies. Congress referred the whole matter of western lands and the western surveys to the same committee of experts from the National Academy of Sciences that recommended the creation of the U.S. Geological Survey. Those scientists recommended a restructuring of land laws in the West to provide the kind of land classification Powell had suggested, but their proposals met intense opposition from western congressmen, who succeeded in blocking reform.

Powell's attempts to reform the land system failed, but they would not be the last. Despite the scale, lavishness, and rapidity of the government's disbursements of the public lands, an immense domain—much of it desert and mountains— remained under federal ownership at the close of the nineteenth century. Continued efforts to bring coherence and efficiency to the use of that land would bring a fundamental change in the land system itself. By the end of the century a consensus emerged that perhaps the federal government should not distribute the entire public domain. The government should retain ownership of this land. This consensus would shape the western landscape in the twentieth century; it would give the federal government a lasting presence in the region.

Readings

Carstensen, Vernon (ed.). *The Public Lands: Studies in the History of the Public Domain.* Madison: University of Wisconsin Press, 1968.

Gates, Paul Wallace. *History of Public Land Law Development.* Washington, D.C.: Government Printing Office, 1968.

Hibbard, Benjamin H. *A History of Public Land Policies.* New York: The Macmillan Company, 1924.

Johnson, Hildegard Binder. *Order upon the Land.* New York: Oxford University Press, 1976.

Opie, John. *The Law of the Land: 200 Years of American Farmland Policy.* Lincoln: University of Nebraska Press, 1987.

Rohrbough, Malcolm J. *The Land Office Business: The Settlement and Administration of American Public Lands, 1789–1837.* New York: Oxford University Press, 1968.

Swierenga, Robert P. *Pioneers and Profits: Land Speculation on the Iowa Frontier.* Ames: Iowa State University Press, 1968.

Wyant, William K., *Westward in Eden.* Berkeley: University of California Press, 1982.

CHAPTER 7

Territorial Government

Federal ownership of the public domain gave the central government a distinctive permanent presence in the West, but for most of the nineteenth century an equally obvious governmental presence came through the territorial system. For a good part of the late nineteenth century the federal government administered much of the American West as a colony of the United States. The territories could not elect their highest officials nor pass their own laws without federal supervision. Only Texas and California skipped the territorial period and immediately entered the Union as states. The rest of the West comprised, for varying lengths of time, the territories. American citizens who lived there gave up some of the rights to self-government that most white males elsewhere took for granted.

Westerners often compared their condition to that of the thirteen colonies before independence. They had a much greater sense of the federal government as an obtrusive presence in their lives than did other Americans. In some ways the comparison with the thirteen colonies was an apt one, for soon after achieving independence from Great Britain the original colonies had erected a colonial system modeled closely on the one that they had just overthrown. The difference, of course, was that western territories, unlike the thirteen colonies, could look forward to eventual statehood and equality with the "mother country."

Even before the constitution was ratified, the United States had, under the Articles of Confederation, set out the basic outlines of the American territorial system in the Northwest Ordinance of 1787. After the ratification of the constitution, Congress reenacted the bill in 1789. The Northwest Ordinance salvaged what its authors thought were the most workable parts of the old British system. To it they added sections designed to protect private property against any attacks that settlers of the new territories might make upon it. They then gave this old administrative framework a new coating of republicanism with clauses to protect basic civil liberties and provide for public education. Powerful congressmen usually selected territorial officeholders, but the president made the appointments. With a few modifications, this law governed the administration of the territories until the early twentieth century.

The framers of the Northwest Ordinance expected territorial expansion to mirror the growth of the old English colonies. They envisioned three stages of development. The first stage, which Congress abandoned before the United States acquired the trans-Missouri West, was more authoritarian than the British colonial system that the colonists themselves had rebelled against. The second stage would begin when there were 5,000 male voters in the territory. At that point the citizens could elect an assembly and a nonvoting delegate to Congress. But Congress still retained considerable authority. Not only did it continue to control the appointment of the governor and judges, but Congress also had to approve the members of the upper house of the assembly— the council. Congress also retained the right to veto any legislation passed by the assembly.

The third stage, and the critical administrative innovation in the bill, came when the territory reached a population of 60,000. The citizens of the territory could then hold a constitutional convention, elect their own officials, and petition Congress for admission to the Union. Here Congress abandoned the precedents of British colonialism and gave the territories what the American revolutionaries had demanded: representation, equality with the "mother country," and home rule, or, in this case, statehood.

This system underwent a significant evolution before Congress organized any territories in the American West. By 1825, Congress no longer required the first stage of government; it made both houses of the assembly elective, and it eased the requirements for voting so much that there was virtually universal white male suffrage in the territories. These changes were embodied in the Wisconsin Organic Act of 1836.

The Wisconsin Organic Act eventually operated like a political cookie cutter, stamping out identical governments across the West. But before it could do so it had to overcome a significant challenge to the whole territorial system. The Northwest Ordinance of 1787 operated on the assumption that the federal government had the duty and responsibility of creating and supervising the government of the territories. Senator Stephen Douglas of Illinois, however, denied the entire premise that underlay the Northwest Ordinance: that territories could only gradually assume the responsibilities of self-government. He asserted a doctrine of popular sovereignty: settlers were a legitimate political community from the beginning and should be allowed to organize their own governments with minimal congressional supervision. Douglas, perhaps the politician most sympathetic to the territorial settlers, advanced popular sovereignty to defuse the real resentments of these settlers, but he also saw it as a way to avoid the growing dispute over slavery in the territories.

The dispute over the governing of the territories—like the parallel dispute over expansion—became part of the larger sectional conflict that was tearing the country in two. In both disputes, the central issue was the spread of slavery. Because of slavery, Congress's usual disinterest in territorial matters gave way to rapt attention. In the late 1840s and 1850s, just as Congress set about organizing the first western territories, the sectional conflict over slavery seemed ready to push the territorial system itself to the verge of collapse. While the territorial system teetered on the edge of disaster in Kansas, it simultaneously had to confront rebellion and four years of military rule in New Mexico, problems with the Mormons in Utah, and the arbitrary actions of territorial governor Isaac Stevens in Washington. If the late 1840s and 1850s had to stand alone, it might appear that the United States was no more capable of effectively governing a western empire than Spain, Mexico, or Great Britain had been.

New Mexico

The initial failure of the territorial system occurred in New Mexico. After his conquest of New Mexico, General Stephen Kearny, following written suggestions by President Polk and his secretary of state, approved the so-called Kearny Code, which combined Mexican, Texan, and American statutes to create a government. In general form, the government of New Mexico resembled other territorial governments then in place. Kearny largely ignored Polk's suggestion that he seek continuity by incorporating as much of existing New Mexican governmental structure and staff as possible. Instead, Kearny appointed the members of the "American party" of Taos and Santa Fe merchants to run the government. Only two native New Mexicans held significant offices (and both of them had strong American connections). Kearny largely ignored ruling Santa Fe families and the powerful priest of Taos, Padre José Antonio Martínez. The general had created an unfamiliar government and staffed it with foreigners.

New Mexicans resisted the new government with more force than they had resisted Kearny and his army. Many New Mexicans bridled at the arrogance of the American soldiers who surrounded them, and they worried about rumors that the Americans would soon undertake a wholesale confiscation of lands, including those of the Pueblos. Actual rebellion came in January of 1847. Taos Indians killed the American governor, Charles Bent, and any other members of the American party they could find. A simultaneous rebellion was supposed to have taken place in Santa Fe, but it failed to occur, and the Americans quickly defeated the rebels of Taos. They tried the leaders of the rebellion for treason and hanged them. A young American, Lewis Garrard, attended the trial. To him, it seemed a travesty to condemn as traitors Indians who were fighting to preserve their lands and community. After watching the judge sentence the rebels to death, he wrote: "Justice! Out upon the word, when its distorted meaning is the warrant for murdering those who defend to the last their country and their homes."

Civil government in New Mexico, whatever its faults, was temporarily buried with Charles Bent. For nearly four years military commanders ruled the region. Little concerned with either civil rights or elections, they established what amounted to a military dictatorship while Congress debated the future status of New Mexico and Texas attempted to annex it. Not until 1850, with the establishment of the Territory of New Mexico, would the military rule of 1,000 Anglo Americans over 50,000 Mexican Americans come to an end. By then far more serious challenges to the territorial system loomed on the horizon.

Slavery in the Territories

For more than a generation most Americans believed that the Missouri Compromise of 1820 had settled the question of slavery in the territories. The Missouri Compromise fixed the latitude of 36°30' north as the future boundary between slave and free territories for most of the Louisiana Purchase (with slavery allowed north of that line only in Missouri). Former president Thomas Jefferson had likened the debate over the expansion of slavery to a fire bell in the night: the compromise had stilled the alarm; the fire, however, continued to smolder. The compromise held until the 1840s, when the acquisition of Texas and the Mexican cession fanned the ashes of the conflict by raising anew the question of slavery in the territories.

The North had a solution to the question of slavery in the territories: the Wilmot Proviso. Passed by the House of Representatives on a hot and humid Saturday night in early August of 1846, the proviso would have banned slavery from all territory acquired from Mexico. The proviso, an amendment to an appropriations bill for the negotiation of peace with Mexico, was the work of northern antislavery Democrats angry at southern domination of their party and fearful that President Polk was saddling them with unpopular proslavery positions. A war to expand slavery, they feared, would cripple the election chances of the Democrats in the North. The proviso passed the House of Representatives on a nearly straight sectional vote, but it died in the Senate, where southern strength (15 slave states to 14 free states in 1847) was greater than that of the North.

The Wilmot Proviso failed to pass, but it became one of those measures the failure of which concealed a larger success. The proviso had raised an issue that politicians could not quiet and that would shape national politics in the 1850s: the nonextension of slavery into the territories. Nonextension did not equal the abolition of slavery. Those who favored nonextension were not advocating eliminating slavery within the South. They were merely arguing that the South should not extend slavery any farther. David Wilmot, the Pennsylvania congressman who introduced the measure, went out of his way to disassociate himself from an opposition to slavery per se. He had, he said, "no squeamish sensitiveness upon the subject of slavery, no morbid sympathy for the slave." The effect of slavery on white labor, not black labor, was what concerned him. Free Soilers— those who wanted to ban slavery from the territories—were not, on the whole, advocates of black equality. Very often they were as racist as their southern opponents. When Free Soilers came to control Kansas, one of their earliest acts was a measure banning the settlement of blacks, free or slave. The quarrel between North and South, it must be stressed, was over the expansion of slavery, not over its existence.

If Free Soilers were not opposed to the existence of slavery in the South, why should they oppose it in the West? Their opposition grew out of what they saw as the lessons of the separate sectional evolution of the North and South. Free Soilers were northerners who regarded the North as a progressive society blessed with abundant opportunities for its citizens. They thought that its people were independent and largely of "the middling sort"—neither rich nor poor. All supposedly had a chance to rise in this society, if not to riches then to the prosperous life of successful farmers and businessmen.

The South, on the other hand, seemed to Free Soilers almost a reverse of the North. Whereas the North was progressive, the South was backward and feudal. Whereas the North was middle-class and egalitarian, the South had extremes of wealth and poverty and was dominated by a small elite. Whereas the North was a land of opportunity, the South was a land where slavery made it almost impossible for white labor to get its just rewards. The North elevated labor and hard work; the South degraded them. Free laborers could not compete against workers who drew no wage and whose work was coerced. Blacks might be victims of slavery, but for those who believed in what historians have come to call the free labor ideology, white laborers were also slavery's victims. The whole society suffered to enrich a few.

But the fear that northerners had of southern success belied their assertions that the section was backward and enfeebled. Southern agriculture was extraordinarily productive. The yield of raw cotton in the South had doubled every decade after 1800; no northern commodity matched that record. About 60 percent of all American exports originated in the South, and the foreign exchange they earned was critical to American economic growth. What northerners took as signs of southern backwardness—the section's lack of urban centers, its lack of industry, its high rates of illiteracy—southerners praised as signs of southern virtue. Farming, they contended, was the highest and most republican of avocations, and education was unnecessary for the mass of people who tilled the soil.

What was more important than the particulars of this debate was that most Americans, North or South, began to see the differences dividing the sections as more significant than the common culture and institutions that united them. When looking south, northerners saw a threat to their own interests. They were worried about slavery's effect on white labor, not on black labor.

The West became an area of critical importance to those who accepted the assumptions of the northern free labor ideology. As they saw it, the driving force of the northern system was its equality of opportunity, and central to that opportunity was the ability of northerners to get cheap land and create their own farms. The expansion of slavery threatened to cut off northern access to cheap land. Northerners would be unable to compete with slaveholders who commanded the unpaid labor of blacks. Without access to the West, opportunity in the North would decline, and the North, too, would begin to evolve into a class society with great extremes of wealth and poverty. Even those northerners who never intended to go West and get a farm thus had an interest in the outcome of the struggle for the territories. For if slavery cut off their access to western lands, then they and their children would eventually find their way of life destroyed. The question, as one orator succinctly put the issue in 1848, "is not whether black men are to be made free but whether white men are to remain free." This issue would become the cornerstone of the new Republican party. Salmon Chase, one of the party's leaders, phrased the issues starkly and effectively. The choice between a free West and a slave West was the choice between freedom and serfdom, freeholds and tenancies, democracy and despotism, education and ignorance, progress and stagnation.

Attempts at Compromise

With so much riding on the issue, congressional attempts at compromise achieved only limited success. The Compromise of 1850, which admitted California as a free state, pared down the exaggerated boundaries claimed by Texas, and organized New Mexico and Utah territories with no restrictions on slavery, solved the immediate problem of administering the Mexican cession. It also gave the South a fugitive slave law that allowed southerners to retrieve escaped slaves even from northern states that had abolished slavery.

The Compromise of 1850 postponed rather than averted the crisis. The issue rose again in proposals to organize territorial governments in Kansas and Nebraska.

Stephen A. Douglas, a Democratic senator from Illinois, was eager to organize the new territories out of lands promised in perpetuity to tribes removed from the East only a few years before. He desired to create the new territories in order to forward his plans for a transcontinental railroad that would begin in his home state. A new territory was necessary, for, as a Missouri congressman asked, how "in the name of God . . . is the railroad to be made if you will never let people live on the lands through which the road passes?"

Douglas realized that he needed southern support in Congress for his plans. Senator David R. Atchison of Missouri let him know what the cost of the support would be. Atchison told Douglas he would see Nebraska "sink in Hell" before voting to organize it as a free territory as the Missouri Compromise demanded. Regarding the slavery issue as a Gordian knot restraining his plans, Douglas, who already believed settlers were fully competent "to judge for themselves what kinds of laws and institutions were best adapted to their conditions and interests," sliced through the slavery controversy with the sword of popular sovereignty: let the settlers of each territory decide whether the territory was to be slave or free.

Douglas forged his sword in Congress, where he sponsored the Kansas-Nebraska Act that organized the two new territories. Douglas realized his action would "raise a hell of a storm" in the North. He may have expected a thunderstorm; he got a tornado. The Kansas-Nebraska Act created a political upheaval that would culminate in the Civil War. With a single measure, Douglas had repealed the Missouri Compromise under the terms of which Kansas and Nebraska both would have been free states, and he had scrapped basic practices of the territorial system. From the beginning of the republic the law had operated on the assumption that the federal government controlled the territories, that it would dictate the organization of government, and that self-rule would come gradually. The Kansas-Nebraska Act made self-rule immediate. It relegated questions of critical national interest—the expansion of slavery—to a few thousand voters in a western territory. It upset the political balance between the North and South.

The North was outraged. It regarded the Kansas-Nebraska Act as a sellout to the South. The issue split the Democratic party and helped galvanize the new Republican party, and Douglas ruefully admitted that he could travel from Boston to Chicago by the light of his own burning effigies. The Democrats lost 66 of their 91 northern congressmen in the 1854 elections.

Kansas

Under the Kansas-Nebraska Act, the voters in Kansas were to decide whether the territory would be slave or free. "Since there is no escaping your challenge," Senator William H. Seward of New York told southern senators, "I accept it in behalf of the cause of freedom. We will engage in competition for the virgin soil of Kansas." Atchison of Missouri told his southern colleagues: "We are playing for a mighty stake. The game must be played boldly. . . . If we win we can carry slavery to the Pacific Ocean, if we fail we lose Missouri Arkansas Texas [sic] and all the territories." Neither side felt it could afford to lose the elections. Both sides organized accordingly.

To make Kansas free, New England abolitionists formed the New England Emigrant Aid Company to finance the movement of abolitionist settlers to the West. The abolitionists garnered much publicity but moved relatively few settlers.

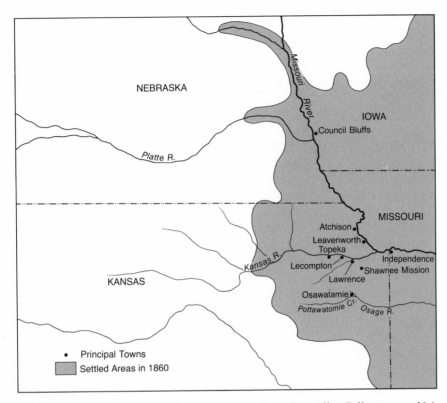

The settlement of Kansas and Nebraska, 1854–60. From Ray Allen Billington and Martin Ridge, *Westward Expansion* (New York: Macmillan, 1982).

About 4,200 settlers came to Kansas from New England, and only about 1,200 of them got help from the New England Emigrant Aid Company. The New Englanders settled largely around Lawrence and Topeka. Most Free Soil settlers came from neighboring states of the Midwest, and although they were opposed to slavery in Kansas, they were not abolitionists.

Southerners, who regarded Kansas as naturally destined for slavery because of its proximity to the slave state of Missouri, were outraged by northern efforts to control the territory. A free Kansas on the border of Missouri would, they argued, create too great a temptation for slaves to escape. They were ready to do what was necessary to make Kansas a slave state. "We are organizing," Atchison told Senator Jefferson Davis of Mississippi: "We will be compelled to shoot, burn, & hang, but the thing will soon be over."

The contest began in November of 1854 when Atchison led a large group of border ruffians across the Missouri to vote illegally in the Kansas elections for a delegate to Congress. Out of 6,318 votes cast in the legislative elections of 1855, a congressional investigation found 4,908 were fraudulent. Despite the fraud, the illegally elected legislature remained seated, and legitimate Free Soil settlers, who by 1855 outnumbered legitimate proslave settlers, refused to accept its authority. They set up a government of their own at Topeka to oppose the proslavery government at Lecompton. Both sides quickly armed to the teeth.

This battery of free state settlers in Kansas ready to defend Lawrence in 1856 was part of the larger breakdown of order in the western territories in the 1850s.

In 1856 proslavery Judge Samuel Lecompte instructed a grand jury to indict free-state government officials for treason and authorized the deputation of Missourians to arrest them. Many of these officials lived in Lawrence, the heart of Free Soil strength in Kansas, and the Missourians laid siege to the town on May 21. Free-state leaders decided against resistance, and the Missourians not only arrested the leaders but also demolished two newspaper offices, plundered houses and shops, and burned the hotel and the free-state governor's house to the ground. Charles Sumner of Massachusetts arose in the Senate to denounce the "Sack of Lawrence" as the work of "murderous robbers from Missouri, hirelings picked from the drunken spew and vomit of an uneasy civilization." Two days later Congressman Preston Brooks of South Carolina assaulted Sumner on the floor of the Senate, beating him over the head with a gold-headed cane 30 times or more. He left Sumner collapsed at his desk, his head soaked in blood.

Kansas became a rehearsal for the Civil War. After the Sack of Lawrence and the beating of Sumner, Kansas descended into civil war. Like some Old Testament patriarch, the Free Soiler and abolitionist John Brown gathered his sons about him and set out to take revenge for the Sack of Lawrence. Telling his followers that we must "fight fire with fire," Brown selected five proslavery settlers living along Potawatomie Creek, none of whom had been involved in violence against free-state settlers, and murdered them, mangling some of their bodies. The combination of the Sack of Lawrence and the Potawatomie Massacre, as Brown's little piece of butchery was called, threw Kansas into chaos.

John Brown became a hero in the North partially because northern settlers had come to despise the Missourians, like those he killed, as nearly subhuman. Even Charles Stearns, perhaps the only pacifist abolitionist in Kansas Territory, thought proslavery Missourians—Pukes, as the northerners called them—were not "men made in God's image" but were "demons from the bottomless pit and may be shot with impunity." To the Missourians, the free-state settlers were "the foreign foe" who sought to crush the South. They were "a pack of evil hypocrites . . . long-faced sanctimonious Yankees." Proslavery settlers claimed that the Free Soilers came to Kansas "for the express purpose of stealing, running off, and hiding runaway negroes from Missouri [and] taking to their own bed and their own arms, a stinking negro wench." Federal troops prevented full-scale battles between the two sides, but they could not stop guerrilla warfare. House and crop burnings, livestock thefts, tarring and feathering, torture, murder, and mutilation of the corpses of the slain all became commonplace. Within a few months 200 more people had met violent death, and the combatants had destroyed two million dollars' worth of property. Kansas became "Bleeding Kansas," and a major issue for the new Republican party. Their unsuccessful candidate in 1856 was John C. Frémont, whose slogan was "Free Soil, Free Men and Frémont."

In the fall of 1856, Kansas Governor John W. Geary—a six-foot, five-inch former mayor of San Francisco—cleverly nationalized both the proslavery and free-state militias and used federal troops to suppress the fighting. He could not, however, suppress the underlying conflict. Overriding his veto, the proslavery legislature arranged for a rigged constitutional convention in 1857 that passed the Lecompton Constitution. That document not only instituted slavery in Kansas but also made it permanent: later voters could not make it illegal. The convention phrased a referendum on the constitution in such a way that a vote for or a vote against both approved slavery. Free Soilers refused to vote, and the proslave settlers submitted the constitution to Congress as the basis for statehood. President James Buchanan accepted it, but Stephen Douglas, denouncing the Lecompton Constitution as a travesty of popular sovereignty, led the opposition in Congress. Congress refused to allow Kansas into the Union as a slave state. In Kansas in 1858 the fighting and the bleeding resumed. In 1861, after the secession of the South, Kansas entered the Union not only as a free state but also as one of the most heavily Republican states in the country.

Utah

As the territorial system collapsed in Kansas, it was also failing in Utah. There, too, settlers eventually appealed to popular sovereignty to uphold another "peculiar institution"—in this case polygamy. There, too, the federal government's right to govern had to be sustained by force. President Buchanan bungled the Utah situation just as badly as he and President Franklin Pierce had mishandled Kansas, but their incompetence should not disguise the real challenge that Utah presented to federal control over the territories.

By the 1850s the Mormons who had settled Utah were one of the most despised and persecuted groups in the United States. Their non-Mormon neighbors had driven them by force from Missouri and Illinois and had murdered their leader,

Joseph Smith. The opposition to the Mormon church that led to violence and persecution in the Midwest came from a conviction on the part of many Americans that the Mormon beliefs and practices were both blasphemous and incompatible with the rights and responsibilities of citizens of a republic. Mormons, it should be pointed out, were not the only people to face such accusations of un-Americanism. Many Americans leveled the same charges against Catholics.

Both Mormons and Catholics believed that God could and did speak directly to the leader of the church to instruct him on issues of faith and morals, although Catholics had not yet made this an article of faith. God spoke more frequently to Joseph Smith and his successor, Brigham Young, the prophet, seer, and revelator of the Mormon church, than to the Pope, but Protestants, who believed that the Bible alone contained the basic truth of Christianity, thought that any such claim of special revelation was blasphemous. Most Americans also believed that the hierarchies of both the Mormon and Catholic churches denied the separation of church and state embodied in the Constitution. Anti-Catholics and anti-Mormons charged that the bloc voting under the direction of church leaders, which indeed did occur, demonstrated the incapacity of such people for citizenship. Many Protestants thought that the fundamental loyalty of Catholics and Mormons was to their church, not to the republic. To be Catholic or Mormon was thus necessarily to be un-American, since American republicanism depended on a free electorate. Finally, Protestant Americans imagined both Mormonism and Catholicism as hives of immorality and perverse sexuality. The lurid stories that circulated about the activities of Catholic priests and nuns and the Mormon practice of polygamy gave such charges wide credence.

That Mormons should be tainted with the brush of un-Americanism is particularly ironic because Mormonism is in many ways the most American of religions. Founded in the United States by a New Englander, it incorporated many of the popular beliefs, religious controversies, and social values of early-nineteenth-century rural New York in its theology. Nonetheless, persecution in Missouri and Illinois did in many ways mold the early Mormon church into an institution designed to survive in a world of enemies. The church engaged in political practices that challenged the constitution, the laws of the United States, and the power of the federal government.

Such practices had brought trouble in Illinois, where Joseph Smith seemed to many a political oligarch in command of a private army that was ready to suppress constitutional rights of free speech and a free press, but in Utah the Mormons nearly brought civil war. They had hoped to avoid conflict with the government by preempting a huge section of the West for a state they called Deseret and governing it themselves. Ironically, the Mormons, whom the Missourians had originally denounced as abolitionists, now adopted the most extreme states' rights doctrines in Utah in order to protect their own peculiar institution—the practice of polygamy. The Mormons established a government that was closer to a theocracy than to the republican norms of the United States. In Deseret, Brigham Young was governor, and the leading officials of the government were also the leading officials of the church. In the words of one historian, they "simply elaborated their ecclesiastical machinery into a government." The government tended to rubber-stamp what church councils had already decided. Although nominally democratic, church leaders often selected members of the legislature without either their consent or their knowledge. Hosea Stout, for example, noted in his diary in 1849: "On Tuesday evening I received a notification to meet in the House of Representatives on Saturday next, I being a member of that Body. By what process I became a Representative, I know not."

The Mormons justified this unique form of government, republican in form, theocratic in practice, with Stephen Douglas's doctrine of popular sovereignty. The settlers of a territory, they declared, knew best what kind of government was suited to their growth and prosperity. But when the Mormons attempted to get Congress to recognize the new territory of Deseret as a state, they failed. Congress paid little attention to the Mormon efforts and eliminated large sections of Deseret from the new territory of Utah that the federal government created in 1850.

Congress, however, was not entirely hostile to the Mormons. The president appointed Brigham Young governor of Utah Territory, and other Mormons or friends of Mormons obtained high office. Along with these appointments came the usual collection of hacks consigned to the territories to make their way in the world. These appointees arrived to find that Brigham Young already controlled all the lucrative federal patronage in the territory, and he was not about to share it with gentiles (as the Mormons called all non-Mormons). The territorial supreme court justices also found that the Mormons had used a loophole in the legislation creating Utah to turn the probate courts, the functions of which were normally limited, into a separate Mormon court system. As a result, few or no cases ever ended up in the federal courts. Disappointed that such a long journey to such a strange place should promise so few material rewards, one of the new officials, Judge Perry Brocchus, denounced Brigham Young and Mormonism at the major Mormon secular celebration, a Pioneer Day picnic. Brocchus, speaking with Young in attendance, showed more courage than good sense and nearly provoked a riot. Having depleted his available supply of valor, he decided to accompany his gentile colleagues when they departed the territory two months later. Brigham Young, with a political astuteness that on this occasion rivaled that of Judge Brocchus, decided the time was ripe to proclaim publicly the practice of polygamy.

All the material for a political conflagration had now been gathered, but surprisingly no one stepped forward to light it. Congress was cynical enough to realize the "flying officers," as Brocchus and his colleagues were called, were more interested in spoils than principles. Given the choice of returning to Utah or resigning, they resigned. The announcement of polygamy brought the predictable denunciation of the Mormons, but President Pierce was reluctant to interfere with popular sovereignty and peculiar institutions in Utah while he was defending them in Kansas. Congress sent new officials to Utah who were as corrupt as the old, and Brigham Young continued to act as if he thought he had to follow the territorial arrangements for Utah only when it suited his convenience.

The new territorial supreme court justices took up the conflict with Brigham Young and the Mormons where the old justices had left off. They tried to force litigation into the territorial courts by declaring the Mormon probate court system unconstitutional. This proved partially successful. Attempts by the Mormon hierarchy to develop industry in Utah collapsed miserably in 1855 and 1856 while the territory was simultaneously beset with a severe winter followed by a drought. Many Mormons, including members of the hierarchy, were destitute and began to accept jury duty or volunteered as witnesses in the hope of gaining some pay

FT. HALL

SALT LAKE
CUTOFF

SALT LAKE CITY

CALIFORNIA
TRAIL

FT. BRIDGER

(FT. LARAMIE)

MORMON
TRAIL

"WINTER QUARTERS"

(COUNCIL BLUFFS)

MORMON STATION

MORMON
CORRIDOR

MOAB

BEAVER
PAROWAN
CEDAR CITY
MOUNTAIN MEADOW
ST. GEORGE
LITTLEFIELD
LAS VEGAS

LEE'S FERRY

TUBA CITY

BARSTOW

SAN BERNARDINO

HOLBROOK

TEMPE
MESA

LUNA

THATCHER

POMERENE

ST. DAVID

PROPOSED STATE OF DESERET, 1849
• MORMON SETTLEMENTS
X MORMON FERRIES
(FT. LARAMIE) NON-MORMON SETTLEMENTS

The Mormon empire. From Warren A. Beck and Ynez D. Haase, *Historical Atlas of the American West* (Norman: University of Oklahoma Press, 1989), map 39.

Brigham Young, appointed governor and then denounced as a traitor, symbolized the federal government's problem of controlling the West in the 1850s.

to relieve their poverty. Young issued tirades against them, and Jedediah M. Grant, a member of the Mormon First Presidency and the mayor of Salt Lake City, called for a general reformation that would weed out the weak. The guilty, Grant asserted, should not only confess their sins but also appoint a place where the faithful might shed the sinners' blood. The faithful might even take sinners' lives under the doctrine of blood atonement.

In the midst of these interconnected crises, all order began to unravel in Utah. Mormon youths broke into the offices of Judge George Stiles of the territorial court and stole and destroyed court records. Rumors of murders and blood atonement exacted by the Danites, or Avenging Angels, a band of murderers who supposedly acted under the command of Brigham Young, circulated in the territory. Once again fearful federal officials fled Utah. The Mormons were clearly defying federal rule in Utah, and this second band of fugitive officials declared that the Mormons were in revolt against the United States.

In 1857, President Buchanan, accepting the accusations of the fugitive officials, began to muster an army to suppress the Mormon rebellion. He had several motives. Congressmen from the new Republican party, whose 1856 platform had called for abolishing the "twin relics of barbarism: slavery and polygamy," put pressure on the president in Congress while an outcry in the press demanded the suppression of the Mormons. Buchanan believed that Democrats and Republicans, northerners and southerners, could unite in an attempt to restore order to Utah, and he could thus divert attention from the crisis over slavery in the territories. He could also deliver a thinly veiled threat against all those extreme advocates of states' rights who urged resistance to federal authority by extralegal means. Even Stephen Douglas, whose doctrine of popular sovereignty the Mormons had adopted for their own ends, rose in Congress to denounce them as "a pestiferous disgusting cancer . . . alien enemies and outlaws engaging in treasonable, disgusting and bestial practices."

Buchanan dispatched 2,500 men, one-sixth of the entire U.S. Army, to suppress the rebellion in Utah. Along with them traveled yet another set of territorial officials. This time the party included a new governor to replace Brigham Young, whom Buchanan neglected to inform of his dismissal from office. The Mormons, meanwhile, prepared to resist. Young proclaimed the territory under danger from a hostile force, which happened to be the army of his own country, and declared martial law. The Mormons abandoned many of their outlying settlements, mustered the Nauvoo Legion—their own militia—and sent out parties to guard the approaches to Utah. After their experience in Missouri and Illinois, Mormons had good reason to fear armed bodies of their fellow countrymen. Nonetheless, all their preparations played into Buchanan's hands, for Young seemed to be acting very much like a traitor in rebellion against the United States.

While the army made its slow and expensive way toward Utah, transcontinental migration continued. Late in the summer of 1857 a wagon train of migrants from Arkansas and Missouri entered southern Utah. The Missourians, angered by the Mormons' refusal to sell them supplies, marked their passage by minor depredations against Mormon fields, abuse of local Indians, and taunts of how they had treated the Mormons in Missouri. In early September of 1857 the Mormons around Cedar City, apparently influenced by a religious revival still working among them and their own mounting sense of siege, decided to cooperate with local Indians who had already commenced an attack on the wagon train. In the midst of the Indian attack, John D. Lee appeared and told the migrants that he had persuaded the Indians to allow the Missourians to depart if they surrendered their arms. When they did so, the Mormons and the Indians at a prearranged signal slaughtered all the adults, men and women, and all those children old enough to bear witness, 120 people in all. The Mormons adopted the 17 children that they spared. Although covered up at the time and blamed on the Indians, the Mountain Meadows Massacre would return to haunt the Mormons later. It revealed the immense potential for violence in the mounting confrontation.

The Mountain Meadows Massacre seemed to foretell a wave of slaughter, yet the "Mormon War" itself was largely free of bloodshed. The army got a late start across the plains in 1857; then delays from the weather and Mormon raiders who stole their livestock and burned the grass they needed to feed their animals slowed them even more. Unable to reach Utah, the army had to spend the winter in the Rockies at the Green River. The delay gave intermediaries such as Thomas Kane, a man who had sympathized with the Mormons since their eviction from Illinois, and Alfred Cumming, the new governor, a chance to negotiate with Young. Young ordered a withdrawal from the Salt Lake valley and planned for resistance, but he also began to moderate his rhetoric. He no longer issued pronouncements that resembled those of the leader of an independent country. In the spring of 1858, as the army renewed its march toward Utah, Buchanan dispatched peace commissioners with an offer of amnesty. Young came to terms, but he had to accept the presence of the federal army in Utah to make sure that he observed the terms of peace.

The "Mormon War," although it suppressed the more flagrant defiance of federal officials, hardly restored efficient territorial government in Utah. The struggle between federal officials and Brigham Young and the Mormon Church would continue for years. In the 1860s, quoting a gentile settler, Mark Twain wrote of Utah: "There is a batch of governors, and judges, and other officials here, shipped from Washington, and they maintain the semblance of a republican form of government—but the petrified truth is that Utah is an absolute monarchy and Brigham Young is king."

A king Young may have been before the Mormon War, but after it he had to settle simply for being the most powerful man in Utah. He never again challenged the federal government so directly. And after his death the Mormons would feel once more the power of the federal government as it moved to stamp out polygamy.

Washington

The troubles in Washington never reached the scale of those in Kansas, Utah, and New Mexico, but they provide yet another example of the larger breakdown of order in the territories. Through the treaties he had negotiated in 1855, Governor Isaac Stevens had provoked an Indian War in Washington Territory that spilled over into Oregon. The actions of territorial officials had so appalled General John Wool, the officer sent to quell the Indians, that he had denounced the governments of both Washington and Oregon for fomenting the war.

In the midst of this war some settlers, some of whom had been former servants of the Hudson's Bay Company and had a long history of friendly relations with the local Indians, remained safely on their claims while their neighbors fled. Governor Stevens accused these people of aiding the Indians, declared martial law, and had them arrested. When Judge Edward Lander of the territorial court ordered them released to the custody of the civil court, Stevens refused. Lander then ordered Stevens arrested for contempt. The governor retaliated by arresting and imprisoning Lander for absenting himself from military duties without leave. When Lander was released, he fined Stevens, but Stevens pardoned himself. This, too, was not how territorial government was supposed to work.

The struggle over slavery in the territories was a quake along the major fault line of American society, a quake that threatened to topple the whole system.

Problems in New Mexico, Washington, and Utah were tremors on secondary faults that further weakened the damaged structure of territorial government. As the country moved toward Civil War, the whole territorial system appeared to be in danger of collapse. Popular sovereignty had proved a spectacular failure as a way to provide a stable and effective government for the territories in the face of sectional conflict. Nor had the federal government proved much more adept in dealing with the smaller crises in New Mexico, Utah, and Washington.

Civil War (1861–65)

The Civil War threatened to topple western governments undermined by the turmoil of the 1850s. Not only did many westerners still hold deep loyalties to the sections from which they came, but they also had scores to settle among themselves. Only one western state—Texas—joined the Confederacy, but it was not at all immediately clear that the federal government would be able to maintain control over other western states and territories.

Although there were secessionist conspiracies in California, the most immediate dangers were in Indian Territory, New Mexico, Utah, and Kansas. In the Indian Territory, the offer of the Confederacy to make treaties of alliance divided the Five Civilized Tribes. Because the elite of these nations held slaves, and because so much resentment lingered over the federal government's failure to protect their rights during the removal crisis, many members of these tribes sided with the Confederacy. Others, however, opposed the slaveholding elite and retained as bitter memories of the actions of the southern states as of the federal government's. Such people tended to side with the Union. Indian regiments fought on each side in the Civil War, but the real tragedy was the miniature civil war that raged within Indian Territory itself. This fighting left homelessness, hunger, and bitterness in its wake, and the pro-Confederate Indians provided an excuse for the victorious federal government to exact further land cessions following the war.

The Civil War also spread into the area southwest of Indian Territory, threatening to overturn the territorial government of New Mexico. Texas, whose own claims on New Mexican territory had come to naught before the Civil War, tried to use the war as a way both to annex eastern New Mexico and to bring the remainder of New Mexico and Arizona into the Confederacy. A small Texas force invaded New Mexico and penetrated into Arizona before being driven out by California volunteers under James H. Carleton and Colorado militia under William Gilpin. Other California volunteers under Patrick Connor replaced regular troops in Utah, where the loyalty of Brigham Young and the Mormons remained suspect.

The bitterest western fighting of the Civil War predictably took place along the Kansas-Missouri border; the region set the standards for brutality during the Civil War. The proslavery settlers became southern guerrillas. The free-state settlers became Jayhawkers. William C. Quantrill—a western drifter and sometime schoolteacher who felt destiny had spared him for great things when he survived a Colorado blizzard that killed his companions— became the most famous southern guerrilla leader. Quantrill had originally sympathized with Kansas free staters, but by 1860 he had chosen the South, and he and his men fought under the black flag—they gave no quarter. His guerrillas, the majority of whom were teenagers, slaughtered and mutilated soldiers and civilians, whites and blacks. In destroying Lawrence, Kansas, in 1863, Quantrill ordered his men to "kill every male and burn every house." Before the day was done they had killed 182 men and boys, shot down before the eyes of their families, and had burned 185 buildings. Jayhawker reprisals in kind left the people of the Missouri border "crazy from fear and terror." Jayhawkers initiated a scorched-earth policy designed to drive out all southerners who sympathized with the guerrillas. The Seventh Kansas Cavalry— Jennison's Jayhawkers—boasted an abolitionist commander, Susan B. Anthony's brother, as lieutenant colonel and John Brown, Jr., as a captain. They murdered and plundered their way across western Missouri. Such attacks created thousands of scattered, individual moments of horror: armed men appearing on a porch at night, farmers tortured and hanged in their own farmyards or shot at their doors, livestock commandeered, and houses burned. Together these moments merged into a general atmosphere of terror.

Texas seceded and Kansas and Indian Territory underwent a bloody agony, but on the whole federal authority held in the West. The challenge to federal authority largely blew itself out on the borders of the West. Elsewhere, the territorial governments weathered the storm. Indeed, during the Civil War the federal government managed to put the disasters of the 1850s behind it and restore stable territorial government.

Territorial Government During and After the Civil War

The triumph of the Republican party and the secession of the South resolved the basic issues of territorial administration. The Republicans banned slavery from the territories. The Lincoln administration brought the remaining unorganized portions of the trans-Missouri West within the territorial system and thus established federal primacy in the region. Congress created Dakota, Colorado, and Nevada territories in 1861 and Arizona in 1863. By 1870, Congress had subdivided the older territories to add the territories of Idaho (1863), Montana (1864), and Wyoming (1868). Only Indian Territory remained outside the territorial system for a time (although Congress made the western part of it into Oklahoma Territory in 1890). In all, Congress created 13 western territories between 1861 and 1888. Only 4 of these—Kansas (1861), Nevada (1864), Nebraska (1867), and Colorado (1876)—achieved statehood during that period.

Within the new territories, the federal government standardized its procedures and exerted a closer supervision over the actions of territorial officials. Congress moved jurisdiction over the territories themselves from the Department of State to the Department of the Interior in 1873. Territorial governors gradually lost many of their discretionary powers, and the comptroller of the treasury examined the accounts of federal appointees often enough to discourage less imaginative kinds of thefts. Mark Twain, who served a brief term as secretary to his brother, the secretary of Nevada Territory, and watched the system in operation, was not so sure that reform made the territorial officials any better, but it did make them more sophisticated: "The government of my country snubs honest simplicity, but fondles artistic villainy, and I think I might have developed into a very capable pickpocket if I had remained in the public service a year or two." As one historian has concluded, increased federal supervision proved more exasperating to officials in the territories than menacing.

As federal supervision grew more standardized and methodical, however, it also grew more distant and general. The federal government wanted no return to the chaos and dissension of the years before the Civil War. It wanted the governors to keep the territories quiet. Officials who created an uproar in the territories, for whatever reason, often found themselves removed from office. Because Congress largely wanted peace and quiet in the West, the citizens of the territories could gain considerable room to maneuver.

Oppressive regimes staffed by outsiders were more a mainstay of western political rhetoric than of territorial government. True enough, offices continued to be filled by outsiders. At the time of their appointment, for example, about 75 percent of the territorial justices who served between 1829 and 1896 were not residents of the territory to which they were assigned. Similarly, two-thirds of the governors who served in the West between 1848 and 1893 came from outside the territory. We must remember, however, that in the territories *most* of the citizens were recent arrivals. Over the territorial period as a whole, most governors continued to live in the territories after they left office. About 75 percent of the governors spent from three or four years to the rest of their lives in the territories when their terms had ended. And starting with Grover Cleveland's first adminis-tration in 1884, presidents began to give preference to territorial residents in appointing governors. Claims that all territorial officials were carpetbaggers who came to loot and run are simply not true.

How qualified were these officials? To staff the new governments the federal government sometimes seemed to send west an endless stream of "political hacks, defeated congressmen, or jobless relatives of congressmen and cabinet members." Or as a Dakotan more pithily put it in a letter to the U.S. attorney general: "You pledged us that we should have good men and good lawyers sent to us as judges, and we get to constitute our Supreme Court an ass, a knave, and a drunkard."

Asses, knaves, and drunkards, both imported and domestic, the West has always had in abundance, and it is a difficult thing to construct a scale to determine if territorial asses and knaves were more asinine or more knavish than those in other parts of the country. We can, however, measure the experience and educa-tion of those who came West. Let us start with the courts. In many ways the territorial judges assigned to the nineteenth-century West were inferior to men who had filled similar positions in the earlier territories and the men and women who would staff the territorial judiciary of the twentieth century. Western justices were politicians. Most of them had run for office and owed their jobs to political patronage. But they were not necessarily political hacks. Most had legal experi-ence, although those serving in the nineteenth-century West had less extensive experience than those who served either before or after them in the territories. Similarly western justices had less education than those who had served in the eastern territories or those who would serve in the twentieth century. Although they compared unfavorably to earlier, and later, territorial officials, the members of the western judiciary were still highly educated in comparison to the general population of the West.

An evaluation of governors establishes a similar pattern. Most governors were neither administratively inexperienced nor incompetent, and those who were incompetent usually quickly lost their jobs. Probably 75 percent had held previous office; one scholar who attempted to assess their qualifications estimated that only 10 percent were poorly prepared for their duties as governor. The general caliber of territorial governors was at least as good as that of contemporary state governors.

A man can be educated and experienced and still be a certifiable ass or a knave. Leaving aside the honest asses for a moment, perhaps the critical question here is the issue of corruption. Cases of obvious corruption are not hard to find. In 1866, Horace C. Wilson, territorial secretary of Idaho, departed office and Idaho with $33,350 of the territory's funds. Wilson, as a contemporary put it, "seems to have been of a very selfish nature," but he only yielded to a temptation that confronted many. A job in the territories was, on the surface, hardly a political plum. The pay was low, job security was nearly nonexistent, living and working conditions were harsh. Not surprisingly, many of those who came looked for ways to make their stay financially worthwhile.

Many, perhaps most, governors in these circumstances engaged in practices that, while not as straightforward or "selfish" as Wilson's departure for greener pastures, seem by twentieth-century standards to involve a clear conflict of interests. The governors maintained private law practices, speculated in land, and organized private corporations that relied on the federal or territorial governments for their success. Before condemning them, however, we should remember that members of the territorial legislatures also often engaged in such practices and that officials usually justified these maneuvers as attempts "to boost" the territory and make it grow. All branches of western government contained opportunists with a flexible morality.

Official opportunism, however, involved more than money. Many officials willingly subordinated their financial ambitions to their political ambitions to return to Washington as senators or representatives once the territory became a state. To succeed, they needed the cooperation of territorial citizens. Most, from necessity, sought some sort of modus vivendi with their new constituents. Possessing little power and liable to removal at any time, they could not afford to court conflict.

Congress usually proved no more assertive in the territories than did the governors. Congress did reject numerous laws passed by territorial legislatures, but far more laws, despite obvious defects, slipped by. Indeed, Congress occasionally intervened to validate territorial laws that the courts had ruled illegal. In theory federal control of the territories was absolute; in practice the declining power of the governors and the rarity of direct congressional intervention left a considerable void in which territorial legislatures exercised much autonomy. Under such conditions, legislatures, elected by the people of the territories, grew increasingly more influential in the post-Civil War West. Governors rarely challenged them, and when they did, they usually lost. Governors had their vetos sustained less often in the western territories than had been true in earlier territories. Congress ignored all but their most flagrant violations of the organic acts that had created the territories and established the rules that governed the legislatures' behavior.

The willingness of Congress to allow citizens of the territories considerable self-government depended, however, on the citizens' doing nothing that would shock national sensibilities. The federal presence in the West usually remained quiescent, but when challenged, the government showed its claws. The Mormons in

Utah insisted on preserving polygamy in the face of federal laws to the contrary, and they found out how powerfully and decisively the federal government could intervene in territorial affairs.

The Federal Government and Polygamy

The federal government rarely intervened forcibly in the western territories following the Civil War. Only two cases stand out. The government intervened to halt violence in New Mexico, and Congress intervened in Utah and neighboring territories to stamp out Mormon polygamy. In 1879 the Supreme Court ruled against polygamy in *United States* v. *Reynolds*, saying that the constitution guaranteed freedom of belief, not freedom of practice. Congress then moved to eliminate the practice. In 1882 it passed the Edmunds Act, which, as interpreted by federal officials in Utah, Arizona, and Idaho, disfranchised all those who either practiced or believed in polygamy. It also imposed heavy fines and imprisonment on those convicted of polygamous cohabitation. The government used the law to drive the leadership of the Mormon church into hiding or prison.

In 1887 the Edmunds-Tucker Act directly attacked the Mormon church as an institution by forbidding it to hold assets over $50,000. The act aimed to break the temporal power of the church by confiscating its considerable property. Despite efforts of the church to evade the act and legal challenges to it, the Supreme Court upheld the act's constitutionality. Four days after the court decision upholding the act, Wilford Woodruff, the president of the church, announced that he had received a divine revelation to obey the law of the United States and thus, implicitly, to end the practice of polygamy when it was contrary to the law. In ending open polygamy, federal prosecution had broken the most distinctive aspect of nineteenth-century Mormonism. But prosecution had done far more. It also had crippled the church's corporate and communal activities, which had restricted the penetration of the free market into Utah. After the 1890s the Mormon church largely lost its appetite for social experiment and grew increasingly more conservative.

Congress and the Territories

Utah politicians eventually learned, as had politicians elsewhere in the West, to coexist, usually quite comfortably, with the federal presence. Patronage wisely, if sometimes illegally, dispensed reconciled local politicians to outside appointees. Particularly in the early years, government expenditures formed the lifeblood of a territory as the federal government heavily subsidized territorial economies. The direct subsidy to the territorial government was relatively small. It came to perhaps 10 percent of the expenses of running territorial governments, with taxes making up the rest. But the government maintained military posts in the territories and spent money to fulfill treaty obligations to Indians. It built roads, provided and staffed land offices, and extended mail routes into newly settled areas. Such expenditures could be sizable. In New Mexico during the 1850s, for example, the federal cost of defending the territory was $3,000,000 a year, with over a thousand civilian workers employed at Fort Union alone. Over 8 percent of the money in circulation in New Mexico came from army expenditures. Colonel Edwin Sumner summarized the situation: "The truth is, the only resource of this country is the

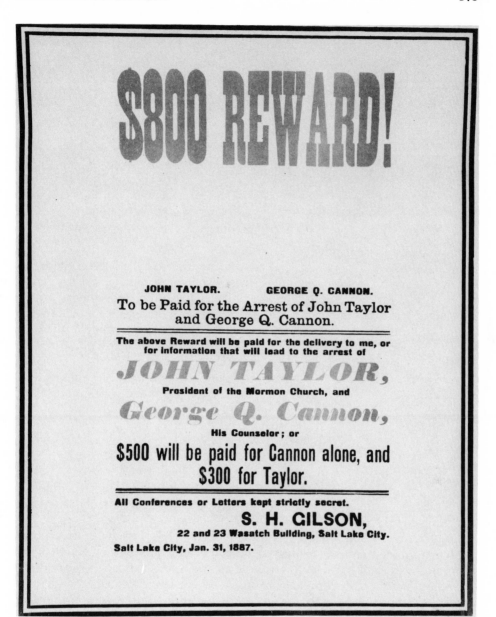

The federal crackdown on polygamy led by 1887 to rewards offered for the capture of the president of the Mormon church. It ended the longest-lasting attempt by white immigrants to establish a radically different set of social practices in the West.

government money. All classes depend on it from the professional man and the trader down to beggar."

For territorial politicians, the ability to make sure that such federal expenditures kept flowing and found their way into the correct pockets depended on main-taining and strengthening one's ties to the party in power in Congress and at the same time trying to destroy the ties of a rival. Under these circumstances, territorial politics often became politics of personality as one faction of officials tried to blacken the reputation of others. In Wyoming Territory, for example, between 1869 and 1872 feuding between Territorial Governor John Campbell and U.S. Marshal Church Howe set off a campaign of mutual vilification. A fair sample is a letter from a Howe supporter describing the Wyoming career of the territorial secretary, a Campbell loyalist named John Lee, as "a series of continued drunken revelries and licentious and shameful debaucheries, in open and unblushing companionship with the lowest creatures of both sexes." With President Grant alternately accepting the defamations of one side or another and directing patronage and offices accordingly, Wyoming politics sometimes seemed a chaotic competition in slander.

Territorial Rings

Territorial government under these conditions of patronage, factionalism, and boosterism came to sport a special adornment: the so-called territorial rings, which were corrupt combinations of business owners and politicians. They existed to turn public expenditures into private profits. They often enjoyed considerable popular support in the territories, because settlers saw them as a means of funneling federal cash into their own pockets. In Dakota Territory, for example, the local Republican party, buttressed by federal patronage, allied itself with officials of the Bureau of Indian Affairs and traders among the Sioux. Together they created an "Indian ring," in this case an organization designed to exploit the Sioux reservation by stealing supplies, embezzling funds meant for the Indians, and controlling contracts. When in 1878 the secretary of the interior, Carl Schurz, attempted to clean up the administration of Indian affairs, he was roundly attacked by friends of the ring in Dakota, and his efforts were stymied. In one of the oddest charges of persecution in American history, supporters of the ring accused the government of persecuting Episcopalians, since, in the afterglow of Grant's peace policy, Episcopalians still controlled the Sioux agencies. Not only was Henry Livingston, the Sioux agent at Crow Creek, acquitted (a result that reportedly astonished him as much as it did the prosecutors), but the citizens of Yankton also gave him a sign of their devotion by electing him to the school board while he was on trial.

Livingston was a crook of modest talents and modest ambitions; he is important not in his own right but instead for what his trial reveals about the attitudes of Dakotans toward corruption. They basically did not regard defrauding Indians as a serious offense as long as the Indians stayed quiet and the benefits of the fraud were circulated throughout the society. In an undeveloped land with few markets and few chances for gain, Dakotans were not about to let the federal government break up an Indian ring that gave contracts to local merchants, ranchers, and farmers just because the agents did well instead of doing good. Western settlers no more valued honesty in government for its own sake than did immigrants in eastern slums who depended on corrupt political machines to help them make a living in a harsh world. In the West, where government was very often the leading industry of a territory, such toleration of corruption is understandable, perhaps even predictable.

These territorial rings prospered throughout the West. They provided a means to bind together members of a local territorial elite and federal officials in the common cause of making money in the territory. In New Mexico, where the famous Santa Fe Ring dominated the territory in the late nineteenth century, corruption provided the means for substantial control over the government by the territorial elite. Federal officials gladly accepted membership in the ring during their stay in New Mexico.

Just as the Indian rings defrauded Indians, so the Santa Fe Ring rose to power by defrauding New Mexicans. In 1879 the ring's original members persuaded Land Commissioner James A. Williamson to approve a survey that extended the so-called Maxwell Grant (acquired, needless to say, by the founders of the ring) from 97,000 to 2 million acres. Several secretaries of the interior had previously rejected such a claim, but Williamson approved it. He coincidentally happened to acquire large ranching interests in New Mexico soon after approving the grant. The validation and extension of this grant and other equally dubious Spanish and Mexican land grants dispossessed many of the original Hispanic settlers of New Mexico. It also prevented incoming Anglo American settlers from homesteading lands thus eliminated from the public domain.

Legacy of the Territorial Period

This combination of federal control, political corruption, and dependence on federal economic support was neither temporary nor fleeting in many areas. Washington spent more than 30 years as a territory. Utah spent nearly half a century, and New Mexico was a territory for over 60 years. The territorial era would not end in the trans-Missouri West until 1912, when New Mexico and Arizona entered the Union as states. It survived outside of the West in Alaska and Hawaii well into the twentieth century.

This long territorial interlude, during which federal government dominated western government, shaped the political realities of much of the western United States. The West lived for long periods under a system in which local political power, while considerable, always needed the approval of outside officials. Many westerners came to associate public office holders with incompetence and corruption. They resented the federal government both for its power and for its failure to use that power to help the West. They simultaneously denounced federal tyranny and clamored for increased federal expenditures in their region. The long territorial period left a legacy of ambivalence toward the federal government that would continue into twentieth-century western politics.

This ambivalence became particularly significant because of the persisting federal presence in the West. Westerners and federal officials alike initially regarded government supervision and stewardship as transitory. With the land allotted and republican governments in place, everyone assumed that the federal government would largely withdraw, its role finished. Theoretically the federal government would eventually have no greater role in Wyoming than it had in New Jersey. That it maintained a much greater role is one of the major elements that sets the West apart from other regions of the United States. Migrants had expected to transform the West into a replica of the East. They only partially succeeded; they created a region that, while sharing the institutions of the nation, forced those institutions into new forms.

Readings

Eblen, Jack. *First and Second United States Empires: Governors and Territorial Government, 1784–1912*. Pittsburgh: University of Pittsburgh Press, 1968.

Fellman, Michael. *Inside War: The Guerrilla Conflict in Missouri During the American Civil War*. New York: Oxford University Press, 1989.

———. "Rehearsal for the Civil War: Antislavery and Proslavery at the Fighting Point in Kansas, 1854–56." In Lewis Perry and Michael Fellman, eds., *Antislavery Reconsidered: New Perspectives on the Abolitionists*, pp. 287–307. Baton Rouge: Louisiana State University Press, 1979.

Gould, Lewis L. *Wyoming: A Political History, 1868–96*. New Haven: Yale University Press, 1968.

Guice, John D. W. *Rocky Mountain Bench: The Territorial Supreme Courts of Colorado, Montana, and Wyoming, 1861–1890*. New Haven: Yale University Press, 1972.

Hall, Kermit L. "Hacks and Derelicts Revisited: The American Territorial Judiciary." *Western Historical Quarterly* 12 (July 1981):273–90.

Lamar, Howard R. *Dakota Territory, 1861–1889*. New Haven: Yale University Press, 1956.

———. *The Far Southwest, 1846–1912*. New York: W. W. Norton & Company, 1970.

McPherson, James M. *Battle Cry of Freedom: The Civil War Era*. New York: Oxford, 1988.

Pomeroy, Earl S. *The Territories of the United States: 1861–90*. Philadelphia: University of Pennsylvania Press, 1947.

Wunder, John. *Inferior Courts, Superior Justice: A History of Justices of the Peace*. Westport, Conn.: Greenwood Press, 1979.

PART THREE

Transformation and Development

LOOKING back from their old age on a period of momentous changes, Anglo American settlers usually saw only the world transformed. They constructed from their memories a simple story of progress: "savagery" subdued, wilderness conquered, civilization planted, wealth created, and progress insured. Perhaps because only the most successful of these settlers had the luxury of writing memoirs or of being interviewed for the innumerable county histories, this remembered West emerges as a fluid, malleable place that people of ambition, determination, and intelligence shaped largely as they pleased.

Comparing their experiences to those of other peoples in other places at other times, many of these settlers assessed their lives rightly enough when they remembered a world of dramatic possibilities. The Anglo American migrants had come as conquerors. They had pushed Indian and Hispanic communities aside, stripping them of most of their resources and autonomy and shoving them toward the periphery of western life. As conquerors, these migrants had been free to reject or ignore most existing western institutions and customs. They had envisioned a West with little or no room for the life that had been previously lived there. In this respect, these western migrants were far different from contemporary immigrants into the eastern United States, who had to adjust themselves to an existing social and economic structure. Anglo Americans in the West felt free to impose their own language, government, economic organization, law, and customs on their adopted land. Anglo American migrants, too, faced a world of tremendous economic possibilities. Except for those women who came West from family loyalty, the vast majority of Anglo American migrants believed that their move would better their economic possibilities and improve their lives. The federal government eagerly cooperated in attempting to make such beliefs reality by dispossessing Indians of their resources and redistributing them among the migrants. The Anglo Americans had an access to resources rarely available to migrants in most modern states.

Yet for all the dramatic possibilities the land seemed to present, westerners had been far more concerned with re-creation than with creation. The goal of the transformation that Anglo American migrants had wrought was ultimately the restoration of the familiar world that they had left behind. They did not want to change the world; they only wanted to improve their position within it. Outside of various small utopian communities that arose in the Pacific Northwest and elsewhere, only the Mormons even tried to alter basic family, economic, and governmental structures prevailing in the East. And the Mormons, after more than half a century of struggle, largely gave up. They preserved a distinctive

This lithograph shows a common image in illustrations of the West: the arrival of the railroad (symbolizing commerce and civilization) and the retreat of the Indian.

religion and ideology, but, except among their own fundamentalist fringe groups, their earlier radicalism disappeared.

This tendency of Anglo American migrants to see their migration in terms of personal betterment within a social and economic structure that basically duplicated the East is a key factor in the development of the West. For the most part migrants left their old local worlds, but they did not leave the national world. They left behind local economies, but they did not leave the national economy. The West reversed the course of development in the East. In much of the East strong local communities and local economies preceded the creation of a national government and a national economy, but the West is a child of a strong national government, and its economy can only be understood as a product of the larger national economy. To overstate things only slightly, western communities—except for preexisting Indian and Hispanic communities—were not creators of the larger world; they were products of it.

For late-nineteenth-century westerners, at least white westerners, the federal presence was only rhetorically an oppressive presence. Government power rested heavily only in those political and economic interstices where there was an insufficiently large Anglo American population with proper "American values" or where the new corporations had not yet penetrated. On an Indian reservation or in an area where little public land had been taken up by settlers; in the capital of a relatively sparsely populated territory; or in Utah, where the Mormons seemed dangerously "un-American," the power of the federal government remained obvious. But in new cities like San Francisco or Omaha or in a town like Butte, with its mining companies, or even in the relatively thickly settled prairie country west of the Missouri, the power of the government was far more remote and far less obvious. The federal government's hand rested lightly on Anglo American settlers. As long as they established republican governments, acquired title to their lands legally, and did not flaunt American cultural norms, Anglo Americans remained free to establish their communities with little federal oversight or supervision.

CHAPTER 8

The Transformation of Western Society: *Migration*

$\mathbf{B}$EGINNING in the mid-nineteenth century, a mass migration transformed the largely Indian and Hispanic West of small villages and tribal communities. The movement of millions of Anglo Americans, black Americans, European immigrants, Mexican immigrants, and Chinese into the American West rearranged the social and physical landscape and altered forever the region's history. Capturing both the broad patterns and individual events involved in this migration presents staggering difficulties. To avoid a narration that simply piles detail upon detail, group upon group, and place upon place, we must resort to analogy and metaphor. The metaphor used here will be that of a stream. If we imagine migration into the American West to be streams of people flowing east, north, and west, then our task is to determine how many people these streams carried, where they came from, and what, so to speak, floated with them on their journey. Mere totals derived from more than half a century of migration are not enough. Since the flow of these streams was punctuated by tremendous floods, brief droughts, and occasional changes of course, these specific episodes must also be noted.

In the nineteenth century the stream of people that flowed from east to west was a river compared to the smaller migrations from Mexico north and across the Pacific from west to east. But this migration was not analogous to a wall of water advancing and flooding all the land as it goes. Even when it is in flood, a stream does not evenly cover the surrounding countryside. A stream in flood (and this migratory stream was in flood for much of the late nineteenth century) overflows its banks and covers the lowest lying ground first. Our metaphorical low-lying ground in the West was, however, often in fact high and mountainous. The migratory stream during the 1840s inundated agricultural lands along the Pacific Coast in California and Oregon and along the Wasatch front in Utah, but it also covered the mountains of California during the Gold Rush of 1849. Afterwards, mineral rushes, like flash floods in the mountains, distributed mining camps through the mountains of Idaho, Montana, Colorado, Utah, Nevada, Arizona, New Mexico, and South Dakota between 1850 and the 1880s.

While the mineral rushes after the Civil War were depositing migrants in the western mountains, the migratory stream was rising gradually and inexorably like some lowland river. It flooded the prairies bordering the Missouri River and moved out onto the Great Plains. On the Great Plains in the late 1870s, the 1880s, and the early 1890s this flood receded but only to advance again.

Even in its flood stage, however, this migratory stream barely touched other areas. Relatively few migrants settled in the Great Basin, that huge interior desert lying between the Wasatch Mountains in Utah and the Sierra Nevada in California. More migrants entered the lands south of the Great Basin, the South-west, but that area remained largely Indian and Hispanic. To the north of the Great Basin the inland empire of eastern Washington and Oregon and southern Idaho had farmers spill in from both the east and west in the 1880s. In ten years farmers opened up 2.5 million acres of land in Idaho, the Columbia Basin of Washington and Oregon, and the Wallowa country of eastern Oregon.

Over the period as a whole, the bulk of the migrants who came west in this stream were farmers, but there are two reasons why it is a mistake to emphasize the rural, agricultural west too heavily. The first is that the most spectacular episodes of settlement, some of the crests of our flooding stream, were mineral rushes. The second reason is that westerners created cities and towns in such numbers that by 1880 the West had become the most urbanized region of the United States.

Mineral rushes peaked quickly and faded, but they produced a form of urban settlement typical of the West. Mining camps and mining towns were urban places: many people lived concentrated in a small area while around them lay thousands of square miles of sparsely populated land. Elsewhere, too, urban settlements were often the first immigrant settlements. In the Rocky Mountains and on the Pacific Coast, and indeed on the Great Plains, towns often existed before farmers and ranchers arrived in any numbers. San Francisco, Seattle, and Denver were important cities even while much of the land around them remained, in terms of permanent residents, unoccupied. Indeed, by the early twentieth century citizens of many cities such as Denver or Seattle worried because there did not seem to be enough farmers around them to sustain their economies.

Patterns of Migration

Watching this migratory stream flow west over half a century or more, we begin to see certain regularities. The stream's course, floods, and droughts become almost predictable. These patterns are admittedly rough; they do not always hold. But they are accurate enough to give us an idea of the overall contours of western migration.

First, native-born migrants, on entering the stream, tended to move to places located on the same general latitude as the place they had left. Settlers from Mississippi, for example, would move to Texas, not to North Dakota, and settlers from Illinois would be more likely to go to Nebraska than to either Texas or North Dakota. In 1850, 83.4 percent of those living outside their state of birth lived entirely or partially within the latitudes of their state of birth. By 1900 the figure had declined, but it still amounted to 74.3 percent.

The reasons for this striking pattern appear to be partially ecological and partly social. Most settlers were farmers, and for most of the nineteenth century both agricultural seeds and animals tended to be locally produced. Many plant seeds are closely adapted to specific latitudes. When seeds are moved to a different latitude, where the seasonal changes in light are different, plant productivity drops. Similarly, the work animals of northerners and southerners differed; each was adapted to a specific climate. Northern farmers relied on horses and oxen, which thrived in the cooler northern climate, while southerners used mules, which were better able to stand the heat of the South. Given these different agricultural patterns, migrants would tend to have the greatest initial success if they stayed close to the latitude of their place of origin.

Farmers, of course, could learn from experience and get new seeds and new work animals, but the ecological factor quickly became a social factor. Farmers who were immediately successful and who continued to employ familiar customs were also more likely to be successful in urging family and old neighbors to join them.

This appeal of the familiar faded only in the late nineteenth century as farmers crossed into the Great Plains. On the plains, ecological factors based on latitude weakened. The major geographical marker on the Great Plains was longitude, not latitude; west of the 98th meridian the land grew increasingly arid. The advantages offered by migration along a line of latitude dwindled, while the challenge of adjusting to the arid West became preeminent.

The second pattern apparent in western agricultural migration was its domination by the middling sectors—relatively prosperous farmers, merchants, and professionals—of American society. The very poor could not afford to migrate west. Although land was free after 1863 under the Homestead Act, the cost of land was only one of the expenses necessary to establish a farm. Farmers had to pay the price of transporting themselves, their families, and their equipment west. They then needed funds to stock a farm and erect buildings. They needed money to support their families until the crops came in. In the 1840s and 1850s, outfitting oneself for a journey to Oregon or California on the overland trails, acquiring land at trail's end, establishing a farm, and surviving until the first harvest came in cost between $750 and $1,500. Similarly, to create a 160-acre farm on the western prairies between 1850 and 1860 cost about $1,000 excluding moving costs; with anything less than $1,000 a farmer's chances for eventual success would diminish. If the poor came west, they had to come as laborers, usually without families. A young man could sign on as an extra hand with a family moving west. Or later he could work for a railroad, mining company, or timber company. Until he had saved some money, however, a poor man could not afford to bring his family west. And even when land was purchased, it usually took two years to develop a farm that could feed a family. Only after three or four years would a significant surplus be available for sale. Poor single women did even worse than poor men. Unless they planned to work as schoolteachers, prostitutes, or domestic servants, migration was very difficult for them. A relatively small number of single women, however, did overcome the difficulties and started their own farms.

A third pattern is the correlation of sharply differing demographic profiles with different economies in the West. Initially, regions dominated by extractive industries, such as mining, lumber, or livestock raising, tended to be overwhelmingly male. Family settlement predominated in agricultural regions. The first transcontinental migrants were farmers bound for Oregon and pre-Gold Rush California. Roughly 50 percent of those moving across the country in this migration of the mid-1840s went as members of family groups. Adult women comprised 15 to 20 percent of all emigrants. The Gold Rush, however, reduced the percentage of people traveling in families to 20 to 30 percent of the migration during the 1850s.

The fourth pattern was the tendency of migration to correlate with larger economic fluctuations in the American economy. Nineteenth-century American capitalism existed with few government controls, and as a result, the economy endured deep and relatively frequent cyclic fluctuations. Periods of rapid growth were followed by recessions and depressions. During prosperous times—the booms—there would be large increases in both western population and farm making. Farmers, eager to expand their operations or provide for their children, sold their eastern farms and used the proceeds to buy new, relatively inexpensive land in the West. During such boom periods, crop prices were often high, work was readily available, and single men and young couples could also accumulate savings and migrate west. During times of depression—the busts—migration would decline and the number of new farms would fall.

The fifth and final pattern was the tendency of settlers to move repeatedly. Americans were a restless people, and frequent movements were typical of American society in the nineteenth century, but western movements carried such mobility to extremes. There was a huge population turnover in new settlements throughout the West. In the gold town of Grass Valley, only 7 percent of the men present in 1850 were still present in 1856. One historian has described the people of San Francisco in the 1850s as "totally rootless"; only 25 percent of those present in 1850 were still there in 1860. Rural areas proved only slightly more stable. Only 34 percent of the people present in Roseburg, Oregon, in 1870 were still there in 1880. In east central Kansas, only 34 percent of those present in 1860 remained in 1870, but stability did increase thereafter. Of those present in 1865, 64 percent remained in 1875. All groups shared in this mobility. Immigrant farmers, it now appears, moved as readily as native-born farmers. A study of French Canadians, Mennonites, and Swedes in Kansas found rates of mobility virtually identical to those of native-born farmers in the area. Only success proved much of an impediment to movement. Usually the wealthiest part of the community tended to stay, whereas the less successful people tended to move on.

The Migrants

Having gotten, as it were, a bird's-eye view of the migratory stream and a rough idea of the patterns of its flow over time, we must switch our focus to its sources. Who took part in the migration west? What, in terms of our metaphor, were the tributaries of the migratory stream flooding the West?

White native-born Americans dominated western migration, but they formed only the main branch of the migratory stream; other powerful tributaries also fed the migration. A very large minority of western migrants were born outside the United States. In 1850, for example, 32 percent of the population of California was foreign-born at a time when only 10 percent of the people in the nation as a whole had been born abroad. And in 1890 there was a higher percentage (45 percent) of immigrants living in North Dakota than in any other state in the country.

The foreign immigrants in this westward-flowing stream tended to be northern Europeans and Canadians. Large numbers of Norwegians, Swedes, Germans, Irish, and Canadians migrated west and formed their own communities. In Kansas, Texas, and later in Oklahoma, native-born migrants dominated agricultural settlement, but north of Kansas immigrants—largely Germans, Scandinavians, and

Irish—became more numerous. In Nebraska, 25 percent of the 123,000 people living in the new state in 1870 were foreign-born. Together with their native-born children, they accounted for 54 percent of the population, excluding Indians. South Dakota, Montana, Wyoming, and Colorado ranked only slightly below North Dakota in their proportion of foreign-born. Immigrants made up between 20 percent and 30 percent of the population of those four states in the late nineteenth century. Even Texas, a state with an overwhelmingly native-born population, still possessed in the hill country northwest of San Antonio a hundred-mile-long district settled by Germans who had migrated between 1844 and the Civil War.

Distinguishing between foreign-born Europeans and native-born whites in this westward flow only partially illuminates the diversity of the migrants. Included among native-born settlers were a smaller number of nonwhites. Slavery and laws banning the settlement of free blacks in states and territories such as Oregon and Kansas restricted black migration to the West before the Civil War. Almost 3,000 blacks (some slave, some free) had migrated to California by 1850, but they failed in their attempt to claim their rights as American citizens. Antiblack legislation in the 1850s relegated them to second-class citizenship, and many left to seek a better life in Canada. Only in Texas, where black slaves worked the fields of the eastern part of the state, was there a substantial black population before 1865.

Migration from the South and East

Migrants in the westward-flowing river of migration were largely white, but Mexicans dominated the northward-flowing stream and Chinese the stream that flowed out of Asia and Australia. Compared to migrants from the eastern United States and Europe, the numbers of both Chinese and Mexican migrants were relatively small. Although an estimated 1 million Mexicans entered the United States between 1900 and the Great Depression, nineteenth-century Mexican migrants were far less numerous. They were, nevertheless, locally significant in southern Texas, Arizona, and southern California. The number of Chinese immigrants is similarly hard to compute. More than 200,000 Chinese traveled to West Coast ports on steamships between 1876 and 1890, but this figure misses the early peak of Chinese migration during the Gold Rush, and more than half of those migrants later returned to China. In 1880 there were 75,132 Chinese in California alone, and the vast majority of the 105,465 Chinese in the United States as a whole lived in the West. Chinese population, however, peaked soon afterwards, for Chinese migration was at the mercy of unique forces. Although American borders remained open to Europeans, Congress in 1882 passed the Chinese Exclusion Act, which virtually ended legal Chinese immigration. Chinese American population declined and would not begin to increase again until World War II.

Despite the ethnic diversity of the migrants, the way in which they decided to migrate and the manner in which they organized their trip show some surprising regularities. In effect, the basic types of migration were all present, if not fully developed, in the first of the great western migrations: the journey west on the overland trails during the 1840s and 1850s.

Table 3

Foreign-Born Whites plus Native-Born Whites of Foreign Parentage in Selected Great Plains States, 1900

Country of origin (total population)	North Dakota (319,146)	%	South Dakota (401,570)	%	Nebraska (1,066,300)	%	Kansas (1,470,495)	%	Oklahoma Terr. (398,331)	%	Indian Terr. (392,060)	%	Texas (3,048,710)	%
Austria	2,014	.6	1,692	.4	8,085	.8	6,329	.4	1,032	.3	356	.1	15,114	.5
Bohemia	3,654	1.1	6,361	1.6	38,471	3.6	7,788	.5	2,698	.7	50	—	22,713	.7
Canada (English)	31,086	9.7	13,058	3.3	19,304	1.8	18,939	1.3	3,600	.9	819	.2	5,446	.2
Canada (French)	6,512	2.0	3,516	.9	3,003	.3	5,547	.4	702	.2	173	—	1,004	—
Denmark	7,139	2.2	10,450	2.6	26,418	2.5	6,687	.5	582	.1	71	—	2,361	.1
England	7,710	2.4	12,402	3.1	33,586	3.1	45,633	3.1	5,540	1.4	2,586	.7	23,722	.8
France	582	.2	835	.2	2,897	.2	5,813	.4	1,048	.3	568	.1	6,304	.2
Germany	32,393	10.1	55,860	13.9	191,928	18.0	131,563	8.9	18,117	4.5	3,446	.9	157,214	5.2
Hungary	1,797	.6	881	.2	882	.1	935	.1	280	.1	40	—	979	—
Ireland	11,552	3.6	16,017	4.0	45,535	4.3	48,525	3.3	5,534	1.4	2,233	.6	25,373	.8
Italy	731	.2	566	.1	1,278	.1	1,543	.1	74	—	734	.2	7,086	.2
Norway	71,998	22.6	51,191	12.7	7,228	.7	3,726	.3	350	.1	98	—	3,045	.1
Poland	2,112	.7	1,146	.3	7,328	.7	1,478	.1	298	.1	357	.1	8,148	.3
Russia	23,909	7.5	25,689	6.4	14,537	1.4	25,048	1.7	5,536	1.4	398	.1	4,048	.1
Scotland	5,664	1.8	3,943	1.0	9,818	.9	14,186	1.0	1,596	.4	1,008	.3	6,839	.2
Sweden	14,598	4.6	17,163	4.3	54,301	5.1	35,219	2.4	1,290	.3	215	.1	9,297	.3
Switzerland	845	.3	1,638	.4	5,852	.5	9,204	.6	1,108	.3	187	—	3,776	.1
Wales	452	.1	1,889	.5	3,098	.3	5,748	.4	439	.1	392	.1	871	—
Other	2,942	.9	7,065	1.8	5,073	.5	6,050	.5	744	.2	410	.1	146,643	4.8
TOTAL	277,690	71.3	231,362	57.6	478,622	44.9	379,961	25.8	50,568	12.7	14,141	3.6	450,343	14.8

Source: U.S. Bureau of the Census, *Census Reports*, vol. 1, *Twelfth Census of the United States, 1900*, pt. 1 (Washington, D.C.: GPO, 1901), pp. cxcvi–cxcvii; for division into first and second generations, see *Reports of the Immigration Commission*, Sen. Doc. no. 756, 61st Cong., 3d sess., 41 vols. (Washington, D.C.: GPO, 1911), 3:512–21. Reprinted from Frederick Leubke, *Ethnicity on the Great Plains* (Lincoln: University of Nebraska Press, 1980), p. 294.

Indians, Chinese, American citizens, and European immigrants all mixed on the roads to the California mines.

The Oregon and California Migrations

Between 1840 and 1860 approximately 300,000 people traveled to the Far West on the overland trails. Of them, 53,000 went to Oregon, 200,000 to California (120,000 during the Gold Rush years), and 43,000 went to Utah. Not all of these people went for the same reasons. The Gold Rush migrants went for quick wealth. Few of them intended to stay in California. The Mormons, on the other hand, sought in Utah a permanent haven from religious persecution. They believed they had divine instructions on how to organize a new and better society. Migrants to Oregon went west in search of farms; they wanted to replicate their existing world in what they thought was a better land.

The first point to be made about this movement is so obvious that it may inadvertently be ignored. All the heads of households—that is, those people who actually made the decision to migrate—believed that they could improve their condition by moving elsewhere. As Jesse Quinn Thornton, an Oregon migrant himself, wrote: "They agreed on one general object—that of bettering their condition, but the particular means by which each proposed to attain this end, were as various as can well be imagined."

The conviction that movement would better a person's condition was by the 1840s a cultural belief deeply ingrained in Americans. Most Oregon or California migrants had moved before either as children or young adults. Such moves tended to come at definite junctures in a family cycle. People were most likely to move at marriage, after the birth of several children, or, finally, when their children began approaching adulthood. All those times were occasions when men and women were likely to feel the need to acquire more land and secure larger opportunities for themselves or their children. The families who took the overland trails tended to be young. The average number of children among them was 3.4, and most of those children were still small; in 22 percent of the cases in the sample, the mother was pregnant with another child.

Oregon and California did not, however, draw people evenly from across the

United States. Ohio, Indiana, Illinois, Kentucky, and Missouri provided the bulk of the migrants. These farmers from the Midwest and upper South, already predisposed by culture and experience to equate movement and prosperity, were eager audiences for the stories about California and Oregon that began to circulate in the 1840s and 1850s. The old image of the West as the Great American Desert, a place where, as journalist Horace Greeley editorialized, it was "palpable homicide to tempt or send women and children over this thousand miles of precipe and volcanic sterility to Oregon," was yielding to the image of an Eden at the end of the trail.

Nationally distributed books and famous public lecturers propagated this new image of Oregon, but the national media were far less influential in recruiting settlers than were local publications and lesser-known speakers. Most migrants felt that the decision to go west was too important to be based on stories circulated by strangers. They wanted information from people they knew personally—from reliable people who had seen the region firsthand. A person who might be skeptical of a traveling lecturer would more likely trust a letter from a former neighbor published in a local newspaper. Local speakers and local correspondents had a credibility among their neighbors that an outsider, no matter how eminent, lacked.

The implications of this system of spreading knowledge were far-reaching. This reliance on individual contacts in deciding to emigrate meant that reliable information did not flow evenly throughout a region. Some neighborhoods acquired a great deal of knowledge about the West and many people migrated. Others knew little and few went. Because people depended on personal contacts for information, migrants tended disproportionately to be kinspeople or former neighbors of earlier migrants. Oregon migrants often traveled west among such kinspeople and old neighbors. A survey of diarists who wrote about their experiences along the overland trails found that 37 percent of them traveled in extended family groups.

Knowing how information was spread does not tell us what information convinced people to move. This is not an easy question. Before the Gold Rush, Oregon and California beckoned because lands there were cheap and fertile. But given the length, difficulty, and expense of the journey, why should anyone have gone all the way to the West Coast? Why did migrants to the Far West not take up the even more fertile and far more accessible land along the so-called Middle Border then opening along the Mississippi? Most farmers looking for new land, after all, did exactly that.

Obviously, more than the existence of good agricultural lands was involved in the transcontinental migration. Those going to the West Coast often added two additional explanations for their decision. The first was health. In the middle of the nineteenth century the Ohio and Mississippi valleys were dangerous and sickly places. Repeated outbreaks of smallpox, influenza, and, most devastating of all, cholera hammered the area, but these diseases were common throughout the United States. More worrisome, because they were more unusual, were endemic diseases, the worst of which was malaria, or, as nineteenth-century Americans called it, the fever and ague. Spread by mosquitos (although no one knew this at the time), the disease took a heavy toll. Victims of malaria suffered annual sieges which disrupted not only personal lives but the life of the community. The onset came in August and September, and the disease left its victims alternately shaking with chills and burning with fever. "Milk sickness" or "puking fever" was a second disease endemic to much of the Midwest. Like malaria it depended on a carrier, and so its transmission remained mysterious. The cause of the disease was poisoning by white snakeroot (*Eupatorium ageratoides*). Humans, of course, did not eat the root, but when they drank the milk or ate the meat of cows that had grazed on the plant, they fell seriously ill.

California may not have been, as Mark Twain asserted, so healthy that you had to leave the state to die, but it and Oregon seemed far preferable to the sickly, malarial Midwest. Certainly anyone willing to be convinced that the West was healthier did not have to look far for reassurance. Before the outbreak of the fearsome cholera epidemics of 1850, 1851, and 1852, some of the medical literature of the time presented health as a by-product of the journey itself. The literature led a reader to believe that no disease had the stamina to make the journey to the coast; germs withered and dropped off by the way.

The second reason buttressing the selection of the West Coast over the Middle Border was its climate. The mild, wet winters of California and Oregon appealed to farmers only too glad to eliminate the necessity of sheltering and feeding animals through a long cold season. In a rural economy this meant the elimination of one of the farmer's most arduous tasks and a considerable savings in money and labor.

California Gold Rush

Moving alongside this migration of midwestern farmers and Mormons in the late 1840s and early 1850s were very different migrants: the Forty-niners, as participants in the first wave of the California Gold Rush called themselves. The Gold Rush had many sources but a common destination: California. On January 24, 1848, James Marshall found gold glinting in the tailrace of the mill that John Sutter, a Swiss entrepreneur, had hired him to build on the American River. Because Sutter knew a gold rush would destroy the little empire he had created in what is today Sacramento, he tried to conceal the news. It was not until May that reports reached San Francisco. News of gold in California reached Hawaii in June and Oregon in August. By fall, Mexico, Peru, and Chile had learned of Marshall's gold. All began to send miners north. Rumors reached the East Coast in August, but not until President Polk confirmed the discovery in a message to Congress in December did the Gold Rush begin in earnest. By 1849, Americans, Europeans, Chinese, Mexicans, and Chileans were flocking to California. How many came is uncertain, but the non-Indian population of the state increased from about 14,000 in 1848 to 223,856 in 1852.

The Forty-niners obtained their information in a different way than did agricultural migrants, conducted their move differently, and had different ambitions. There is a recurring metaphor in the descriptions of gold rushes that underlines these differences. Chroniclers of gold rushes tended to compare the miners to sick or insane people. "Gold fever" was what nineteenth-century Americans in general called the reaction created by news of the discovery of gold. Gold, as the Sioux holy man, Black Elk, bitterly recalled, was "the yellow metal that makes Wasichus [whites] crazy."

This metaphor of lunacy recurs repeatedly in descriptions of the California

Gold Rush. Most observers described the effect produced by the news of the discovery as a sort of temporary derangement. In April of 1849, according to one of Sutter's employees, Sutter's own workers "seemed to have gone insane." In May displays of gold in San Francisco reduced that town from approximately 1,000 people to less than 100 as its inhabitants stampeded for the mines. A visiting U.S. naval captain, watching this nearly hysterical exodus to the mountains, wrote that "nothing but the introduction of lunatic asylums can effect a cure."

The careful consideration, the weighing of reliable evidence, typical of the Oregon migrations was not a large part of the California experience. People did not believe the first rumor they heard, but once the discovery of gold was verified by President Polk in his message to Congress and gold was actually put on display, pandemonium ensued. From the East people departed for California on any ship that could float, while from the Midwest they set out on the overland trails. News spread not through the intricate local networks that lured people to Oregon, but through the national media. The net drawing people to California was as wide as the one drawing migrants to Oregon was narrow.

The broad net that drew people into California had, however, a fine mesh: it filtered out women and children, who together numbered only about 5 percent of the Gold Rush migrants. Relatively few women proved as adamant as Luzena Wilson of Missouri, who insisted on coming west when her husband determined to set out for California in 1849. "I would not be left behind," she later recalled, "I thought where he could go, I could, and where I went I could take my two little toddling babies." Those women who entered the net, however, sometimes regretted it. "This is the Paradise of men," Martha Hitchcock wrote back home in 1851, "I wonder if a paradise for poor *Women* will ever be discovered."

Later rushes were, in a sense, only echoes of California. Tens of thousands of men from the area east and south of Missouri flocked to Colorado in 1859. There they joined a much smaller number of veteran miners from California. In 1859 and 1860 about 10,000 miners crossed the Sierra Nevada from California at news of gold and silver discoveries in the Comstock Lode of Nevada. Then in 1862 perhaps 20,000 people rushed to Idaho at news of mineral strikes there. Some of these same people were undoubtedly among the approximately 30,000 people who moved to Montana beginning in 1864. Such rushes could, as they did in California and Nevada, take sparsely populated regions and give them enough people to make them states seemingly overnight.

Types of Migration

With this brief account of early migration on the overland trails before us, we can classify the different types of migration and create models of migration. The first type we can call, for lack of a better name, community or kinship-based migration. Native-born migrants to Oregon exemplify it as well as anyone.

This community model of migration had several characteristics. It combined a basic satisfaction with a way of life and a deep dissatisfaction with present opportunities for living that life. It was fueled by the belief that people can improve their own condition by seeking new opportunities elsewhere. People involved in this kind of migration organized their trip around existing kinship and community ties. They depended on personal networks of communication that are not open to the whole society: letters, conversations, speeches, materials carried in local newspapers.

The second type of settlement, far less common than community settlement, can be called utopian. The Mormons provided the best example of it in the entire history of the West. Utopian migrants were not so much interested in maintaining an existing way of life in a better place as they were in creating a new and better way of life. Their new way of life differed from that of the dominant society, and people who participated in utopian settlements usually sought some kind of separation from that society.

In the largest and most successful of the utopian experiments in the West, the Mormons withdrew into the desert away from the corrupt East, where they had been persecuted. The Mormons thought a perfect society possible because of the spark of divinity that they believed all people carried. To achieve a greater perfection, they were willing to change many of the basic institutions of American society. Many nineteenth-century Mormons would replace monogamy with polygyny. They would replace individualism and democracy with communalism and authoritarianism. Utah would become Zion, the seat of God's kingdom on earth.

The third type of migration was one that would grow increasingly important after the Civil War, and it is the hardest to label and distinguish. Because it is still typical in the West, we will call it modern. The migration to California during the Gold Rush was a manifestation of this kind of migration. These migrants did not look on their destination as either a site for re-creating an existing way of life or of establishing a new and better one. Instead, the purpose of migration was simply to accumulate property that could be transferred somewhere else. Very often the migrants saw the move as temporary. Once they made sufficient money, they intended to return home.

Whereas the first two types of migration tended to depend on narrow and personal networks of information in selecting destinations, the modern type depended on mass or public information. News of the Gold Rush, for example, was available to everyone in newspapers and public documents. Similarly, whereas the first two types of migration were usually organized around extended kinship networks, community networks, or churches, modern migrants tended to move in units no larger than families, and very often they moved as individuals.

These models only partially fit the migrants who traveled east and north. There is too little information on Mexican migration during the nineteenth century to generalize, but Chinese migration combined aspects of both the community and modern forms. Chinese migration resembled the community model in that news of the Golden Mountain—California—spread through local networks established among the impoverished peasants and workers of Guangdong Province, from which 70 percent of the early Chinese migrants came. Letters from Chinese in San Francisco drew some to the Golden Mountain. Sixteen-year-old Lee Chew was typical of others. He came to California after seeing a man of his village return rich from the "country of the American wizards."

But Chinese migration also resembled the individual migration of the Gold Rush, of which it was a part. Chinese men left their families and came to California for what they hoped would be a short and profitable stay. They purchased tickets on steamships from credit brokers, who either charged them extravagant interest or took a share of the profits. On arriving in California, they discovered that to get to the mines they required further loans from Chinese merchants in San Francisco and thus further interest. The Chinese came as free laborers, not as coolies or slaves, but they were free laborers who carried their own small mountains of debt to the Golden Mountain.

These Chinese migrants maintained a demographic profile typical of the Gold Rush well into the late nineteenth century. In the 1870s only one in every 13 Chinese in California was a woman. Chinese continued to hope that they could make a fortune and return home to die wealthy and respected, surrounded by their children and grandchildren.

After the Civil War, all three types of migration, and the Chinese variant of them, persisted, but they did not contribute equally to the migratory stream. On the whole, native-born settlers, with the exception of black Americans and perhaps southern whites, followed the modern paradigm of migration. European immigrants—along with these black and white southern native-born Americans—continued to follow the community or kinship paradigm. And in rare instances, isolated examples of utopian settlement occurred.

Foreign Immigration as Community Migration

The persistence of community or kin-based migration into the West is particularly clear in the case of Norwegian migrants who settled in large numbers on the grasslands of western Minnesota and the Dakotas. Norwegians became one of the most important of the migrant groups of the American West. Nineteenth-century Norway was second only to Ireland in its per capita rate of emigration.

By far the best data we have on Norwegian immigrants comes from Balestrand, in the province of Sogn og Fjordane in western Norway. The motives for this migration were deeply grounded in the peasant culture of Norway, but the reasons that caused people to leave may, at first glance, appear confusing. Norwegians did not come to the American West to get rich, nor did they come because they were growing poorer at home. In what appears to be a paradox, peasants in Sogn og Fjordane grew dissatisfied with Norway even as their standard of living increased.

This apparent paradox between rising standards of living and increased desire to emigrate revolved around landownership. When nineteenth-century emigration occurred, agriculture in Balestrand was flourishing and the general population was enjoying an increased level of wellbeing. But despite economic growth, primogeniture—an inheritance pattern that gave the farm intact to the eldest son—and an increasing population combined to create a landless class which, while relatively well off, had no hope of obtaining land. That class faced a future as cotters, or landless tenants, in a society which placed great value on landholding. America offered an escape. Here land was available, and Norwegians believed a familiar society could be reestablished on an adequate land base.

Still, migration to the United States represented a real risk, and the people of Balestrand described the first immigrants to America in the same way that people talked of the Forty-niners who rushed off after gold. They were daring but mad. Substantial migration did not occur until these early migrants established local networks of communication to draw others after them. The immigrants wrote home and convinced others to follow.

The first Norwegian immigrants to the United States came from the ranks of the more prosperous peasants. Children of landholders took their share of their inheritance and departed to purchase lands across the sea. Successful peasant farmers, too, sold their farms to go to a land where there was promise of land for all their children. But for the landless, there was also hope. Immigrants already in America often loaned their poorer kinspeople the money for passage. Successful farmers in the new land, eager for workers who spoke their language and shared their culture, paid the passage of immigrants in exchange for a term of labor in a country where land was cheap and labor expensive. In America, landless Norwegian peasants believed, work paid. Immigrants wrote home that a frugal laborer could save enough in several years to buy land, something that was nearly impossible in Norway.

Once in America, Norwegians relied on the same kinship and regional networks that had brought them to the United States to expand their settlements. The availability of new lands farther west allowed Norwegian immigrants to escape the problem of recurring land shortages as existing communities filled. Groups, often composed largely of young married couples, hived off from older communities. As in the earlier migration to America, these migrants sought to combine new opportunities for landholding with life in a familiar Norwegian community.

Existing Norwegian communities in Wisconsin and Minnesota thus served as stepping-stones to new lands farther west. Balestrand immigrants who settled in Deuel County, South Dakota, for example, first lived for a time in the Norwegian settlements of Arendahl and Camp, Minnesota, before making the relatively short move into the Dakotas.

This kind of movement did not represent a step into a totally strange land. Norwegians and other ethnic groups maintained ties with their kin and fellow emigrants who lived in widely scattered enclaves. Not only did people exchange letters, but newspapers printed in a group's native language circulated from community to community. These informal networks effectively spread information about new opportunities in the West and steered people into existing ethnic communities. Such networks, like the communities they served, were largely closed to outsiders. Norwegians, Germans, German Russians (that is, Germans whose ancestors had settled in Russia a century earlier), and Swedes all developed similar networks to steer kin, friends, and fellow religionists into relatively homogeneous communities.

Although they came from very different environments and cultures, Norwegian settlers migrated in ways similar to those that brought earlier native-born settlers into Oregon. Norwegians after the Civil War, however, had far less in common with most native-born migrants to the West. Outside of the South, native-born migrants were relying less and less on kin- and community-based migration networks.

The Growth of Modern Migration Networks

Migration westward after the Civil War and the coming of the railroads differed in fundamental ways from most of the earlier transcontinental migrations. Some of these alterations are obvious. The length of the journey, how it was made, and the time the move took all changed. After the construction of the railroads, journeys that had taken months now took days or, at the most, weeks. Most migrants now shipped their belongings and farm equipment in special immigrant cars and rode the railroads west to the point nearest their new land. Many settlers still traveled by wagon, but they now covered much shorter distances, since they drove only from the railroad to their claim. There was obviously less need to rely on the assistance of friends and family in making such a move.

Nor were migrants as dependent on personal information in making their move. A public and open communication network—mass advertising by railroads, states, and territories as well as mass-circulation newspapers and magazines and traveling exhibits at state and county fairs—became increasingly ubiquitous in the late-nineteenth-century United States. The railroads, once they made their selections, sought to sell the lands granted them as quickly possible. They were particularly active in soliciting immigration. The Union Pacific, Northern Pacific, Burlington, Santa Fe, and other lines vigorously promoted their lands in the prairie and plains states. They not only sought native-born settlers but also sought to stimulate foreign immigration. In 1882 the Northern Pacific alone distributed over 600,000 pamphlets in English, Swedish, Dutch, Danish, and Norwegian. Migrants tended to rely more and more on these public sources and less on personal information.

Western governments equated population growth with economic growth and development, and they, too, sought to stimulate immigration. Dakota Territory started to promote immigration as early as 1862, but it was not until the late 1860s that both governmental agencies and private groups advertised the virtues of western lands nationally and internationally and hired traveling agents to promote the western states and territories.

Because they were intended to encourage the sale of lands, the pamphlets distributed by the railroads, states, and territories were not necessarily any more reliable than the accounts of Oregon or California that had appeared in newspapers before the Civil War. At their worst, they exaggerated both the fertility and climate of the West, particularly by promoting the idea that aridity was not a problem, since rain would increase as the land came under cultivation. But some pamphlets did give relatively accurate assessments of the difficulty of settlement. A Santa Fe pamphlet of 1879, for example, warned against any married man coming to Kansas without at least $800 to $1,000 to start a farm.

Why then did native-born farmers respond to this wave of national publicity with more enthusiasm than they had to the earlier campaign for Oregon? They responded so partly because promotion had become more sophisticated. Railroads quickly discovered the utility of cultivating the small-town press. Railroads sponsored free excursions by reporters into the West to view their lands. Having been abundantly liquored and extravagantly fed, reporters were hardly likely to be very critical of the lands their hosts wanted them to promote. The stories about western lands that reporters and editors churned out on their return home were usually little more than advertisements for the railroads.

Migrants were not, however, simply seduced by slick boosters, for they could now often visit and look firsthand at the lands they intended to buy. Earlier settlers could not travel to Oregon and inspect the land there before making their decision to move. They had to rely on information from others. After the completion of the railroads, however, settlers could with relatively little trouble take a ride on the Northern Pacific, the Santa Fe, or the Kansas Pacific and examine the lands that were available. The railroads even sold special land exploring tickets. If the buyer purchased at least 160 acres of railroad lands, the cost of the ticket was deducted from the price of the land.

It was in the interest of the railroads to sell their land grants quickly and at reasonable rates.

African American Migration Networks: Exodusters

Yet even as this modern system of migration expanded, the older forms did hold on among some native-born groups. Black American migration networks, in general, seem to have remained community- or kinship-based, closely resembling those of many European immigrants. In this case, too, information traveled through letters that were read aloud in churches. Circulars praising western lands passed from hand to hand, and advocates of migration held public meetings in existing black communities to solicit migrants.

In the years of repression following the end of Reconstruction, community-based settlement among blacks shaded over into utopian settlement. First from Kentucky and Tennessee and then, in 1879, from Louisiana, Mississippi, and Texas, thousands of blacks sought a better life in the West. Fleeing the aftermath of Reconstruction, many former slaves developed an almost millennial belief in a refuge in Kansas, and that state became the destination of the largest and most notable of the post-Civil War migrations of former slaves.

Benjamin "Pap" Singleton stirred and directed this millennial fervor. Singleton saw himself as an instrument of God's will in Kansas, and he thus joined Joseph Smith and John Brown in thinking that God had special plans for that region. Already 70 years old in 1879, he was a man who had grown old in slavery, but he labored mightily to create black settlements in the West. His efforts were such that he could declare, with only some exaggeration, "I am the whole cause of the Kansas migration."

Singleton and his followers envisioned Kansas as the site of a struggle to unite all blacks in a massive effort to improve their common lot. They envisioned a black society segregated from but coexisting with neighboring whites. The vision of Singleton and others took shape gradually. Singleton himself founded two colonies, and several other black colonies grew up in the state. The largest of them, with about 700 people in 1880, was Nicodemus, founded by black Kentuckians in Graham County, Kansas, in 1877. It was from these settlements that circulars, letters, and speakers went east to attract new settlers from existing black communities in the South.

In 1879, following brutal murders and general repression of blacks during southern election campaigns of 1878, Kansas fever took hold in Louisiana, Mississippi, and Texas. Some 6,000 blacks migrated to Kansas between March and May 1879, and as many as 20,000 may have fled the South for Kansas and Kansas City, Missouri, in 1879–80. Singleton was influential, but this explosion of Kansas fever depended on no single leader. It briefly became a mass millenarian movement feeding on faith. Kansas was an escape from terrorism and poverty in the South. Southern whites, fearing a loss of cheap labor, tried, often violently, to halt the movement. The migration continued anyway and was broken only by the refusal of steamboat captains to carry migrants across the Mississippi. When transportation became available later in the year, the migration resumed on a smaller scale before slowly dwindling out. In 1880, Kansas contained 15,000 blacks, most of them Exodusters, as veterans of the exodus from the South were called.

No other single black migration west in the nineteenth century would match the size, suddenness, or millenarianism of the Exodusters, but black migration would continue to follow the patterns of early Kansas migration. Small communities of blacks, often separated by great distances, appeared throughout the West—in Nevada, Utah, the Pacific Northwest, and elsewhere. They often arose where specific job opportunities lured small groups of blacks, who then persuaded relatives or friends to join them. Sometimes such settlements arose as successful blacks sponsored others. In 1859, Clara Brown, who had purchased her own freedom from slavery, persuaded a group of gold prospectors departing for the West to hire her as a cook. Once in Colorado, she started a series of laundries, and with the proceeds she outfitted 34 of her relatives for a trip to Denver after the Civil War. Afterwards, she sponsored other blacks who sought to come West. Supplementing this piecemeal migration by free blacks and former slaves was the settlement of discharged black soldiers in the West later in the nineteenth century. Black soldiers formed a considerable segment of the western army, and some of these men chose to stay when their enlistments expired.

Migration: The Journey Itself

In terms of our metaphor, we have now looked at both the course of migration and the tributaries that fed it. We know something of where people went and how they, as groups, entered the migratory stream. What remain to be examined are the connections that continued to link these migrants with the larger American society as they undertook their journey.

The standard image of western migration applies only to the migration from east to west: a line of wagons moving off toward the setting sun. Leaving "civilization" behind, the migrants are venturing into the unknown. They are people about to be thrown back onto their own resources. They depend only on each other to survive. In terms of our metaphor, it is as if the migratory stream carves its own deep canyon, traveling along in isolation until it reaches its destination. If we think about this image for a moment, we realize that it is not very applicable to later migration, when railroads took migrants west. Whatever validity the image may have depends on early migration by covered wagons, the supreme manifestation of which was the overland trails. An examination of conditions along the overland trails, therefore, can give us some idea of how self-reliant and isolated from the larger society migrants in fact were.

Over time several overland routes developed to the West, but the major routes until the coming of the railroads always remained the Oregon Trail along the south side of the Platte River and the Mormon Trail on the north side. Both trails merged to go through South Pass in Wyoming before the Mormon Trail branched south to Utah. The Oregon Trail eventually presented a series of options before all the cutoffs reunited on the Snake River and then proceeded west to the Columbia and the coast. A traveler to California could either take one of the cutoffs west of South Pass and then descend to the Humboldt River or follow the Mormon Trail, picking up the Humboldt farther on.

Along these trails, all migrants shared a basic technology and faced the same physical hardships. The journey itself was arduous and moderately dangerous. The death rate on the trail was about 3 percent, or about 10,000 people in all, compared to a death rate of 2.5 percent in American society as a whole. Certainly the major danger to western migrants in folklore—Indian attack—was rare. By available records, between 1840 and 1860, Indians killed 362 whites on the trail, whereas whites killed 426 Indians. Other migrants died at the hands of white outlaws, who, disguised as Indians, were responsible for atrocities—including the torture of children—blamed on Indians. Accidents accounted for more deaths than did Indian attacks, but most deaths—90 percent—were caused by disease. Diphtheria was nearly endemic on the trail and killed many children, but the major killer was cholera. The cholera epidemic of 1850–52 killed half of all the people who would die on the trails between 1840 and 1860.

Clara Brown helped organize African American migration into Colorado.

Ft. Vancouver The Dalles
Oregon City
Ft. Boise
Soda
Springs
Ft. Hall
LANDER CUTOFF
Yreka
HUDSPETH
CUTOFF
South Pass
Ft. Laramie
Shasta City
Pilot
Peak
SUBLETTE
CUTOFF
Ft. Kearny
Ft. Bridger
Salt Lake
City
Sacramento
HASTINGS
CUTOFF
Independence
Stockton
Santa Fe

- - - - - Oregon Trail (1834–1858)
———— California Trail (1841–1859)
—·—·— Santa Fe Trail (Ca. 1800–1880)

Overland trails. Based on Warren A. Beck and Ynez D. Haase, *Historical Atlas of the American West* (Norman: University of Oklahoma Press, 1989), map 32.
Copyright © 1989, 1991 by the University of Oklahoma Press

Technologically, there was little to differentiate the overland travelers from each other. The migrants overwhelmingly transported their goods by covered wagons pulled by oxen, or, less often, by horses and mules. Most migrants overestimated the capacity of their animals to pull heavy loads over mountains and across deserts. To lighten the load, men walked alongside their teams. Although women rode more often, many of them also walked. Few families were lucky enough to have sufficient horses to ride west.

For most migrants, the elimination of passengers became merely the first of progressive attempts to lighten their wagons. The way west was a thoroughfare littered with abandoned goods and dead animals. One army officer gave a partial enumeration of the debris along the trail: bar iron, large grindstones, baking ovens, cooking stoves, kegs, barrels, harnesses, clothing, bacon, and beans. Even iron safes and a diving bell appeared along the trail. In one 40-mile stretch of the Nevada desert in 1850, a migrant counted 2,000 abandoned wagons. The oxen pulling them had died or given out.

The long line of wagons carrying household goods west is one of the most evocative western images, but there were other ways to travel west before the railroads. One was by packing what you could carry on your back, and during the Gold Rush many did pack west. During the Gold Rush, too, entrepreneurs organized special express wagon trains that promised a rapid trip to the coast with all the necessities supplied. Such trips, however, usually proved neither profitable for their organizers nor rapid for the passengers.

In 1856, Brigham Young and the Mormon church created yet another mode of travel. Attempting to cut back on the costs of the migration, the church ordered converts moving to Utah to pile their belongings onto handcarts and to push them across the plains and over the mountains. The experiment failed. The last party to depart suffered numerous breakdowns, ran short of food, and finally got caught by early winter snows. Before a relief party from Salt Lake City reached them, 225 people died. It was the greatest single disaster in the overland migrations, and it ended the handcart experiment.

Just as they shared the same technology, so too did all of the migrants have to make their journeys within the same set of environmental limits. No party could depart from Independence or Saint Joseph, Missouri; Council Bluff, Iowa; or other jumping-off places for the journey until the spring and early summer. New grass had to sprout on the plains and prairies and be high enough to feed their stock before they could depart. All had to cross the last high western mountain ranges—the Sierra Nevada and the Cascades—before fall snowstorms closed the passes. All had to endure the same heat and cold; all had to eat the same dust stirred up by thousands of human and animal feet and churning wheels.

This journey west did not transform the beliefs or attitudes of the migrants. On the trail, they applied existing gender and social roles to arduous new conditions. Differences in conduct existed, but these reflected differences between groups that existed before they started their journey, not differences brought by the journey itself. Since Mormons differed from other groups in their social organization, for example, their social experience on the trail was also different. Mormon migration tended to be more hierarchical, authoritarian, and highly organized than that of other immigrants.

When families traveled together, they apportioned work along strict gender

Given the size of the teams and what appears to be an absence of oxen, this photograph of a wagon train probably was not a picture of Oregon- or California-bound emigrants.

lines, and this tended to work to the advantage of men. On the trail men could forgo much of their ordinary work, since the daily labor of farm or business was now impossible. Their nearly sole duty was transportation: driving the wagons, caring for stock, selecting the route, and making necessary repairs. Being up at four to harness stock and walking beside a loaded wagon all day was arduous labor, made worse by periodic turns at nighttime guard duty, but women fared even worse.

Once the trains stopped and the animals had been set out to graze, men could rest, but women had far rarer periods of leisure. They got up before the men to prepare breakfast and cleaned up after them. When the wagons stopped, women served lunch, and in the evening they cooked dinner and prepared the lunch for the next day. Women hauled water and collected firewood and buffalo chips to cook the evening meal while men rested. After dinner, women had to air supplies to prevent mildew and mend clothes. When the train was delayed and water was available, they washed clothes. Child care was their ultimate responsibility, but on the trail those women who could delegated the care of younger children to the older ones. Women had, in the words of one, "no time for sociability." Men worked with other men and hunted with other men, and a sense of camaraderie developed among them; women were confined to the family and isolated.

The only exception to the stability of social roles on the trail occurred when travel involved the absence of women in the trains of Gold Rush migrants. Then some men had to take on "women's work." Resentment over having to do work usually left to women occurs repeatedly in the trail diaries of the all-male parties of the Gold Rush.

Conflict was as much a part of trail life as cooperation. Except among the Mormons, units of migration larger than kinship or neighborhood groups tended to be fragile things. Before departing, many groups compiled elaborate constitutions and voted on leaders for the journey, but few such parties completed the trip intact. Most emigrant companies and wagon trains fractured and split repeatedly.

The dissolution of parties could be dangerous in the early years of overland migration, but following the Gold Rush, when the trails were "wide and busy highways" so polluted with travel debris and dust that "overlanders donned goggles to see," a traveler who left a train was hardly likely to be marooned in the middle of the wilderness. During the 1850 migration it was not unusual for several thousand migrants to pass Fort Laramie in a single day. Indeed, the overland trails during these years are best considered a single, vast migratory society. Selfishness, violence, and predatory opportunism were not unknown, but more often the members of this community exchanged information, helped those in distress, provided services, and traded with each other.

Changing Nature of Migration

In one sense travelers clearly left American society behind when they departed on the overland trails, but in another quite real sense they encountered extensions of the society repeatedly on the trail itself. The American state and the larger American economy met them at nearly every turn. Both the federal government and individual entrepreneurs provided the migrants with the protections, goods, and services that they both needed and demanded.

The most obvious governmental presence was the U.S. Army. The relative paucity of Indian attacks on western immigrants did not lessen the migrants' fear of attack. They demanded protection from Indians, and protection they received. The government deployed over 90 percent of the minuscule U.S. Army in western posts during the 1850s, and it negotiated numerous treaties to secure safe passage for travelers on the overland trails. Both migrants and government officials presumed that it was the federal government's responsibility to insure safe passage across the West.

Protection was merely the beginning of services extended migrants by the government. Migrants expected accurate information at the posts about the best routes and current conditions, a service codified in Frémont's reports and maps. They expected, and received, emergency medical aid and emergency supplies. Migrants often obtained the right to use blacksmith shops at the posts. By the late 1850s military surveys had shortened and improved the eastern sections of overland trails, and congressional appropriations had enabled the military to undertake similar work from Fort Kearney west. In western Washington and Oregon other military roads conducted the migrants on the last stages of their trip.

Just as the migration spurred a greater federal presence, so too did it provide incentives for merchants and entrepreneurs to open up businesses in the West. From the beginning these entrepreneurs tended to see the migrants as so many

Ferries and other conveniences quickly appeared along the Oregon Trail. This is a camp scene at the Elkhorn River Ferry.

sheep lined up for fleecing. Francis Parkman, after witnessing transactions at Fort Laramie in 1844, reported that the migrants were "plundered and cheated without mercy." He calculated merchants' profits at Fort Laramie that summer at about 1,800 percent. The relationship between merchant and migrant was thus often less than cordial.

The enterprises that served the earliest emigrants had existed before there was an Oregon Trail. Fort Laramie at the confluence of the Platte and Laramie rivers, Fort Hall near where the Snake and Portneuf rivers met, and Fort Boise at the mouth of the Boise River all were initially fur trading posts which later found new sources of profit in the annual migrations. Jim Bridger and Louis Vasquez glimpsed the new opportunities that the migration presented as early as 1841. When they established Fort Bridger on the Green River, their goal was to trade with emigrants. Former mountain men and Taos traders soon began to undertake annual summer journeys to sell riding animals, draft animals, and food supplies along the trails. Later, as cutoffs emerged, these and other merchants competed for access to the shifting flow of migrants. All of these traders happily sought to charge whatever the market would bear.

A well-provisioned migrant who avoided the loss of stock might escape extravagant charges for supplies, but almost inevitably migrants found that they had to pay for other services offered along the trail. Entrepreneurs quickly established ferries and eventually built bridges across the major rivers. As early as 1843 there was a ferry across the Kansas River. In 1847 the Mormons established a ferry across the North Platte, and in 1848 they added one across the Green River. It was better to pay than to risk the dangers and unforeseen delays of river crossings.

When the Gold Rush increased the scale of migration, businesses along the trails increased proportionately. By 1850 virtually all the significant rivers and creeks on the eastern prairies and plains had been spanned by bridges or were served by ferries. By 1853 the Platte itself had been bridged. Farther west, competition rapidly emerged at the ferry sites. During the peak Gold Rush years of 1849–53 demand for service was so high that wagon trains often backed up for two or three days at the ferry crossings. Tempers grew short in the jostling crowds waiting during the long, hot summer days, and arguments over places in line sometimes degenerated into brawls and murders. These bottlenecks spawned more than violence by concentrating emigrants. Seasonal enterprises blossomed. Migrants could exchange (at a considerable loss) lame stock for fresh, buy supplies, get blacksmith work done, get drunk, or gamble. The larger forts did not just provide supplies, but, like Fort Kearney, which by this time boasted four "eating houses," also provided travelers with other services not usually connected with overland travel.

Central to this expansion of mercantile capitalism were the Mormons. The Mormons had ironically migrated with the desire to avoid further contact with gentiles, and they themselves had initially constructed an economy with strong communitarian elements, but the Gold Rush left them very close to the main line of western migration. The Mormon capital of Salt Lake City became a stopping point on the trail and a center of trade. It was a place where, in the words of one migrant, "it cost nothing to get in, but a great deal to get out." Even this assessment of a stop in Salt Lake was probably sanguine, for getting there involved a detour across a collection of Mormon ferries and bridges that cost between $14.50 and $20 per wagon.

The Mormon leadership remained ambivalent about the prospect of large numbers of gentiles traveling through Utah. But since the migrants clearly came and gentile merchants from the East had set up shop in Salt Lake City to serve them, the Mormons might as well profit, too. The Mormons sold fresh food to the migrants tired of flour, bacon, and salt pork. They exchanged fresh stock for old and sold supplies to those forced to winter in Utah. Unlike the traders further east, however, the Mormons wanted goods, not cash, in return. They preferred to barter for manufactured goods that were otherwise unobtainable. To increase their supply of scarce goods, the Mormons also sent out scavenging parties to bring back the goods abandoned by the migrants. These parties, knowing the common emigrant tactic of disguising caches of goods as graves, traveled east, digging up graves as they went.

To the west of Salt Lake City lay the most forbidding stretches of the California Trail, but there, too, by 1850 businesses and services abounded. California traders appeared on the Carson, Truckee, and Humboldt rivers ready to charge prices high enough to leave emigrants with fond memories of Taos and Mormon traders. Some of these outposts became permanent settlements when their proprietors deemed it too expensive to transport their stock back to California.

Between 1840 and 1860 the increase in migration, the protection offered by the federal government, and the presence of emigrant-oriented businesses transformed overland travel. Where once rivers had to be forded, now they could be crossed by ferries and bridges. Where once there were only scattered fur trading posts, now there were military posts, stores, blacksmith shops, and even hotels and restaurants. The young American state and a growing commercial economy were everywhere in evidence.

Together, the state and the merchants made the migrants simultaneously safer and more resentful. The great disasters of the overland trails were, by and large, early disasters. The Donner party of 1846–47 fell victim to a series of stupid decisions, improvident delays, factional quarrels, and bad advice that in no way set them apart from the mass of emigrants. They, however, traveled before merchants existed to profit from their bad fortune, before promoters of new routes regularly sent out guides to lure emigrants to their trails, and before a substantial military presence existed to rescue them. The Donner party got caught in early snows in the Sierra Nevada and progressed from hunger to starvation to cannibalism. Finally, after an initial party failed to secure help, a party of 15—ten men and five women— set out in a desperate midwinter crossing of the Sierra Nevada. Two men and all five women survived by eating their dead companions. Help arrived, but before the ordeal ended 42 people had died; 47 survived.

After 1849, emigrants did not have to rely only on such heroic efforts to summon aid, for parties from California were eager to provide it. The motives of those rescue parties were not selfless. Both California and Oregon were eager to facilitate immigration and to avoid the bad publicity generated by trail disasters. New communities west of the Cascades and Sierra Nevada wanted to direct emigrant traffic through their towns and regularly announced new cutoffs and sent out guides with supplies to bring the emigrants in. Emigrants whose oxen were exhausted, whose food supplies were nearly gone, and who worried about early winter snows were often only too eager to follow. Some of the new trails, such as the Lassen Cutoff to California and the Applegate Trail, were hardly improvements on existing routes, and their promoters were roundly denounced by unhappy immigrants. But no one was left to die on these new routes. The willingness of existing communities to send out rescue parties, often at considerable cost to themselves, averted disaster. At the end of a long trip such rescuers might well have been asked, as they were by a member of the Donner party, whether they were from heaven or from California.

Migrants, even in the earliest phase of migration, did not leave their society behind them. They met it at virtually every turn. The stream of migration did not travel through deep canyons cut off from the outside world. It passed through an open and accessible country. Those thirsty for profits came to drink from it, and those who wanted increased populations tried to divert it.

The Decision to Migrate

To look at the final and most intimate aspect of migration, the individual decision to migrate, it is necessary to abandon the metaphor of a migratory stream. Real streams are the creation of topography and climate. The water that makes them up does not have much choice in the matter. Water that falls from the sky does not choose to combine with other drops and flow into a stream and follow the stream to a river and the river to a sea. But in our metaphorical migratory stream, the drops—individual people—did choose to join it. Real streams are purposeless and impersonal, but in our migratory stream actual migrants have purposes; their goals are personal. And it is here that the metaphor fails. It cannot help us organize what we know about why some people decided to go to the West.

Before looking at this final question, however, another caution must be inserted. All decisions are contingent on circumstances. People decided to migrate, but not all people did. Women, as we shall see, often had to abide by male decisions in the making of which they did not share. Nor were all things possible for all people. Some people could in practice no more go to the West than they could go to Venus. A decision not to migrate could be prompted by the certain knowledge that there was no money to pay for the move. People did not always control their own lives or the circumstances in which they lived. The challenge is, with these cautions in mind, to find the links between the larger historical conditions that induced migration and individual decisions to migrate.

Few people, outside of those Indians who were coerced to leave their eastern homelands and remove into Kansas, Nebraska, and Oklahoma, came west because of force. Most people freely decided to move. Their moves, as we have seen, correlated with measurable economic patterns and climatic fluctuations, but in the end it was neither the economy nor the climate that determined what they did. They decided, given a particular set of circumstances and a choice among a limited range of options, that a move to the West was the best response they could make to conditions confronting them. They made decisions, and then they made journeys. When large numbers of people made the same decisions, the result was mass migration.

We have remarkably little information about how these decisions were made, but what we have indicates that it was in all three migratory streams a male decision. Our best information comes from the overland migration to Oregon in the middle of the nineteenth century. This migration was largely a family migration, but within the families husbands almost universally initiated the move. One study of Oregon Trail diaries did not find a single case in which the idea to move had come from a woman. Indeed, three-quarters of the women in the sample opposed the move; most often they cited the necessity of leaving parents or other family members whom they would most likely never see again.

But paradoxically, the reluctance of women to leave family members that led them to resent migration in the end caused them to consent to go. For women, above all, sought to keep families together. Unable to keep extended families together, they agreed, if reluctantly, to keep the nuclear family intact. They accompanied their husbands and usually confined their opposition to the men's decision to their diaries. Forced to leave existing homes and associations, these women packed the wagons with particularly valued family heirlooms, cuttings from ornamental gardens, and other objects of more sentimental than utilitarian value. All of these things were meant to put "the stamp of some domestic past on the new west."

Those women who did publicly object to the move had few weapons to use if the husband was determined to go. When a man threatened to go alone, women had little choice but to agree, for in nineteenth-century rural society there were very few opportunities for a woman seeking to earn an independent livelihood. Elizabeth Cress, who, having followed her husband from North Carolina to Illinois, refused to move any farther, learned that defiance meant desertion. And desertion equaled destitution. Asking her parents for help, she wrote, "My old man has left me & has gon [sic] to Californa and took my wagon and left me and my Children in a bad situation."

Men held the customary authority in these decisions and, as Elizabeth Cress found out, could inflict the ultimate penalty by deserting their wives, but in most families, although the husband decided, he tried to win his wife's consent. Some women gave it eagerly; far more gave it reluctantly. But in virtually all cases women could only consent or vote against the decision. The decision itself was made by men.

In conveying that decision men often had trouble articulating exactly what led them to decide to leave. Enos Ellmaker had a "fine [Iowa] farm" with "much improvements yet I was not satisfied with the country." He moved to Oregon. Like James Ross, who moved from Illinois to Nebraska after the Civil War, he thought he could do "better" farther west.

Dissatisfaction on the one hand and the hope of doing better on the other: these were the obvious parameters of most decisions to move. But dissatisfaction and hope were as much emotional as rational responses to conditions. Two people similarly dissatisfied with their current conditions and similarly hopeful about the future would not necessarily agree that a move west was in their best interests. People did not make the decision to move simply because times were hard or because they wanted a better life. Within this context, something else had to tip the scale, precipitating the decision to move. The arguments of others, grandiose hopes or ambitions, the promise of aid in the migration—these and numerous other factors could prompt the final decision to migrate.

Such decisions often did not come easy. Milton Bowie was, his son remembered, "eking out an existence" on 80 acres of Texas "blackjack land" in the mid-1890s when his own father, already in Oklahoma, wrote him asking him to sell the land and to come and file "on good land" in Oklahoma Territory. But Bowie's wife, Ada, refused to go, saying, "There's nothing up there but Indians and rattlesnakes and blue northers and prairie fires." Johnson Isaiah Bowie, Milton's father, persisted in his urgings to move, and after putting in another crop, Milton Bowie himself took a wagon up to the Cheyenne country to "see about it." When he came back two months later, he had made the decision; he had already filed on land in Oklahoma. Many decisions were probably like Bowie's. Growing out of dissatisfaction, they coupled hope, fear, and some connection with people already in the new country. Migrants hammered out these decisions in family disputes and discussions, relying on such information as they could gather. But in the end, men decided.

Doing "better" was by its very nature an ambiguous rationale. Doing better for the Bowies was a combination of a failing farm and hope of better land in Oklahoma. Doing better for Enos Ellmaker, however, involved improving on what was already a successful Iowa farm. Doing better virtually always contained hopes of material gain, but the gain in question could involve anything from simply owning instead of renting land, to accumulating some property, to getting rich. Farmers most often thought of better in terms of more fertile lands and larger farms. The promise of free or inexpensive or more fertile land swayed their decision to move. They accepted the West as a "land of opportunity." There, as Forty-niner Charles Boyle wrote about California in his first diary entry, he could eradicate "the detested sin of being poor."

The conviction that the West was the best place to seek material improvement remained a perennial factor in individual decisions to move west. It was shared by Americans and immigrants, by whites, blacks, Mexicans, and Chinese. "All I know," a Chinese immigrant later recalled, "was that *gam saan haak* [travelers to the Golden Mountain] who came back were always rich." When asked his motives for coming, a black migrant to Kansas in the 1870s answered: opportunity. "That's what white men go to new countries for isn't it? You do not tell them to stay back because they are poor." Going west for material improvement, if a man was a farmer or if he was young and in a hurry to gain wealth by finding gold or silver, was a rational decision. In the West lay cheap land and precious metals.

But because people do more than seek wealth, because life is not just a series of rational decisions, because life's critical decisions are made within a tangle of hopes, fears, and motives not fully known even by the person making the decision, this kind of rational assessment goes only so far. For Mormons like Joseph Grafton Hovey, "called" by Brigham Young to make a settlement in Iron County, Utah, rational decisions to accumulate wealth had far less to do with his move than his commitment to "forsake all and go build up the Kingdom of God." And to many others who decided to seek opportunity in the West, they went west rather than elsewhere because family or friends had preceded them or would accompany them. For many the decision itself was but a single step in a chain of decisions, one in a series of moves that eventually brought them west. When Bill Humphrey sold his barbershop in Roberts, Illinois, in order to join a group of farmers moving to West End, Dakota Territory, he probably thought it no greater a decision than prior ones that had led him from West Virginia to Kentucky to Illinois. A barber in Illinois, he became a barber in Dakota Territory. Such decisions, at once small and momentous, created the immigrants who transformed the West. We do not in our stereotypes of pioneers think of barbers moving west, but among people seeking to re-create familiar worlds barbers are certainly more typical and more necessary than mountain men.

Readings

Crockett, Norman L. *The Black Towns*. Lawrence: Regents Press of Kansas, 1979.

Faragher, John Mack. *Women and Men on the Overland Trail*. New Haven: Yale University Press, 1979.

Gjerde, Jon. *From Peasants to Farmers: The Migration from Balestrand, Norway, to the Upper Midwest*. New York: Cambridge University Press, 1985.

Hudson, John C. "Migration to an American Frontier." *Annals of the Association of American Geographers* 66 (June 1976):242–65.

León, Arnoldo de, and Kenneth L. Stewart. "Lost Dreams and Found Fortunes: Mexican and Anglo Immigrants in South Texas, 1850–1900." *Western Historical Quarterly* 14 (July 1983): 291–310.

Luebke, Frederick C. *Ethnicity on the Great Plains*. Lincoln: University of Nebraska Press, 1980.

Mann, Ralph. *After the Gold Rush: Society in Grass Valley and Nevada City, California, 1849–1870*. Stanford: Stanford University Press, 1982.

Painter, Nell Irvine. *Exodusters: Black Migration to Kansas After Reconstruction*. New York: W. W. Norton, 1976.

Rice, John G. "The Role of Culture and Community in Frontier Prairie Farming." *Journal of Historical Geography* 3 (April 1977): 155–72.

Takaki, Ronald. *Strangers from a Different Shore: A History of Asian Americans.* Boston: Little Brown and Company, 1989.

Tsai, Shih-Shan Henry. *The Chinese Experience in America.* Bloomington: Indiana University Press, 1986.

Unruh, John D., Jr. *The Plains Across: The Overland Emigrants and the Trans-Mississippi West, 1840–1860.* Urbana: University of Illinois Press, 1979.

CHAPTER 9

Transforming the Land

THE movement of migrants into the West disrupted both existing human communities and existing ecological communities. The two processes were intertwined. When western migrants destroyed native plants and animals, inevitably they undercut the economies and cultures of the peoples who used those plants and animals to procure food, clothing, and shelter. When they exterminated buffalo, diverted streams, and planted or grazed holy grounds, they were subverting different ways of understanding and ordering the world.

Nineteenth-century whites, Indians, and Hispanics held different understandings of nature—that is, the land and the plants and animals it supported. To most whites nature existed largely as a collection of commodities. God, they believed, had created nature for individual human beings to use, and it was their duty to make use of it. Logically enough, they valued plants, animals, and minerals according to their utility, and to call something useless was to question its right to exist in a human-dominated environment. Only those members of the natural world that served human needs could be secure in the world that white migrants sought to create. The only possible source of reprieve available to species that failed to qualify as "useful" was to inspire feelings of beauty, reverence, awe, or sublimity in the people who beheld them.

The cultural baggage Anglo Americans carried into the West was heavy but not necessarily permanent. Farmers, loggers, or miners intent on making a profit did not ponder their relation to the land, but many did, at least briefly, note its grandeur. "The landscape of those pristine prairies," the child of one early settler in Kansas wrote, "was a power so tremendous that no wholly well man could escape its enchantment." Early scientists and explorers in the West felt the same enchantment, and it sometimes carried them away from the utilitarian ends for which their investigations were intended. Within three months of his arrival, George Davidson of the California Coast Survey had reversed his disparaging comparisons of California to New England. "Nature only served an apprenticeship when she made the East," he wrote. "A master hand fashioned the charm of the Sierra Nevada." California scientists in particular began to view nature, in the words of one scholar, as "a laboratory rather than a warehouse of salable goods." Because of their study of the West, many of them began to speak the language of ecological interdependence.

Native Americans' beliefs about nature varied widely, but as a whole they can be distinguished from whites' attitudes by their tendency to endow nature with a spiritual dimension largely lacking in white thought. Plants and animals were no more a simple commodity than were humans. They were conscious beings whom Indians endowed with symbolic and religious significance. Indians and whites contended over the same land, but they perceived different landscapes.

The Hispanic peoples of the West tended, like Anglo Americans, to see nature as a set of commodities and resources, but unlike Anglo Americans, many Hispanics saw these resources as the possessions of communities as well as individuals. Particularly in northern New Mexico, people regarded the land as a communal resource. It was a source of livelihood for all rather than the individual possession of a few. This system was hard on the land; between grazing and cropping, the fields of a village received little rest. But villagers also developed a deep reverence for the lands that gave them life. For Hispanics as well as Indians, the ability of Anglo Americans to determine how the land was thenceforth to be used posed a dual threat, economic and cultural.

Although the changes that migrants made in the land altered existing cultures, the Anglo American migrants were not the first to initiate environmental change in the West. Nature is no stranger to disruption and change. Even without human intervention, natural populations fluctuate over time. Climatic shifts, often dramatic, expand the possibilities for some species and limit others. Nature is not always in balance; catastrophes occur, and species disappear, sometimes by the thousands. But in the midst of this flux, the general evolutionary movement tends toward diversity. Like whites, Indians and Hispanics deliberately interfered in the evolutionary course of natural systems. They encouraged the species they desired, and they introduced new species across the West.

Rather than initiating change, Anglo American migrants altered the direction of that change and increased its pace. White migrants introduced, purposefully or accidentally, many new species of plants and animals. Such introductions promised greater diversity, but Anglo Americans actually pushed the land toward greater uniformity. When farmers viewed a native prairie in bloom or saw deer, elk, or buffalo grazing in the distance, they were likely to look through the scene before them and see beyond it a future landscape of corn fields, wheat fields, or cattle. The farmer sought to replace the diversity of the prairie with the more limited species of the field. What a farmer meant by "improved land" was simplified land.

Farmers, however, failed to simplify as drastically as they wished. Unwanted species survived in spite of their best efforts. Some of these became the "pests" or "weeds" of the farmers' fields, although more often than not such pests were as much newcomers as the farmers themselves. Indeed, they had accompanied the farmers in their migration. "Weeds" were a generic name for plants already well adapted to be pioneer species on the very lands disturbed by the farmers' plows or by the grazing of their domesticated animals. These weeds traveled along the roads that farmers cleared. They came with the migrants' crop seed and animal feed. Similarly, "pests" were animals, such as the rat, which, while unwanted, had long ago become as much the traveling companions of Europeans as had horses or cows.

As the impressive success of rats and weeds in the West indicated, environmental change involved more than purposeful changes in the land; it also involved the unintended consequences of human actions. Migrants inadvertently initiated ecological changes that slipped beyond their control. Most often these unintentional changes frustrated the migrants, but sometimes they actually aided their settlement. The epidemics that carried off millions of Indians were, for the most part, the accidental introductions of Europeans. Without these epidemics, Indians almost certainly would have retained their hold on a far greater portion of North America. And if they had survived in greater numbers, the whole history of the continent would have proved far different.

A less grisly but equally uncontrolled ecological invasion took place in the grasslands. Euro-American migrants purposefully introduced a variety of exotic grasses to North America. These grasses had evolved under grazing pressure from horses, cattle, and sheep, and they could withstand having animals pastured upon them. Some of these grasses, such as bluegrass, gradually spread beyond the immediate limits of European settlement. They were present when the first settlers arrived, and when European domestic animals destroyed the native grasses that had not evolved to withstand heavy grazing pressure, the exotic grasses spread and took their place. The spread of bluegrass or wild oats or soft chess, which provide excellent forage, seemed harmless, but such exotics often proved temporary dominants as overgrazing continued. Under continued heavy grazing pressure, other, less palatable forbs and grasses replaced them. In California this process of invasion and replacement had transformed the remaining grasslands by the twentieth century. Remnants of the native grasslands occurred only along railroad rights-of-way, in graveyards, or in other areas protected from the plow and domestic stock.

European species spread relatively easily across much of North America because of similarities in climate between this continent and Europe. One historian has aptly called much of North America a Neo-Europe—that is, a region environmentally very similar to the migrants' European homelands. Because of this similarity, North America (and other Neo-Europes such as New Zealand) eventually came to share many of the plants and animals of Europe.

Yet the larger successes of this environmental invasion that spread exotic species across the continent often hid disturbing failures. Not all of North America was as humid or as temperate as Europe. The eastern United States was environmentally very similar to Europe, but much of the West was not. The West resisted attempts of migrants to create near replicas of their European or eastern North American homelands. When migrants stubbornly persisted in modifying western ecosystems in order to make them like those of the East, they set in motion a process of ecological change that often brought undesired consequences for both the land and the people living upon it.

Environmental Changes

Anglo Americans began to change the western environment long before they actually settled it. Mountain men, for example, eliminated beaver throughout wide sections of the West, and fur traders hunted sea otter to near extinction along the Pacific Coast. And because such animals existed as part of a larger, interdependent ecosystem, their demise initiated other changes. Along the California coast the virtual elimination of sea otters in the 1830s allowed the abalone and sea urchins upon which the otters fed to increase greatly in number. And because abalone and sea urchins, in turn, grazed on kelp, their increase meant a decrease in kelp. Because coastal waters with abundant kelp support greater fisheries than waters without much kelp, less kelp meant fewer fish. And so an unexpected causal chain linked the elimination of otters to an increase in abalone to a decrease in fish.

All of this affected humans. From the 1860s onward, Chinese fishermen harvesting the abundant abalone of the coast unknowingly benefited from the earlier slaughter of otters by fur traders. During the late nineteenth century, however, other fishermen began to accuse the Chinese of depleting not only the abalone fisheries but also fisheries in general. Fisheries were declining, but climatic factors unrelated to Chinese activities were largely responsible for the decline. Indeed, the Chinese, by eliminating abalone and thus increasing the growth of kelp, were actually helping to increase the fisheries. Nevertheless, whites drove the Chinese from the fishing grounds and believed that they had saved the fishing, as fish increased at the end of the century. The fish returned not because of a decline in Chinese fishing pressure but in response to the decline of abalone; the simultaneous elimination by hunters of marine mammals, such as seals and sea lions, that preyed on fish; and more favorable climatic variations. In this case, ecological, social, and environmental change intertwined to influence the lives of humans who never understood the ramifications of their own actions.

The complexity of this kind of change became even more tangled when immigrants to the West not only eliminated native species but also introduced exotic species. Such introductions had already shaped the western environment long before the mass migrations of the nineteenth century began. Corn and beans arrived from Mexico long before the first whites appeared; the horse preceded Europeans over great sections of the West. Sheep and cattle were more intimately connected with the arrival of Europeans, but many Indian peoples had made these animals their own and established them in some western ecosystems well before the late nineteenth century.

The number of new species introduced into the West increased dramatically as the century progressed. The farmers moving into the West brought with them a myriad of plants, animals, insects, and microbes that permanently altered existing natural systems. Most of these new species probably would not have survived if they had arrived alone. They were not intrinsically superior to existing western species; they succeeded because they were better adapted to the changes that the new migrants made in the land. The Euro-American migrants who plowed the land, cut timber, and grazed livestock weakened existing ecosystems and created nurseries for the invaders. A farmer plowing under native plants was quite consciously giving introduced plants an advantage just as a farmer poisoning wolves gave introduced livestock an advantage.

A farmer's fields were beachheads for invading plants and animals. Like the Indians before them, but on a much larger scale, migrants created their own landscapes. A Pacific Northwest botanist would later characterize the ecological changes white migrants brought to that area as the most cataclysmic series of events in the region since the Ice Age. Similar statements could describe changes in other areas of the West.

When immigrants in the West spoke of these changes, they did so in terms of conquering nature. Speaking for millions like him, a farmer in Washington Territory during the 1850s asserted that the main purpose of settling the land was "to get the land subdued and the wilde [sic] nature out of it. When that is accomplished we can increase our crops to a very large amount and the high prices of every thing that is raised heare [sic] will make the cultivation of the soil a very profitable business." In essence, farmers were to tame nature and yoke it to the task of turning a profit for the farmer.

In practice, conquering nature was neither easy nor fully achievable. The farmers were at best apprentice ecological alchemists; although they sought to make nature yield gold, their efforts produced transformations of a different sort. Some farmers could flee their failures, but those who remained had to live with an altered nature that sometimes exacted retributions of its own. Declining crop yields, increased flooding, and mounting soil erosion forced changes on the farmer. Social change and natural change thus often proved to be reciprocal; changes in the land produced changes in society, and vice versa. The Great Plains provide an excellent vantage point to begin an examination of this particular pattern of change.

The Great Plains

The western prairies and the Great Plains often appeared forbidding to migrants, but they are not necessarily an inhospitable place for human beings. Plains nomads and horticulturists knew this land in loving detail and lived on it successfully. German Russians, fresh from the steppes of the Ukraine, found the grasslands a familiar and comfortable place. Migrants used to the forests of eastern North America or of northern Europe, however, found it terrifying. Beret, a character in O. E. Rölvaag's novel *Giants in the Earth*, called it "the great stillness where there was nothing to hide behind." Finding the plains forbidding, many settlers helped to transform it.

The transformation of the Great Plains began with the near extinction of the bison. The decline of the species began before the arrival of white settlers. The range of the buffalo, or bison, as it should properly be called, once extended well east of the Mississippi and west of the Rockies, but the huge herds of historical times grazed the short-grass plains. How many buffalo grazed the plains will never be known. Bison numbers probably peaked at about 25 million animals. Current estimates put the southern herd (that is, the herd south of the Platte River) at from 6 million to 7 million animals in the mid-nineteenth century, and as late as 1870 the southern herd still numbered well over 3 million animals. The herd north of the Platte was probably somewhat smaller.

Hunters had eliminated those bison east of the Mississippi by the end of the eighteenth century, and bison largely had disappeared from the prairies west of the river in the early nineteenth century, but even in the West the bison may have begun to decline before the advent of widespread hide hunting for the fur trade. The plains bison herds always existed in tenuous equilibrium with disease, wolves, hunters, weather, and accidents. By the 1840s bison were in trouble, not so much from overhunting, although that was increasingly a factor, as from a combination of drought, habitat destruction, competition from exotic species, and introduced diseases. During periods of drought, such as the one that struck the Great Plains in the late 1840s, bison had to compete with Indian horse herds and wild mustangs for food and water in critical riverine habitats. Drought seems to have contributed to the "big die-up" of 1867, when millions of bison supposedly starved between the Concho and Brazos rivers. At the same time,

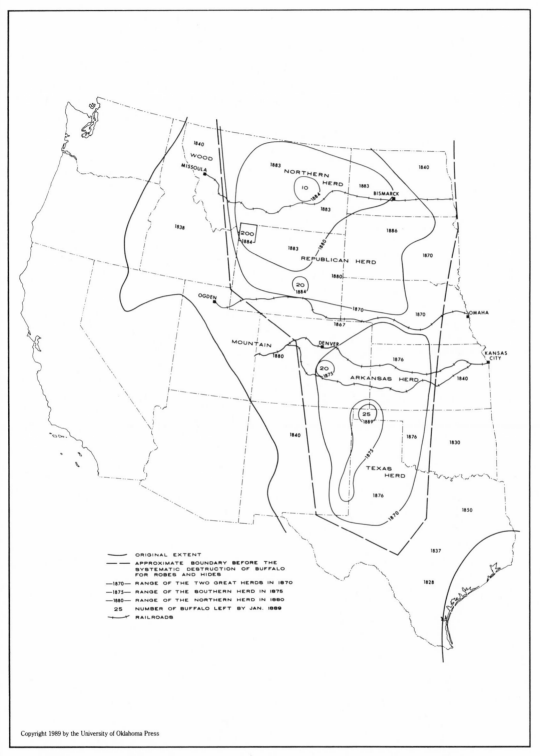

The bison herds. From Warren A. Beck and Ynez D. Haase, *Historical Atlas of the American West* (Norman: University of Oklahoma Press, 1989), map 10.

livestock taken by Indian raiders and cattle driven across the plains by white migrants spread tuberculosis and brucellosis to the buffalo herds. The creation of the overland trails and the spread of white settlement to the edges of the Great Plains drove the bison from critical riverine habitat and denied them the peripheral tall-grass habitat on which they depended as a refuge from drought and hunting. The result was a buffalo population already unable to maintain its numbers when the white hunters struck.

The first commercial pressure on the western herds came with the development of a significant market for their robes and for pemmican—a mixture of pounded dried buffalo meat, fat, and berries that kept for years. Pemmican became a staple high-energy food on the plains, and the fur companies purchased large quantities of it to feed their trappers and *engagés* in the subarctic. Indians increased their kills of buffalo to supply pemmican and robes. Also in the 1830s and 1840s new hunters appeared to prey on the herds. The removal of eastern Indians to lands west of the Missouri brought an influx of people who soon became skilled buffalo hunters, making seasonal forays onto the plains.

Coupled with this commercial hunting was a second kind of hunting. The opening of the overland trails started an onslaught on the buffalo by migrants, soldiers, and various eastern and European sportsmen. These people killed bison in numbers far beyond what they could ever use. They hunted largely for sport and left the carcasses to rot on the plains. The consequences of this hunting disturbed both the plains nomads and horticulturists. By mid-century various Indian groups, particularly those along the Missouri River, the Platte River, and the Santa Fe Trail, began to complain of dwindling numbers of buffalo.

The coming of the railroads sounded the death knell for the herds. The railroads provided a new means of getting the bulky skins to market at the same time that a new tanning process made it possible for eastern tanneries to turn the hides into a cheap leather for straps and machine belts. Previously the market for hides had been confined to buffalo robes. Hunters had to kill the animals during the winter when their fleece was thick, and they could profitably kill no more than Indian women were willing to process into robes. Turning the hides into leather, however, removed these bottlenecks; hunters could kill as many animals as they could skin, and they could kill them at any time of the year.

With a new market, a new means of transportation, and a new hunting season that stretched throughout the year, professional buffalo hunters moved onto the southern plains in the early 1870s. Killing bison to feed the railroad crews expanded to hunting for hides and for tongues, which were salted and shipped to market. The southern hunt peaked between 1872 and 1874. In all, the hide hunters took an estimated 4,374,000 buffalo during these years. To that number has to be added the Indian kill of approximately 1,215,000 on the southern plains during this same period, as well as the smaller number of bison killed by settlers and sportsmen. In the 1870s Congress passed a bill protecting the bison, but President Grant vetoed it.

The scale and procedures of this slaughter made it a kind of industrial hunting unlike anything seen in the West before. Hide hunters worked on foot. Their preferred method was to get downwind of the buffalo, a species with very poor eyesight. Once positioned, the hunter killed the animals at long range with high-powered rifles. A herd often went peacefully and serenely to its death. As long as the animals did not smell the hunter or were not startled, they kept grazing, oblivious to the other bison dying around them. A lone hunter might kill a hundred animals at a single stand before the herd stampeded. The most skilled hunters took 2,500 to 3,000 buffalo in a single year. One party of 16 hunters is supposed to have killed 28,000 buffalo during a few months in 1873.

Hunters, seeking to kill the maximum number of animals in the minimum of amount of time with the least amount of labor, learned to focus their efforts around water sources. They hunted the animals that tried to get to the water by day, and then they lit bonfires at night to keep the thirst-crazed bison at bay. The next day they resumed the slaughter. An English traveler along the Arkansas River in 1873 reported that "for some thirty or forty miles along the north bank of the Arkansas River . . . there was a continual line of putrescent carcasses, so that the air was rendered pestilential and offensive to the last degree. The hunters had formed a line of camps along the banks of the river and had shot down the buffalo, night and morning, as they came to drink." Tourists supplemented the work of the professional hunters by routinely shooting down buffalo as their trains ran through herds grazing alongside the tracks.

The efficiency of the killing was not matched by efficient use of the dead animals. Virtually all the meat rotted. Some hunters initially did not even know how to skin the animals properly, and they thus wasted the hides. Other hunters killed more bison than they could skin. Contemporary sources estimated that at the peak of the hunt in 1872, three to five buffalo were killed for each hide that reached market. By 1875 the southern herd had largely ceased to exist.

The destruction of the smaller northern herd came later. In 1876 the Northern Pacific Railway reached Bismarck, North Dakota, and began pushing its tracks west into the buffalo country. In that same year the army began the campaigns that broke Sioux control of the northern plains. In 1880 the assault on the northern herd commenced in earnest. By 1882 there were an estimated 5,000 white hunters and skinners at work on the northern plains; by the end of 1883 the herd had vanished. The slaughter was so thorough and so quick that not even the hunters could believe what they had done. In the fall of 1883, many outfitted themselves as usual. But there was nothing to hunt except piles of bones bleaching in the sun and wind.

The Consequences for Indian Peoples

The elimination of the buffalo by white hide hunters cut the heart from the Plains Indian economy. Various military commanders encouraged the slaughter of bison for precisely this reason. Without the buffalo, Plains Indians could not effectively resist American expansion. But the disappearance of the buffalo had a meaning for Indian peoples that was more than economic. The buffalo were not just a source of tepees and robes, of meat and tools. The animals were crucial to the cosmology of both the plains nomads and the horticulturists. In 1871, for example, with the buffalo already growing scarce on the central plains, Quaker agents tried to persuade the Pawnees not to hunt the buffalo that season. The hunt was certain to be unrewarding, and it would just as certainly be dangerous, because the Sioux were determined to drive the Pawnees from the remaining buffalo grounds. The Quakers urged the Pawnees to concentrate on farming; with the buffalo gone, they would in the future have to depend solely on their agriculture for support.

The Pawnee chief Peta-la-sharo tried to explain why, given the Pawnee under-standing of the world, the Quaker position made no sense. The hunt had to continue. Without the buffalo, he told the Quakers, there could be no agriculture. Offerings of buffalo meat were central to the Pawnee ceremonies, and it was only these ceremonies that ensured the continuance of the natural cycles that allowed humans to live on the planet. Without buffalo there would be no annual renewal, and the corn could not grow.

Indians like the Pawnees would hunt buffalo until the very end, both because they had to and because they did not believe that their hunting had anything to do with the animals' disappearance. The Sioux, for example, recognized that the buffalo were growing less numerous, but they believed that the buffalo were withdrawing underground because they had been mistreated. They would return and allow themselves to be hunted only when all hunters accorded them the ritual respect that was their due. Whites were unlikely to give them such respect, but in 1890 when the Ghost Dance religion spread to the Sioux, it promised a world where the dead would live and whites would disappear. Then the buffalo would return. Such a return was perfectly logical, given Sioux beliefs. A world purged of the whites would be a world that was hospitable to buffalo. But whites would not vanish. The buffalo would not return. And the disappearance of the buffalo marked the final blow to the old life. In the words of the Crow warrior Two Leggings: "Nothing happened after that. We just lived. There were no more war parties, no capturing horses from the Piegan and the Sioux, no buffalo to hunt. There is nothing more to tell."

Cattle

The elimination of the great free-roaming herds of bison created an ecological vacuum on the Great Plains. Cattle moved in to fill that vacuum. The first cattle appeared even before the buffalo had vanished. During the overland migrations, traders, who bought exhausted or injured cattle and oxen from overland migrants, and teamsters, who used oxen to haul supplies for the army, both discovered that cattle could winter on the plains. These traders and teamsters created the first cattle herds on the plains, but the real stocking of the Great Plains came after the Civil War, when Texans began the long cattle drives that would spread the famous Texas longhorns throughout the West.

The expansion of cattle onto the Great Plains was no more a purely ecological phenomenon than was the elimination of bison. Both were intimately connected with the growth of the American economy and the expansion of the railroads to the west. Economy, culture, and ecology all combined to create conditions that led to an explosion in the numbers of cattle.

The Texas longhorns were a new breed descended from a cross between the criollo cattle introduced by the Spanish and Anglo American introductions such as the English longhorn. Ambitious Texas ranchers had begun efforts to market these cattle in the 1850s, but the Civil War cut the state off from its markets. The longhorns increased until they probably numbered about 5 million head. As commercial beef cattle, the longhorns were a butcher's nightmare— "eight pounds of hamburger on 800 pounds of bone and horn." These long-legged animals, whose horns often spread five feet from tip to tip, put on weight slowly and did not reach full weight until they were eight to ten years old. Even when fully

Their coloring and bulk indicate that these longhorn cattle were most likely a mixture of Texas Longhorns and other breeds.

mature, the animals remained lean, weighing only about 1,000 pounds, and their meat was stringy and tough. But cattle raisers tolerated such commercial deficiencies because of the animals' hardiness. Longhorns could travel far on little water. They could defend themselves against predators, and as long as the herders tolerated winter death rates that ranged as high as 20 percent, they required no winter feeding. They were in this respect ideal animals for driving north and west to stock the range.

The longhorns had, however, an additional liability which would have a significant influence in shaping the cattle industry in the West. Texas longhorns carried with them a small tick that transmitted splenic fever, commonly called Texas or Spanish fever. Longhorns endured the tick and the fever with equanimity, for they, from long exposure, were largely resistant to the disease. The tick died during northern winters, and cattle buyers could safely ship their cattle east for fattening after the frost. But spring, summer, and fall cattle drives from Texas exposed domestic stock to the tick, and the passage of Texas cattle through a farming region meant devastation to dairy herds, oxen, and breeding stock. As early as 1851, Missouri had banned Texas cattle, and the state instituted a more effective ban in 1861. Following the Civil War in 1867, Kansas established a special quarantine line east of which the cowboys could not drive their herds. Cattle towns thus had to lie somewhere west of thickly settled farming regions, and when farmers appeared around them, the town merchants who depended on the drives usually undertook measures to compensate farmers for any stock they lost to Texas fever.

Abilene, Kansas, was the first of the cattle towns created by the convergence of the longhorns, the railroads, and ticks. In 1867 an Illinois entrepreneur named Joseph McCoy, beating out rivals who had much the same idea, established a shipping point for cattle at the small town of Abilene, located where the Kansas Pacific Railroad crossed Mud Creek. Connected to Texas by the Chisholm Trail through Indian Territory, Abilene became the first of the cattle towns. The heyday of the long drives, and with it the heyday of the cattle towns, had begun. Every summer for nearly twenty years the herds moved north. Cattle towns such as Wichita, Caldwell, and Dodge City succeeded Abilene and competed to attract the herds and the cowboys who drove them. The towns could make money from both.

Cattle Ranching and the Land

Even as Kansas cowtowns and Texas cattle raisers began their profitable partnership, cattle raising was expanding onto huge expanses of grassland beckoning to the north. Many of the cattle driven from the prolific bovine womb of Texas were bound for pastures on the Great Plains. The nearly legendary Colonel Charles Goodnight blazed trails to stock the ranges of Colorado and New Mexico. John Iliff, a Colorado cattleman who became known as the "cattle king of the plains," had begun as one of the traders buying out footsore and exhausted oxen and cattle from emigrants, fattening them on bunch grass, and selling them to miners. Goodnight himself eventually pushed cattle into the heart of the Comanche country by establishing the first ranch in the Texas Panhandle. His outfit at Palo Duro Canyon was 250 miles from the nearest railroad or supply base.

Others pushed cattle farther north. Of the 630,000 cattle driven across the Red River in 1871, western Nebraska and southern Wyoming got about 100,000. The government provided a market for other cattle by purchasing nearly 50,000 head annually by 1880 to feed western Indians, but the trail herds consisted largely of young cattle going north to fatten on the western ranges. As railroads advanced, they created new shipping centers and thus opened more and more land for cattle raising. The Missouri, Kansas and Texas Railroad reached northern Texas in 1873, giving Texas cattle ranches there a direct link with Kansas City. Meanwhile, the Texas Pacific ran west across the state to El Paso. The Santa Fe and the Denver and Rio Grande opened up New Mexico and much of the southern plains. The Union Pacific reached Cheyenne, Wyoming, in 1867, and by the end of the 1870s, Sydney in Nebraska and Pine Bluffs, Cheyenne, and Rock River in Wyoming had become the leading shipping points for cattle on the Union Pacific. By 1880 there were, excluding milk cows, approximately 4 million cattle in Kansas, Nebraska, Colorado, Wyoming, Montana, and the Dakotas, and the boom was accelerating.

The early 1880s combined relative prosperity, a nation hungry for beef, and an expanding railroad network on the plains. The cattle industry reached the apex of its boom. Cattle shipments had declined during the depression of the mid-1870s, but they picked up again by 1876. Eastern and European capital flooded into the West nearly as rapidly as did the cattle themselves. Calves sold at $5.00 and mature steers marketed at $45.00 to $60.00 in 1883. To ensure that the calves became steers, ranchers had only to invest in horses and the wages of the cowboys who rode them, a few dugouts, and some primitive corrals. It seemed impossible to lose money. Grass, the major ingredient for transforming calves to steers, was free. Few ranchers bought the land they grazed their cattle on. Even when the larger cattle companies began to drill deep wells to provide water for previously unusable rangelands, their total capital costs remained relatively low. Tales of dependable profits of 40 percent annually filled the newspapers and livestock journals and attracted numerous eastern and European investors. New cattle companies multiplied; 20 new companies with a capitalization of $12 million were organized in Wyoming alone in 1883.

As the price of cattle skyrocketed, the type of cattle grazing on the western plains began to change. Cattle from the ranges of eastern Oregon, descendants of the cattle immigrants brought west before the Civil War, now advanced into the Great Basin and Montana. And eastern cattle, called "pilgrims" or "barnyard stock," joined the longhorns on the range. This was the first step in a concerted attempt to bring improved breeds to the western grasslands and "breed up" the longhorns into a superior grade of cattle that fattened more quickly and carried more meat. Ranchers crossed white-faced Herefords, so prominent in the West today, with the longhorns. The appearance of these new and more valuable cattle made the Texas longhorns less welcome. Longhorns driven north in the summer still carried Texas fever with them, and the disease could decimate the newer stock. State by state and territory by territory, the West closed its boundaries to new drives from Texas. In 1885, Kansas shut its borders to Texas cattle between March 1 and December 1 of every year.

This cattle boom rapidly and seriously overstocked the ranges. By the mid-1880s there were an estimated 7.5 million head of cattle on the Great Plains north of Texas and New Mexico. With cattle raisers betting on limitless grass and a market that would eagerly consume all the beef they could produce, ranchers stocked the plains with more cattle than the land could support. The cattle industry raced toward economic and ecological disaster. It arrived at both nearly simultaneously.

The combination of overstocked ranges and the new fences designed to shut out competitors was instrumental in the ecological disaster that cattlemen produced on the plains between 1885 and 1887. With the exception of the winter of 1880–81 at the beginning of the cattle boom, the winters on the Great Plains during the early 1880s were mild. Easy winters allowed the survival of the eastern cattle that joined the longhorns on the range. But each winter in which cattle prospered meant greater grazing pressure the next year, and further introductions of cattle increased the pressure still more. For the grasslands, the result was a decline in the most heavily grazed plant species—buffalo and grama grasses—and an increase in unpalatable species of woody plants and forbs. Poor grasslands meant undernourished cattle less able to endure the rigors of winter cold.

Disaster first struck the southern plains, where overgrazing had severely damaged the grasslands. In 1870, 5 acres of land could support a steer; in 1880, the same animal needed 50 acres to survive. Cattle raisers nevertheless continued to put new animals onto the depleted ranges until some areas held four times as many cattle as they could adequately support. In the fall of 1885, 200,000 cattle evicted from Oklahoma for illegally grazing on reservation lands in Indian Territory arrived on the already overgrazed grasslands of Colorado, Kansas, and the Texas Panhandle. And that winter the weather failed to hold. During one of

A western roundup during the golden era of the range cattle industry.

the most severe winters in the history of the area, the cattle starved and froze to death. The fences designed to protect the pastures became death traps as cattle drifting before the storm ran into them, piled up against them, and froze to death. Ranchers suffered frightful losses; some claimed to have lost 85 percent of their herds, but the average loss was much less.

The next year disaster struck the northern plains. There, too, overgrazing had seriously reduced the ability of the land to feed cattle. In some areas where 5 acres had sufficed to feed a steer, it now took more than 90. The summer of 1886 was dry and hot. This weather not only retarded the growth of the already overgrazed grasses, but it also forced cattle to congregate around remaining water sources. The lands around these creeks and waterholes were so heavily trampled and grazed that nothing grew on them. The cattle entered the winter weak and in poor condition. Beginning with a blizzard in November, winter gripped the northern plains and pummeled them unmercifully. Howling winds and bitter cold that dropped temperatures as low as −46 degrees Fahrenheit kept ranchers and their cowboys confined to their houses and bunkhouses. On the range the cattle died. In the spring the cowboys found the rotting corpses of cattle piled in coulees and lying in rows against the fencelines. The losses varied widely. Some ranchers lost nearly all their herds. An overall estimate of losses is difficult to make, for many ranchers, as it turned out, had no idea how many cattle they owned. Losses appear, however, to have averaged 30 percent and in some places far more. Even those animals that survived were weak, emaciated, and often maimed, with their tails, ears, and feet frostbitten. Hardened ranchers were revolted. Granville Stuart wrote years later: "A business that had been fascinating to me before, suddenly became distasteful. I never wanted to own again an animal that I could not feed and shelter."

In 1887 ecological disaster only fed economic disaster. With the country entering a depression and prices dropping, creditors frightened by the losses began calling in their loans. The ranchers, both to pay back their creditors and to reduce pressure on their denuded ranges, had to sell on a falling market. They succeeded only in driving prices down even lower and driving themselves into bankruptcy.

In the wake of the cattle, their competitors, sheep, inherited much of the plains. Sheep raising, long the basis of the New Mexican economy, had expanded in the shadow of cattle following the Civil War. Sheep needed less water, were able to forage farther from water sources, and ate forbs that cattle would not touch. Sheep raising first expanded within the old Hispanic borderlands of California, New Mexico, and Texas, but it spread in the 1870s to the Columbia Plateau and into Utah and on into Wyoming and Montana. These northern herds were improved wool-producing breeds—Rambouillets and merinos— and not the common all-purpose *churros* of the Southwest. Cattlemen fought this expansion. They believed sheep ruined the range for cattle, and they considered sheep inferior animals raised by inferior men—Hispanics, Basques, and later Mormons.

Despite wide fluctuations in wool prices on international markets, sheepherders, however, survived and spread into new regions as cattle ranchers declined. The first stages of the ecological changes brought on by overgrazing actually helped sheep even as they hurt cattle. On the Columbia Plateau, for example, sheep thrived on the invading forbs, which were only marginally palatable for cattle. Sheep raisers, too, resorted to transhumance, grazing their animals in the mountains in summers and in the valleys in winters, more quickly than did cattle raisers. Sheep in the western mountains were, in John Muir's words, hoofed locusts that devastated the fragile mountain environment, but for a period the sheep thrived. In both Wyoming and Montana sheep raising replaced cattle ranching as the leading agricultural activity by 1900. Montana became the leading sheep-raising state in the country.

The ecological and economic catastrophe that crippled the cattle industry on the Great Plains was neither an accident nor a case of simple bad luck. It would be repeated a few years later in a still harsher environment: the Great Basin. Ranchers first moved cattle into Nevada from California in order to feed the miners of the Comstock Lode. In 1871 a dry winter in California brought thousands of additional cattle into Nevada, and the exodus continued as Californians, shifting from cattle ranching to growing cereal grains, drove their herds out of the Central Valley and over the Sierra Nevada. The building of the Central Pacific Railroad opened up the California markets to Nevada ranchers in the 1870s. In this high desert country with its scattered water sources, ranchers found it easy to control grazing land by monopolizing water. There they imitated sheep raisers in adopting transhumance. Herders wintered their cattle on the deserts and then drove them into the mountains to feed in the summer. Acquiring only the land necessary to control water sources, these ranchers depended on their ability to graze their cattle on the public domain.

The Great Basin lands that their cattle grazed were sagebrush grasslands. Silver gray in the desert sun, seeming to turn purple in the dusk, they were a deceptively desolate landscape. The sagebrush that dominated them was only marginally palatable for cattle, but beneath the sagebrush grew an understory of perennial bunch grasses. Cattle depended on these grasses for their survival, and the grasses made the land far richer than it appeared. As the number of cattle increased, however, the sagebrush-grass communities suffered. They became "stark, shrub dominated landscapes without sufficient understories to support anything but marginal livestock production." Eventually this ecological vacuum would be filled by the Russian thistle—the common western tumbleweed—which was the first of the alien weeds to invade the sagebrush country, and by cheatgrass. They filled the niche left vacant by the declining native grasses.

By the late 1880s too many cattle grazed on the denuded pastures. The summer of 1889 was very dry, and the cattle entered the winter in a weakened condition. The winter storms began in December of 1889, and during the first months of 1890 temperatures dropped to as low as −40 degrees Fahrenheit. By spring some ranches had lost 75 percent of their cattle; others reported losses of 50 percent. Dead cattle were supposedly so thick along the Mary's River fork of the Humboldt that a person could walk upon the corpses for 100 miles. To try to escape the stench of rotting cattle, cowboys had to cover their noses with bandannas.

As on the Great Plains, the death of cattle created openings for sheep. Ranches that had 150,000 cattle in 1890 grazed only 30,000 a decade later. All around them sheepherders, Basques and Mormons from Utah and southern Idaho, Scots from Washington and Montana, dared the violence of cattlemen and moved onto the ranges. The damage done by sheep and cattle, although great, was not simply a function of grazing pressure. During years of above-normal rainfall, native plants could sustain more pressure than during years of drought. The worst damage came when drought and overgrazing coincided. The way in which grazing pressure and climatic cycles intersected in the destruction of some grazing lands can be seen in northern New Mexico. Between 1820 and 1835 when Indian depredations in New Mexico had been minimal, Hispanic herders had heavily stocked the sheep ranges. This overstocking, however, seems to have done little damage because rainfall was normal or above normal. When sheepherders and cattle ranchers restocked this region in the 1880s and 1890s following the subjugation of the Indians, the damage was severe. This period was drier than usual, and the rain that did fall tended to come in the form of brief, violent cloudbursts that accelerated the cutting of arroyos, gullies formed by runoff. Arroyos lowered the water table, further weakening vegetation already under stress from constant grazing and drought.

The result was a radical change in vegetation and a major increase in erosion. Native grasses died back and were replaced by less productive grasses and by yarrow and fleabane, which sheep and cattle found unpalatable. Tracts that had been grasslands became dominated by sagebrush. In mountain ranges like the Sangre de Cristos, grazing first disrupted and then destroyed the original flora. Invaders such as sheep fescue and Kentucky bluegrass came to dominate the alpine grasslands.

The decline in the productivity of grasslands and the disasters that befell the Great Plains and Great Basin ranchers ended the old open-range system of free-ranging cattle gathered in yearly roundups that had been inherited from the Spanish and Mexicans. Those large cattle ranches that survived the 1880s and

1890s gradually gave way to smaller operations that grew hay in irrigated fields or relied on drought-resistant sorghum to provide winter feed for their cattle. Ranchers also introduced new exotic grasses such as crested wheatgrass and relied less and less on the natural vegetation of the range. This change came gradually. It began in the late nineteenth century, but it dominated the industry only during the early twentieth century. Its importance, however, cannot be underestimated. Ranchers replaced reliance on the natural production of the land with reliance on a managed and transformed environment.

Like so many other adjustments to the West, the adaptation of ranchers to the new limits would depend on government. As Joseph McCoy, the father of Abilene, Kansas, wrote, the cattleman considered himself "an independent sovereign, and as such capable of conducting his affairs in his own way," but he found that he could not do so in this land. Ranchers needed and wanted government intervention to secure the water necessary for irrigation to grow hay. And they needed, but did not always want, government intervention to control the number of animals that grazed on the public lands.

Agriculture and the Environment

Like stock raisers, farmers changed the western environment, and for them, too, the consequences of the changes were often sobering. The human relationship to the land would not be the simple story of the transformation of the "wilderness" into a garden.

Aridity presented farmers with the greatest challenge that they faced in the West. Moving west across the prairies, white farmers left the tall-grass lands, where big and little bluestem and other prairie grasses grew as high as horses' bellies. On these prairies only thin ribbons of trees bordering the streams challenged the endlessly swaying grass for possession of the land. There was, and is, no exact boundary between the prairies and the Great Plains. There is only a transition zone, an area from 100 to 150 miles wide, the exact location of which shifts with climatic cycles but which is centered roughly on the 98°30' line of longitude. This transition zone begins in the east, where the bunch grasses— buffalo grass, blue grama, and others—first appear among the tall grasses. Approaching the western boundary of the zone, the bunch grasses dominate, and there the Great Plains begin. This change in ground cover is itself only the most visible reflection of aridity. As one moves west, average annual precipitation declines. On the Great Plains precipitation averages only between 15 and 20 inches a year, or half the amount in the Mississippi Valley. Not enough rain fell to grow either corn or wheat by the methods then practiced by eastern farmers.

For John Wesley Powell, the explorer who became the country's most incisive thinker about the arid West, this nearly invisible boundary was the most critical marker in the West. Powell placed the boundary, marked only by a gradual change in vegetation that reflected an absence of a few inches of rain over the course of a year, at the 100th meridian. On the eastern side of this line old ways of farming and farm making were still possible. On the western side, he believed, attempts to farm as people did in the East would bring only tragedy. Farmers, however, initially crossed Powell's line with disdain. They believed that nature was malleable, that rainfall would increase. Willingly deceived by a combination of their

The J. C. Cram family pose with canaries, house plants, and a pile of antlers outside their sod house in Loup County, Nebraska, in 1886.

own hopes and the fervent assurances of boomers and promoters, farmers were prepared to domesticate the plains. They would reproduce the farms of the prairie and forest lands farther east.

Such false hopes should have been quickly disappointed, but these farmers were also, it turned out, the victims of coincidence. Their movement out onto the plains during the 1880s happened to coincide with the beginning of one of the periodic wet cycles of the plains. Farmers proceeded west seemingly surrounded by evidence that rain was indeed following the plow. Farming itself, they thought, was altering the climate.

But even in the flush days of their settlement, when the rains fell and the crops grew, farmers had to adjust to a land far different from the land most of them had left behind. In this treeless land the old symbols of Anglo American farmers were out of place. The log cabin yielded to the sod house and dugout. A dugout was no more than a cave dug into the side of a ravine or a hill with the opening covered. Such shelters were inexpensive, fireproof, and quick to construct; a 10-foot by 14-foot dugout cost about $10.00. Dugouts were also, unfortunately, sometimes equally quick to flood or collapse. Sod houses were more elaborate, substantial, and costly; a normal family dwelling ranged from $80.00 to $100.00. Settlers plowed a field to cut the sod into one-foot by two-foot bricks and then used these bricks to build their houses. Sod houses were sturdy buildings; many survived as sheds or stables long after a family moved into a frame house. Yet unless they were walled and plastered, they were also damp and dirty places. As one Nebraska girl put it, "There was running water in our sod house. It ran through the roof." Settlers shared their homes with mice, centipedes, spiders, and the snakes that crawled out of the walls and roofs.

Nature on the plains seemed particularly oblivious to human desires. The theory that rain followed the plow assured farmers that nature would become kinder and that droughts and aridity would vanish. This arid, treeless, seemingly barren place would be as wet, forested, and bountiful as farmers allowed it to be. They had only to cultivate and wait. Farmers needed such a faith that the land would change, because this land regularly confronted them with scourges most Americans associated with biblical Egypt instead of the nineteenth-century United States.

The first scourge was the climate. The interior West was hotter and drier in the summer, colder in the winter, and windier at virtually any time than the eastern states. And as the altitude increased, conditions grew more harsh. According to settlers on the high plains of Wyoming, there were only three seasons in that region: winter, July, and August. Such a division makes July and August, with their sometimes searing heat and constant winds, seem more pleasant than they were. In Glendive, Montana, in 1893 there was a 164-degree range in temperatures from a summer high of 117 degrees to a winter low of 47 degrees below zero. The winters brought blizzards that sometimes lasted for days, and east of the Rockies, the summers brought tornados.

And then there were the grasshoppers. Grasshoppers, to be fair, were not confined to the Great Plains; they spilled over onto the adjoining prairies. In a bad year, such as 1874, the grasshoppers swarmed into the northern prairies in such numbers that farmers mistook them for storm clouds massing on the horizon. When the insects alighted, they sounded like hail. They fell from the skies until they lay four to six inches deep on the ground. Their weight on trees snapped off limbs, and when trains tried to move over them on the tracks, their crushed bodies greased the tracks and left the engine's wheels spinning uselessly. Grasshoppers ate the crops; they fouled the water. Attracted by the salt left from human sweat, they even ate tool handles.

But for each agricultural drawback of the grasslands, both plains and prairie, there was a compensating virtue. The grasslands were demanding, but they also promised rich rewards. They were a place where land was relatively inexpensive and well suited to grain production. The absence of wood made heating and fencing more difficult, but there was no backbreaking work to clear forests. Although prairie land could be broken only during a few weeks in the late spring, steel plows allowed farmers to bring the prairies into production relatively quickly. In 1860 the amount of labor involved in clearing an acre of prairie was only 5 to 10 percent of the labor involved in clearing forest land. Nor did a farmer have to break the prairie himself; specialized work teams broke the land for a fee.

As the century progressed, technological improvements on everything from seed drills to combines repeatedly cut the amount of labor required to plant and harvest. The grasslands might have been distant from markets, but with their open, level fields they were ideally suited for the mechanized agriculture that was transforming American farming. On the plains and prairies farmers could produce staple crops more cheaply than in the East, and in good years this land yielded abundantly. During the Dakota wheat boom of the 1880s a family, once it had brought the land into production, could make enough money to pay off its farm and equipment with one or two harvests.

When, however, the rains failed—as inevitably they did—the result was a life as constricted and cramped as the plains were vast. From 1889 into the 1890s drought gripped the plains, and the exodus into this land reversed itself and flowed back east. Some Great Plains counties lost half their populations between 1890 and 1900. One family's pithy summary of such a life was supposedly left written on a sign they posted on their abandoned cabin in Blanco County, Texas: "Two hundred miles to nearest post office; one hundred miles to wood, twenty miles to water, one mile to hell. God bless our home. Gone to live with the wife's folks."

Yet some immigrants did adjust to the cycles of rain and drought, or at least they survived the years when rain was scarce. In most places a few always stayed on through the droughts and the depressions. They hung on and waited for the next boom. "Living in Nebraska," so the old joke went, "is a lot like being hanged; the initial shock is a bit abrupt, but once you hang there for a while you sort of get used to it." Settlement never completely died; it always revived with the next boom and the influx of new migrants.

As farmers realized that the climate would not change simply because they plowed the plains, they turned to other methods of adjusting to this land. Ditch irrigation began as early as 1873 on the southern plains, and irrigation proved locally important in areas such as Garden City, Kansas, in the 1880s. But over most of the area the solution seemed to be dry farming. Hardy Campbell, who believed that he had worked out a way to make agriculture practical on the plains, preached dry farming as the solution to farmers' woes. He urged farmers to give up attempts to grow corn. They should turn to drought-resistant grains like Turkey Red, a hard winter wheat, and sorghums. They should plow deeply in the fall and pack the subsoil. In the summer they should plow repeatedly to create a dust mulch, and they should always leave part of their fields unplanted to conserve moisture.

The years between 1900 and 1920 were good ones for farmers on the plains. Rainfall, despite some droughts, was above average, and wheat prices were high. Not all the settlers succeeded, and many of them turned to stock raising or combined it with farming, but those farmers who did persist acquired larger and larger holdings. In 1920 the average holding in the high plains counties of Kansas, Colorado, and Texas was 771 acres. The increasing mechanization of farming made such large farms possible. The value of implements and machinery on the northern plains rose by 240 percent between 1900 and 1920. These years saw the advent of tractors and machine-powered combines that allowed farmers to plow up and harvest more and more of the native grasslands with less and less labor, but the real boom in tractors would come in the 1920s.

This renewed agricultural expansion, well underway before the outbreak of World War I, boomed as the war created new markets for wheat. Farmers put nearly 5 million new acres of land in field crops on the northern Great Plains. The boom spurred the development of "suitcase farming," in which farmers who lived elsewhere commuted to lands only during critical times in the cycle of planting and harvesting. The farm as a home was clearly separate from the farm as a business. Wheat poured in from the plains, and farm machinery poured onto them.

Wheat farmers achieved the height of their prosperity during World War I, but as grain prices and land prices fell during the 1920s, only the largest and most mechanized farmers continued to prosper. Ida Watkins, who was known as the

"Wheat Queen," made a profit of $75,000 on her 2,000 acres of wheat in 1926. And her operation was small compared to that of Hickman Price, whose 34,500 acres required 25 combines at harvest time. Times were hard on most smaller farms during the late 1920s, but farmers could take some solace in their seeming success at having eliminated the environmental obstacles to commercial agriculture on the plains. By the late 1920s the plains seemed domesticated. Farmers continued to plow with abandon, clearing 5 million additional acres on the southern plains between 1925 and 1930. They increased the scale of farming because only large-scale farming seemed to promise success.

Plains farmers realized that they had problems in the 1920s, but they thought the challenges they faced were only organizational and economic, not environmental. Earlier farmers had failed, these plains farmers thought, because they had lacked the techniques of dry farming and could not operate on the scale made possible by the new technology. If a farmer knew the proper techniques, nature had no choice but to respond and to yield food and profits. These farmers did not see the land as part of a complex ecological system; it was merely a form of capital that could be made, despite itself, to yield a profit. Or so it seemed in 1930, on the eve of the Dust Bowl.

Farming in the Far West

The environmental processes of invasion and adjustment obvious on the Great Plains were at work in less dramatic form across the West. Farming inevitably involved changes in the land, although these changes might seem relatively insignificant at the time. When farmers in western Washington and Oregon struggled to restrict native plants and animals and introduce invaders, their efforts initially seemed inconsequential, because most of the land remained dominated by huge forests of fir, spruce, hemlock, and cedar. But the success of the farmers gradually made major changes in the environment. Farmers locally exterminated wolves, elk, and bear. They increased the numbers of sheep, pigs, and cattle. They continued the task begun by the British of spreading invaders such as oats, wheat, and potatoes.

Nature, however, did not prove as malleable as they wished. Many exotics failed to take hold. Tomatoes, melons, corn, and sweet potatoes, for example, did not find western Washington hospitable. Invaders such as the Canadian thistle moved in like unwelcomed guests and stayed. Canadian thistle was always regarded as a noxious invader that lessened crop yields, but even desired companions in settlement sometimes turned on the farmer. In parts of western Washington the pig became an ecological monster that first destroyed the patches of camas—a native root that Indians depended on for food—and then turned on the farmers' fields.

This process of invasion and change was not a simple shock followed by restored stability. Farmers could not restore stability when their own involvement in the market mandated constant change and readjustment to meet the demands of the marketplace. Farmers in the Northwest soon found themselves in competition with farmers of California. In western Washington, California imports forced farmers to abandon grain and potatoes and switch to sheep raising. When sheep proved cheaper to raise east of the Cascade Mountains, the farmers switched to new varieties of grain and to potatoes, and when these failed, some began leasing their fields to Chinese tenants. Each change in crops brought changes to the land. Overgrazing of pastures by sheep allowed thistle and velvetgrass to intrude, reduced the productivity of the land, and increased the cost of sheep raising. Wheat production produced bountiful yields in some areas for a while, but often at a cost of increased erosion and declining yields. The land became a shifting kaleidoscope of plants and animals as the market forced the farmers to act and local ecological systems reacted in ways farmers could not predict and that sometimes proved disastrous for them.

California

In California farmers operated on a larger scale. In the Tulare Basin of the southern part of the Central Valley of California, for example, farmers began to replace cattle ranchers. They turned the basin landscape into what a modern scholar has called "wall to wall wheat." This transformation involved a dramatic alteration in the area's ecology. Domesticated grazers replaced the antelope and the Tule elk. Farmers destroyed native vegetation. But farmers went beyond such predictable changes to alter the entire shape of the landscape.

The most spectacular environmental alteration of the basin involved Tulare Lake. At its maximum historical extent the lake covered about 760 square miles; by the early twentieth century its remaining waters were impounded within a single township: 36 square miles. To irrigate their lands, farmers tapped the Kings, Kaweah, and Tule rivers and Deer Creek. Inexorably, the lake began to die. By 1890 its remaining waters were too saline to support fish, and the lake, once "copious with fish," became barren. By the early twentieth century the teeming migratory fowl of the area had disappeared as farmers claimed the lake bed itself.

Irrigation did produce abundant crops, but it also brought major ecological problems. The water that once flowed into the lake now went through irrigated fields directly into a water table that rose dramatically. The high water table, in turn, thwarted the normal leaching of salts from the soil. Salt deposition is a by-product of irrigation, and unless the salts are leached or washed from the topsoil, the land becomes alkaline and unproductive. Alkalization became so serious in some areas by the 1890s that the land had to be abandoned.

The general process of change experienced in the Tulare Basin occurred at different rates throughout the interior valleys of central and southern California. Anglo Americans took over from the *californios* in spreading cattle and sheep into the valleys. The carpets of flowers that John Muir noted in the spring became food for livestock, and then as wheat farming spread, the native vegetation vanished beneath the plow.

Farmers and Miners

Farmers in the Central Valley not only had to confront the consequences of the ecological changes that they themselves induced, but they also had to confront the consequences of ecological changes brought by others. During the 1870s and 1880s farmers along the Sacramento River and its tributaries and miners in the Sierra Nevada were locked in a legal and political battle with far-reaching environmental implications. At issue was the right of miners to continue hydraulic mining—the technique of using water cannons to blast away hillsides of gravel and expose the gold-bearing deposits beneath. In effect, hydraulic mining took

This Carleton Watkins photograph of the Malakoff Diggins in Nevada County, California, about 1871 reveals the devastation caused by hydraulic mining. (Amon Carter Museum, Fort Worth)

mountains and washed them into rivers. In places the accumulated debris filled mountain canyons to a depth of 100 feet and more. Year by year, with every snow melt and flood, this mass of gravel and rock moved down out of the mountains into the river systems. By the late 1860s it was clogging rivers, raising their beds and causing floods that spread rocks and gravel out into the valleys. Already hundreds of acres of fruit orchards were dying. And as the debris raised the beds of the rivers, floods threatened not only farms but cities as well. Marysville and Yuba City had to erect a series of levees that soon reached to the housetops. The river actually flowed above the streets of these towns.

Raising the banks of rivers to protect the cities and towns that bordered the streams became a task as endless as it was expensive. Each spring brought new debris from the mountains, and each new deposit required a rise in the levees. The debris also created shoals in the rivers that soon closed the Sacramento and its tributaries to all but the smallest boats. Any break in the dikes was disastrous. When they gave way in 1875, water and debris buried Marysville. In 1878 great floods covered virtually the entire lower Sacramento Valley, leaving Sacramento and Marysville as islands behind their dikes. And in 1881 the levees failed again. Later examinations by army engineers revealed that by the 1890s the debris had totally buried 39,000 acres of farmland and partially damaged another 14,000 acres.

When farmers demanded compensation for damages and an end to the dumping of mining waste in the streams, they were in a tricky situation. Legally their only recourse was to sue for damages, but they could not sue because they could not prove which mine had provided the particular debris that had killed their orchard or buried their hen house. Miners, in any case, contended that because they had begun operations before farms existed in the valleys, they had a vested right to dump debris. Miners and their supporters in San Francisco, where most of the mine owners lived, argued that the farmers took their land with full knowledge of mining practices. To solve their problem, farmers turned in the late 1870s to political remedies, seeking bills to prevent the befouling of rivers and streams.

The result was a long legal and political battle in California over the environmental consequences of dumping mining debris into Sierra Nevada streams. The struggle ended in a victory for the farmers. Several factors aided the farmers in their fight: a changing economy (in which the value of agriculture loomed larger than that of mining), the rising toll of damage as the debris not only ruined farmland but also rendered river water useless for human and animal consumption, and, finally, the arrival of the debris at San Francisco Bay, where it threatened to produce serious shoaling in that body of water. As technical solutions to dispose of the debris failed, a consensus developed for eliminating hydraulic mining entirely. In 1884 the courts in *Woodruff* v. *North Bloomfield et al.* ruled the mines a public nuisance and issued a permanent injunction against dumping. Although enforcement would take several years, the decision proved to be a major victory for farmers over miners, and it established the legal precedent for shutting down a polluting industry entirely.

Hydraulic mining would return briefly to California, but only after Congress in the Caminetti Act of 1893 gave the state the power to regulate the miners. The industry proved incapable of making a profit without fouling the rivers, however, and it never again became an important factor in the California economy. More significantly, the Caminetti Act created the Sacramento River Commission, which had power to "improve" the Sacramento to eliminate flooding. The act, ironically, marked the beginning of a process that would largely eliminate free-flowing rivers in California, creating instead a complex of dams and canals.

While hydraulic mining came under increasing regulation, underground mining proceeded unimpeded. William Wright, who wrote under the pen name Dan De Quille, described the mines of the Comstock Lode of Nevada as the "tomb of the forests of the Sierras." An estimated 600 million feet of timber went to support the mines, and 2 million cords of wood fueled the mining towns, denuding the hills and mountains. Few saw this as anything but progress. Even when in the mid-1880s the sulfurous smoke of the smelters of Butte, Montana, so darkened the streets of the town that pedestrians could sometimes not find their way, most people regarded the murk as evidence of the town's prosperity and success. Unsuccessful mining camps, after all, had no problems with smoke.

Most westerners thought that they had successfully "conquered" nature by the early twentieth century. They believed that they had learned hard lessons but that the land had been subdued. The free-grazing cattle ranges had yielded to the smaller operations that depended on winter feeding and, where possible, transhumance. The attempts to maintain the magical quarter-section of 160 acres as the ideal farm and to cultivate it by eastern methods had failed, but proper crop selection, large farms, a new technology, and dry-farming techniques seemed to have created a potential for bonanzas in the West. To most western farmers, the real struggle no longer seemed to be with the land but instead with making the farmer a better businessperson. Financing the farm, selecting efficient technologies and remunerative crops, and marketing the yields were to them the critical issues. Few were concerned about the consequences their actions had on the land.

Readings

Dale, Edward E. *The Range Cattle Industry*. Norman: University of Oklahoma Press, 1930.

Dasmann, Raymond F. *California's Changing Environment*. San Francisco: Boyd and Fraser, 1981.

DeBuys, William. *Enchantment and Exploitation: The Life and Hard Times of a Mexico Mountain Range*. Albuquerque: University of New Mexico Press, 1985.

Dykstra, Robert R. *The Cattle Towns: A Social History of the Kansas Cattle Trading Centers, Abilene, Ellsworth, Wichita, Dodge City and Caldwell, 1867–85*. New York: Atheneum, 1976.

Flores, Dan. "Bison Ecology and Bison Diplomacy: The Southern Plains from 1825 to 1850." *Journal of American History*, September 1991.

Kelley, Robert L. *Gold vs. Grain: The Hydraulic Mining Controversy in California's Sacramento Valley*. Glendale, Calif.: Arthur H. Clark Company, 1959.

McEvoy, Arthur F. *The Fisherman's Problem: Ecology and Law in the California Fisheries, 1850–1980*. New York: Cambridge University Press, 1986.

McGregor, Alexander C. *Counting Sheep: From Open Range to Agribusiness on the Columbia Plateau*. Seattle: University of Washington Press, 1982.

Miner, Craig. *West of Wichita: Settling the High Plains of Kansas, 1865–90*. Lawrence: University Press of Kansas, 1986.

Ottoson, Howard W., et al. *Land and People in the Northern Plains Transition Area*. Lincoln: University of Nebraska Press, 1966.

Paul, Rodman. *The Far West and the Great Plains in Transition, 1859–1900*. New York: Harper & Row, 1988.

Preston, William L. *Vanishing Landscapes: Land and Life in the Tulare Lake Basin*. Berkeley and Los Angeles: University of California Press, 1981.

Smith, Duane A. *Mining America: The Industry and the Environment, 1800–1980*. Lawrence: University Press of Kansas, 1987.

Smith, Michael L. *Pacific Visions: California Scientists and the Environment, 1850–1915*. New Haven: Yale University Press, 1987.

White, Richard. *Land Use, Environment, and Social Change: The Shaping of Island County, Washington*. Seattle: University of Washington Press, 1980.

Worcester, Don. *The Texas Longhorn: Relic of the Past, Asset for the Future*. College Station: Texas A&M University Press, 1987.

Young, James A., and B. Abbot Sparks. *Cattle in the Cold Desert*. Logan, Utah: University of Utah Press, 1985.

CHAPTER 10

The West and the World Economy

THE achievement of American workers, capitalists, farmers, and managers in transforming western lands awed their contemporaries. They had made the grasslands yield wheat and cattle, they had turned the western forests into lumber, and they had made the western mountains surrender gold, silver, and copper. And they had done all this with astonishing speed. This was an economy that instead of advancing in carefully calibrated stages from subsistence to commercial production had rushed headlong into the world markets. Most Anglo Americans in the West showed no interest in subsistence production; self-sufficiency held as little attraction for them as did isolation. These were things to be endured, if necessary, for a few years and then transcended. When they encountered Indian or Hispanic villagers concerned largely with producing only what they themselves could use, Anglo American settlers scorned those economies as relics of backwardness and barbarism. Indians and Hispanics, they believed, used western resources inefficiently and so deserved to lose them.

The transformation of the western economy was a product of rather effete financiers as well as hardy pioneers; the proper economic symbols of this economic expansion into the West were the railroad and the telegraph. They tied the larger world and the West in a tight embrace. Across the telegraph wires came the instructions and information that coordinated eastern financial markets and western production sites. Along the railroads traveled the raw materials of the West and the finished manufactures of the East.

In many ways the basic outlines of the western economy that persist in some areas down to the present day began in the economic transformation that followed the Civil War. An extractive economy in a world market; an economy plagued by excessive competition and a shortage of capital; an economy dependent on government aid, outside capital, and outside expertise: these qualities still mark large sections of the West. Once they marked all of the trans-Missouri West.

Perhaps because the growth of this extractive economy depended on "natural" products—cattle, wheat, gold, lumber, silver, and copper—it is easy to think of the evolution of the economy itself as natural and inevitable. It was neither. It was the result of conscious economic choices, and as it grew, it eliminated earlier competing economies. The creation of the extractive economy that came with the railroads produced losers as well as winners, and it is best to begin with the losers, who are too often ignored.

The Destruction of Communal Economies

The greatest losers in the capitalist transformation of the West were those people who tried to maintain existing communal economies. Although the economies of Indian and Hispanic villages were themselves linked to world markets by the fur trade and the trade in cattle hides, these links had not changed their basic subsistence orientation. Indian and Spanish villagers still produced virtually all of their own necessities; people depended on the labor of kinspeople or slaves or peons rather than on wage labor.

Most participants in these village economies did not willingly change their way of life following American conquest. Instead, the Anglo Americans forced change upon them by commandeering the resources they depended on. The federal government willingly assisted the invaders by opening up to outside use resources—whether land, buffalo, water, minerals, or timber—previously controlled by Indians and Hispanics. In an 1853 article entitled "Washington Territory—The Future," the *Olympia Columbian* captured the expectation of Anglo American settlers that the government would advance their prosperity at the expense of Indians: "Of the Indians now in our midst and around us in every direction, and in large numbers, but a miserable remnant will remain, and they, confined within such narrow limits as Government may allot to them in some obscure locality, will ultimately succeed in dragging out to a bitter end their wretched existence."

Anglo Americans in the West thought the Indian's fate was the price of progress; it was the Indian's problem and none of their own. They expected their government to take land from Indians and give it to whites. They expected, too, more indirect aid in reallocating resources, as when federal troops protected buffalo hunters who slaughtered buffalo for market and, in the process, made it impossible for nomads to continue their accustomed way of life.

Many Indian economies quickly buckled under this assault. Other Indian peoples, however, retained functioning communal economies into the twentieth century. Those who survived the longest were concentrated in the Southwest, because there whites initially made the fewest demands on Indian resources. Both the Pueblos and the Navajos managed to maintain farming and herding economies that remained largely peripheral to the larger American economy until well into the twentieth century. A few Indian economies adjusted to the new economic world growing up around them. In the 1870s and 1880s the Makahs of Washington Territory became successful commercial fishermen and sealers. They had five native-owned schooners that sailed as far as Alaskan and Japanese waters in pursuit of seals.

The Assault on Mexican American Resources

The Hispanic response to incorporation into the world economy was more mixed than that of Indians. The owners of large ranches in California, New Mexico, and Texas and claimants to princely land grants from the Mexican and Spanish governments welcomed the additional economic opportunities that American conquest brought. Here, seemingly, were new markets for their livestock and new buyers for their lands.

The rancheros and their employees and dependents soon learned, however, that for them the dangers of the new economy far outweighed the opportunities. Disaster came first to California. The 1848 Treaty of Guadalupe Hidalgo had promised the *californios* citizenship and the "free enjoyment of their liberty and property," but it became apparent that they would enjoy neither. The first signs of the inferior status Americans intended for them came with the Gold Rush. *Californios* joined the rush and did well in 1848, but by 1849 Anglo American miners had begun to organize against "foreigners" in the diggings. Among the "foreigners" they included the *californios*, who had lived in California their entire lives and who were, by the treaty, American citizens. Labeling the *californios*, together with Chileans and Sonorans from Mexico, "greasers," Anglo American miners assaulted them and sometimes killed them. Those who were allowed to compete with whites did so only at a considerable disadvantage. Hispanics, along with the Chinese, had to pay $16.00 a month under the Foreign Miners' Tax of 1850. White immigrant miners did not usually have to pay the tax. The tax and the assaults drove most *californios* out of the mines.

Banishment from the mines was the prelude to a series of catastrophes. As Anglo Americans and foreign immigrants flooded into northern California, they began squatting on the large ranchos around San Francisco, killing the cattle and cultivating the land. By 1853 every rancho within a day's ride of San Francisco Bay had produced its crop of squatters. The Land Law of 1851, passed by Congress to make sure that all Spanish and Mexican land grants in California were valid, forced the rancheros into extended litigation to validate their claims.

In the litigation over the grants, the rancheros seemingly did quite well, but their victory proved an empty one. The Supreme Court eventually upheld all but 700,000 acres of the 14 million acres of the land grants, but the process took years, and by the time the commissions and courts validated the grants, squatters, moneylenders, and the very attorneys whom the rancheros had hired had drained the rancheros of their resources. Even if ultimately successful in court, a ranchero often found his herds and orchards destroyed and himself deeply in debt for the costs of defending his land. He was also by law obliged to pay the squatters compensation for the improvements they had made on his land. He had to sell off much of his property to pay the debts he had accrued in its defense or to cover tax bills.

The stories of the rancheros differed only in the details and the scale of the losses. The Peralta family lost its 19,000-acre Rancho San Antonio to Horace Carpentier, who first swindled the family and then bought the property at a sheriff's sale. On the site Carpentier founded the townsite of Oakland. Farther south, at the foot of the bay, the Berreyesa family lost its lands and saw three family members lynched and three more driven insane. It was a family, as one survivor recalled, that "most justly complained of the bad faith of the adventurers and squatters and the treachery of American lawyers."

While northern California landowners succumbed to the Anglo American assault, those in the south initially prospered, but they did so in an atmosphere of increasing racism and conflict. The mines provided a booming market for southern California cattle, but prosperity provided its own traps. With success seemingly assured, rancheros spent and borrowed freely, accumulating a debt burden that depended on continued prosperity. By 1855 imported cattle began

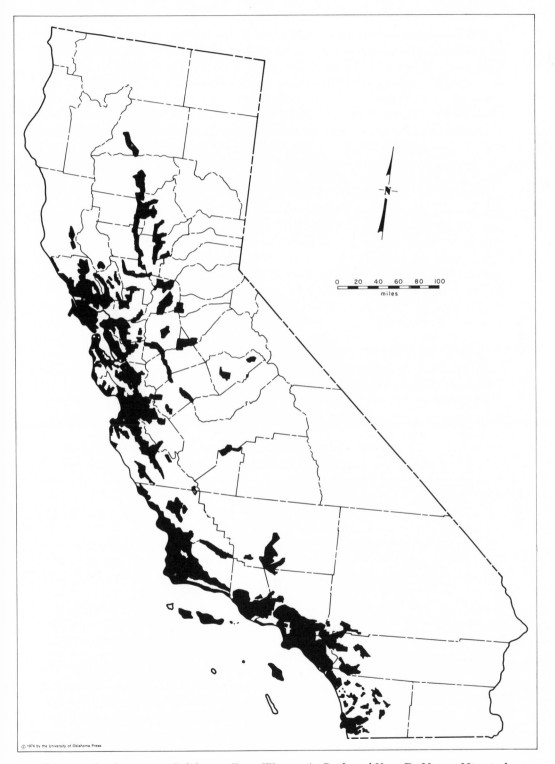

Mexican land grants in California. From Warren A. Beck and Ynez D. Haase, *Historical Atlas of California* (Norman: University of Oklahoma Press, 1974), map 24.

to push prices down, tax bills mounted, and heavy debt burdens became unman-
ageable.

What finally killed the southern ranchos, however, was drought. Between 1862
and 1864 the rains virtually ceased in southern California. In Los Angeles County
seven out of every ten range cattle were lying dead by the end of 1863; possibly
3 million were dead by 1864. In all, about 40 percent of the state's livestock died.
With their herds gone, in debt to lawyers and merchants, and unable to pay their
taxes, the rancheros had by 1864 begun selling the land that remained to them.

The collapse of the ranchos meant dislocation for both the elite *californios* and
the poorer classes who worked for them. Some of the sons and daughters of once
wealthy families married into incoming Anglo American families; others sank
into poverty. Only their memories of better times distinguished them from the
numerous vaqueros, sheepherders, and skilled rural workers whose jobs vanished
with the ranchos. In towns such as Santa Barbara, Los Angeles, and San Diego,
the immigrating whites who gained ownership of the ranchos and the communal
lands converted them into farms and orchards. This in turn meant a decline in
the demand for the labor of the free shepherds and vaqueros. Many *californios*
tried to maintain their hold on these traditional skilled jobs of Mexican California
by seeking work in the Central Valley, but their attempts only turned them into
migrant workers traveling far from home. As white migrants moved into Los
Angeles, *californios* became a minority confined to barrios—segregated ghettos—
within their own homeland. They declined from 82 percent of the population in
1850 to 19 percent in 1880.

The experience of Hispanics in New Mexico differed from those of California
not so much in kind as in degree. New Mexico remained predominantly Hispanic
and Indian in population. Anglo Americans and other European ethnic groups
were a definite minority. A very small Hispanic New Mexican elite acted as
brokers between the majority of the people and the newcomers and thus managed
to retain an influence that the *californios* and Tejanos quickly lost. Members of
that elite held offices in the legislature and served as delegates to Congress. They
also participated in the Santa Fe Ring and took part in the land frauds that marked
the New Mexico territorial period.

Although some members of the elite prospered, most Spanish-speaking New
Mexicans struggled to maintain their lands and way of life. The small landholders
and communal villagers of northern New Mexico suffered crippling losses first
through the frauds that deprived many villages of their lands and then, more
seriously, by the refusal of Congress and the Court of Private Land Claims,
established in 1891, to grant them title to their traditional communal holdings.
Most villagers managed to retain their small irrigated plots, but the courts refused
to recognize their rights to the *ejidos,* or communal grazing lands, that belonged
to the villagers as a whole. As these lands fell into the hands of large cattle
companies, the villagers could no longer maintain their own herds. To replace
herding in the economy, men began to migrate out of the villages to seek seasonal
work in the mines, railroads, ranches, and farms of Colorado and New Mexico.
By the early twentieth century whole families were becoming migrant workers.

The Hispanics of Texas shared elements of both the Californian and the New
Mexican experience. Before American conquest, elite Mexican families between
the Nueces and the Rio Grande held the land through a system of *derechos,* or

rights. Under Mexican law families or lineages and not individuals owned these lands. Under American law, however, the lands became subdivided among heirs, who could sell them without regard to family claims. Land became a commodity— a thing for sale on the market. Mexican Texans lost control of their land through outright fraud and coercion and because of their reluctance to transform their ranches into capitalist enterprises.

In the case of the Mexican Texans it is often hard to draw a sharp line between fraud and legal dispossession. Legal mechanisms cloaked theft. For example, in 1877 the Hidalgo County sheriff sold 3,000 acres of the Hinojosa grant for $15.00 in order to cover tax arrears. Legal authorities also had other means of achieving illegal ends. Mexican Texans called the Texas Rangers *los rinches de la Kineña*— "the rangers of King Ranch"—because they believed the rangers used the law to help wealthy Anglo ranchers expropriate the land of their neighbors. But if fraud and law hurt the Mexican Texans, so too did the mechanisms of the market. As cattle ranching became more highly organized and highly capitalized, marginal Mexican Texan ranchers could not compete. They lacked the money to build wells, improve breeds, or invest in fencing. They lacked the profits to pay taxes on the land. When drought hit or cattle markets collapsed, these rancheros were liable to lose everything.

Mexican Texans and more recent Mexican immigrants remained a majority (73 percent) in South Texas during the last half of the nineteenth century, but they became an increasingly impoverished majority. By the late nineteenth century, when South Texas became a center of large-scale commercial agriculture, Mexican Texans had become a group of unskilled rural laborers.

Utah

In Indian villages and in the Hispanic villages and ranches of Texas, New Mexico, and California, existing communal economies retreated before an expanding capitalist economy that enjoyed the backing of local and federal governments. In the West the defenders of the communal economy, with one major exception, were nonwhite. That one exception was the Mormons.

Outside of some small utopian colonies, the Mormons made the only sustained attempt among incoming whites to avoid incorporation into the world markets. Joseph Smith, the founder of Mormonism, had enunciated a law of consecration and stewardship which presaged Karl Marx's dictum, "From each according to his abilities, to each according to his needs." Early attempts to put this law of consecration and stewardship into practice failed, but when the Mormons settled in Utah, Brigham Young tried once again. Young imagined a nearly self-sufficient Utah with an economy based on cooperation rather than competition.

Young regarded economic independence as essential for the security of the Mormon church. American armies, Young said, could never conquer Utah, but American merchants would reduce it to dependency by making Mormons rely on imports from outside. The Mormons, to be sure, traded with Americans from the beginning, but Young envisioned this early trade with transcontinental migrants as a temporary expedient until the Mormons could produce the required goods themselves. In order to provide basic necessities, Young ordered the Mormons to create their own beet sugar, textile, and iron industries. The Mormons attempted all of them; they all failed miserably. The cotton mission, sent south to Saint

George in Utah's "Dixie" in 1861 to create a textile industry, produced little cotton. The cotton mill lacked both adequate machinery and skilled workers. Despite their efforts, Mormons continued to require outside imports.

The Mormons never succeeded in severing the umbilical cord that bound them to the larger American economy, but increasing signs of their dependence only led them to redouble their efforts. The completion of the transcontinental railroad through Utah in 1869 and the effects of the financial depression of 1873 on Utah's business spurred Young to take new measures for independence. A successful cooperative movement in Brigham City, where 400 stockholders from nearly every family in the community had pooled their resources and virtually severed links with the outside economy, seemed to provide the necessary model.

In 1873, Young announced the creation of the United Order of Enoch. In the first of these orders, organized in Saint George in 1873–74, members pooled their labor, knowledge, and property and became subject to an elected board of management. Each person received stock in the order commensurate with his contribution. He pledged himself to stop importing goods, to boost local manufacturing, and to do business only with members of the order. In addition to the United Order of Enoch, the Mormons created three other similar orders. Together, they eventually included 150 communities.

Yet by 1877, when Brigham Young died, most of the orders had failed. The arrival of the railroads and the discovery of valuable minerals put too much pressure on the faithful. Gentiles gladly took up commercial opportunities the Mormons refused, and the church recognized that by forbidding Mormons to work the mines and build the railroads it was delivering up much of Utah's wealth to non-Mormons. And so Mormons, with church permission, began to dig silver and to lay track. Many Mormons responded eagerly to these opportunities. They quickly became part of the larger economy that Young had sought to banish.

But not all Mormons yielded. On the small desert farms of Utah and neighboring territories, many Mormon families remained remarkably self-reliant well into the twentieth century. Their self-reliance was, however, no longer a mark of Utah's independence; instead it was a sign of the territory's poverty and the unusual religious discipline of its citizens. Desert farms produced little surplus to sell. The church persuaded its members to refrain from tobacco and alcohol, the common luxuries of the West, and to wear only simple, locally made clothing. Desert and church thus complemented each other. The desert denied farmers the ability to purchase outside luxuries, and the church told them such things were sinful.

National and International Markets

The arrival of the railroad, the development of mines, and the creation of large corporate ranches were all aspects of an expanding world economy that neither Indian or Hispanic villagers, traditional rancheros, nor the Mormon church were able to stand against. Inexorably and relentlessly, resources once ignored or consumed within the West began to flow out of the area; manufactured goods began to flow into it.

A pile of rusting tin cans outside a western worker's shack gave the economic facts of life. What westerners produced they usually did not consume, and what they consumed they did not produce. Trees felled in western forests became masts for European ships and boards for Asian and South American buildings. The gold and silver mined in western mountains circulated throughout the world. The cattle that grazed western plains and prairies fed eastern and European cities. The grain western farmers grew competed on world markets with grain from Europe, Australia, and South America. Prospectors, cowboys, lumberjacks, and mountain men became quintessential western figures, but they were agents in a system of production and trade centered in the eastern United States and western Europe.

At its most elemental level, this system of production, like all systems of production, sought to apply human labor to the natural world in order to transform natural objects into finished products for human use. Anglo Americans transformed land, grass, plants, rock, and timber into resources. During the late nineteenth and most of the early twentieth centuries, western economic development consisted largely of identifying such resources, extracting them from nature, and transporting them elsewhere. Westerners did not usually participate in the final molding of resources into finished goods. With the notable exception of the workshops and factories of California, manufacturing usually took place outside the West.

The western economy was, therefore, primarily an extractive economy, and the number of workers west of the Mississippi engaged in agriculture, mining, and lumbering and other forms of primary (that is, extractive) production increased by more than 84 percent between 1870 and 1910. Nationally by 1910, one out of every three workers found employment in extractive industries such as agriculture, mining, logging, and fishing; in the West, a far higher percentage of workers worked in primary industries. Only the Far West conformed to national trends; elsewhere in the region from 40 to 60 percent of western workers mined, farmed, herded livestock, or fished.

A significant minority of western workers found employment in service industries. Service industries essentially are everything left over after primary resource production and manufacturing are eliminated. Doctors, lawyers, prostitutes, domestic servants, storekeepers, and railroad engineers were all service workers. The most important components of western service industries were workers connected with transportation, particularly the railroads. Without a huge and expensive transportation network, the productions of mines, forests, and fields remained useless. Transportation brought western products to market and thus linked the West to the larger economy. The transportation industry directly employed numerous workers, and indirectly, through associated jobs in trade and finance, created employment for many more.

Requirements of the Extractive Economy

With a basically extractive economy, the West, first of all, needed markets for its commodities. Westerners did not consume most of what they produced; there is no such thing as a subsistence logger or miner, and indeed, there are no subsistence wheat farmers. Second, the West needed sufficient labor and sufficient capital—that is, the means to procure the technology, factories, and wages necessary to produce goods or services. Operating within a capitalist economy, westerners obtained capital by promising (but not always delivering) returns on labor and investments greater than workers or capitalists could obtain elsewhere.

Table 4
Distribution of Labor Force in the United States by Percentage

Region	Agriculture	Mining	Forestry	Manufacturing	Services
1870					
U.S.	51.48	1.49	0.26	21.14	25.41
Plains	61.63	0.50	0.26	14.91	22.67
S.W.	73.67	0.31	0.16	7.04	18.8
Mountains	33.59	29.54	0.84	12.94	26.07
Far West	25.73	18.03	1.63	18.20	36.00
1890					
U.S.	40.62	1.97	0.54	24.3	32.31
Plains	51.57	1.29	0.33	16.42	30.35
S.W.	63.94	1.14	0.30	9.11	25.45
Mountains	26.53	12.71	1.18	19.99	39.57
Far West	28.85	4.44	2.30	22.55	41.32
1910					
U.S.	32.46	2.53	0.45	27.92	36.46
Plains	40.85	1.82	0.29	19.99	37.01
S.W.	57.67	1.77	0.36	12.37	27.78
Mountains	29.93	8.47	0.67	20.48	40.43
Far West	20.1	2.84	2.04	26.95	47.6

Third, the West needed a transportation system that could convey these resources to market. In the manipulation of these seemingly simple requirements lay the history of economic development in the West.

The markets the West served were in many cases as recent creations as the western economy itself. A combination of rapid world population growth, urbanization, improvements in transportation, and European imperialism had together produced a rapidly escalating demand for basic commodities and an expanding world market centered on Europe and the United States.

Consider the example of wheat. After 1880, wheat became the major agricultural export over much of the Great Plains, California, and the interior Pacific Northwest. In 1890 these regions produced 50 percent of the wheat grown in the United States. By 1910 farmers in these areas had increased their share of national production to 65 percent. Cities, of course, had imported wheat long before the late nineteenth century, but they had imported it from neighboring areas. As late as 1850 the East Coast of the United States produced 60 percent and Britain 75 percent of their own wheat. In the late nineteenth century both the scale of this demand and the source of the imports changed. Between 1876 and 1880, U.S. grain exports doubled. This rapid rise in demand resulted from an increase in world population of more than 50 percent during the half-century preceding World War I. Population growth increased demand, and a drastic fall in transportation costs allowed cities to buy wheat from areas thousands of miles away. European migrants to Australia and Argentina as well as the western United

States colonized new lands and planted wheat upon them. They sold the wheat to those who remained behind.

In this new economic world of increased demand and increased production a seeming miracle occurred: western farmers received a higher real price for their wheat even as eastern consumers paid less for it. The price of wheat on the world market fell during the late nineteenth century, but in real terms (that is, in terms of actual buying power) farmers received more for their crop than ever before. To be sure, farmers did not get better real prices every year. In the West the real price received by farmers fluctuated periodically, but on the whole it rose between 1867 and 1913. The source of this seeming paradox lay in declining transportation costs, declining production costs, and declines in the price of goods purchased by farmers. All of these fell even more rapidly than the price of wheat declined on the international markets. Again, it must be emphasized that the rise in the real price that farmers received for wheat was an overall trend. Periodic and serious declines in the real price paid western farmers for their wheat did occur in the early and middle 1870s and in the late 1880s and early and middle 1890s.

This demand for western wheat and the price offered for it clearly influenced the economic expansion of western agriculture. In Nebraska, Kansas, and the

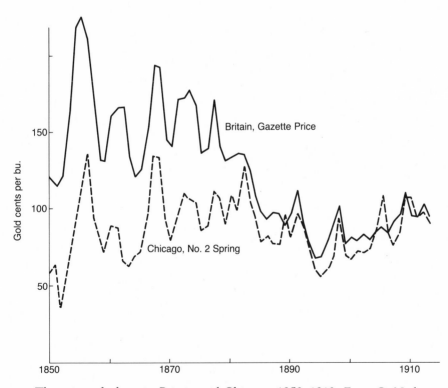

The price of wheat in Britain and Chicago, 1850–1913. From C. Nick Harley, "Western Settlement and the Price of Wheat, 1872–1913," *Journal of Economic History* 38 (December 1978): 867.

Dakotas the rapidity of settlement and the expansion of farming correlated with the local price of wheat. As one economic historian has summarized the data, "The price of wheat . . . tied the American West firmly into the world economy." Virtually from the outset, farmers in seemingly isolated places of Nebraska or the Dakotas decided what to produce on the basis of other decisions made in Chicago, New York, Boston, or London markets.

All western commodities shared wheat's reliance on national and international markets. Silver, gold, copper, timber, and cattle prices responded to fluctuations in international supply and demand and decisions made by governments and large capitalists. The yield of a crop of wheat in South Dakota depended on the vagaries of weather and the skill and hard work of the farmer. But the profit that farmer received from the crop depended on the yields of other farmers elsewhere in the world, English economic policies, the currency policy of the United States, the rates railroad corporations decided to charge—in short, a myriad of decisions by people in faraway places over whom the South Dakota farmer had no control.

Railroads

Before the West could produce basic commodities for national and international markets on a large scale, western producers had to have a way to get these commodities to market. They needed a transportation system capable of carrying heavy loads over long distances at a cost that was low enough to allow the materials to be sold at a profit at journey's end. In the arid West, a land of few navigable rivers and vast distances, there simply was no other practicable way for producers to have access to national and international markets. Without the railroads, commercial agriculture, most mining, cattle raising, and timber production for a national market remained unprofitable. The modern western extractive economy began with the railroads.

The railroads did not advance steadily across the continent. In the West, the railroads extended their lines in two great spurts. Federal land grants initiated the first burst of western railroad building in the middle and late 1860s. Competition and system building—the attempt of the railroads to capture the trade of larger sections of the West with new lines—spurred the second burst of building in the 1880s. In 1886, Kansas and Nebraska had less than half their 1913 railroad mileage, but three years later Kansas had 90 percent of the mileage it would have before World War I, and Nebraska had more than 80 percent of its prewar mileage. The first expansion of the railroad system depended on federal subsidies; the second depended on access to capital raised by eastern investment bankers.

Building and Financing the Railroads

In the mid-nineteenth century, railroads confronted westerners with a frustrating paradox. Except in unusual circumstances, development would be slow and unrewarding without railroads, but until development took place, railroads could not make a profit (for they would have neither freight nor people to haul), so there was little incentive for private capitalists to build them. To escape from this dilemma, westerners looked to the government, particularly the federal government, which, they contended, should provide the aid necessary to build the railroads.

Each level of government had its appointed task in encouraging railroad building. Boosters expected states, counties, and towns to provide yard and station sites, donate rights-of-way, exempt the roads from taxation, and, above all, to fund bond issues the proceeds of which would help to build the railroads. The bulk of the aid, however, came from the federal government in the form of land grants and loans. The nature of these grants changed over time. In the 1850s railroad land grants went to the states bordering the Mississippi, and the states then distributed them to the railroads. During the 1860s, the federal government usually made direct grants to the railroads that it intended to aid.

The great goal of these later grants was to build a network of railroad lines across the continent. Congress matched its lavish ambitions with lavish grants. The first grant went in 1862 to the Union Pacific. It was followed by grants to the Central Pacific; the Atchison, Topeka and Santa Fe; the Northern Pacific (which was the largest of all); the California and Oregon; the Atlantic and Pacific; the Texas and Pacific; and numerous smaller lines. In addition, Texas provided its own generous land grants to those railroads building within its boundaries. Not until 1871 did the Texas and Pacific Act bring the trans-Mississippi grants to an end, and not until the late 1870s did the local subsidies largely cease. Congress did demand something in return for the land grants. It mandated that the railroads use American iron and steel for their tracks, and Congress required the railroads to carry troops and the U.S. mail at special rates.

To buy rails, employ workers to lay them, and purchase locomotives and cars the companies needed more than a congressional guarantee that title to land would be transferred to them when their roads were complete. Only the Union Pacific and Central Pacific were lucky enough to get federal loans to begin the project, and even then such loans did not meet the costs of so daunting an endeavor as a transcontinental railroad. The railroads had to attract private capital, either by selling stock, that is, a share in the company, or by selling bonds—borrowing from private investors, with tracks, locomotives, cars, and (with congressional permission) land grants as collateral to secure the loans. The Union Pacific, for example, obtained its construction capital by selling approximately 11 million dollars' worth of stock, by receiving 27 million dollars in government loans, and by raising 30 million dollars through the sale of its own bonds.

Because they were so expensive to build, railroads became the first enterprises to require extensive capital from outside their region. By the 1850s the source of such capital was New York, which had eclipsed Boston and Philadelphia as the center of American finance. Investment banking firms emerged to link American companies seeking funds with eastern and European investors. Western railroads depended on New York financiers; their stockholders and bondholders were overwhelmingly in the East and Europe.

Particularly during the railroad building boom of the 1860s and early 1870s the New York financial markets were highly competitive. When compared to other potential investments, transcontinental railroads were not particularly appealing. Many people, including experienced eastern railroad owners, did not believe that the transcontinentals would ever, in fact, make money. Their capital requirements were too high; their potential returns were too low. Many doubted the security offered by the railroads on their bonds.

To combat skepticism and to raise money in competitive financial markets, the

This W. H. Jackson photograph of a Union Pacific bridge in Weber Canyon, Utah, displays modern technology amidst a spectacular natural setting. It was this combination that made western railroads seem so symbolically as well as economically significant.

railroads promised high returns on their securities in much the same manner that "junk bond" promoters of the 1980s promised high returns on risky investments. To secure such returns, the railroad corporations heavily discounted the actual purchase price of their stocks and bonds. A certificate that was offered for $100 (par), for example, usually sold for substantially less. Thus, for every $10 million in bonds it sold and paid interest on, the Union Pacific actually received only $6.3 million from the people who bought the bonds. The railroads also happily sold stock as long as the market would absorb it regardless of the real assets of the road. When the market refused to absorb all of it, the railroads used stock instead of money to pay contractors and other suppliers. The huge amount of railroad stock that resulted from these procedures was thus "watered": the face value of the stocks far exceeded the real value of the roads.

This kind of financing made the fiscal basis of these railroads as rickety and jerry-built as the lines themselves. With stock issued in excess of actual value, and with everything on the lines mortgaged, the railroads staggered under a tremendous load of debt. Even during good times, most railroads did well to pay the interest on their debts. All of this served to get railroads built, but it made them fragile enterprises.

This system of financing the transcontinentals invited fraud, and many promoters, speculators, politicians, and bankers gladly accepted the invitation. The possibility of federal grants and loans brought intensive lobbying of Congress for additional railroads, and the lobbying brought bribery and corruption. But the greatest corruption and the greatest scandals resulted from stock manipulation. The most notorious of these scandals revolved around the Crédit Mobilier, a company founded in 1864 with an elegant name and a deceitful purpose. Essentially it was a construction company owned by some of the major stockholders of the Union Pacific and by other prominent investors. The participants used their influence within the Union Pacific to vote the Crédit Mobilier lucrative construction contracts to build the road. The payments were so lavish that the Crédit Mobilier was guaranteed a profit even though the Union Pacific might operate at a loss. The promoters of the Crédit Mobilier reaped a profit of from $13 million to $16 million on an investment of $4 million. To secure continued congressional support for their operations (the profits of which partially came from government loans), the promoters established a slush fund. The resulting corruption touched dozens of congressmen, a secretary of the treasury, two vice-presidents, a leading presidential contender, and an eventual president. It caused a scandal that remained an issue in four presidential elections.

The owners of the Central Pacific Railroad used a similar scheme to secure their fortune. T. D. Judah, an engineer, created the Central Pacific. Judah used the possibility of land grants to persuade four Sacramento merchants—Leland Stanford, Collis P. Huntington, Mark Hopkins, and Charles Crocker—to incorporate the Central Pacific Railroad Company in 1862. These men together made a relatively modest investment of, at most, $60,000. They had successfully conspired to squeeze Judah out even before his death left them in complete control of the railroad, and they set up their own separate construction company. They voted themselves construction contracts that paid them $90 million for work that cost them only $32.2 million. By 1876 their wealth and power were so great that Californians came to refer to them simply as the Big Four. Their prosperity came at some cost to the initial financial strength of the railroad itself, but the Central Pacific recovered from its initial dose of debt and, linked with the Southern Pacific, became the dominant economic power on the West Coast.

The huge cost of building these railroads and the overcapitalization of the railroads set the stage for financial disaster. Eastern bankers and investment houses cooperated in the debacle that followed. Hoping for huge commissions and speculative profits of their own, investment banking houses both sold railroad stocks and bonds and invested in railroad securities themselves. The most important of these investment bankers was Jay Cooke and Company. In 1870, Cooke agreed, for a hefty fee, to undertake the financing of the Northern Pacific by selling $100 million of its bonds, a huge offering for the time. By terms of the agreement, Cooke had to provide funds to begin construction of the road. In return he acquired a potential majority interest in the Northern Pacific, which possessed the largest land grant of all. Congress had granted the railroad an area roughly the size of New England, but the road could not claim title to that land until it built its line and surveyed the grant. Cooke thus had little to offer for security of the bonds, but with substantial favors to prominent politicians he managed to get Congress to agree to allow the railroad to mortgage its land grant before the road was built.

By this agreement Jay Cooke thoroughly intertwined the fate of his company with that of the Northern Pacific. The bond offering and his advance to the Northern Pacific were so large that if he failed to sell the bonds, he was ruined. Cooke tightened the link to the Northern Pacific by making other investments, the success of which depended on the completion of the railroad through Minnesota and surrounding regions. To fund necessary construction, the Northern Pacific drew larger and larger drafts on Cooke's firm, but meanwhile Cooke had overestimated his ability to sell the risky bonds on a glutted market. To stave off disaster, Cooke sought more government aid. When he failed to get it, his banking house collapsed in September 1873, and its fall triggered a panic. The stock market crashed. Other investment houses and brokers with heavy investment in railroads failed. As the banks collapsed, the country fell into a depression. By 1875 the Northern Pacific itself was bankrupt, as were numerous other western railroads.

The end of this first burst of railroad building left the West with an impressive but ramshackle transportation network in the 1870s. There was, on the one hand, much to praise. Once construction had begun, railroad crews had built the new roads faster than seemed possible. They broke records for track laid in a day and then broke them again. They built across the highest mountain range in the continental United States and across forbidding stretches of desert.

In a relatively short period, the railroads created the skeletal structure of the western transportation system. This is not to say that all these railroads reached their destinations before bankruptcy overtook them. Of all the transcontinentals chartered and granted aid by Congress and the states, only the Union Pacific and Central Pacific actually succeeded in linking the eastern United States and the Pacific Coast. On December 2, 1863, the Union Pacific began building west from Omaha. At its peak the railroad employed 10,000 men (many of them Irish immigrants) to lay its track. On May 10, 1869, at Promontory Point, Utah, the Union Pacific linked up with the Central Pacific, which Chinese laborers had built eastward from California. By 1865, 80 percent of the workers on the Central Pacific were Chinese, and thereafter 10,000 to 11,000 of them laid track across mountains and deserts.

None of the other transcontinentals got near the Pacific Coast. The Kansas Pacific did well to reach Denver in 1870. The Atchison, Topeka and Santa Fe also aspired to the Pacific without reaching it. To the south, the Atlantic and Pacific; the Texas and Pacific; and the Buffalo Bayou, Brazos and Colorado, which would be absorbed by the Southern Pacific, struck out for the sea but ended up far short. The Northern Pacific expired at Bismarck, North Dakota. A spurt of railroad building in the prairie states and Texas during the late 1860s and early 1870s contributed many other roads, while small networks of railroads began to radiate out from Denver, Portland, and Salt Lake City.

There was also another aspect of the railroad network that soon became all too apparent: much of the track could not dependably carry freight. Despite all the effort that went into them, these lines were poorly constructed. Railroad technology remained primitive. Iron rails rusted quickly, and untreated wooden ties rotted between them. Engineers made curves too sharp, and workers laid ballast improperly so that the roadbeds collapsed. On the whole, the western railroads may have been no more shoddily built than those in the East, but

The announcement of the opening of through trains on the Union Pacific Railroad.

nonetheless, most of them demanded almost immediate rebuilding. The Santa Fe, for example, had to replace its entire line within 15 years of its original construction. By the time the Union Pacific made its juncture with the Central Pacific, the line already needed nearly 7 million dollars' worth of repairs, and the worst sections of its tracks could barely support a locomotive. By 1887 the original builder of the Union Pacific, General Grenville M. Dodge, was describing that road as "two dirt ballasted streaks of rust."

The collapse of the railroads in the larger wreckage of 1873 fueled what would become the chronic resentment of westerners toward both the railroads and their eastern and foreign bondholders. Towns, counties, and states that had bought bonds to finance the railroads found their bonds worthless and the tax dollars used to pay for them wasted. Being only minority stockholders and lenders without first mortgages, they found easterners and Europeans taking actual control of the roads. With the railroads bankrupt, westerners hostile, and eastern and European investors wary, railroad building slowed drastically following the panic of 1873.

The Consolidation of the Western Railroad System

The problems with financing railroads that had led to their bankruptcy in 1873 were not open to easy solutions. Although well-financed and well-managed railroads could operate profitably, the western railroads still staggered under their debt loads. The excessive book value created by its watered stock and its weak financing prevented the Union Pacific, for example, from being profitable in the 1870s, but if the railroad's returns had been calculated in terms of actual money invested in the corporation (and not in terms of the inflated figures of its watered stocks and discounted bonds), then the Union Pacific would actually have averaged profits of over 11 percent a year during the decade. Smart businessmen and investors recognized that well-financed, well-constructed railroads could become profitable enterprises in the West.

By the 1880s, with the economy improving across the United States and the railroad companies reorganized, the West was ready for a new burst of railroad building and a rapid expansion in railroad mileage. Much of this building took the form of feeder lines. Without them, the transcontinentals would have been trunks without branches. Railroad builders laid over 40,000 miles of track west of the Mississippi during the 1880s, for a total of 72,473 miles by 1890. States such as Kansas, Nebraska, and Texas nearly tripled their mileage. These feeders tapped the great western hinterland. Ostensibly independent, they were usually linked to parent companies. The Spokane and Palouse to the wheat fields of eastern Washington and the Corbin roads to the Coeur d'Alene mines of Idaho, for example, were feeder lines sponsored and controlled by the Northern Pacific. Competing railroad networks opened up new territories and then invaded each others' territories in attempts to drain off each others' business.

The growth of feeder lines and the expansion of the railroad system sprang from basic changes in the American railroad industry. Railroads with their large debt load had very high fixed costs. They had to pay interest on their debts whether their trains ran full or nearly empty. Because roughly two-thirds of their total costs were fixed, in the sense that they did not vary with the amount of traffic carried, railroads had a great deal of incentive to fill their cars by cutting rates. Although the railroads would not make money with low rates, they would lose less than they would by carrying no freight at all. A little loss was better than a big loss.

To avoid the ruinous competition for freight between railroads that this situation caused, the railroads created pools. They agreed to standardize their rates and divide up existing business among themselves. The earliest and most successful of these pools was the Omaha Pool, organized in 1870, by which the roads agreed to divide equally the receipts from all Chicago-to-Omaha business after deducting operating expenses. Other more complex pools followed, such as the Southwestern Railway Rate Association in 1876, the Western Trunk Lines Association in 1883, the Transcontinental Traffic Association in 1883, and the Pacific Coast Association.

The problem with such pools was that the railroads had no legal way to enforce the agreements; they depended on the good faith of their members. Such good faith virtually always proved to be lacking. To remedy the problem, some railroad managers sought to have Congress pass legislation to make the rules of the railroad associations legally binding, but instead the Supreme Court eventually ruled that the Sherman Antitrust Act of 1890 had made such associations illegal.

Pools were, in any case, particularly vulnerable to speculators such as Jay Gould, who bought into railroad companies, ignored pooling arrangements, and tried to buy or win control of smaller lines that fed the main lines of their rivals. Gould himself attempted to build a national railroad system by bringing numerous lines under single ownership, and he forced his rivals to do the same if they wished to protect their traffic. The so-called Gould system of the 1880s brought many previously independent railroads in Missouri, Arkansas, Indian Territory, and parts of Kansas and Texas under Gould's ownership.

Gould built his system around the Missouri Pacific. At first he merely amalgamated existing lines, but in the 1880s Gould built thousands of miles of new track in order to tap the territories of his rivals. It was unclear whether Gould expected to force his rivals to buy him out or whether he thought that by maintaining high traffic volume he could eventually profit, but his operations soon became precarious. Like the older transcontinentals, the Gould system was deeply indebted, badly overcapitalized, and vulnerable to falls in rates. Many of the original lines were poorly built, and Gould's later investments only partially corrected the problem.

Gould's national system soon collapsed, but he maintained a smaller system in the Missouri border region and Texas, and with it he began a railroad war in the West. With pooling arrangements in shambles, the major lines felt that if they did not expand rapidly, rivals like Gould would steal their existing business. They desired to secure their own territory and expand into that of their competitors. The Southern Pacific emerged as perhaps the most successful of the lines that attempted to create such a profitable consolidated railroad system. By the 1870s the Big Four of the Central Pacific had secured a monopoly over rail transportation in California. Their success created the Southern Pacific as the southern extension of the Central Pacific. To disguise the joint ownership of the two railroads and the monopoly control they exerted over transportation in California, the Big Four created separate management for the two roads.

The Southern Pacific soon outstripped its parent road. The Octopus, as it was known, became far and away the most powerful, and the most hated, railroad on

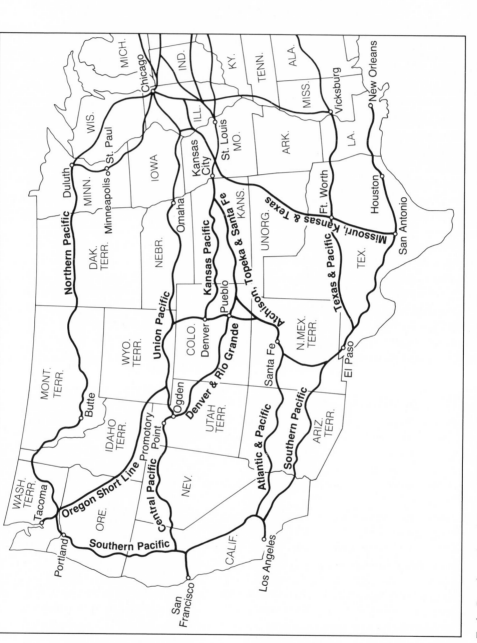

Early Pacific railroad lines, 1887. Based on a map in John Blum et al., *The National Experience* (San Diego: Harcourt Brace Jovanovich, 1985).

the West Coast. As it grew bigger, it grew more voracious. California could not contain it. In 1882 the Southern Pacific, building east, met the Texas and Pacific near El Paso, thus creating a new transcontinental route from which numerous branch lines extended out like tentacles.

The movement of the Southern Pacific to the east brought it into competition with the Atchison, Topeka and Santa Fe, which was seeking a route west. Initially the two roads compromised, joining together at Deming, New Mexico, to create yet another transcontinental link. The alliance was, however, temporary. Frustrated by its dependence on the Southern Pacific for use of the track necessary to reach the Pacific Coast, the Santa Fe attempted to secure its own independent route. After a prolonged fight to secure a right-of-way, it succeeded in doing so during the mid-1880s and thus challenged the Southern Pacific's monopoly in the latter's southern California heartland. By 1887 the Santa Fe was the largest railroad system in the world.

The Union Pacific, too, chafed under the Southern Pacific and Central Pacific's monopoly of tracks to the coast. Through an arrangement with the Oregon Railway and Navigation Company, the Union Pacific secured an independent route to the Pacific by building north from Granger, Wyoming, to the Columbia and then on to Portland.

By the time that Union Pacific reached the Pacific Northwest, however, the Northern Pacific had created the first transcontinental link in the region. In 1879 the Northern Pacific, seeking to avoid forfeiting its federal charter and land grants, resumed its long delayed approach to the West Coast. The line did so through the agency of Henry Villard, who demonstrated how power in the West sprang from being trusted by people with money in the East. A German immigrant who, after careers as a newspaperman and a civil service reformer, had forged close ties with German and Boston investors, Villard had come to Oregon as the representatives of bondholders worried about their investments in Ben Holladay's enterprises. As agent for these investors, he acquired Holladay's properties, united them with the Oregon Steam Navigation Company, which monopolized traffic on the Columbia River, and created the Oregon Railway and Navigation Company in order to build a railroad into the interior.

This proved to be only Villard's first step. Using his standing among eastern and European investors, Villard organized a blind pool (that is, a pool whose subscribers invested money without knowing what Villard proposed to do with it). With the money, he acquired control of the Northern Pacific, which had already resumed its western advance. In 1883 the Northern Pacific finally joined its tracks with those of the Oregon Railway and Navigation Company to complete a transcontinental connection between the Pacific Northwest and the East.

Villard's triumph proved short-lived. Four months later, in a stockholders' revolt, he lost control of the Northern Pacific. The pendulum now swung from monopoly to bitter competition as the Northern Pacific and the Oregon Railway and Navigation Company fell into separate hands. It was in 1884 that the Oregon Railway and Navigation Company joined with the Union Pacific's branch line, the Oregon Short Line. Then in 1887 the Northern Pacific gained independent access to the coast by completing a direct route through the Cascade Mountains to Tacoma on Puget Sound.

In 1893 the last of the nineteenth-century transcontinentals, the Great Northern, reached Seattle. The only railroad built without major government aid, the Great Northern was ultimately the most successful western railroad. Although the Great Northern, like all western railroads, depended on eastern and European banks and investors for capital, its founder, James J. Hill, was a manager and businessman, not a speculator turned railroad builder like Gould nor a financier and publicist turned railroad builder like Villard. A bluff, matter-of-fact Scots Canadian, he oversaw his railroad with an exacting eye for detail.

The Great Northern, which evolved out of the earlier Saint Paul-Minneapolis and Manitoba Railroad, was from the beginning a well-built, superbly engineered, and conservatively financed line. Hill did not build railroads to obtain land grants or secure insider contracts or to manipulate stock, but instead to carry profitable traffic. He designed his line to carry plains wheat, Rocky Mountains copper, and Pacific Northwest lumber cheaply and efficiently, and he constantly sought ever greater efficiency. The Great Northern increased the tonnage on its average cross-country train from 179 tons in 1890 to 281 tons by 1897.

Not only could the Great Northern carry more freight than its rivals, but it also had a far lower debt load and less outstanding stock. In 1893 the Great Northern, with 3,682 miles of track, was capitalized at $147 million, whereas the Union Pacific, with 8,148 miles of track, was capitalized at $427 million and the Northern Pacific, with 5,216 miles of track, was capitalized at $370 million. The Great Northern was an extremely profitable railroad. In part, profits came from careful management, but they also came from cutting workers' wages when hard times permitted and from keeping rates high for farmers when they had no other options for shipping their wheat.

In the race to capture territory and enlarge systems in the 1880s, the railroads became even more dependent on specialized eastern banking houses such as J. P. Morgan and Company; Kuhn, Loeb; August Belmont; and Kidder, Peabody & Company for the money they needed to finance their expansion. When the economy fell into depression in the 1890s, the Union Pacific, Northern Pacific, and Santa Fe all slid back into bankruptcy. Their bondholders, J. P. Morgan and other investment houses, stepped in to reorganize them. Morgan at first tried to reinstitute a pooling system by calling leading railroad managers to New York to form the Western Association and set standard rates. Morgan told them that his and other firms would not tolerate construction of parallel lines nor the extension of new lines without the approval of the executive committee of the association.

Morgan soon learned the limits of voluntary cooperation, and the courts reiterated their stand against rate fixing; instead of cooperation, he joined in a new attempt at consolidation. In the early twentieth century Edward C. Harriman, a small, deceptively meek looking broker who had taken control of both the Union Pacific and the powerful Southern Pacific, attempted in alliance with the New York banking house of Kuhn, Loeb to add the Northern Pacific to this holdings. James J. Hill, with the backing of J. P. Morgan, made the same attempt. The result was a compromise, the formation of the Northern Securities Company, which would have controlled the Northern Pacific, the Great Northern, and the Burlington Northern. The Supreme Court, however, dissolved the company under the Sherman Antitrust Act in 1904. Hill retained control of the Great Northern and Northern Pacific, while Harriman controlled the Union Pacific and Southern Pacific.

By the early twentieth century four railway systems—the Gould roads (17,000 miles); the Rock Island group, including the Santa Fe (25,000 miles); the Hill roads (22,000 miles); and the Harriman lines (25,000 miles)—controlled the West. But these systems had themselves really become creatures of the eastern investment bankers, who dominated the boards of western railroads and their financial decisions, and of the professional managers who ran the railroads and made their operating decisions.

The railroads both created the infrastructure for the emerging western economy and set the patterns for its development. Without the railroads the rest of the western extractive economy would not have been possible. With their combination of power and financial vulnerability, their dependence on federal aid and eastern and European capital, their technical achievements and often shoddy construction, the railroads in many ways typified the western economy that they supported.

Railroads and the Western Economy

The building of the transcontinentals and their feeder lines created the basic infrastructure for economic development of the West in two ways. First, the railroads themselves were an engine of economic development. Their building and operation provided a substantial market for both the timber industry and western coal mines. The building and maintenance of the railroads consumed prodigious amounts of wood for bridges, stations, fences, fuel, and, above all, railroad ties. From the 1870s until 1900, the railroads used 20–25 percent of the annual timber production of the United States. The net consumption of wood for railroad ties alone was staggering. In one year, 1890, the railroads needed an estimated 73 million ties to maintain old lines and build new ones. The demand slackened only as cement replaced wood for construction, coal replaced wood for fuel, and the railroads began to treat the ties chemically to prevent insect damage. Ties that had previously lasted from 5 to 10 years could now be used from 35 to 50 years. While the demand lasted, however, it proved a significant spur to lumber production on the West Coast and in Idaho.

The early replacement of wood by coal to power the railroad steam engines stimulated the development of western coal mines. There was virtually no coal production in the West in 1870, but by 1890 productive mines existed from the plains states to the Pacific Coast. Although these mines never represented a large share of national production (comprising only about 10 percent of the national output in 1910), they did eliminate the need to import eastern coal.

Railroads provided a second stimulus for economic development by greatly enlarging access to eastern and European markets. Not all western commodity production required the railroads in order to succeed. Western lumbermen, for example, had depended initially on the San Francisco market and had grown by shipping their timber to markets throughout the Pacific Basin. In the 1850s some Puget Sound mills successfully shipped cut lumber to Hawaii, and others explored markets in Hong Kong and other China treaty ports, Australia, and South America. These early sales laid the basis for the cargo trade—the overseas export of lumber. They helped stimulate the continuing growth of the lumber industry. Miners had also worked deposits of gold and silver before the arrival of the railroads. But they could only profitably develop the richest deposits because of the astronomical cost of supplies and equipment and the expense of shipping out gold and silver by wagons and pack trains.

Large-scale industrial mining of low-grade ores demanded railroad transportation. The trains lowered the heavy cost of transporting the latest mining technology and the supplies into the mines. Before the railroads, for example, George Hearst paid $30,000 in freight costs alone to get a single 80-stamp mill (that is, a mill with 80 stamps to crush the ore) into the Black Hills. On the Comstock Lode, mine owners expected the railroads to cut production costs in half, because the trains allowed mine owners to move large quantities of low-grade ores to the smelters. In 1881 the arrival of the railroads at Butte, Montana, permitted that town to escape its dependence on dwindling silver production and turn to its abundant copper. Only railroads could haul the ore on the scale efficient development demanded. No wonder the U.S. Geological Survey reported in 1884 that the creation of new western mines "may be regarded as the direct result of the rapid extension of the railroads in the Rocky mountains."

Still, the arrival of the railroads could not ensure export markets for all western commodities. Lumber mill owners, for example, hoped that the arrival of the transcontinentals would allow them to ship wood to the lumber-starved Great Plains. Such markets, however, developed very slowly. The transcontinentals did not provide low enough rates for West Coast timbermen to compete in markets east of the Rockies. In the 1880s Michigan lumber continued to dominate the market as far west as Idaho. Only during periods of railroad rate wars were West Coast lumbermen able to penetrate the markets of the plains and prairies.

Even if their grandiose dreams of new markets failed to reach immediate fruition, timbermen still benefited from the arrival of the railroads. Railroads did not initially expand the market for Pacific Northwest timber by bringing the timber to the buyers, but they did bring buyers to the timber. The railroads spurred a dramatic rise in population in the Pacific Northwest, and this, in turn, stimulated a building boom. The railroads not only created this market, but they also gave loggers the means to supply it. By the 1880s loggers had stripped the shorelines of navigable rivers and harbors of their commercially valuable trees. Small local railroads allowed loggers to leave the shore and to exploit the vast forests in less accessible areas.

Eventually the railroads did begin to give the lumbermen of Washington, Oregon, and California access to the national market that they yearned for. As the last of the great pineries of the upper Midwest fell before the logger's saw and ax, western timber found a national market. By 1906 the new railroad trade took as much lumber from the Pacific Northwest as did the older seaborne cargo trade.

The Search for Capital

Just as railroad construction depended on raising capital, so too did exploitation of western minerals, grasslands, farmlands, and forests. Business owners, confidence men, local boosters, elected officials, and lawyers traveled, wrote, begged, and beseeched easterners and Europeans to invest money in the West. For many of these boosters there was no promise that was too extravagant and no return that was too far-fetched.

With one major exception, this search for capital took place in the East and in Europe. The exception was California. The Gold Rush gave California a

Table 5

Lumber Production by Major Political Subdivision

(in million board feet)

Year	California	Oregon	Washington	British Columbia
1849*	5,000	16,853	4,080	. . .
1859	196,000	41,169	77,125	1,750†
1869	353,842	75,193	128,743	25,000†
1879	326,340	177,171	160,176	50,000†
1889	528,554	444,565	1,061,560	67,612
1899	737,760	734,181	1,428,205	252,580

Sources: F. L. Moravets, *Production of Lumber in Oregon and Washington, 1869–1948,* Forest Survey Report no. 100 (Portland: U.S. Forest Service, Pacific Northwest Forest and Range Experiment Station, 1949); Richard H. May, *A Century of Lumber Production in California and Nevada,* Forest Survey Report no. 20 (Berkeley: U.S. Forest Service, California Forest and Range Experiment Station, 1953); H. N. Whitford and Roland D. Craig, *Forests of British Columbia* (Ottawa: Canada, Commission of Conservation, Committee on Forests, 1918); Edmond S. Meany, Jr., "History of the Lumber Industry of the Pacific Northwest to 1917." Reprinted from Thomas Cox, *Mills and Markets: A History of the Pacific Coast Lumber Industry to 1900* (Seattle: University of Washington Press, 1974), p. 301.

*Lumber production for Oregon in 1849 includes only those counties of Oregon Territory located south of the Columbia River; Washington production figures for 1849 are for those counties of Oregon Territory north of the Columbia River.

†Author's estimates based on scattered, fragmentary sources, primarily reports published in *Canada Lumberman.*

regional economic preeminence that it never lost. Money made either in the mines or from serving the miners flowed into San Francisco, and San Francisco money, in turn, helped finance mining development in the Comstock Lode in Nevada. Profits from Nevada silver returned to San Francisco to fund further development of copper in Montana, silver in Utah, and gold in the Black Hills of the Dakotas. San Francisco money helped to finance the early timber industry of both California and the Pacific Northwest.

San Francisco's merchants proved more reluctant to invest in manufacturing. The capital necessary to start the initially small industrial enterprises came from local sources, but it was more likely to come from the small savings of skilled workmen or loans from William Ralston's California Bank (before its bankruptcy).

The caution of San Francisco's merchants eventually cost them dearly, because San Francisco between 1860 and 1880 grew into a major manufacturing city. High freight rates from the East to California gave some protection to manufacturers producing for the local markets of the West Coast. Most of these manufacturing establishments remained small, but some grew to impressive size. Claus Spreckels made the California Sugar Refinery in San Francisco into one of the three firms that controlled the nation's sugar business by the 1890s. And although the Southern Pacific was an octopus strangling California farmers, it was also, until Harriman took the railroad over late in the century, a resident-owned California octopus. California's economic prominence and seeming self-sufficiency led Englishman James Bryce to observe that "California, more than any other part of the Union, is a country by itself, and San Francisco is its capital."

Still, Californians at their wealthiest could not finance all of their own projects, let alone the host of new economic enterprises elsewhere in the West. Throughout most of the West money remained scarce. Western interest rates ran as high as 24 percent a year, while loans obtained in the East in the early 1880s paid only about 8 percent interest. Serious borrowers and promoters turned to the East and to Europe for capital. This capital was of two sorts. Easterners and Europeans made direct investments by buying stock in companies that exploited western resources. European and eastern investors and banks also loaned money to western corporations or individuals.

Mining exemplified the relentless search of westerners for capital and the extent to which they often squandered the capital they did obtain. Once miners exhausted the rich surface placer deposits of California and began to go underground, the industry needed outside funds to continue. Miners quoted the Mexican proverb that it took a gold mine to develop a silver mine, and added that it took a bank to develop the gold mine. Miners went to great expense simply to ascertain whether a mine even held minerals. As one amazingly frank mining prospectus declared, mining was "essentially a lottery," but there were many investors ready to play. People did, after all, get lucky. George Hearst, the father of William Randolph Hearst, was "pretty near broke" at 49. At his death he was a millionaire. "If you're ever inclined to think that there's no such thing as luck," Hearst said, "just think of me." In this lottery, however, large investors tended to be the luckiest. They could hire their own agents, often professional mining engineers, to investigate particular mines before investing.

Without careful investigation and considerable luck, investments evaporated, but with proper information, investors could make fortunes. There was a rush of eastern investment in Colorado mines in the 1860s. Many of the mining schemes were frauds. Most investors got little or no return on their funds. Even where gold existed, miners could not solve the technical problem of removing the sulfur that prevented the separation of the gold from the ore, so the mines did not pay. But a second investment boom centered on Leadville provided enough capital to produce $70 million in silver between 1879 and 1883 and to employ thousands of men in and around the mines. In Butte, Montana, Boston capitalists joined Californians in financing the copper industry, and the French and British invested heavily in silver. Most of the money vanished into the mines. Only one in nine of the British companies ever returned a profit.

Many promoters found that it was far more profitable to mine investors than to mine ore. Promoters often pocketed up to 50 percent of the capital they raised, and the value of the capital stock of mining companies often far exceeded either their assets or their potential profits. In 1895, for example, there were 126 Colorado companies supposedly working the Cripple Creek District. They registered over $461 million in capital stock, or $50,000 more than the entire district produced in gold between 1890 and 1953.

The grandiose claims of mining promoters rendered investors cynical but not immune to temptation. Mine investments were a form of gambling. The lure of immense returns from relatively small investments proved hard to resist. A mythical list of officers for the Hunkidora Silver Mining Company parodied the kind of mining proposals that one Colorado mine owner said were "sent over the country broadcast to catch suckers":

Park City, Utah (now a ski resort) was one of the many nineteenth-century mining towns
that served as industrial outposts in the mountain West.

Officers

President—Honorable Jeremiah Blowhard

Treasurer—Honorable Gideon Graball

Secretary—Honorable Simon Smoothface

General Superintendent—Miner Botch, Esquire

Directors

Major General D. Bility

Brigadier General Melisher Cervis

Honorable Tim Trumphet, Member of Congress

Honorable Verily Hardup

Adjutant General P. Q. Lation

Legal Advisors

Sneak, Quibble, and Steele

The country may have been "full of more petty propositions in the way of
mining stocks than Hell is full of imps," and the very word *mine*, as one Montana
judge said, may have been "almost synonymous with conspiracy to defraud," but
the Hunkidoras of the world still found their investors. The odds were great, but
fortunes beckoned.

The cattle industry shared mining's dependence on outside capital. During the
heyday of open-range ranching in the 1870s and 1880s, the industry probably had
a higher proportion of European investment than any other western business.
Between 1876 and 1880 the annual import of American beef into Great Britain
increased by 15 times and provoked a wave of interest in western cattle raising.
The British alone invested, either directly or through commission firms, an

estimated $45 million in the western livestock industry, with perhaps $25 million of that amount going into Texas. The investment companies that managed these sums created ranches that extended like small European principalities across the public lands. In 1883 the Prairie Cattle Company, a Scottish company, consisted of three divisions, the first of 3,500 square miles, the second of 4,032 square miles, and the third of 400 square miles. The spectacle of European corporations extralegally controlling such huge tracts of western land and impeding the settlement of American farmers and small ranchers provoked a reaction that produced the Alien Land Law of 1887 and a similar measure in Texas in 1892. The Alien Land Law banned the ownership of land in the territories by foreign corporations and by those who did not intend to become citizens. The law, however, proved largely a statement of pious intentions. Ten years later there had apparently not been a single forfeiture of land under its provisions.

Despite the extent of European investment, even in the cattle industry most investment appears to have come from the East, particularly New York and Boston. Investment peaked between 1882 and 1886. Wyoming then had 93 cattle companies, with a total capitalization of $51 million, while Colorado had 176 companies capitalized at $74 million. Much of this investment was lost in the collapse of the cattle industry following the bitter winters and the economic downturn of the late 1880s. Most investors liquidated what assets they could and brought their money back east.

The timber industry followed a slightly different pattern. San Francisco companies controlled the timber harvest from the redwoods of Monterey Bay to the south and Humboldt Bay to the north up to the Douglas fir forests along Puget Sound. The giants of the early Puget Sound lumber industry—Puget Mill Company, Tacoma Mill Company, and the Port Blakely Mill Company—all depended on San Francisco capital, had their business offices in San Francisco, and maintained lumberyards there.

The challenge to California's domination of the forests came from the Midwest. Twenty-one timber holding companies bought up tracts of redwoods for later use between 1880 and 1902; ten of these companies were from the Great Lakes states. And in January of 1900 the Weyerhaeuser Corporation bought 900,000 acres of timberland from the Northern Pacific Railroad, immediately making Weyerhaeuser the dominant force in the timber industry of the Pacific Northwest. California no longer controlled the industry, but San Francisco capitalists continued to be active into the twentieth century. They created Crown Zellerbach from smaller northwestern companies in 1928, and this giant dominated West Coast logging during the 1930s.

The western search for capitalism so prevalent in mining, ranching, and lumbering extended to farming. The older tradition of eastern investors accepting mortgages on western farms continued into the late nineteenth century. At first glance, mortgages might seem unnecessary in the West because the federal government provided free land through the Homestead Act. But 160 acres of raw prairie or plains land did not constitute a farm. To work it and live on it, a farm family needed work animals, a wagon, plows, harness, seeders, a house, and a well. A farmer needed barbed wire fencing, barns, and outbuildings. To break the first 40 acres of a 160-acre homestead and put it into production cost about $1,000.

Many farmers lacked the funds necessary to develop their farms; to obtain them, they mortgaged their lands. With the proceeds of the mortgage they could buy necessary stock and equipment. Many nineteenth-century observers took mortgages as a sign of desperation, thinking that people borrowed because their farms could not support them. But mortgages could just as easily have been cited as signs of success. Farmers, confident of the future, borrowed in order to bring their farms into production more quickly.

Unlike railroads, which borrowed millions of dollars, individual farmer borrowed hundreds or thousands, so the means by which a farmer raised money differed substantially from the ways railroads raised money. Railroads had J. P. Morgan and Kuhn, Loeb. Farmers had farm mortgage companies and individual agents who served as middlemen between eastern and European investors and western farmers, soliciting capital and making loans. By 1880 there were some 40 major agencies or companies lending money in Kansas. Capital poured into Kansas and Nebraska at such a rate in the late 1880s that the manager of one loan company complained that he could not obtain mortgages fast enough to fulfill the demand. According to one sample of investors on the prairies and plains, the people who provided this capital were largely small investors, almost half of whom were women. Approximately 70 percent were Americans; the other 30 percent were Europeans, largely English. The enthusiasm of these people for mortgage investments drove down interest rates, which stood at 12 percent in Kansas and Nebraska during most of the 1870s but dropped to about 8 percent by the late 1880s and early 1890s. The actual price paid by the farmer was somewhat higher, as commission costs added from 1 to 3 percent to the total interest payments. These levels were still higher, however, than those prevailing in the East.

The private borrowing by western farmers and the public borrowing necessary to offer incentives to western railroads resulted in a growing burden of indebtedness. Western states led the union in public debt per capita by the 1880s, and the faster a state's growth and the greater its railroad mileage, the more imposing the debt. Kansas, for example, had the fifth highest public debt per capita in the Union in the 1880s (the first four states being farther west). Kansas also had mortgages on a higher percentage of land than did any other state in the country, while the per-capita private debt of the state's citizens was four times the national average. To carry such debts the West had to believe in a future of assured prosperity, but such a future was not to be.

The farm crisis that hit the West in the late 1880s and early 1890s struck both debtors and mortgage companies hard. Most of them failed during the early 1890s. An estimated 90 percent of the farmers in western Kansas were unable to meet their loan obligations in the early 1890s, and even in central Kansas approximately 45 percent of the farmers were in default on their loans. The mortgage companies foreclosed, but they could not easily resell the lands to recoup their loans. Their capital became tied up in unproductive land, and taxes on these lands drained their remaining assets.

Organizing Production

The debt loads carried by a Kansas farm and a transcontinental railroad marked both farmer and railroad manager as people dependent on outsiders to finance

These corporate employees of the Prairie Cattle Company gathered for a group photograph at the home ranch at Dry Cimarron, New Mexico, in the late 1880s.

their business. The railroad train hauling Kansas wheat also marked a common dependence on outside markets to sustain the western economy. But between the Kansas farmer who freighted his wheat to the nearest railroad and the representatives of the company who eventually oversaw its shipment there were also sizable differences. Farming remained a form of household production. Farmers, using largely family labor, worked their own crops on their own land and sold their own products. Railroads were large modern corporations. There were many family farms but virtually no family railroads. Western ingenuity created Dorsey S. Baker's Walla Walla Railroad, a one-man operation that on leaving Walla Walla, Washington, depended on gravity to propel it down its first five miles of track; only when trains reached Whitman did they acquire a locomotive. But such railroads existed to be sold to others with more money. The chairman of the board of a railroad never stepped into a locomotive to take it down the tracks, but everyone expected the owner of a farm to work his own land. Within the capitalist economy of the West, in short, were a variety of ways of organizing production.

The vast majority of businesses in the West were small, owner-operated endeavors, but we will defer a discussion of them until the next chapter and concentrate here on those businesses that operated on a larger scale. For outside of farming and ranching, it was these larger businesses that, together with the railroads, would most significantly shape the western economy. Unlike the railroads, many of these businesses started small, but like the railroads, they found that their need for capital brought them increasingly under the sway of eastern bankers, investors, and industrialists.

Mining provides probably the best example of how small operating units became consolidated into larger and larger properties. Mining ventures began as individual claims on western mountainsides. Ultimately a mining company might extend its shafts thousands of feet below the surface and employ thousands of men. The prospector who staked a claim often worked only with hand tools; the companies that developed a mine needed million-dollar smelters. The most lucrative role in mining was financing the development of a claim. Financiers and speculators were more likely to reap rewards than were working miners or prospectors. Although virtually all mines began as small individual claims, relatively few mine owners began as working miners.

Still, the hope of rising from rags to riches that drew men to the mines was not entirely illusory. When owners or operators of western mines are compared to industrial leaders in the East, the rags-to-riches ideal of western mining obviously has some truth. The so-called bonanza kings—the men who grew rich in mining—had a decidedly less privileged background than the eastern business elite. One sample of western mine owners found them more likely to be foreign-born (30 percent in the West to less than 10 percent in the East), less educated, and more likely to have experienced poverty in their youth than eastern business leaders. Some, like Marcus Daly, fit the poor-boy-made-good stereotype exactly. Daly was a poor, uneducated Irish immigrant who began his career as a working miner and ended it as a millionaire copper king in Butte, Montana.

Daly's secret, and that of other bonanza kings, was to buy promising claims in times of depression and find the funds to develop them as prices rose or as new technologies appeared. Downturns in the national economy and technical difficulties involved in working western quartz insured that there would always be falls in the value of mining claims. Bonanza kings transformed the numerous small individual claims that originally characterized a mining district into larger working mines. If a mine owner wished to avoid endless litigation or limited yields as the vein played out, he had to acquire numerous claims.

The combination of properties was only the first step in consolidation. Most entrepreneurs lacked the capital to develop their mines. They had, therefore, to seek outside investors and incorporate their mining company. Very often they had to hire those with the technical knowledge necessary to run the mines. And when a mine started producing, opportunities for further consolidation appeared. Minerals do not emerge pure from the ground. Mills and smelters have to pulverize and refine ores until they obtain pure ingots. And in addition to the mills, smelters, refineries, and sampling and assaying works, the mines required timber for the underground props and coal to power their machinery. There had to be waterworks for the mills and railroads to transport low-grade ores. Such things did not come cheaply. As early as 1863 the Gould and Curry mill on the Comstock Lode cost nearly $900,000.

Integrating mines, mills, smelters, railroads, and other enterprises into a single company tempted some developers from the beginning. William Ralston of the Bank of California reaped a fortune from Nevada's Comstock Lode in the early 1870s. Ralston, and the so-called "bank crowd" that gathered around him, controlled mines, but their real source of strength was the Union Mill and Mining Company, with its 16 quartz mills, the Virginia and Truckee Railroad, and the Carson and Lake Tahoe Lumber Company. Although Ralston himself ended his days as a financial failure and a probable suicide, he had demonstrated that the consolidation of properties from mines to mills to railroads promised great returns. For a surprising number of years the final refining of minerals often continued to take place in the East, but mining was gradually to become an enterprise with its various processes increasingly concentrated within a limited area and in limited hands.

How consolidation produced the early giants of the western mining industry can be glimpsed by following the investments of three San Francisco capitalists: George Hearst, Lloyd Tevis, and James Ben Ali Haggin. In the 1870s all three were already wealthy: Hearst from mining; Haggin from ranching, irrigation, and land speculation; and Tevis from banking. Together they made investing in western mines as close to an exact science as it would ever come. In 1872 the three had bought the Ontario, the richest silver mine in Utah. And in 1877 they purchased the Homestake Mine in the Black Hills of South Dakota. They had acquired one of the largest ore bodies on the continent, and they moved to control production from mining to milling. As other neighboring mines exhausted rich ore bodies on the surface and had to raise capital to go deeper and get less lucrative ore, the Homestake bought them out, thus enlarging its own ore reserves. This combination of vertical integration and consolidation gave the Homestake a life span beyond that of any other American mine. Between 1878 and 1962 the Homestake produced bullion worth $715 million.

Part of the profits from the Homestake went toward the development of another Hearst-Haggin-Tevis property, the Anaconda Copper Mining Company, that would carry consolidation of the mining industry to an even higher level. Marcus Daly had originally bought the Anaconda claim as a silver mine for $30,000. Not having the funds to develop it, he brought in Hearst, Haggin, and Tevis. Daly sold 75 percent of the claim to the three San Franciscans for what it had cost him; he retained a quarter-interest in the mine and became its supervisor. The silver mine turned out to be the richest copper mine yet discovered. Developing the copper, however, involved an investment of millions of dollars in concentration and smelting plants, in a timber company, in coal mines, and eventually in a railroad to haul ore. By the mid-1890s the company not only owned huge reserves of ore, coal, and lumber, but also the world's largest reduction works and a modern refinery. It owned farmland and city lots; it owned railroads and hotels; it owned waterworks and electrical works.

Anaconda had grouped together a spectacular mine and its auxiliary industries, but this stage of consolidation was by 1900 itself yielding to even more gigantic combinations. Like the combinations emerging among the railroads, mining corporations began to dominate an entire region or an entire sector of the industry. Large, heavily capitalized national corporations such as the American Smelting and Refining Company, Phelps Dodge, and the Amalgamated Copper Company dwarfed the older operations. These corporations in turn were sometimes controlled by even larger organizations; Standard Oil, for example, controlled the Amalgamated. When the Amalgamated Copper Company swallowed Anaconda, it consolidated the entire Butte copper industry. When the Amalgamated dissolved, Anaconda reappeared as a much enlarged corporation.

Much the same process of consolidation occurred in the lumber industry. By the 1850s productive capacity had outstripped demand in the western lumber mills, and demand never caught up during the rest of the century. To get or retain business, the mills cut prices and offered rebates. The result was a chaotic industry. Many relatively small mills competed so ruthlessly that even during the best years most mills could not run at full capacity for prolonged periods.

Mill owners, like railroad owners, needed ways to protect themselves from the punishing effects of competition and overproduction. They, too, tried to form pools—organizations that would fix prices and regulate the running time of mills. Puget Sound and Portland mill owners and the mill owners of the California coast all tried, and failed, to create organizations that would set prices and diminish competition. Members broke the agreements, and outsiders undersold those companies that maintained the agreements.

At the end of the nineteenth century the lumber industry remained in chaos. Many of the small mills could not adjust to the new railroad trade or afford the technology necessary to modernize their mills. Competition had pushed many of them to the brink of failure. Most of the older mills eagerly sold out to new mill owners from the Great Lakes. The midwestern lumbermen transformed the industry and made it the domain of giants. They largely abandoned attempts to control the production of the mills; instead, following the example of Frederick Weyerhaeuser, they sought to control access to the timber itself. Those firms that did not acquire extensive timber holdings faced extinction. Future efforts to increase prices and control production would center on timber supplies.

Western Economic Development and the Larger Economy

By the beginning of the twentieth century the linkages between the western economy and larger world and national economies were firmly in place. The West possessed an extractive economy that depended on outside markets, outside capital, and, most often, skills and technologies imported from the outside. Westerners had learned to look anxiously to eastern and European markets and investors. Outsiders controlled their economic fate.

Some westerners, however, found certain opportunities in the dependence that their distance from markets and their own lack of capital imposed on them. In mining, in cattle, in railroads, and in other industries eastern investors and even more sophisticated eastern bankers learned some difficult lessons about doing business in the West. Distance facilitated the efforts of those who found fraud an easy road to affluence. It hindered efforts of corporate ranchers and mine owners to keep close track of their businesses. Fraud, distance, and poor oversight brought wasted investment. Inefficiency thrived and productivity suffered. The West desperately needed capital, but many of the investments made in the West yielded nothing but promises and gaudy stock certificates. Bankrupt mining companies, cattle companies, and railroads abounded in the West. The money invested in them enriched some shrewd westerners, but it did not develop the West.

Fraud, of course, was a two-way street, and westerners could be corrupted as well as corrupt. Large western corporations such as railroads that had to do business in many separate jurisdictions, each with its own rules and laws, sought to simplify the situation. They sought uniformity of a sort by bribing local officials to ignore disagreeable laws or to pass ones favorable to the railroads or other corporations. Such corruption, like other forms of fraud, added to the cost of doing business without increasing production.

Nineteenth-century westerners never overestimated the rationality of the economy, underestimated the gullibility of investors, or placed excessive faith in the honesty of businessmen and politicians, and we should not make this developing economy more rational than it was. In the long run, the failure of so many western investments and the ubiquity of corruption had its costs. It certainly contributed to the skepticism of eastern investors about putting more capital into the West, where returns proved so uncertain.

The result was an economy not only of perceived opportunity, but of considerable resentments. Westerners felt starved for capital and controlled by outsiders, while many eastern investors were from past experience reluctant to trust their money in western enterprises. They felt safe only when businesses were closely supervised from the East.

Particularly as mining companies and lumber companies imitated railroad companies and became larger and larger enterprises controlled by eastern corporations, the western economy began to seem like a marionette controlled by eastern puppeteers. In the less-populous western states such as Montana, Wyoming, and Nevada the sense of economic domination by outsiders was deeply felt. When the twentieth-century Montana newspaperman Joe Howard referred to his state as being "at the end of the cracked whip," he expressed this sense of subjection and control. In Nevada by the early twentieth century 100 corporations and individuals, most of whom either lived or were incorporated outside the state, owned 75 percent of the privately held land in the state. A 1918 study revealed that two-thirds of the state's industries were absentee-owned. Westerners clamored for investment, but even boosters sometimes chafed under the results, because control of their economic destiny lay elsewhere.

To understand this resentment it is necessary to shift focus away from the links that tied the western economy to the outside world and away from the larger corporations and their ties with eastern capital and to look at the West of small farmers, ranchers, businesspeople, and wage workers, for these were the people who ardently sought outside development and who often resented the results.

Readings

Arrington, Leonard. *The Great Basin Kingdom: Economic History of the Latter-Day Saints, 1830–1900*. Lincoln: University of Nebraska Press, 1958.

Bogue, Allan G. *Money at Interest: The Farm Mortgage on the Middle Border*. Reprint, Lincoln: University of Nebraska Press, 1969.

Cash, Joseph. *Working the Homestake*. Ames: Iowa State University Press, 1973.

Chandler, Alfred D. *The Visible Hand: The Managerial Revolution in American Business*. Cambridge: Belknap Press of Harvard University Press, 1977.

Coelho, Philip R. P., and James F. Shepherd. "The Impact of Region Difference in Prices and Wages on Economic Growth: The United States in 1890." *Journal of Economic History* 39 (March 1979): 69–86.

Cox, Thomas R. *Mills and Markets: A History of the Pacific Coast Lumber Industry to 1900*. Seattle: University of Washington Press, 1974.

Fahey, John. *The Inland Empire: Unfolding Years, 1879–1929*. Seattle: University of Washington Press, 1986.

Ficken, Robert. *The Forested Land: History of Lumbering in Western Washington*. Seattle: University of Washington Press, 1987.

Fleisig, Heywood. "The Central Pacific Railroad and the Railroad Land Grant Controversy." *Journal of Economic History* 35 (1975):552–64.

Gressley, Gene M. *Bankers and Cattlemen*. New York: Alfred A. Knopf, 1966.

Harley, C. Knick. "Western Settlement and the Price of Wheat, 1872–1913." *Journal of Economic History* 38 (December 1978):865–78.

King, Joseph E. *A Mine to Make a Mine: Financing the Colorado Mining Industry, 1859–1902*. College Station: Texas A&M University Press, 1977.

Larson, Henrietta M. *Jay Cooke, Private Banker*. New York: Greenwood, 1968.

Perloff, Harvey S.; Edgar S. Dunn, Jr.; Eric E. Lampard; and Rich F. Muth. *Regions, Resources, and Economic Growth*. Baltimore: Johns Hopkins University Press, 1961.

Peterson, Richard. *The Bonanza Kings: The Social Origins and Business Behavior of Western Mining Entrepreneurs, 1870–1900*. Lincoln: University of Nebraska Press, 1977.

Pitt, Leonard. *The Decline of the Californios: A Social History of the Spanish-Speaking Californians, 1846–1890*. Berkeley: University of California Press, 1970.

Robbins, William. "'At the End of the Cracked Whip': The Northern West, 1880–1920." *Montana: The Magazine of Western History* 38 (Autumn 1988): 2–11.

Schlebecker, John T. *Cattle Raising on the Plains, 1900–1961*. Lincoln: University of Nebraska Press, 1963.

Spence, Clark. *British Investments and the American Mining Frontier, 1860–1901*. Ithaca, N.Y.: Cornell University Press, 1958.

CHAPTER 11

The Economic Structure
of the West

THE late-nineteenth-century western economy was a study in contrasts. On the one hand it was very much a creature of the world economy: its sources of capital, the markets for western production, and most of the products that westerners consumed all lay outside the West itself. On the other hand, western communities and western producers lived and worked far from the centers of this larger economy in remote, isolated, and rugged areas. Often living in rude shacks and dugouts, western workers and farmers lacked many of the basic refinements of life in the East. What many families called home often amounted to only a small rectangular space of 300 square feet. Yet when the miner left his shack and went to work, he employed the latest in industrial technology. When the farmer stepped outside his sod shanty, he often used the most modern farm machinery. Social paradoxes also abounded. The West was identified with individual opportunity and personal advancement, but quite early in its history the region contained class-conscious workers who believed their lot could be improved only if the condition of all workers changed.

Perhaps the greatest contrast in the western economy came in the organization of production itself. Both small, family-run enterprises and large private companies and public corporations developed side by side in the nineteenth-century West. It was not always clear which kind was going to dominate various sectors of the economy. Granted, by the late nineteenth century the Hill and Harriman empires had established the gargantuan scale of the railroad industry, but other parts of the economy were still contested by lilliputians. Indeed, in two major sectors of the resource economy—cattle raising and farming—corporate operations actually lost out to smaller family-run units.

Organizing Production

Large corporations originally dominated the cattle industry of the Great Plains, Southwest, Great Basin, and California. In the years following the Civil War, a wave of European and eastern investment in cattle produced corporations of awesome size. The enormous XIT Ranch in Texas, owned by Chicago investors, covered 3 million acres. Outside of Texas, cattle companies used the public domain without purchasing it, so their scale is best measured by the size of their herds. In 1877, P. B. Weare began the Weare Land and Livestock Company after making a fortune exporting other products of the plains and prairies: first, prairie chickens; then buffalo robes; and finally, through his grain-brokerage business, wheat. By 1881 he had 50,000 head of cattle grazing on public lands in three territories. Even larger was the Sparks-Harrell operation in Nevada and Idaho, which at its peak supposedly had 150,000 cattle grazing on 3 million acres.

In western farming, the so-called bonanza farms served as the agricultural equivalents of the cattle companies. In the 1870s and 1880s the bonanza farms of the Red River valley of North Dakota and Minnesota and the Central Valley of California with their fleets of machines and platoons of laborers seemed the future of western farming. They were business operations, in the words of one historian, typified by "large scale and sometimes corporate organization, absentee owners, professional management, mechanization, and specialized production."

Bonanza farms required access to large, easily developed tracts of land, a ready supply of capital, and relatively cheap transportation. In North Dakota and Minnesota, the arrival of the Northern Pacific Railroad at Fargo opened the Red River valley up to wheat production while the Northern Pacific, trying to escape its financial obligations, allowed its investors to exchange their depreciated securities for land from the Northern Pacific land grant. In 1875, George Cass and Benjamin Cheney, officials of the Northern Pacific, hired Oliver Dalrymple to develop lands they acquired from the company about 18 miles west of Fargo. Dalrymple broke and planted 1,280 acres the first year. The next year he produced 75,000 bushels of wheat and invested in his own farm while continuing to manage the adjoining farm of Cass and Cheney. By the mid-1880s, Dalrymple's various operations had 32,000 acres in wheat and 2,000 acres in oats.

Dalrymple and his imitators divided these massive farms into managerial units ranging in size from 1,280 to 5,000 acres. Each unit had its own foreman, equipment, and seasonal laborers, with a superintendent supervising the farm as a whole. Heavily mechanized and dependent on seasonal migrant labor for planting and harvesting, Dalrymple's farms employed 500 men for planting and up to 1,000 for harvests.

California wheat farms operated on a similar scale. In the 1850s wheat began to replace livestock in the Central Valley around Sacramento and Stockton as well as in the Santa Clara Valley around San Jose, and California wheat production first boomed during the Civil War. The Confederate navy had cut California off from the East, forcing the state to rely more heavily on its trade with England. Wheat became the major export, and Isaac Friedländer made a fortune as a grain broker when he brought ship owners, bankers, and farmers together to organize grain exports to Great Britain. Following the war, the building of the Central Pacific and the Southern Pacific opened new areas for cultivation. The Central Pacific land grants, coupled with the confirmation of title to the ranchos of the Spanish and Mexican eras, put large blocks of these lands into relatively few hands. In 1870, 100 individuals owned 5,465,206 acres of land in ten California counties, or an average of 54,652 acres per person. By 1880, Dr. Hugh Glenn may have been the largest wheat grower in the world. His 66,000 acres of land in Colusa County stretched for 16 miles along the Sacramento River. It took more than 60 headers and six giant threshers to harvest his more than one million bushels of wheat.

By the mid-1880s California led the nation in wheat production. California's absentee wheat farmers ran huge, heavily mechanized operations that created rural landscapes devoid of the familiar features of the nineteenth-century American countryside. A traveler would search much of the Central Valley in vain for farmhouses, barns, schools, or villages. There was only a huge expanse of grain waving in the sun. The only visible figures were likely to be the farm workers who did most of the planting and harvesting.

Yet for all their size, both the corporate ranches and bonanza farms yielded to smaller family-run operations. By the 1890s even the great XIT was eagerly soliciting farmers to buy its lands. Production by capitalists employing wage labor was losing out to household production in which the same people who owned the means of production also provided most of the labor.

In an era that saw mechanized large-scale production based on wage labor dominate other areas of the economy, why did agriculture and ranching not follow suit? There are several reasons for this apparent anomaly. First, household production in the West was not merely an archaic form of peasant farming. Household farmers also benefited from the technological changes transforming American agriculture during the nineteenth century. The invention of reapers, gang plows, and other improved agricultural implements, by decreasing the amount of labor needed to farm, made it possible for a family to provide virtually all the labor needed to run a relatively large farm. With the new machinery, household farmers cultivated more acres than ever before and produced much larger surpluses. Household farms, with their sophisticated technology and relatively small demand for labor, were thus economically feasible, while the very idea of a household railroad was laughable, and "household" mining operations were of only minor and transitory importance.

The second and probably most important reason for the triumph of household production was its flexibility under harsh conditions. Both capitalist and household farms can prosper in good times, but a capitalist farm must earn profits even during bad times. If it does not, the owners will liquidate it and reinvest their money elsewhere. If prices for wheat fell, bonanza farmers had to cut costs. They could, for example, try to force workers to work longer hours for less pay. They might try to lower costs by keeping old machinery longer. But if such measures failed, eventually bonanza farmers ceased production. Bonanza farming was a way of making money, not a way of life.

On a household farm, by contrast, farming was both a way of making money and a way of life. Family members had a greater stake in the farm, and they could more easily consume less and work harder in order to allow the enterprise, which was also their home, to survive. They did not need annual profits to survive; they needed only enough to maintain the family and the farm. During periods of declining wheat prices, such as the late 1880s and early 1890s, many household farms failed, but a much higher percentage of bonanza farms went under. With greater returns on capital available elsewhere, capitalists liquidated their enterprises and cut their losses. Household farmers drove themselves, their wives, and their children to work even harder. Household farmers won out over bonanza farmers because they could better tolerate misery when times were bad.

Cattle ranching faced a comparable situation. With the gradual decline of the open range following the disasters of the 1880s and the increasing penetration of the plains by farmers, cattle ranching depended on the ability of the rancher to feed livestock during the winters. By 1900, although the vast majority of cattle obtained the bulk of their food from the open range, only 5 percent of the cattle on the plains relied on the open range for *all* their food. Ranchers increasingly fed their cattle with hay grown on irrigated lands, and they had to be willing to continue improving their stock so that they used this feed efficiently.

The turn to more intensive ranching gave smaller ranchers an advantage over the large operations. These smaller ranchers increased their reliance on Herefords, the breed that would dominate plains ranching for the next half-century. Herefords fattened more quickly and were sold younger. Ranchers thus produced higher-quality beef on fewer acres, which allowed the small cattle raisers to compete more effectively with larger operators. These smaller ranchers remained capitalists who depended on hired labor, their cowboys, but who operated on a much smaller scale than in the past. Their ranches were more likely to be family-owned operations rather than corporate operations established by eastern money and run by hired managers.

Small Businesses

Ranches and farms resembled the vast majority of western businesses in that they remained relatively small. Corporations were the towering giants of the economic forests, but small businesses formed an abundant understory.

Small businesses filled several economic niches in the West. Some businesses took over specialized tasks within the extractive industries dominated by corporations or large companies. In the nineteenth century, for example, most large lumber mills did not do their own logging; instead, they bought logs from independent loggers. On the Pacific Coast, small manufacturers thrived because of the region's isolation. By 1868, for example, San Francisco boasted 15 iron foundries and machine shops to serve western mining regions. Other manufacturers served local consumer markets. Some of them, such as Levi-Strauss, dry goods merchants and clothing manufacturers of San Francisco, would grow into national enterprises, but most of these businesses could prosper only as long as freight rates remained high enough to banish eastern competition. These Pacific Coast business owners had much to lose from the rise of large manufacturing corporations in the East which might be able to overcome the cost of shipping and penetrate their markets.

The Far West initially boasted another important business group: the merchant wholesalers. In antebellum western cities such as San Francisco, Portland, or Salt Lake City, merchant wholesalers formed the dominant local economic power. They controlled the import and export of goods. But when economic development accelerated in much of the West after the Civil War, the dominance of merchant wholesalers began to yield to direct marketing by manufacturers who maintained their own sales and distribution networks. By the late nineteenth century eastern manufacturers took over an increasing share of the wholesale trade, and the merchants went into decline. Wholesalers and jobbers did not disappear; they held on well into the twentieth century in grocery, drug, and hardware trades, but they lost control over most manufactured goods.

The decline of wholesale merchants left only retail merchandising securely under the control of local entrepreneurs. And even here, with the rise of large mail order houses such as Sears, Roebuck and Company, retailers suffered from corporate competition. Retailers necessarily had one foot in the local economy and another in the national economy, which supplied most of the goods they

San Francisco in the 1890s had maintained its position as the only major manufacturing center in the West.

sold. Particularly in mining towns, mill towns, or important railroad centers, such small businessmen depended indirectly on the corporations for their prosperity. When their customers worked for railroads, mining companies, or mill companies, the retailers' fortunes varied with corporate wages.

Small businesses that lived by the corporations could also die by the corporations. Sometimes the death came from direct competition, as when corporations took over the tasks formerly performed by small businesses. In the logging industry, for example, mill companies in the late nineteenth and early twentieth centuries increasingly did their own logging, thus eliminating many of the independent logging companies. In mining towns, mine companies opened company stores and coerced their workers to shop there. At other times the death of small businesses came indirectly. A corporation that cut wages and impoverished a local community destroyed the small businesses that depended on the patronage of workers. As the merchants of Grass Valley had realized early, small-town merchants in a mining town lived not off the mines but off the miners. Mine profits usually left the area, because owners were Californians, easterners, or Europeans; wages, at least the wages of stable, permanent workers, stayed and were spent at local businesses.

Although hardly the most significant local businesses, saloons were certainly the most notorious and in many places arguably the most prevalent kind of retailing outlet in the West. A saloon was many things in a western town. It was a welcome social center in towns where many workers lived in filthy and cramped rooming houses. Sometimes it was a social problem. But it was also and always a business enterprise and a retail establishment. Saloons can serve as an example of how retailers tied together local consumers and regional or national suppliers. Saloon keepers were businesspeople in search of profits. They were particularly abundant businesspeople both because westerners were remarkably thirsty and because opening a saloon initially called for only a small investment. When a veteran of the Arizona mining camps estimated that ten dollars invested in a "modest stock of mingled water, chemicals, and alcohol" could start profits flowing, he probably underestimated the investment and overestimated the profits. But he did underline the appeal of liquor retailing in western towns and cities.

Western saloons varied in size, luxury, and cost. The assets of small saloons in

Notice the abundance of small retail businesses in this street scene from Helena, Montana, in the late nineteenth century.

Saloons were probably the most common western retail business. This is the Long Branch
saloon (later made famous in the television series "Gunsmoke"), in Dodge City, Kansas.

crude shacks or tents ran from $500 to $700 in the Rocky Mountain mining
camps. Most saloons had from $1,000 to $2,000 in assets. A few had substantially
higher values: from $7,000 to $10,000. All of these saloons were tied into the
larger economy by their need for alcohol, a product that few produced themselves.
Until the 1880s beer, which spoiled quickly, was a local product, but then
improvements in bottling and pasteurization allowed national breweries to
emerge. In the last two decades of the century the railroads increasingly carried
Schlitz, Pabst, Blatz, and Budweiser from German breweries in Wisconsin and
Missouri into the West.

In carrying beer, the railroads integrated beer into the existing distribution
system for other alcoholic beverages. In the Rocky Mountains the railroads carried
alcohol to wholesalers in Denver, Boise, Helena, Tucson, Corinne, Durango,
and other distribution centers. From there freighters carried it to saloons in the
camps and towns. Freight rates were high, but this only encouraged the importation of alcohol, because its value was high relative to its weight. The freight for
a hundredweight of flour that sold for $20.00 to $30.00 and a hundredweight of
whiskey that retailed at between $200 and $300 was, after all, the same.

Although many saloon keepers could begin business with a small investment,
staying in business entailed greater costs. As towns and camps stabilized, the cost
of doing business rose with customers' expectations. Glasses, billiard tables, and
elegant furnishings demanded money, as did increasing rents, licenses, bonds,
and taxes. Saloon keepers had to invest to compete, and to compete, like other

merchants they also had to extend credit. The result, with a mobile population, was a certain measure of bad debts.

In a competitive business in a mobile society, saloon keepers proved to be as transient as their customers. In Leadville, Colorado, a relatively stable mining camp, only about 5 percent of the saloon keepers in the 1880s remained in business for six years or more. Why so few survived is relatively clear from the tax assessments. At any given time, 80 to 85 percent of the saloon keepers in Leadville had either no assessable personal property or real estate or had property valued at less than $500. They could not make the investments necessary to survive. Not surprisingly, the larger and more prosperous saloon keepers were the more stable ones. They all began business with considerable amounts of capital: their average first assessment was $4,300.

Those smaller saloon keepers who survived, and even thrived, were thus the survivors of a far larger group. In Leadville, out of a large group of men with little capital and laboring backgrounds who opened saloons, a little under 10 percent survived either to establish middle-sized saloons or else to maintain their small gin mills over a period of years.

Labor

Many saloon keepers, and presumably other small merchants, came from the ranks of labor. Many returned to those ranks when their businesses failed. Wage labor occupied a somewhat paradoxical position in the West. In the nineteenth-century West, most people did not work for wages. The exclusion of the vast majority of women from paid employment put a large minority of the adult population outside of the wage labor system. Household farms depended on family, not wage, labor. Small merchants and most professionals were self-employed. Yet wage labor was, nonetheless, the keystone of western economic development, because the corporations that dominated and shaped the western economic structure depended on wage labor.

Some people participated in both the wage labor system and the household system. Men often left their farms to work seasonally for wages just as some miners supplemented their wages by working individual leases in the mines. Unmarried women might work as teachers, seamstresses, laundry workers, and domestic servants, while some married women combined household work and wage work. Married black women were particularly likely to combine the two. The vast majority of these black women worked as domestics or laundry workers. Fewer Hispanic women worked for wages. A sample of four cities found a little over 10 percent of all women between ages 20 and 50 employed in 1880. These figures, however, do not include women such as the Hispanic women in the Southwest, who worked as part-time *vendadoras* selling foods, handicrafts, and household wares in the markets. Not surprisingly, women who were widowed or abandoned were far more likely to have full-time occupations.

Work for most married women, however, remained closely connected with the home: feeding their families, taking care of the children, and maintaining the house. By necessity, girls and young women might be pressed into agricultural labor, but the gender boundaries of work still remained clear to them. Susie Crockett of Oklahoma remembered that although "I could help the boys with the plowing or trapping, they would never help me with the sewing." Women's profit-making ventures remained almost universally home-oriented. Many urban women took in boarders. Most farm and ranch women produced butter or eggs for market or engaged in small domestic manufactures. The contrast between the domestic confines of even the remunerative labor of women and the wider world of men was not lost on many farm and ranch women. "A man that is cowhunting with a lively crowd has no idea how long and lonesome the time passes with his wife at home," a Texas ranch woman confided to her diary. "A man can see his friends, hear the news and pass time . . ., while his wife is at home and sees and hears nothing until he returns from a long trip tired and worn out." The lines between men's and women's work gave way only when men fell ill or died, when they left to work for wages or deserted their family, or when Mormon men left for their missions. Then women very often had to take over the complete economic responsibility for the family.

In the mining town of Cripple Creek, Colorado, in the early twentieth century married women rarely worked outside the home. Whereas men defined their economic position according to their jobs or their wealth, women defined their economic position according to their relation to men. For many union men, a woman working outside the home was a disgrace, because it meant that a man "wasn't a good worker; he was lazy, he wasn't able to take care of his family." Working-class women in Cripple Creek by and large accepted such a view. If women were to earn money, they should keep it quiet and not embarrass their husbands.

The reality of a working-class woman's life was hard labor. When one Cripple Creek woman was asked what she expected of marriage, she replied: "Just what I got. A lot of hard work." Married women in Cripple Creek tended vegetable gardens, kept chickens or perhaps a cow, made clothing, and did housework. About 20 percent provided income by keeping boarders, and others took in laundry. Women's work, in short, usually revolved around serving men. This was true of married women, who at the minimum took care of their husband and often took in boarders, and of unmarried women who worked as waitresses or laundresses. Those women workers who fell out of the ranks of "good women" and became dance-hall girls or prostitutes even more obviously served men.

In this larger world of male and female work, wage labor took a privileged place in the West. Occasional wage labor allowed marginal household operations to survive, and the most vigorous sectors of the developing economy depended entirely on wage labor. Mines, railroads, and smelters all employed wage laborers in large numbers. By 1890 the major Butte mines employed 300 to 900 men each, and the Anaconda employed 3,000 in mining and smelting. Not all of these workers were adults. Western coal mines employed young boys at the "picking table," where they separated coal from slate and stone. Others worked underground. In 1889 an average Utah coal mine had 29 children working underground; an average Wyoming mine had 19.

To attract workers, western employers offered wages that were significantly higher than those in the East. Even after the higher cost of living in the West has been factored in, western workers earned a higher real wage than those elsewhere in the country. Relatively well paying work is not, however, the same thing as steady work. The severe cyclical fluctuations of nineteenth-century

Table 6

Real Wages by Occupation and Region in 1890

(in cents per day)

Variable	New England	Middle Atlantic	East North Central	West North Central	East South Central	South Atlantic	West South Central	Mountain	Pacific
Baker	199	192	218	218	219	173	202	182	258
Blacksmith	243	258	242	251	271	231	292	297	292
Bricklayer	318	368	396	398	422	306	375	463	477
Cabinet Maker	238	260	220	255	260	214	282	302	243
Carpenter	231	255	240	244	258	208	311	297	293
Common Labor	147	145	156	160	115	97	145	215	176
Farm Labor*	135	119	—	—	71	—	83	—	—
Farm Labor†	132	105	120	129	82	70	94	130	135
Machinist	227	248	255	262	282	256	355	280	284
Mason	308	332	362	346	368	279	378	405	431
Moulder (Iron)	218	251	263	258	269	260	298	293	308
Painter	207	260	238	244	244	183	268	285	268
Plumber	285	292	307	355	352	267	326	366	352
Stonecutter	297	345	373	384	351	276	394	411	392
Tinsmith	222	249	240	248	255	240	276	302	279
Mean‡	234	259	255	275	260	206	278	325	302

Source: Philip Coelho and James Shepherd, "The Impact of Region Difference in Prices and Wages on Economic Growth: The United States in 1890," *Journal of Economic History* 34 (March 1979): 77.

*These data are from the *Aldrich Report.*

†These data are from the United States Department of Agriculture, Bureau of Statistics.

‡These means are the means for all observations from the *Aldrich Report* within a region. They are not column means; and they do not include wages of farm labor from the USDA source.

capitalism, the completion of large projects such as the railroads, seasonal variations in lumber or harvesting—all of these things periodically threw large numbers of people out of work. Many, but not all, could retreat back into household production, but a large portion of the nineteenth-century western labor force was, from necessity, mobile. Unemployed workers gathered in the newer mining camps of the west, on the ranches and orchards of the Central Valley of California, in timber towns like Everett, Washington, or in urban districts like Skid Road in Seattle or Larimer Street in Denver either to seek work or to wait out the seasonal lags in the economy. These places preserved traces of the earlier predominantly male West of mining camps and ranches long after sex ratios had evened elsewhere in the West. Male migrant workers were largely responsible for giving the West the highest percentage (10 percent) of single-member households anywhere in the country.

Working Conditions

Western workers, like workers throughout the United States in the nineteenth century, often contributed their health, their limbs, and even their lives to economic development. To examine the workplaces of western mines, mills, and forests is to enter a chamber of horrors. The technologies that increased productivity also increased the carnage of the workplace.

The worst working conditions probably existed in the mines. As the quartz mines of the West reached deeper and deeper into the ground, both the temperature and water level in the tunnels rose. On the Comstock Lode temperatures in the mines reached well over 100 degrees, and at 2,000 to 3,000 feet below the surface they went to over 150 degrees. Miners worked in breechcloths and wore thick shoes to protect their feet from scorching rocks and steaming rills of water. They had to refresh themselves constantly at water showers and ventilating tubes. Men died directly of the heat, dropping dead as they worked, or indirectly by catching pneumonia when they rose, dripping sweat, into subfreezing temperatures above ground.

The poor ventilation in the mines compounded the danger. The levels of carbon dioxide caused headaches, dizziness, and drowsiness that increased the risk of accidents. If enough gas accumulated, miners fainted and suffocated. Carbon dioxide was, however, only one ingredient in a lethal brew that also included unburned nitroglycerine, quartz dust, and, in some mines, silver and lead compounds. Probably half the miners on the dry levels of the mines contracted silicosis, which badly impaired their breathing and eventually disabled them.

With the simple act of breathing becoming a danger to health, miners had entered a lottery of death. Miners died in explosions, cave-ins crushed them, fires incinerated them, machinery maimed them. The mining cages that lowered and raised workers in the mines crippled and killed. A spell of dizziness, a tool that caught on a support or a rock wall could throw a miner off balance so that he was either crushed by the cage itself or else plummeted to his death.

New technologies eliminated some dangers and added others. Machine drills proved to be four times as effective as hand drills, but the dust they created cut the miners' lungs and caused phthisis, which in turn opened the miners up to tuberculosis. In one Colorado mining district phthisis was the chief or contributing factor in 30 percent of all miners' deaths. Promoters promised that dynamite

Machine drills such as this one made mining both more efficient and far more dangerous.

would eliminate the unburned gases common after an explosion of nitroglycerine and was less likely to explode accidentally, but dynamite proved susceptible to premature or delayed explosions and left behind sometimes fatal amounts of carbon monoxide.

In the hardrock mines of the West in the late 1870s accidents annually disabled 1 out of every 30 miners and killed 1 out of 80. In the course of his career a miner who spent a lifetime in the mines had a good chance of being permanently or temporarily disabled in an accident, and he might very well be killed. The fatality rate in Colorado was almost 6 per 1,000 workers in the mid-1890s, falling to 2 or 3 per thousand in the early twentieth century. It was over 8 per 1,000 in Montana in 1896 and, adjusted to count only underground miners, 9.3 per 1,000. Between 1899 and 1906 the rate averaged between 2.8 and 3.5 per 1,000 in the western mining states, but it rose again in some states thereafter.

Metal and coal mining remained the most hazardous industries in the twentieth-century United States. Death rates among American miners were far higher than those suffered by European miners, and statistics underestimated the death rate among underground miners because they included all workers employed around the mine and not just those working in the tunnels. Such rates, too, counted only immediate fatalities; they did not include those who died of pneumonia or phthisis or silicosis that they contracted in the mines. In Butte, a sample of over 1,000 miners taken between 1916 and 1919 found that 42.5 percent had miner's consumption and another 6 percent had tuberculosis. These respiratory illnesses did not just kill the old; in Butte, the average age at time of death from respiratory illness in 1906–1907 was 42.7 years.

Lumbering's risks rivaled the carnage of the mines. In Washington, five times as many workers died in the mills and the woods than in any other sector of the economy. At the Port Blakely mill alone in 1904 there were 142 accidents, and such accidents were often gruesome as saws took off fingers, hands, and arms. In the woods loggers died under falling trees. Logging cables snapped, dismembering nearby workers. As in mining, increased mechanization meant increased danger.

Agricultural workers did not share the relatively high wages of miners or mill workers, but in addition to squalor, discomfort, and deprivation they, too, suffered increasing danger to life and limb as farming became more mechanized. Working largely as seasonal harvest hands instead of permanent employees, they received neither adequate food nor shelter. They worked under the hot sun and slept on straw. The working conditions were so bad that farm owners themselves used them as an argument for admitting Chinese, Filipino, and Mexican immigrants. No white worker, they argued, would put up with such conditions, and they even scorned those white workers who did as degraded people who deserved no better.

Dual Labor System

The denigration of agricultural labor in the Far West because of its domination by nonwhite workers was a sign of what came to be a pervasive labor structure across the West: a dual or two-tiered labor system. The top tier consisted of managerial positions and skilled work and was the domain of white workers. The bottom tier consisted of arduous but unskilled, low-paying jobs such as farm labor or railroad construction. This bottom tier was disproportionately the domain of nonwhite workers.

Bottom-tier jobs became, almost by definition, minority jobs because employers argued that minorities were racially suited to them. Thus Chinese, Mexicans, Filipinos, and other nonwhite workers were supposedly suited to agricultural stoop labor by their small size, tolerance for heat, stoicism, minimal wants, and lack of ambition. Conversely, whites argued that minorities lacked the qualities— ambition, skill, and intelligence—necessary for better jobs.

Those white workers who took bottom-tier jobs suffered a loss of status in the eyes of other whites for failing to procure "white man's work," but their situation was never quite the same as that of minority workers. Irish immigrant workers, for example, laid track for the Union Pacific Railroad, a bottom-tier job, but most Irish moved on to better jobs. The Chinese, and later Mexican Americans, did not. Minorities were the only groups who occupied lower-tier positions permanently.

Although excluded from the most lucrative jobs, minority workers struggled against their condition. Chinese fruit pickers in Santa Clara County, California, in the 1880s and hop pickers in Kern County, for example, went on strike when farmers would not meet their demands. Even more often minority workers tried to find cracks in the system that they could wedge open to increase their opportunities.

The experience of the Chinese is illustrative of the mixed results of such struggles. Gold had brought the Chinese to California, and despite persecution, the miners' tax, and their restriction in many regions to working claims already abandoned by whites, the Chinese held on as independent placer miners as long as possible.

Chinese workers provided the main labor force for the construction of the Central Pacific Railroad.

When not even the Chinese could make these claims pay, they abandoned mining and became a large, mobile pool of unskilled laborers. About 10,000 Chinese found work building the Central Pacific across California and Nevada and on into Utah between 1866 and 1869. With the completion of the railroad, some Chinese moved on to other mining areas of the West, and others became tenant farmers and agricultural laborers in the Central Valley. Many, however, remained available for railroad work. In 1882 when the Northern Pacific began to build its line through the Pacific Northwest, it recruited 15,000 Chinese to work in Washington Territory alone, with another 6,000 engaged in construction in Idaho and Montana.

Chinese workers made various attempts to escape from their relegation to hard and dangerous labor, but such attempts met fierce resistance. When during the 1860s and 1870s, for example, Chinese entered and soon dominated the California fishing industry, both California and the federal government passed laws limiting Chinese fishing and banning the export of their catch. Harassed and threatened, the Chinese largely surrendered the fishing business to whites.

In rural areas the Chinese confronted similar obstacles, and there, too, despite their efforts they found themselves on a downward economic slide. Former miners either as tenant farmers or owner operators became truck gardeners, growing fresh produce for local markets, only to descend within two decades to agricultural laborers because of rising land values, sporadic rural persecution of the Chinese, and the Chinese Exclusion Act, which cut off immigration. Given the small number of Chinese women in California, lack of new immigrants meant an aging and declining male population.

The rural Chinese who achieved financial success did so as merchants, large tenant farmers, and labor contractors. They capitalized on their ability to act as intermediaries, negotiating with whites for land while organizing the labor of their fellow countrymen. Chin Lung, the "Chinese Potato King," immigrated from China in 1882 or 1883. After learning English in a class conducted by the Chinese Baptist Church, he leased land in the Sacramento Delta, an area reclaimed with Chinese labor, and hired up to 500 Chinese workers to cultivate his potatoes. Chin Lung and those like him succeeded in large part because of the dual system of labor and not in spite of it. Without large numbers of Chinese forced into agricultural labor, they would have been unable to command large numbers of laborers at low wages. Chin Lung eventually returned to China, and no other Chinese matched his success, for the Chinese Exclusion Act eliminated the rural laborers that men like the Potato King needed to succeed.

Declining opportunities in rural areas and the threat of violence made the Chinese an increasingly urban work force. The Chinese population of Sacramento tripled between 1860 and 1880, but far more Chinese moved to San Francisco, which by 1870 held 30 percent of the state's Chinese population. There they worked in laundries, in domestic service, and in factories, dominating the textile and tobacco industries. The Chinese formed perhaps 25 percent of the wage workers in California in the early 1870s. As late as 1900, the industries dominated by Chinese workers paid only 60 to 70 percent of the average annual wage in San Francisco.

The dual labor system had far-reaching consequences for the West. Because it divided workers on the basis of race and secured white workers a certain advantage, white workers had reason to maintain a racial rather than a class solidarity. Most white workers thought they had less in common with nonwhite workers than with white employers.

There was additionally a second obstacle to workers' developing a class-conscious view of themselves. Most laborers did not think of themselves as permanent workers. Many shared the widespread American belief that a person's class status was temporary, not permanent. This belief formed part of an ideology, for which Abraham Lincoln served as both spokesman and symbol, that historians have called the free labor ideology. Because American society promised success to all those willing to work, it had become, or so its proponents claimed, a basically middle-class society with few rich and few poor. A man (for these ideologues presumed workers would be men) might start out working for a wage, but if he worked hard and persistently, he would eventually own a farm or business of his own and come to employ others who were themselves also striving toward economic independence. The free labor ideology denied the significance of class. If working for wages was simply a transitory condition, then a self-conscious working class became an impossibility.

Social Mobility

The free labor ideology promised social mobility, and social mobility depended on economic growth. Like the railroads that made growth possible, economic development in the West was a rickety wonder. Sometimes it traveled at amazing speeds, but sometimes it failed to move at all. Dazzling in its scope and staggering in its reach and power, it was also inefficient and wasteful. And just as a traveler on a railroad might be either a passenger in a luxurious Pullman car or a tramp clinging to a precarious perch while suspended beneath a boxcar, so the rich and the poor got quite different rides as the economy moved forward.

Most westerners equated the vast physical transformation of the West—the opening of farms, the cutting of forests, the mining of minerals, and the building of cities—with progress. As proud of their collective triumph as they were, their ultimate judgment was more personal: Had they achieved individual success?

This question of individual success and opportunity goes to the heart of American conceptions of the West. Americans have long identified the West with opportunity, a place where people could go and grow up with the country. But was success more easily achieved in the West than in the East? Was there more opportunity? The dual labor system certainly guaranteed that there was not equal opportunity for Indians, blacks, Chinese, and Hispanics. But evaluating the economic success of the mass of white western migrants, and comparing it to opportunities in the East are difficult tasks. Often all historians can recover are the labels—carpenter, miner, merchant, lawyer—attached to people in census returns or city directories or the values of property contained in tax records, wills, or censuses. These all, to be sure, measure something, but they do not necessarily measure success. For in large part success is an individual judgment. A western carpenter, for example, may have worked his whole life, raised a family, and obtained the respect of his fellows. He might consider his life a success. A historian, however, might dismiss this same life as a failure because the carpenter began life as a carpenter and ended it as a carpenter. He never got a "better" job; he never advanced up the class ladder. When we attempt to measure something like social mobility, we assume all workers would automatically change jobs in order to advance to more rewarding or prestigious work.

Along with these basic conceptual difficulties are other more immediate problems. It is difficult to trace people in the records. Westerners, for example, moved repeatedly: Does the departure of someone from a given area mean failure or a better chance of success elsewhere? These are not trivial problems, but we can still get a rough picture of the economic possibilities that the West held for Anglo American migrants.

Historians have found that opportunity in both the nineteenth- and the twentieth-century West was not as great as popularly believed. Current studies for portions of the West indicate that wealth was no more evenly distributed in the West than in the East. A study of northern California counties in 1860, for example, found that in the most remote counties, far from markets, and with few advantages to draw wealthier migrants, wealth was most evenly distributed. But this was because people were poor together, not prosperous together. In the most prosperous counties and in the urban areas, the distribution of wealth roughly paralleled that of the East. And as more migrants entered the state, the concentra-

Table 7
Occupational Mobility Among Manual Workers, 1870–90

Direction of Mobility	Native Whites	Immigrants	Blacks
1870–80			
Upward mobility to a white-collar or higher position	15% (34)	32% (60)	— (16)
Upward mobility within manual class (i.e., from unskilled or semiskilled to skilled position)	38% (16)	6% (34)	— (14)
Total upward mobility	32% (34)	35% (60)	— (16)
No significant mobility	64% (34)	65% (60)	88% (16)
Downward mobility within manual class (i.e., from skilled to semiskilled or unskilled position)	6% (18)	— (26)	100% (2)
Number in sample	34	60	16
1870–90			
Upward mobility to a white-collar or higher position	20% (20)	30% (40)	— (14)
Upward mobility within manual class (i.e., from unskilled or semiskilled to skilled position)	50% (8)	17% (24)	— (12)
Total upward mobility	40% (20)	40% (40)	— (14)
No significant mobility	50% (20)	57% (40)	86% (14)
Downward mobility within manual class (i.e., from skilled to semiskilled or unskilled position)	17% (12)	6% (16)	100% (2)
Number in sample	20	40	14

Source: Robert M. Tank, "Mobility and Occupational Structure on the Late-Nineteenth-Century Urban Frontier: The Case of Denver, Colorado," *Pacific Historical Review* 47 (May 1978): 199.

Note: The percentage of the subsample that was occupationally mobile was arrived at by dividing the number of men who experienced occupational mobility by the number of men who had the potential to be occupationally mobile (shown in parentheses). Thus the denominator in the calculations to determine the percent of manual workers upwardly mobile to a white-collar or higher position represents all the manual workers in the subsample, since all manual workers had the potential to rise to a nonmanual position. However, the denominator in the calculations to determine upward mobility within the manual class includes only men working in unskilled or semiskilled occupations and excludes skilled workers, since they did not have the potential to be upwardly occupationally mobile within the manual class. Since the denominator varies from one calculation to another, the columns do not total 100 percent.

tion of wealth at the top increased. This was true of large cities such as San Francisco, where between 1850 and 1880 a relatively small elite garnered a larger proportion of the available wealth. And it was only slightly less true of smaller towns such as Roseburg, Oregon, where in 1880, 20 percent of the population controlled 80 percent of the wealth.

The uneven distribution of wealth, however, does not rule out the possibility that most people gained a more modest success. Current studies seem to show, however, that most nineteenth-century westerners advanced only slightly or not all during their working lives. The same study of northern California found that in terms of property, most middle-aged men had little to show for their life's work. In 1870 the poorest 50 percent of men appearing in the census had anything from 0 percent to 1.3 percent of the total property held by 45-year-olds as a whole. Northern California—largely rural and cut off by poor transportation from major urban centers—cannot, however, serve as a representation of the entire West. Were conditions different elsewhere?

San Francisco was at the center of the western economy, but it was only briefly a place where people could rapidly climb the social ladder. In the early days of the Gold Rush, many San Francisco merchants did experience what has been called shipboard mobility. Departing the East with a small stock of goods, they could establish themselves as merchants literally on arrival. They might depart a small shopkeeper and arrive a wholesale merchant. But the price of such upward mobility was the chance of nearly as rapid a fall. In the tumultuous speculative economy of the 1850s many lost fortunes as quickly as they had gained them. The stabilization of the economy narrowed the opportunities for either rapid economic ascents or descents. After the early 1850s, San Franciscans as a whole experienced no greater career opportunities than did the people of eastern cities. And despite the rise of some industrial owners and managers from the working classes, most blue-collar workers experienced less social and economic advancement than did those in the East.

The opportunities available in San Francisco seem to have been relatively typical of western cities. In Omaha, Nebraska, between 1880 and 1920, 75 percent of blue-collar workers began and ended their working lives in the working class. Similarly, in Denver, Colorado, between 1870 and 1890, 67 percent of native-born manual workers, 63 percent of immigrant workers, and 100 percent of black workers achieved no significant upward mobility. These mobility rates were about the same as those in the East. It appears that although in some industries such as mining an elite of owners and managers may have, to a disproportionate degree, risen from the ranks of immigrants and workers, in most places and in most occupations, rags to riches stories were as rare in the West as in the East.

Table 8
Percentage of Total Real and Personal Estate Owned by 45-year-olds in Selected Counties of California, 1870.

County	Richest Tenth	Second	Third	Fourth	Fifth	Poorest Half
El Dorado	64.6	23.5	8.4	2.9	0.6	0.0
Humboldt	78.6	9.7	4.9	3.7	2.1	0.9
Marin	88.5	9.2	1.6	0.4	0.2	0.0
Mendocino	56.1	19.0	12.0	7.7	4.1	1.0
Napa	76.8	10.3	6.5	3.4	1.6	1.3
Nevada	80.6	12.4	5.1	1.9	0.0	0.0
Sacramento	72.4	16.9	7.0	2.6	0.8	0.0

Source: Robert A. Burchell, "Opportunity and the Frontier: Wealth-Holding in Twenty-six Northern Californian Counties, 1848–1880," *Western Historical Quarterly* 52 (April 1987): 183.

Most western migrants had to be content with very modest gains from a lifetime of labor, but in certain places at certain times there were extraordinary opportunities for certain groups. In late-nineteenth-century Denver, for example, many skilled workers, particularly immigrants, did advance into the middle class of management and small proprietorships. In Denver, too, immigrant nonmanual workers, like their skilled fellow immigrants, found considerable occupational opportunity. Indeed, those European immigrants who arrived with a skill or with enough money to start a business often did better in the West than they did in the East. Germans, and particularly German Jews, were far more successful in San Francisco than the general population.

Class Consciousness and the Creation of a Working Class

Despite individual opportunities at certain times and places to advance in wealth and status, most people who began their lives in the western working class, despite a lifetime of hard work, seem to have ended their lives in the working class. But just because large numbers of people spent their lives in manual labor did not mean that they automatically came to reject the assumptions of the free labor ideology and came to think of themselves as a single, coherent working class.

Class, like any social grouping, is a cultural creation; it does not spring from work itself but from how people organize work. A self-conscious working class demands not just common labor, but also a common sense of identity, a common set of interests, and a common set of values. The more homogeneous a group of workers is, the easier class consciousness is to achieve.

In the West the creation of class-conscious workers was thus a struggle against both the diversity of the work force and an ideology that put a person's fate solely in the individual's own hands. Although not all immigrants and nonwhites in the West were blue-collar workers, such workers were disproportionately immigrants, children of immigrants, and nonwhites. In the Comstock Lode of Nevada, for example, Cornish (that is people from Cornwall in England) and Irish workers each made up one-third of the mining work force. Only 20 percent of the miners were native-born. Later, in the Cripple Creek district of Colorado, only about 30 percent of the miners were immigrants, but this is partially because the miners forcibly kept newer immigrant groups out of the mines.

As the exclusion of eastern and southern Europeans and Hispanics at Cripple Creek demonstrates, ethnic solidarity often seemed more important than working-class solidarity. A Cornish miner was proud to be a miner, but he was often so particularly proud to be a *Cornish* miner that his class consciousness did not extend to other miners, let alone other workers. Nearly any Saturday night in Grass Valley or Virginia City brought evidence of the divisions among miners. The Cornishmen brawled regularly with the Irish and Germans in saloons or in the streets. They were equally quick to assault Chinese, who, the Cornishmen feared, would be used by mine owners to break the Cornish hold on underground labor. The Cornishmen attacked the Chinese not for what they had done but for what others might do with them.

Given these divisions, mining towns in California, Nevada, Montana, and Colorado often seemed a collection of separate ethnic working-class communities whose overarching class consciousness was tentative and fragile when it existed at all. Thus Cornish and Irish miners in Grass Valley in 1869 united against the mine owners in 1869, but German and native-born miners mobilized, unsuccessfully, to oppose them. And in Gilpin County, Colorado, Irish and native-born workers refused to join a predominantly Cornish union. The sides, however, could easily be reversed. The Cornishmen, for example, initially served as strikebreakers against Irish and native-born miners on the Comstock Lode in Nevada. And at Cherry Creek, Nevada, a union was organized specifically "to counteract the manifest preference given by mine managers to the Cornishmen." In Butte, Montana, "the Gibraltar of Unionism," the Irish thoroughly dominated the miners' union and used it to gain preference for Irish workers.

These barriers were not, however, impenetrable, at least as far as western Europeans were concerned. As early as the 1860s and 1870s, miners from various communities in the Sierra Nevada and Rocky Mountains began to organize local unions that spanned ethnic boundaries. Ethnic divisions still arose, but now they focused on newer immigrant groups, as when in 1888 the Irish and Cornish miners of Gilpin County, Colorado, having overcome their own earlier differences, jointly attacked Italian strikebreakers as "a horde of men who belong to the lowest class in the civilized world." When the Italians of Gilpin County joined the union, the animosity largely dissipated, but this was not always the case.

The ability of class consciousness to overcome ethnic and racial divisions remained limited into the twentieth century. Most unions not only continued to exclude blacks, Chinese, and Hispanics, but they also excluded southern and eastern Europeans. The Butte Miners Union dissolved partially because of conflicts between the Irish and eastern Europeans, whom one Butte newspaper described as "European Chinamen." A self-conscious "white man's camp" like Cripple Creek, Colorado, drove out Slavs, Italians, Greeks, Hispanics, Chinese, and Japanese because workers feared they would undermine the wage structure. One miner wrote, "The Dagoes, Japs, or Chinese will walk in and take a chance with those cheap guys who today are willing to work for $2.50 or $2.00 a day." Another resident of Cripple Creek remembered that "if there was any threat to anyone coming into the camp and working for cheaper wages, like if your Spanish people would come in, they were driven out of town, the town guns would stone 'em out. They wouldn't let 'em come in at all." Class solidarity and union organization thus were strongest among western European immigrants and native-born American workers. Only rarely did these workers extend class sympathy to other groups of workers.

Job stability also served to divide workers. In the cities and towns of the West, skilled workers—carpenters, teamsters, bricklayers, engineers, conductors, railroad shopmen, printers, and others—and those industrial workers holding steady jobs often set themselves apart from the mass of transient and unskilled workers. Skilled workers often formed a prosperous part of local communities. In Washington state at the turn of the century, for example, 40 percent of these workers owned their own home and 80 percent were married. In San Francisco, even after accounting for a higher cost of living, the average white male worker earned 20 percent more than his counterparts in New York or Chicago. Similarly, the skilled railroad workers of a town like Emporia, Kansas, were not markedly different from their nonrailroading neighbors. They were apparently less likely to own a home only because the nature of their job led them to change locations so often. In Butte, an Irish working-class community developed where high wages and steady work gave men an opportunity to own homes, marry, and raise families.

Unions

Skilled workers created the strongest unions in the West because they were harder to replace than unskilled workers and because most shared a craft background that placed a high value on the worker's independence. Cornish miners, for example, jealously guarded the right to make decisions about how, and at what pace, their highly skilled and dangerous work was done. They often refused to work with a supervisor present. Many Cornish miners in the early industry coupled wage labor with prospecting and the leasing and working of idle claims. Whether working for wages or for himself, the miner vehemently guarded his independence.

The unions that developed among craft workers and among the more stable mining communities developed a devotion to the so-called bread and butter issues of wages and working conditions later typical of the American Federation of Labor (AF of L). These working-class conservatives tended to seek accommodations with their employers, particularly when, as in Butte, they shared ethnic ties with them. Many had visions of a better society, but the reforms they supported tended to be ameliorative and not revolutionary. They wanted not so much to overthrow capitalism as to increase the power of organized workers as a counterweight to corporate interests and to protect the gains they had already made. Such workers often had substantial middle-class support, as the great railroad strikes of 1877 and 1894 demonstrated.

For a time, the economic structure of some western areas reflected the strength of workers and their unions. Butte, Montana, became a bastion of unionism, albeit often a conservative unionism in the late nineteenth and early twentieth centuries. The Butte Miners Union was the largest mining local in the West, and it imposed a closed shop in the Butte mines. The miners further enhanced union power in Butte by affiliating with 34 other unions to form the Silver Bow Trades and Labor Assembly, which by 1891 boasted nearly 6,000 members. Between 1898 and 1922, San Francisco became perhaps the quintessential union town in the nation. The closed shop—that is, a business that promised to hire only union labor—prevailed in most of the San Francisco job market as San Francisco businesses accepted unionism. Confined to a peninsular city of only 46 square miles, typical San Francisco businesses such as drayage, shipping, and construction could not escape unions by moving elsewhere without abandoning the city's superb port. Since most businesses were small or middle-sized and competed in a regional market, paying good wages and accepting union work rules made sense. Unions created an even playing field within San Francisco, and San Francisco's businesses were in no danger of being undersold by larger but distant eastern firms. In any case, businessmen were too bitterly divided among themselves to make common cause against the unions.

The creation of even a partial working-class identity and the growth of labor unions introduced a new component into the economic structure of the West. Workers attempted to negotiate as a group instead of as individuals. They sought collective power over both the compensation they received from their work and the conditions under which they labored. Given the dangers connected with mining, lumbering, railroading, and other occupations, the conditions of work mattered as much as the pay.

In many ways, unions, particularly in the mining industry, waged a defensive struggle. The shortage of skilled labor and the richness of many early western mines combined to give the hardrock miners in the West a legacy of high wages. Miners organized and fought both direct wage cuts and attempts to introduce lower-paid Chinese workers into the mines. The unions, too, worked as benevolent societies that compensated for the carnage in the mines by paying benefits to sick and injured miners and giving aid to the widows and orphans of the deceased.

These miners' unions, however, differed from urban craft unions in an important respect: they contained the seeds of industrial unionism. Industrial unions sought to organize all workers in an industry into a single union rather than dividing them up into various craft unions (carpenters, machinists, teamsters, and so on). Despite their ethnic and racial prejudices, the miners' unions cultivated a vision of workers as a single group with a single set of interests.

As with most unions, miners' unions tended to prosper in good times and decline in bad. Depressed prices for silver and lead in the mid-1880s brought a strong challenge to the $4.00-a-day wage that the unions had established. By 1883, mining companies were attacking the $4.00 standard in Arizona, southern Colorado, Utah, and Idaho. In Tombstone, Arizona, and Wood River, Idaho, the miners' resistance was bitter and violent, but it failed to prevent a decline in wages. Only on the Comstock Lode of Nevada did miners preserve both the $4.00-a-day wage and the eight-hour day. When a brief recovery of mineral prices in the late 1880s gave way to a slide first in silver prices and then in lead and copper prices in the early 1890s, mine owners again attempted to reduce the miners' wages. Once more miners resisted, and this time the battle lines hardened.

As mine owners cut wages in Utah, Colorado, and Montana in the early 1890s, the individual mining unions sought to create a federation that would strengthen the efforts of individual unions. Meeting at Butte in 1893, they organized the Western Federation of Miners (WFM). The new federation allowed assistance from working locals to be funneled to those on strike and also provided a corps of organizers to enlist nonunion miners. But the WFM represented more than a simple tactical move by existing unions. Convinced that the organization of the American economic and political system favored capitalists over workers, the militant unionists who controlled the WFM decided that only fundamental changes in society as a whole could improve their situation.

The initial strength of the WFM originated in Butte itself. Butte was paradoxically, given WFM radicalism, a stronghold of conservative unionism. Marcus Daly and later Anaconda exerted significant influence within the Butte local, which itself never struck, but the local did provide substantial aid in organizing the WFM. Although mine owners outside of Butte opposed the WFM at every step, the federation numbered more than 200 locals by the end of the century. The years from 1899 to 1903 were the golden age of the WFM. It grew into the most powerful single union in the West.

The WFM loomed so large in the West because it combined size and militancy with a radical ideology and an impressive local network of self-help organizations. The WFM sought to transform the economic structure of the West. Its leadership scorned the contemporary craft unions of the AF of L and withdrew from that organization in 1897. Ed Boyce, the influential Irish-born president of the WFM from 1896 to 1902, said that he considered western workers to be 100 years ahead of those in the East. He condemned the AF of L and its members for their conservative stance during the depression of the 1890s, when "4,000,000 idle men and women are tramps upon the highway, made so by the vicious system of government that will continue to grind them further into the dust until they have the manhood to get out and fight with the sword or use the ballot with intelligence." In 1897 Boyce delivered a speech to the WFM meeting in Salt Lake City urging unions to form rifle clubs and provide every member with a modern gun so that "in two years we can hear the inspiring music of the martial tread of 25,000 armed men in the ranks of labor." By 1901 the WFM had become avowedly socialist, demanding "a complete revolution of present social and economic conditions to the end that justice may be meted out to all people of the earth."

This kind of rhetoric tended to drown out the WFM's simultaneous promise to work peacefully with employers until workers were strong enough to change the system and also to obscure their impressive efforts at self-help. While struggling against capitalism, the union sought, more immediately, to improve the health, working conditions, and living conditions of its members. At least 25 affiliates of the WFM established local hospitals, and the mining unions spent more time and money on mutual aid—caring for the sick, injured, widowed, and orphaned and burying the dead—than on any other activity. This mutualism, this daily struggle to control the circumstances of their working lives, was the root of the miners' socialism.

As militant, class-conscious, and well-organized as the WFM was, it, like earlier miners' unions, most often acted defensively. In practice, the WFM was too busy defending itself against capitalists to have much time left over for overthrowing capitalism itself. The WFM engaged in nearly constant battles to maintain wage scales and working hours and to regain ground that miners had lost in the depression. The only real issues upon which the federation could mount an offensive were the drive for an eight-hour day and protective legislation to govern working conditions in the mines. By 1910, miners and smelter workers had achieved the eight-hour day, either by legislation or by contract, in most of the mining towns of the West. Their success on protective legislation was more mixed, but they did manage to get legislation controlling the silica dust that caused silicosis.

Such victories, however, only partially offset a series of disasters. Lost strikes at Cripple Creek and Coeur d'Alene and the indictment of WFM leaders for the assassination of former Idaho governor Frank Steunenberg all rocked the WFM. In Nevada, Arizona, Montana, and Utah the WFM suffered defeat after defeat in the early twentieth century. Striking miners faced federal troops and state militia as well as small private armies of gunmen hired by the mine owners. Meanwhile, their own federation grew more and more divided. In Butte ethnic and political divisions tore apart that once powerful local. In 1911 the WFM rejoined the AF of L, the very organization it had formerly so despised, and in 1916 it changed its name to the International Union of Mine, Mill and Smelter Workers (IUMMSW).

The IUMMSW proved no more able to stand against the increasingly large and powerful western corporations than had the WFM. In Arizona the Phelps-Dodge Corporation emerged in the early twentieth century as one of the new generation of mining conglomerates. Doggedly antiunion, the company in 1917 exploited ethnic and racial divisions to break a strike of workers belonging to rivals IUMMSW and Industrial Workers of the World (IWW) at company mines in Jerome and Bisbee, Arizona. Denouncing the strikers at Bisbee as an assortment of "inferior" Mexicans, aliens, and traitors, armed deputies on July 12 rounded up 1,200 strikers, loaded them onto trains, and dumped them in the desert near Hermanas, New Mexico.

The Industrial Workers of the World (IWW)

The IWW, which shared the IUMMSW's defeat at Bisbee, was the prodigal son of the WFM just as the IUMMSW was its direct heir. The WFM helped create the IWW in an attempt to organize a militant, class-conscious, and openly political labor federation that would compete with the AF of L. In 1905, William Dudley Haywood (known as "Big Bill") of the WFM called to order in Chicago the "Continental Congress of the working class," and the IWW was born. The WFM was initially the only functioning union within the IWW, but in an internal dispute that prefigured later fights that wracked the organization, the WFM withdrew from the IWW in 1906. Haywood did not follow. He resigned from the WFM in 1907 and devoted himself to the IWW.

The Wobblies, as members of the IWW were called, were syndicalists. They advocated one big union of all the world's workers that would in some vague manner usher in a working-class millennium. The Wobblies made the IWW into one of the most colorful, radical, and ultimately ineffective labor organizations in American history. Their free-speech fights proved more successful than their strikes. Because local authorities often reacted to the presence of Wobbly organizers by jailing them, the Wobblies had to fight to be heard. Wobblies practiced civil disobedience, courting arrest by public speaking until the jails could hold no more. Elizabeth Gurley Flynn, "the Rebel Girl," became one of the most prominent of the Wobbly national leaders. She excelled in these free-speech fights, and from them she drew much of the inspiration for the American Civil Liberties Union, which she co-founded years later.

Wobbly organizers promoted their millennium with the same religious fervor as did the Christian evangelists with whom they often competed for the bodies and souls of poor working people. Even the Wobblies' songs, written by songwriters such as Joe Hill and gathered in their famous "Little Red Song Book," were often parodies of the hymns with which the Salvation Army serenaded down-and-out workers. Joe Hill composed his famous "Preacher and the Slave" to the tune of "In the Sweet Bye and Bye"; it captured the Wobblies' vocal disdain for middle-class values and hypocrisy:

> Long-haired preachers come out every night,
> Try to tell you what's wrong and what's right,
> But when asked how 'bout something to eat
> They will answer with voices so sweet:
>
> Chorus:
> You will eat, by and bye,

> In that glorious land above the sky;
> Work and pray, live on hay,
> You'll get pie in the sky when you die. . . .

The IWW attracted the fierce loyalty of the migratory workers of the West who were in many ways the backbone of the western extractive economy. They cut timber and worked in sawmills, built and repaired the railroads, harvested the crops, and worked the less skilled jobs available in the mines. Most of these workers were semiskilled or unskilled. In the Southwest and California, many of them were nonwhite, but in the late nineteenth century, particularly on the Great Plains, in the Rocky Mountains, and in the Pacific Northwest, many were European immigrants. They moved from job to job because their work was often by its very nature seasonal, and long bouts of unemployment in the mines and mills interrupted their working life. Between jobs, migratory workers were the men who rode the rails looking for work. If they were lucky, they traveled in empty boxcars or gondolas; if not, they suspended themselves beneath the cars, where they hurtled along ten inches above the roadbed. William Z. Foster, who became head of the American Communist Party, had been a western migratory worker; so too, for a period, was William O. Douglas, the future Supreme Court justice. Usually single, often foreign-born, and owning little beyond what they carried with them, these men were an alienated and potentially revolutionary segment of the western working class.

The Wobblies survived because they understood the nature and the needs of the migratory working force whom the AF of L organizers usually ignored. Wobbly union halls became dormitories, social clubs, mess halls, and mail drops for migratory workers. Wobbly union cards became a pass to ride the trains unmolested. The social network the Wobblies created explains how the IWW could hold worker loyalty despite the nearly constant defeats Wobbly unions endured.

Ironically, one of the few successful strikes the Wobblies organized in the West led to their demise. Capitalizing on longstanding worker discontent with long working hours, horrible conditions, and low pay, the Wobblies virtually shut down the Washington and Idaho timber industries in the summer of 1917. The strike, however, took place in a nation at war. The United States had just entered World War I, and the armed forces demanded timber for cantonments, railroad cars, and ships. But above all, they needed Sitka spruce for the biplanes of the period, and Sitka spruce was available only in the Pacific Northwest. The government jailed the union leaders.

The Wobblies returned to work but continued the strike on the job. They acted as if they had been granted an eight-hour day, quitting work after eight hours or putting in only eight good hours in a ten-hour day. They engaged in ingenious slowdowns and sabotages. They crippled lumber production nearly as effectively as they had while on strike. The government attempted to pressure lumbermen to concede the eight-hour day, but it failed. To procure necessary production, the government organized the Loyal Legion of Loggers and Lumbermen and demanded membership from all those who wished to work in the woods; the government also delegated 25,000 troops, the Spruce Production Division, to work in the woods as needed. In exchange for breaking the union and disciplining the workers, the government mandated, and the lumbermen accepted, an eight-

The crowding, the sweat, the dirt, and the primitive conditions of this western Washington bunkhouse about 1904 made it and the bunkhouses of other logging camps fertile grounds for IWW recruiters.

hour day for the industry. The loggers had won their central demand, and reforms in working conditions and wages followed, but the government had, nonetheless, broken the Wobbly unions and jailed their leaders. Between 1917 and 1919, Idaho, Washington, California, Oregon, and other states passed criminal syndicalism laws aimed at the Wobblies. The laws made illegal membership in any organization "advocating crime, sabotage, violence or unlawful methods of terrorism" as a means of accomplishing reforms.

With the end of the war, fear of Bolshevism swept the nation following the Russian Revolution, and this fear brought the Wobblies under renewed attack. In 1919, American Legionnaires attacked a Wobbly hall and lynched Wesley Everest, a Wobbly and a war veteran with a distinguished record. This killing was part of a more general reaction against labor radicalism that followed World War I. As the government arrested and deported many radical leaders, others, including Big Bill Haywood, jumped bail and fled to the Soviet Union.

The Wobblies were largely a spent force in the Pacific Northwest after World War I. When workers in Seattle staged a general strike that shut down that city in support of striking shipyard workers, it was the Central Labor Council, an organization of AF of L unions, that led the strike. Wobblies participated and supported it, but they did not lead it. They received credit nonetheless, as many

Americans rather hysterically identified the strike with the Wobblies' apocalyptic "General Strike" that would usher in the revolution. The Seattle general strike, flawless in its immediate execution but vague in its purposes, lasted for only four days in February of 1919. Its failure allowed Mayor Ole Hanson to announce that he had saved the country from revolution and had dealt a severe blow to organized labor in Washington.

The Western Economy

The failure of the Seattle general strike was a sign of the realities of the western economy. Unions and corporations both represented attempts to organize the western economy into bigger and bigger units. Only the corporations were able to consolidate their success. The labor councils of cities like San Francisco and Seattle became, for a time, powerful forces in the economy of the region, but the failure of the Seattle general strike and the fall of labor from power in San Francisco revealed their inability to counter the power of the corporations in the western economy and in western politics.

Yet it is best to keep in mind that corporate power had its limits. Large corporations controlled transportation and the extractive industries. They largely broke the attempts of their own workers to exert control over wages and working conditions. But they did not dominate all of the economy. Retailing, farming, and ranching were still largely the domain of small businesses. And even in the sectors that they did dominate, corporations had not overcome the problems of competition. The railroads, mining companies, and timber companies that loomed so large in the western economy would soon enter a period of prolonged crisis brought on by overproduction and glutted markets.

Middle-class westerners often resented these companies that dominated the economic landscape, but corporations had succeeded in persuading most of the middle class that their real interests lay in supporting the companies against the workers who challenged them. A victory for the corporations, they argued, would signal easterners that the West was a safe place to invest. The result would be a flood of capital into the West and prosperity for all. But the flood of capital never seemed to appear, and increasingly in the twentieth century disappointed westerners would look to government rather than private investors to supply the capital that they needed for development.

Most westerners saw the rapid development of the West as their greatest triumph. They calculated their achievement in the terms that development itself mandated: tons of ore, miles of rail, bushels of wheat, heads of cattle. They converted all of these things into dollars, and there is no doubt that their achievement was great. They physically transformed the West and poured its resources out to a waiting world. But in calculating the cost of this effort they dismissed things that cannot be reduced to dollar values. No one subtracted crippled and dead miners or mill men from the gross national product. No one thought of the diminished opportunities for Indians, Hispanics, or Chinese as a cost worth assessing. Few thought that the mountain valleys ruined by hydraulic wastes or buffalo rotting on the plains represented a cost that offset the gold the mines produced or the cattle the ranches raised. Measuring these costs would come later.

Readings

Burchell, Robert A. "Opportunity and the Frontier: Wealth-Holding in Twenty-six Northern Californian Counties, 1848–1880." *Western Historical Quarterly* 52 (April 1987): 177–96.

Chan, Sucheng. *This Bittersweet Soil: The Chinese in California Agriculture, 1860–1910.* Berkeley: University of California Press, 1986.

Cox, Thomas R. *Mills and Markets: A History of the Pacific Coast Lumber Industry to 1900.* Seattle: University of Washington Press, 1974.

Decker, Peter R. *Fortunes and Failures: White-Collar Mobility in Nineteenth Century San Francisco.* Cambridge: Harvard University Press, 1978.

Derickson, Alan. *Workers' Health, Workers' Democracy: The Western Miners' Struggle, 1891–1925.* Ithaca, N.Y.: Cornell University Press, 1988.

Dubofsky, Melvyn. *We Shall Be All: A History of the Industrial Workers of the World.* Chicago: Quadrangle, 1969.

Fite, Gilbert. *The Farmer's Frontier, 1865–1900.* New York: Holt, Rinehart, and Winston, 1966.

Friedmann, Harriet. "World Market, State, and Family Farm: Social Bases of Household Production in the Era of Wage Labor." *Comparative Studies in History and Society* 20 (October 1978):545–86.

Gardner, A. Dudley, and Verla R. Flores. *Forgotten Frontier: A History of Wyoming Coal Mining.* Boulder: Westview Press, 1989.

Jameson, Elizabeth. "Women as Workers, Women As Civilizers: True Womanhood in the American West." In *The Women's West.* Ed. Susan Armitage and Elizabeth Jameson. Norman: University of Oklahoma Press, 1987.

Lingenfelter, Richard E. *The Hardrock Miners: A History of the Mining Labor Movement in the American West, 1863–93.* Berkeley: University of California Press, 1974.

Peterson, Richard. *The Bonanza Kings: The Social Origins and Business Behavior of Western Mining Entrepreneurs, 1870–1900.* Lincoln: University of Nebraska Press, 1977.

Tank, Robert M. "Mobility and Occupational Structure on the Late-Nineteenth-Century Urban Frontier: The Case of Denver, Colorado." *Pacific Historical Review* 47 (May 1978):189–216.

West, Elliott. *The Saloon on the Rocky Mountain Mining Frontier.* Lincoln: University of Nebraska Press, 1979.

Wyman, Mark. *Hard Rock Epic: Western Miners and the Industrial Revolution, 1860–1910.* Berkeley: University of California Press, 1979.

CHAPTER 12

New Communities and the Western Social Order

NINETEENTH - CENTURY migrants into the West established what amounted to a new world on top of the existing world of Indian and Hispanic villages. In some ways these worlds shaded into each other. Like Indian and Hispanic communities, most Anglo American and immigrant communities were family-based. To maintain order, they both relied on informal but highly effective means of social control such as gossip, moral sanctions, and the ability to bestow or withhold personal aid in times of need. In all of these communities women remained subordinate to men. And in all of them, although the tasks assigned to each sex differed, there were definite divisions of labor by sex. In this sense, gender effectively determined social and economic roles.

That Indians, Hispanics, and the newer migrants all organized communities was not automatic. The physical proximity of people does not insure communities; human relationships create communities. A community arises as an outgrowth of the face-to-face activities of daily life. Community depends on a variety of intimate, familiar contacts. Members of a community know and recognize each other; they share a certain kind of social experience. Emotional bonds, mutuality, or sharing—whether it be of experience, property, or emotions—mark the life of community members. Such mutuality can develop only among relatively small groups and only when there is some permanence to the myriad of individual relationships that community life involves. Mutuality defines a community, but an emphasis on mutuality should not obscure the divisions that exist even in small communities. Gender and class divisions split white communities just as gender and clan divisions often split Indian communities.

Because communities are small, it does not follow that communities and villages are synonymous. Cities can contain numerous communities. And although a community usually does belong to a particular place, it can also be mobile and transient. Communities can move if their members move together. This was as true of Norwegian settlers hiving off to form a new settlement as it was of nomadic bands of Sioux or Comanches. It is this ability of a community to be mobile that sometimes allows communities to persist even when the society has high rates of mobility. Small groups of kinspeople, friends, and former neighbors did flow along with the general stream of settlement and then precipitate out as a small intact community. Such migratory communities existed throughout the West.

Having already seen how ties of kinship and community shaped the Oregon migration, it should be no surprise, therefore, for us to find settlers in Oregon's

Willamette Valley clustered according to place of origin and kinship. At least 45 percent of the Willamette Valley's rural households had kinship ties with at least one other household group in 1850, and if more complete information were available the connections would undoubtedly prove to be far greater. In antebellum Oregon kinship ties and the ties between former neighbors created the basis for the neighborhoods of the new settlements. Among German Jewish immigrants, kinship ties similarly formed the foundation of new communities. Bernard Goldsmith, who settled in Portland, eventually brought seven younger brothers to join him.

This pattern of community formation often created neighborhoods and villages that tended to be clannish and closed. The existence of such rural communities helps explain why there is a correlation between persistence in a community and economic success. Members of an existing community would certainly be more likely to welcome and aid new migrants who were their kinspeople or friends than they would strangers. The different receptions offered to kinspeople and strangers, in turn, made it far more likely that those with prior connections within a community would stay and those without such connections would leave. A single New England man in a Kentucky settlement in Oregon, for example, might have worked a season or two as a laborer, but chances were that he would not stay permanently. Without access to credit, cooperative labor, and aid, it would have been difficult for him to establish a farm.

Immigrant Communities

Immigrant farming settlements on the prairies and plains can serve as an example of the complexity of successful community creation. To an outsider such communities seemed the simple result of common ethnicity, but the filters that sifted community members were, in fact, far finer. Within European rural areas, dialect, culture, and social practices varied considerably over short distances. A random group of Swedes in the Dakotas might have very little in common. But Swedes usually segregated themselves as finely as possible by province and even parish of origin. They thus formed cohesive communities linked together by multiple ties of religion, kinship, dialect, and custom. In the Dalesburg Community in Clay County, South Dakota, for example, settlers from upper Dalarna settled together, as did those from the Bothnian Coast and those from Östergötland. In some cases definite subcommunities formed as settlers grouped themselves according to the very parish they came from in the home country. Evidence from Minnesota indicates that the more homogeneous a Swedish migrant community was at its creation, the lower was its future rate of emigration.

Such finely selected communities were rarer in western cities, but they did occur. Irish immigrants to Butte, Montana, came heavily from the west of Ireland, particularly from County Cork. Of the 1,700 people who migrated to the United States from the single parish of Eyeries in the township of Castletownbere in Cork between 1870 and 1915, 1,138 made their way to Butte. As late as 1917 a parish priest could write back to Ireland that "everyone here is from Castletownbere."

Chinese immigrants to San Francisco were largely from Guangdong province,

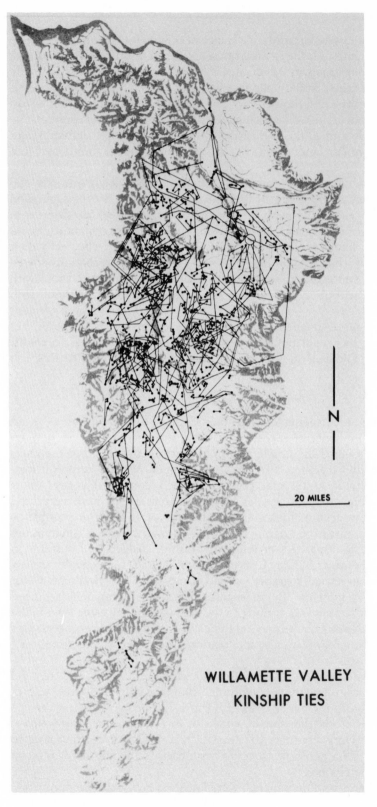

**WILLAMETTE VALLEY
KINSHIP TIES**

Willamette Valley kinship ties. From William Bowen, *Willamette Valley: Migration and Settlement on the Oregon Frontier* (Seattle: University of Washington Press, 1978), p. 52.

20 MILES

N

and they organized themselves both into *fongs*—groups with ties of kinship, clan, and village originating in Guangdong—and into *huigans*, which were traditional organizations formed by people from the same province or districts while away from home. *Huigans* had become in China a typical form of merchant organization, and in California the *huigans* became known as companies; the six *huigans* that affiliated together in San Francisco became known as the Six Companies.

The affiliation of the Six Companies, with its full-time officials, evolved into a kind of governing body for the California Chinese, and the California *huigans* had branches in virtually all western Chinatowns. The leadership of the Six Companies settled disputes between individual Chinese and among the companies themselves, formulated strategies for defense against Anglo American persecution, represented laborers in disputes with employers, and arranged the public celebrations of the Chinese communities. Usually headed by successful merchants, the Six Companies maintained houses for transient laborers and altars for religious worship. The combined organization nurtured, protected, and governed a self-contained community life largely shielded from outside interference.

High rates of mobility in these immigrant communities did not necessarily destroy such community ties. Migration became a part of the natural life of the communities. Among Norwegians, for example, a move west often signified adulthood, marriage, or the formation a new household. Such moves represented less an abandonment of the home community than a hiving off. Migrants often departed in the company of neighbors. And if their goal was not the formation of a new community, then their destination was most likely another Norwegian community that contained kinspeople or former neighbors. Thus, even though a community might have relatively high turnover in population, it could still remain relatively homogeneous and cohesive.

Mormon Communities

Mormon communities shared similar traits of high turnover and community cohesiveness. Mormons, attempting to settle as rapidly as possible the various farming oases of the Great Basin, engaged in the most systematic attempt at community creation in the West. Although most Mormons moved voluntarily to areas that seemed agriculturally promising, the church itself planned other colonies and "called" or assigned people to them. In doing so, Brigham Young could draw on an allegiance no other institution in the West could command. Joseph Grafton Hovey, for example, responded to his call by writing in his diary for November 6, 1850: "The President Called out some Hundred to go and make a Settlement in Iron county on the Little Salt Lake. I Joseph being called to go also not withstanding my hard labours since I have been in the valley. I am willing to forsake all and go build up the Kingdom of God . . . there seams to be no stopping place for a man but he must do the will of God." A move such as Hovey's hardly represented a dissolution of a community or an obstacle to creating a new one.

Mormons quickly created cohesive, homogeneous communities organized around the church. Church leaders supervised the settlements, reminding settlers that brotherhood and cooperation should characterize their efforts and that they were engaged in a religious as well as a secular pursuit. They often cooperatively built schools, canals, irrigation ditches, meeting houses, and homes and distributed the land. By the end of the nineteenth century the Mormons had created 500 such communities stretching from Alberta, Canada, to Chihuahua, Mexico, and from Bunkerville, Nevada, to the San Luis Valley of Colorado. These were remarkably orderly places. In 1851, George A. Smith, the leader of the Iron County mission, wrote that the Fourth of July celebration in the new town of Parowan had been placid, with "not a gun fired, nor a drunken man seen in the streets." Smith's seemingly casual remark about the quiet streets of Parowan highlighted exactly what set the kin-based and utopian settlements of the West apart from the mining camps, cattle towns, and cities with which they shared the region. It was the noisy, chaotic, and sometimes violent streets of these places that caused many Americans to worry about the lack of community and social order in the West.

"Modern" Migration and Community Formation

Not all western migrants moved in the well-defined and secure streams that governed kin-based and utopian settlements. Part of the high rates of mobility in the West came from individuals, particularly single males and poorer workers and farmers (both male and female, single and married), who were not rooted in any western community. Single males were particularly prevalent in urban areas. In antebellum Oregon, for example, men outnumbered women everywhere, but in the countryside where families labored on farms, the percentage of men (58 percent) was smaller than in the cities (69 percent). Far more dramatic differences, however, existed in the mining camps and, at least seasonally, in the cattle towns.

The large numbers of single, mobile men who came west presented the greatest challenge to western community formation. Nineteenth-century writings on the American West reflect a pervasive fear that such unattached men would never permanently settle. Failing to form community ties of their own, they seemed to present a constant danger to those communities that did establish themselves in the West. "Left by themselves, men degenerate rapidly and become rough, harsh, slovenly—almost brutish," Reverend William Goode wrote after visiting the Colorado mines. The dangers presented by a society of rootless men appeared most clearly to those whom Victorian society thought naturally pious and pure: middle-class women. Protestant women organized various "home" missionary societies that pursued a double goal in the West: they sought to reassert Christian social order based on Victorian family values of piety and purity and also to establish the moral authority of women vis-à-vis men.

The anxiety that this population of rootless young males generated in the larger society is in some ways surprising, for such males seemed to be conforming to the prevailing social ideologies of late-nineteenth-century America: individualism and laissez-faire. Nineteenth-century Americans assumed that progress toward the best possible society would result from the actions of individuals who were free to pursue their individual welfare unburdened by any but the most basic institutional restraints. But what nineteenth-century Americans celebrated in economic and social theory, they feared as a social fact when they seemed to encounter it in the West. A western mining camp seemed to carry individualism and laissez-faire capitalism to their logical, and threatening, conclusion. When confronted with such unfettered individualism, many Americans immediately prescribed community, family, and stability as necessary antidotes. Mining camps and cattle towns, precisely because of the anxiety they generated, provide us with the best window on western attitudes toward community and the steps that westerners took to create communities.

Creating Community: The Problem

The Gold Rush created in California a phenomenon that other mining camps, logging camps, and cattle towns would replicate during the remainder of the nineteenth century: a largely male, highly mobile work force, the members of which were either single or separated by great distances from their wives and children. In 1850 the population of California was an astonishing 93 percent male. Young male adults between 20 and 40, for example, made up 90 percent of the population of the mining camp of Grass Valley in 1850. Americans conceived of community as necessarily based on families, but given California's demographic profile, such communities clearly were impossible.

How could a community emerge when these young male miners not only lived outside of families, but also consulted only their own prospects for wealth in deciding whether to move or stay? No one seemed to set down roots. Approximately 90 percent of those present in Grass Valley in 1850 were gone by 1856. This restless search for wealth and the physical mobility it engendered among a group of single men had produced a society of incredible rootlessness, diversity, and fragility.

Even under these extreme conditions some links based on kinship and prior locale did form. About 32 percent of households sampled in Grass Valley, for example, contained male kinsmen, and men tended to associate with others from the same town, state, or region. Men worked beside and fought beside those of similar origins; they fought against and segregated themselves from those of different origins. Without wives and daughters, however, such connections were sterile. Since only 3 percent of the men in Grass Valley had families present in 1850, the self-perpetuating family-based communities of rural areas could not arise. And women who did enter these camps often seemed at risk. Abby Mansur wrote home from Horse Shoe Bar, California, of the career of a Mrs. French, who, on leaving her husband, stopped "first with one man and then with another" but, getting pregnant, moved in with a man "that is married and has a wife and 4 children at home." Mansur concluded, "That is the way the men do here." Communities failed to emerge from this mobile, fragmented mass of single men.

How then did communities form in mining camps? We must differentiate between community and mere order—that is, the imposition of rules for the transfer of property, the institution of government, and so on. Order existed in early mining camps. An early mining camp was a modern libertarian's dream world, for there, in a society that existed only to create wealth, government served only to secure and protect property. Miners created their own mining law and their own local governments, but by and large government enforced only the basic rules necessary to establish claims to gold, silver, and other minerals. The mining camp had no larger community goals, and except for the saloon, few community institutions. As one Nevada City storekeeper put it, "the sociable man is lost in the money making."

Miners did not create such a minimal society out of ideological conviction. They could not shed their past lives and values as easily as they had shed their eastern clothes. They had been raised in families and communities whose social life involved far more than accumulating property. Most of them shared a common belief in a Victorian moral order in which community revolved around domesticity and the home and in which "true" women who were pure and pious made the home a haven from the world. But in the mining camps the home, "true" women, and censorious public opinion were largely absent. As a result, as Julian Rolph observed of Montana: "Men without the restraint of law, indifferent to public opinion, and unburdened by families, drink whenever they feel like it, whenever they have the money to pay for it, and whenever there is nothing else to do. . . . Bad manners follow, profanity becomes a matter of course. . . . Excitability and nervousness brought on by rum help these tendencies along, and then to correct this state of things the pistol comes into play." Miners tolerated this half-world because they believed that they would only reside there temporarily. Far from envisioning a future spent outside familiar community boundaries, they intended to reenter those old communities as wealthy men.

The ultimate intention of miners did not change the immediate reality of their situation; they lived at least temporarily in a society where the search for wealth overwhelmed everything from labor to love, reducing them both to commodities. Perhaps the most telling sign of the fragility of normal social ties is miners' acceptance of sex as a mere commodity, something to be bought and sold. A miner could purchase sex as readily as he purchased a shovel, and the purchase of one signified no greater commitment to the seller than the purchase of the other. Prostitution usually has emerged on a large scale where there are large ratios of men to women, where the men are rootless and mobile, and where sufficient money is available to pay for sexual favors. It also prospered in nineteenth-century America because of the prevailing cultural myth of female passionlessness: "normal" women did not enjoy sex. Culturally and socially, the mining camps provided an ideal situation for prostitution to prosper. In the Comstock Lode of Nevada, where the towns of Gold Hill and Virginia City boomed in the 1860s and 1870s, in 1860 there were 2,306 men to only 30 women. The growth of prostitution in such a place was striking. A decade later, when the Comstock Lode contained a more sexually balanced population, men still outnumbered women by two to one and prostitution continued to flourish. As late as 1875, at least 1 in 12 Comstock women was a prostitute.

In all, probably more than 50,000 prostitutes worked the American West during the late nineteenth century. Prostitutes in the mining and cattle towns worked in bordellos, saloons, and dance halls; they walked the streets; and they worked out of narrow one-room adobe or wood shacks called cribs. There was a hierarchy of prostitutes. The elite worked in bordellos; the most lowly walked the street or worked in the cribs. Unlike most hierarchies, in this one most women started out at the top of their profession and descended as they aged.

The Demimonde and Community

The ubiquity of prostitution and the absence of families in these largely male communities undercut the normal community structure of homes presided over by the "true" women that governed Victorian family life, but conceivably alternative communities could have developed. Prostitutes might have formed a community among themselves, or a community of sorts might have developed among the prostitutes, their pimps, and their customers. Western myth often pretends that such communities did form. In these myths prostitutes have hearts of gold. They nurse the sick and contribute to charity, and men in the bordellos pay for sex but have real affection for those who sell.

In the West neither of these potential communities seems to have emerged; prostitution was a business in which women exchanged sex for money. A few women succeeded at it and accumulated property. In Helena, Montana, for example, women dominated prostitution in the 1870s and 1880s not only in the obvious sense that they provided the sexual services, but also in the sense that they ran the brothels and owned the buildings in which they worked. Successful prostitutes in Helena in 1880 earned from $179 to $339 a month at a time when a saleswoman obtained $65 a month. Some used their earnings to accumulate wealth. In the 1880s a madam, Josephine Hensley, or "Chicago Jo," came to control the Helena demimonde. She owned most of the property in the tenderloin district of saloons and brothels. But in the 1880s the prosperity of Helena's prostitutes began to diminish. Most independent prostitutes became renters instead of owners of property. And by the 1890s men instead of women controlled the vice trade as pimps took over from the madams. As the pimps took over, violence, suicide, and accidental death became more prominent features of life of prostitutes in the demimonde.

Violence appeared late among prostitutes in Helena, but violence and poverty seem to have marred the lives of most prostitutes in the West well before the 1890s. Many women had become prostitutes to escape lives already deteriorating into disaster. They entered brothels either to combat economic hardship or to flee from unsatisfactory marriages, or after having been abandoned, divorced, or widowed. Often they had children to support. Prostitution usually only accelerated the course of disaster. With sex stripped of affection and commitment, they and their customers shared only a mutual distrust. Although some prostitutes did manage to form friendships that sustained them through crises, their relationships more often seem to have been ones of rivalry, competition, and jealousy.

The ties prostitutes formed with their male customers and pimps proved just as fragile. These men offered them more violence than aid. Beatings and even murders of prostitutes rarely commanded the attention of the law. Many prostitutes married and many did bear children while continuing to ply their profession, but few of them succeeded as either wives or mothers. Most faced lives of poverty, alcoholism, disease, violence, and drug addiction. Many ended their lives by suicide.

What made prostitution notable in the West was not its existence, for it existed throughout the United States, but its centrality to early social life in these largely male camps and towns. Prostitution and gambling were the center of the demimonde. The demimonde existed in most places as a subterranean counterworld to normal bourgeois life, but in the early mining towns, and later in cattle towns, the demimonde was above-ground and dominant. Prostitution would not retain its eminence in most of these towns, but neither would it entirely disappear. Gradually, emerging communities restricted prostitutes to certain districts. Segregated but not banished, they served at once as sexual outlets for men, as a source

"Chicago Jo," successful madam of Helena, Montana, was one of the relatively few women to prosper in the demimonde.

of revenue for the towns and cities that fined and taxed them, and as a warning of the penalties paid by women who did not conform to the social roles demanded of them in American society.

Formation of Communities

Prostitutes, gamblers, and saloon owners existed as a kind of antithesis to what Harriet Behrins, who came to California in 1851, called the "refined home life" of Victorian America. Behrins later remembered walking to church on her first Sabbath in California when she passed two men dangling dead from the building where the San Francisco vigilantes had hanged them; saw bulls, "decorated with gay ribbons, on the way to the Presidio, to fight to the death," running through the streets with "a mob at their heels"; and walked by saloons and gambling houses with doors open to "tempt the weak ones." Her heart "became heavy with the knowledge of so much evil" and a longing for the home life she had left behind.

For Behrins and other proselytizers for family and community, prostitutes, gamblers, and saloon owners became the symbol of a society without community. The bordellos, gambling halls, and saloons yielded towns like Leadville, which the novelist Mary Hallock Foote dismissed as a "senseless, rootless place." Mining towns, an Idaho schoolteacher declared, were "the hardest place to live upon principle I ever saw, and the young are almost sure to be led away." For reformers, the Victorian family and the Protestant church became the only means to stabilize a rootless and dangerous social world.

Reformers, who drew heavily from middle-class merchants and middle-class Protestant women, propounded stability instead of transiency, "respectable" women instead of prostitutes, thrift instead of gambling, temperance instead of saloons, and the family instead of the world of single men. Merchants and women worked in concert in most reform efforts, but their aims were not always fully harmonious, for the struggle to impose morality involved a simultaneous struggle over who would be the arbiters of morality: men or women.

Merchants, a group seemingly the most likely to subscribe to the ideology of the free market, were among the first to try to curb the sway of the market over the social life of the West. As more permanent towns emerged, merchants mounted campaigns for moral reform which they saw as the essential beginning for community life. Merchants were the ones, after all, who had made the earliest and greatest commitment to and investment in a town. To profit on their investment, they needed stability. If a town failed or lost out to rival towns, its merchants lost. But their interest was not simply mercenary. Like other men in mining camps, they had never intended their departure from community life to be permanent. "We are here," a Dodge City, Kansas, editor proclaimed in 1885, "to live and get rich." He summarized aptly enough the dual ambition of many middle-class town dwellers. But if they were going to live in mining towns or cattle towns, then they would have to create communities within them.

Community for these Victorian merchants meant women and families, and women and families demanded common standards of respectability to thrive. Middle-class citizens quite naturally measured a town's respectability and stability by its ability to repress "immorality." Crime, prostitution, opium dens, saloons, and bawdy theatres all were in a sense business activities, but they were also marks of what was, according to contemporary American standards, a prevailing immorality that threatened their desire for a stable community life. How could families thrive in such an atmosphere? And without families, there could be no community. Vice, therefore, had to be controlled.

Moral reform became the centerpiece of self-conscious middle-class attempts to create community. But those who attacked drugs, prostitution, liquor, gambling, and crime took a second significant step. They did not just define and attack "immorality"; they associated immoral activities with particular ethnic and racial groups. Thus in California an attack on murderers and robbers could become an attack on Mexican Americans, who Anglo Americans asserted were inherently violent criminals. Similarly, attacks on drugs and prostitution often became attacks on Chinese, who were supposedly drug addicts infected with special strains of sexually transmitted disease. Some Mexican Americans indeed committed crimes, and some Chinese did use opium, but reformers jumped from these verifiable observations to the conclusion that all crime, all drug problems, and all prostitution were the fault of particular ethnic groups. They then made these ethnic groups the symbolic targets of reform. Such efforts were far more successful at punishing or driving off minority groups than in eradicating the evils under attack.

If minorities became associated with vice in this scheme, "true womanhood," at least white womanhood, was associated with virtue. Certainly this is how many middle-class women in the West saw their role. Eliza Farnham, in her influential 1856 book *California, Indoors and Out*, wrote: "There is . . . no honorable woman but is a missionary of virtue, morality, happiness and peace to a circle of careworn, troubled, and often, alas, demoralized men."

Farnham was drawing on a version of womanhood that had achieved cultural dominance in the mid-nineteenth-century United States. Historians have labeled this ideology as the cult of true womanhood or, more briefly, domesticity. Men had once governed the home, but as they moved outside of it to work, middle-class women became the guardians of hearth, children, and domestic values. In Puritan New England men had been responsible for the religious instruction of their wives and children. Now, as churches became increasingly feminine in membership, Americans agreed that women were naturally more moral and religious. The country confused culture with nature, and women were pronounced to be frail, retiring, moral beings whose proper sphere was home, church, and children.

The cult of true womanhood proved particularly useful in attempts to restrict the demimonde and to build up middle-class, family-oriented communities in places like Grass Valley and Nevada City, California, or, later, Dodge City or Caldwell, Kansas. As merchants and professionals in these towns established permanent businesses there, many either sent for their families or went east to marry and returned with a wife. In terms of numbers, these men with families remained heavily outnumbered by single men. In Grass Valley only 7 percent of working men lived with wives in 1860, and in Nevada City the number was only 13 percent. Similarly, in their early years Dodge City, Caldwell, and Wichita, Kansas, were all bachelor towns. But once established, even a small number of families encouraged the emergence of a community life separate from the demimonde, and these communities mounted an assault on the demimonde itself.

As the number of families in such towns increased, they formed a self-conscious social circle. They organized their own clubs; they held their own dances. Western white women in particular seemed determined to create churches and schools for their children as soon as possible. In the first years of a mining or cattle town, women on their way to church and children on their way to school could not avoid some contact with prostitutes, gamblers, and rowdy drunks. In 1879, for example, Leadville, Colorado, boasted 120 saloons, 19 beer halls, and 188 gambling houses and private club rooms and only four churches. Married women encountered, and often quarreled with, prostitutes on the streets, and they feared that prostitutes might influence their daughters. Occasionally brothels and middle-class homes bordered each other. Merchants, professionals, and their wives demanded restriction of the demimonde of prostitutes, gamblers, and saloon owners that they found all around them. They wanted a world in which the emerging Victorian ideal of an innocent and sheltered childhood could exist.

Protestant Churches

The attack on the demimonde and the Protestant missionizing of the West were intimately linked. Protestant churches regarded the salvation of the "New West" as part of their Christian and patriotic duty. Combining secular and religious millennial themes, ministers proclaimed that if the West became safely Protestant, the republic would thrive. If it did not, American liberties would end. Protestants had to save the West from Mormons and from Catholics, but most of all they had to save it from its own moral decay. In all, the various Protestant mission boards may have poured $76 million into the western churches.

Ministers arrived in the West to save souls, establish churches, and reform society—tasks which for them remained inseparable. They were not people to downplay the challenge. Presbyterian Alexander T. Rankin described Denver in 1860 as a city that put "no restraint on human passion." The common saying in Kansas in the 1870s was that there was "no Sunday west of Junction City and no god west of Salina." In 1880, Baptist James Spencer thought he could postmark the letters he sent from Butte as coming "from Hell." Although early ministers sometimes held their initial services in saloons and gambling halls, ministerial assaults on gambling, prostitution, and saloons usually marked the opening volley of the Protestant campaign to redeem the West.

Such moral offensives usually met stiff resistance from opponents, who either identified ministers with a demasculization of the West or who equated them with the very gamblers and confidence men the ministers opposed. Colorado Congregationalist James Walker recalled that "the minister was 'sis' to the average cowman." Ministers were also "Gospel sharks," "Gospel sharps," or "sky pilots." When a traveling salesman asked Utah's Episcopal bishop how long he had been "peddling salvation," he clearly granted no privileged status to missionary endeavors.

But ministers also found allies in their crusade who, while just as skeptical of theology as the opponents of religion, regarded churches as socially beneficial. Josiah Royce, the Harvard philosopher and native Californian, recalled that in Gold Rush California "there was from the first, the characteristic American feeling prevalent that churches were a good and sober element in the social order, and that one wanted them to prosper, whether one took a private and personal interest in any of them or not." This attitude that churches signified civility, permanence,

This collection of Dodge City photographs features its churches in order to emphasize the city's progression from cowtown to stable community.

and a belief in progress, and thus were necessary elements of a stable, orderly, prosperous society, became what California Methodists by the 1870s approvingly called "business Christianity." Its equivalents could be found in the common desire of western town boosters, Christian and non-Christian alike, to encourage church buildings as a sign of town stability and prosperity. As the *Albuquerque Morning Democrat* editorialized in 1893, "a church does as much to build up a town as a school, a railroad, or a fair." Indeed, so ecumenical could be the appeal of a Protestant church as a sign of stability, order, and urban health that Jewish merchants in many western towns often contributed to Protestant church building funds. In nineteenth-century Texas, the growth in church membership paralleled the rise of commercial farming and economic prosperity. Texans and other westerners became more churchgoing as they became more prosperous and settled.

The Protestant moral crusade in the West became significant as early as the 1850s, when reformers sought temperance, Sabbatarianism (the restriction of public activities on Sunday to religious worship), and the restriction of gambling in California. Most of these measures failed to achieve their ends completely, but they did gradually succeed in restricting the demimonde to specific sections of town, where officials taxed and fined gamblers, saloon owners, and prostitutes to cover the cost of their own policing.

Later, in the cattle towns of the Great Plains, the same pattern partially repeated itself. There, too, Protestant reformers rooted in the churches also spoke for a community based on families and stability. There, too, some merchants argued that moral reform would yield the social stability necessary for prolonged prosperity. But in the cattle towns, unlike the mining towns, such a position split the business community because it seemed to threaten the immediate economic interests of the town. Minerals are not mobile. Miners had to come to gold and silver deposits no matter what rules a town enforced. Cattle, however, are mobile, and if cattlemen did not think a town was receptive, they could go elsewhere. Many businessmen were wary of eliminating the services cowboys demanded. They opposed movements to prohibit the sale of alcohol, resisted Sabbatarianism, and tried to block restrictions on gambling. But in Kansas the reformers won a sweeping statewide victory in 1880 when the people amended the constitution to provide for total prohibition of liquor by 1881. The enforcement of such laws became thereafter a leading issue in the cattle towns. Some saloons continued to operate openly; other liquor sellers created "blind tigers," where they sold liquor covertly.

Eliminating vice formed the first phase of the middle-class drive for stable communities; the second phase was the inculcation of virtue. Churches became the leading institutions for shaping public morals in the West, but paradoxically their public activities usually won them more influence than members. That many found reasons to support the churches without joining them was reflected in the West's continuing status as the region with the largest unchurched population. Many western towns boasted an abundance of churches and a paucity of church members. The presence of numerous competing Protestant denominations spread the churchgoers thin. Instead of competing for the churchgoing population, Protestant ministers came to cooperate. In the West, outside of the southern Great Plains, theological differences tended to take on lessened significance. When Protestants desired sectarian battles, they could always demonize the Catholics and Mormons; they had no need to attack each other. In many western towns, Sunday schools—interdenominational bible study classes—tended to attract more people than did the churches themselves. In California, Thomas Starr King, a San Francisco Unitarian minister, symbolized this generic interdenominational Protestantism. King, who attained astonishing popularity before his death at the age of 40 in 1864, made the Anglo American settlement of California a culmination of God's plan as well as a vindication of the movement for equality and dignity of labor. He linked California to American destiny and Christian destiny. He assured Californians there was an ordering force behind the seeming chaos of the Gold Rush.

Comparative Protestant unity and a focus on moral and social instead of theological issues gave the churches considerable influence on western society. But in the establishment of a western social order, the women of the congregation, as well as the ministers, emerged as critical figures. From the Victorian home there emanated a powerful constellation of values that united women, domesticity, and virtue.

Some middle-class Protestant women pushed the premises of Victorian culture that associated women, religion, and virtue to their logical conclusion: If women were more pure and moral than men, then should not women exercise moral authority within society? Throughout the West, in rescue homes for Mormon polygamist women or Chinese prostitutes, in homes for unwed mothers, and in temperance crusades, Protestant missionary women attempted to exercise this moral authority. Missionary women gradually formulated a critique of male-dominated social orders and their consequences, but as white Protestant women they initially dared attack only those men already beyond the bounds of Victorian

The Victorian home was the center of a powerful constellation of values that at once confined women and gave them cultural and social power in the West.

society. They branded Chinese and Mormon men, for example, as immoral defilers of women because Mormons and Chinese were already pariahs in the nineteenth-century West and thus relatively safe targets. But in efforts to help polygamist wives, Chinese prostitutes, and unwed mothers, Protestant missionary women had identified unrestrained male lust as the major force victimizing women. Their attack on male lust led some of them to a critique of their own society.

The missionary impulse of Protestant women in the West took the conventional Victorian female virtues of piety, purity, and domesticity and made them subversive. As Winifred Spaulding of the Woman's Christian Temperance Union in Colorado wrote in 1892, the "making of a Christian home is the highest sphere of woman," but to create such a home, women must have a "sturdy, independence of spirit" that would allow them to reject vice. And if marrying a bad man was the only choice available to a woman, it was better that she should not marry at all. In such common situations "noble minded girls" should "support themselves and make their homes with other girls." Starting from the conventional premise, Spaulding had justified both a female moral authority higher than male moral authority and independent lives for women. Although most Protestant women did not go as far as Spaulding, their own efforts to secure piety and purity often led them into conflict with their male allies in reform.

Male reformers feared women were taking too much control and escaping their "place." Such quarrels between men and women reformers surfaced throughout the West. They split missionary efforts at the Industrial Christian Home for polygamist women in Utah (an effort never very successful to begin with), and they caused difficulties when the Methodist Church General Conference in 1888 rejected Angie Newman of the home missionary societies as a delegate to that body because she was a woman. Most middle-class men accepted the conventional Victorian belief that "true" women and the home formed the basis of society, but they grew uncomfortable when women began to assert their own moral authority.

By associating women with piety and purity, the cult of true womanhood clearly linked women with morality and religion; but the connection of women with education was less obvious. Male Protestant ministers often took the initial steps in bringing education, particularly high school and college education, to the West, and many of the first schoolteachers were male. School boards tended to take whoever was immediately available, and standards were rough and ready. Organizers of Denver's first school recruited Oliver Goldrick after he entered town in a Prince Albert coat cursing his team in Greek, Latin, and Sanskrit.

The availability of schools and teachers varied wildly. In 1870, Nevada had only 38 schools, or about 7 for every thousand school-aged children, while the figures for Montana and Nebraska were among the highest in the nation. In general, western states did well in getting urban children into the classroom and poorly in getting rural children into the schools.

Because western population was sparse, fewer taxpayers provided for the schools than in the East, thus increasing individual tax burdens. Between 1880 and 1920 the West spent more per capita on education than any other region. California's willingness to tax for education produced probably the best nineteenth-century school system in the nation. Elsewhere results were mixed. A Montana official in 1873 found most schoolhouses "a terror to behold."

The widespread perception that male schoolteachers in the West took the jobs because, as one Californian wrote, they were "too lazy to work, hadn't the ability to gamble and . . . couldn't scrape a little on the fiddle" created particular opportunities for women teachers. Wages, while higher than in the East, were not high enough to hold qualified male teachers. And when the Leadville, Colorado, school board had to urge the prosecution of an instructor for "shooting at scholars," the classroom was ripe for domesticity.

Even more so than in the rest of the country, a vast majority of the Anglo American public schoolteachers in the late-nineteenth-century American West were women. This connection between women teachers and the American West had originated in the middle of the nineteenth century. Beginning in 1846, the National Popular Education Board began to recruit single women in the Northeast to teach in the West. At that time the "West" was largely the Midwest, but during the next ten years women teachers recruited by the board did go to Oregon, Kansas, and Nebraska.

These teachers went west both from a real missionary idealism and also because young adulthood otherwise promised to be a bleak and empty period of their lives. The National Popular Education Board drew heavily from New England, where many young women faced a dilemma for which their upbringing had given them little preparation. In a society that expected women to marry young, changing

As this Idaho school scene shows, the successful movement of women into western school teaching was one aspect of an imperial vision of the home which stretched domesticity to create new possibilities for western women.

demographic and economic patterns had created a situation in which New England women could no longer count on marriage as soon as they reached adulthood. To many rural New England women looking for alternatives, teaching promised to provide not only an independent income, but also a chance to help "civilize" the West. Catharine Beecher, who developed the plan to send eastern teachers to the West, thought Protestant women teachers would redeem the region. And the general agent of the board, former governor William Slade of Vermont, insisted that the organization recruit only women because Slade believed it was women's special task to "rescue" a West where men had abandoned all else in a quest for wealth. Without women's moral influence as teachers, wrote Sarah Josepha Hale, editor of *Godey's Lady's Book* and one of the most prominent formulators of the cult of true womanhood, western "gold will prove a curse and not a blessing."

By extending the logic of the cult of true womanhood, middle-class western women in the late nineteenth century had little trouble in establishing the classroom as a domain as rightfully theirs in nineteenth-century terms as the kitchen or parlor. Classrooms seemed, after all, to be but extensions of the home and thus rightfully under the control of women. Once women established their right to teach, however, their concerns came to have less to do with civilizing the West than with carving out more opportunities for the young western women who became teachers. If Colorado serves as an adequate representative of western teachers in the late nineteenth century, women soon began to see teaching as a career. They no longer thought of it as merely a prelude to eventual marriage or as a temporary mission to save the West. Teaching allowed young women to become independent, if poorly paid, professionals at a time when virtually all other professions remained closed to them. In Colorado at a time when men outnumbered women in the state by a ratio of four to three, women teachers married and bore children at far lower rates than did other women. If faced with a choice between marriage and a profession, many Colorado teachers chose their profession. A movement into the classroom that grew out of the belief in women's inherent domesticity thus began to give women options that extended beyond the normal life course of maturity, marriage, and childbearing.

The cult of true womanhood came to play an ironic role for middle-class women both in the West and elsewhere in the United States. Domesticity made women and the family the necessary basis of order and "civilization" and gave women a central role in imposing that order. But domesticity allowed western women to expand their social role in unanticipated ways. Central to the cult of true womanhood was the idea that women's natural sphere was the home, but in the West, and elsewhere, women developed an imperial vision of the home. They were quick to extend its boundaries not only into the classroom but also into the culturally defined male sphere of business and commerce. In rural areas women supplemented family income by selling eggs and making and selling butter, and women in the mining towns also worked. In Grass Valley in the 1860s and 1870s the women in the majority of married households supplemented their husband's income by sewing, washing, or, most commonly, taking in boarders. Again, these tasks fit within the culturally defined female domestic sphere, but by making these jobs commercial, women blurred the boundaries between women's sphere of home and men's sphere of remunerative labor. Even as the basic American Protestant cultural order of families and strict gender divisions of labor rose in the West, small cracks had begun to appear in its foundation.

Chinese settlements in the West, which shared none of the ideological underpinnings of Anglo American communities, had to face many of the same challenges to community as did the western mining camps, cities, and cattle towns of which the Chinatowns were often a part. How, from a transient mass of young single males, could people establish a community tied to a set of values geared to something beyond the acquisition of wealth?

The Chinese approached the problem from a cultural perspective quite alien to the cult of true womanhood and Victorian morality in general, but neither could the Chinese transplant traditional communities in the West. They had, first of all, to live in the midst of a dynamic capitalist economy unlike anything in China. Second, few members of gentry families migrated. There could be no class of landowning literati in Chinese communities; instead, merchants appropriated the highest rungs of the social ladder. Finally, few Chinese women migrated to the United States, thus severely limiting the number of families.

Chinese tongs had a complicated relation to prostitution. Most tongs (a word that means hall or parlor) were benevolent societies of the kind common enough among other groups in the West. Some, however, were secret societies, and a few were criminal organizations run by the so-called highbinders, or hatchet men, involved in the opium trade and prostitution. These secret societies became powerful organizations in America that became visible to outsiders only when their feuds erupted into violent tong wars. Such wars became increasingly prevalent in San Francisco in the 1880s.

The eruption of the tong wars and the increasing denunciations by Anglo Americans of opium addiction and Chinese prostitution eventually led to a concerted attack on the Chinese tongs and demimonde. Prostitution was as prevalent in Chinese settlements as in white settlements. In 1860 virtually all Chinese women in northern California were prostitutes. In 1870, 61 percent of the 3,356 Chinese women in California were listed as prostitutes, a figure that declined to 46 percent in 1880. Christian home missionary efforts to create rescue homes for Chinese women sold into prostitution were the most visible aspects of this attack on the demimonde, but other measures came from native-born members of the Chinese community. Organized in groups such as the Chinese Society of English Education, the Chinese Students' Alliance, and the Chinese Native Sons, Chinese Americans moved in the 1890s to stamp out prostitution in the region's Chinatowns. By then, however, an increase in the number of Chinese women in California had made prostitution less central to Chinese American life. Second-generation Chinese Americans, too, were instrumental in breaking the power of the violent tongs. In this they had the aid of Chinese consuls, who cooperated with the Anglo American authorities in repressing the gangs, even arresting and imprisoning the gang members' relatives and associates in China. Although employing different cultural methods, the Chinese, too, repressed the demimonde and established communities.

Community and the Larger World

Communities aspired to create order, predictability, security, mutuality, and familiarity. They promised a known, bounded world. But given the scale and complexity of western society, few individuals could spend their entire life within the sheltering bounds of a community. A Pueblo village, a Scandinavian farming community, a Kansas town, or a neighborhood of immigrant workers in San Francisco all might try to live by their own values and customs, but they were small islands always being flooded by a larger governmental and economic sea or invaded by members of adjoining communities.

Western towns often contained several distinct communities. Emporia, Kansas, a division center on the Santa Fe Railroad, for example, contained at least three distinct communities: one of successful businessmen, professionals, and their families; another of white workers, both those employed by the railroad and others; and, finally, a third and smaller community of blacks. Even these units might not fit a strict definition of community, for within them people tended to associate with specific work, neighborhood, or class groups. Similar divisions appeared in other towns and cities across the West. Western communities, indeed, tended to fall into distinct constellations separated by location (rural or urban), class, religion, and race.

Members of any communities, some more often than others, inevitably had to embark upon the sea surrounding their neighborhood, village, or township. And at sea, the rules that obtained within island communities proved inappropriate. Governments and corporations, and for that matter other hierarchical organizations such as the Catholic church, were different social species. With its land offices, Indian agencies, and military posts, the federal government imposed a social organization whose scope was as broad as the scope of the community was limited and whose rules were as universal as a community's rules were particularistic. To belong to a community depended on personal relationships with other community members, but obtaining land from the government, at least theoretically, involved not personal relationships but fulfilling certain broadly applied legal requirements. Rule-bound and universal, government bureaucracies differed fundamentally from a community world of personal relationships. It is no wonder that local communities often resented government officials for being an alien force beyond their control.

Similarly, much of the new western economic system challenged community control. A small general store, for example, usually existed within a community of which the owner was a part. Store owners, particularly in bad economic times, felt intense local pressure to treat their customers as the friends and neighbors that they also were. These friends and neighbors asked for, and often got, credit on the basis of their personal relationship with the owner and not on the basis of their ability to pay. The store lived and died with the community. But what was true of a general store was not true of a railroad corporation or a mining company. Railroad or mining corporations transcended communities and were largely impervious to the concerns of any single community.

Once they left the boundaries of their communities, westerners entered a different social and moral universe, and they acted differently toward those they met there. They rarely applied to outsiders the relatively generous standards of mutuality that applied within the community. In this wider, anonymous world people were not known in terms of personal relationships as friends, brothers, sisters, husbands, wives, neighbors, or children; they fell within larger categories devoid of personal connections. They were buyers or sellers, customers or employees, "whites" or "Chinese" or "Indians." Westerners in moving beyond their community went from being individual, known persons to being interchangeable members of a larger and anonymous society.

Different standards applied. People who might, with no feelings of guilt, fraudulently obtain land from the federal government would think of cheating their neighbors only with guilt and foreboding. Workers who stole valuable ore from a mine would not think of stealing from each other. People who ruthlessly destroyed game and undercut the subsistence system of Indians would willingly contribute to help their own neighbors in need.

Voluntary Organizations

The limits of community did not mean that personal relations outside the community turned life into a war of all against all, but it did mean that individuals were more likely to consult self-interest in their transactions with strangers than they were in their dealings with relatives or neighbors. This pursuit of self-interest inevitably led them into further involvement in voluntary organizations. Such organizations—which we have already seen in Protestant churches and Chinese American *huigans*—became the primary means for organizing self-interest in the world beyond the community or in a world where communities were weak.

Voluntary organizations, whether labor unions, chambers of commerce, literary societies, fraternal organizations, or churches, could unite people who shared similar individual ambitions—whether these ambitions be business profits, higher wages, or salvation—and enable these people to pursue their goals more effectively. Self-interest in such cases bound people from different communities and different classes behind a common cause, and in some cases

voluntary organizations such as churches and labor unions became a seedbed
for community. Although initially they were strangers, members of voluntary
organizations might establish personal relations. If they began to see each other
socially, aided each other in matters unrelated to the organization's goals,
and married each other's relatives, then the voluntary organization spawned
communities.

Voluntary organizations thus could do two things. They could partially transcend small, localistic communities by attracting members from several (but not
all) such communities, and they also could create new communities where none
existed before. In Butte the Ancient Order of Hibernians became one of the
means for distilling a stable Irish American working-class community from a much
larger mass of Irish American workers. Churches organized in a mining camp,
cattle town, or railroad town also brought together, in the words of Josiah Strong,
"many [who] did not know each other, as Christians even," and made them into
a community. Strong later became a leading American nativist and reformer, but
in 1872 and 1873 he was a young Congregational minister in Cheyenne, Wyoming, who self-consciously used his church to bring his congregation and other
town residents to a recognition of their shared social and moral values and
their common interests. The church, itself a voluntary organization, not only
created community but also gave birth to other voluntary organizations that
worked for a town library, a town park, temperance, and an end to prostitution.
Literary societies, particularly prevalent on the Great Plains, could likewise
fulfill particular goals while encouraging a larger sense of community. Literaries,
with their recitations, dialogues, and musical numbers, obviously sought to
communicate a common culture, but they were also occasions for visiting and
entertainment.

Cripple Creek, Colorado, was a town split by ethnic, class, sexual, and religious
divisions, but voluntary organizations partially bridged them. The Cripple Creek
district, with approximately 20,000 people over the age of 16, boasted over 100
chapters of 40 different lodges and fraternal orders, ranging from the Knights of
Columbus to the Masons, Elks, and Knights of Pythias. These lodges performed
social and welfare functions for their members, and they organized socials and
dances. Some of these lodges were exclusively male or female, but others were
mixed-sex organizations or, like the Masons, had male and female chapters that
often held joint events. Similarly, within the lodges there was considerable cross-
class mixing. People seeking business contacts, recreation, or insurance or welfare
benefits from the lodges were all pursuing individual interests, but in their pursuit
of these interests they created the lodges that knit together the various communities of Cripple Creek and brought together people who otherwise would have
remained distant.

In San Francisco, merchants similarly united across ethnic and religious boundaries to pursue their common interest in promoting the primacy of the city in
trade. Their cooperation was little different from Jewish-gentile cooperation
elsewhere in the West when Jews and gentiles mingled in Odd Fellows or Masonic
lodges or when Jewish reformed rabbis and liberal Protestant ministers shared
pulpits. Such cooperation, however, did not mark the merging of the two groups.
Anglo merchants who daily dealt with Jewish merchants nonetheless banned the

Jews from their exclusive clubs. Jews who prided themselves on their good relations with gentiles would nonetheless virtually banish members of the community who married gentiles.

Rural-Urban Divisions

Cripple Creek and San Francisco were collections of urban communities; their lodges and other organizations expressed a collective urban identity and interest. But early migrants into the West did not arrive as prefabricated urban or rural dwellers. Instead, such identities emerged as the migrants built towns and developed farms. Given the mutual economic dependence of farmers and town dwellers, there was no particular reason to expect hostility between the two groups simply because of occupational and residential differences. But hostility arose quickly during times of economic crisis. Urban and rural communities, while generous to their own members, quarreled bitterly over how to deal with nonmembers—that is, all those who did not belong to their particular face-to-face world. Such disputes became chronic on the Great Plains as farmers and townspeople sought to respond to the suffering brought by recurring droughts. Within the community relatively generous standards of aid initially applied, but as local resources were exhausted, larger efforts had to be mounted which involved both urban and rural communities. Self-interest, as expressed through various voluntary organizations, replaced personal generosity.

In 1874, for example, drought caused a significant division between urban Wichita and the rural communities around it. Although the drought caused considerable suffering, the farmers around Wichita voted down a tax hike for the relief of the destitute. The farmers argued that any increase in taxes would only increase the problems of all the other drought-stricken farmers. Instead of public aid the farmers proposed forming relief committees to solicit private aid in the East and in Kansas itself. At this point the rural-urban conflict spawned a division between men and women in Wichita. The Wichita Ladies Aid Society immediately set out to relieve the suffering brought by the drought. Merchants and urban property owners, however, were outraged at the bad publicity such efforts generated. They thought it encouraged images of "droughty" Kansas and discouraged settlement. One Wichita editor reacted by denying the existence of suffering except among "lazy louts, dead beats, and shirks" and argued that the sooner they left, the better off the county would be. Although a state investigation found that of the 5,000 rural residents of Sedgwick County (which contained Wichita), roughly 2,000 of them, half of them children, lacked food and clothing that winter, the existence of real suffering was almost beside the point. The editor contended that townspeople had to resist any talk that kept out new immigrants. The Ladies Aid Society pursued their relief efforts but "not without . . . hinderances [sic] . . . and much criticism." Community values were real, but such values did not easily extend beyond the narrow bounds of the community itself. In times of crisis the lines that divided various communities emerged more clearly.

In the Wichita example urban communities pitted themselves against rural communities, but just as notable in such disputes as the divisions is the ability of various rural communities to make common cause. Farmers came to see themselves not just as members of a particular rural neighborhood, but as *farmers* with special interests as *farmers*. Various voluntary organizations, including the Grangers (1870s), the Farmers' Alliance (1880s), and the Populist party (1890s), tried to nurture this common identity.

Racial Divisions

Ethnicity, rural and urban divisions, and class all divided western communities, but race certainly formed the most prominent division in western society. As we have seen in so many other cases, culture and history are more important than biology in explaining race. Race in the West began as a cultural fiction, but the first chapter was written in Spanish instead of English. The elites of New Mexico and California, who were more often mestizo than Spanish, created a myth of pure Spanish descent to validate their status and ensure their rule over people who, in fact, shared a similar descent. They imposed fictitious racial categories to buttress a social order already in place.

Anglo Americans and white ethnic immigrants also used race as a way to insure their own privileged status in the social order. Some racial beliefs amounted to little more than an intolerance of people with different skin color, religion, or language, but others carried with them a far more systematic set of ideas. Their "racialism" (as distinct from twentieth-century "scientific racism") relied on an assertion that God had created a superior "Anglo Saxon" race destined to conquer and subordinate all others. Racialism contended not only that nonwhites were inferior to whites, but also that they were permanently inferior. Providence, racialists asserted, had doomed these inferior peoples to disappearance or slavery.

Extermination and subordination thus formed the heart of racialism, and it proved a persuasive doctrine to many whites who sought to explain and justify white expansion at the expense of nonwhite peoples. The decline of Indian peoples, the enslavement of blacks, and the conquest of Mexico all became evidence of the inevitable fate of inferior races who resisted superior races.

Westerners usually divided the nonwhites in the West into four distinct races: the Indians, the Mexicans (as they called both Mexican Americans and Mexican immigrants), the "Mongolians" (as they called the Chinese and sometimes all Asians), and blacks. Until lumped together by whites, none of these groups except, perhaps, blacks had ever thought of themselves as a single race before. Hispanics (as we will call both Mexican Americans and Mexican immigrants) far from considering themselves a single race had subdivided themselves according to racial distinctions of their own. The creation in the white American mind of an Indian race also imposed homogeneity on a people who usually thought of themselves as made up of numerous distinct peoples or nations. The Chinese similarly had many divisions of their own and were, in any case, as ethnocentric as any white Americans. They thought of themselves as a superior people and would never have lumped themselves into a single race with other Asians.

As used in the West, the concept of race created a confusing system of classification. Sometimes it seemed to rest on biology, using, for example, skin color and other features to distinguish Indians as a single group. At other times, however, racialists described people who were of mixed descent as a single race. The many blacks who had some white ancestry were still black. Hispanics, too, were a mixture of people of Native American, European, and African descent, but racialists lumped them together and labeled them as a single race. This confusion of criteria illustrates how much race was a cultural construction and not simply a recognition of biological "facts."

Having created "races," racialists could then ascribe characteristics to them which were demeaning and derogatory. According to the ruling racialist mythology, for example, both Indians and Mexicans were dark, dirty, without morals, incapable of sexual restraint, cruel, vindictive, and lazy. Racialist stereotypes could easily be joined to sexual stereotypes. Whether condemned as sensual and lascivious or as ugly drudges, nonwhite women had to bear unfavorable comparisons to Anglo American "true" womanhood. Racialists distinguished between racial groups according to both their particular mix of undesirable traits and their usefulness for whites. Thus, "useful" Hispanics and blacks often ranked ahead of "useless" Indians. At other times, "brave" Indians ranked ahead of "cowardly" blacks and Hispanics. In time, the particular groups classified as races and stigmatized as racially inferior would themselves both adopt and redefine this racial identity.

Not all whites accepted the tenets of racialism. Virtually all nineteenth-century white Americans were racially prejudiced—that is, they thought that nonwhites were inferior to whites. We must remember, however, that racialism was more than mere prejudice. It was an assertion that not only were nonwhites inferior, but they were *permanently* inferior. God and nature had doomed them to be either the slaves and servants of whites or to disappear. Many whites rejected racialism's assertion that nonwhites were permanently inferior people whose only choice was between extinction or slavery. Instead they believed that "inferior" peoples could, with help, redeem themselves by imitating white Americans. Racial differences for these assimilationists were neither innate nor permanent. They gave these differences a distinctive cultural interpretation.

The Christian reformers who governed U.S. Indian policy, for example, did not seek either the biological extinction or the permanent subordination of Indian groups. Instead they sought to destroy the Indian customs that they thought were the cause of Indian inferiority. Having taught Indians proper "American" values and gender roles, the larger society could assimilate them just as it assimilated European immigrants. For the reformers, assimilation was the alternative to extermination, and they argued that it was the proper course by drawing on both democratic ideology and Christian morality.

If either the racialists or the reformers had been able to achieve their goals, the distinctive social arrangements of the western United States would have proved unnecessary. If the racialists, for example, had succeeded, they would have simply eliminated nonwhites or reduced them to permanent servitude. If the assimilationists had succeeded, they would have eliminated any separate identity for western minorities.

But in fact neither racialists nor assimilationist reformers proved able to succeed completely in their plans. Racialism ran into serious problems when nonwhites failed to fade away or accept subordination as predicted. The Chinese presented a particular challenge: instead of declining in the face of white competition, the Chinese increased in numbers during the 1850s, 1860s, and 1870s. Persecution and discrimination failed to stop either Chinese population growth or the ability of the Chinese to garner wealth from the most humble endeavors.

The Chinese aroused such deep racial hatred in the nineteenth-century West precisely because they seemed to be a threat to the economic success of white migrants. According to racialism, this was not supposed to happen. Nonwhites were not supposed to be able to compete with whites. The Chinese seemed less an obstacle to be swept away, like Indians or Hispanics, than dangerous rivals.

The Chinese provided racialism with its first glaring contradiction. When by the turn of the twentieth century Japanese, Hispanics, and eventually even Indians began to increase in numbers, racialism as an ideology capable of explaining the world collapsed. Racialists then became scientific racists who set about the interesting task of explaining in biological terms the apparent contradiction of how "inferior" races were "outbreeding" and threatening to overwhelm "superior" races. The old imperialist, optimistic beliefs of the racialists had become the defensive, fearful (but very dangerous) beliefs of the racists.

Assimilationists, however, proved no more successful. They devoted their greatest effort to assimilating Indians. In spite of enormous efforts, increasing coercion, and the willingness to use violence when necessary, they did not succeed in totally destroying the cultures or identities of Indian peoples or in assimilating them fully into American society. Separate minority communities, particularly Indian, Chinese, Hispanic, and black communities, continued to exist if not to thrive in the West.

Racial Relations

Despite their differences about whether nonwhites were permanently or temporarily inferior, racialists and reformers both agreed that they should be treated differently than white Americans. How differently they were treated varied from place to place and from group to group, but no nonwhite group could move into full citizenship with the ease of white immigrants. Even after the passage of the fourteenth, fifteenth, and sixteenth amendments to the Constitution ending slavery and guaranteeing blacks citizenship, African Americans still faced discrimination and segregation in the West. Similarly, Mexican Americans became citizens with the Treaty of Guadalupe Hidalgo ending the Mexican War, but in much of the Southwest they found their suffrage and political rights curtailed often by the simple expedient of allowing only English-speakers to vote.

Other groups did not obtain even the narrow and crabbed citizenship available to Mexican Americans and blacks. The United States denied citizenship to the Chinese, and later the Japanese and other Asians, on the basis of a 1790 federal law limiting naturalized citizenship to white persons. These policies created a body of foreign nationals living within U.S. territory. Admittedly, many foreign nationals also lived elsewhere in the United States, but in the East such foreign nationals were largely white. Only in the West were the conditions of foreign nationality and race so intimately intertwined. This linkage placed the status of racial minorities in the American West partially beyond the control of the various state and territorial governments. Race relations became to a significant degree foreign relations, regulated by treaties between independent foreign nations and the United States. Minority communities not only differed internally from surrounding white communities, but they also differed in their relationship to the federal government.

It is this peculiar condition of minorities that did much to create a unique social structure in the West. The territorial minorities of the West—Indians and

Mexican Americans—had special status by virtue of treaty. Mexican Americans derived their rights from the Treaty of Guadalupe Hidalgo. Indians, as members of domestic dependent nations, were citizens of semisovereign nations within American boundaries. The United States acknowledged their limited sovereignty in separate treaties. The tribes, in theory, dealt directly only with the federal government.

Beyond the conquered groups, other minorities also had their status regulated by treaty. The Chinese, and after them the Japanese, were also foreign nationals. Although their children became citizens if born in this country, the immigrants had no choice but to remain resident foreign nationals, and disputes involving them often involved federal negotiations with the Chinese or Japanese government. Similarly, most Mexican immigrants into the West also remained foreign nationals. Most of them intended to return to Mexico at some later date and never applied for citizenship. Disputes over these immigrants and their status, particularly during the twentieth century, often came to involve federal negotiations with the Mexican government. Thus, for different reasons race relations in the West involving Indians, Chinese, Japanese, and Mexican immigrants and their communities became a species of international relations.

Transformation of Minority Communities

Loss of resources and the effect of the dual labor system transformed the existing minority communities of the West. The pace and course of change differed somewhat among various Indian groups and *californios*, Hispanic Texans, and Hispanic New Mexicans, but all found that they could no longer maintain their preconquest rural communities.

In California, Hispanics became a predominantly urban population. Even men who spent much of the year traveling as rural seasonal laborers maintained their families in the cities and towns. Those Hispanics who chose to work as well as live in the cities became unskilled workers, taking over the jobs left open when whites drove the Chinese from southern California. Hispanics became ditch diggers, street graders, and harvest workers. By 1880 about 80 percent of the Hispanics in Santa Barbara were unskilled workers, and many of them lacked employment for at least part of the year. Only 11 percent of workers with non-Spanish surnames held such jobs.

A somewhat different pattern held in Texas and New Mexico. Anglo Americans did not become a majority in New Mexico or in southern Texas, where native Hispanic Texans and more recent Mexican immigrants composed roughly three-quarters of the population during the last half of the nineteenth century. Particularly in New Mexico, dispossession came gradually, but the general trend moved inexorably toward proletariatization as existing communities lost control of their land and Hispanic Texans and New Mexicans faced reduction to rural unskilled wage labor. From being a group of farmers, small ranchers, skilled agricultural laborers, and craftspeople they gradually declined into a group of unspecialized laborers. In Texas by 1900 native Mexican Texans and Mexican immigrants made up nearly 99 percent of this unskilled general labor pool. This was the dual labor system in action.

The result of the process of the creation of *barrios* (that is, of segregation into separate urban enclaves) and dispossession was a transformation of Hispanic communities. In South Texas the arrival of Anglo American ranchers and the commercialization of cattle ranching forced the Tejano elite to either conform to the new commercial order or to lose their land. Most Tejano ranchers continued to regard their land and ranches as a family patrimony necessary to maintain their existing way of life rather than a business. As a result, taxes, fraud, the costs of legal battles to validate their claims, enclosure of watering holes, and fluctuating cattle prices made the Tejanos unable to maintain their land in the face of Anglo American competition. The landed elite and the smaller rancheros failed to pass their land on to their children. The propertied classes of Tejano society failed to reproduce themselves.

Despite far-reaching change, much of the daily life of communities initially remained familiar. Peonage continued in South Texas, but landless, indebted laborers worked for Anglo ranchers who became patrons in place of the old Tejano elite. Taking care of their workers' necessities, paying them wages, and giving them a *jacal* and provisions when they grew old, the Anglo ranchers themselves became partially Mexicanized, adopting the paternalism, reciprocal obligations, and permanency that characterized the older labor system. The children of the old rancheros did not necessarily sink into peonage. More often they became *vaqueros*, or cowboys, workers who sought and often maintained a greater independence until ranchers abandoned the open-range system. As openings for vaqueros declined, they and former peons became a floating pool of unskilled labor forced into railroad construction work and field work.

A variant on this same process affected the villages of northern New Mexico. There the loss of village lands forced an emigration of men seeking seasonal work. As one Hispanic New Mexican woman remembered, by the 1920s, "when the men came back, they were kind of like guests." In the villages of northern New Mexico, extended kinship patterns remained strong, but women, not men, took the major responsibility for maintaining them.

This feminization of local social and economic networks was also true of urban areas such as Los Angeles. By 1880 in a city like Los Angeles approximately 30 percent of urban Hispanic households were headed, at least seasonally, by a woman. The fathers had either left to look for work, deserted their families, or died, for in a city such as Los Angeles the death rate for Hispanic men was twice that for women. As economic conditions deteriorated in California, Mexican American women and their children also entered the labor force in increasing numbers as domestics, harvest workers, and cannery workers.

Although most Indian communities managed to maintain a diminished land base, they faced similar challenges and changes. Some Indians attempted to link their communities to the larger economy through farming or, as in the Pacific Northwest, fishing, but these efforts largely failed. In the Pacific Northwest, for example, better capitalized whites gradually laid claim to Indian fishing grounds and banned the Indians from sites they had fished for generations. They continued to fish less productive sites for subsistence, but they now also worked seasonally in the hop fields and lumber camps of western Washington to supplement the reduced proceeds of their fishing.

Most Indians by the early twentieth century had learned to scrape together a minimal living by mixing hunting, fishing, gathering, and gardening with casual labor and payments from the federal government. These payments represented money owed Indians under treaties, funds won in land settlement cases, or rent from allotments leased to whites. When all else failed, the government would provide rations to those in desperate need. Taken together, these sources of income managed to sustain most Indian communities in abysmal poverty. Indians became at once the poorest and the most dependent of western minorities. Most Indians escaped integration into the dual labor economy, but the price was economic marginalization. By the early twentieth century most reservations had no functioning economy at all.

Such marginalization necessarily meant disaster for many Indian communities. Strong Indian communities remained in the Southwest among the Navajos and Pueblos, but at their worst, southwestern reservations, like many more reservations elsewhere, could become sinks of misery. By the twentieth century the Jicarilla Apaches on their high, mountainous reservation in New Mexico had attained a level of suffering as deep as that found anywhere in the West. The government had allotted the reservation, and whites soon gained access to most of its prime resources. White squatters and homesteaders claimed the best agricultural land, and officials leased the Jicarillas' winter grazing lands to Anglo and Hispanic herders. The government sold off part of the reservation's timber and deposited the proceeds in noninterest-bearing accounts in the federal treasury.

Until drought hit in the mid-1890s, the Jicarillas survived by combining food rations, annuity payments due them by treaty, some livestock raising, and handicraft production. A few obtained jobs in the Indian police, the only regular jobs available at the agency. But with the drought, the Jicarillas' herds died and the Indians nearly died with them. Their population fell from 815 in 1900 to 588 in 1920. They lived on corn tortillas and black coffee. The government responded callously. In 1911 officials cut Jicarilla food rations in half. Poorly housed and poorly fed, the Jicarillas sickened; by 1912 an estimated 75 percent of the tribe had tuberculosis, and the disease made it even harder for the Jicarillas to end their free fall into misery. Even when temporary work became available, about 61 percent of the Jicarilla men were too sick to take advantage of it. Those who could work found that their employers routinely paid them less than non-Indians for equivalent work. In such circumstances community became difficult to sustain.

Communities in Context

By the late nineteenth century all communities in the West existed within the framework of an increasingly modern and centralized society. All communities had to deal with economic and political units far more powerful than the local world of neighbors and kinspeople. But within this framework, not all communities were equal. Minority communities had the most limited ability to control their fate within the larger world of a market economy and an emerging modern state. White communities were far more likely to find opportunity in the powerful economic and political forces unleashed by western conquest, migration, and development. In this new world, communities and individuals struggled to maintain themselves or advance, but they also struggled against each other.

This struggle was often violent. Community efforts at self-protection, as well as individual attempts at self-aggrandizement, spawned a West of open and often raw conflict. The political system managed to contain and channel much of this conflict, but the West became noted for the conflicts that politics could not contain. Communities could and did arm to protect or advance their interests. A vigilance committee was as much a voluntary organization as was a merchants' association or a labor union.

Readings

Bender, Thomas. *Community and Social Change in America*. Baltimore: Johns Hopkins University Press, 1986.

Bowen, William. *The Willamette Valley: Migration and Settlement on the Oregon Frontier*. Seattle: University of Washington Press, 1978.

Butler, Anne M. *Daughters of Joy, Sisters of Misery: Prostitutes in the American West, 1865–90*. Urbana: University of Illinois Press, 1985.

Dykstra, Robert R. *The Cattle Towns*. New York: Atheneum, 1976.

Emmons, David M. *The Butte Irish: Class and Ethnicity in an American Mining Town, 1873–1925*. Urbana: University of Illinois Press, 1989.

Fischer, Christiane. *Let Them Speak for Themselves: Women in the American West, 1849–90*. Hamden, Conn.: Archon Books, 1977.

Frankiel, Sandra Sizer. *California's Spiritual Frontiers: Religious Alternatives in Anglo-Protestantism, 1850–1910*. Berkeley: University of California Press, 1988.

Gjerde, Jon. *From Peasants to Farmers: The Migration from Balestrand, Norway, to the Upper Midwest*. New York: Cambridge University Press, 1985.

Goldman, Marion S. *Gold Diggers and Silver Miners: Prostitution and Social Life on the Comstock Lode*. Ann Arbor: University of Michigan Press, 1979.

Griswold del Castillo, Richard. *La Familia: Chicano Families in the Urban Southwest, 1848 to the Present*. Notre Dame, Ind.: University of Notre Dame Press, 1984.

Guarneri, Carl, and David Alvarez. *Religion and Society in the American West*. Lanham, Md.: University Press of America, 1987.

Hine, Robert V. *Community on the American Frontier: Separate but Not Alone*. Norman: University of Oklahoma Press, 1980.

Horsman, Reginald. *Race and Manifest Destiny: The Origins of American Racial Anglo-Saxonism*. Cambridge: Harvard University Press, 1981.

Jeffrey, Julie Roy. *Frontier Women: The Trans-Mississippi West, 1840–1880*. New York: Hill and Wang, 1979.

Kaufman, Polly Welts. *Women Teachers on the Frontier*. New Haven: Yale University Press, 1984.

León, Arnoldo de, and Kenneth L. Stewart. "Lost Dreams and Found Fortunes: Mexican and Anglo Immigrants in South Texas, 1850–1900." *Western Historical Quarterly* 14 (July 1983): 291–310.

Lotchin, Roger W. *San Francisco, 1846–1856: From Hamlet to City*. New York: Oxford University Press, 1974.

Luebke, Frederick C. *Ethnicity on the Great Plains*. Lincoln: University of Nebraska Press, 1980.

Mann, Ralph. *After the Gold Rush: Society in Grass Valley and Nevada City, California, 1849–1870*. Stanford: Stanford University Press, 1982.

May, Dean. *Utah: A People's History*. Salt Lake City: University of Utah Press, 1987.

Montejano, David. *Anglos and Mexicans in the Making of Texas, 1836–1986*. Austin: University of Texas Press, 1987.

Muller, Dorothea R. "Church Building and Community Making on the Frontier, A Case Study: Josiah Strong, Home Missionary in Cheyenne, 1871–73." *Western Historical Quarterly* 10 (April 1979):199–216.

Pascoe, Peggy. *Relations of Rescue: The Search for Female Moral Authority in the American West, 1874–1939*. New York: Oxford University Press, 1990.

Paul, Rodman W. *Mining Frontiers of the Far West, 1848–1880*. New York: Holt, Rinehart and Winston, 1963.

Petrik, Paula. *No Step Backward: Women and Family on the Rocky Mountain Mining Frontier.* Helena: Montana Historical Society Press, 1987.

Pritchard, Linda K. "A Comparative Approach to Western Religious History: Texas as a Case Study, 1845–1890." *Western Historical Quarterly* 19 (November 1988):413–30.

Rice, John G. "The Role of Culture and Community in Frontier Prairie Farming." *Journal of Historical Geography* 3 (April 1977): 155–72.

Rohrbough, Malcolm J. *Aspen: The History of a Silver-Mining Town, 1879–1893*. New York: Oxford University Press, 1986.

Szasz, Ferenc Morton. *The Protestant Clergy in the Great Plains and Mountain West, 1865–1915*. Albuquerque: University of New Mexico Press, 1988.

Tsai, Shih-Shan Henry. *The Chinese Experience in America*. Bloomington: Indiana University Press, 1986.

Underwood, Kathleen. "The Pace of Their Own Lives: Teaching Training and the Life Course of Western Women." *Pacific Historical Review* 55 (November 1986): 513–30.

West, Elliott. *Growing Up with the Country: Childhood on the Far Western Frontier*. Albuquerque: University of New Mexico Press, 1989.

CHAPTER 13

Social Conflict

IT is not surprising that conflict and violence pervade the history of the American West. Anglo Americans conquered Indians and Mexicans and kept those people subordinated by force. The inevitable hostility between conquerors and conquered nurtured a particular strain of violence, but other strains also developed and thrived among the Anglo Americans and other immigrant groups. Differences in race, ethnicity, class, religion, and earlier sectional loyalties created friction, and friction often sparked conflict.

The most significant western conflicts sprang from basic social and economic divisions that mobilized large groups of westerners against each other. Whites rioted against the Chinese and on occasion hunted Indians like animals. Between 1890 and 1920 open class warfare sporadically raged in the mining towns of the Rockies and later in the mill towns of the Pacific Northwest. Outlaw gangs not only disrupted the peace of the Missouri border, Montana, Oklahoma, and Texas but also sometimes found significant public support for their depredations. Vigilantes claimed their victims in virtually every western state and territory. Cattle raisers killed sheepherders, and small and large stock raisers battled each other from Wyoming to New Mexico.

When most Americans think of the West, they think of it in terms of conflict but not in terms of these clashes of social groups. Instead, they conjure up images of individual violence: two gunmen confronting each other on a deserted street of a dusty town. Western myth has preempted history in explaining conflict in the West. Myth takes a West of Indian hunting and violent strikes, of fence cutting and range wars, and translates it into a West of rugged and armed individualists: gunfighters, outlaws, and sheriffs. Myth makes all conflict personal and resolves all conflict with violence. The stock figures of myth and folklore—mountain men, gunfighters, cowboys, Indian warriors, scouts, and prospectors—come onto the scene armed and dangerous. They seek a climactic, individual showdown.

Explaining the bloody conflict in the West in terms of personal violence is perhaps appealing to Americans because it allows them to escape asking uncomfortable questions about social conflict. Despite the bloodletting of the Civil War, nineteenth-century Americans took great pride in the ability of their political system to defuse, or at least ameliorate, social conflicts. Americans believed in rule of law, not in the rule of force and violence. Western myth, in effect, validated the larger belief in a society of social peace. Violence existed, the myth said, but the violence was personal, and it largely vanished as society imposed law and order. But if, contrary to the myth, the social order itself sometimes encouraged violence, then the easy reading of western history as the imposition of peace and the rule of law upon a lawless and violent land loses its meaning.

The reality of social conflict in the West creates another reading of western history. It is a more mixed story of how law and government repressed some violence and provoked other violence. The American political system did succeed in diverting many social conflicts into peaceful political channels, but in the West these channels were often not deep enough to contain all the enmities diverted into them. Complete diversion was impossible if only because the political system itself excluded significant groups of westerners—Indians, Hispanics, Chinese, Japanese—from political participation.

Violence, therefore, occurred when social conflict spilled outside normal political channels, but this is only a partial explanation for violence, because violent conflict sometimes proved an integral part of the political system itself. When farmers or miners or even some outlaws denounced the political system as either corrupt or the tool of their class or sectional enemy, they were often perfectly correct. At certain times local, state, and federal officials did employ the coercive power of the government against one class, race, or ethnic or interest group in order to promote the interests of other classes, races, or ethnic or interest groups. Violent confrontations often resulted.

Unlike movie makers, novelists, or storytellers, historians cannot reduce real social conflicts into a series of individual confrontations between symbolic combatants: the classic showdowns between two armed men in the empty street of a western town. Folklore and myths have their own logic and meaning that historians must respect (and which will form the material for another chapter). Historians, however, must also distinguish between personal violence and crime on the one hand and large-scale social conflicts on the other.

Personal Violence

Conflict in the American West formed a spectrum on which personal violence and crime formed one extreme and social violence another. At the center was a much murkier area where the two categories mixed and overlapped. Personal violence did exist, but only within quite specific social boundaries. It never overwhelmed the social order.

People who believe that the nineteenth-century West was a perpetually violent and lawless place, where the only sure protection for individual life and property was a special aptitude for personal violence, usually have relatively specific places in mind. They do not contend, for example, that Norwegian farmers in North Dakota habitually squared off with Colt .45s to settle the ownership of an ox or a wagon or that German Mennonites in Kansas regulated their farm boundaries by slicing each other with bowie knives. They locate violence in a more narrow realm. The most violent places, the ones on which they base their case, were the domains of young, single men, and these young men were often drunk. In cattle towns and mining towns, if anywhere, we should find the West of lawless and heroic individuals, men devoted to the cult of personal violence.

The violence practiced by men against other men is fairly well documented. Two studies of largely male towns, one an examination of cattle towns (including Dodge City and Ellsworth, Kansas) and the other a study of two California mining towns, address the question of crime and male personal violence. No one would mistake Dodge City or Ellsworth or the mining camps of Aurora and Bodie, California, for Quaker villages. All of them were rough and violent places.

Cattle-town residents who had their town invaded each summer by drunken young men certainly had reason to worry about a certain amount of unpleasantness. But recognizing the potential for violence, they systematically and prosaically did their best to limit the danger. Although restricting possession of handguns remains an emotional issue in the twentieth-century West, nineteenth-century cattle-town residents resorted to gun control without much hesitation. Wichita and other towns outlawed the carrying of handguns within the city limits and established police forces to patrol the towns and enforce the ordinances.

These police forces often contained noted gunfighters, but the officers had little taste for individual showdowns. They acted as part of an organized body of police, the bulk of whose duties was quite ordinary. Sheriffs and marshals rarely faced down gunfighters, but they regularly knocked down and dragged away drunks. Controlling and disciplining the inebriated was, in fact, their main duty. When they lacked sufficient drunks to look after, the police inherited an assortment of other civic duties. Police officers, for example, often doubled as street commissioners. The terms of employment offered Wyatt Earp and Wild Bill Hickok, both of whom served as cattle-town police officers, stipulated that during the off-season when the cowboys had returned to Texas, Wild Bill and Wyatt might pass their time repairing sidewalks and removing dead animals from the streets.

Gun control and regular police forces were, by and large, successful in curtailing violence. There were never more than five murders in any given cattle town during a single year despite the presence, on both sides of the law, of gunfighters like Clay Allison, Doc Holliday, Ben Thompson, John Wesley Hardin, Bat Masterson, and Wyatt Earp. Only Hardin and Earp actually killed men in the cattle towns. Hardin, while drunk, fired through the wall of his hotel room to silence (in this case permanently) a man whose snoring was keeping him awake. Earp, as a law officer, killed two men (one of them a "special" policeman) by mistake. During the peak years of the cattle towns, the average number of homicides was only 1.5 a year for each town.

This restricted (at least when compared to myth) number of murders did not result from the potential murderer's fear of quick and violent retaliation. When murders did occur, cattle-town residents did not demand excessive punishment. Cattle-town merchants feared that executing a cowboy just because he had killed another cowboy might discourage Texans from returning and spending their money. Juries were prone to dismiss murder as a youthful indiscretion or as the unfortunate consequence of too much to drink. Only three persons ever received the death penalty for a killing in the cattle towns, and all of them eventually had their sentence commuted. When the victims of murder were cattle-town residents, the citizenry did take retaliation more seriously, but still they hanged only one murderer when an Abilene lynch mob executed a local tailor.

In terms of personal violence the mining camps of Aurora and Bodie were even rougher and rowdier than the cattle towns. As in the cattle towns, men got drunk and fought. The usual criminal charge in Bodie and Aurora was "drunk and disorderly." Man Eater McGowan, the terror of Bodie, typified the mining camps' barroom brawlers. Man Eater, a rough-and-tumble fighter, got his name from his

Two soldiers, victims of Wild Bill Hickok, lie dead on a Hays, Kansas, sidewalk.

nasty habit of chewing on his opponents' ears and noses. Before being permanently exiled from town, he bit the sheriff's leg, broke a pitcher over a waiter's head, threatened to chew off the justice of the peace's ears, and got in an assortment of more mundane fistfights. Like Man Eater, most brawlers relied on their teeth and fists, but such fights did have a greater potential for damage in Bodie than they had in the cattle towns because the miners were armed. Fistfights escalated into gunfights far more often in Bodie and Aurora than they did in Dodge City or Ellsworth.

Bodie was, as nineteenth-century Californians put it, a shooter's town. Forty-four confrontations ended in shootings between 1877 and 1883, but most of these involved a relatively small group of men, the so-called Badmen of Bodie, who were young, quarrelsome, touchy, and armed. During its boom years Bodie had 29 killings that would qualify as murder or voluntary manslaughter. When converted to the form of modern crime statistics, this gave the town an annual homicide rate of 116 per 100,000 population. By way of comparison, the highest rate in the United States in 1980 was Miami's figure of 32.7 per 100,000. The rate for the United States as a whole in 1980 was 10.2 per 100,000. No eastern city in the 1880s had a rate remotely close to Bodie's.

These killings, because they took place largely between willing combatants, many of them known toughs, excited little alarm. The courts in Bodie and Aurora only convicted one man of murder. More than that, however, died for murder. When badmen attacked the weak, old, innocent, or female, lynch mobs often intervened before the courts could pass sentence. For most people, everyday public life remained secure.

We know that a woman, or at least a woman who was not a prostitute, was relatively safe on the streets of Bodie or Dodge City, but we do not know how safe women were at home. Violence against prostitutes—usually in brothels or cribs—appears to have been relatively common, but in the few towns in which historians have conducted systematic studies, reported rapes and assaults against women who were not prostitutes were relatively rare. Such studies do, however, have two large gaps. They do not reflect exceptional waves of violence, such as the rape of Indian women that was a common auxiliary of warfare, nor do they reflect private or domestic violence. Evidence from literary memoirs is, of course, unreliable for determining the extent of domestic violence, but in the absence of other evidence it can at least record attitudes toward such violence. If the evidence from works such as Mari Sandoz's Old Jules, Agnes Smedley's Daughter of Earth, Meridel Le Sueur's The Girl, and Tillie Olsen's Yonnodio is at all indicative of actual social attitudes, then such violence was socially condoned, and thus conceivably unreported, in the West.

As the Bodie example demonstrates, personal violence certainly could reach extraordinary levels in the West, but it remained confined to very narrow social milieus. When armed and drunk, young men often proved lethal, but most often they killed each other. Restraining this violence was not, however, difficult. Those towns such as the cattle towns that disarmed young men lowered the rates of personal violence considerably. Those towns such as Bodie and Aurora that did not disarm men tended to bury significantly more of them. Society as a whole was able to control personal violence when the community desired to do so. Western myth has taken this personal violence of saloons and brothels, which did exist, and used it to obscure a far more pervasive social violence. And indeed, when looked at more closely, much of the personal and criminal violence of the West was actually part of larger social conflicts. Vigilante movements demonstrate how instances of crime and personal violence shaded into collective conflicts.

Vigilantes

In the West of myth, and in actual western communities, there were times when personal violence and crime rose to levels that a community refused to tolerate and that the constituted authorities seemed unable to control. When rustling became so pervasive in Kimble County, Texas, that the thieves outnumbered the honest ranchers, the Texas Rangers literally rounded up the entire male population of the county in order to separate the law-abiding from the lawless. Constituted authorities stepped in in Kimble County, but very often such situations produced vigilantes—people who claimed to operate outside the law in order to enforce the law itself. Between 1849 and 1902 there were at least 210 vigilante movements in the American West; together they claimed 527 victims, most of whom died by hanging. The most lethal of these movements, an 1884 vigilance committee in eastern and northern Montana, claimed 35 victims. Only Oregon and Utah lacked significant vigilante movements.

Vigilantes contended that when constituted authority broke down to such a degree that the communities were threatened with destruction by criminals, an armed citizenry had to take over to preserve order. There were situations in which such an account of vigilante behavior was largely accurate. Vigilantes did sometimes confront flagrant and spectacular breakdowns of law and order. In the early 1860s, for example, the Plummer gang of Montana murdered and robbed with impunity because its leader, Henry Plummer, was also the sheriff of Bannock. The Bannock-Virginia City vigilante movement of 1863–65 dispatched the Plummer gang and established a classic model of what has been called "socially constructive" vigilantism: citizens organized, dealt straightforwardly with a problem of disorder beyond the control of the constituted authorities, and then disbanded. To justify such actions, vigilantes invoked the doctrine of self-preservation and claimed that they were only observing the fundamental doctrine of American republicanism: the right of the people to assume sovereignty when government proved incapable of protecting their rights and property. Although vigilantes overrode legally constituted officials, they did not reject the duties and procedures of those officials. Instead they mimicked them: they captured criminals; conducted formal, if illegal, trials of the accused; and punished the guilty, usually by hanging.

Although virtually all vigilantes claimed that they dealt with conditions similar to those in Montana, most vigilante movements confronted far more ambiguous situations. Western law enforcement was often not so much nonexistent or corrupt as inefficient and expensive. Vigilantes sometimes seemed to be more frustrated with the cost of suppressing crime than with crime itself. In such cases they stormed jails to hang men already in custody, thus saving the town or county the cost of a formal trial and execution. Most residents of Golden, Colorado, for example, praised an execution conducted by a local vigilante group for having saved the county $5,000 or $6,000.

Every community in which vigilantes supplanted local law officials did not necessarily face an alarming crime wave. Vigilantes sometimes used crime only as an excuse to crack down on what the upper and middle classes saw as a more diffuse and pervasive threat to prevailing moral standards and their own social dominance. Sometimes vigilante movements arose when there was no convincing evidence of any breakdown of law and order. The San Francisco vigilance committees of 1851 and 1856, among the earliest and most widely imitated vigilante movements in the West, can serve as a case in point. The San Francisco Vigilance Committee of 1856 was also among the largest, numbering from 6,000 to 8,000 members, far above the usual vigilante membership of 100 to 300. The San Francisco vigilantes claimed to be reacting against a crime wave sweeping the city, but the evidence does not reveal any unusual crime wave in San Francisco in 1855–56. The vigilantes were, in fact, not so much interested in suppressing crime as in taking political control of the city from the dominant faction of Irish Catholic Democrats. The vigilantes—who were largely Protestant and native-born—smashed their political opposition by exiling its leaders from the city.

Both the socially constructive vigilante movements and movements such as the San Francisco Vigilance Committee shared a common social structure. They almost universally drew their leaders from the local social elite; the middle levels of the community supplied their rank and file. Their victims almost uniformly came from the lower levels of the community; most often their victims were criminals, but sometimes their only crime was to have challenged the social dominance of a local elite and thus to have excited the wrath of the vigilantes. Thomas Dimsdale, whose *The Vigilantes of Montana* became a classic and laudatory account of vigilantes, revealingly denounced their victims not just as criminals but as "low, brutal, cruel, lazy, ignorant, sensual, and blasphemous" people. These were qualities that he apparently considered to be as deserving of violent repression as murder and theft.

Vigilante movements stand at the midpoint on our spectrum of conflict and violence in the West. Their emphasis on suppressing crime and criminals clearly connects them with the mythic West of gunfighters, while their roots in larger social divisions point toward the collective violence of large social groupings. The tendency of some vigilante movements to label entire social groups as criminal is particularly significant. Such accusations carry us deeper into the collective side of our spectrum, where real criminal episodes can also mask deeper social conflicts.

Anglo-Hispanic Conflict: Banditry

Perhaps nowhere do the issues of crime and vigilantism become more embroiled in large-scale social conflict than in the clashes involving Anglo Americans and Hispanics in the Southwest. From virtually the beginning of the American occupation of the region questions of banditry and racial conflict became linked. In the early 1850s, following the Foreign Miners' Tax and the expulsion of *californios* and Mexicans from the mines, bandits began preying upon the miners. Many of the bandits were known to be Anglo Americans or European immigrants, but the majority of them appear to have been Hispanic.

As the robberies and killings grew in number, the various groups of bandits involved in this outbreak gradually took on a single identity. Whites asserted that at the center of the robberies and murders was a mastermind whose first name they always gave as Joaquin and whose last name was variously Muriati, Murieta, Ocomorenia, or others. A Cherokee Indian gold miner turned journalist, John Rollins Ridge, completed the fusion of numerous actual Hispanic bandits into a single mythic figure. He created the bandit leader Joaquin Murieta and in doing so gave California its foremost folk legend. Supposedly whipped and expelled from the mines by American miners who also raped his wife and hanged his brother, Joaquin Murieta, according to Ridge, set out to take his revenge. The myth symbolized ethnic conflict as a response to personal injustice, and a Cherokee Indian invented Joaquin Murieta as a champion of the oppressed.

The Murieta stories recognized that California banditry had its roots in oppression of Hispanics even as they transformed this social conflict into the exploits of a single man. Implicit in such stories was the recognition of a collective conflict. Whites and Hispanics feared criminals, but more than that they feared each other. The general mood was captured by a California traveler in 1854. "When I see a Mexican approaching," he wrote, "I cock my rifle and cover him with it. At the same time calling him to raise his hand away from his lasso which hangs at his saddle-bow. In this way I keep my rifle on him until he has passed and gone beyond lasso distance."

Such attitudes brought Los Angeles to the brink of race war between 1850 and 1856. There were 44 homicides in Los Angeles County between August 1850 and October 1851, an extraordinary number considering that the total population of the area was less than 2,300. These killings, in turn, caused vigilantes, predominantly Anglos, to organize. But their efforts, and those of the regular judicial system, to suppress crime fell disproportionately on *californios* and Mexicans. Anglo killers seemed to slip free, while the vigilantes and courts routinely dispatched Hispanic killers. The vigilantes, too, were often not particular about whom they lynched. With the cooperation of leading *californios* they hanged many legitimate bandits, but they also hanged many quite innocent *californios* and Mexicans.

The racial conflict that in California took the form of clashes between Hispanic "bandits" and Anglo American "vigilantes" took on a similar form in Texas. The Texas Rangers, although they evolved into a fairly conventional state police force, originally existed partially as a force to combat Indians and "Mexicans"— both Tejanos and Mexican immigrants. Whites readily excused the excesses of the rangers as they went about their task of keeping Indians and Mexicans as well as criminals in line, but Tejanos despised the rangers. They regarded them as an armed force designed to intimidate and legally plunder Hispanics in the interests of an Anglo elite.

In Texas, Tejanos came to see both state and local police forces as agencies of their own oppression. In 1859 in South Texas, which was overwhelmingly Hispanic in population, Juan Cortina, the 35-year-old son of a prominent Tejano family, saw the sheriff of Brownsville, Texas, Bob Spears, pistol-whipping a drunken vaquero who worked for his mother. Cortina shot Spears. Two months later, Cortina returned to Brownsville with 60 riders, freed all the Hispanic prisoners in the jail, sacked the stores of white merchants, and executed four Americans who had killed Hispanics and had gone unpunished. A virtual civil war—the Cortina War—between Cortina and his followers and the Texas Rangers resulted. The rangers, unable to capture Cortina, who also evaded Mexican troops on the other side of the border, retaliated indiscriminately against all Hispanics in the region.

Social Banditry

Cortina, to the extent that he was a bandit at all, was what historians have called a social bandit. Driven outside the law because of some act sanctioned by local conventions but regarded as criminal by the state or local authorities, the social bandit has been forced to become an outlaw. Members of the local community, however, still consider the social bandit an honorable and admirable man. Robin Hood was the archetypical social bandit, and Hispanics considered Juan Cortina to be one too. Outbreaks on the scale of Cortina's war would not occur again, but a tradition of border social banditry lingered on into the early twentieth century. Many men honored after their deaths as social bandits, such as Billy the Kid, were simple criminals, but some, like the now famous Gregorio Cortez of Texas, seem indeed to have fulfilled the criteria for social banditry. Falsely accused of horse theft in 1901, Cortez killed a sheriff and undertook a spectacular, if ultimately unsuccessful, flight against enormous odds that made him a Hispanic folk hero.

White-Hispanic conflicts in which the dominant group denounced its opponents as criminals or used repression of crime as an excuse to attack an entire group or community demonstrate how fine a line there sometimes was between crime and collective social violence. Such episodes also occurred between various groups of whites who were divided by sectional, ethnic, or economic interests. These clashes, too, sometimes yielded instances of social banditry.

Sectional conflict along the Kansas-Missouri border produced a famous and prolonged clash that paralleled the Anglo-Hispanic conflicts of the Southwest. At the end of the Civil War the Kansas-Missouri border had clearly established itself as the bloodiest region in the West. Already the scene of the eviction of the Mormons from Missouri during the 1830s and the battles of Bleeding Kansas during the 1850s, the area grew even more sanguinary as during the Civil War both southern guerrillas and their northern opponents hoisted the black flag that denoted no quarter. The guerrilla raids of William Quantrill and the reprisals of Kansas Jayhawkers and Union troops left a legacy of hatred that survived the war. When, following the Civil War, former Confederate guerrillas—Jesse James, his brother Frank, and the Younger brothers—began a series of robberies and killings, the lines between crime and social violence blurred as thoroughly as they did in Texas.

Jesse James and his supporters portrayed the James-Younger gang as social bandits; their victims, and those who had supported the Union during the Civil War, branded them as simple criminals. The James gang was both. In western Missouri years of social conflict had eroded public trust in the impartiality and honesty of law enforcement. Jesse James could credibly picture himself as a man persecuted for his political beliefs. He and the leading members of the gang came from prominent rural families. They were criminals, but they were criminals who could command widespread social support from both former Confederates and those who resented the increasing power of banks and railroads in the countryside. Jesse James hardly lost support when his usual targets were banks and railroads, two of the most hated institutions in the rural West in the nineteenth century. The jury that acquitted Jesse's brother, Frank James, for crimes he surely committed was made up of "well-to-do thrifty farmers."

Other western outlaws, such as the Doolin-Dalton gang in Oklahoma and Sam Bass in Texas, also managed to garner popular support in areas plagued by social conflict where respect for law enforcement had been seriously eroded. In Oklahoma Territory, the home of the Doolin-Dalton gang, settlers distrusted U.S. deputy marshals, whom they regarded as little better than criminals themselves. During the land rush, deputies used their offices unfairly to secure the best lands, and settlers believed that they arrested settlers for minor crimes in order to collect the fees they gained by persecuting "poor defenseless claim holders." Many accounts of the Doolin-Dalton gang attacked the deputy marshals and portrayed the outlaws as social bandits. The *Ardmore State Herald* made this kind of connection explicit:

Their life is made up of daring. Their courage is always with them and their rifles as well. They are kind to the benighted traveler, and it is not a fiction that when robbing a train they refuse to take from a woman.

It is said that Bill Doolin, at present the reigning highway man is friendly to the people in one neighborhood, bestowing all sorts of presents upon the children. It is his boast that he never killed a man.

This is fully a romantic figure as Robin Hood ever cut.

Social banditry and vigilantism demonstrate the connections between the individual violence of the West and larger social divisions within the West. These social divisions were, however, rarely clear-cut. Some *californios*, for example, cooperated with vigilantes. Similarly, many former Confederates tried to hunt down the James gang. As we move along our spectrum beyond banditry and vigilantism, however, the social dimensions of such conflicts grow even clearer, while the complicating factor of criminal activity fades.

Indian Hunting

Collective violence in the West claimed far more victims than did personal violence. During the boom period of Aurora in the early 1860s, for example, 17 people in the mining camp died from personal violence: gunshot wounds, beatings, or knife wounds. Such carnage was impressive for a town the size of Aurora, but collective violence in the area dwarfed it. Between 1861 and 1866 nearly 200 Indians and 30 whites died in interracial violence in the vicinity of the town. Many, perhaps most, of these Indian and white casualties were not the victims of warfare.

This fighting between Indians and whites around Aurora neither began nor ended as warfare. Paiute Indians, their native food sources destroyed by cattle, killed the cattle that whites grazed on their lands. Whites hunted and killed Indians. Indians murdered whites in retaliation. When federal troops became involved at the height of the conflict, the fighting took on aspects of war, but because federal troops engaged in mass executions of Paiute prisoners, the line here between warfare and murder is a fine one.

Because federal troops were involved, the fighting between whites and Paiutes around Aurora and in the Owens Valley, while clearly an example of organized conflict between the races, straddles the line between social violence and warfare. But other conflicts between Indians and whites in the Far West were less problematic. Warfare involves organized violence conducted by separate political entities; collective violence represents outbreaks of killing conducted by distinct social groups in a single society. When whites and Indians clashed in much of California and Oregon, federal troops were not involved, and Indian victims often lived and worked among whites. This fighting was not warfare; it was Indian hunting—the stalking and killing of human beings as if they were animals.

In wars, Indians, who usually defined themselves as warriors, confronted either federal troops or state militia. The army and militia were relatively disciplined commands representing the organized violence of the American state. In warfare, too, Indians and whites usually formed clearly distinct groups that were physically separate from each other. Warfare was hardly free of atrocities. Troops, as they did at Sand Creek, could run amok, and commanders could order the slaughter of captives. But the goal of this fighting was the subjugation and not the extermination of Indian peoples. Indeed, it is possible to go further than this and say that perhaps the most effective sympathizers with Indians in the western United States came to be career military officers. This was not true of the high command—Generals Sherman and Sheridan despised Indians—but it was true of many officers who actually led troops against Indians in the West. These "humanitarian generals," men such as Generals John Pope, George Crook, and Oliver O. Howard, acted in the tradition of General John E. Wool. They fought Indians, but they thought that far more wrongs rested with the whites than with their enemies. They rationalized their own conduct by arguing that unless they defeated Indians and placed them on reservations, Indians faced extermination at the hands of white settlers.

The Indians who were killed in battle, hanged, murdered, or exiled in the wars of resistance were no less dead or despoiled from having met their fate at the hands of duly constituted authorities, but in this situation whites could at least attempt to justify their actions by their own legal code. In southern Oregon and California, however, there was often not even the color of legality. People simply murdered Indians. The Indians they murdered often lived among them, working on ranches, farms, towns, or mining camps.

As the Owens Valley fighting demonstrates, the line between many wars of resistance and Indian hunting is admittedly a fine one. In the Rogue River region of Oregon, for example, where Indians resisted first fur trappers and then miners encroaching on their lands, sometimes there was war and sometimes there was Indian hunting. In August 1853, whites in Jacksonville, Oregon, hanged a seven-year-old Indian boy, justifying the murder on the grounds that "nits breed lice." In California such incidents became hardly worthy of comment.

Murders of Indians occurred everywhere, but the manifestations of organized racial violence—organized civilian campaigns to eradicate or enslave entire groups of Indians—were largely West Coast phenomena. These campaigns only marginally involved federal troops and most often did not involve soldiers at all. The worst episodes of Indian hunting occurred in California, where the state's Indian population declined from approximately 150,000 (a number already less than half of the population there at white contact) to about 30,000 in 1870. Whites hunted Indians down first to secure a labor force and later simply to eliminate the threat they thought Indians posed to their property. Citizens raised subscriptions to pay bounties on Indian scalps and heads. Extermination, its advocates claimed, was necessary because treaties and reservations did not stop Indian depredations and interference with white activities.

Whites killed an estimated 4,500 Indians in California between 1848 and 1880. This is a minimal estimate, for many attacks certainly went unrecorded. Nor does the number include those Indians whom violence drove away to starve or die of disease. Most of those killed died at the hands of civilians, not soldiers.

As mentioned above, the earliest Indian hunting was intended to secure a labor force for California's ranches and farms. Gold Rush California had a labor shortage, and during the 1850s and 1860s Americans adopted and modified the Spanish and Mexican practice of peonage to force Indians into the labor system. Although the California constitution outlawed slavery, the legislature passed in

1850 "An Act for the Government and Protection of Indians" that provided for the indenture—forced labor—of loitering or orphaned Indians, regulated their employment, and defined a special class of Indian crimes with appropriate punishments. In effect, the law enabled Americans to arrest any Indian not already working for whites. Whites could then pay the bail of these Indians and force them to work until they had earned enough to cover their bail or fines. If the Indians then attempted to leave, they were unemployed under the law and were once more liable to arrest. When the Americans coupled these indentures with other laws providing for Indian apprenticeship, they could legally compel unpaid labor from Indians.

In southern California this law allowed the perpetuation and expansion of the Mexican system of peonage that had developed following the end of the missions. Indians came to make up the bulk of the labor force on cattle ranches of the area, and a substantial proportion of the work force in the towns. In Los Angeles in 1860, the majority of Indians lived either in non-Indian households as servants or in nonfamily households.

In northern California, Americans transformed peonage into something very close to slavery. During the first two years of the Gold Rush, many Indians worked for white miners. They received no wages, only food and clothing. Incoming white miners, imbued with both hatred of Indians and anger at the advantage Indians gave their masters, ended the system by murdering and running off Indian laborers. Indians thereafter largely became agricultural laborers or house servants. The indenture and apprenticeship acts created lucrative opportunities for whites who could secure Indian workers by force.

In the 1850s and 1860s white gangs raided villages, kidnapped the occupants, and sold them to farmers and ranchers. Selling human beings is no longer peonage; it is slavery. Indian women and children were particular targets. The kidnappers often killed the parents of the children they seized. When children tried to escape, whites often hunted them down and killed them. California did not repeal the law that encouraged such crimes until 1863. With Indian indentures illegal, whites could not legally compel Indians to labor, and the incentive to kidnap and sell Indians vanished.

Before it ended, however, this system of forced labor helped to destroy the existing village life of many California Indians. By 1860 a little more than half the 32,000 Indians remaining in the state lived among whites. Already dwindling under the effects of epidemics and white attacks, many communities now had their children stolen and their women removed. When working for Anglo Americans or *californios*, relatively few Indians lived in family units. They often lived sexually segregated lives in which reproduction and the raising of children were not feasible. And so their population continued to fall.

The repeal of California's Indian legislation ended slave raiding, but it did not end Indian hunting, because there remained a second rationale for killing Indians: the suppression of Indian raiding. Some California tribes, such as the Yokuts, were already accomplished raiders at the time of the American conquest. They raided American ranches just as they had earlier raided Mexican ranches. Other groups, who had not previously raided, began to raid as invading whites deprived them of access to their usual resources. White cattle replaced wild game; pigs ate the acorns that were an Indian staple; miners ruined the salmon streams. When

Indians killed white livestock, angry whites retaliated by killing Indians. Reciprocal murders followed, with guns matched against bows and spears, until the whites
began campaigns of systematic extermination that lasted until the Indians were
dead or had fled.

These campaigns became grim vendettas; each side retaliated against the other
with such atrocities as they could muster. But for every white, often a woman or
child, who died, whites indiscriminately killed a hundred or more Indians—men,
women, and children. A gruesome murder of a family or of women and children
at home alone aroused strong emotions on both sides, and it is not hard to
understand how angry men, either Indian or white, would set out to take quick
and harsh revenge. But the attacks by whites went beyond such moments of
passion. Some men became professional Indian killers, hunting human beings as
they would animals. These murderers enjoyed their work and were admired for
it.

Hi Good and Robert Anderson were two Indian hunters. They operated in the
Yahi Indian territory of California near Mount Lassen. By 1872 the Indian hunts
they and others staged had virtually wiped out the Yahis, a subgroup of the Yanas.
One small band remained in hiding for years until its last member, Ishi, left his
native canyons in despair in 1911. The Yanas as a whole declined from 2,000–
3,000 people when the Americans arrived during the Gold Rush to fewer than
50 by 1872.

Good and Anderson's favorite tactic was to locate a Yahi camp, surround it,
and shoot the inhabitants as they emerged at dawn. In one of these attacks Good
spared a young boy whom he found lying in a stream because the child had six
toes. Good kept him as a servant for years. When the child was a teenager, he
took a rifle and stepped into the bushes beside the road that led to the house
where he and Good lived. The trees around the houses were still decorated with
Yahi scalps. When Good walked by, the boy stepped out and blew off the back
of Good's head. He then waited for the whites to come, having, after all, no
people to flee to. When the whites came, they hanged him. Anderson drew a
moral from the story: you cannot trust an Indian, he wrote, no matter how much
you do for him.

The California experience serves to make the logic of the humanitarian generals
alluded to earlier more compelling than it otherwise might seem. Where the
federal government, either the Bureau of Indian Affairs or the army, did not
control relations between whites and Indians, conditions became a nightmare.
Genocide was never the official policy of the U.S. government, but it was the
wish of many, although hardly all, Anglo American settlers. When left to their
own devices, they could on occasion put it into practice.

Indian hunting was only the most dramatic manifestation of the collective racial
violence in the West. No minority group totally escaped such confrontations.

Racial Violence: The Chinese

Next to the Indians, the Chinese probably were the victims of the most direct
racial violence. But whereas California Indians faced organized violence that
compelled them to labor, the Chinese faced violence that sought to prevent them
from laboring. The Chinese worked only at the sufferance of whites. As long as
white labor was scarce, or as long as whites found no use for a resource that the

Chinese exploited, most whites were content to leave the Chinese alone. Few whites, for example, had wanted the arduous, unappealing, and dangerous job of building railroads through the Sierra Nevada. As the Chinese moved into new areas of urban labor, however, they began to seem a real threat in occupations white workers expected to control. The Chinese, white workingmen argued, drove whites from positions by agreeing to work for less. They could work for less, the argument went, because they were racially inferior semislaves who lived hopelessly degraded lives. If allowed to displace whites, they would not only soon force everyone down to their standard of living, but also strip the country of its wealth by sending most of their earnings back to China.

Anticoolie clubs, which began to spring up in California during the late 1860s and blossomed in the 1870s, set out to end this threat by enforcing a ban on Chinese labor. These clubs sought laws against Chinese labor and organized economic boycotts of Chinese-made goods, but they did not confine themselves to political and economic action. Club members physically attacked Chinese in the streets; they were suspected of arson at factories that employed Chinese. Not only workers but also tradespeople, who saw their businesses threatened by larger manufacturers employing Chinese labor, joined these clubs. In time, manufacturers themselves turned against the Chinese as Chinese merchants attempted to open factories in competition with white-owned factories.

By the early 1870s anti-Chinese agitation became an almost irresistible way for politicians to attract the votes of workers. The Chinese provided a scapegoat for the economic troubles that beset California during its depression of 1872–75. First the Democrats and then Dennis Kearney and the Workingman's party seized on the anticoolie movement as a route to political power, while in the countryside the Caucasian League both agitated against the Chinese and led a campaign of terror against them. The new California constitution of 1879 denied the vote to the Chinese and forbade their employment on any state or local public works project. The anti-Chinese movement then turned to securing a federal ban on Chinese immigration. In 1882 the movement achieved its goal when Congress passed a bill that forbade the immigration of all Chinese laborers for a period of ten years. Congress regularly extended the ban thereafter.

This victory did not end agitation against the Chinese. White workers continued to blame them for any deterioration in their own wages and working conditions. In the mid-1880s a wave of violence that extended from the Pacific Northwest and northern California into Wyoming rocked Chinese communities across the West. White mobs drove the Chinese from Eureka, California, and from Tacoma and Seattle in Washington. A mob burned the Chinese section of Rock Springs, Wyoming, to the ground and killed 25 Chinese. Such attacks, coupled with immigration restriction, served to reduce drastically the total Chinese population in the United States. Many migrants returned to China, and new migrants could not enter to replace them. The Chinese population of California fell by at least one-third between 1890 and 1900.

The violent reaction of white workers against the Chinese clearly worked to enforce the existing racial division of labor, but most white workers saw their attacks as defensive. They believed that employers would use the Chinese to drive

Both class and racial antagonisms erupted in Seattle's anti-Chinese riot of February 8, 1886. Workers and their middle-class allies evicted the Chinese from the city.

down their wages and reduce them to a status no higher than that of the Chinese workers themselves. The 1885 attacks upon the Chinese by white miners in Rock Springs, Wyoming, arose, for example, from white miners' anger at attempts by the Union Pacific to replace white workers in the company coal mines with Chinese workers at lower wages. If the Chinese worked for less, one logical tactic might have been a campaign to organize the Chinese to demand wages equal to those paid whites. Anticoolie organizers argued that this was impossible. They asserted that the Chinese, because of their racial makeup, could never share the values or ambitions of white workers. They were, the theory went, a lesser people content with a lesser wage, and if they were not content to remain in menial jobs unwanted by whites, then they had to be banned.

Economic Conflict

Racial conflict in the West never vanished, but it was at its height in the years just preceding and following the Civil War. By the late nineteenth century, racial conflicts tended to become thoroughly embroiled with class and economic conflicts. In San Miguel County, New Mexico, for example, a bitter dispute developed in 1889 between Hispanic villagers who attempted to defend their communal grazing lands from Anglo cattle ranchers and merchants who claimed that the lands were not communal but were partible—that is, they could be divided and sold. When ranchers fenced the land, masked and armed horsemen— *las gorras blancas* (the White Caps)—destroyed the fences, and as the conflict escalated, they broadened their attacks to include railroads, lumber operations, and Anglo businesses. Although the movement initially had support from the largely white Knights of Labor, it soon came to be primarily the resistance of communal *campesinos* against Anglo capitalist intrusions. It was at once an economic conflict and a racial conflict.

Other examples of this kind of ambiguous social conflict, both economic and racial and ethnic, abound. White riots against the Chinese obviously contained racial and economic aspects. So, too, did the El Paso Salt War of 1877. The war resulted from attempts by local Anglo American politicians to claim ownership of the salt beds 110 miles west of El Paso. Hispanics had traditionally used these beds as a communal resource. When Judge Charles Howard claimed ownership and tried to ban the Hispanics, they rose up against the Anglo Americans, killing Howard and four other Anglos. American troops had to enter the area to reassert political control.

Making a precise distinction between racial and economic elements in such incidents is hopeless, but nonetheless, economic elements increasingly seemed to dominate as the nineteenth century wore on. Certainly the economic system provided causes enough for conflict even without racial tensions.

A certain amount of economic conflict was basic to laissez-faire capitalism. In the West, as elsewhere in the capitalist economy, competition theoretically acted as the mainspring of the economy. Producers competed for markets. The most efficient producers eliminated the least efficient. The result of such competition, which nineteenth-century social theorists liked to compare to evolutionary competition, would be material progress.

Even the most enthusiastic proponents of competition, however, intended to keep it within bounds. When advocates of laissez-faire capitalism proposed unrestrained economic competition, they did not mean to be taken literally. Businesses were not to battle like rough-and-tumble brawlers. Economic adversaries instead should abide by a kind of Marquis of Queensbury economic code. Just as in boxing the object was to win without resort to kidney punches, eye gouging, or rabbit punches, so economic rivals should fight it out without engaging in theft, fraud, sabotage, or deceit. Laissez-faire might translate as "let it be," but the code always presumed that the state should not let everything be. It had to enforce certain standards.

In the actual economic life of the West, however, competitors did not completely conform to laissez-faire expectations. Sometimes they proved to be reluctant gladiators who tried to avoid any conflict at all. Railroads, timber companies, and mining companies, for example, all attempted to avoid competition by forming pools to control their markets. On the other extreme, economic adversaries competed, but they readily indulged in the economic equivalent of a rabbit punch or an eye gouge whenever they thought such tactics might succeed. On the Comstock Lode in 1878, disputes between the Alta Mining Company and the neighboring Justice Mining Company led to the recruitment of so-called shotgun miners to fight for the contested ore body. The miners themselves prevented this particular dispute from going further, but a similar controversy several years earlier had killed several miners.

The railroads occasionally decided possession of preferred routes by mustering armed employees instead of lawyers. In 1878, for example, the Atchison, Topeka and Santa Fe held the rights to a pass into the Leadville mining district against the Denver and Rio Grande with the support of armed workers and supportive citizens.

At their most extreme, such business rivalries threw entire areas into turmoil. In Lincoln County, New Mexico, a dispute over a life insurance policy, a business rivalry between two firms—Tunstall and McSween versus Murphy and Dolan—and cattle stealing combined to create the Lincoln County War in 1878. The ensuing violence encapsulated most of the brief and bloody history of Billy the Kid, who served as a gunman for Tunstall and McSween. New Mexican territorial authorities of the Santa Fe Ring, who sympathized with the Murphy-Dolan faction, did little to end the fighting, leading President Rutherford B. Hayes to declare the county in a state of insurrection and to intervene to restore peace.

Wars such as the one in Lincoln County were not good for anybody's business, and economic violence rarely involved powerful businessmen recruiting hired killers against each other. Violence was far more likely to occur when powerful economic groups found themselves in conflict with groups of small producers or with their own workers.

Conflict on the Cattle Ranges

Large cattlemen were probably the most prone to violence of any economic interest group in the West, although the scale of their violence would not equal that of mining companies against their workers. Cattle ranchers' predilection for violence largely resulted from the tenuousness of their own legal claims to the land. Driving competitors away seemed more certain than fighting them in courts. The most famous conflicts involving cattlemen sprang from large ranchers' ultimately unsuccessful attempts to maintain their illegal monopoly on the public domain.

Farmers challenged the cattlemen, but contrary to western myth, their attempt to farm was not the source of most violence. Farmers did cut the fences of the large ranchers, and ranchers did attempt to drive out farmers, but most violence resulted from competition between livestock raisers, not between cattle raisers and farmers. Such violence fell into two principal categories: conflicts between cattle raisers and sheepherders and conflicts between large and small ranchers.

Conflicts between cattlemen and itinerant sheep grazers occurred throughout the West but were probably most virulent in the Southwest, the Great Basin, and the Pacific Northwest. Like so much other economic violence, these conflicts often had racial, religious, and ethnic overtones. In New Mexico, although cattlemen attacked all shepherds who threatened their range, most sheep owners were Mexican Americans, whereas most cattlemen were Anglo Americans. In Lincoln County, New Mexico, during the 1880s the Lincoln County Stock Growers Association first warned sheepmen out and then, if their threats were ignored, killed the flocks. In Nevada and southern Idaho the conflict was not racial, but it was often religious and ethnic. There the shepherds were Mormons and Basques, and the cattlemen, Anglo Americans. The owners of the Sparks-Harrell ranch, for example, drew a deadline across the Goose Creek basin in the 1890s and declared no sheep could proceed beyond that line. When the shepherds insisted, the company hired gunmen who were instructed to kill if necessary. In 1896 two employees of the ranch shot and killed two young Mormon sheepherders after an argument over their intent to cross the deadline.

Large ranchers also turned to violence in their disputes with small cattlemen. Fences often provided the immediate point of conflict. Large ranchers fenced off large sections of the public domain. Small ranchers, who could not hope to pasture their animals on their relatively small claims, cut the fences to provide their cattle with access to the public lands. In central Texas the result was the Fence-Cutters' War of 1883–84, which resulted in deaths in Clay County and near open warfare in Brown County. Only the passage of a state law making fence cutting a felony in 1884 ended the fighting.

The peak of violence between large and small stock owners occurred in Wyoming when members of the Wyoming Stockgrowers Association moved to eliminate small ranchers who they believed were rustling their stock. The roots of this violence lay in quarrels over the ownership of mavericks— unbranded calves found without their mother on the open range. The big ranchers who made up the association had been in the habit of simply appropriating the mavericks and dividing them up among themselves, but during the cattle boom their own cowboys began branding mavericks to form their own small herds. As the editor of the *Laramie Sentinel* put it, this created the necessity for the "big thieves" to find a way they "could head off the small thieves." Various attempts by the Wyoming legislature, which was dominated by the Wyoming Stockgrowers Association, to settle the issue failed to defuse the hostility between large and small cattle ranchers.

In the late 1880s, as the big ranchers staggered under the double blow of declining prices and the legacy of the bitter winter of 1886–87, their conflict with the small ranchers deepened. Most of these small ranchers were former cowboys who had homesteaded land and established small herds of their own. They regarded the big cattlemen as illegal monopolists of the public domain; the big ranchers considered the former cowboys to be rustlers who had helped themselves to the ranchers' stock. Rustling certainly did occur, but not on the scale big ranchers contended. In Johnson County—an area controlled by small ranchers— there were only 13 cases of cattle stealing in the peak year, 1889. It is also true, however, that juries rarely convicted accused rustlers. In 1889 the courts dismissed all the cases in Johnson County.

To defeat the "rustlers" of Johnson County, the big cattlemen moved beyond the courts. They began in 1889 by lynching James Avrell, a local homesteader, and Ella Watson, a prostitute known as Cattle Kate because she exchanged sex for stolen cattle. The courts dismissed the case when the four leading witnesses to the crime failed to appear to testify. In 1891 leading members of the Wyoming Stockgrowers Association escalated the conflict with the small ranchers even further. They began to organize a "lynching bee" to clean out "rustlers" in Johnson County. They set out to recruit gunmen in Texas even as unknown persons began to lynch and dry-gulch suspected rustlers in the county itself.

On Tuesday, April 5, 1892, a special train left Cheyenne for Casper carrying 25 Texas gunmen and 24 "regulators": ranch owners, managers, foremen, and detectives. No cowboys took part in the expedition; their employers apparently feared that they sympathized with the small ranchers. The invaders carried a death list of people they planned to execute or drive off.

The result of the expedition was a murderous fiasco. The little army of gunmen shot one "rustler" but then took a whole day to take a cabin held by his companion, the aptly named Nate Champion. After finally setting fire to the cabin and murdering Champion, the invaders marched into a county that was by then armed and ready to meet them. Eventually they fortified themselves in a ranch where 200 local settlers besieged them. In what is probably a telling piece of evidence about marksmanship in the Old West, the invaders and settlers shot at each other for three days before the cavalry arrived to end the fighting, and no one was killed on either side. One Texas gunman, who in the excitement shot himself in the groin, did die later.

Class Conflict

In 1892 when the Johnson County War erupted, confrontations between groups of armed westerners determined to defend their economic interests were becoming increasingly common. But unlike the Johnson County War, most of these confrontations involved open class conflict between workers and their employers. By the 1890s and on into the early twentieth century, western miners, in the words of one historian, "literally waged armed war with their capitalist adversaries."

In the same year that armed groups of small ranchers confronted the hired gunmen of large ranchers in Wyoming, armed miners confronted the gunmen of mine owners in the mining towns strung out along the canyons of the Coeur d'Alene River of Idaho. The Mine Owners' Protective Association (MOA) had hired Pinkerton and Thiel detectives to infiltrate the local miners' union and, allegedly, to act as agents provocateurs. One of these detectives, Charles A. Siringo, actually became secretary of the Gem Miners' Union local.

The Coeur d'Alene strike had begun when the MOA reduced wages. The miners walked out, and the owners, vowing never to hire a union man, set out to break the union. They perfected a set of tactics that would become increasingly common over the next two decades wherever the unions commanded significant local support. Knowing local officials to be unsympathetic, the mine owners, while maintaining their own armed force of guards, claimed that local authorities could not preserve order and appealed to the governor of the state for militia. If the governor refused, the mine owners turned to the federal government and courts for marshals and, if possible, troops.

Such tactics proved effective in Coeur d'Alene. Although initially peaceful, angry miners, frustrated over the length of the strike and the federal injunctions that the mine owners obtained against them, took up arms in July 1892. They assaulted the Frisco and Gem mines, destroyed the Frisco mill, and captured all

The reality of class conflict in the West: armed coal miners at Trinidad, Colorado, about 1913.

the guards and scabs. They then marched on the Bunker Hill and Sullivan mines, and, after capturing the company's ore concentrator, which had cost $500,000, they secured the dismissal of all the scabs there. The fighting left six men dead.

The miners had won a pyrrhic victory. The MOA now easily obtained a declaration of martial law. Six companies of the Idaho national guard marched in and made wholesale arrests of union members and of local businessmen and lawyers who sympathized with the union. The soldiers herded more than 300 men into crude stockades or "bullpens." Eventually, in 1893, the Supreme Court overturned the convictions of those who were convicted of crimes rising out of the strike, but by then the MOA had largely broken the union.

One of the greatest achievements of the mine owners in the late 1890s and early twentieth century was their success in driving a wedge between middle-class and working-class members of the mining towns. Many of the people in the bullpens of Coeur d'Alene in 1892 had been merchants and lawyers who had backed the strike. Middle-class men and women who sold the miners goods and provided services often sympathized with their customers. Such support became rarer and rarer in the late 1890s and the early twentieth century. Labor violence in many places became not just a struggle between laborers and their employers, but also a struggle between classes that convulsed communities.

Two strikes at Cripple Creek, Colorado, illustrated the changing relations between the workers and the middle class. At Cripple Creek in 1893 the miners' union fought a bitter and violent strike when mine owners attempted to increase

The intervention of the armed forces of the state often decided western labor struggles as it did in Cripple Creek in 1893.

the working day in the mines from eight to ten hours. Armed miners confronted armed deputies, with casualties on both sides. The miners seized mines, banished scabs, and dynamited one mine. The miners, however, obtained significant middle-class support. Governor Davis Waite, in one of the few cases in which a state government proved sympathetic to striking miners, helped negotiate a settlement and used the state militia to prevent further violence rather than breaking the union. When the strike ended, Cripple Creek returned to normal. Both business and the miners prospered.

The second strike came a decade later. It arose because the Western Federation of Miners (WFM) was an industrial union pledged to protect not only the underground miners who were victorious in 1893 but also the less skilled and more vulnerable mill and smelter workers. The 1903 strike arose over the refusal of the Colorado Reduction and Refining Company to allow the WFM to organize its mills. The WFM and the underground miners of Cripple Creek backed the smelter workers, and a strike ensued.

The strike was long and complicated, but bitterly antiunion mill owners defeated the WFM because they could rely on an antiunion governor to send troops and because the miners gradually lost the support of the local middle class. Governor J. H. Peabody of Colorado twice dispatched the militia to Cripple Creek over the protests of local officials. They came the second time not to preserve order but, in the words of their commander, "to do up this damned anarchistic federation." In doing up the WFM, militia officers refused to obey court orders or honor writs of habeas corpus. But the critical blow to the union was the rise of a local Citizens' Alliance. As the lengthy strike progressed, merchants found it impossible to extend any more credit to miners. The union then opened cooperative stores, a move that alienated local shopkeepers. This dispute gave conservative elements in the community an opening, and by the end of August they had organized the Citizens' Alliance, with largely compulsory membership among local businessmen. The Citizens' Alliance operated as a vigilante organization and was determined to break the union and the strike. By March 1904, members of the Citizens' Alliance had begun forcibly deporting union leaders and strikers from the town.

The conflict exploded in a series of ugly incidents in June of 1904. That month, shortly after nonunion men reached a railroad station to board a train, someone blew up the railroad depot, killing 13 men. The Citizens' Alliance blamed the WFM; the WFM blamed agents provocateurs hired by the mine owners. But initiative lay with the Citizens' Alliance, whose members forced, at gunpoint, the resignation of the sheriff and other local officials sympathetic to the WFM. The militia and the Citizens' Alliance then began the wholesale arrest and deportation of union members, while Cripple Creek employers introduced a permit system designed to deny employment to all union workers. The Citizens' Alliance broke the union, but in doing so they in effect also broke themselves. Two years later Cripple Creek had nonunion miners and lower wages, but business was stagnant, buildings were vacant, and real estate values had declined by half. Wealth continued to pour from the mines, but merchants of towns relearned too late that they indeed lived not off the mines but off the miners.

The Cripple Creek strike was only one of a series of violent confrontations that shook the West at the turn of the century. Throughout the West striking miners faced federal troops and state militia, as well as small private armies of gunmen hired by the mine owners. Although the WFM bore the brunt of the violent conflict with employers, the conflict extended beyond the hardrock mines. One of the bloodiest incidents occurred in 1917 in coal mines of Ludlow, Colorado, that were owned by John D. Rockefeller. After a bitter strike in which the wives and daughters of the largely Greek, Slavic, and Italian miners played as active a role as did their husbands, strikebreakers, militia, and deputies attacked the tent colony that strikers had erected after their eviction from company housing. The strikers resisted, and as the battle raged, the attackers set fire to the tents. The attack killed 39 people, including two women and 11 children who suffocated in a pit underneath a burning tent.

The Ludlow Massacre was particularly notorious because so many women and children were among the victims, but neither attacks on armed strikers nor murders of union organizers were unusual in the first years of the twentieth century. Nor were they confined to mining. They occurred also in the lumber industry. The Wobblies in particular developed, and reveled in, a fearsome, if largely unwarranted, reputation. They often preached industrial sabotage but rarely practiced it. They were more often the victims of violence than its instigators. Armed gunmen hired by the employers, militia, federal troops, and vigilantes from citizens' alliances repeatedly assaulted IWW organizers. In Butte, Montana, in 1917, vigilantes lynched Frank Little, a one-eyed, part Indian, antiwar Wobbly

These two photographs, one before and the other after the militia's attack on the strikers' tent colony at Ludlow, Colorado, demonstrate the ferocity of official violence in the West.

organizer. And in the lumber mill town of Everett, Washington, in 1916, local officials attempted to shut the city to Wobblies and Wobbly organizers. When Seattle Wobblies came anyway, vigilantes deputized by the town sheriff met their boat at the dock. Who fired the first shot remains unclear, but in the ensuing gun battle at least five Wobblies and two deputies died, and at least 51 other people were wounded.

Violence and the West

The endemic social violence of the West was not a mere sideshow to western history, nor something that was overcome as the West became "civilized." Instead, violence was an intrinsic part of western society, and it was thus intimately connected with the processes that created western communities and situated them within the larger western social order. Both the powerful and the weak resorted to violence, but they did not achieve equal success. The state tended to quickly suppress social bandits, *las gorras blancas*, and armed workers. Vigilantes, citizens' alliance gunmen, and California Indian hunters either succeeded without molestation or with the aid of agencies of the state. On the whole, extralegal violence of whites against minorities met far less official opposition than did the violence of minorities against whites.

This privileged access to extralegal violence not surprisingly paralleled a similar uneven access to political and economic power. Politics remained the major arena for resolving the conflicts of class, race, community, and economic interest. The frequency of social violence demonstrates that politics could not resolve all social conflicts, but politics, not violence, played the major role in mediating between the diverse interests and communities of the West.

Readings

Beckham, Stephen Dow. *Requiem for a People: The Rogue Indians and the Frontiersmen.* Norman: University of Oklahoma Press, 1971.

Brown, Richard. *Strain of Violence: Historical Studies of American Violence and Vigilantism.* New York: Oxford University Press, 1975.

Byrkit, James W. *Forging the Copper Collar: Arizona's Labor-Management War of 1901–21.* Tucson: University of Arizona Press, 1982.

Daniel, Cletus E. *Bitter Harvest: A History of California Farmworkers, 1870-1941.* Berkeley: University of California Press, 1981.

Jensen, Vernon H. *Heritage of Conflict: Labor Relations in the Non-Ferrous Metals Industry up to 1930.* Ithaca, N.Y.: Cornell University Press, 1950.

Kroeber, Theodora. *Ishi in Two Worlds: A Biography of the Last Wild Indian in North America.* Berkeley: University of California Press, 1976.

Larson, Robert. "The White Caps of New Mexico: A Study in Ethnic Militancy in the Southwest." *Pacific Historical Quarterly* 44 (May 1975): 171–86.

Lingenfelter, Richard E. *The Hardrock Miners: A History of the Mining Labor Movement in the American West, 1863–1893.* Berkeley: University of California Press, 1974.

McGrath, Roger D. *Gunfighters, Highwaymen, and Vigilantes: Violence on the Frontier.* Berkeley: University of California Press, 1984.

Papanikolas, Zeese. *Buried Unsung: Louis Tikas and the Ludlow Massacre.* Salt Lake City: University of Utah Press, 1982.

Rosenbaum, Robert J. *Mexicano Resistance in the Southwest: The Sacred Right of Self-Preservation.* Austin: University of Texas Press, 1981.

Saxton, Alexander. *Indispensable Enemy: Labor and the Anti-Chinese Movement in California*. Berkeley: University of California Press, 1971.

Schwantes, Carlos. *Coxey's Army: An American Odyssey*. Lincoln: University of Nebraska Press, 1985.

Tyler, Robert L. *Rebels of the Woods: The I.W.W. in the Pacific Northwest*. Eugene: University of Oregon Press, 1967.

Utley, Robert M. *Billy the Kid: A Short and Violent Life*. Lincoln: University of Nebraska Press, 1989.

White, Richard. "Outlaw Gangs of the Middle Border: American Social Bandits." *Western Historical Quarterly* 12 (October 1981): 387–408.

CHAPTER 14

Western Politics

IN the nineteenth- and early-twentieth-century West, politics served as the handmaiden of economic development. This linkage of politics and development distinguished the West from the East and South in degree more than in kind, but differences in degree are nonetheless significant. Precisely because western politics has been so thoroughly developmental politics, the West rarely forged any kind of larger regional political unity. There has been no western equivalent of the solid South. Various states, communities, and sections in the West competed for the same capital—whether private or federal; they thus saw each other as rivals as well as allies. Even periods of protest by westerners against eastern domination tended to accentuate the region's internal divisions as much as highlight its differences from the East.

The West thus rarely had a consistent set of internal political alliances, let alone a consistent regional ideology, but it did develop certain distinctive political characteristics that provide coherence of a sort. First and foremost was the search for outside capital that dominated western political efforts. Second, the western electorate differed from the electorate in the East and South. In most western states and territories women obtained the vote earlier than elsewhere in the country, while white westerners simultaneously excluded most racial minorities from political participation. This particular combination of including women and excluding minorities marked the West as unique. Third, ethnocultural issues revolving around religion, ethnicity, and morals were usually less prominent in the West than elsewhere. Fourth, party loyalty in the West was markedly weaker than in the South, Northeast, and Midwest. The national parties—the Democrats and Republicans—that dominated the western political landscape have usually had weak local organizations. Western politics became a politics of personality. Indeed, the major contribution of westerners to national politics was an almost limitless resourcefulness in finding new ways to weaken party ties. Fifth, for a brief but important period in the late nineteenth century westerners did participate in a movement that transformed the politics of the whole region: Populism. And as an attitude, more than as a specific program, Populism has had a lasting legacy for the West. Sixth, and finally, westerners have anchored politics firmly to the federal government. Westerners have not resolved and, given the economic and social realities of the West, could not resolve most issues within their state governments. Resolution of political issues in the West has repeatedly required federal intervention.

The dependence on the federal government has been the central reality of western politics. The weaknesses of western political parties, the huge landholdings of the federal government within the region, and the long period during which the West was an economic colony of the East have all tended to diminish state power and increase federal power. From the building of the transcontinental railroads through the Bureau of Reclamation's irrigation efforts in the West, the government provided the only alternative to total dependence on eastern or foreign capital. As a result, successful western politicians have been those able to secure federal favors for significant constituents or constituencies. In the East, politicians sought to prevent federal interference with the power held by corporations; in the South, they sought to prevent federal interference with an established racial order. In the West, politicians sought federal intervention to open up Indian reservations, build railroads, and guarantee cheap and docile labor; above all they have sought to control federal land and resource policy. In Congress, western politicians have usually traded away their votes in national political controversies in return for support on the issue that mattered a great deal in the West but not so greatly in the East or South: land and resource policy.

Political Pattern I: The Electorate

In most of the United States during the nineteenth and early twentieth centuries the electorate was overwhelmingly white and male. On the surface the exclusion of minorities from the political arena in the West hardly made the region distinctive. Texas, for example, simply extended the southern disfranchisement of blacks to Mexican Americans. Between 1902 and 1918 whites in South Texas enacted a poll tax, approved the whites-only primary, eliminated interpreters at the voting booths, and denied naturalized citizens assistance from election judges until they had been citizens for 21 years. Together these measures drastically reduced the number of Hispanic voters. White Texans justified such measures by arguing that the Hispanics were "a class of foreigners who claim American citizenship but who are as ignorant of things American as a mule."

Disfranchisement of minorities elsewhere in the West differed from disfranchisement in Texas because tactics such as the poll tax or a whites-only primary proved unnecessary. Western minorities—Indians, Chinese, Japanese, and most Mexican immigrants—could not vote because they were not citizens. The law prohibited Chinese and Japanese immigrants from becoming citizens, and Indians could become citizens only by renouncing their tribal ties. Mexican immigrants could become citizens, but the proximity of their homeland, to which most hoped to return, kept most from seeking citizenship. In El Paso, for example, about 90 percent of the Mexican immigrants retained their Mexican citizenship. When the Mexican Revolution broke out, Mexican immigrants in the United States eagerly supported it. To this immigrant generation "politics meant the Revolution and one's country meant Mexico." Only in New Mexico did Hispanic voters possess significant political power. Indeed, Anglo fear that the Hispanic New Mexican majority would exercise too much political power was one of the factors blocking efforts to attain statehood in the 1890s.

Minorities more often entered the western political arena as objects of political action instead of participants in it. Denis Kearney, an Irish-born drayman, mastered the art of turning hatred of the Chinese into a tool for attacking the economic and political elite. Anti-Chinese agitation had been a staple of San

Francisco and California politics long before Kearney appeared on the scene in 1877, but he was the first to recognize its full political possibilities. Kearney himself was not a worker; he was a businessman who entered politics because the condition of the city streets made his draying business difficult. His anger over potholes, however, soon yielded to his anger at the Chinese and the rich.

Kearney linked the rich and the Chinese in the same way that poor white southerners before the Civil War had linked rich planters and their slaves. In both cases the argument ran that nonwhites were the means by which rich whites exploited poor whites. Thousands gathered in the sand lots (or empty building sites) of San Francisco to hear Kearney denounce the millionaires on Nob Hill for using the Chinese to drive down wages. By 1878 Kearney and his Workingmen's Party of California (WPC) had become a major political force in San Francisco and elsewhere in California. The WPC briefly solidified working-class and lower-middle-class immigrant voters against the Chinese, the rich, and the older parties. In near panic Republican and Democratic leaders nominated a joint slate in the election for the California constitutional convention in 1879. Their "nonpartisan" ticket elected 81 of 152 delegates. The WPC elected 51.

The meteoric rise of the WPC made possible their equally dramatic fall. Henry George, who became California's most famous radical reformer, was not surprised. The WPC, with its focus on the Chinese and its attacks on the corruption of politics by the rich, could not institute, and indeed did not have, "any shadow of reform which will lessen social inequalities or purify politics." The WPC ended up advocating the most conventional and the most fruitless of American reforms: "Elect honest men to office and have them cut down taxation." Honesty and harassment of the Chinese hardly amounted to a program to transform the social order.

The decline of the WPC did not bring a decline in anti-Chinese feeling; harassment of Chinese simply returned to more conventional channels. Political repression was usually not the repression of choice in the West. Cultural prejudice, economic discrimination, and, if necessary, extralegal violence proved sufficient to maintain the dual labor system that relegated nonwhites to menial work. Politics contributed to economic inequality, but it did so passively by *not* raising the dual labor system as an issue. When outright racial repression of Hispanics, Chinese, and Mexicans took place, it was most often the work of private groups ranging from vigilantes to mobs to Indian hunters. The official agencies of the government once again contributed to repression by *not* doing anything, by allowing private groups to gain their ends with little or no interference.

Women's Suffrage

The domination of western politics and the western electorate by whites remained constant throughout the late nineteenth and early twentieth centuries, but within that white electorate a major shift took place: millions of women gained the vote. A large majority of the first states and territories to grant women the vote were in the West. Before the country as a whole ratified the nineteenth amendment that gave women the vote nationally in 1920, women had secured the vote in Wyoming (1869), Utah (1870), Colorado (1893), Idaho (1896), Washington (1910), California (1911), Arizona (1912), Kansas (1912), Oregon (1912), Mon-

Women in Washington campaign for suffrage in 1910.

tana (1914), and Nevada (1914). In some of these states women could initially vote only in local and school board elections, but the entries they made into the electoral system grew wider and wider.

Why, and even how, women got the vote in the earliest territories remains something of a mystery. Certainly it was not pressure from women themselves. When in 1869 Wyoming Territory granted white women the vote, there were only a little over 1,000 non-Indian women over ten years old in the entire territory. One writer for *Harper's Weekly* suggested that the very scarcity of women had won them the vote. "Wyoming gave women the right to vote," he wrote, "in much the same spirit that New York or Pennsylvania might vote to enfranchise angels or Martians."

In Utah the motives were clearer. The Mormons gave women the vote to protect polygamy and to preserve their own social order from attack. In the 1860s the vast majority of Americans regarded polygamy as both sinful and degrading to women. By granting women the vote, Mormons sought to counter such external attacks. Women's suffrage, Mormons thought, would demonstrate the high standing accorded women in Utah and their own consent to the existing order. Women's votes would help preserve the very institution that gentiles argued degraded women. The Mormon leadership badly needed these new voters. In 1870 new mining ventures and the completion of the transcontinental railroad introduced large numbers of non-Mormon voters into Utah at the same time as a sharp split occurred in church ranks over Brigham Young's policies. In Salt Lake City, in particular, the church worried about losing political control to an alliance of gentiles and dissident Mormons. Mormon women would add significantly to the church's electoral strength, while the few "gentile" women would add little strength to the anti-Mormon bloc. Although they had little to do with securing passage of suffrage legislation, many Mormon women did become enthusiastic political participants until the Edmunds-Tucker Act of 1887, as part of Congress's assault on polygamy and the Mormon church, abolished women's suffrage in Utah. The Utah State Constitution would restore the vote to women in 1895.

Although the two initial victories came with little participation by women, the suffrage movement that rolled over the West later in the century was very much a women's movement. During the last quarter of the century the West began to produce a group of skilled and articulate suffrage leaders: Abigail Scott Duniway of Oregon, who started her women's rights paper, the *New Northwest*, in 1871; Caroline Nichols Churchill of Colorado, who published the *Colorado Antelope* during the 1890s; and Jeannette Rankin of Montana, who would become the first woman elected to Congress.

Abigail Scott Duniway, the first and most influential of the western suffragists, proved that western women were more politically adept in the West than were better-known eastern leaders such as Susan B. Anthony and Anna Howard Shaw. Duniway was an agrarian reformer before she committed herself to suffrage, and she was and remained an ardent Oregon booster who believed that the "new country" was the best country. An ambitious businesswoman who used her lecture tours to speculate in town lots across the Pacific Northwest, she promoted a range of reforms that went well beyond suffrage. She demanded equal economic rights for women and protection for their property. Socially, she called for divorce reforms, shared responsibility for housework and child care, and better education for women. A self-conscious westerner, she saw her natural constituency as "women of the border": farmers' wives, countrywomen, and working-class women. She addressed them and eastern audiences in a direct, forcible, "offhand" manner that many regarded as peculiarly western. She maintained her fight in the face of heartbreakingly narrow defeats in Oregon and lived to see victories in Washington and Oregon.

Ultimately, Duniway and other suffrage leaders had to rely on male voters and male legislatures to grant women the vote. And since many male voters had convinced themselves that women did not really want the vote, suffragists had to persuade them otherwise. In Colorado the difference between an overwhelming defeat for women's suffrage in a referendum in 1877 and the successful passage of a suffrage amendment in 1893 was the effective organization of women in the interval between the elections. Rather than start new organizations, Colorado women mobilized existing organizations. Middle-class women's clubs, women members of labor unions, and the Woman's Christian Temperance Union (WCTU) all joined for the suffrage battle. The small number of women who actively worked for suffrage in 1877 had allowed opponents of suffrage to claim that most women were apathetic or hostile to the reform. With women laboring tirelessly and effectively, and with the aid of the Populists and organized labor, suffrage triumphed in 1893.

In a sense women's suffrage in the West was the sum of state victories, but analyzing each state does not explain the regional pattern. Why did women gain the vote in the West far more readily than in the East? If western women had

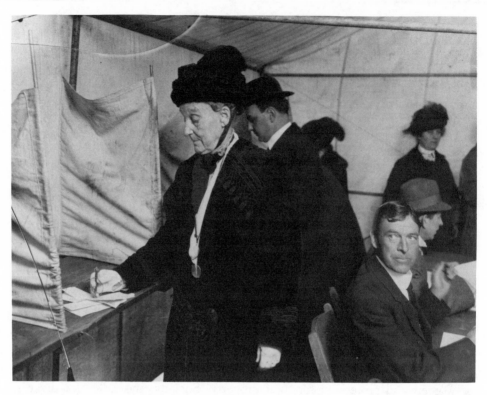

In 1914, after years of leading the struggle for women's suffrage in Oregon, Abigail Scott Duniway was finally able to vote in a state election.

dramatically different attitudes toward gender roles than eastern women had, or if western men regarded women differently than did eastern men, the problem would not be so perplexing. But there appears to be little variation in sexual stereotypes. In Kansas, for example, when voters granted women the vote and elected women to office, they still expected them to observe the conventions of the cult of true womanhood. Campaigning unaccompanied by a male escort or when pregnant cost women candidates votes and elections.

The regional distinctiveness of the West in granting women the vote may be connected with another distinctive pattern of western politics: the lack of strong ethnocultural foundations in the Rocky Mountain and Pacific Coast states. In the East women's suffrage became part of a wider range of cultural issues that divided native-born Protestants and immigrant Catholics. Suffrage efforts often collapsed when immigrant Democratic voters feared that women's suffrage would lead to prohibition and other laws striking at immigrant and Catholic mores.

Abigail Scott Duniway believed suffragists had to prevent a linkage of temperance and women's suffrage in the minds of male voters. Duniway blamed the 1906 defeat of a referendum on suffrage in Oregon on eastern middle-class women and the WCTU, whose campaign had wedded the two issues. When prohibition and suffrage became entwined in Washington state, women's suffrage also went down to an initial defeat there. Similarly, a strong antisuffrage vote from immigrant, "wet" (that is, antiprohibitionist) San Francisco defeated women's suffrage in California in 1896 and came close to defeating it in 1911.

The Pacific Coast states seem, however, to be exceptions. In most of the West during the nineteenth century voters did not connect the two issues, largely because Catholic-Protestant and immigrant–native-born divisions were far less pronounced than in the East. After 1910 western voters did connect women's suffrage and temperance, but by then prohibitionist sentiment was apparently strong enough in most of the West to be an asset instead of an obstacle to women's efforts to get the vote.

Even with such explanations, however, the West's willingness to grant women the vote still ends up as something of a mystery. It represented a combination of peculiar local conditions in Utah and Nevada, the work of a strong network of western women's organizations in other states, and the lack of ethnocultural obstacles that hobbled suffrage campaigns elsewhere in the country. Perhaps, too, since the western community was so often the work of women, the moral arguments of suffragists had a stronger and more immediate appeal in the West. If women were more moral, more generous, and more virtuous, then was not the best way to reform politics and society to give them the vote?

Political Pattern II: The Weakness of Ethnocultural Politics

A twentieth-century political cliché holds that people "vote their pocketbooks," but in late-nineteenth- and early-twentieth-century elections Americans tended more often to vote according to ethnocultural factors: their section, religion, and ethnicity. Voting became an exercise in identification with a community, a culture, and a past; politics, like religion, was part of a voter's identity. The two were often intimately related. To be a Democrat, for example, was a function of being Irish and Catholic or of being white and southern. To be a Republican was the logical consequence of being a northern, native-born Protestant. The political parties functioned as "political churches." They mobilized the support of what one historian has called "distinctive, but mutually antagonistic, coalitions of ethnoreligious groups."

Most nineteenth-century westerners were migrants, and they carried their political loyalties and habits west, but their party affiliations took shallow root across the Missouri. Comparing voting patterns in the Rocky Mountain and Pacific Coast states to those of the states of the Northeast reveals a weaker commitment to political parties. In those sections of the West 10 to 12 percent of voters between 1876 and 1900 split their tickets; that is, they voted for candidates of more than one party in a single election. The figure was low, but it was still more than five times the average in the Northeast. Similarly, only 8 to 11 percent of western voters switched parties from one election to the next, but this was more than three times the percentage of northeasterners who switched parties. Fewer westerners than easterners, in short, had deep commitments to the existing parties.

More significant than the number of voters who switched parties was the number who failed to vote at all in certain elections. Only about 50 to 55 percent of far western voters were core voters—those who stuck with their party no matter what candidates it ran. By comparison, from 66 to 79 percent of northeastern

Table 9
Estimates of Party-Vote Consistency

Period	President to President		President to Off Year	
	West	North	West	North
1876–1900	40.8	69.3	37.0	58.3
1900–32	37.3	55.9	29.8	42.3
1932–44	55.3	61.9	34.5	47.6
1944–64	55.2	59.5	40.5	50.5
1964–84	47.6	46.9	37.0	36.0

Source: Paul Kleppner, "Politics Without Parties. The Western States, 1900–1984" in Gerald Nash and Richard W. Etulain, eds., *The Twentieth Century West* (Albuquerque: University of New Mexico Press, 1989), p. 301.

Note: Entries are mean percentages of the electorate repeating the same partisan choice at successive elections.

voters were core voters. The remaining western voters either usually did not vote (about 25 percent) or deserted their party during some elections.

Weaker party loyalty in the West resulted, at least partly, from the lack of animosity between Protestants and Catholics and between native-born Americans and white immigrants in the West. In 1890 the West actually had a higher percentage of immigrants than did the Northeast and nearly as high a percentage of Catholics, but election results, particularly those in the Rocky Mountain and Pacific Coast states, failed to reflect religious and ethnic identity as clearly as elections in the Northeast did. Religious and cultural issues were sometimes prominent in western elections—the issue of public schools versus Catholic schools in New Mexico, for example—but such issues did not form the basis for permanent party loyalty to the same degree that they did in the East. On the whole the issues that provided a focus for ethnocultural politics were weak in the West. Before the 1920s, only prohibition formed a rallying point for western ethnocultural politics. And even prohibition, as we saw with regard to women's suffrage, eventually took a form that was not particularly compatible with ethnocultural politics.

Prohibition

In nineteenth-century America prohibitionists tended to be evangelical Protestants—that is, Protestants in denominations that stressed a personal conversion experience. Catholics tended to oppose prohibition. Prohibitionists were often rural; antiprohibitionists were urban. And in many states, Republicans tended to be prohibitionists while Democrats, outside the South, were likely to be antiprohibitionists. But these divisions, although present, were never as strong in the West, and they blurred substantially throughout the country after 1910. Ethnocultural explanations for the national prohibition movement work best for the nineteenth century, when the movement was weak in the West; they work less well in the early twentieth century, when it was strongest in the West.

Because few Anglo Americans were present in the region, the early American temperance movement of the 1840s and 1850s had little effect on the American

West, but the second wave of the movement achieved its first major triumph in Kansas. In 1878 voters passed an amendment to the Kansas constitution prohibiting the importation, sale, and manufacture of liquor. The battle over the measure bore all the hallmarks of an ethnocultural conflict. Catholics, Germans (both Lutheran and Catholic), city dwellers, Irish and eastern European immigrants, and residents of the disproportionately male western counties tended to vote against the amendment. Evangelical Protestant farmers tended to vote for it.

The triumph of the prohibitionists in Kansas sparked similar efforts in other western states and threatened to split some state Republican parties along ethnocultural lines. But in the end, North and South Dakota were the only western states to follow the "Kansas plan," and South Dakota soon thought better of it and repealed prohibition in 1896. The threat of prohibition to reorganize politics along ethnocultural lines faded nearly as quickly as it arose.

Prohibition itself, however, was not a movement that died easily, and in the early twentieth century it reappeared and carried most of the West before it. The target of this new prohibitionist offensive was no longer the drinker—often Catholic, immigrant, and working-class—but instead the saloon. The saloon had acquired the reputation of a mother of vices ranging from drunkenness and prostitution to crime and political corruption. Many western states, including California and Washington, passed local-option laws that allowed localities to ban the manufacture and sale of liquor. Oklahoma had entered the Union in 1907 with prohibition embedded in its constitution. Other states, too, enacted strict laws that banned the consumption as well as the sale of liquor. In 1914 the voters of Oregon, Washington, Colorado, and Arizona voted to go completely dry. Utah, Idaho, Montana, Nevada, Wyoming, and Texas also enacted some form of prohibition. The West had thus become a bastion of prohibition even before the United States ratified the eighteenth amendment in 1919 and made prohibition national.

This last prohibition campaign succeeded in the twentieth-century West because it had transcended its evangelical Protestant roots without losing its hard-core Protestant support. Kansas ironically produced the great symbol of the older rural religious prohibition, Carrie Nation, just as the base for prohibition broadened in the early twentieth century. Deeply religious and possessed of a foolhardy courage, Carrie Nation attacked saloons directly and flamboyantly. Walking into illegal saloons with a hatchet, she reduced both dives and elegant clubs to rum-soaked wrecks. She enjoyed her work: "I tell you, ladies, you don't know how much joy you will have until you begin to smash, smash, smash. It is wonderful."

But Carrie Nation was an old-fashioned prohibitionist. New organizations— the WCTU and the International Order of Good Templars—adopted both more modern arguments and more effective reform tactics. The average Templar shared with Carrie Nation only a hostility to alcohol and the saloon. The Templars denounced drink as the source of social evil, but they fought it cheerfully. With their bands, picnics, dances, and debates, the order provided its members with a gathering place and social activities that mimicked the saloon even as they displaced it. Unlike Carrie Nation and older temperance workers who saw alcohol as the only cause of social problems and the individual drinker as the key figure in a moral drama, Frances Willard and the WCTU argued that drinking was the result as well as the cause of social problems. WCTU members denounced the social and economic conditions that spawned both poverty and drinking.

Carrie Nation and her hatchet were out of place among the reformers of the WCTU and the cheerfulness of the Templars, and she could find little comfort among other branches of the temperance coalition. Temperance workers had always argued that drinking ruined one's health, but temperance advocates of the early twentieth century pushed this theme of health so steadily that they sounded more like advocates of a modern antismoking campaign than fundamentalist Protestants. And finally, many advocates of prohibition advanced economic arguments that drinking hurt economic productivity and discouraged growth. When an Everett, Washington, newspaper editor wrote in 1910 that the vote in an upcoming election to ban saloons would hinge on whether saloons hurt or helped the city's growth, he was emphasizing an aspect of the issue foreign to Carrie Nation's concerns.

These newer arguments, and the real social problems associated with the saloon, brought sufficient Catholics and workers into the "dry" camp to impose prohibition on cities that one would expect to have stayed "wet." Voters in Everett, a working-class mill town, and in San Jose, California, a city with a large percentage of Catholics, endorsed prohibition. The issue of saloons bitterly divided the Washington State Federation of Labor. Workers as radical as the Wobblies argued that saloons functioned to enslave labor.

Appeals to reform, health, and economic efficiency dominated successful prohibition campaigns in most areas of the West; Protestant evangelicalism and ethnocultural divisions explained the success in some others. Sometimes the two strains of prohibition combined. When breweries in Texas, knowing that Mexican Texans and blacks tended to oppose prohibition, contributed funds to pay their poll taxes, racism, anti-Catholicism, and reform fused in the prohibitionist attempt to stop minority voting. In South Texas, reformist, modern, Anglo American farmers pushed prohibition as part of a larger campaign to overcome the political bosses supported by "immoral" Mexican Texans.

Yet despite the ethnocultural overtones found in early prohibition campaigns in Kansas and in later campaigns in Texas, prohibition never became a vehicle for dividing western politics on ethnocultural lines. Prohibition in the West succeeded by phrasing its arguments in terms of "modern" values such as efficiency, health, and progress. Prohibitionists also reduced their claims. Prohibition would not singlehandedly remake society, but as one in a series of necessary reforms it would help create a progressive, prosperous, and modern America.

Political Pattern III: Mass Voting Patterns

Since ethnocultural politics shaped the voting patterns of the late-nineteenth-century United States, the failure of ethnocultural politics to take firm root in the West necessarily set western voting patterns apart. Late-nineteenth-century western voters were less loyal to political parties. They were more volatile—liable to follow third parties that rose on the basis of a single issue or cluster of issues and then faded. Westerners tended to respond to charismatic leaders more than to stable political organizations.

Western politicians could not create material incentives for loyalty as effectively as could their eastern counterparts. National patronage existed in the West, but western politicians had trouble controlling it. As long as an area remained a territory, for example, the selection of the governor and other top officers and the patronage they could bestow remained beyond the grasp of local voters. One party might carry the territory, but if the other party won the presidency, it could appoint territorial governors and control most territorial patronage. The long territorial periods of many western states weakened partisanship among western voters. Since the major goal of politics was to boost the territory and to gain personal advantage, it was best to remain flexible in one's loyalties. Devout party loyalty had few practical payoffs. Without deep ideological or cultural commitments to the existing political parties, western voters found it easy to switch parties in pursuit of immediate, pragmatic interests.

This same flexible political loyalty easily shaded over into other issues. The Mormons, although far more given to authoritarian politics than other westerners, were in effect being quintessentially western when in the 1890s the church hierarchy asked half of the faithful to become Republicans despite earlier Republican attacks on polygamy. Congress would rule on Utah's admission into the union, and the church needed to be acceptable to both parties. Political loyalty among many other westerners probably had no deeper roots than it did among Mormon voters.

Political Pattern IV: Local Politics

With neither ideology, ethnocultural affiliations, nor patronage able to tie the voters to national political parties, western politics largely remained a politics of local boosterism and individual gain. If business and politics were twins throughout the country, they were Siamese twins in the West. Western politics involved intense competition for the funds, services, and favors available through government. In this westerners differed from other sections of the country only in being less easily deflected by ideological or ethnocultural concerns in their rush toward the pork barrel.

Politically, the arrival of Anglo Americans in the West had been like a stone hitting glass. The huge geographic entity of the West split into thousands of smaller jurisdictions: territories and states, counties, townships, cities, and villages. Battles between these jurisdictions became the heart of early western politics. Westerners who yawned through debates on the nation's tariff policy could devote months of rapt attention over debates about which village would become the county seat or where the legislature should locate the insane asylum. Bond elections to raise money to secure a railroad connection were of far more concern than American foreign policy. Equally parochial concerns dominated the attention of voters elsewhere in the country, but the political and economic rawness of the West gave its concerns an urgency and uniqueness. After all, elsewhere in the country the location of capitals and county seats, state institutions, and transportation routes had already been decided.

In most rural areas of the West, political leadership centered on the courthouse rings of the village. A courthouse ring was an alliance of local politicians and merchants interested in the distribution of political favors and in using those favors to boost their own businesses and other financial interests. In most places these political leaders were the "town fathers," men who had founded the towns and promoted them. They were men such as General Delevan Bates of Aurora,

Hamilton County, Nebraska, who during his career led efforts to obtain the county seat for Aurora, helped build the courthouse, secured the Republican Valley Railroad for the town, and advanced the money to buy land for the town's high school. Bates and other town fathers had tied their careers, public and private, to the growth of their towns, and they reaped both political and economic rewards when their towns thrived. A second group, the "old settlers," those who had come to the town and the region surrounding it early and had set down roots, supported the town fathers both politically and economically. The old settlers were usually synonymous with the most prosperous settlers. Throughout much of the West, those who stayed the longest in a place were, after all, those who had accumulated the most property there.

The town fathers and old settlers did not always form a unified political group within the village; some were Democrats and some were Republicans. Personal animosities and rivalries often divided a town's leaders, and party labels were only a reflection of those animosities. Both parties drew their leaders from this village elite, for the successful businessmen of the village were always better organized, more sophisticated, and more fully informed than the farmers of the surrounding countryside. The village elite could, and usually did, put aside their differences in order to promote the collective economic well-being of their town over that of rival towns. These men were small capitalists who had invested all their money locally. If the town failed, they failed with it.

Urban Politics

In cities and mining towns, as opposed to the farming villages, the logic of politics did not change, but the people most likely to hold office did. In the small mining towns of the Rockies and Sierra Nevada, miners often elected men from their own ranks to local office. There union men and union sympathizers could dominate politics as fully as town fathers and old settlers did in the agricultural towns. Such men might have stronger class-based ideologies than rural politicians, but daily politics still consisted of attempts to get economic concessions and favors for their constituents.

What distinguished urban politics from rural politics was the scale. A city contained a far more elaborate administrative framework with far more favors to bestow. It also contained far more people and thus far more competitors for political spoils. In the nineteenth century a single political organization or a single political boss rarely controlled an entire city. Politicians governed the city through a network of alliances. A successful politician was a broker, a person able to arrange deals between competing interests. Politics built up from the neighborhood and ward level, and the ward boss was probably the most familiar urban political figure. The further a politician got from the ward, the more adept he had to be at keeping competing factions together.

Within these fragmented politics a machine arose when a politician succeeded in creating a coalition of ward organizations. Such nineteenth-century machines were rare, but Christopher ("Blind Chris") Buckley succeeded in maintaining a shaky San Francisco machine for eight years. Buckley, initially working out of his saloon, organized 47 Democratic party political clubs scattered through San Francisco's 12 wards to control the seven supervisors necessary to pass an ordinance and the nine needed to override the mayor's veto. Buckley, who held no office himself, did not dictate how San Francisco's Democratic supervisors should vote on most issues. He only wanted to control votes on those issues immediately profitable to him.

Politics became a business, and "the boss business," as he once called it, paid Buckley well. Those who wanted to acquire franchises to build trolley lines or provide water for the city had to pay Buckley off. Merchants and corporate leaders would have preferred to save the expense, but as Collis P. Huntington of the Southern Pacific put it, "If you have to pay money to have the right thing done, it is only just and fair to do it." Blind Chris Buckley knew business leaders would come around. "It was surprising," he later remembered, "to see how universal was the desire among men of substance, firms, and corporations, to get on the right side of politics." Martin Kelly, a San Francisco Republican politician, sought to unseat Buckley during the 1880s and gain control of San Francisco politics, but he objected to Buckley's control over political profits and not his methods. Kelly, too, thought receiving money for political favors was natural and just: "When men of wealth come to us [politicians] for gifts which meant golden fortunes for themselves, does any fool suppose we didn't ask for a modest 'cut'? Of course we did. Was it not equitable and just?"

Despite the money flowing in, Buckley's political machine was fragile because his machine benefited only those with their hands on the controls. It had relatively little patronage to dispense. Holding office in one of Buckley's clubs brought status, but it brought little else. Buckley, as well as his opponents, subscribed to San Francisco's "dollar limit." They would not tax property at a rate higher than a dollar for each $100 of assessed valuation. The dollar limit caused San Francisco to be starved for funds to build sewers and streets, maintain schools, construct hospitals, or build parks. Buckley's machine met its demise not from being too lavish with public funds but from being too parsimonious. San Francisco's middle class demanded the public investment necessary to solidify the city's commercial preeminence and to guarantee themselves decent streets, sewers, parks, schools, and fire and police protection.

Political Corruption

The everyday western politics of locality, economic interest, and personal ambition usually flowed in the predictable channels, but sometimes these local politics burst the ordinary channels and attracted national attention. In the 1890s the Clark-Daly feud of Montana demonstrated to a fascinated nation how western local politics worked and how bizarre these politics could become. William A. Clark and Marcus Daly were both millionaires many times over. Both had made their wealth in mining. Both had helped develop the Butte-Anaconda region. Both had originally entered politics to protect their economic interests, yet they had also developed political ambitions that extended beyond fattening their bank accounts. Marcus Daly wanted Anaconda—a town that he had created and that depended on the Anaconda Mine for its existence—to be the state capital. William Clark, who one detractor described as "about as magnetic as last year's bird's nest," had at least one uncontrollable passion: he desperately wanted to be a U.S. senator.

During the 1890s while Populism, labor conflict, depression, and foreign war wracked the state and nation, politics in Montana revolved around the ambitions

William Andrews Clark of Montana, who detractors said had the charisma of a last year's bird's nest.

of Clark and Daly. The two men hated each other. Without Clark, Daly could have made Anaconda the capital. Without Daly, Clark could have been a senator. Each denied the other his wish. Only the most blatant mutual economic interests brought them together. As mine owners, they briefly cooperated in attempts to insure U.S. Treasury coinage of silver, but usually they fought. Both were Democrats, but party loyalty meant little. Daly would, and did, support Republicans to defeat Clark. Clark gladly sought Republican support and bribed Republican legislators to secure his election to the Senate.

Their battle culminated in the 1899 election for U.S. senator, an office then determined by the vote of the legislature. Clark bought the election, paying off the legislators who selected the state's U.S. senator and anyone else who could help his campaign. Buying a seat in the Senate was hardly unknown. As one of Mark Twain's characters in *The Gilded Age* explained, "We would have to go without the services of some our ablest men, sir, if the country were opposed to— to—bribery. It is a harsh term. I do not like to use it." But Clark's tactics were so flagrant that the members of the U.S. Senate had to use the "harsh term." They ruled the election null and void "on account of briberies, attempted briberies, and corrupt practices." Clark's methods proved too much for the Senate to swallow, but they went down easily enough in the Montana legislature. In 1900 that body reelected him to the U.S. Senate, and that time the Senate accepted him.

In their pursuit of personal ambition and local interests Clark and Daly engaged in an extreme version of typical western politics. They brought to their battles resources, ruthlessness, vindictiveness, and a level of corruption beyond the means of their contemporaries. By twentieth-century standards many western politicians were corrupt, but very few were so flamboyantly and extravagantly corrupt as Clark and Daly.

Clark and Daly were, in effect, the wild horses of western political corruption. They were big enough and powerful enough to break out of the political corral. Most corrupt western politicians were, however, more like political mules than wild horses. When confined to the political corral and harnessed to local develop-ment, they remained unpleasant but unremarkable and predictable offspring of the union of business and politics. Most business leaders did not harbor Clark's and Daly's political ambitions. They preferred to work more quietly and effectively, if no more honestly, in securing government favors or in preventing unwanted government intervention in the affairs of business.

Corruption was as prevalent in western county courthouses and state legislatures as in its city and town halls. States and towns needed railroads and outside capital; corporations, in turn, wanted local favors, subsidies, and protection from unwanted regulation. Both sides were willing to pay for favors when they had to. The railroads, as the largest and most complex of western corporations, became particularly active in creating political coalitions to serve their interests. So successfully did they influence politics that at times it became difficult to discern if elected officials took their obligations to their constituents more seriously than they did their duties to their political sponsors. John H. Mitchell, a late-nineteenth-century U.S. senator from Oregon, frankly confessed that the politics of the railway magnate Ben Holladay "are my politics and what Ben Holladay wants I want." Where the citizens of the state of Oregon fit into this cozy arrangement Mitchell left unclear.

Railroads and other corporations frequently bought the votes of elected officials, but such ad hoc bribery was a crude and ultimately expensive way to gain political ends. Where corporations had permanent interests they forged more permanent alliances, which served both their interests and those of a given locality and its politicians. The Southern Pacific in California, the Union Pacific in Nebraska and Wyoming, and other railroads and corporations elsewhere in the West established networks of political influence. So far-reaching did some of these become that Collis P. Huntington of the Southern Pacific complained, "Things have gotten to such a state that if a man wants to be a constable he thinks he has first got to come down to Fourth and Townsend streets [that is, Southern Pacific headquarters] to get permission."

John Thurston, the counsel for the Union Pacific, developed a particularly successful railroad machine in Nebraska. Because Omaha formed the eastern terminus of the Union Pacific, that railroad always had a particular interest in Omaha politics as well as a wider interest in Nebraska politics. A Republican, Thurston nonetheless worked easily with the Democratic politicians of Omaha. Both recognized that their mutual interests in keeping the Union Pacific in Omaha were far stronger than party divisions.

The maintenance of such railroad factions needed constant attention. The railroad used passes and corporate patronage to cultivate politicians in the towns and villages along its line, but Thurston could not count on politicians automatically obeying the railroad leadership. Politicians accepted railroad passes and fees and cut deals with Thurston, but they had loyalty to the railroad only insofar as the railroad served their personal interest or the interest of their locality. When the railroads became unpopular because of their rate structures, these men tended to drift away and even become cautious reformers who sought to regulate the railroads and limit their influence in politics.

Reform Politics

The flip side of railroad factions were antirailroad factions, which usually lay near the center of any western political reform movement. In many states antirailroad politics found a home in ephemeral parties such as the Greenbackers of the late 1870s and early 1880s and the Union Labor party of the late 1880s. But in most states the two national political parties usually contained antirailroad factions.

Opposition to the political and economic power of the railroads was part of a core of grievances common to most western reform movements. Reformers also usually demanded inflationary policies to help debtors plagued by the persistent currency deflation that followed the Civil War, and they attacked the unequal distribution of the tax burden. The antirailroad reformers achieved some success in the 1870s and 1880s. Several states formed railroad commissions, but given the railroads' monopoly over rate information and the economic condition of the roads, the commissioners usually found it hard to make effective policy or to oversee rates.

In no western state was the railroad a bigger issue than in California, where reformers fought for three decades to restrict the power of the Southern Pacific. The Octopus, its opponents claimed, strangled the state's economy and fouled its politics. The Democrats began the campaign against the Southern Pacific in 1869, and the war continued over the next 30 years with a strong faction within the Republican party joining the antirailroad Democrats. Angered at high rates and the Southern Pacific's flagrant interference in politics, Californians often exaggerated the railroad's political power and internal unity, but exaggeration did not constitute fabrication. The railroad had real economic and political power.

In the 1870s the California legislature established a regulatory commission to oversee railroad rates, but like other railroad commissions it proved a disappointment to reformers. Railroad regulation was too large a task for part-time commissioners unfamiliar with the intricacies of the railroad business. The Southern Pacific's ability to appeal commission decisions, and thus delay regulations, stymied real reform. Reformers in both major political parties launched a renewed antimonopoly crusade in the 1880s to increase state control over the railroad. And in the 1890s large numbers of California farmers, businesspeople, and workers joined a "fight to the death" against the Octopus.

The campaign against the Southern Pacific system during the 1890s produced two major political battles. The reformers, first of all, demanded that the Central Pacific repay the large debt that it owed the U.S. government for the loans originally made to build it. Because the Southern Pacific had absorbed the Central Pacific, this attack on the Central Pacific was also an attack on the Southern Pacific. The reformers also supported the city of Los Angeles in a second battle: Los Angeles's fight to secure a harbor at San Pedro. The Southern Pacific wanted to force the city to build its harbor at Santa Monica, where the railroad could monopolize rail traffic. Both battles ended in at least partial defeat for the railroad.

The loans owed by the Central Pacific to the U.S. government came due between 1896 and 1899. The principal on the loans amounted to $25,885,120, and the security for the loans was the tracks and equipment of the railroad. Leland Stanford and Collis P. Huntington initially contended that the government should forgive the debt because of the great good the railroad had brought the nation by linking the Pacific Coast with the East. Important California politicians and the state's leading newspapers, however, demanded that the government foreclose on the mortgage when the debt came due and assume control of the railroad. This would split the Central Pacific from the Southern Pacific and thus create competing railroads in northern California. Faced with intense opposition in California, Huntington switched tactics and asked that the debt be refinanced at 3 percent interest over the next 50 years. Antirailroad politicians in Congress defeated two attempts to refinance the debt, and the issue finally ended in a compromise that forced the Central Pacific to pay the debt in 10 years at 3 percent interest.

The Los Angeles harbor fight, which reached a critical stage in 1896, pitted railroad forces against a coalition of Los Angeles business people who sought to build a harbor at San Pedro free from domination by the Southern Pacific and its allies. Despite unanimous recommendations by expert commissions in favor of the San Pedro harbor, Huntington used his influence with congressional committees to block federal appropriations for the harbor. Although San Pedro received a small grant, Huntington got an appropriation ten times as large for Santa Monica. Los Angeles politicians and business interests fought back and secured a third congressional commission empowered to make a final decision. When in 1897 this commission designated San Pedro as the harbor, the Southern Pacific apparently suffered a major defeat. The Southern Pacific and the Los Angeles and Salt Lake railroad companies, however, quickly moved in and ended up controlling most of the San Pedro harbor frontage.

At best the Southern Pacific suffered only partial defeats in the debt and San Pedro controversies, but that these battles occurred at all demonstrated the growth of united and effective antirailroad coalitions. That in the end both controversies were resolved in Washington instead of California was also revealing. The ultimate locus of western political power was not in the West itself. Opposition to the Southern Pacific was local, but to check the corporation, politicians and businesspeople had to resort to the federal government. This was the irony of western politics. Resolutely local in its focus, western politics nonetheless could not usually resolve major disputes locally. The quest for development necessarily meant involvement with distant corporations and a distant federal government.

Political Pattern V: A Sectional Party, the Populists

The relationship of western politics to national politics, of western development to national development, and of the West to the nation became central concerns of the western electorate in the 1890s. During the 1890s a distinctive sectional party of the West and South, the Populists, flared briefly but brightly and then disappeared. Despite electoral victories, the Populists had only limited success in implementing their program. Nonetheless, the Populist party was quite significant for western politics. First, it represented a regional political movement in which the West and South joined in a political challenge to the dominant Northeast. Second, it specifically raised the issue of the West's economic subordination to the Northeast and demanded solutions that involved the political intervention of the federal government in the running of the national and regional economy. Third, it initially represented a political revolution within the West as farmers struggled to win political control back from the small-town elites of the courthouse rings. Like a bursting bomb, Populism at once illuminated and changed the political landscape.

According to the Populists, bankers, eastern investors, western middlemen, and the railroads conspired to rob western farmers of the just rewards of their labor. Capitalists, vaguely identified as the "money power" or "plutocracy," reaped the wealth that farmers created. Western and southern Populists might be vague about the alternate identity of the money power, but they were quite specific about its abuses and local agents. The Populists resented the railroads for a rate structure that was high compared to that of the more competitive East and that discriminated against agricultural shippers. They resented the middlemen who controlled the grain elevators and obtained more profit from storing a farmers' crops than the farmers did for growing them. They resented the bankers and mortgage companies whose interest rates exceeded those of the East. They resented a gold standard that caused a steady deflation that hurt borrowers. Deflation forced debtors to repay loans with money the actual purchasing power of which exceeded that of the original loan. Western Populists were commercial farmers who had expected that a life of hard work, thrift, and care would lead to independence and comfort. For many of them hard work had led only to debt, anxiety, and failure. They resented their own lack of success, and they resented, too, those bankers, middlemen, and railroad managers who seemed to garner the profits that rightfully belonged to the farmer.

The economic grievances of the farmers were quite real, but because many grievances were longstanding, they cannot explain the fervor of the Populist response in the early 1890s. Railroad rates had, for example, been higher in the 1870s, and so had interest rates. The Greenbackers had launched an earlier attack on the gold standard and a contracting money supply without winning the political support that the Populists achieved. The unrest of farmers in the 1890s involved more than just railroad rates or interest rates reaching an intolerable level.

The farmers were responding to what they perceived as trends in the economy and their declining ability to adjust to them as much as to specific economic burdens or injustices. Those states in which Populism and farmer protest reached the highest levels were the states where prices for agricultural commodities fluctuated most radically. Wildly fluctuating prices made it impossible for farmers to make rational decisions on how to farm. Corn prices, for example, fell sharply in 1888, causing many farmers to decide that the rational approach was not to sell corn but instead to use the cheap corn to fatten cattle. They accordingly used cheap corn to build up their herds only to face a drought in 1890. That year the corn crop failed, corn prices rose 300 percent, and farmers had to sell their cattle at a loss. Farmers seemed to lose if nature favored them and their abundant harvests drove prices down or if nature frowned on them and shortages drove prices up.

Similarly, it was not just railroad rates that angered Populists, but also the seemingly unpredictable and irrational fluctuations of those rates. The long-term trend in transportation rates during the late nineteenth century was downward. The cost of shipping wheat from the prairies and plains to New York and Liverpool tended to fall in real terms between 1870 and 1897. Sharp short-term rises in rates were exasperating to farmers precisely because of their expectation of declining rates. When railroad rates rose sharply from 1890 to 1894 even as grain prices fell, farmers felt manipulated and betrayed.

The economic hardships and frustrations of the late 1880s and the 1890s confronted most western farmers, but not all of them became Populists. The farmers who tended to become Populists were those who not only faced economic hardship but who also lived at some distance from the towns or in counties with few or no villages over 1,000 people. Populist farmers thus had less direct contact with the boosters and courthouse rings that dominated local politics in the West than did non-Populist farmers. These boosters and courthouse politicians were the major groups trying to maintain loyalty to the older parties in the midst of the Populist rebellion, but they found poor and isolated farmers hard to hold. On the margins of existing political networks, these farmers were ready to break free of those networks in a time of economic crisis. The farmers did not believe that the existing system could cure their problems. They stood ripe for defection and a new politics.

Only when taken together do economic problems, isolation, and alienation from existing political networks predict an affinity for Populism. One without the others was less likely to produce Populists. But even together they did not always produce Populists. In Nebraska, for example, the most rural and isolated parts of the state—the far western counties—were poor but they were not the most Populist. Because they lacked railroads and were still in the process of bringing their lands into cultivation, the farmers there saw railroads not as a cause of their poverty but as a cure for it. They tended to vote for exactly the kind of booster whom the Populists disavowed.

The Roots of Populism: The Farmers' Alliance

The political solutions and organization of Populism grew out of an earlier nonpolitical organization, the Farmers' Alliance. The Farmers' Alliance was not confined to the West; in most ways it was stronger in the South. It reached its fullest development in Texas—that part southern, part western state—which served as a refuge for farmers dispossessed by the crop-lien system of the Old South. Under the crop-lien system, a farmer gave a furnishing merchant a lien on his crops as security for credit at the merchant's store. By charging interest on the goods advanced to farmers and by charging higher prices for those goods than for goods bought with cash, merchants forced farmers deeper and deeper into debt. Eventually many farmers lost their farms, ending up as tenants on land they once owned. In 1877 a group of Texas farmers founded the Knights of Reliance to combat both livestock thieves and the crop-lien system. The new organization soon changed its name to the Farmers' Alliance.

The Farmers' Alliance grew slowly until the appointment of S. O. Daws as "traveling lecturer" in 1883. Daws organized farmers around a cooperative crusade that envisioned independence for Texas farmers through cooperative stores, cooperative grain elevators and cotton yards, and cooperative purchasing that would replace the furnishing merchant and other middlemen. This cooperative crusade spread across the southern states and, as a campaign against middlemen, into the West. It raised hopes, but it did not achieve its ends. Indebted farmers still had to deal with the furnishing merchants as long as they owed them money. And middlemen quickly organized against the cooperatives. Merchants threatened to withhold their own business from any wholesalers who sold to the cooperative organizations of the alliance members.

The Farmers' Alliance instilled in farmers a sense of their own power and common exploitation; when attempts to exercise this power through the cooperative crusade failed, many alliance members turned to politics as the only hope for securing low-interest credit, for escaping debt, and for eliminating exploitation by railroads, bankers, and middlemen. The alliance program thus became a political program. In its Saint Louis convention of 1889 the Farmers' Alliance called for currency reform, government ownership of the railroads and telegraph, equitable taxation, governmental economy, and a subtreasury plan. To implement these proposals, farmers would obviously have to control state and federal governments.

This alliance platform was a mixture of old and new reforms. Only the subtreasury was a purely original idea. Nationalizing the railroads to make them the equivalent of public roads upon which any common carrier could operate was hardly a novel demand in the West. Such a plan envisioned running the railroads along the lines of a modern superhighway; the government would own and maintain the track, and any licensed shipping company could use the tracks. Not only Populists but many Democrats and Republicans as well supported such a reform.

The subtreasury system advocated by the alliance was its most innovative, complicated, and controversial suggestion. Under this plan the government would erect in every agricultural county warehouses in which farmers could store their crops. The farmers could secure a loan of up to 80 percent of the local market value of these crops, paying 2 percent annual interest on the loan when they redeemed the crops. Their certificates of deposit on their crops would be negotiable—that is, they could be bought and sold. Farmers could sell their certificates at any time of the year with the value determined by prevailing market prices. Essentially, these certificates would serve as money just as greenbacks had served as cash during the Civil War. The subtreasury proved particularly attractive because it addressed several problems facing farmers. Proponents claimed that it would stabilize prices and eliminate uncertainty. Because certificates were negotiable, they represented an inflationary device that would increase the money supply. Finally, the plan provided farmers with low-interest loans at harvest, the most critical time of the year, and would thus help break the influence of the furnishing merchant in the South.

The political program of the alliance galvanized the West. Farmers who had never fully believed in the cooperative crusade accepted the logic of a political solution. They flocked into the Farmers' Alliance in Nebraska, Colorado, and the Dakotas in the late 1880s.

The Populist Revolt

The Populist party itself metamorphosed out of the Farmers' Alliance in Kansas. Urged on by orators such as "Sockless Jerry" Simpson and Mary Lease, Kansas Populists emerged from their alliance chrysalis in 1890 and swept the state. The Populists captured five congressional seats in Kansas and 96 out of 126 seats in the state legislature, and they placed a Populist in the U.S. Senate. In Nebraska, too, alliance candidates captured the legislature, and they made smaller but significant inroads in the Dakotas.

These victories led to the creation of a national Populist or People's party in 1891. The first national Populist convention convened in Omaha in 1892 to nominate James Weaver for president. The new party adopted a platform that added a graduated income tax, an eight-hour working day, and immigration restriction to the core alliance demands. The last two planks were attempts to lure eastern as well as western workers into the party.

The Populist preamble phrased their revolt in national terms, but the initial battlegrounds were local. Although many townspeople in the West sympathized with the farmers' grievances, both townspeople and farmers realized that Populism threatened the interests of the towns. When alliance men and women began to organize their own cooperative stores or grain elevators and to demand representation in the local, state, and national government, local merchants and political leaders were immediately alarmed. The farmers might denounce a distant "money power" or trust, but their most accessible targets were inevitably the merchants and politicians of the villages and county seats. As one Populist farmer wrote to the editor of the *Hayes County* (Nebraska) *Republican* in 1890, "We're going to have a paper here before long and then things will pop. We'll have an Alliance Store too, at Hayes Center and back these merchants off the track. You just wait till we control things and we'll make you town fellers hump yourselves."

In Nebraska voting patterns in rural precincts and town precincts had once been nearly identical; they now diverged. After 1890 the Republicans could capture nearly 20 percent more votes in the towns than they could in the rural districts. Despite their sympathy with farmers' problems, which after all threatened their own economic well-being, the town politicians and merchants resisted the

Populist challenge to their political leadership and their control of the local economy. They largely remained Republican.

Rocky Mountain Populism

Farmers formed the core Populist constituency, but farmers alone could not have provided the electoral totals that the Populists secured in Colorado, Idaho, and Nevada. In those states the Populist party became a coalition of farmers and miners. Because the Rocky Mountain Populists had to attract the votes of an emerging industrial working class if they wished to be a majority party, mountain Populists tended to sponsor a wider array of reform measures than did those of the plains and prairies.

To attract working-class voters, many of whom were miners, Rocky Mountain Populists emphasized the silver issue. The Populists wanted to inflate the currency, which they thought Congress had artificially contracted to serve the interests of "the money trust." Because the money supply did not keep pace with population growth, prices fell as scarcer dollars became more valuable. Debtors, such as farmers who had mortgaged their land, had to repay their debts in currency more valuable than the currency that they borrowed. Some Populists, adopting the old Greenback solution, wanted a fiat currency, similar to our present system, in which money is backed by neither gold nor silver but is issued by the government in amounts necessary to meet the needs of commerce and is backed only by the government's credit. Other Populists, however, believed that the government could solve the currency problem simply by authorizing the unlimited coinage of silver.

The whole silver question had arisen quietly enough in 1873 when Congress voted to demonetize silver—that is, no longer to allow owners of silver to present it at the mint for automatic coinage. Although Populists and western radicals would later denounce demonetization as the "crime of '73," few people either noticed or opposed demonetization at the time. The market price of silver in 1873 was actually higher than the price paid by the mint, so nobody turned in silver to be coined. The rich silver strikes in the West in the 1870s and 1880s, however, soon flooded the country with silver, and its value dropped from $1.32 an ounce in 1872 to $0.87 in 1892. Two compromise measures, the Bland-Allison Act of 1878 and the Sherman Silver Purchase Act of 1890, provided for limited purchase of silver by the government at market prices, but the purchases were too small to prevent further contraction of the currency. The "Silverites"—those who wanted the full remonetization of silver—pressed for free and unlimited coinage of silver at the pre-1873 ratio of 16 to 1 to gold. The ratio of 16 to 1 signified that the amount of silver backing a silver dollar weighed 16 times the amount of gold in a gold dollar. Farmers hoped for indirect benefits from remonetization of silver. If the government had to issue a dollar for every 16 ounces of silver, the result would be inflation, which would help agricultural debtors. Miners favored the proposal for the more direct reason that it would shore up the mining industry and protect their jobs and wages. Mine owners, needless to say, also advocated free and unlimited coinage.

Remonetization of silver had such universal support in the mountain states that even state Republican and Democratic parties broke with the national parties and endorsed it. But Republicans and Democrats were in an awkward position, because in 1892 both national Democrats and national Republicans nominated candidates who advocated strict adherence to the gold standard. This allowed the Populists in Colorado to ride the silver issue into office.

The coalition of miners and farmers at the heart of Colorado Populism set it apart from Kansas and Nebraska Populism. Colorado Populists were much more likely to be working-class and foreign-born town dwellers. Allied to the farmers of the Colorado plains, the miners briefly became a formidable political force. Under Governor Davis Waite, the Colorado Populist party grew increasingly uncompromising in its defense of the rights of labor, thus alienating those more conservative Coloradans who voted Populist largely because of the silver issue. The result was Waite's and the Populists' defeat in 1894.

Populist Politics

Governor Waite went down to defeat with the Populist banner still flying above him; his defeat foreshadowed the defeat of more compromised Populists later in the decade. To speed electoral success, western Populists in 1892 often combined or fused with the minority party in a given state, usually the Democrats, in order to defeat the majority party, usually the Republicans. Local fusion brought the Populists some immediate political success, but it weakened their overall organization and effectiveness. Populists on fusion tickets subordinated the Populist platform to the task of gaining office. The combination of weak organization, the inexperience of many legislators, and opportunism made it difficult for Populists to enact legislation, particularly when the Republicans continued to control at least some branch of most state governments. Populist legislators advanced a variety of reforms from railroad regulation to women's suffrage, but their lack of success often disappointed their followers.

When in 1896 the Democratic presidential nomination went to William Jennings Bryan of Nebraska, a westerner, a Silverite, and a man sympathetic to the farmers, leading western Populists called for fusion on a national level despite the opposition of most southern Populists. After a bitter fight in their own convention, the Populists decided to back Bryan even though the only part of the Populist platform that Bryan accepted was the unlimited coinage of silver.

Bryan fought the 1896 campaign on the silver issue. On election day he carried all the states west of the Missouri and south of the Ohio except Oregon, California, and North Dakota, but the Republican candidate, William McKinley, carried all the states east of the Mississippi and north of the Ohio, where the population, and thus the electoral votes, was centered. Although fusion tickets in the West put Populists in office throughout the region, they were now officeholders without a national party. As middle-of-the-road or antifusion Populists had predicted, Populist fusion with the Democrats and concentration on the silver issue ended the party's independent existence. Bitterly split by the issue of fusion, and having abandoned much of its own platform, the party found it difficult to reorganize and reclaim voters whom it had urged to vote for a Democratic presidential candidate. Although many of their ideas survived them, as a party the Populists would never again be an important factor in western politics.

Despite their shortcomings and failures, the Populists represented a significant moment in western and national political history. Many of their specific proposals were not new. And in some respects, they were merely an economic interest

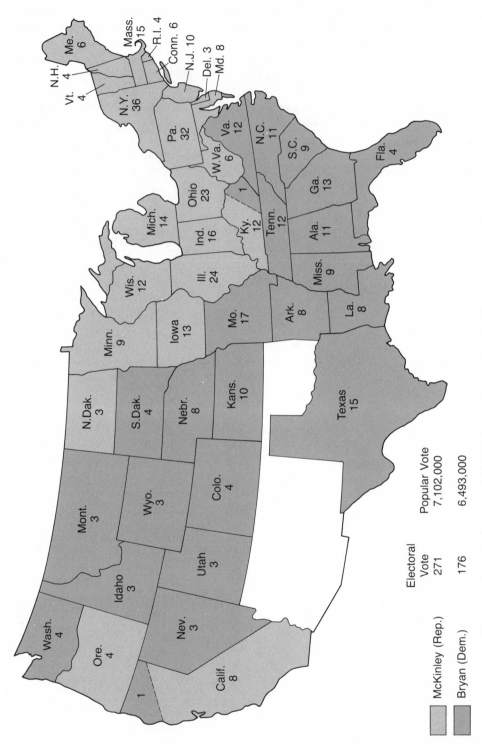

Mass. 15
R.I. 4
Conn. 6
N.J. 10
Del. 3
Md. 8
Me. 6
N.H. 4
Vt. 4
N.Y. 36
Pa. 32
Va. 12
W.Va. 6
N.C. 11
S.C. 9
Fla. 4
Ohio 23
Ga. 13
Mich. 14
Ind. 16
Ky. 12
1
Tenn. 12
Ala. 11
Wis. 12
Ill. 24
Miss. 9
Minn. 9
Iowa 13
Mo. 17
Ark. 8
La. 8
N.Dak. 3
S.Dak. 4
Nebr. 8
Kans. 10
Texas 15
Mont. 3
Wyo. 3
Colo. 4
Utah 3
Idaho 3
Nev. 3
Wash. 4
Ore. 4
1
Calif. 8

	Electoral Vote	Popular Vote
McKinley (Rep.)	271	7,102,000
Bryan (Dem.)	176	6,493,000

The presidential election of 1896. Copyright © 1991 by the University of Oklahoma Press.

group, like the railroads, who sought to control government in order to regulate an excessively competitive economy that was driving them toward ruin. They drew their major support from entrepreneurial farmers and organized workers who wanted the reform, not the abolition, of capitalism. But the Populists did inject demands for sweeping economic reform and popular participation into national politics, and they articulated a new, if often hazy and fleeting, vision of a cooperative western society. Farmers declared their unwillingness to leave politics to a village elite, currency to bankers, and economics to businessmen. The Populist response to this hardship was profoundly democratic. Populists were unwilling to select passively between choices presented them by others; they formulated choices of their own.

Western Political Patterns in Twentieth-Century Politics

The political patterns developed during the nineteenth century continued to mark the West of the twentieth century. As other states adopted women's suffrage, and as ethnocultural politics and party loyalty declined nationally, the West appeared less unusual. Yet in its relation to the federal government and its search for local development, western politics continued to remain distinctive.

After Populism, western radicals never again mustered such widespread popular support. Indeed, in the early twentieth century only two states produced relatively long-lived radical political movements comparable to the Populist insurgency. In Oklahoma, socialists built on the grievances of tenant farmers and workers to establish not only a state Socialist party, but also an indigenous political culture of shared beliefs, organizations, and rituals to sustain it. By 1908 the Oklahoma Socialist party was the largest socialist party in the United States. Between 1912 and 1916 the Socialists controlled about 25 percent of the vote in southern Oklahoma, but World War I destroyed the party. The party declined rapidly in the wake of the Green Corn Rebellion—a brief and confused uprising by tenant farmers persuaded that their young men would be drafted and they would be reduced to farm laborers by a capitalist war. Given the general crackdown on all those who opposed the war, however, the Socialists were open for persecution no matter what they did. The Green Corn Rebellion probably only hastened the inevitable.

In North Dakota the Nonpartisan League shared much of the Oklahoma socialist experience. A. C. Townley, a former Socialist, organized native and immigrant Scandinavian farmers to protest conditions that would have seemed familiar to the old Populists: unfair pricing and grading in the grain trade, lack of political representation for farmers, and political and economic domination by outsiders, in this case the railroad and grain interests of Minneapolis. The Non-Partisan League called for state ownership of grain elevators, flour mills, and packing houses. It demanded state grain inspection and insurance programs and a state-operated bank, the Bank of North Dakota. Using grass-roots organizing to capture the majority Republican party of North Dakota, the league controlled the state government from 1917 to 1921. Like other radical organizations in the West and elsewhere, however, the league fell victim to federal persecution. Accused of treason and Bolshevism, the league failed in its attempt to expand into neighboring states, and government prosecutions ultimately destroyed its base in North Dakota. After the Oklahoma Socialist party and the Non-Partisan

Table 10
Patterns of Partisan Strength, 1900–84

	Democratic Percent of Vote				Partisan Lead*			
	West	Mntn	Pacific	North	West	Mntn	Pacific	North
1900–16	36.9	42.5	32.7	36.5	−11.4	−3.7	−17.4	−14.2
1918–30	22.6	40.1	17.7	36.7	−23.0	−13.3	−29.2	−17.7
1932–44	52.0	57.3	49.6	50.9	15.6	15.9	15.3	4.0
1946–66	46.2	48.8	45.2	49.7	−1.6	−1.9	−1.6	.7
1968–84†	40.3	34.6	42.3	45.2	−13.8	−25.1	−9.8	−4.5
1970–82‡	52.3	48.8	53.5	54.4	6.5	−.6	9.0	13.1

Source: Paul Kleppner, "Politics Without Parties: The Western States, 1900–1984," in Gerald D. Nash, Richard W. Etulain, eds., *The Twentieth Century West* (Albuquerque: University of New Mexico Press, 1989), p. 297.
*Democrat minus Republican percent of vote, so negative signs indicate Republican lead.
†Presidential contests only.
‡Off-year congressional contests only.

League flared and were stamped out, no mass-based western radicalism replaced them.

Western Progressives

The decline of the third parties left Democrats and Republicans in control of the western political landscape. In terms of presidential politics, the first three decades of the twentieth century witnessed Republican dominance everywhere in the West except Texas and Oklahoma (states whose southern heritage kept them Democratic) and Arizona. Except for 1916, when Woodrow Wilson got 50.6 percent of the western votes, the Republican majority held in every presidential election until 1932. On closer examination, however, this Republican dominance was not as strong as it seemed. The Republican party itself was so split along ideological lines in the early twentieth century that at times it nearly composed two distinct parties. Republicans might carry the West in presidential elections, but after 1916 the Democrats gained ground in local and state elections, particularly in the Rocky Mountain states.

The real battle in the West was less between Democrats and Republicans than between progressives in both parties and conservatives who dominated the powerful traditional wing of the Republican party. Western progressives were but part of a diverse national movement devoted to eliminating corruption in government; controlling special interests, be they corporations or immigrant political machines; and reorganizing American society along more efficient social and economic lines in order to insure both prosperity and the assimilation of new immigrants. The progressives believed in an activist government capable of solving social and economic problems. After 1916 western Democrats became both more progressive and an increasingly formidable force in state and local elections. In the Rocky Mountain states after 1916 the Democrats usually controlled about half of the congressional delegations. They made gains even in Utah, where Mormon church leaders had in 1900 reached an agreement with

Mark Hanna, the Republican national chairman, that in exchange for a guarantee against federal harassment the church would encourage its members to vote Republican. Under the guidance of Senator Reed Smoot, the church hierarchy and the Utah Republican party became virtually synonymous. But the conservative church hierarchy could not always deliver the votes of the Mormon faithful, and the Democrats and progressives maintained a considerable influence in state politics.

The progressive wing of the Democratic party arose from several sources. In the Rockies and Nevada, the Democrats had absorbed many of the so-called Silver Populists, and these voters gave Democratic politics an anticorporate/prolabor tilt that tended to attract lower-income groups. Lower-income voters, however, tended to vote far less often than did the middle- and upper-class voters from whom the Republicans drew much of their strength. Only when their candidates successfully mobilized these lower-income voters or attracted Republican progressives could the Democrats compete with the Republicans. In North Dakota progressive Republicans unhappy with conservative control of their own party threw their support to the progressive Democrat John Burke, who served as governor from 1906 to 1912.

In Texas, the progressive Democrats harnessed much rural reformist sentiment against courthouse rings and corrupt, rancher-dominated politics of South Texas. The progressives dominated the Democratic party from about 1911 into the 1920s. There was a dark side to this progressivism. Among the successes of Democratic progressivism in Texas was the disfranchisement of Hispanics. The economic transformation of South Texas from ranching to farming brought an accompanying political battle between the old rancher-dominated machines and the newer farmers. Since Mexican Texans voted for the machines, the progressive farmers, already convinced of Hispanic racial inferiority, deprived them of the vote.

More often than not, however, western progressives achieved power through the Republican party instead of the Democratic party. Western Republicanism was thus Janus-faced. One face was progressive. Behind it were men such as Hiram Johnson in California, George W. Norris in Nebraska, and William Allen White, "The Sage of Emporia," in Kansas. The other face was conservative and laissez-faire. Many progressive Republicans had once been part of the conservative wing of the Republican party. Both Norris and White had, for example, begun their careers as opponents of the Populists.

These progressive Republicans parted ways with their party's conservatives after 1910 over so-called good government issues. Progressives sought a series of reforms that combined an enthusiasm for material progress represented by the new industrial economy and an appeal to an older, more homogeneous Protestant and Anglo Saxon America. They wanted to bring honesty and efficiency to government and to enforce an older Protestant morality. They sought to create social conditions that would enable all citizens to attain a life of material comfort, and to achieve those ends they had to end the influence of "special interests" such as the Southern Pacific.

Hiram Johnson, in his California gubernatorial campaign of 1910, underlined the divisions among Republicans in delivering one of the country's more memorable political denunciations. His target was the conservative Republican publisher of the *Los Angeles Times*, Harrison Gray Otis. "Otis sits there," Johnson told a crowd in Los Angeles, "in senile dementia with gangrened heart and rotting brain, grimacing at every reform, chattering impotently at all things that are decent, frothing, fuming violently, gibbering, going down to his grave in snarling infamy." The split in the Republican party became so deep that western progressives led the move to bolt the Republican party and form a Progressive party in 1912.

Progressive Republicans were particularly strong on the West Coast and on the Great Plains. Johnson won the California governorship. Oregon followed progressive Republicans such as William S. U'Ren and elected progressive Democrats such as Oswald West (1910). Progressives had captured the Washington Republican party by 1910. In Nebraska, Kansas, and South Dakota the progressives controlled the Republican party by the end of the first decade of the century largely by drawing on the votes of farmers made prosperous by rising prices for their crops.

The progressives maintained an ambiguous relationship with both business and organized labor. On the one hand the progressives denounced corporate political influence, campaigned for municipal ownership of utilities, and supported bureaucratic regulation of business. But they were never antibusiness. They obtained considerable business support and spoke admiringly of successful business leaders who had built efficient organizations.

The probusiness attitudes of California progressives, however, tended to weaken as the movement evolved, and their connections with labor increased. Early progressives were unwilling to back most of organized labor's political agenda, and in most labor disputes, business-minded progressives—or the "goo-goos," as their critics in organized labor called the "good government" people—could be counted on to come down on the side of capital, but after 1910 they became increasingly dependable allies of labor.

Progressives and Labor: The Union Labor Party in San Francisco

The progressives hoped for the votes of union laborers, but their own relations with the unions were often rocky. The progressive mayor of San Francisco James D. Phelan (1896–1901) recognized that the progressive plans for municipal improvement would "give employment to labor and circulate money" and should, therefore, attract workers' votes. Union workers did vote for Phelan, but union leaders found themselves excluded from the higher levels of progressive politics in San Francisco. They discovered that Phelan's union sympathies were limited. The crisis came in 1901 when Phelan authorized police to escort nonunion teamsters and their wagons through the streets during a strike. Workers deserted Phelan, and union leaders of the Building Trades Council organized member unions into the Union Labor party.

In terms of issues, the Union Labor party in San Francisco differed from the progressives only in its commitment to the closed shop, in the number of workers and union leaders whom it nominated for office, and in the political inexperience of its leadership. Sensing a leadership vacuum in the new party, Abe Ruef, a lawyer from San Francisco's Jewish mercantile elite, secured the Union Labor nomination for mayor for his friend and former business associate, Eugene Schmitz. Schmitz, an affable native San Franciscan, was Catholic and of Irish and German ancestry and headed the musicians' union. He was an ideal candidate for a coalition of workers and small businessmen.

Although both progressives and conservatives denounced the Union Labor party as a machine, they overestimated its powers. Ruef never exercised even Buckley's shaky control, although he and Schmitz did imitate Buckley's willingness to take payoffs. Ruef took bribes from businessmen seeking franchises and from the owners of the city's "French restaurants," as the fancier brothels were known. Ruef and Schmitz shared this graft with working-class officeholders, but higher union officials found themselves once more excluded. Schmitz's immense personal popularity with San Francisco's workers allowed him to slight union leaders.

Progressive journalists and conservative business leaders combined to bring Schmitz and Ruef down. In 1906 and 1907 attacks on the Union Labor party culminated in convictions for corruption that put Schmitz and other leaders in jail but did not touch the utility corporation executives who had paid the bribes. Ruef, who testified against Schmitz, fell from power.

With Ruef and Schmitz gone, union leaders at last took over the leadership of the party and turned the Union Labor party into a political vehicle for the powerful Building Trades Council (BTC) and other San Francisco unions. In 1909 the party returned to power, electing BTC President Patrick McCarthy, a former carpenter from County Limerick, Ireland, the mayor of San Francisco. Electing union leaders, however, proved easier than governing San Francisco. Afraid to push too radical a labor program for fear of alienating more conservative workers and middle-class members of its constituency, the Union Labor party often seemed to promote no program at all. Its own union constituency began to see it as ineffective, and that gave the progressives their opening.

As the Union Labor party struggled in San Francisco, progressives in the state legislature were on the verge of giving organized labor a surprising string of victories. Between 1911 and 1913 the legislature passed a workmen's compensation act, an eight-hour day for women, a child labor law, and a factory inspection act. These were all prounion measures, and they were greater legislative victories than workers had ever achieved before. Workers who had previously tended to vote against progressive candidates began to vote for them, offsetting a decline in progressive Republican strength in middle-class southern California. In San Francisco a progressive, James Rolph, succeeded McCarthy as mayor. Unlike Phelan, Rolph supported the unions and the closed shop.

The alliance between progressives and workers had its ideological basis in a disillusionment with individualism. Individualism had lost meaning in a society of powerful corporations and bureaucracies in which individuals clearly did not determine their own fate. The progressive willingness to sponsor labor legislation that governed working hours and conditions struck at the heart of conservative individualism and the conservative notion of freedom of contract. Oregon in many ways led a national movement to regulate working hours and conditions. There in 1903 progressives passed legislation providing for a maximum ten-hour day for working women. They argued that in negotiations between individual workers and corporations the parties were so unequal in strength that the state had to limit contracts in order to prevent the weaker party from suffering grave harm. In *Muller* v. *Oregon* (1908) Louis Brandeis, later to become an extremely influential Supreme Court justice, successfully defended Oregon's legislation before the Supreme Court by demonstrating that excessive hours of labor had detrimental effects on women workers.

Progressivism was a national movement, and in most ways its ideology varied little from east to west, but western progressivism did differ from eastern progressivism in its devotion to direct democracy and its disdain for party discipline. Democratic Senator Harry Lane of Oregon was typical of western progressives in his willingness to ignore his party's platform and decisions. Parties, George Norris of Nebraska complained, robbed a man of his political freedom. Indeed, Norris bolted the Republican party so many times during his long and distinguished political career that Arthur Capper of Kansas described him as "a perambulating Declaration of Independence."

Instead of party decision making, the progressives favored measures which put political choices directly before the voters in statewide elections. The famous Oregon System was in many ways the quintessential western progressive reform. Engineered by the progressive Republican William S. U'Ren, who never held a major office himself, the heart of the Oregon System was the initiative, which allowed a direct ballot vote on specific measures put on the ballot by petition, and the referendum, which allowed voters to vote on bills referred to them by the legislature. Oregon voters ratified constitutional amendments providing the initiative and referendum in 1902, and Oregon later added direct primaries (1904), the Corrupt Practices Act (1908), and a recall amendment (1908). Widely copied throughout the West, all of these measures intentionally weakened political parties.

The progressive willingness to ignore party dictates made the seeming Republican domination of western politics somewhat illusory. Republican majorities were often divided majorities. The Republicans often could not muster the internal consensus necessary to mediate disputes among themselves or their constituents. Competing groups did not value party loyalty highly enough to subordinate their demands to electoral success. And with party loyalty weak, it became very difficult to forge coherent programs. The Oregon System and California's labor legislation were the exception rather than the rule. Leaders tended to act as individual political entrepreneurs. Although this could lead to the brief spurts of legislative success achieved by Hiram Johnson or U'Ren, it rarely led to orderly politics. Very often state governments were immobilized and incapable of enacting, or even agreeing on, legislative programs.

In the face of a popular issue or a charismatic candidate, Republican domination crumbled. Woodrow Wilson in 1916 and two Progressive party candidates, Teddy Roosevelt in 1912 and Robert LaFollete in 1924, used their considerable personal popularity to bring out significant numbers of western lower-income voters who usually stayed at home. These elections shook the ground underneath the Republican party, revealing how shallow its western foundations were.

With state governments weak and divided, regional cooperation became almost impossible. All the states bordering the Colorado River, for example, eagerly anticipated its development, but the division of the waters engendered a political free-for-all that subsided only when the federal government mediated the Colorado River Compact in 1922. And even this compact, as incorporated in the

Teddy Roosevelt on the way from Laramie to Cheyenne, Wyoming, in 1903.

Boulder Canyon Act of 1928, proved incapable of halting disputes between Arizona and California over allocation of Colorado River water. Virtually constant federal intervention proved necessary. The result of the development of the river, in the words of a historian who studied the compact, was "the emergence of the government in Washington as the most powerful authority over the Colorado River and, by extension, over other interstate and navigable streams as well."

With weak western state governments and an increasingly powerful federal government, it is not surprising that leading western progressive politicians abandoned state politics for national politics. The real locus of western political power had after all rested in the Senate since the nineteenth century. Because each state, regardless of population, got two senators, Wyoming was, in the Senate at least, the political equal of New York, and the West became the political equal of the Northeast and Midwest. The West's senate votes gave it an influence worth courting, but its small population guaranteed that the region's strength would remain confined to the Senate. Western progressive such as Hiram Johnson from California, George Norris from Nebraska, and William Borah from Idaho became powers in the U.S. Senate. Unlike equally powerful senators from the South, these western senators sought to promote federal activity in their section rather than limit it.

Western progressivism weakened but did not disappear in the 1920s. Progressives continued to win important victories against renewed conservative opposition. In California progressive Republicans elected C. C. Young as governor in 1926 and kept the California state government an active agent in social welfare and economic development throughout the decade.

In some western states during the 1920s, however, progressive politics acquired a belated and disturbing ethnocultural tint. The rise of the Ku Klux Klan made religion, ethnicity, and associated "moral" issues the center of politics in Colorado and Oregon during the 1920s. Western Klansmen selected the issues they needed to meet local appetites from the wider national Klan menu of law and order, racism, anti-Semitism, anti-Catholicism, and 100 percent Americanism.

Many progressives such as Democratic Governor William Sweet of Colorado opposed the Klan, but for other progressives Klan issues often proved surprisingly compatible with the progressive rhetoric of moral righteousness and attacks against an arrogant and unresponsive political and economic elite. In some communities the Klan approached what one historian has called a "hooded progressivism." Opposition to corrupt politics or outside control translated into opposition to Catholic voters supposedly controlled by the Pope and thus incapable of true American citizenship. Opposition to alcohol translated into opposition to Irish or Italian Catholics who violated prohibition.

The Klan dominated Oregon and Colorado politics, but the dominance proved to be fleeting. At its height in the early and middle 1920s the Klan enlisted more than 35,000 members in Colorado and 14,000 in Oregon, with Portland having the majority of Oregon's members and Denver the majority of Colorado's. Colorado elected a Klan governor and a majority of Klansmen in the lower house of the legislature in 1924. In Oregon the Democratic progressive Walter M. Pierce won election in 1922 as governor with Klan support, and Klan members controlled the legislature. That same year Oregonians passed the Klan-supported Compulsory School Bill, an initiative measure requiring all children to attend public school. Aimed at eliminating Catholic education, the bill was later ruled unconstitutional.

In its self-proclaimed crusade to defend Protestantism, Americanism, and the white race, the Klan foundered quickly. In order to organize urban and small-town Protestants, the Klan had used perceived dangers of immigrant crime, Jewish or Catholic conspiracies, and successful attempts by blacks or Mexican Americans to escape their "place." But anti-Semitism and anti-Catholicism lacked a deep foundation in the West, and when the supposed menaces failed to materialize, the issue collapsed. Westerners remained interested in subordinating racial minorities, but the Klan was extraneous to this task. The dual labor system had existed before the Klan and continued to exist afterwards.

The Klan failed, too, because like other political groups that captured state governments, it found itself unable to implement its programs. In Oregon as well as Colorado, Klansmen were unable to turn electoral gains into real change. Unable to exercise effective power, faced with an increasingly well organized opposition, and plagued by scandal, the Klan lost its electoral hold as quickly as it had gained it. Once weakened, the Klan faced the mundane dangers that plagued any secret society. What initially seemed exotic soon only seemed silly. Hooded men and burning crosses had been mysterious in the early 1920s; by the late 1920s they were banal.

Two high leaders of the Colorado Klan confer during the Klan's Colorado heyday.

Sectional Politics

By 1930 westerners had created neither a western political party nor a western political ideology, but they had at least created a western political agenda and a western political style. Few westerners retained the radical Populist vision, but they did retain a suspicion and resentment of the East. Many of them would still join crusades against railroads, banks, and large corporations not because they disapproved of either capitalism or large corporations in principle, but because these economic organizations symbolized eastern control, control by outsiders. Outsiders had not promoted the development of the West in the ways westerners thought the West deserved. Many western voters retained the Populist perception of the West as a colonial area exploited by the capitalist East. Most westerners, however, were also capitalists, or at least aspired to be, so western politics did not become so much a clear rebellion against capitalism as a more diffuse politics of resentment. Westerners were more prone to think of solutions to their economic problems in terms of congressional pork-barrel politics than of radical economic reform. Voters and politicians alike sought to increase the West's share of wealth. Frustrated by dependence on eastern banks and corporations, they worked for a greater share of federal expenditures in order to reduce western reliance on eastern capital. They needed the federal government, but they also feared federal control.

When in the twentieth century Western politicians turned from seeking eastern capital to seeking federal funds, they underwent no great ideological transformation. Their goal was the same: rapid development. Like the Populists, twentieth-century western progressives wanted federal aid in overcoming their economic dependence on the East. But these politicians, enamored with bureaucrats and experts, abandoned the democratic, cooperative thrust of Populism; they retained only its emphasis on an activist federal government.

Readings

Aldrich, Mark. "A Note on Railroad Rates and the Populist Uprising." *Agricultural History* 54 (July 1980):424–32.

Argersinger, Peter H. "Ideology and Behavior: Legislative Politics and Western Populism." *Agricultural History* 58 (January 1984): 43–58.

Bader, Robert Smith. *Prohibition in Kansas: A History*. Lawrence: University Press of Kansas, 1986.

Clanton, O. Gene. *Kansas Populism: Ideas and Men*. Lawrence: Regents Press of Kansas, 1969.

Clark, Norman H. *The Dry Years: Prohibition and Social Change in Washington*. Seattle: University of Washington Press, 1965.

Goodwyn, Lawrence. *Democratic Promise: The Populist Moment in America*. New York: Oxford University Press, 1976.

Gould, Lewis L. *Progressives and Prohibitionists: Texas Democrats in the Wilson Era*. Austin: University of Texas Press, 1973.

Green, James. *Grass Roots Socialism: Racial Movements in the Southwest: 1895–1943*. Baton Rouge: Louisiana State University Press, 1978.

Hundley, Norris, Jr. *Water and the West: The Colorado River Compact and the Politics of Water in the American West*. Berkeley: University of California Press, 1975.

Issel, William, and Robert W. Cherny. *San Francisco, 1865–1932: Politics, Power, and Urban Development*. Berkeley: University of California Press, 1986.

Kazin, Michael. *Barons of Labor: The San Francisco Building Trades and Union Power in the Progressive Era*. Urbana: University of Illinois Press, 1987.

Kleppner, Paul. "Politics Without Parties: The Western States, 1900–84." In *The Twentieth-Century West: Historical Interpretations*, pp. 295–338. Ed. Gerald D. Nash and Richard W. Etulain. Albuquerque: University of New Mexico Press, 1987.

———. "Voters and Parties in the Western States, 1876–1900." *Western Historical Quarterly* 14 (January 1983):49–68.

La Forte, Robert Sherman. *Leaders of Reform: Progressive Republicans in Kansas, 1900–1916*. Lawrence: Regents Press of Kansas, 1974.

McDonald, Terrence J. *The Parameters of Urban Fiscal Policy: Socioeconomic Change and Political Culture in San Francisco, 1860–1906*. Berkeley: University of California Press, 1986.

McGuire, Robert A. "Economic Causes of Late Nineteenth Century Agrarian Unrest: New Evidence." *Journal of Economic History* 41 (December 1981):835–51.

Malone, Michael P. *The Battle for Butte: Mining and Politics on the Northern Frontier, 1864–1906*. Seattle: University of Washington Press, 1981.

Morlan, Robert L. *Political Prairie Fire: The Nonpartisan League*. Minneapolis: University of Minnesota Press, 1955.

Moss, Rosalind Urbach. "The 'Girls' from Syracuse: Sex Role Negotiations of Kansas Women in Politics, 1887–90." In *The Women's West*, pp. 253–64. Ed. Susan Armitage and Elizabeth Jameson. Norman: Univesity of Oklahoma Press, 1987.

Mowry, George. *California Progressives*. Berkeley: University of California Press, 1951.

Myres, Sandra L. *Westering Women and the Frontier Experience, 1800–1915*. Albuquerque: University of New Mexico Press, 1982.

Parsons, Stanley. *The Populist Context: Rural Versus Urban Power on a Great Plains Frontier*. Westport, Conn.: Greenwood Press, 1973.

Pollack, Norman. *The Populist Response to Industrial America*. Cambridge: Harvard University Press, 1962.

Pomeroy, Earl. *The Pacific Slope*. New York: Alfred E. Knopf, 1966.

Sarasohn, David. "The Election of 1916: Realigning the Rockies." *Western Historical Quarterly* 11 (July 1980):285–306.

Stefano, Carolyn. "Networking on the Frontier: the Colorado Women's Suffrage Movement, 1876–1893." In *The Women's West*, pp. 265–76. Ed. Susan Armitage and Elizabeth Jameson. Norman: University of Oklahoma Press, 1987.

Teaford, Jon C. *The Unheralded Triumph: City Government in America, 1870–1900*. Baltimore: Johns Hopkins University Press, 1984.

Thompson, John. *Closing the Frontier: Radical Response in Oklahoma, 1889–1923*. Norman: University of Oklahoma Press, 1986.

Turner, James. "Understanding the Populists." *Journal of American History* 67 (September 1980):354–73.

Wright, James Edward. *The Politics of Populism: Dissent in Colorado*. New Haven: Yale University Press, 1974.

PART FOUR

The Bureaucratic Revolution in the West

A quiet revolution began in the West in the 1880s and continued beneath the tumult of the Populist Revolt into the twentieth century. The essence of the revolution was simple enough: the federal government no longer saw its basic role as transferring public resources to private ownership; instead, it asserted permanent public ownership of portions of the remaining public domain and began to manage and supervise use of those lands. The accomplishments of this revolution appeared gradually throughout the West in public dams, national forests, and national parks, all manned by the growing cadres of the managerial state. Gradually as the revolution succeeded and entrenched itself during the twentieth century, the National Forest Service, the National Park Service, the Bureau of Reclamation, the Bureau of Land Management, and numerous other federal agencies grew to oversee the federal domain. They eventually dwarfed the older bureaucracies that represented the initial federal presence in the West: the Bureau of Indian Affairs, the U.S. Geological Survey, and the General Land Office (which finally disappeared entirely).

This revolution had ramifications throughout western politics and society. It found both allies and opponents. Its allies tended to be located in the emerging regional power bases of the West: the cities and corporations. By the 1880s the cities had solidified their positions as centers of population and economic control. The cities themselves arose from processes that were driven by both market and state. Although the popular image of the West was, and remains, one of scattered populations and isolation, the West in fact very quickly became an urban region whose cities held sway over vast hinterlands. By 1880 the West beyond the Great Plains was the most urbanized region in the country.

The western universe began to take the shape of a collection of discrete solar systems, and the suns of these systems were cities. First San Francisco, Denver, Salt Lake, Portland, and Omaha and later Dallas, Houston, Seattle, and Los Angeles emerged as significant regional centers within the West. The size of the hinterlands these urban centers controlled varied drastically. The brightest sun in the nineteenth-century western universe was San Francisco, which was by 1880 already the ninth largest city in the United States. With a population of 234,000, it dwarfed all other western cities. Second-place Denver had only 35,000 people; ranking third was San Francisco's own satellite, Oakland, with 34,000 people. Indeed, in 1880 the population of San Francisco and its urban planets—Oakland, Sacramento, San Jose, and Stockton—was greater than that of all other major western cities combined. After 1880, additional new cities arose to challenge, and in some cases overshadow, their slightly older rivals. By the early twentieth century Los Angeles was the center of the West.

Within their own urban solar systems, these cities served as administrative, commercial, and cultural centers. The boundaries of their hinterland—that is, the region over which their economic hand extended—had little to do with political boundaries. San Francisco, for example, exerted such financial and cultural influence on Nevada that in the 1870s and 1880s two of Nevada's senators, William Sharon and his successor, James Fair, actually resided in San Francisco, as did, for that matter, both of California's senators. In a similar if less dramatic fashion, the economic and cultural influence of Salt Lake City extended over the Idaho border into heavily Mormon southern Idaho and eventually south into the Mormon colonies of northern Arizona and western Colorado. In the twentieth century, urban governments, like city governments elsewhere in the country, moved from being merely regulators of public life to promoting growth. They, often in cooperation with federal bureaucracies, sought to manage not only urban space but also the hinterlands that they regarded as necessary for urban prosperity.

Corporations tended to be more fickle allies of the federal bureaucracies, but on the whole, they, too, proved sympathetic to federal management; certainly they were more sympathetic than were small businessmen. Large and small resource users in the West, all pursuing their own calculus of self-interest, split over particular proposals. Small farmers on the whole strongly supported federal irrigation projects and national forests originally designed to protect the watershed. Small stock grazers and small lumbermen tended to oppose the new federal presence, which tended to thwart their own ambitions for expansion. Larger stock raisers and the big timber companies, however, realized that federal supervision could serve their interests by helping restrain the overproduction that plagued their industries, by restricting the expansion of potential competitors, and by allowing them to turn their greater financial resources into privileged access to the federal domain.

In western political life the revolution produced a mounting sense of frustration. This was not because specific programs lacked political support in the West, but instead because bureaucracies, national in origin and inspiration, often acted beyond western control. Until the late nineteenth century, westerners could treat the looming federal presence as temporary. It presumably would retreat as the territories became states, as Indians were assimilated and reservations disappeared, and as the government carved the vast public domain into individual private holdings. When this failed to happen, western politicians tended to react like disappointed heirs. While it was true that the resources were by no stretch of the imagination theirs—the public domain belonged to the nation as a whole—they had expected that someday the public lands would be left in the care of western states and their citizens. To be deprived of what they regarded as their patrimony left most western officials petulant and angry.

The triumph of this managerial revolution put the West and the East in very different relations to the federal government. The federal presence was incomparably greater in the West, and regional and local affairs involved negotiations with federal agencies that would be unimaginable in the East for decades to come. Whatever else western politicians were, they had to be adept negotiators with federal resource managers. And in time many of them learned to master the art of rhetorically denouncing federal interference while securing the federal programs and dollars that sustained their region.

CHAPTER 15

At the Centers of Power

POWER, whether political or economic, consists of the ability to compel or persuade other human beings, or nature, to do what one wishes. Power shapes and transforms. When people exercise power they enable some things to happen and inhibit others. Power is wielded by individuals, but in modern society power resides in institutions.

Everyone exercises some power, but power tends to aggregate, and in the twentieth-century United States three concentrations of power have emerged: the federal bureaucracies (including the armed forces), the cities, and the corporations. The growth of the American West has coincided with the appearance of these large concentrations of power, and this coincidence has inevitably shaped the region. Things or attitudes that appear peculiarly western are often, in fact, marks of the West's status as the most urban region in the United States (that is, the region with the greatest percentage of people living in towns and cities) or the region where federal bureaucracies have the greatest sway. Concentrations of power have shaped the modern West perhaps more than any other region of the United States.

Corporations, federal bureaucracies, and western cities all existed in the West at the turn of the century, but their days of greatest influence lay ahead. In the twentieth century indigenous western corporations arose alongside eastern corporations. Both federal bureaucracies and urban governments shed their role as passive regulators in order to emphasize active service. The federal government no longer simply distributed resources, allowing title to slip into private hands; it now managed resources for optimal growth, retaining title itself. City government, as in San Francisco, no longer aimed simply at keeping taxes low; instead it sought to promote growth and provide the services necessary to sustain it. Both bureaucracies and cities sought to control nature on a scale never before attempted, and in controlling nature they necessarily increased their control over human beings.

The Oil Industry

The oil industry contained the vanguard of powerful new western corporations in the twentieth century. In the early twentieth century the uses for oil were expanding even as existing petroleum reserves in the East dwindled. Petroleum powered locomotives and factories; it provided asphalt for roads; and later it fueled the cars that ran upon them. It eventually heated the homes of those who drove the cars. Wildcatters, men who prospected for oil—black gold—as Forty-niners had for actual gold, discovered new deposits in the West, and eastern corporations moved to dominate the new western oil fields. That corporations dominated oil as they had all other extractive industries in the West was hardly surprising. But the organization of the oil industry was, in fact, different from other extractive industries. Eastern developmental capital did not translate to eastern control to the extent that it had in other western extractive industries.

There were essentially two oil industries in the West. The first was east of the Rockies, primarily in Kansas, Texas, Oklahoma, and, to a lesser degree, Wyoming. The Standard Oil Company, which monopolized the nineteenth-century oil industry of Pennsylvania and Ohio, had begun serious explorations in Kansas in the 1890s. But exploration and production quickly shifted south to Texas, where Spindletop field, discovered in 1901, was one of the richest in the world, and to Oklahoma, where there were major discoveries between 1904 and 1914. By the late 1920s Texas and Oklahoma had emerged as the leading oil-producing states in the country. A motorist could drive through 150 miles of West Texas without losing sight of oil derricks, and the biggest discoveries were yet to come. In 1930, Columbus Marion ("Dad") Joiner, a wildcatter who had worked in the oil fields for years, discovered the massive East Texas field. Beneath it lay a 200-square-mile pool of oil.

These new western oil fields cost John D. Rockefeller's Standard Oil the nearly complete national monopoly that it had achieved over oil transportation and refining. Although Standard of New Jersey became the major stockholder in Humble Oil of Texas (later Exxon), the state of Texas intervened to thwart Standard Oil's attempts to regain its dominance. The Texas Populists had left as part of their legacy antimonopoly laws that prevented any corporation from engaging in more than one aspect of the petroleum business. A corporation could produce, transport, refine, or wholesale oil, but it could not, as Standard Oil had done in the East, do all of them. Well before the United States Supreme Court broke up the Standard Oil Company as an illegal monopoly in 1911, the Texas courts had dealt the giant company serious setbacks. Texas repealed its antimonopoly laws in 1917, and the Texas Oil Company (now Texaco) went on to become a major integrated producer. But by then Texas independents—that is, large companies specializing in one aspect of the oil business—had already established themselves as important competitors in the field.

Having nurtured the independents with antimonopoly laws, Texas continued to support them by other means. Independents continued to proliferate, because the number and extent of oil discoveries in the state made it impossible, at least in the short run, for the integrated companies to achieve an oligopoly. These smaller companies survived under the wing of the Texas Railroad Commission, which received authority from the state to regulate the industry. As a result, a large percentage of the revenues of Texas oil remained within the state. Through a combination of wages, leases, taxes, and the purchase of equipment and services, the industry pumped huge amounts of money into the region; revenues from oil leases on state lands provided much of the money for the university system in Texas.

In California, the second major oil-producing region, development took a different course, but the result once more was the growth of strong western corporations and the retention of substantial profits within the region. Between 1900 and 1926 California produced more oil than any other state in the country,

Oil was the greatest of the twentieth-century West's extractive industries. This early-twentieth-century oil well was near Douglas, Wyoming.

but California's distance from both eastern markets and other oil-producing regions meant that its oil went largely to markets in Washington, Oregon, Arizona, Nevada, Alaska, and Hawaii. Only small amounts of California oil ever reached the East Coast, and virtually no outside oil came in.

California's early prominence in the industry rested on fuel oil, used to power furnaces, factories, ships, and trains, instead of gasoline. Fuel oil proved lucrative for small oil producers because it needed little refining. And since California lacked coal reserves, fuel oil quickly replaced imported coal on railroad locomotives, on ships, and in the state's factories. The location of oil fields relatively near the large Los Angeles and San Francisco markets also reduced the amount of capital necessary to enter the industry, as transportation costs were limited. Small companies could survive in California because large corporations such as Standard Oil could not secure bottlenecks on transportation or refining and drive out competitors as they had in the East. Nor could the giants move in outside oil to drive down prices and destroy smaller companies. The transportation costs were too high. Standard Oil of California (separated from its eastern parent by the antitrust decision of 1911) and Royal Dutch Shell Petroleum Company did become major powers in the California oil industry, but they were unable to eliminate the California independents, which joined together to create major new oil companies. Early operators in Ventura County combined to form the Union Oil Company in 1890, and small companies in the Kern River field formed the Associated Oil Company in 1901. As a result, of the three largest companies operating in California—Standard Oil, Union Oil, and the Southern Pacific (which had acquired the Associated Oil Company)—only Standard Oil was primarily a creation of outside capital, and it established its corporate headquarters in San Francisco.

It was western expertise, too, that ran western oil fields. California was the first western state to invest in its higher education system, and engineers, chemists, and geologists trained at Berkeley and Stanford discovered new oil fields, greatly increased the efficiency of production, and found new uses for petroleum. By 1920, Oklahoma, and later Texas, rivaled California in training petroleum geologists and engineers, but their educational systems as a whole remained narrow as California's continued to grow and broaden. It created a pool of experts and an educated labor force that no other western state could rival.

The oil companies represented a new kind of western extractive industry—one developed, in part, by western capital and western expertise as well as by western labor and western resources. When after 1920 the market for petroleum products began to shift from fuel oil to gasoline, California oil companies had accumulated both the financial resources and the expertise to make the transition. They constructed enough modern refineries by 1929 to make petroleum refining California's largest manufacturing industry. The state's share of oil production fell steadily after 1923 as new fields elsewhere came into production, but California had already used its petroleum profits to spin off new industries that helped make the state into a major manufacturing center. By 1929 California ranked eighth among the states in manufacturing output, and manufacturing accounted for one-third of California's income.

Mineral Policy

Outside of Texas and Oklahoma, where private, state, and Indian lands contained oil, most western oil lay beneath public lands. And because of the peculiarities of western mineral law, oil, like coal and precious minerals, was initially available almost literally for the taking. The ready availability of oil helped created great corporations, but these corporations eventually had to confront federal bureaucracies trying to exert stricter controls over the public lands and their resources.

Well into the twentieth century the Mining Law of 1872 remained the basic legislation regulating the production of minerals on public lands. By giving miners the unrestricted right to prospect and mine on federal lands, this law put mining largely outside of public control and left it free to respond to market forces. A payment of from $2.50 to $5.00 an acre (depending on the mineral) allowed miners to patent a claim of up to 160 acres and maintain such a claim in perpetuity simply by performing at least $100 worth of work on it a year. The law bestowed a phenomenally generous gift of public resources to private entrepreneurs. Unlike Spanish, British, Mexican, or Australian mining law, American law reserved no portion of a public resource for public use. In 1880 the first public lands commission reported to President Hayes that "while 20 acres of lode mineral land on the Comstock lode at $5 per acre are sold for $100 . . ., as in the case of the Consolidated Virginia and California mines, [they] may yield more than $60,000,000."

Coal and later oil lands fell outside of the Mining Law of 1872, but only during the early twentieth century did the federal government begin to exert greater control over their exploitation. Until 1920 the Coal Lands Act of 1873 gave

discoverers of coal lands a preferential right of purchase at a set price ranging from
$10 to $20 per acre, depending on location. The railroads proved particularly
adept at using these laws to monopolize western coal lands. They drove independent mine operators out of business by the simple expedient of charging them
high rates for carrying coal while subsidizing their own mines. By the turn of the
century two subsidiaries of the Denver and Rio Grande Railroad owned all or
nearly all the operating coal mines in Utah, while in Wyoming the Union Pacific
had obtained a virtual monopoly in coal production along its route.

Theodore Roosevelt made revision of the 1873 law one of his top legislative
priorities. He forced the return of some fraudulently obtained coal lands to the
public domain, and then, when Congress refused to act quickly on his proposals
for a leasing law, he withdrew 66 million acres of coal lands from entry in 1906.
Roosevelt's successor, William Howard Taft, withdrew 3 million acres of public
oil land in California and Wyoming from entry in 1910. Until then, claimants
had been able to acquire oil lands in much the same way that they bought mineral
lands.

The withdrawals launched a long battle for reform only settled with the Mineral
Lands Leasing Act of 1920. For the first time the federal government instituted
a policy of leasing instead of selling coal and oil lands. Under the law, the secretary
of the interior issued oil prospecting permits valid for two years and covering a
maximum of 2,560 acres. If the prospectors discovered oil, they could lease up to
25 percent of the 2,560 acres for 20 years for an annual royalty of 5 percent. The
leasing policy represented a major deviation from the older federal policy of simply
giving resources away to entrepreneurs who wanted to develop them. Leasing
allowed the government to collect royalties on coal and oil production on federal
lands, but these royalties remained quite low. Coal lands commanded a minimum
royalty of $0.05 a ton, with the usual price somewhere between $0.10 and $0.15
a ton. Revenue was, however, not the main goal of the legislation. Proponents
supported leasing as a way to regulate resource production and make it more
efficient. The government could curtail wasteful overproduction by holding back
on leases and prospecting permits. And as was the case with other federal regulatory programs, some of those who were to be regulated welcomed the regulation.
The bigger oil firms all backed the legislation as a way to stabilize the industry.
Oil producers in particular wanted predictable and stable prices. Overproduction
and ruinous competition forced them to operate at a loss and sometimes forced
them near bankruptcy. They could not make rational judgments on acquiring or
developing new properties if they could not predict future price and production.

Federal Power

The increase in federal control over oil and coal on public lands was only a single
aspect of rising federal power in the West. Beginning in the 1890s, the central
government ceased to be a nursemaid to the future states and a prodigal distributor
of resources to the country's citizens and corporations. Washington instead became a manager of western land, resources, and, inevitably, people.

The enlarged federal role in the West paralleled progressive attempts to rational-
ize western resource use and to make the exploitation of those resources as
"efficient" as possible. The men who molded much of the western bureaucratic
structure—in effect the captains of bureaucracy—were remarkably charismatic

figures for the founders of institutions whose staffs have most often been described as "faceless" and whose functioning demands the establishment of routine and the interchangeability of personnel. In the nineteenth century, bureaucracies took shape under the one-armed Civil War veteran John Wesley Powell, who led the first expedition to run the Colorado River, and the brilliant Clarence King— mountain climber, scientist, and a man who defied the conventions of his century by marrying a black woman. In the early twentieth century the most influential bureaucrats were Gifford Pinchot, who wrestled, boxed, and swam with Theodore Roosevelt and cooperated with him in creating the modern National Forest Service, and William Mulholland, an Irish immigrant and self-taught engineer who created the Los Angeles Department of Water and Power, an agency which in a very real sense made modern southern California possible.

For all their own individuality, Powell, King, Pinchot, Mulholland, and dozens of lesser figures spoke a common language and sought a common goal: the *efficient* development of the West. By the twentieth century, widespread fraud, waste, and inefficiency in the lumber industry, overgrazing in the cattle industry, disap- pointingly slow growth in irrigation, and increasing disparities in the distribution of wealth throughout the West all alarmed a new generation of national leaders. Progressive conservationists shared a perception of the West that emphasized deficiency and scarcity instead of abundance. They feared an approaching timber famine; they recognized an arid West where rainfall would never increase enough to water crops; they saw a public domain with insufficient grasses to support the number of domestic animals placed upon it. They saw efficiency and scientific expertise as the cure. When they spoke of efficiency, progressive bureaucrats meant eliminating waste to gain the maximum benefit from each blade of grass, each tree, and each lump of coal and organizing production so that the nation would not run out of necessary raw materials. In the national forests, or by extension anywhere on the public lands, this meant producing, as Gifford Pinchot explained, "the largest amount of whatever crop or service will be most useful, and keep on producing it for generation after generation." Americans had to learn to husband and conserve.

In 1903, President Roosevelt appointed a Public Lands Commission to review all public land laws and report on their operation and effect. The commission never officially finished its work, but it did articulate a principle basic to the new conservation program: public ownership. Only under continued public ownership could managers exert the control necessary to insure the efficient development of the resources of the public lands.

Public ownership did not necessarily mean that the government would retain title to all remaining public lands. Some lands would be open to entry—but often at higher prices and with stricter enforcement of the exact requirements of the law. The Interior Department and the Department of Agriculture were determined to make sure that valuable resources such as coal, oil, phosphate, and sites suitable for waterpower development would not be open to homesteading or to purchase as agricultural lands. President Theodore Roosevelt's administration (1901–1909) mounted a sustained effort to inventory the public lands, determine the resources they held, and implement systems of management. Having withdrawn waterpower sites from entry, for example, the Roosevelt administration allowed their development only under a permit system. Users would have to pay fees in order to use these sites to produce electricity.

Management clearly required employing managers, and the selection of such managers opened up a pandora's box of political controversy. The progressives feared that federal management of public resources could become a political pork barrel from which victorious politicians would reward their friends with jobs and leases. Citing the widespread corruption in those government agencies wherein employees gained their positions by political connections, progressives argued for specially trained experts who by virtue of their education and professionalism would be devoted to efficient, businesslike management. And college-educated experts did come to staff the major new bureaucracies of the progressive era: the National Forest Service, the National Park Service, and the Bureau of Reclamation. There was, however, a trade-off for the detachment, honesty, and expertise of these officials; theoretically, at least, as long as elected officials supervised public lands there existed a modicum of democratic control, but now the possibility for such control became more remote. Bureaucrats who made critical decisions on the use of public resources did so without any direct supervision by the people or their elected representatives.

Water Rights

The immediate focus of western conservation was on the rivers. Aridity defined large sections of the West. Unless westerners could redirect water to where they needed it, they would have to adjust to the western landscape instead of reshaping and developing that landscape to suit their wants. Before rearranging the West's rivers and streams, however, westerners had first to decide who owned them and thus had power over them.

The exact legal nature of private ownership of water was in flux when Anglo American settlers moved into the West. Under the English common-law doctrine of riparian rights, rights to water accompanied rights to the land along a riverbank: all landowners who bordered a stream had a right to use water flowing past their lands. They could not, however, appreciably diminish it, contaminate it, or change the course of the stream through which it flowed. Such traditional riparianism—which practically confined the water to household uses and watering livestock—guaranteed the navigability of rivers (which in the West were often not navigable to begin with) while it stood in the way of economic development in an age of waterpower. Dams inevitably flooded lands upstream and interfered with the flow downstream. Before the Civil War, the American courts had already begun to adjust the common law to emerging capitalism by allowing an appropriative right for "productive use," largely by industrialists, to take precedence over undisturbed enjoyment by the riparian landowner. Appropriative rights did not depend on owning any land along a stream.

Appropriative rights in the West were thus a local implementation of a larger national modification of the law, not a western innovation. California miners added a new twist to appropriative rights when, to settle the disputes that arose when there was not enough water for every potential user, they made the rule that "the one first in time is the first in right." Western courts, eager to encourage mining, supported this right of prior appropriation.

The rights of appropriators, however, were not absolute; they had to apply water to a beneficial use. They had to "use it or lose it." In a drought, the person with the oldest water right could take his or her full appropriation even if this left none for the person with next right. In the 1880s when Colorado, claiming state ownership of water rights, abrogated all riparian right to surface waters within its boundaries and took over enforcing appropriative rights, the doctrine of prior appropriation came to be known as the Colorado Doctrine. It established prior appropriation as the exclusive water right. Although the federal government questioned the states' right to claim ownership of all water, the Colorado Doctrine quickly dominated the Rocky Mountain states.

Elsewhere in the West a modified riparianism held on for some time. California contained both humid and arid lands, and the courts tried to reconcile both riparian rights and the rights of prior appropriation. In *Lux* v. *Haggin* (1886) the California supreme court rejected the logic of the Colorado Doctrine by asserting that the federal government was the original owner not only of the land but also of the water of the public domain. When the federal government transferred land title, the riparian right to water went with it unless there were preexisting rights of prior appropriation. Neither right was absolute. *Lux* v. *Haggin* thus laid the basis for the California Doctrine, an uneasy marriage between riparian rights and prior appropriation.

Lux v. *Haggin* was not a popular decision in California. By upholding partial riparian rights—favored by livestock interests—it inhibited the permanent diversion of large amounts of water away from the river. But in hindsight that was not necessarily such a bad thing. Nineteenth-century irrigation systems were inefficient, and contiguous irrigation wasted far less water through evaporation and seepage than did the use of water far from the river.

There was, finally, a third water doctrine in the West. It found its fullest expression in Wyoming, where the state constitution gave the state title to all water and allowed state administrators to reject water claims and override existing appropriations not in the public interest. Nebraska, the Dakotas, and Oklahoma all followed Wyoming's lead in claiming full control over water.

Emphasizing only the differences between the Colorado, California, and Wyoming doctrines can, however, obscure their shared instrumental and utilitarian approach to water. Legislators and judges throughout the West rewarded those who used water and denied rights to those who allowed water to flow on to the sea. They assumed that water flowing freely through its natural channels was "wasted," as if this water did not sustain the ecosystems of the West. The courts and legislators all conceived of water as a resource, an instrument of production and not as an elemental part of natural systems that, when deprived of water, would collapse.

Demand for Federal Water Development

These legal battles might seem far removed from the growth of federal bureaucratic power, but in effect they unintentionally set the stage for increasing federal control. Proponents of irrigation believed that neither the huge wheat farms that dominated the California landscape nor the large cattle ranches that dominated the High Plains could survive in the face of irrigation. Irrigation demanded intensive labor and close attention to detail and in return gave high yields. It supposedly insured that small farmers would inherit the earth.

Californians thought they had beheld the ultimate triumph of small-scale irrigation when William Chapman established the Central California Colony near Fresno in 1875. Chapman divided his land into 20-acre farms, constructed irrigation works, and set out saplings and vines. New settlers could purchase a farm for $1,000. Among those who did were four San Francisco schoolteachers, one of whom, Minnie Austin, put part of the land in raisin grapes. Austin established raisin growing in California, and by 1886 she was shipping 7,500 boxes a year. She symbolized the promise irrigation held for enterprising people of limited means. They could, it seemed, create prosperous small farms where baronial estates had stood.

Irrigationists, however, deluded themselves in thinking that the Minnie Austins could stand alone. Without large capitalists such as William Chapman there would have been no Minnie Austins to make the desert bloom. Minnie Austin and her neighbors lacked the resources to build the irrigation systems necessary to provide the water from any but the smallest and most easily tamed streams. In the 1870s and 1880s private corporations moved in to divert the rivers, dig the ditches, and deliver the water to small farmers. In return they hoped for large profits from the water's sale. In the early 1880s, for example, the Northern Colorado Irrigation Company constructed the 85-mile High Line Canal for $650,000, and similar enterprises developed land in Wyoming, New Mexico, and Idaho.

The water these companies delivered tended, however, to be expensive. The farmers not only paid for the water they received, but also paid a kind of rental fee for using the dams, ditches, and canals that brought them the water. The quarrels between the irrigation companies and their customers over the cost of water were often long and acrimonious and usually spilled over into the political arena. Many companies, too, overestimated the rate of settlement; when settlers failed to appear as quickly as the company anticipated or refused to buy the expensive water, the companies went bankrupt. By 1900 one estimate put 90 percent of the private canal companies in financial distress. Most sold out, often on credit, to their water users. Such financial failures did not encourage further private investment in irrigation systems.

With corporate efforts unable to sustain small-scale irrigation, irrigationists turned to the states. State water bureaucracies had already appeared in the West. Beginning with Colorado's irrigation acts of 1879 and 1881, Colorado, Wyoming, and other states began to create water divisions, water commissioners, and state engineer's offices to determine and enforce water claims during drought years, to adjudicate excessive claims, and to allocate water. But irrigationists wanted more than regulation; they wanted promotion and funding.

In 1887 the California legislature passed the Wright Act, which provided an alternative way of financing an irrigation network: the irrigation district. In order to promote irrigation, these districts could condemn (that is, force the cession of) all individual water rights, reallocating them among their members. Once established by a two-thirds vote of the electorate within the proposed district, the act gave an elected board of directors power to construct an irrigation project.

This panorama of irrigated farms in Washington's Yakima Valley shows the irrigationists' dream of small, fertile farms.

The directors could fund the project by bond issues that were secured by taxes imposed on all the agricultural lands within the district. The district would distribute water proportionate to the amount of taxes each landowner paid the district.

Irrigation districts, in California and elsewhere, developed very slowly. Directors overestimated water supplies, underestimated costs, miscalculated how much water they had to provide, and mismanaged construction. They borrowed money and defaulted on their payments. During World War I the demand for food stimulated a revival of irrigation districts but in a notably less democratic form. The large landholders now obtained an influence over district affairs commensurate with their holdings within the district, and most states instituted stricter regulation of the water districts in order to reassure eastern bondholders that their investments were safe. In California these revamped irrigation districts accounted for nearly two-thirds of the expansion of irrigated land between 1910 and 1930.

The initial failure of irrigation districts left promoters in a quandary. By the mid-1890s western irrigation had reached a plateau, with about 7 million acres under irrigation, and it seemed that irrigation of the arid lands would proceed no farther. Irrigators had tapped most of the smaller streams capable of watering the land without expensive engineering projects. If irrigation was to expand, it would, it seemed, have to depend on large projects, but private capital had proved incapable of building such projects at a profit, and the irrigation districts seemed incapable of doing so efficiently. Yet amidst the droughts and failures of the late 1880s and early 1890s, irrigation seemed more important than ever for western agricultural growth.

In the 1890s irrigation found its prophet, William Smythe, whose book *The Conquest of Arid America* became the bible of a new crusade for an irrigated West. Smythe proclaimed the old dream of irrigation as the road to a democratic, egalitarian West of small farmers. The West would take urban dwellers displaced or alienated by new industrial organization and technology, put them back on the land, and make them irrigated farmers. To build the irrigation network necessary for these farms, Smythe wanted federal assistance.

National Reclamation Act (Newlands Act)

The failure of the Desert Land Act had brought demands at the First National Irrigation Congress of 1891 (a gathering that included more engineers, lawyers, real estate agents, and journalists than farmers) that Congress cede the arid lands to the states for development. Congress refused, but in 1894 it did pass the Carey Act, which gave each desert state 1 million acres. Under the law each state could hire a construction company to build irrigation works at a guaranteed profit. The state would then sell this land itself to the farmers at a nominal cost and in addition charge them their proportionate share of the costs of the irrigation work. Except in Idaho and Wyoming, however, the Carey Act was largely a failure. The states were unwilling to risk trying to do what private capitalists had failed to achieve.

It was this history of partial failure by corporations, irrigation districts, and the states that drove proponents of irrigation to turn to the federal government for aid. Once they had linked irrigation to federal aid, westerners stood around like the groom at a shotgun wedding; their own desire had delivered them up to a partnership they had never wanted. In 1899, George Maxwell, a lawyer from Sonoma, California, created the National Irrigation Association to lobby for a federal takeover of water development. In 1901 a Nevada congressman, the aptly named Francis Newlands, introduced a bill to place money from the sale of western public lands into an "arid lands reclamation fund" for the construction of irrigation projects. The law allowed the government to sell tracts of irrigated lands no larger than 160 acres within the projects. The settler would pay for the land in ten annual installments, with the price determined by the cost of the project—the dams, canals, gates, and ditches. The purchase money would return to the fund to create other projects.

This bill, the National Reclamation or Newlands Act, written and promoted by westerners and serving regional western interests, garnered significant eastern support in Congress. The support was not from eastern workers yearning for farms, the supposed beneficiaries of the bill. Instead it came from representatives of eastern manufacturers who saw in an expanded agrarian West new markets and an outlet for discontented workers from the industrial East. Conservative easterners and western boosters thus combined to pass an act that gave the federal government control over a critical aspect of western development. The act established a new western bureaucracy—the Bureau of Reclamation (as it was renamed in 1923)—that set out to develop the irrigated West that private capital, local irrigation districts, and the states had failed to create.

One historian, Donald Worster, has with excusable hyperbole called the National Reclamation Act "the most important single piece of legislation in the history of the West." It marked a new approach to the development of the arid lands, and it became a landmark in the larger resurgence of federal power in the West that has made the modern West so much a creation of "state power, state expertise, state technology, and state bureaucracy." Smythe and his allies achieved the federal aid they desired, but they never achieved the ends for which they sought it. Called upon to create a land of small farmers, federal managers and experts entered the West and created a land of powerful bureaucracies and large, eventually corporate, farmers far different from Smythe's agrarian vision.

Yet despite its eventual importance, the Bureau of Reclamation failed for 25 years either to irrigate on the scale it desired or to create the kind of irrigation districts the Reclamation Act envisioned. The bureau did not turn large amounts of the public domain into small farms. And the land it did develop was sometimes not on the public domain. In the Salt River Project of 1905 in Arizona the bureau purposefully secured water for privately held lands in order to gain credit for a successful project. At other times the bureau fully intended to develop land on the public domain, but as soon as bureau engineers showed an interest in a tract, speculators rushed in to buy up the land, hoping to resell it at a large profit.

The government retained its announced goal of providing homes on small farms, but in violation of its own charter the bureau also provided irrigation to large landowners. The agency's director, Frederick Newell, threatened to enforce the 160-acre limitation on all lands developed by federal projects, but the bureau rarely did so. Nor was there much public pressure to enforce the limit; neither the eastern poor nor, for that matter, the children of western farmers lined up to acquire land on the federal projects where living conditions were harsh, the land expensive, and bureaucratic requirements usually confusing. By 1923 the federal projects had added only a little over a million acres to the irrigated lands of the West, which by then, thanks to a resurgence of the irrigation districts during World War I, totaled about 20 million acres.

In terms of acres irrigated, substantial success for the Bureau of Reclamation would not come until the 1930s, but the mere existence of the bureau had increased the potential for bureaucratizing the West. The bureau represented a relatively complete section of the road to federal control. The road did not as yet carry much traffic, but it stood ready to handle substantial freight later on. The Bureau of Reclamation was only part of the federal bureaucracy that irrigation justified; initially far more successful and influential was the Forest Service.

Genesis of the Forest Service

Initially both the national forests and the Forest Service arose from the desire of western irrigators to protect their water supply. From experience farmers feared that lumbering, overgrazing, and fires would destroy the mountain forests that regulated the flow of water into the rivers. The result would be heavy spring floods, rivers dry by the summer when farmers needed the water most, increased erosion, and silting that would clog their irrigation ditches and streams. Congress's conference committee report on the General Land Law Revision Act of 1891 had cited the need to protect western watersheds as the rationale for forest reserves when it had given the president the right to establish forest reserves by proclamation.

In the 1890s, with little fanfare or controversy, President Benjamin Harrison created 15 forest reserves totaling over 16 million acres. During his second administration Grover Cleveland added more than 21 million acres of new reserves, but neither Harrison or Cleveland created any effective mechanism for managing these lands. Not until 1897, when the Forest Management Act gave the secretary of the interior the power to regulate the use of the reserves, did federal management begin in earnest. The act paved the way for federal officials to regulate grazing, commercial lumbering, and hydroelectric power generation within the forests. Unlike the public domain of unsold and largely unsupervised lands, the national forests would become subject to planned and regulated development under the auspices of the federal government.

The significance of the new law, however, paled in importance beside the man who came to enforce it, Gifford Pinchot. A professional forester born in New England and trained in Germany, Pinchot in 1898 became director of the Division of Forestry within the Department of Agriculture, and in 1901 got the division elevated to bureau status. Making his office an advocate of scientific management of forests, he launched a bureaucratic raid to have control of the national forests transferred from the General Land Office in the Interior Department to his own office. Pinchot argued that forestry was "tree farming"; trees were a crop that took "more time and less attention than corn," but still a crop, and thus the national forests belonged with Pinchot's tree farmers in the Agriculture Department. In 1905, Pinchot succeeded in getting the national forests put under his jurisdiction. The Bureau of Forestry became the National Forest Service.

Once in control, Pinchot interpreted the Forest Management Act of 1897 quite broadly. He began to exact user fees for grazing within the national forests, to enforce stricter competitive bidding in timber sales, and to staff the Forest Service with young, professionally trained foresters schooled at Yale and other universities. Pinchot's new managers found plenty to do as the national forests expanded rapidly in the early twentieth century. When Theodore Roosevelt became president in 1901, there were 41 reserves with 46,410,209 acres. By 1907, Roosevelt had increased the system to 159 national forests containing 150,832,665 acres. Even with these withdrawals, however, nearly 80 percent of the commercial timber in the United States remained under private ownership.

Gifford Pinchot established a basic pattern of federal bureaucratic management in the region by dividing potential opponents of regulation and winning over established economic interests. The battles over conservation seemed to pit eastern experts and bureaucrats against western settlers and entrepreneurs, but both westerners and their opponents turned out to be divided. Indeed, many westerners never thought of conservation as a unified set of programs. They supported or opposed particular programs not out of ideology but according to calculations of how those programs affected their own immediate interests. They supported some programs and sought to derail others.

Those westerners connected with either large economic units (such as corporations) or large urban units (that is, cities, which worried about the security of their water supply) tended to support the growing trend toward federal management, while those westerners associated with small economic units (unirrigated farms or small businesses) and smaller population units (rural areas or villages) tended to oppose such management. In other words, those sectors of western society rising in power and influence supported the growth of federal management, and those who were in decline opposed it. Rural westerners waged much of the battle against conservation, but even they did not stand united. Irrigation farmers, who wanted and needed federal aid, and large ranchers generally supported the early conservation movement.

The national forests served as the lightning rod of federal management; they caught the full wrath of western rural opposition. The national forests embodied the very essence of restricted access in order to promote efficiency; they enraged those who still envisioned the West as a region where opportunity was synonymous with unrestricted access to resources. Conservation, they believed, would victimize not only small operators but also the West as a whole by halting economic and population growth. Many cattlemen, proclaiming their rights as "free-born American citizens," refused to pay grazing fees instituted by the Forest Service in 1906; others threatened to hang federal "tree agents" from the trees they came to protect. The Hispanics of New Mexico, who saw incorporated within the national forests much of the communal grazing lands already fraudulently taken from them by speculators, also bitterly resented the reserves. In Colorado and Wyoming arsonists set forest fires to protest forest reserves. In a single South Dakota protest in 1897, 30,000 people gathered to object to a new forest reserve in the Black Hills. The protesters found ready support in the state governments, and in the early twentieth century, elected officials in Colorado, Wyoming, Washington, Montana, New Mexico, and indeed most other western states attacked growing federal control and did their best to halt it.

In numbers and local political influence the opponents of federal management in the West initially exceeded the proponents, and western delegations in Congress reflected this. Western congressmen often led the opposition to forest reserves, denouncing them as an obstacle to regional development. Colorado Senator Henry Teller sarcastically denied that the West needed "the fostering and kindly hand of the National Government. We want it taken off." His constituents were harsher. They saw "Czar" Pinchot as at best "an impractical dreamer" and at worst a "rapacious, venal, petty despot"; his rangers were "cossacks" enforcing a tyranny. Occasionally, as in the Park Range of northwestern Colorado after the imposition of the grazing tax of 1906, resistance became violent. Opponents of conservation grossly underestimated the damage that westerners had perpetrated on the forests and the grazing lands, but they did accurately gauge the political results of conservation. Elias Ammons, a leading opponent of conservation and federal management in Colorado, wrote that the state would be divided between "two systems of government," one run by "its people" and the other the domain of "some bureau in Washington."

Pinchot managed to split this opposition. When the government dropped attempts to prohibit grazing on the reserves, the number of opponents dwindled. The majority of large stock raisers welcomed the chance to end unregulated competition for land and to gain some legally defensible rights. Many of them wanted to see management of livestock extended to the rest of the public domain through leasing. Supporters among cattle raisers grew even more numerous as federal regulations gave preference to local cattle owners over itinerant sheepherders in allocating grazing rights in national forests. Ability to get a grazing permit from the Forest Service could now often make or break a rancher or sheepherder. Those who obtained permits tended to support the program; those who did not had to rely on private lands or the still unregulated public domain or give up ranching.

Similarly, in the timber industry, opposition to the forest reserves centered on small operators. Charcoal makers and small mill owners who produced railway ties or lumber for local markets saw their access to wood cut off as the Forest Service regulated cutting in the forests. They accordingly denounced federal management. The larger timber companies, with their sizable private holdings, came to support the forest reserves. The National Forest Service, by restricting previously open access to public timber, seemed to offer an opportunity to overcome the industry's problem of chronic overproduction. Timbermen also eagerly cooperated with the states and federal government to promote programs to halt forest fires and pushed for other government policies that would reduce their taxes. Although lumbermen and the U.S. Forest Service would differ on specific measures, their mutual interest in a managed timber economy usually remained paramount, and Pinchot underscored his determination not to lock up resources permanently, but instead to guarantee their efficient use.

By the second decade of the twentieth century, the western anticonservationists had lost the battle to prevent federal management. They could hinder and limit the management of western land, but they could not drive the managers out. In 1907, for example, western anticonservationists in the U.S. Senate combined with eastern conservatives to strip the president of his unilateral power to create any more forest reserves in Oregon, Idaho, Washington, Montana, Colorado, or Wyoming. Roosevelt accepted the bill, but only after creating 21 new national forests on the day before he signed the act.

Western politics long retained its antifederal, anticonservation, individualist rhetoric, but like so much western rhetoric, this talk masked a very different reality. The West had become managed, and westerners had shifted their attention to capturing the management process. In managing the forests, forest rangers determined carrying capacities—the amount of livestock that could graze the land without diminishing the regeneration of grasses and forbs. They assigned grazing permits and collected grazing fees. Westerners learned to bargain with and influence the federal bureaucracies; they learned to operate inside of them. They sought to control what they could not prevent and to turn federal agencies into servants of western interests. By 1910 the Forest Service had established local forest advisory boards made up of prominent resource users, and such boards exerted considerable influence on Forest Service decisions. The Forest Service preferred to work with the larger producers. Regulating a few large ranchers or timber companies was, after all, easier than regulating scores of small ranchers or timber companies.

National Parks

One of Gifford Pinchot's favorite aphorisms was, "Wilderness is waste"; it neatly summarized the utilitarian emphasis of early-twentieth-century conservation. It also exemplified the dilemma faced by advocates of nonutilitarian preservation of the public lands in the National Parks. The National Parks came under federal management not because progressives or western interest groups thought the government could make the lands more productive, but because they believed those lands to be useless in terms of the extractive economy of the West.

Proponents of the parks originally urged their creation because of a national fascination with the monumental scenery of the West. The United States was a young nation lacking both an ancient history and a cultural tradition rich in art, architecture, or literature. Americans looked to scenery as compensation for the cultural riches they lacked. They hoped nature at its most monumental would provide the inspiration, the sublimity, and the glimpse of timelessness that American culture had not yet achieved. It became a matter of national pride that the new country set apart areas such as the Yosemite Valley of California or the Yellowstone country of Wyoming as symbols of national greatness. These "earth monuments," proponents claimed, rivaled in grandeur the monuments of Europe's antiquity.

The monumentalism that inspired the national parks was far removed from modern environmentalism. When the Yosemite Act of 1864 created what was for all practical purposes the first national park (even though the federal government initially ceded the park to California for administration), the result was an exercise in "scenic nationalism." The legislation took no steps to preserve the totality of the Yosemite Valley, but instead emphasized its monuments: the sheer cliffs of the valley and the giant sequoias. The same values prevailed when Congress created Yellowstone, the first federally administered national park, in 1872.

Monumentalism meshed easily with the prevailing utilitarian attitudes toward the West that found their expression in the National Forest Service and the Bureau of Reclamation. Well into the twentieth century, western national parks tended to contain only the highest, most rugged and extreme land forms. They were lands economically "worthless" except for their scenery. Unless an area was useless for other purposes, or as Ebenezer Bryce more pithily put it in describing Bryce Canyon in Utah, "a hell of a place to lose a cow," its chances of preservation as a park were slim. Any place where a cow could take some comfort was too valuable to be reserved for a park.

Monumentalism fit, too, with the growth of tourism in the West and the railroads' desire to promote it. Railroads sought passengers, and if large numbers of easterners and Europeans desired to travel west to view natural wonders, they would travel on the railroads. Although the railroad itself would not provide access to the park until 1883, Jay Cooke and the Northern Pacific Railroad sponsored attempts to get Congress to make Yellowstone a national park. In the early twentieth century Louis W. Hill, the president of the Great Northern Railroad, promoted Glacier National Park as a rival of Yosemite and Yellowstone. The Great Northern paralleled the southern boundary of the new park, which Congress created in 1910, and had a virtual monopoly over passenger traffic to it.

Despite the railroads' enthusiasm for the parks and the government's reservation of new sites, there did not as yet exist at the beginning of the twentieth century a national park *system*. The parks remained largely unmanaged and vulnerable. Poachers hunted protected park animals, and promoters lobbied from railroad rights-of-way across Yellowstone. The most eloquent advocate of parks as fully preserved areas of natural splendor, and the most widely heard critic of their current condition, was John Muir of California. "Nature-struck tramp," self-trained geologist, and mystic, Muir shared neither the prevailing monumentalist rationale for parks nor the conservationist approach to nature. Instead of reducing nature to human scale—justifying its preservation because of its ability to fulfill human needs, he measured humans against nature and usually found them wanting. He desired more than spectacular monuments; he wanted nature preserved in all its diversity. He wanted nature protected so that humans might momentarily escape their human condition by mystical communion with forces greater than themselves.

In time Muir tramped most of the West Coast and even parts of Alaska, but Yosemite was his great love. Muir came to loathe the way that sheep—or as he called them, "hoofed locusts"—destroyed the vegetation in the Sierra Nevada surrounding Yosemite. He and Robert Underwood Johnson, an editor of the eastern magazine *Century*, launched a brilliant publicity campaign to return Yosemite to federal jurisdiction and to expand the park to include the adjoining backcountry. Muir partially succeeded in his immediate goal— creation of an expanded national park—but he did not completely displace the monumentalist rationale for parks. Many supported him because the expanded park would preserve vulnerable monuments—groves of sequoias that would otherwise fall to the axe.

Scenic nationalism and the economic "worthlessness" of an area still largely determined the eligibility of a piece of land for national park status. If the land seemed adaptable to more profitable uses, preservationists had difficulty protecting it. The Lacey Act of 1906 helped the preservationists but at the same time compounded their problems. The Lacey Act created a kind of halfway status for some public lands by allowing the president, without congressional approval, to set aside "historic landmarks, historic and prehistoric structures and other objects of historic or scientific interest" as national monuments. Teddy Roosevelt had aroused a good deal of controversy when he used the act to reserve 800,000 acres of Arizona Territory as Grand Canyon National Monument in 1908. National monuments were closed to private land entries, but, unlike national parks, many of them remained under the Forest Service. And the Forest Service administered them as multiple-use areas—that is, it allowed grazing and lumbering on them.

Although the government set aside an increasing amount of land as national parks or national monuments, much of this land remained vulnerable. After a series of preservationist successes that included the return of Yosemite to federal supervision, the creation of neighboring Sequoia National Park, the establishment of Mount Rainier National Park in Washington (1899), and the granting of national park status to Crater Lake in Oregon (1902) and Glacier National Park (1910), the tide turned. Federal reclamation service engineers and forest rangers cast covetous eyes on the timber and water the parks contained. They demanded that the government return resources inadvertently included in existing parks to the national forests or to the public domain. And they, along with mining and timber interests, urged even greater scrutiny to make sure that exploitable resources remained outside of future parks. Under the Wilson administration the Forest Service in particular began to enjoy considerable success in its war against the parks. The Forest Service and its allies stripped Olympic National Monument of half its land in 1915 and reduced the size of the new Rocky Mountain National Park by two-thirds before its approval in 1915.

Bureaucratic Battles

As the clash between the Forest Service and preservationists demonstrated, the fight over whether there would be a federally managed West had largely yielded to a battle among the managers themselves over the nature of management. The issue had become a question of which bureaucracies promoting which ends would manage the land. In the most spectacular of these early-twentieth-century bureaucratic fights westerners played a central role. The particular dispute centered on the way the government would develop hydroelectric sites on public lands, but the larger issue was the extent of federal management. The antagonists were Gifford Pinchot, the symbol of conservation, and Secretary of the Interior Richard Ballinger, a westerner and a champion of western business interests.

Under the Roosevelt administration, Secretary of the Interior James Garfield had applied the same permit system for hydroelectric sites on the public domain that Pinchot had instituted for those in the national forests. Private operators could develop waterpower sites on the public domain only under federal license and under federal supervision. When President William H. Taft came into office, although he maintained the vast bulk of the management system in place in the West, he allowed Ballinger to reduce federal supervision of hydroelectric development and to advocate ceding waterpower sites to the states. Pinchot, who, because the Forest Service was in the Department of Agriculture, remained outside of Ballinger's jurisdiction, attacked both this policy and then Ballinger himself. He eventually used accusations that Ballinger had improperly helped several corporations obtain Alaskan coal lands to discredit the secretary. Taft sided with Ballinger and fired Pinchot in 1910.

Pinchot reacted so strongly against Ballinger because the secretary of the interior, in attacking a portion of federal management, seemed to be attacking its entire rationale. Pinchot was perfectly willing to countenance private development and profit, but only under the supervision of federal rules and experts who would ensure efficient development. Ballinger distrusted such management and sought to limit it. Pinchot succeeded in making Ballinger appear to be the tool of corporate interests, but Ballinger, in fact, represented the smaller entrepreneurial interests of the West. Most corporations were willing to accept conservation; Ballinger instead spoke for groups that had in most cases opposed conservation from the outset. Ballinger, like Pinchot, lost his position in the end, but his downfall mattered less than the nature of his battle with Pinchot. Westerners like him were opposing programs *within* the bureaucracies that they had been unable to stop from coming into being.

Hetch Hetchy

In this complicated, divided West bureaucratic infighting quickly became a western skill far more practiced and polished than gunfighting, and this infighting produced the most famous of the early conservation battles. In 1913, after considerable controversy, the Taft administration decided to allow the city of San Francisco to dam and flood the spectacular Hetch Hetchy Valley of Yosemite

National Park. Taft made the final decision on a controversy that had revealed divisions among the conservationists as deep as any among their opponents. To John Muir and most members of the Sierra Club, an organization that he helped found, Hetch Hetchy was a "temple" about to be destroyed by the "devotees of ravaging commercialism." The government should preserve the valley because it was beautiful. To San Francisco's public officials, many of whom were also conservationists, and to their sympathizers, including Gifford Pinchot, the scenic grandeur of the valley was, in Pinchot's words, "altogether unimportant compared with the benefits to be derived from its use as a reservoir."

In the battle over Hetch Hetchy, Pinchot and the conservationists believed that they confronted two sets of enemies: preservationists such as Muir and western entrepreneurs and speculators who cared nothing about Hetch Hetchy but who sought to stop the creation of municipally owned water and power companies. Muir and his allies pointed out that there were other possible reservoir sites for San Francisco, but conservationists and most urban progressives rejected the sites because they were in the hands of private developers who could hold the city at ransom. Conservationists believed that for the public good, San Francisco had to develop Hetch Hetchy. One side made preserving Hetch Hetchy a symbol of ethical, spiritual, and aesthetic standards; the other made destroying it a symbol of the victory of the public good—also a matter of ethics—over the greedy interests of private developers. Both sides phrased the issue in terms of a managed West. Utility and public development won; preservation of nature lost.

The loss of Hetch Hetchy was a clear triumph of utilitarian values, and it badly frightened the advocates of national parks. The decision implied that whenever bureaucrats or businesspeople discovered other uses for national park lands, these lands, too, would be lost. Utilitarian arguments could, however, save as well as dismember parks. With the loss of Hetch Hetchy, proponents of the parks realized that the national parks could not be defended on scenic merit alone. Those advocates of the parks, too, began to make economic arguments. Tourism, long promoted by the railroads, now became the chief rationale of the parks. Advocates argued that the national parks promoted economic growth of their own through the visitors that they attracted. These visitors would, according to proponents of the parks, come in increasing numbers as the nation grew more urban, for only amidst unspoiled nature could Americans escape from the urban and industrial life that surrounded them. By linking the national parks to economic growth and national health, those in favor of preserving the parks succeeded in meeting the utilitarian arguments of their opponents. They coupled their own brand of utilitarianism with an antimodernist critique of industrial civilization to create a hybrid, but effective, justification of the parks that would serve for the next half-century.

No matter how effective such arguments proved in ideological combat, advocates of the parks largely remained outside of government; in the new bureaucratic West they would inevitably lose policy battles to opponents in the Forest Service, the Bureau of Reclamation, and other agencies who operated within the government. The preservationists needed their own bureaucracy. In 1916 they obtained it with the creation of the National Park Service.

The driving force behind the National Park Service was Stephen Mather. A Californian and a Sierra Club member, Mather had become an avid mountaineer

This early-twentieth-century picture advertising Denver shows the way in which boosters attempted to make the western landscape an engine for growth.

after climbing Washington's Mount Rainier in 1905. Every summer thereafter he climbed peaks and traveled the backcountry of the Sierra Nevada, and in 1912 he encountered John Muir in the Kings River canyon. The meeting with the 80-year-old Muir stirred Mather to help preserve the old man's beloved Sierra Nevada from loggers, miners, and dam builders. Mather was a successful and well-connected businessman as well as a mountaineer. When his name came up in a search for an assistant to the secretary of the interior in the Wilson administration, Mather was asked his opinion about conditions in the parks, and he answered critically. Secretary of the Interior Franklin Lane responded, "If you don't like the way the national parks are run, why don't you come down to Washington and run them yourself?" Mather did.

Mather went to Washington in 1914, and before he resigned in 1928 he had created the National Park Service. Often spending his own money to acquire lands or pay assistants, he organized a publicity campaign to drum up public support for the parks and lobbied for a park service capable of administering them. In 1916 there were 12 national parks, with three more under consideration, and 19 national monuments under the Interior Department's jurisdiction. This domain of 4.6 million acres received only the barest custodial care and no coordinated administration at all. To achieve a new bureau capable of administering the parks, Mather had to overcome both conservative congressmen reluctant to create a new government agency and the determined opposition of the Forest Service, which wanted utilitarian management of the public lands and opposed preservationism of any kind.

Mather overcame this opposition through a masterful lobbying campaign. He mobilized the General Federation of Women's Clubs to lobby for the parks. He coordinated publicity in national magazines such as *National Geographic* and the *Saturday Evening Post*. The result was a compromised preservationism, one that reflected Mather's own pragmatic mix of mountaineer and businessman. He had to agree to allow grazing in all the parks but Yellowstone. And knowing the parks depended on public support, Mather promoted the building of roads and the creation of lodges within the parks. The parks could lease lands to private concessionaires in order to accommodate visitors. The very accessibility of the parks and the abundance of modern accommodations in them would later cause immense problems, but in those early years they seemed necessary to preserve the parks themselves.

Urban Power

In the Hetch Hetchy controversy one of the new centers of power in the West, the federal bureaucracy, allied itself with another, the cities. By 1920 it was clear that in terms of numbers and wealth, the future of the West lay with the towns, the cities, and their suburbs. Already in the late nineteenth century the West had become more urban than the nation as a whole, and it would remain so throughout the twentieth century. Two Wests—one urban, one rural—had emerged. The urban West began just south of the Canadian border with what would become the Seattle-Everett-Tacoma metropolis on Puget Sound. This was the most northerly of a series of urban nodes that protruded irregularly out of the western landscape. Other smaller urban clusters lay to the east and south. By 1920, Washington, Oregon, and Idaho were 50 percent or more urban; their populations had been approximately 60 percent or more rural in 1900. From Portland, the urban center of Oregon, the urban West skipped south to appear again in San Francisco, Los Angeles, and San Diego. Urban areas protruded again in Tucson, Albuquerque, El Paso, and Denver, which by 1920 had 256,000 people. From there the land remained largely rural until Wichita on the eastern plains and San Antonio, Dallas, and Houston in Texas. The population of Dallas grew from less than 43,000 people in 1900 to 260,000 in 1930, and Houston's grew even faster, rising from 27,000 in 1900 to almost 300,000 by 1930. In Oklahoma people clustered in Tulsa and Oklahoma City, which had 120,000 people by 1925 and 189,000 by 1930. Only the Great Plains lacked important cities. To the east, the last urban nodes occurred at Topeka and Omaha.

These cities—mere specks within the larger western landscape—formed a series of dots which when connected formed the outlines of a vast, if broken, urban arc. Within this arc lay other smaller, scattered urban concentrations such as Salt Lake City, which had 118,000 people by 1920; Boise; and Butte. Grudgingly and gradually before 1920, and increasingly rapidly, but no less grudgingly, after 1920, the rural West was losing influence, wealth, and people to these cities.

California's cities grew the most rapidly, and California itself became more and more distinctive and powerful within the region. The San Francisco-Oakland area and Los Angeles were, in terms of population, the two greatest urban concentrations in the West. In 1900 their combined urban areas already contained 40 percent of the state's population. Los Angeles grew from 50,000 people in 1890 to 1.2 million by 1930; by then it had replaced San Francisco as the leading metropolitan center in the West. California was far and away the largest, richest, most developed, and most influential western state.

California's economic growth matched its population growth. During World War I war orders stimulated California manufacturing. California factories doubled their production between 1914 and 1919, and among these factories were airplane manufacturers, who built their plants in Los Angeles and San Diego in order to capitalize on the good weather. But the stimulation provided by federal orders was only part of the story. Unlike the economies of Seattle and Portland, which rose because of federal orders for ships during World War I and fell thereafter, Los Angeles and San Francisco sustained their growth.

Amadeo P. Giannini, the founder of the Bank of America, symbolized the ability of California businesspeople to create their own sources of capital. Building on the small investments of Italian immigrants and small businessmen in San Francisco, Giannini transformed the Bank of Italy into the Bank of America and opened hundreds of branch banks. By 1929, Giannini and other California bankers controlled more than $4 billion dollars in capital and could finance much of California's rapid expansion.

California produced new industries from oil refining to food processing that turned the state's raw materials into finished goods. Its large urban areas attracted other manufacturers. As the automobile became a defining element of the California way of life, auto makers such as Ford, General Motors, and Chrysler opened subsidiary assembly plants on the West Coast, and tire companies, including Akron and B. F. Goodrich, did the same. Because most of this growth took place in southern California, Los Angeles, not San Francisco, became the industrial center of the state. Around these major industries clustered numerous smaller companies and retail outlets associated with the automobile.

Industrializing California freed itself of dependence on eastern universities as quickly as it escaped the thrall of eastern factories. In Stanford and the University of California the Golden State produced the first major universities in the West. Economically and politically, the West as a whole remained a colonial appendage of the East, but California had broken free, and a new and more complex West would be the result.

Hollywood was, perhaps, the most visible sign of this triumph. In the Hollywood movie studios, transplanted easterners, many of them Jews who sought opportunities denied them elsewhere, created an industry that shaped the state's image and then turned that image into a source of profit. By 1929 motion pictures were the country's tenth largest industry, and they were quintessentially a southern California industry. The national fascination with the movies fortified southern California's identification with glamour, leisure, and romance. The movie industry drew more than a quarter of a million tourists to Hollywood each year. The West, the site of so many American fantasies, had made fantasy itself into a western business.

Urban West

Twentieth-century California was urban, but urban in a new way. At the turn of the century the urban West, like the urban areas of the nation as a whole, had consisted of unruly, unplanned, and chaotic cities. But just as the federal government was making the public domain a far more managed place, so were other groups preparing to manage the cities. They acted to channel and control the excesses of western boosters.

Western cities had long been the domain of the boosters, people who aspired to be human magnets. Boosters lived to attract others, and to attract others boosters sometimes necessarily deceived them. But the boosters just as relentlessly deceived themselves. When western speculators drew a town plat, filed it in a county courthouse, and imagined a great future, they believed fervently in their own creations. Feeding on their own hopes, they added extensions to their nonexistent towns in order to accommodate people who they believed were always just about to arrive.

Boosters sought to make towns grow for a simple reason: they wanted to make lots of money. Growth pushed up property values, and then all those who owned land could float on the rising financial tide. Most urban promoters failed, but when they did succeed in boosting an area, they induced a sort of speculative frenzy that made victims of common sense, new migrants, and the less agile of the speculators themselves. In Los Angeles the completion of the Southern Pacific's transcontinental railway link in 1881 failed to induce a boom, but when in 1887 the Santa Fe Railroad arrived to compete with the Southern Pacific and fares plummeted, local boosters sniffed opportunity. Bargain railroad fares and professional "boomers" from the Midwest brought crowds of tourists, potential residents, and curiosity seekers. There were brass bands and parades, sideshow attractions, and free lunches. There were land auctions in circus tents. People stood in line to buy city lots. It was a boom borne on warm winds and hot air, and in 1888 people stopped buying as prices rose too high; Los Angeles landed with a thud. Within two years population dropped by roughly 37 percent. Property values, too, fell dramatically, but they remained higher than they had been in 1880, and the boosters were ready to try again. By 1890 Los Angeles had a chamber of commerce whose high-pressure efforts to sell the city nationwide became a model of their kind. During the next two decades, William May Garland, the "Prince of Realtors," subdivided and sold Westlake, Ocean Park, Hermosa Beach, and Beverly Hills. His successors, Frank Meline, I. N. Van Nuys, and Harry Culver created similar developments throughout the Los Angeles Basin. Other boosters, of course had celebrated themselves by giving their towns their names, but after Culver City, Harry Culver had enough subdivisions left over to hold contests to name the rest. The promoters of Azusa came up with its exotic name as an acronym for A to Z in the USA.

Every city in the West had its own version of Los Angeles's boosters, boomers, and real estate agents and a local business community that dreamed of rising land values and new customers. Such boosters cooperated with local political leaders; indeed the two were often identical. These politicians and merchants planned on how to attract growth, but they did not plan on how to manage the growth they solicited. The normal result was cities of narrow and often unpaved streets, poor public services, and ramshackle buildings. Denver in 1900 had 800 miles of streets, but only 24 miles were paved. San Francisco and Seattle seemed trapped between steep hills on one side and tidewater on the other. Most western cities lacked adequate water supplies for future growth; they were without open spaces, without efficient sewer systems, without proper provisions for public health, and without adequate public transportation. These were cities that could not absorb

The promoters of Montrose, a Los Angeles development, throw a barbecue in 1910 for potential buyers, who arrive by car and buggy.

the people they solicited and yet feared being left behind by rivals in the race to grow. By the 1890s, for example, San Francisco looked nervously south at Los Angeles. Portland, while unusually handsome and well built for a western city, worried that Seattle, booming as the entrepôt for the Alaskan gold rush, would soon eclipse it as the premier city of the Pacific Northwest.

In the twentieth century boosterism became a joint endeavor of local government and business leaders, and it grew less raw. It became more the domain of the advertising executive and less that of the huckster. Lavish exhibitions on specially constructed fairgrounds, built partially with public funds, replaced the old circus tents and sideshows. Portland's Lewis and Clark Exposition in 1905 attracted 1.5 million visitors. It followed the Trans-Mississippi Exposition in Omaha in 1898. Seattle put on the Alaska-Yukon-Pacific Exposition in 1909. San Francisco held the Panama Pacific International Exposition in 1915, the same year that San Diego opened the California-Pacific Exposition. The cities regarded each out-of-town visitor to these fairs as a potential immigrant or investor.

The city officials and the members of the business elite who cooperated in staging the expositions also realized that they had to plan cities to absorb the future growth they hoped to promote. The usual western rhetoric about individualism was particularly empty in the cities. By their very nature people in cities were interdependent. Urban residents ran collective risks and had collective responsibilities. Urban residents did not and could not grow their own food, secure their own fuel, obtain their own water, or even dispose of their own waste. Increasingly few urban residents even lived close enough to their place of work to provide their own transportation. Self-sufficiency had never been the reality for most people in the West; within the city it was by definition an impossibility.

The implications of city planning, particularly when cities grew in an arid environment, extended far beyond their boundaries. Farmers were glad to have nearby urban markets, but in the arid West they were hardly eager to have cities compete with them for scarce water. Western cities such as San Francisco and Los Angeles developed increasingly "imperial" ambitions—they attempted to determine their own development and the development of their sometimes vast hinterlands. They needed outlying areas as sources of raw materials, as consumers of their manufactures, and as recreational sites for their citizens.

The symbols of this new commitment to city planning were the numerous urban plans commissioned by western cities from largely eastern planners. The designs for remaking western cities, by and large, came from urban planners of the national City Beautiful movement, which advocated not only attractive and liveable cities, but also functionally integrated cities in which people, traffic, and goods all moved smoothly and easily. City planner Daniel Burnham's plan to rebuild San Francisco and Edward H. Bennett's plan for Portland in 1911 both envisioned comprehensive park systems and new street systems that would move traffic more quickly, divide the cities into coherent districts, and beautify them. Landscape architect Frederick Law Olmsted and his brother, John C. Olmsted, submitted plans in 1903 for Seattle's boulevard and park system, and Seattle itself established a Municipal Plans Commission in 1911.

The plans of Burnham, Bennett, and Olmsted for the most part remained confined to paper. City officials could imagine their cities transformed, but actual transformations eluded them. They lacked the funds and the authority. The great city plans finally survived only as monuments to municipal ambitions, not as actual accomplishments. Even when the disastrous earthquake of April 18, 1906, and subsequent fires virtually destroyed San Francisco, the city did not rebuild according to Burnham's plan.

Burnham's San Francisco did not rise from the ashes of the old San Francisco, but the city still continued to move incrementally towards greater planning and municipal control. Before the late 1890s, municipal government in San Francisco had devoted itself to keeping taxes low and services modest. This was as true, perhaps even more true, of "machine" governments as of business governments. In the late 1890s, however, the progressive reformer and Democratic mayor of San Francisco James Phelan united his coalition of merchants, middle-class residents, and unionized workers on the basis of the benefits that would accrue to all of them from an expanding public sector.

Each of the elements of Phelan's coalition sought different things. The members of the neighborhood improvement clubs tended to be residents in the newer middle-class residential areas of the city, and they wanted streets and sewers built and maintained by the city as well as police, fire, and educational services extended to their areas. Because of ceilings on property taxes, the city was unable to provide these services. The merchants, organized by 1894 in the Merchants' Association, wanted to "beautify and healthify [sic] San Francisco, make it attractive to strangers and pleasant to its residents, and thereby increase its business and add to the value of the property." They, too, wanted sewers and streets and also parks and suggested using city bonds to pay for them. Finally, workers in the older neighborhoods wanted better schools for their children, and they gladly anticipated the employment Phelan promised would result from public expenditures. Phelan himself summed up the advantages to be gained by the expansion of municipal services: "When we have made our city sanitary and our schools fit . . . we will draw a population and every accession will pour into the veins of trade new blood and new energy, and with the growth of the city based upon such a new foundation, every man, woman, and child, especially industrial employment, should feel and enjoy the benefit."

Phelan and progressive reformers like him emphasized adequate water, sewer, utility, educational, and transportation systems as the foundations of urban growth. They were interested in the plans of the City Beautiful movement, but they really desired a city efficient. As a first step they wanted to provide basic city services. As a second step, their plans encouraged zoning laws to designate some areas as commercial, others as residential, and still others as industrial. This new planning would not eliminate ugliness or regulate architecture; it would, however, establish minimum standards of construction through building codes. The stress on health, on sewage systems, on parks, and on schools in this expansion of municipal services tended to involve middle-class women in the campaign to change the city. The doctrine of domesticity had given women responsibility for the home, and both in the West and nationally, middle-class women by logical extension claimed responsibility for what they described as "municipal housekeeping": urban sanitation and urban beautification.

This progressive alliance for the expansion of municipal services had to face the troubling question of how to pay for these new services. Their original answer was that they would do so by eliminating waste and corruption; they would purge city governments of useless workers who drew excessive salaries for doing nothing. When they came to power, however, Phelan and most other reformers were unable to find the waste they had announced. Increased municipal services, it turned out, meant increased taxes. But the need for increased taxes to expand services not only created potential political discomfort, but also meant that promises of rapid extension of basic services had to wait on increased revenues. Taxes in San Francisco did increase, as did services, but Phelan and his successors were unable to fulfill both the promise of new services and lower taxes through increased efficiency.

As reformers succeeded in overcoming the parsimony of municipal governments and convincing voters that governments had to anticipate the needs of a growing city in order to provide for future growth, the modern service city came into being. As in the federal bureaucracy, passive regulation gave way to active service. Fueled by a willingness to borrow and an ability to tax, municipal governments during the first three decades of the twentieth century took over from private companies the task of providing basic services from water and electrical power to transportation for their citizens. Even more intensively than the federal bureaucracies, they reshaped nature, controlled human actions, and increased their power.

Municipal ownership proved attractive to westerners for many of the same reasons it was attractive to easterners: it seemed to promise an escape from the corruption and the inefficiencies of the existing franchise system in which private companies purchased the right to provide city services. Private companies obtained franchises to provide trolley service, water, or electricity for all or part of an urban area. These companies often bribed city officials to get such a franchise and provided inferior service once they had it.

Municipal ownership also proved attractive for more particularly western reasons. It represented an escape from dependence on eastern capital; it seemed a path to local control and power. Westerners could tolerate rather large doses of corruption and inefficiency, but corruption seemed most galling when the corporations doing the corrupting, such as the United Railroads in San Francisco or the Seattle Power Company, were owned by easterners. Together, the combination of corruption, poor service, and outside ownership created local resentments that municipal ownership promised to soothe.

The emergence of modern city services accompanied this push for municipal control. When James Rolph became mayor of San Francisco in 1911, he capitalized on widespread discontent with the franchise system to expand the new Municipal Railway, the first municipally controlled streetcar line in the nation but one which controlled only a portion of San Francisco's trolley routes. He similarly led San Francisco's battle to secure Hetch Hetchy for a reservoir, thus taking the first step toward a municipally owned water system.

In Seattle, George Cotterill led an attack on the franchise system in that city and was elected mayor in 1912. Cotterill's election culminated a drive for municipalization; its greatest advocate and symbol was the city engineer, R. H. Thomson. Seattle had already secured a municipal water system when in 1900 it began a long battle with Seattle Electric, which held a virtual monopoly on local power and transportation. In 1902 the city constructed its first municipal power plant, and under Thomson it eventually succeeded in creating a municipal power system. Thomson, for all his accomplishments, was not a man of overwhelming environmental sensitivity. He believed Seattle was in a pit, and he meant to dig the city out. He sluiced much of Denny Hill north of downtown, and the ridge between First Hill and Beacon Hill to the south, into the tideflats bordering the city. He created in the process the world's largest manmade island, Harbor Island.

The push for municipal ownership did not succeed everywhere; it often ended in compromise. In Denver, Robert Speer came to office as head of a coalition designed to stop a new city charter that would have provided for municipal ownership of utilities, restricted saloons, banned gambling, and extended the civil service system to the police and fire departments. Although opposed to municipal control, Speer expanded the sewer and street system and brought in a city planner to outline a boulevard and park system.

In Denver, Speer sought to regulate rather than municipalize utilities. Denver, and also Wichita, encouraged the consolidation of smaller companies and gradually turned the franchise system into a system of regulated public utilities such as Denver Gas and Electric and Kansas Gas and Electric Company. Both companies provided lower rates and fewer power interruptions than did their predecessors. Such consolidation seemed necessary because reliable energy sources were becoming as much a requirement for growth as adequate water was. Particularly during the energy-short years that stretched from about 1915 into the 1920s, cities such as Wichita, Dallas, Oklahoma City, and Los Angeles solicited new business on

The regrading of the hills of Seattle was an example both of R. H. Thomson's joy in moving earth and of the new urban planning that arose in western cities during the early twentieth century.

the basis of their proximity to reliable oil and gas supplies, while Denver stressed its access to coal. As energy supplies increased and utilities grew more efficient, the focus of urban energy policy changed. In the 1920s utilities no longer worried about how to supply necessary power; they worried about having enough consumers to use the power available. The success of their campaigns to get people to use more energy marked the beginning of the energy-intensive cities of the West.

The creation of new consolidated utilities, however, could create monsters that possessed a power far greater than that of the old franchise holders. In San Francisco eastern bond companies engineered mergers that created the gigantic Pacific Gas and Electric Company (PG & E), a regional power company that became the largest utility on the Pacific Coast. By 1915, PG & E ranked among the top five utilities in the country. During the 1920s Mayor James Rolph, largely because of his own political and business ties with the bankers who owned PG & E, failed to secure a municipally owned power system in San Francisco.

Private corporations in other western cities also managed to retain ownership of critical elements of the urban infrastructure—gas, telephones, and sometimes electricity and transportation. In Los Angeles, Henry Huntington, nephew of

Collis Huntington of the Southern Pacific, controlled the city's trolley lines, and initially he followed the usual procedures of franchise owners. He kept his cars in such poor repair that they claimed several hundred casualties a year. But Huntington also knew how to plan transportation networks to both guide and capitalize on the city's growth. Early in the twentieth century he created the Pacific Electric Railway system and then the Los Angeles Inter-Urban Railway Company. Electric railway systems, Huntington realized, did not respond to growth; they created it. As he proclaimed in 1904, they "must anticipate the growth of communities and be there when the homebuilders arrive—or they are very likely not to arrive at all, but to go to some section already provided with arteries of traffic." By combining his railway company with utility companies and with land purchases that made him probably the largest landowner in southern California, Huntington created a real estate and transportation empire. The Los Angeles interurban opened up Huntington's holdings in Venice, San Marino, Huntington Beach, and Seal Beach for development, and then Huntington utility companies provided gas and light.

Los Angeles: Capital of the West

The various threads creating a powerful modern west—boosterism, corporate growth, the aggressive growth of municipal services, and expanding federal power—came together in a dazzling fashion in Los Angeles, the city that would dominate the twentieth-century West. At the turn of the century Los Angeles's future seemed threatened by potential water shortages and an inefficient private water company. The Los Angeles Basin lacked the water necessary to support a city whose size was commensurate with the ambitions of local boosters. Fred Eaton, a former engineer for the company and the head of the Republican City Central Committee, persuaded the local business community that the only way to banish the specter of drought was to municipalize the city water supply and search for new sources of water. The current badly managed private system, he argued, could hardly meet the city's present needs, let alone make the investments necessary to bring water vast distances.

The agency that took over the city's water system, the Los Angeles Department of Water and Power, became to Los Angeles what the Bureau of Reclamation was to the arid West. At its head was William Mulholland, an Irish immigrant and largely self-educated engineer, who controlled the agency from 1902 until 1928. In the early twentieth century Mulholland and the Department of Water and Power demonstrated the new realities of urban power. With the cooperation of the Bureau of Reclamation, Mulholland secured Los Angeles's future by destroying the economic future of the Owens Valley, a rural valley below Mount Whitney on the eastern side of the Sierra Nevada. First peacefully, and then amidst a flurry of violence, the department transformed an entire rural county into a dependency of Los Angeles. Agents of the Department of Water and Power bought out local water rights from people who initially thought they were selling their rights to the Bureau of Reclamation in order to secure a local irrigation system.

Federal officials cooperated with Los Angeles's plan to secure water, but Los Angeles paid for the project. Mulholland and local business leaders secured funding for each new phase of the Los Angeles water system through bond elections. They assured voters that without the new water Los Angeles would cease to grow. In Mulholland's words, "If we don't get the water, we won't need it." This was certainly true enough, at least for the first stage of the Owens Valley project, but Mulholland and his allies buttressed their case for additional projects with the more dubious claim that Los Angeles would soon face renewed shortages after water from the Owens Valley arrived. In fact, Mulholland's plans secured water surpluses that allowed, without Mulholland's collaboration, powerful Los Angeles businessmen such as Harrison Gray Otis and Henry Huntington to add to already large fortunes by speculating in San Fernando Valley lands. These arid, low-priced lands became valuable when surplus Owens Valley water, twice the amount actually used by residents of Los Angeles, flowed into them with the completion of the first aqueduct in 1913. Mulholland's success also allowed the city itself to grow both in population and size by annexing surrounding districts. Los Angeles would not sell water to consumers in these areas until they became part of the city.

The city acquired the ability to generate power as a by-product of its water system. Water coming from the Owens Valley watershed to Los Angeles fell 8,000 feet in 360 miles, thus allowing the city to generate electricity by installing dams and turbines. To insure city control of that electricity, Mulholland had to overcome opposition from local businessmen who were usually his allies. The potential profits from power generation on a system already constructed with public funds were too lucrative for businessmen to give up easily. The Bureau of Water and Power entered into a long and bitter struggle with two private utilities, Los Angeles Gas and Electric and Southern California Edison. Mulholland argued that municipal control over the power generated by the aqueduct was the only way to subsidize the operations of the expensive water project. Taxpayers agreed that business should not reap profits from power that would otherwise allow the city to keep taxes down. In the end, the Bureau of Water and Power controlled power as well as water.

Water spurred growth, and growth spurred the demand for yet more water. In the early 1920s, Los Angeles officials moved to secure more Owens Valley water (and also to increase power generation from the project). The city obtained additional water rights, this time to Mono Lake, and acquired access to Colorado River water. Once again Los Angeles obtained far more than its residents needed. When a new Metropolitan Water District that eventually served much of southern California provided Colorado River water in 1941, Los Angeles had no need for it. The city's 1940 Mono Lake extension provided all the water Los Angeles required. Although the city was entitled to half of the water brought from the Colorado, that water instead went to develop the surrounding communities. Even booming southern California could not initially absorb the surplus. After its first ten years of operation, the district only delivered 18 percent of the water it was capable of supplying. The rest remained available for future growth in southern California. Southern California thus matured with water relatively cheap and abundant. The new residents of southern California had little sense of inhabiting a desert. Most of the residents outside the city limits of Los Angeles did not realize that should it wish, Los Angeles could demand its unused allocation of water from the Metropolitan Water District, leaving other southern Californians high and dry.

Ironically, Mulholland, who diverted so much water into southern California, saw his career disappear underneath a flood. In 1928 the Saint Francis Dam, a local storage reservoir, collapsed, sending a hundred-foot wall of water through the Santa Clara Valley. The flood obliterated three towns lying in its path and claimed more than 400 lives. Mulholland, who had pronounced the dam safe the very day of its collapse, took full responsibility for the disaster. He resigned in disgrace.

The massive engineering feats of the Department of Water and Power demonstrated the necessity for the expenditure of public funds to secure private growth. The result of such expenditures was growth on a scale that western cities had never before witnessed. In the early twentieth century, Los Angeles overtook San Francisco as the West's largest and richest city. It was a city of migrants from the American Midwest, from Texas, from Japan, and from Mexico, but the white native-born migrants dominated numerically and culturally and made the city over in their own image.

Los Angeles, and indeed southern California in general, has been one of the most spectacular American inventions of the twentieth century. Envisioned first as a Mediterranean land of orchards, endless sun, and perpetual health, its promise of perpetual well-being brought an influx of consumptives. The California sun could do little for many of them, though, and they coughed away their last days in the land of palms and health. By the early twentieth century this initial image of southern California as a giant outdoor sanatorium had yielded to a second, more romantic creation. Building not so much upon the actual past of ranchos and missions as on their literary reincarnations in novels such as Helen Hunt Jackson's *Ramona* (1884) or in the works of literary promoters such as Charles Fletcher Lummis, the editor of *Land of Sunshine/Out West*, boosters portrayed southern California as a pastoral Hispanic paradise in order to build a mass urban society. D. W. Griffith gave this mythic Hispanic California even greater circulation in a series of mission films he made in 1910 and 1911. In this California of fiestas, pageants, weird neomission architecture, and romance, the only acceptable Hispanics were padres and conquistadores. Field laborers and the workers who built Henry Huntington's interurbans had no place.

Boosters originally designed these images of a Mediterranean California and a Hispanic California to appeal to a leisured class: retired people and winter vacationers from the more prosperous farms and towns of the Midwest. Boosters advertised southern California not only as a land of opportunity but also as a land of leisure. It was a place where people could enjoy life and cash in the dividends of a lifetime of work. Boosters lured the farmers and small townspeople of the rural Midwest with promises of sunshine, warmth, and relaxation. And in the prosperous agricultural economy of the early twentieth century, retired midwesterners could afford to move to California. They did so by the hundreds of thousands.

Los Angeles prospered on more than the cumulative spending of the sick, the elderly, and the leisured. The oil business was booming, and Hollywood and the entertainment industry were prospering. The migration to California widened beyond the Midwest. Missouri and Texas now followed Illinois as the leading birthplaces of those Californians born outside the state.

These midwestern and Texas migrants shaped Los Angeles. American intellectuals, even those who, like Upton Sinclair, lived in southern California, reacted sourly to the results of this migration. Beneath the facade of palms, orange groves, and mission architecture they found Los Angeles dull, homogeneous, selfish, and parochial. Sinclair, prominent muckraker, political radical, successful novelist, and eventual candidate for governor, wrote: "The country has been settled by retired elderly people, whose health has broken down, and who have come here to live on their income. They have no organic connection with one another; each is an individual desiring to live his own little life, and to be protected in his own little privileges. The community is thus a parasite upon the great industrial centers of other parts of America." A former southern Californian, Willard Huntington Wright, dismissed Los Angeles in 1913 as the work of the "rural pietist obsessed with the spirit of village fellowship, of suburban respectability."

When they noticed such attacks at all, midwestern migrants into Los Angeles resented them, but the attacks themselves were admissions of how thoroughly the new migrants dominated the city. These migrants were not at the margins but instead at the center of life in the West's largest and most powerful city. The new migrants did not control the new corporations, but culturally, socially, and increasingly politically, Los Angeles was theirs.

Physically, Los Angeles took the form of a series of connected villages. Builders avoided the hills and constructed homes on the flatlands, a terrain comfortable and familiar to midwesterners. They created a cultural and social atmosphere that was equally familiar and comfortable. They had left the Midwest to seek warmth and relaxation. They preferred life in a city for its conveniences and diversions. But within Los Angeles they frankly intended to maintain small-town morality and small-town customs. Reverend Dana W. Bartlett, born in Maine and reared in Iowa, spoke for them in wanting to "ruralize the city." A home in a residential suburb epitomized his and other migrants' vision of ideal living. Here each family had land, a house, and a garden without the cold, isolation, or hard work of a midwestern farm. In Los Angeles, with its single-family homes and endless residential communities, the midwestern migrants seemed to have achieved their vision of a ruralized city.

Loyalty to small-town values did not, however, really re-create a Midwest stripped of its climatic and social shortcomings. The midwesterners did not transport intact communities to new places any more than had immigrants from foreign lands. The migrants formed but small segments of the midwestern communities they had left. Sinclair and Wright, after all, could not both be correct. Los Angelenos could not be both detached and isolated individuals *and* promoters of "village fellowship." Sinclair and Wright saw only extremes. For them either Los Angeles represented the final breakdown of community, the ultimate realization of anomie or rootlessness, or else it represented the rigid replication of a midwestern small town in a Mediterranean land that deserved better. The midwesterners, like other migrants, were, however, doing something else. They were creating

Holt Avenue in Pomona showed how midwestern immigrants of the early twentieth century created a Midwest with palm trees in California.

new western communities from their previous social experience and from elements they found at hand in southern California.

Los Angeles only appeared midwestern. Unlike any other city of its time, Los Angeles consisted of detached houses. In 1940 half the population of Los Angeles lived in single-family houses. Its nearest rival among large American cities in terms of single-family housing was the midwestern metropolis of Chicago, but Chicago had only 15.9 percent of its population living in detached houses. Los Angeles did not feel like a midwestern town. The city had few parks, courthouse squares, or other public places. The streets were largely empty of pedestrians, and the mobility of the residents kept ties between neighbors weak. The churches failed to attract members; only one in five people in Los Angeles affiliated with a congregation in 1927. Wright's village fellowship thus certainly took a bizarre form in Los Angeles, where inhabitants were often strangers to each other. They had retired away from family and friends, and loneliness and isolation became their chronic complaints.

Upton Sinclair recognized this isolation and breakdown, but his view was as partial as Wright's. Midwesterners in Los Angeles created new kinds of associations and identities based on previous residence. To conquer isolation, midwesterners created state societies in which membership depended on earlier residence in another state. These societies blossomed in Los Angeles in the early twentieth

century, with Iowa's being the largest. Monthly contacts at society meetings did
not re-create the older communities the migrants had left, but then migrants
never fully intended them to. Instead, they became a means of enabling the
migrants to meet others like themselves and forge new connections within Los
Angeles. Similarly, although midwesterners did not always re-create midwestern
congregations within southern California, they provided recruits for new Los
Angeles congregations that were sometimes very different from the churches they
had left behind. Some became Pentecostals, followers of the flamboyant Aimee
Semple McPherson; others joined mystical cults such as "Mankind United,"
"Mighty I Am," or the "Pre-Astral Fraternity of Love."

Sinclair and Wright both captured part of what was happening in Los Angeles,
but they failed to make full sense of it. Obsessed with the idea that these were
small-town people, they neglected the ways in which those people were creating
a mass society. In Los Angeles people were retreating ever more deeply into their
personal lives, but these were oddly public personal lives. Radios, cars, and movies
allowed people to be of, while not in, a public. Reverend Robert ("Fighting Bob")
Shuler became one of the nation's first radio preachers, the "Savonarola of the
Southland." His church "congregation" numbered 42,000, but his real congregation was the hundreds of thousands of listeners who heard him assail Catholics,
Jews, dancing, jazz, and evolution. As Fighting Bob recognized, small-town
prejudices could in a city of a million people find mass audiences and become
something far more potent.

The less people knew about each other, the more public appearances mattered.
Compulsive concern with figure, clothing, and style made sense in a world where
what strangers thought of you mattered a great deal, but where people only
thought about what they could see at a glance. Aimee Semple McPherson grasped
their goal of a good life in which God rewarded faith with the material blessings
and abundant leisure that seemed to typify Los Angeles. Intellectuals like Sinclair
and Wright could, then and later, easily ridicule Los Angelenos as philistines, as
people whose great cultural contribution was Forest Lawn, a cemetery where, in
deference to local prudery, the reproduction of Michelangelo's David wore a fig
leaf, but they were successful philistines who had obtained what they wanted.
They dominated Los Angeles; their tastes created its form and its culture. They
took the boosters at their word and remade the city into a sort of mission Midwest.
White, native-born, Protestant, and largely middle-class, they created a city that
reflected both their origins and what they took to be California's native appeal.
Who, after all, was there to resist them? Earlier Anglo migrants had long before
subordinated the *californios*. The economic elite of Los Angeles welcomed them,
profited from them, but the elite possessed little vision of the future of the city
except as a source of wealth. Their only contenders for determining the shape of
Los Angeles were other migrants, and since most other migrants were nonwhite
immigrants, they were easily shunted aside.

By the end of the 1920s the federal bureaucracies, the corporations, and
the great cities of the West had established their ascendancy. California
epitomized the new order of things. As a locus of the new power centers, the
state was clearly shedding its colonial status. The rest of the West would not
be able to follow immediately, but the emergence of California as a national

economic and political force underlined the potential results of the shift in power within the West. But not all of the West, nor all westerners, shared in the new power. In the early twentieth century, most continued to live on the peripheries of power.

Readings

Abbott, Carl. *Portland: Planning, Politics, and Growth in a Twentieth Century City.* Lincoln: University of Nebraska Press, 1983.

Albright, Horace. *The Birth of the National Park Service: The Founding Years, 1913–33.* Salt Lake City: Howe Brothers, 1985.

Andreano, Ralph. "The Structure of the California Petroleum Industry, 1895–1911." *Pacific Historical Review* 39 (May 1970):171–92.

Cohen, Michael. *The Pathless Way: John Muir and American Wilderness.* Madison: University of Wisconsin Press, 1984.

Dunbar, Robert G. *Forging New Rights in Western Waters.* Lincoln: University of Nebraska Press, 1983.

Fox, Stephen. *John Muir and His Legacy: The American Conservation Movement.* Toronto: Little Brown and Company, 1981.

Franks, Kenny A. *The Oklahoma Petroleum Industry.* Norman: University of Oklahoma Press, 1980.

Hays, Samuel P. *Conservation and the Gospel of Efficiency.* Cambridge: Harvard University Press, 1959.

Hudson, John C. "The Plains Country Town." In *The Great Plains: Environment and Culture,* pp. 99–118. Ed. Brian W. Blouet and Frederic C. Luebke. Lincoln: University of Nebraska Press, 1979.

Hughes, Thomas. *Networks of Power: Electrification in Western Society, 1880–1930.* Baltimore: Johns Hopkins University Press, 1983.

Johnson, Arthur M. "California and the National Oil Industry." *Pacific Historical Review* 39 (May 1970):155–70.

Kahn, Judd. *Imperial San Francisco: Politics and Planning in an American City, 1897–1906.* Lincoln: University of Nebraska Press, 1979.

Kahrl, William L. *Water and Power: The Conflict over Los Angeles' Water Supply in the Owens Valley.* Berkeley: University of California Press, 1982.

Larsen, Lawrence H. *The Urban West at the End of the Frontier.* Lawrence: Regents Press of Kansas, 1978.

McCarthy, G. Michael. *Hour of Trial: The Conservation Conflict in Colorado and the West.* Norman: University of Oklahoma Press, 1977.

McDonald, Terrence J. *The Parameters of Urban Fiscal Policy: Socioeconomic Change and Political Culture in San Francisco, 1860–1906.* Berkeley: University of California Press, 1986.

Meinig, Donald W. "American Wests: Preface to a Geographical Interpretation." *Annals of the Association of American Geographers* 62 (June 1972): 159–84.

Monkkonen, Eric H. *America Becomes Urban: The Development of U.S. Cities and Towns, 1780–1980.* Berkeley: University of California Press, 1988.

Nash, Roderick. *Wilderness and the American Mind.* New Haven: Yale University Press, 1982.

Pisani, Donald J. "Enterprise and Equity: A Critique of Western Water Law in the Nineteenth Century." *Western Historical Quarterly* 18 (January 1987):15–38.

———. *From the Family Farm to Agribusiness: The Irrigation Crusade in California and the West, 1850–1931.* Berkeley: University of California Press, 1984.

Rose, Mark H., and John G. Clark. "Light, Heat, and Power: Energy Choices in Kansas

City, Wichita, and Denver, 1900–1935." *Journal of Urban History* 5 (May 1979):340–64.

Rowley, William D. *U.S. Forest Service Grazing and Rangelands: A History*. College Station: Texas A&M University Press, 1985.

Runte, Alfred. *National Parks: The American Experience*. Lincoln: University of Nebraska Press, 1981.

Sale, Roger. *Seattle: Past to Present*. Seattle: University of Washington Press, 1976.

Starr, Kevin. *Material Dreams: Southern California Through the 1920s*. New York: Oxford University Press, 1990.

White, Gerald T. "California's Other Mineral." *Pacific Historical Review* 39 (May 1970):135–54.

Williamson, Harold F. *The American Petroleum Industry*. 2 volumes. Evanston, Ill.: Northwestern University Press, 1959–63.

Worster, Donald. *Rivers of Empire: Water, Aridity, and the Growth of the American West*. New York: Pantheon Books, 1985.

CHAPTER 16

On the Peripheries of Power

GEOGRAPHY only partially defined the boundaries between the centers and the peripheries of power in the early-twentieth-century West; the divisions were also social. Geographically, the centers of power were urban; the peripheries of power were rural. Socially and institutionally, aggregations of power centered in large, modern organizations: bureaucracies and corporations. More traditional social organizations, from villages to tribes, saw power slip away. Because periphery can refer to either a geographical space or a social space, neither geography nor social position defined it fully. There were people living in cities—centers of power—who were largely powerless. Similarly, there were people living in rural areas— peripheral regions— who had significant amounts of power.

Relative powerlessness was already familiar to a large number of westerners by the twentieth century. They belonged to groups defeated or subordinated during the nineteenth century. Indians, Asians, Mexicans, and Mexican Americans were the predictable inhabitants of the periphery.

Powerlessness was, however, unfamiliar and surprising to westerners who belonged to groups that had come into the West as conquerors. Anglo American farmers and ranchers of the rural West and the immigrant workers of western cities and towns all thought that the conquest of the West had assured them a future of rising prosperity and increasing control over their lives. They had conquered the West and seemingly shaped the land to their will, yet these people, too, found themselves losing their ability to shape events.

The eroding power of the rural West proved particularly bitter because it most affected those people who seemed to exemplify the ostensible values of the West: individualism, self-reliance, and republican independence. Those rural westerners who maintained access to power and influence were those who abandoned the older values, those who instead of resisting the rise of large corporations and the new bureaucracies cooperated with them and tapped into the power of the cities and the large organizations. They prospered while those who battled the new centers of power saw their fortunes decline.

The periphery tended to be rural, but more to the point, it tended to be localistic and decentralized. The groups without power or losing power lacked connections with each other. They tended to remain separate and mutually isolated. Occupied by minorities, immigrants, and rural and working-class Anglos, the peripheries of power comprised a more diverse social and cultural landscape than did the centers of power. The people at the periphery shared little more than a mutual alienation from the new progressive outlook with its emphasis on efficiency and a managed world. Efficiency and planning were not values that evoked much enthusiasm on the periphery among Navajo sheepherders, itinerant loggers, or New Mexican villagers. All brought other concerns and other logics to their work and use of the land. These concerns were particular and local, but Navajos who let their sheep die of old age on the range, New Mexicans who valued the communal life of their villages more than personal advancement, or fiercely independent loggers who seemed to care not a whit for an efficiently managed forest were all out of touch with the new progressive creed. Yet their common estrangement led nowhere, because they remained as alien to each other as they were to the new managers of the bureaucracies and corporations.

The fight against conservation, the struggle to control the railroads, the prolonged attempts of rural state legislators to limit the governmental powers of cities—all of these seemingly unrelated struggles were episodes in a larger battle against centralization. It was a doomed struggle, for even when opponents of the new centralized institutions won, they did so at the cost of setting up other institutions to counter the bureaucracies or corporations that they opposed.

Labor unions demonstrated that to achieve even a modicum of power, the powerless, too, had to organize and centralize. In early-twentieth-century San Francisco, and to lesser degrees in Los Angeles and Seattle, workers created organizations that exercised considerable influence over public life. Only in the 1920s did these organizations fail, and only then did business push western urban workers fully into the periphery.

Studying the periphery thus involves looking at groups that, though once prosperous, were sliding into dependency—groups that had long lacked power and that, while they might respond to their plight creatively, almost always acted defensively. And finally, such study involves groups that, although lacking in power, were engaged in attempts to grasp it, to seize the initiative, and to redefine the West itself. To give this examination more coherence, it is best to treat the rural and the urban Wests separately.

Rural West

The twentieth century has not been kind to the rural West. Isolated from the seats of economic and political control, its people have become increasingly dependent on those centers. But the decline of the rural West has been gradual and only obvious over the long run. Indeed between 1900 and 1920, the rural West never seemed more prosperous. With the rise in farm prices that began at the turn of century and continued until 1920, western farmers, and indeed all American farmers, appeared to have entered a golden age.

During the years before World War I, the rural West grew at a phenomenal rate. The Midwest seemed to form a vast reservoir of migrants ready to venture farther west. Iowa and Minnesota, along with the western states of North and South Dakota and Nebraska, provided the bulk of migrants to the Columbia Plateau country. Smaller numbers of people from eastern Kansas, Nebraska, and the Dakotas joined foreign, largely European, immigrants on a movement onto the High Plains. Other midwesterners, breaking the usual patterns of migration along lines of latitude, moved into South Texas.

The numbers involved in these migrations were immense. In the so-called Winter Garden area of South Texas the breakup of the cattle ranches into commercial farms led to a quadrupling of the population from 80,000 to 320,000 between 1900 and 1930. Nearly a million people, many of them farmers, migrated into Washington, Oregon, and Idaho between 1900 and 1910. The populations of Washington and Idaho doubled in a decade, and Washington enjoyed a growth rate six times that of the nation as a whole. So great was the influx of outsiders that by 1910 only two out of every ten Washington residents had been born there. The northern High Plains of Kansas, Nebraska, and North and South Dakota gained over a million people between 1900 and 1920. The most spectacular increases took place in the western counties as settlers took up "surplus" Indian lands made available through allotment and homesteaded the public domain. Indeed, more people took up land under the Homestead Act between 1900 and 1920 than during the entire late nineteenth century.

Oklahoma, too, boomed as whites took up Indian land following the demise of Indian Territory. In the late nineteenth century, thousands of whites had lobbied Congress to open up the territory and, to increase the pressure, had physically invaded it and held it until they were evicted by U.S. troops. David Payne became the best known of these "boomers" and a symbol of their cause. Potential settlers were Payne's shock troops, but railroads financed his efforts and gave him legal aid. By their charters, some railroads stood to gain large land grants should Congress dissolve Indian Territory; others sought rights-of-way through the territory. Together with commercial interests in Kansas City and Saint Louis, the railroads led congressional lobbying efforts to open up Oklahoma while other corporations, particularly cattle companies, that enjoyed special privileges within Indian Territory lobbied to preserve the lands of the Five Civilized Tribes. The boomers and their corporate allies proved stronger. The Oklahoma land rushes made the old Oklahoma Territory and the newer reservations to the west the domain of white farmers.

The small-scale speculation typical of all American agricultural migrations accompanied this movement. Many "settlers" on the plains took up land only in the hopes of reselling it at a profit. Schoolteachers, domestic workers, cowboys, merchants, doctors, publishers, and virtually everyone else in these areas staked a claim, built a tarpaper-roofed claim shack, and waited to sell out to others.

This booming, bustling movement of farmers and small merchants into the arid regions on both sides of the Rockies seemed a vindication of older methods of settlement. Dry farming techniques of deep plowing and summer fallows seemed to have tamed the resistance of the arid lands. Men and women seemed able to forge their own destinies on the western lands. The disasters of the late nineteenth century seemed to recede in the wake of this triumphal advance.

Utopian Settlement

Amidst the commercial farmers and small-time speculators of the early twentieth century there came another far less numerous group of settlers who, while shunning the economic individualism of other settlers, shared their optimism. The West continued to serve as a magnet for both religious and secular utopians. Some, such as the Mennonites, simply sought to maintain a separate, religion-based way of life. Others hoped to resurrect an older Jeffersonian dream of transforming the urban poor into rural freeholders. Still others desired to transform a corrupt world by creating a model of a better life.

Most of these rural utopians came to their tasks with fervor; few of them came with necessary agricultural skills and knowledge. The Mennonites were one of the few groups to combine both, and they proved the most successful and lasting. Jewish utopians brought equal dedication but no equivalent agricultural knowledge. In the nineteenth century the Hebrew Emigrant Aid Society and other organizations attempted to assist Jewish immigrants from eastern Europe in establishing agricultural communes in Oregon, Kansas, North and South Dakota, and Colorado; the communes proved to be interesting fiascos. A twentieth-century attempt at Clarion, Utah, to create a Jewish agricultural Zion in the midst of the Mormon Zion extended the record of failure into the twentieth century. The Salvation Army's colonies in Colorado and California, designed to return the urban poor to a healthy life in the West, demonstrated the ecumenical nature of agricultural failure. The Salvation Army colonies proved as disappointing as the Jewish communes.

Secular utopias fared little better. The West had a considerable history of failed attempts at cooperative settlement by the 1890s. The Union Colony of Greeley, Colorado, begun in 1870, had been the most famous of an array of cooperatives created by temperance and labor groups and socialists. Their failures did not deter others. In 1896 the Brotherhood of the Cooperative Commonwealth planned to socialize the state of Washington by creating a model community that would inspire imitation in state after state until the whole country embraced socialism. The campaign began and ended with the creation of a settlement called Equality on 280 acres along the shore of Puget Sound. At its height Equality had 300 members. By 1903 it had only 38.

By 1903 the Home colony had stolen the utopian limelight. The settlers at Home were cooperative anarchists, and at one time there were 500 of them. They shunned violence and embraced a toleration that their own diversity tested daily. Home included vegetarians and omnivores, atheists and religionists of various stripes. Some lived in families, while others shared "mutual living arrangements." It all proved too much for Emma Goldman when she paid the colony a long visit in 1898. America's leading anarchist, who had "a heart that embraced the world," did not embrace Home. Its members, she thought, had withdrawn from changing the world and were more interested in "vegetables and chickens than in propaganda."

What Emma Goldman objected to among the anarchists was a trait that they shared with the Salvation Army settlers and the residents of the Jewish cooperatives: they all thought of the countryside, particularly the western countryside, as a haven against industrial society. Philanthropists and reformers conceived of this idealized rural West not as a place of increasing powerlessness, but instead as a place where people could regain control over their lives.

This romanticization of the western countryside also colored far more individualistic attempts at agricultural settlement. Returning the urban poor to the land was always a major theme in propaganda for irrigation projects, but in the Pacific Northwest urban promoters employed the same back-to-the-land rhetoric to encourage settlement on the dank, dripping lands west of the Cascade Mountains. Fearing that the logged-off lands surrounding Everett, Tacoma, and Seattle would become an unproductive wasteland, boosters tried to induce the urban poor of Washington's cities and unemployed loggers to farm them. The promoters of the

Equality colony, whose apartment house is shown here, was one of the numerous utopian colonies that sprang up around Puget Sound during the late nineteenth and early twentieth centuries.

movement were urban, middle-class citizens who sought to make the cities a safer, and more profitable, place for themselves by draining off the poor and discontented. The boosters imagined an idyllic urban hinterland of small farmers who happily supplied the cities with milk and vegetables and purchased urban products in return. When the Forest Service attempted to reforest the cut-over land, back-to-the-land advocates denounced them on the grounds that the government was trying "to grow trees on land that should grow men." The back-to-the-land movement in the Pacific Northwest produced neither trees nor men; instead, it perpetuated a cycle of human and environmental destruction. Farms failed, and on the scarred lands farmers left in their wake the Douglas fir often failed to regenerate.

Changes in Agriculture

Back-to-the-land movements and utopian colonies both operated on the assumption that cities and industrialization did harm and that the countryside and agriculture healed. They misjudged the nature of early-twentieth-century rural life. Modern capitalism, not a pastoral idyll, reigned on western farms. Poor urban migrants stood little chance of succeeding in agriculture at a time when farmers welcomed a new industrialized agriculture and sought to bring modern capitalism to the land. The countryside had its victims, too, and many of those who seemed successful in the early years of the century would soon join their ranks.

Giant stumps which dwarf the cow grazing among them illustrate the difficulties of bringing logged-off lands into production.

The most successful farmers who settled the Great Plains, the Columbia Plateau, or South Texas in the early twentieth century realized that the new agricultural technology made large-scale farming not only profitable but also necessary. The ideal of a 160-acre farm by the early twentieth century had died and been buried on the arid lands of the West. In 1909 the government passed the Enlarged Homestead Act, which offered dryland farms of 320 acres to each settler. Such farms quickly became small by plains standards. A study of 22 High Plains counties in Colorado, Kansas, and Texas found the average farm to contain 771 acres in 1920 and 813 in 1930. In the dryland wheat areas of the Big Bend region of eastern Washington in 1929, farms averaged 1,000 acres, and those of the Palouse country averaged 600 acres. In South Texas the size of farms did decline, but this was an artifact of the breakup of the big ranches and not the establishment of small-scale farming. In these boom years fossil fuel began to replace animal and human power as the primary energy source for agriculture. As the new machines displaced horses in eastern Washington at the outbreak of World War I, French army officers traveled the countryside buying surplus horses for military transport in France.

The machines drastically curtailed the amount of human labor necessary to produce food. Whereas in 1830 it had taken 58 hours of work to plant and harvest an acre, by 1930 it took only 3 hours on some sections of the Great Plains. The flat expanses of the Great Plains and the rolling lands of the Columbia Plateau were ideally suited to mechanized agriculture, and tractors— International Harvesters, Farmalls, Cases, and John Deeres—by the 1920s became as familiar a part of the plains landscape as buffalo had once been. The wheat lands seemed a source of wealth and a shining example of the ability of American farmers to manipulate nature for their own benefit. These farmers hardly seemed victims or people in decline.

But there were dangers that came with success. Debt was the companion of mechanization. From 1910 to 1920 the cost of equipment on a typical Kansas farm tripled from $292 to $980. Farmers borrowed to buy, and they could not afford to pay interest on machines that lay idle. They had to use their new machinery as fully and productively as possible, and big farmers could use machines more efficiently than small farmers. When farmers bought tractors, they enlarged their acreages by purchasing or renting the farms of neighbors who could not afford to buy the new technology. When after World War I wheat prices began to fall, farmers had to increase the scale of operations even more in order to maintain profits. Less profit per acre meant cultivating more acres, not fewer.

At its most extreme, market pressures created a kind of capitalist farming that severed any connection between farm and home. The irrigation propagandists and the back-to-the-land enthusiasts spoke of home and land being synonymous, but agriculture for profit divorced the two. In extreme cases the farm became merely a production site without permanent residents. Suitcase farmers and side-walk farmers rented land and showed up several times a year to sow and to harvest. They were ready to take the harvests in the good years and abandon the land in the bad. By the 1930s roughly half the farmland in Greeley County, Kansas, was farmed by people who lived outside the county. Many other nearby counties had 20 to 30 percent of their land cultivated by absentee owners as suitcase farming boomed in western Kansas and eastern Colorado.

The growth in farm size and the appearance of suitcase farmers meant a West in which fewer and fewer people lived in rural regions. When a wheat farmer in the Pacific Northwest could drive his harvester five miles in a straight line without leaving his own land, then the number of farms the area could hold was clearly limited. On the Columbia Plateau the last reservoirs of good, cheap land vanished as land prices in the wheat belt of Washington quadrupled in a decade. By 1913 Governor Ernest Lister of Washington complained that if he had to place even a thousand new farm families, he would be at a loss to tell them where to find good land ready for the plow.

Equally clear signs of changing conditions appeared on the Great Plains. Between 1912 and 1918, North Dakota ceased public efforts to attract immigrant farmers. There were too many immigrants for the land available. Rural boosters in the more arid regions put their hopes for small farms and future growth in irrigation, but in the early twentieth century many rural districts throughout the West reached their peak populations. The High Plains states of Montana, Colorado, Wyoming, North and South Dakota, Kansas, and Nebraska reached a collective peak in 1920 when their farm population stood at about 2.6 million people. By 1950 it had declined to 1.7 million. The total population of the area did not decline, for some towns and cities continued to add people, but rural decline matched urban advance closely enough so that the total population inched up only slowly. The population of the central and northern High Plains was 6 million in 1920, but only 6.7 million in 1950. Individuals might continue to prosper, but the region as a whole was in decline.

By the 1920s scale was the key to economic survival in the rural West. Farming had become a large-scale operation that demanded access to capital and technology. Throughout the West, the most marginal farmers lost their land, gave up, and became part of the rural work force or migrated into the towns and cities. Nowhere was this trend clearer than among the Mexican Texans and New Mexicans of the Southwest.

The expansion of commercial farming into South Texas amounted to an invasion of a pastoral, paternalistic society by an agrarian, capitalist society. Racial differences compounded economic and social differences. The older residents of South Texas were overwhelmingly Hispanic; the new settlers were largely Anglo midwesterners drawn by the climate and the possibilities of year-round agriculture. The newcomers despised the society they found as backward and corrupt. They were intent on transforming it. They challenged the political dominance of Anglo ranchers who acted as *patrones* and political bosses to Mexican Texan vaqueros and peons and set out to strip remaining Mexican Texan landholders of their ranches.

Incoming Anglo farmers gained a foothold as some ranchers, Anglo and Mexican Texan, willingly sold their land at large profits. The newcomers expanded their hold when they took control of local government and increased taxes to pay for public improvements. By taxing undeveloped land at the same rate as developed land, they put ranchers at a disadvantage, for an acre of rangeland yielded far less income than an acre of cropland. More ranchers sold their land to escape the increasing tax burdens.

As the newcomers stripped Mexican Texans of their votes and began to strip them of their lands, the Mexican Texans resisted. The result was virtual civil war in Texas between 1915 and 1917. Both Texas Rangers and U.S. Army troops battled Mexican Texans and Mexican revolutionaries raiding from across the border. The fighting claimed hundreds, perhaps thousands of lives, and it only accelerated the decline of Mexican Texan landholding. The rangers, in cooperation with land speculators, coerced Mexican Texan villagers into signing over their lands. By 1920, many Mexican Texans who had managed to retain their lands since the Texas Revolution found themselves reduced to tenancy or to labor alongside thousands of Mexicans recruited from across the border.

The continuing reduction of the Hispanic people of northern New Mexico into a rural work force was more gradual and less violent than the suppression of Mexican Texans. Annual labor migrations out of the villages of northern New Mexico to the sugar beet fields of Colorado had become a well-established part of regional life, but in the 1920s dwindling landholdings, falling cattle prices, increasing Anglo settlement, and rising taxes gave the migrations increased urgency. Whereas once only males had migrated, now entire families had to work together in order to get enough money to pay taxes on their land, buy necessary supplies, and finance their next annual migration. The economic pressures proved too great for many; they lost their land and joined Mexican newcomers in the migratory work force. Landlessness relegated these former villagers to the bottom of the dual labor system. They shared in the misery of life in the fields of the new commercial farms, whose owners contended that such conditions were what their Hispanic laborers wanted and expected, but they shared little else. In the farm labor camps the Hispanic New Mexicans often could not reproduce their old, tight village communities. It is no wonder that many New Mexicans sought a better life in the cities. There, too, however, common resources disappeared, and each family depended on the wages that its members could bring in.

Indians

The most powerless people of the rural West were Indians. On the reservations in the early twentieth century, even after allotment, the federal government exercised arbitrary power with an impunity matched nowhere else in the United States. Agents imprisoned people without trial, schoolmasters separated children from parents, and federal authorities broke up religious ceremonies and destroyed ritual objects. In 1908, Z. Lewis Dalby, an attorney conducting an investigation of the Montana Crow reservation for the Bureau of Indian Affairs, told Plenty Coups, an influential Crow chief, that "your position here as chief is not an official or necessary position. You have such influence as the Department of the Interior is willing that you should exercise. If the Department of the Interior finds that you are exercising that influence to the detriment of the Crow Indians then your influence will be taken from you."

For Indians the old possibilities of an autonomous life, free from American control, had ended, but this did not mean that Indian communities had ended or that Indians would vanish. Anglo Americans tended to see Indian responses in black-and-white terms. Indians were either conservatives who resisted change—the people agents called "traditionalists" or "longhairs"—or else Indians were the progressives who sought to imitate whites and assimilate into the larger society. There were probably a few Indians who fit such stereotypes, but most fell into a much greyer area.

Carlos Montezuma, seemingly the most "progressive" of Indians, exemplifies the ambiguities. Montezuma was an unusual man who lived an unusual life. Born a Yavapai in southern Arizona and named Wassaja (meaning "a beckoning" or "a signaling"), he was captured as a small child by the Pimas, who sold him to an Italian immigrant photographer named Carlos Gentile. Gentile had Wassaja baptized and gave him a new name: Carlos Montezuma. By the twentieth century Montezuma had gained a college education, had become a doctor in Chicago, and had emerged as a prominent leader in the Society of American Indians, a pan-Indian organization devoted to Indian betterment and dominated by people like Montezuma—that is, college-educated Indians living in the larger society.

A successful man and never a humble man, Montezuma in effect saw his own life as a parable for other Indians. Like him, Indians had been captured and thrust into white society. Their salvation would come if they, like Montezuma, adopted the culture of the larger society. They must speak English, attend public schools, and live amidst the surroundings of white civilization. But Montezuma, much like Richard Henry Pratt, whom he ardently admired, coupled his disdain for Indian cultures with a deep belief in Indian abilities. Proud of Indian capacities, he scorned reservations, which he regarded as prisons, and despised the Bureau of Indian Affairs, which he viewed as an un-American tyranny that was abusing Indians and holding them down. In 1916 he founded the newsletter *Wassaja*, the masthead of which bore the slogan, "Let My People Go."

Montezuma's assimilationism, however, was not undiluted. Even as he emerged as a national pan-Indian leader, Montezuma became involved with the Yavapais. For the first time since his capture, he returned to visit them in 1901. In the first decade of the twentieth century the Yavapais were struggling to preserve their reservation at Fort McDowell and their water rights in Arizona. The Bureau of Indian Affairs (BIA) supported efforts by the Bureau of Reclamation and the city of Phoenix to claim the water. By 1910 the progressive Indian Montezuma was backing Yavapai resistance. His allies in this fight were conservatives, the Indians who maintained the old dances and customs Montezuma disdained. Although the word would come later, Montezuma began to see the reservations not as prisons but as "homelands"— sovereign Indian land bases that he wanted somehow to free from BIA domination. In his own last days the Chicago physician, the assimilated Indian, would journey "home," sick with tuberculosis, to die in a brush shelter at Fort McDowell on January 31, 1923.

Montezuma's dream of reservations purged of the BIA remained, however, an impossibility in the early twentieth century. Indians living on the reservations lived under federal domination, and the communities that existed on them would have to govern themselves within the boundaries and limits established by the federal government. The new political structures Indians created during those years were not ones they would have chosen themselves, but neither were they a simple submission to federal dictates. They represented a new form of Indian politics and governance that was a response to conquest itself.

Because on virtually every reservation there obtained different traditions of governance, these new political structures varied from tribe to tribe. Even under similar conditions people with similar cultural backgrounds could proceed in different directions. The Crows and the Arapahos, both northern plains Indians and both faced with allotment and loss of land, chose different methods to reconstruct a narrowed sphere of autonomy under federal domination.

Among the Crows of Montana, as among many other groups, older tribal leaders initially retained their influence by mediating between the demands of the government and the desires of their followers. But because such leaders could only survive as long as the government saw them as useful, they ran the danger of appearing to be mere puppets and losing influence among their followers. Engaged in a difficult balancing act, these older leaders often faced a challenge from a new group: younger Indians, bilingual, educated in the government schools, who were more familiar with white society than the older people and angry at their own exclusion from patronage and influence.

The complicated struggle between the young insurgents and older chiefs resulted in the creation of a tribal business committee, dominated by the younger men, that negotiated leases and other agreements with outsiders and served as a forum for settling internal disputes. By the mid-1920s the Crows had evolved a general council in which all reservation Crows assembled to make important decisions. Business committees and general councils were not aboriginal forms of social organization. They were direct responses to the limits of the reservations that attempted to come to terms with, and reverse, the powerlessness of the Crows.

By accepting certain restrictions on their actions, the Crows sought to avoid additional outside interference.

The Arapahos took a different route and reached an accommodation with more of the older elements intact. The prereservation Arapahos depended on age hierarchy, in which men and women advanced through a series of stages of life, each with its responsibilities, to govern their communities. Ceremonial elders, endowed with religious authority, reinforced these social obligations. But as the priests died and the BIA agents repressed religious activities, the ceremonial elders found it difficult to pass on knowledge of the necessary ceremonies to younger men. The Arapahos responded by accepting as elders men without the requisite knowledge and, in the words of Loretta Fowler, an anthropologist who studied their adjustment, "altering or reinterpreting the ceremonies to fit the abilities of the men available to direct them." By allowing young men to take on responsibilities at a much younger age, the elders prevented the young from mounting a challenge to their own authority as the agents encouraged them to do. Similarly, the elders accepted the validity of the new peyote religion, which allowed youths to have visions without apprenticing themselves to elders. Use of peyote, a hallucinogenic cactus, became an alternative way of praying.

In the twentieth century the Arapahos took a further step. They replaced their "chiefs" with six "business councilmen." They did so willingly because they were eager to have the BIA perceive them as progressive and thus worthy of aid and favors, but in fact the business councilmen hardly represented a dramatic break with earlier practices. White officials believed the councilmen to be elected, but actually they were usually selected by tribal elders. The business council worked not to undermine the old ways but to maintain the social fabric of reciprocity and sharing. The whites, as Lone Bear, who had been a chief and had worked his own farm, explained: "They do not understand things, and they undertake to think for a man living here. They think their own way and think they can change the Indians in accordance with their own way of living. They think the Indians can make money and have money like they can, but that is impossible."

Lone Bear, and men and women like him, changed and accommodated. They were not the stubborn conservatives of the agents' imaginations; they adjusted, but they did so in order to try to maintain a basic fabric of life and not to become like whites.

Urban Migration

White migrants who took up the "excess" reservation lands of the Crows and other Indians were themselves after World I but a dwindling minority of migrants into the West. The urban West drew off most of the streams of incoming migrants. These streams—originating in the West's own rural regions, in the eastern United States, in Europe, in Asia, and in Mexico— remained distinct. They did not spill migrants promiscuously over the West. Each group of migrants tended to select a relatively limited set of destinations. Asian immigration, for example, did not penetrate much beyond the West Coast and was always heaviest in California. Unlike earlier Chinese migrants, however, the Japanese formed only a small community in San Francisco, where they met intense hostility from organized labor; most Japanese moved south to cluster in and around Los Angeles. Mexican immigrants concentrated in Texas, Arizona, and southern California. Hispanic

American Horse of the Sioux becomes an American citizen in this 1907 photograph labeled, without irony, "Naturalizing American Horse."

New Mexicans tended to move to Denver. Many migrants coming directly from eastern and southern Europe moved to mining towns in the Rocky Mountain West, but much more often their destination was to larger cities. Italians, for example, moved into San Francisco and to a lesser degree into Denver.

Because migrants concentrated in certain places, specific cities became identified with specific groups of immigrants. San Francisco attracted far more European immigrants than did Los Angeles, but Los Angeles drew far more midwesterners, Japanese, and Mexicans. Seattle, Tacoma, and Salt Lake City received disproportionate numbers of Scandinavians. Some of these Scandinavians came directly to the West; others arrived only after first settling in the Midwest.

All migrants were strangers to their new homes, and in this obvious way all were initially peripheral to western urban society, but they did not all stay peripheral. They were moving into booming cities, and many migrants found opportunities and attained an influence that moved them out of the periphery. Midwesterners dominated Los Angeles politically, set its cultural and social tone, and prospered economically. Some immigrant groups, such as Jews and Scandinavians, also quickly integrated themselves into western urban society.

Success and power clearly were possible for newcomers, but success and power did not come evenly to all groups. The Japanese prospered economically, but only within narrow agricultural and commercial niches left open to them by the dominant society. Italians and Mexicans made more money than they could have made in their home country, but because they planned to return home to establish themselves on farms or in small businesses, they remained on the peripheries of western society.

Relegation to the Periphery: Migration and Race

The prime candidates for powerlessness in the early-twentieth-century urban West were nonwhites. The urban boosters who so eagerly sought immigration wanted only white immigrants. Above all, white westerners sought to deter Asian immigration. In 1902 western Sinophobes secured an open-ended extension of the existing congressional ban on Chinese immigration. Because the immigration laws allowed only relatives of Chinese Americans to enter legally (although others entered by claiming to be related to American residents or by sneaking over the border from Canada or Mexico), only a trickle of Chinese immigrants continued to make their way into the West.

As the United States choked off Chinese immigration, California faced an increase in Japanese immigration. The Japanese government had prohibited the emigration of its citizens until 1884, when it permitted temporary laborers to work on Hawaiian sugar plantations. Not until 1899, however, did significant numbers of Japanese begin to emigrate to the West Coast. In the 1890s and early twentieth century they came as contract laborers whom Japanese middlemen recruited briefly from Japan and then more regularly from Hawaii. By 1906 some 14,000 Japanese laborers were employed as section hands on western railroads, and during the height of the harvest season 38,000 worked in the fields, mainly in California. California union leaders and politicians denounced the Japanese in the same terms that they had denounced the Chinese. In the words of San Francisco Mayor James Phelan, they were "not the stuff of which American citizens can be made." Since American law banned Japanese immigrants from obtaining American citizenship on the grounds that they were not "free white" persons within the meaning of the 1790 Naturalization Act, Phelan's was a self-fulfilling prophecy. Not until American-born children (the Nisei) of Japanese immigrants (the Issei) became citizens would the Japanese be able to make any attempt to grasp full political rights.

This virtually unanimous hostility to California's Japanese residents, never more than 3 percent of the state's population, worried the federal government. Federal officials had little solicitude for the immigrants themselves, but they feared the effect such laws and agitation might have in Japan, which had emerged as a major power in the Pacific, an area of the world where the United States sought influence. When San Francisco in 1906 attempted to segregate Asian schoolchildren, President Theodore Roosevelt objected because he feared that such actions would sour U.S. relations and trade with Japan.

Roosevelt, however, also feared the political repercussions of protecting the Japanese in California, so he tried to escape his dilemma by negotiating in 1907 the so-called Gentleman's Agreement with Japan. The Japanese government agreed to refuse passports to laborers, but it would allow the wives and children of migrants already in the United States to join their husbands and fathers.

Japanese immigrant laborers, who could not become citizens, succeeded the Chinese as unskilled workers in the West's dual labor system.

Thousands of Issei used a loophole in the agreement to secure so-called picture-book brides in Japan until the federal government called a total halt to further legal Japanese immigration in 1924.

To a degree, the Japanese prospered in the West, but only within the narrow economic terrain the larger culture allowed them. The Japanese worked out what was probably the most specialized, and tenuous, relation to western urban society of any group in the West. Although they were relatively numerous in Seattle, their accommodation to western society centered on Los Angeles, which contained the largest and most important of the Japanese communities in the United States. By 1930 over 35,000 Nisei and Issei lived there.

White westerners not only excluded the Japanese from certain jobs through informal discrimination, but they also tried by law to prevent the Japanese from establishing themselves in certain occupations. The Japanese succeeded by exploiting small niches within local economies that had been ignored by others. Near San Pedro, for example, Japanese fishermen from the same prefecture in Japan formed a small village to catch, dry, and export abalone to their home country. They later obtained financial backing from whites and expanded their operations.

The most successful Japanese activities, both in Los Angeles and elsewhere, were truck farming and the flower and nursery business. Japanese farm laborers leased lands, and by applying skills and techniques developed in the labor-intensive peasant agriculture of Japan, they succeeded in a kind of specialty agriculture few others had even attempted. They changed crops to meet market demands, located their fields close to or even on empty fields within the city or rented land, and set up a distribution system to market crops quickly. The small size of their plots limited their expenses, but through intensive interplanting— that is, growing compatible crops on the same land and thus getting several harvests—and close and careful labor, they achieved spectacular productivity. In 1920 Japanese immigrant farmers produced 10 percent of the dollar volume of California agriculture on 1 percent of the farm acreage. By maintaining a spartan existence, they accumulated capital.

Their very success bred resentment. White Californians made the Japanese scapegoats for the woes of California's white small farmers and of labor. They argued that Japanese living standards were so low that whites could not compete. That they were skilled and progressive, as a San Francisco labor leader admitted, only made them all the more threatening. The Japanese became the "Yellow Peril." The state reacted to agitation against the Japanese by passing alien land laws in 1913 and 1920. The laws banned purchase of land by anyone not eligible for citizenship—basically the Japanese—and prohibited the leasing of land to Japanese farmers for longer than three years. The laws against purchase were ineffective, because the Japanese were largely truck farmers who tended to rent, and not buy, land. When the Issei did wish to purchase land, they avoided the provisions of the law by vesting the titles in their American-born children. The Issei could evade the laws against leasing through the same subterfuge. When the California legislature attempted to control loopholes in the law by prohibiting Issei parents from acting as guardians of their Nisei children, the courts ruled their efforts unconstitutional.

Although many Japanese were economically successful, they worked within a clear caste system that kept them out of the most profitable occupations. Denied access to the jobs at the center of the new economy—professional jobs, government jobs, and managerial positions within the large corporations—they still managed to start small businesses with capital accumulated through farming and fishing. These businesses remained largely restricted to the retail trade. The Issei created a very successful, but a necessarily narrow, ethnic economy.

Economically confined, the Japanese were also socially segregated. Whites banned Japanese from public golf courses and swimming pools in Los Angeles. Deed restrictions and restrictive covenants excluded them from the better housing developments. In Whittier, the Japanese could not live "outside certain sections where it is agreed by community custom they shall reside." When the Japanese spread outside of Los Angeles's Little Tokyo, they largely lived in dingy residential areas.

The restrictions placed upon the Japanese and their need to prosper in often marginal occupations created occasions for conflict, not only with whites but with other minority groups as well. When Mexican workers struck Japanese berry farms around Los Angeles in 1933, the farmers and virtually the entire tightly knit Japanese American community reacted fiercely. Red baiting and unified action by the growers broke the strike. In the face of a challenge by their workers, Japanese growers made common cause with white growers to battle the largely Hispanic unions around Los Angeles from then until the end of the Depression.

Japanese unity against threats from outsiders, however, concealed deep generational differences between the Issei and the Nisei. In Little Tokyo the ambitions of the Nisei, citizens and American-educated, to share in the larger American world and to protest their exclusion from that world came into conflict with the accommodations to discrimination made by the more conservative Issei. Although bound into a single community, the experience, values, hopes, and ambitions of Issei and Nisei differed.

Filipinos, Armenians, and Indian Sikhs also made their way to California, but they came in smaller numbers. They, too, faced hostility. Recruited as agricultural laborers, the Filipinos provoked the same reaction from nativists and labor unions as had the Chinese and Japanese. By 1930 roughly 30,000 Filipinos were working in California. A mixture of racial antipathy and white laborers' fear for their own jobs sparked four anti-Filipino riots between 1929 and 1939 and brought pressure on Congress to restrict Filipino immigration. The Tydings-McDuffie Act of 1934 limited immigration from the Philippines to 50 people a year. Significant immigration would not resume until after World War II.

Mexicans formed the most numerous group of nonwhite immigrants, but until the 1930s they did not provoke the same hostility as did Asians. They faced discrimination, but few westerners wished to banish a people that had become a critical source of labor for the West's farms, railroads, and mines. When during World War I the draft, coupled with a literacy test and a head tax under the 1917 immigration law, impeded the migration of needed Mexican workers into the West, the government granted exemptions to the 1917 law rather than face a labor shortage. It renewed these exemptions every year until 1920. Between 1920 and 1930, 459,287 Mexican immigrants legally entered the United States, most of them going to California. They became the single largest immigrant group of that decade. Others, seeking to avoid the long waits for immigration permits and to escape the fees, simply crossed the borders illegally. By 1930 roughly one million Mexican immigrants lived, legally or illegally, in the United States, most often in the border states of Texas, Arizona, New Mexico, and California.

White westerners did not want to halt Mexican immigration, and they could not have done so if they had tried. The federal government could not control the long Mexican border. Yet if westerners did not want to keep Mexican immigrants out, neither did they want them to stay permanently. White westerners welcomed Mexicans only as temporary laborers who would return home when their employers no longer required their services. The growth of substantial resident Mexican communities in twentieth-century western cities thus bred worry and distrust among Anglo Americans.

During the early twentieth century Hispanics became a largely urban people. Rural communities persisted, and large numbers of seasonal agricultural laborers came up from Mexico and returned, but by 1930 slightly over half the Spanish-speaking population in the United States lived in urban areas even though all or part of the family might migrate seasonally for agricultural harvests.

From Texas to Los Angeles and north to Denver, western cities had their barrios and *colonias*. El Paso, whose smelters employed thousands of immigrants, was perhaps the most thoroughly Mexican city in the United States. Mexicans made El Paso so obviously an immigrant city that it acquired the unlikely title of the New York of the Southwest. Elsewhere, too, Mexicans moved into cities, finding their niche at the bottom of the urban dual labor system. In San Antonio they worked at shelling pecans, becoming in the process probably the most underpaid and exploited group of workers in the United States. In 1910, San

Antonio contained the largest number of Mexican immigrants of any city in the West.

Southern California celebrated its Hispanic heritage while simultaneously despising actual Hispanics. As Anglos appropriated the region's mission heritage, Hispanics found themselves shunted further and further onto the periphery even as they increased in number. In the early twentieth century Mexicans moved to Los Angeles, where Henry Huntington's agents recruited them to build his interurban railways. Hispanic communities in and around Los Angeles contained more than 90,000 people by 1930, and recent immigrants greatly outnumbered the old *californios*. The immigrants originally settled in the barrio around the plaza, but labor camps built to house workers for the construction of Huntington's interurbans evolved into smaller satellite barrios. During World War I the residents of the old plaza community began to shift east of the Los Angeles River, creating a new *colonia* that became the center of Mexican immigrant life in Los Angeles. Not bothering to differentiate between native-born Mexican Americans and immigrant Mexicans (who certainly made distinctions among themselves), Anglos lumped them together as "Mexican."

Overcrowded, with poor sanitation and few public services, many of the barrios were death traps. Conditions in Los Angeles did not match those in El Paso, where, for example, immigrants had no running water, no sewers, and poor sanitation. But Los Angeles and El Paso shared high rates of sickness and disease. In Los Angeles County the infant mortality rates for Mexican immigrants only once dropped below 10 percent of births between 1916 and 1929, and in the flu epidemic of 1918 the rate rose to an astonishing 348 deaths per 1,000 births. During that same period infant mortality rates for whites in Los Angeles never rose above 80.5 per 1,000, and in 1918 the rate was only 71.3 per 1,000. There was no greater reflection of marginality and powerlessness than the inability to keep one's own children alive while the children of neighboring communities lived.

Nationally, African Americans bore the brunt of racial discrimination, but in the Far West part of this burden was deflected onto other, more numerous western minorities. Southern blacks formed a relatively small if quite visible component of the urban migration to the West Coast in the early twentieth century. Los Angeles became the center of this migration, and by 1900, Los Angeles had surpassed San Francisco as having the most populous black community in California. Between 1915 and 1930 black migration, predominantly from Texas, increased the number of African Americans in Los Angeles to 39,000, and by 1940, Los Angeles held 25 percent of all blacks residing west of the Great Plains. Within Los Angeles white discrimination confined blacks to a few restricted areas, but blacks still encountered far more favorable conditions than they had known in Texas. Residents of the ghettos of central Los Angeles and Watts earned enough and saved enough so that a sizable minority—about one-third of the population—were able to own their own houses. Home ownership and the relative well-being it represented set the ghettos of Los Angeles apart from black ghettos elsewhere.

Los Angeles, in this sense, may be indicative of a pattern that distinguished African American experience in many western cities before World War II from that in the East. In Seattle, too, African Americans, while denied employment opportunities, gained relatively full civil rights and achieved high levels of home ownership. And in Seattle the slowly growing black population did not become as fully segregated as in Los Angeles. It gained the time and the relative freedom to transform rural southern black culture into a vital urban culture rooted in church, family, and the kinds of voluntary organizations familiar to other native-born westerners.

Ethnicity and the Urban West

Race played a critical role in determining the fate of minorities in the West, but because race itself is partially a social construct, it is impossible to draw firm lines between racial minorities and ethnic minorities. Before the late nineteenth century, European immigrants into the West had faced relatively little hostility, but after 1900 racists across the United States began to narrow the definition of white. In 1893 the Building Trades Congress in Salt Lake City passed a resolution urging the city council to have contractors hire "white men" rather than "dagoes" for municipal work. A more limited definition of white had arrived in the West. This hostility to immigrants from southern and eastern Europe mounted throughout the 1890s and the early twentieth century. Denouncing Slavs, Jews, Italians, and Greeks as racially inferior and inassimilable, American nativists sought to restrict their immigration as they already restricted Asian immigration.

By 1917, when they passed a literacy test over President Woodrow Wilson's veto, restrictionists had begun to achieve some success in curtailing European immigration. In 1921, Congress passed a quota law, and in 1924 it passed a second, much stronger quota law. When finally implemented in 1929, the 1924 law proved particularly crippling to eastern and southern European migration of Jews, Slavs, Italians, Greeks, and other "inferior" peoples who were the particular targets of restrictionists.

The obvious question, given this hostility and the limits on opportunity, is why did southern and eastern European migrants, and indeed nonwhite migrants, continue to come? The answer for the groups that suffered the greatest hostility—Mexicans, Japanese, and Italians—is that changes in their home country had uprooted them. Migration to the United States had become but an additional step in an existing pattern of labor migration. Having participated in earlier migrations closer to home, they believed that migration to the United States would also be temporary. Their powerlessness, their poverty, their life on the periphery of western society—these things they could endure, for they planned to return home with enough savings to establish themselves on a farm or with a small business.

The proximity of the United States made temporary labor particularly tempting for Mexicans. At home the policies of President Porfirio Díaz and a rising population had combined to force many peasants off the land. They became part of a mobile labor pool, the members of which tended to migrate to northern Mexico, where a sparser population and larger farms in need of labor created higher wages. Faced with mounting competition from new migrants, northern laborers in turn moved to take the still higher paying jobs in the United States. By American standards the average pay of Mexican immigrants was quite low, only one-fourth of what white native-born workers received. Mexican workers, however, initially tended to compare their wages to the still lower pay of their home country.

Like the Mexicans, most Issei originally intended only a brief and profitable stay in the West. Most immigrants before 1907 were *dekasegi*—men who thought they would return home in a few years with funds to enlarge the family farm or to create a place for themselves in Japanese society. Men migrated without women or families. In 1910 there were five and one-half times as many Japanese men as women in California. It was a society of itinerant male laborers. Many men did return to Japan with their savings, but after 1907, immigrant leader and newspaper publisher Abiko Kyutaro succeeded in persuading many Issei to give up the *dekasegi* ideal. Kyutaro envisioned a permanent future for the Japanese in America. A Christian convert whose own mother had died at his birth, Kyutaro lacked strong ties to Japan, where he felt his own ambitions had been stifled. He urged the Issei to establish a permanent social and economic stake in American society. As migrants decided to remain in the United States, their families in Japan, using the migrants' photographs and inflated descriptions of their success, arranged marriages for them, and "picture-book" brides arrived in the United States married to men they had never met. The discrepancies between touched-up pictures and actual husbands and between exalted descriptions and American realities often shocked and disappointed the brides. As the Issei married and had American-born children, the sex ratio grew more even, but before World War II it never entirely evened out.

Many European immigrants also shared the Japanese and Mexican tendency to see life in the United States as only a temporary interlude in their lives. Twentieth-century interviews with immigrants who had remained in Nevada found that only about half had intended to stay in the United States. Most of the Italians of San Francisco originally thought of themselves as sojourners in the West. By 1920, San Francisco's Italians were the largest immigrant community in a city where until the 1940s the foreign-born and their children outnumbered native-born Americans of native-born parents. Much of the Italian community still anticipated eventually returning to Italy. Approximately 75 percent of all emigrants leaving Italy between 1908 and 1923 said that they expected to return, and 60 percent of all Italian immigrants actually did return home within a few years. In some years the number of returnees outnumbered the immigrants to the United States.

For Italians the move to San Francisco merely extended an existing pattern of labor migration. Moving to California differed from earlier moves to other sections of Italy or to other European countries in distance, duration, and the greater degree of cultural discontinuity, but not in causes, methods, or intent. Most migrants, 70–80 percent of the whole, were young males without families. Most had previously taken part in other labor migrations within Italy. They sought to make money to acquire land in their home villages.

That so many immigrants intended to return to their homelands had significant implications for the position of immigrants within western society. It influenced their rates of political participation and citizenship. It influenced how immigrants spent or invested their savings. It influenced how they viewed each other and the kinds of organizations they formed.

But life is more than intentions, and human beings end up doing what they never planned to do. Although intending to return home, migrants remained in the West. As the years slipped away, people who intended only to be sojourners became residents. Failure as well as success rooted them in places they had only intended to visit. Mexicans, Japanese, and Italians who never quite managed to

Italian fishing boats with lateen masts at Fisherman's Wharf in San Francisco during the early twentieth century.

accumulate the savings necessary to buy land at home, or who found that land at home was not available at any price, tended to stay on. Their youth gave way to middle age, and they found that they had spent most of their lives in a foreign land. Some, like Pietro Torrano, an Italian immigrant to San Francisco who originally worked to save money to return home, discovered that the American business begun as a means of returning to the old country had become an end in itself. Work mattered more than the old home. They no longer desired to return.

Others never lost the desire to return, but a web of new ties entwined them and kept them in the West. Interviewed years later, many immigrant women in Nevada recalled their migration with regret. But even those who still longed to return to their homeland after many years would not do so. Most had children who had no desire to move to a country they had never known. The very families of immigrants were made up of people born in the West, people who considered the region their home, and people who had no wish to leave it.

As immigrants not only came but stayed as well, new American ethnic communities emerged in the urban West as they did elsewhere in the United States. These communities seemed homogeneous and "foreign" to outsiders; they seemed small pieces of Italy, Japan, Mexico, or Scandinavia transported to the West. They were nothing of the sort. They were American creations. Attempts to preserve old ways certainly abounded. Jews started Hebrew schools. Mexican Americans formed *mutualistas*, which promoted mutual assistance as well as a variety of other social and cultural activities. Japanese immigrants created *gakuen*, or Japanese language schools, to maintain both language and customs. But insofar as such organizations tried to duplicate the culture of the old country, they failed. Instead they introduced old-country elements into new American ethnic identities. Residents of American ethnic communities did not so much transport cultures as create them from a combination of elements carried from various sections of the old country and new elements they found in the United States.

Far from being bastions of traditional old-country life holding out against the progressive American tide, the immigrant communities were hotbeds of conflict and change. When surveying the barrios and *colonias* of El Paso, San Antonio, Santa Barbara, Denver, and Los Angeles, Anglos missed the often mutually antagonistic groups who lived there and lumped them together as "Mexicans." By the 1920s Hispanic New Mexicans had begun identifying themselves as Spanish Americans to differentiate themselves from the Mexican immigrants. In 1930, Santa Barbara, California, had two separate barrios. One held the old *californio* population; the other contained Mexican immigrants. Throughout California, Mexicans and *californios* formed separate and often antagonistic groups. In Texas, Mexican Texans found to their dismay that Anglos immigrating into South Texas refused to differentiate them from Mexican laborers, while in the barrios of Denver, Mexican Americans (*manitos*) disdained the Mexican immigrants (*surumatos*), whom they blamed for the increasing discrimination Mexican Americans encountered. Only gradually, as Mexican immigrants spent their lives and raised their children in the United States and as their children intermarried with Mexican Americans, did immigrant and native-born Hispanics forge from their similarity of culture and common working-class identity a distinctive Chicano culture.

Working out American ethnic identities involved both the internal relations of an ethnic group and the relation of the new ethnic group as a whole to the larger society. Members of ethnic communities sought access to power, and Anglo Americans resented their efforts. This resentment and fear was partially cultural. Precisely because ethnic minorities created *American* cultures and did not merely transplant existing cultures, they laid implicit claim to the ability to define what being an American, what being a westerner, consisted of in what was the newest and least culturally secure section of the country. Anglo Americans, themselves self-conscious newcomers, feared that their ability to monopolize the definition of Americanism was at risk.

This very newness and the contested nature of Americanism created opportunities for those immigrant groups who could define themselves as white and gain membership in the middle class. The experience of western Jews provides a specific example of how the creation of ethnic identities was part of this larger construction of larger western and American identities. The largely middle-class German Jewish communities established in San Francisco and Portland since the mid-nineteenth century seemed to outsiders tight-knit groups. But they had long been capable of spectacular religious quarrels among themselves. In 1880, for example, Rabbi Mayer May of Portland shot a member of his congregation in a quarrel over religious school instruction. The congregation paid the rabbi to leave Portland.

During the early years of the twentieth century other divisions compounded these religious controversies. The German Jewish communities in western cities

Table 11

Mexican-Born, Mexican-Heritage, and Total Urban Population
in Four Cities and Counties, 1900–50

	Los Angeles	Tucson	Sante Fe	San Antonio
1900				
Mexican-born	1,613	3,520*	48	4,752*
Total population	170,298	14,689*	5,603	69,422*
1910				
Mexican-born	11,793	4,457*	103	13,226*
Total population	504,131	22,818*	5,072	119,676*
1920				
Mexican-born	29,757	4,261	138*	28,444
Total population	576,673	10,354	7,236	161,379
1930				
Mexican-born	53,684	1,199	14*	1,745
Mexican-heritage	97,116	10,235	834	82,373
Total population	1,238,048	32,506	11,176	231,542
1940				
Mexican-born	36,840	2,874	102	22,530
Total population	1,504,277	35,752	20,325	253,854
1950				
Mexican-born	71,620	2,220	106	33,831
Total population	1,970,358	45,454	20,325	408,442

Source: U.S. Department of Commerce, Bureau of the Census, Twelfth to Seventeenth Censuses, volumes on population as follows: *Twelfth Census*, vol. 1; *Thirteenth Census*, vols. II, III; *Fourteenth Census*, vol. III; *Fifteenth Census*, vol. III; *Sixteenth Census*, vol. II; *Seventeenth Census*, vol. II. Reprinted from Richard Griswold del Castillo, *La Familia* (Notre Dame: University of Notre Dame Press, 1984), p. 95.

Note: Only the 1930 census distinguished between the Mexican-born and the Mexican-heritage populations. In that census they enumerated "all persons born in Mexico or having parents born in Mexico." This excluded almost all third-generation Mexican Americans, including a large number of Hispanos who were enumerated with the white population. *Fifteenth Census: Population*, vol. 2, p. 27.

*County-based data.

felt an obligation and a distant kinship with the new and poor eastern European Jewish immigrants flooding into the United States at the turn of the century. Most German American Jews, however, resented and were ashamed of the newcomers whom they set out to aid. These immigrants seemed nearly as backward, superstitious, ignorant, and exotic to the German Jewish community as they did to gentiles and thus represented a threat to the identity German Jews had already forged. A common religion did not automatically create community, and Jewish "communities" in Portland and San Francisco became collections of competing congregations divided by degrees of orthodoxy and by national origins.

Western Jews had, in effect, entered into a contest among themselves over what being an American Jew meant. They eventually forged a common identity, thanks in large part to community-wide organizations such as B'nai Brith, which began as a Jewish imitation of Masonry. In a very American way, Jews created voluntary organizations to forge a community identity.

In the process of creating an American Jewish identity, Jews rearranged their relations with each other in ways that created new patterns of thought and action. This change was uneven. Jewish merchants in Portland, for example, reconstructed familiar European mercantile roles, but for their wives and daughters residence in Portland meant far-reaching changes. American-born Jewish women in Portland found they had far more options for employment outside the home (at least before marriage), and they had more power to make independent decisions about marriage partners, family structure, and civic participation than their mothers had possessed in Germany or eastern Europe. Women to a large degree assumed responsibility for charity and welfare work among Portland's Jews. They, together with men, created an ethnic middle-class Jewish community with new gender roles.

The changing role of women as well as the mercantile activity of men in turn forged increased connections with the larger society. Middle-class Jews gained influence within that society not as Jews but as merchants or reformers. Opportunities and connections outside the community then served to further accelerate change within the community.

In some ethnic communities this escalating process of change could nearly completely alter older expectations and ways of acting. In Seattle, for example, Scandinavian women largely discarded older roles and responsibilities. Most young Scandinavian women came to Seattle without family ties and supported themselves as domestics. In doing so, they participated in existing Scandinavian migration and labor patterns for single women. Their average age at marriage (their mid-20s) also conformed to Scandinavian norms. But with marriage they abruptly broke from older patterns. First of all, nearly 40 percent of the Norwegian and Swedish women married outside their own ethnic group. Second, in Scandinavia women had continued to work outside the home after marriage; in Seattle married Scandinavian women rarely did. Seattle's Scandinavian women adhered much more closely to native middle-class American cultural patterns than they did to Scandinavian expectations.

Italians did not forge such middle-class connections and habits as quickly or easily. In part this was a result of their sometimes ambiguous status as "whites"; in part it resulted from the nature of their immigration. Most Italian immigrants were young males who intended to stay but a short time. These immigrants made some effort to take up familiar occupations. Although Italian market gardeners were a visible part of San Francisco life, and the city became famous for its Italian fishing fleet, relatively few Italians became fishermen and truck farmers in the Bay Area. Only about 10 percent of the male workers fished or farmed. Immigrants had to accept what the western economy offered. Most aspired to a future as small merchants, but, despite the seeming ubiquity of Italian fruit and vegetable stands or corner groceries, relatively few succeeded. Most Italian immigrants became unskilled or semiskilled workers outside the unionized core of the economy.

The Italians were initially as socially marginal as they were economically marginal, but after 1910 increasing numbers of male migrants began to send for the families they had left behind. Other immigrants returned home only to fail to obtain land or to find permanent work in Italy, whereupon they decided to return permanently to the United States. The trend toward family immigration thus quickened, but it still usually took three to nine years before an immigrant brought over his wife and children.

By 1920 the city's 24,000 Italian immigrants and their 22,000 children made the Italians San Francisco's single largest national group, but despite their growing numbers, the Italians remained peripheral to the life of the city. There was no real "Italian" identity among immigrants from Italy; they organized around their regions of origin. Not until 1916, with the creation of the Italian Welfare Agency, was there a nonregional Italian organization in San Francisco. A common identity as Italians did not really develop until the immigrants came to regard regional loyalties as a bar to their economic advancement in the United States. Amadeo P. Giannini, founder of the Bank of Italy, which would become the Bank of America, achieved his first success by convincing immigrants that money pooled in his bank could do more to help Italians in San Francisco than money distributed among numerous regional mutual aid societies. By the 1920s his bank had become what the newspaper *L'Italia* called "the national institution of the Italians of California."

Giannini's bank did more than make Giannini rich and help create a sense of identity; it also created jobs for Italians. Italian workers, whether single women making chocolate for Ghirardelli and Company or the male tellers at Giannini's Bank of Italy, worked for nonunion businesses owned by their compatriots. Like the Japanese, the Italians evolved an ethnic economy, but it was one that by the 1920s was beginning to produce major businesses with power in the larger economic world. As Italians forged a more coherent Italian American identity, as they created businesses at the heart of the western economy, and as their children moved into skilled or white-collar jobs, Italians as a whole began to move toward the center of life in San Francisco.

As these experiences indicate, not all immigrant groups found themselves consigned permanently to the periphery of western life, and not all immigrant groups remained isolated and self-contained. Western urban areas, and indeed western and American identities, were dynamic and changing. There were, however, barriers to this dynamism besides race. Those ethnic groups that grasped for power from a working-class instead of middle-class base proved, in the long run, less successful.

Power and Class

Late-nineteenth- and early-twentieth-century San Francisco was a city of European immigrants, and by the early twentieth century San Francisco had arguably the most powerful labor movement in the country. German American and Irish American workers dominated this labor movement, and they had attained for labor political and economic power on a scale unmatched elsewhere in the United States. Organized labor, particularly the powerful Building Trades Council, found a place in the power structure that elsewhere fell almost exclusively to business and to the new government agencies. The power of labor during the years before World War I created avenues of opportunity for northern European immigrants and their children.

The goal of labor in San Francisco was to maintain the city, and indeed

The absence of vehicles on the streets of Seattle during the General Strike of 1919 revealed the power of the western urban labor movment at the very moment that the movement was about to go into precipitous decline.

California, for what German-born labor official Paul Scharrenberg called "us and our kind of people." "Our kind of people" for San Francisco unionists were German Americans and Irish Americans. Irish and German immigrants made up half of all the immigrants in the city in 1900, and they and their children made up 38 percent of the city's population. Most were workers and their families, but many were small merchants who lived in working-class neighborhoods, depended on workers for their business, and sympathized with workers' views. San Francisco's politicians, too, were by and large Irish and German. And the Irish controlled the Catholic church at a time when 80 percent of all San Franciscans who declared a religious affiliation were Catholic.

The success of Irish American and German American workers in attaining economic and political power in San Francisco did not make the city a paradise for immigrants in general. The building trade unions maintained their power by securing a closed shop. To work in most trades, a person needed union membership. By controlling apprenticeship programs, the unions could restrict the number of available workers and secure high wages. Because apprenticeships and jobs went first to the Irish and German San Franciscans, outsiders had difficulty obtaining union membership and jobs. The unions, needless to say, excluded the Chinese and Japanese, but the Italians fared little better.

By World War I, however, the Building Trades Council, the heart of labor's power in the city, was in decline. With the local economy stagnant in the years before the war, the unions had found it difficult to match the strength of major new national corporations, such as Bethlehem Steel, that moved into the area.

Large corporations with factories in more than one locale had the ability to transfer production elsewhere in case of strikes. More serious still was the building slump during World War I when war production brought civilian construction in San Francisco to a near standstill and badly hurt union membership in the construction trades. But most serious of all was the failure of the unions to maintain their own independent electoral power base in San Francisco. Relying more and more on their alliance with California progressives, they no longer elected union men to the courts and municipal offices. The prolabor press, too, went into gradual decline.

After World War I, the unions were vulnerable to an assault by business groups that successfully united in the Industrial Association of San Francisco (IASF). Enrolling about a thousand member companies—including the biggest corporations in California, the IASF was determined to break the closed shop. In San Francisco, the climactic battles were already underway as the association organized. Union leaders, some of them tinged by corruption, offered ineffective resistance to employers' organizations that refused to sell building materials to any contractor who recognized union work rules. Lockouts and union breaking were the employers' sticks; their carrots were promises of welfare capitalism under which employers would provide benefits such as insurance formerly provided by unions. By 1923 the IASF bragged that 85 percent of San Francisco's workers were under the open shop. For the first time in San Francisco's history, organized labor lost ground during a period of prosperity. Wages in San Francisco's construction industry, once among the highest in the country, fell until by 1930 they were among the lowest for similar-sized cities. In a city once dominated by immigrants and organized workers, large corporations had convincingly demonstrated their power and control. There were escapes from the periphery, but there were also retreats back to it.

The Peripheries of the West

The poverty, the suffering, and the human costs of powerlessness were quite real in the West, but they did not transform the peripheries—either urban or rural—into a uniform grey landscape of despair. Because marginalized groups were isolated, they were also unique and distinctive. Crow Indians, residents of a Los Angeles barrio, Issei farmers, and Italian immigrants all were at the margins of western society, but culturally and socially they shared little else. The margins of society were never devoid of people of initiative or imagination. Those on the margins did not always seek the same success as did motivated members of the dominant social groups, but they did seek a success that they defined in their own terms, and they desired control over their own communities. Their struggles for that control and success were just beginning in the first decades of the century.

Readings

Athearn, Robert G. *High Country Empire: The High Plains and Rockies.* Lincoln: University of Nebraska Press, 1960.

Camarillo, Albert. *Chicanos in a Changing Society: From Mexican Pueblos to American Barrios in Santa Barbara and Southern California, 1848–1930.* Cambridge: Harvard University Press, 1979.

Cinel, Dino. *From Italy to San Francisco: The Immigrant Experience*. Stanford: Stanford University Press, 1982.

Daniels, Roger. *The Politics of Prejudice*. Berkeley: University of California Press, 1962.

De Graaf, Lawrence B. "The City of Black Angels: Emergence of the Los Angeles Ghetto, 1890–1930." *Pacific Historical Review* 39 (August 1970): 323–52.

Deutsch, Sarah. *No Separate Refuge: Culture, Class, and Gender on an Anglo-Hispanic Frontier in the American Southwest, 1880–1940*. New York: Oxford University Press, 1988.

Fowler, Loretta. *Arapahoe Politics, 1851–1978: Symbols in Crises of Authority*. Lincoln: University of Nebraska Press, 1982.

Garcia, Mario. *Desert Immigrants: The Mexicans of El Paso, 1880–1920*. New Haven: Yale University Press, 1981.

Goldberg, Robert A. *Back to the Soil: The Jewish Farmers of Clarion, Utah, and Their World*. Salt Lake City: University of Utah Press, 1986.

Hewes, Leslie. *The Suitcase Farming Frontier: A Study in the Historical Geography of the Central Great Plains*. Lincoln: University of Nebraska Press, 1973.

Hoffman, Abraham. *Unwanted Mexican Americans in the Great Depression*. Tucson: University of Arizona Press, 1974.

Hoxie, Fred. *A Final Promise: The Campaign to Assimilate the Indians, 1880–1920*. Lincoln: University of Nebraska Press, 1984.

Ichioka, Yuji. *The Issei: The World of First Generation Japanese Immigrants, 1885–1924*. New York: Free Press, 1988.

Iverson, Peter. *Carlos Montezuma and the Changing World of American Indians*. Albuquerque: University of New Mexico Press, 1982.

Kazin, Michael. *Barons of Labor: The San Francisco Building Trades and Union Power in the Progressive Era*. Urbana: University of Illinois Press, 1987.

LeWarne, Charles. *Utopias on Puget Sound, 1885–1915*. Seattle: University of Washington Press, 1975.

Meinig, Donald. *The Great Columbian Plain: A Historical Geography*. Seattle: University of Washington Press, 1968.

Melendy, H. Brett. "California's Discrimination Against Filipinos, 1927–35." In *Racism in California*, pp. 141–52. Ed. Roger Daniels and Spencer C. Olin. New York: Macmillan Company, 1972.

Montejano, David. *Anglos and Mexicans in the Making of Texas, 1836–1986*. Austin: University of Texas Press, 1987.

Nelson, Paula M. *Homesteaders and Town Builders in Western South Dakota, 1900–1917*. Iowa City: University of Iowa Press, 1986.

Ottoson, Howard W., et al. *Land and People in the Northern Plains Transition Area*. Lincoln: University of Nebraska Press, 1966.

Romo, Ricardo. *East Los Angeles, History of a Barrio*. Austin: University of Texas Press, 1983.

Takaki, Ronald. *Strangers from a Different Shore: A History of Asian Americans*. Boston: Little, Brown and Company, 1989.

Toll, William. *The Making of an Ethnic Middle Class: Portland's Jewry over Four Generations*. Albany: State University of New York Press, 1982.

Webster, Janice Reiff. "Domestication and Americanization: Scandinavian Women in Seattle, 1888–1900." *Journal of Urban History* 4 (1978):275–90.

PART FIVE

Transforming the West

IN the West of the 1930s, federal bureau-
cracies, powerful corporations, and cities (which contained large numbers of
immigrants into the West) all served as conduits for outside influence. Few
westerners alive in 1930, however, would have believed how quickly events
beyond the West would change the region over the next fifteen years. The Great
Depression and World War II devastated much of the world, but they also allowed
parts of the West to escape their colonial dependence on the East.

The main agent of the liberation from dependence on eastern capital was the
federal government. The Depression and World War II changed the parameters
of permissible federal political and economic activities. Fifteen years of crisis
enabled the government to create an economic infrastructure for the region,
bankroll its corporations, and fund a military establishment that guaranteed
regular infusions of jobs and money into the western economy. As the West
Coast, the Southwest, and portions of the Rocky Mountains region boomed and
grew in population, western politicians became national power brokers on a scale
that eclipsed the modest accomplishments of the progressives.

And yet, even as the consequences of the Depression and World War II changed
the West, the changes came in a manner very much shaped by the western past.
An analogy can be made with something else that occurred during these years.
In the Southwest the early twentieth century was a period of recurring drought
and gullying. Oraibi Wash in the Hopi country was only 20 feet wide and 12 feet
deep in 1897; by the 1930s it was, on the average, 150 to 300 feet across and 30
to 35 feet deep. The Oraibi Wash of the 1930s was obviously no longer the Oraibi
Wash of the 1890s. In a real sense, the new wash was the result of climatic
factors—changes beyond the land itself. But on the other hand, there is no
understanding the vast new wash without referring back to the older landscape
that channeled the runoff. There is no understanding the runoff without looking
at how westerners—Anglo Americans, Hispanics and Indians—used the land.
The Oraibi Wash of the 1890s in a real sense shaped the wash of the 1930s, but
it could not have done so unless much greater changes had taken place beyond
Oraibi.

What was true of Oraibi Wash was true of the West as a whole: the climatic
change of the Depression and World War II instigated change, but that change
flowed through familiar channels. It is a measure of the power that corporations,
cities, and the federal bureaucracy had already amassed during the first three
decades of the twentieth century that the near economic collapse of the United

States and the entry of the nation into a world war only widened and deepened their holds on the region.

When the war ended, the West's relationship with the outside world had changed. The East's influence over the region had faded. But to many westerners it seemed that the West had merely switched masters. That liberation from eastern capital meant only that the federal government exerted an even greater power over the destiny of the region. And so, not surprisingly, the hostility toward eastern capital and the often radical rhetoric that had accompanied it gradually gave way to a hostility toward the federal government voiced with a new and often reactionary rhetoric.

CHAPTER 17

The Depression

On October 24, 1929, the New York stock market crashed. Oddly, given the West's own speculative bent, most western commentary on the crash had a moralizing tone. Congenitally hostile and distrustful of Wall Street, westerners acted as if speculation in Wall Street stocks differed qualitatively from speculation in mining stocks or commodity futures. Westerners reassured themselves that only eastern speculators (the bad kind) would suffer from the collapse of stock prices. As an editorial in one Texas trade paper, the *Cotton and Cotton Oil News*, put it, the resources of the United States had not been lessened by "a single ton of ore or coal, or a single bushel of grain, or a bale of cotton, or by a single industrial building." Coal, grain, and cotton were the solid things that westerners depended on and produced; as long as such resources remained, then the western economy must be secure.

Yet for westerners to put their dependence on resources alone was as silly as their denunciation of easterners as speculators. Resources were useless to the West without outside markets. The West did not and never had used its own ore or consumed its own grain. These were commodities, and commodities needed markets. Western commodity producers had long been a part of a capitalist market, and the stock market crash signaled that something was very wrong in capitalist markets.

The solid things—the ore, grains, and cotton—that westerners placed their confidence in became actual liabilities in the years after 1929. Westerners borrowed to produce them and then could not sell them at a price sufficient to repay their loans. By 1931 the declining markets for western products had left every section of the region with a surplus of commodities and a deficiency of work and money. Between 1929 and 1933 the gross national product declined by more than 35 percent, and domestic private investment fell 90 percent. Residential construction was down to 18 percent of what it had been in 1929. Roughly 30 percent of the work force was unemployed (the government at that time kept no accurate count), with many more only partially employed. From the outset of the Depression until Franklin Delano Roosevelt's inauguration in March 1933, about 5,500 banks with $3.4 billion in assets had closed. Proportionately, the West suffered more than the nation as a whole. The decline in real income in the West was greater than the national average; 12 of the 20 states with the greatest declines in income were in the West, including 7 of the top 10.

The Depression hit the West so hard that many sections would not get back on their feet until World War II. With so little opportunity for profit or productive work, the flow of capital and people from the East that had fueled western development for nearly a century slowed to a dribble. The Rocky Mountain states, the Southwest, and the Great Plains states actually declined in population between 1929 and 1939. With the economy of the country in ruins, economic activity in the West fell by more than half between 1929 and 1933.

The 1920s: Uneven Prosperity

The initial equanimity of western editorialists in the wake of Wall Street's troubles seems particularly misplaced, because important sectors of the western economy had weakened badly during the 1920s. The cities may have prospered, but the agricultural and extractive economy of the rural West showed signs of severe distress well before the stock market crash.

These economic problems were not new; western producers of basic commodities found world markets glutted and prices in decline. Western wheat farmers had watched crop surpluses mount and wheat prices fall throughout the 1920s. Washington farmers, who received $1.83 a bushel for wheat in 1920, got $0.38 a bushel by the end of the decade. Western farmers produced still more wheat to make up for lower prices, and when, as in Montana, drought cut yields, the result was catastrophic. Half the farmers in Montana lost their farms to foreclosure between 1921 and 1925. As they had in the nineteenth century, economic problems spawned political solutions; the McNary-Haugen Bill proposed federal purchases of surplus crops and their sale abroad. Every western congressional delegation supported the bill, but Calvin Coolidge's veto killed the measure. Farm problems worsened in the 1930s. By 1931–32 virtually all the farmers participating in a study by the Nebraska College of Agriculture were operating at a loss. And they represented the previously more prosperous and successful farmers. In North Dakota average per capita income during the Depression fell to $145, less than half the national average.

Ranchers suffered as well as wheat farmers. Cattle prices fell by more than half between 1918 and 1922. In Wyoming, where there had been well over a million cattle worth nearly $74 million in 1919, there were only about 800,000 cattle worth $23 million in 1925. In the West as a whole there was a gradual improvement in the cattle business after 1925, but then prices fell by 66 percent between 1928 and 1931.

The extractive industries fared no better. The output of Colorado mines declined during the 1920s. Like other neighboring Rocky Mountain states, Colorado had already begun a long economic slide that by 1930 had reduced the Rocky Mountain region's annual per capita income to a figure well below the national average. It continued to fall during the Depression. In Colorado, per capita income dropped by 40 percent between 1929 and 1933. In the Pacific Northwest the lumber industry, which accounted for half the wages earned in Washington and Oregon by the 1920s, suffered first from declining prices after 1923 and then from a slowing of the construction industry after 1927 that anticipated the Depression. With the Depression itself came a rapid decline in production between 1929 and 1933. Like the lumber industry, the oil industry suffered from overcapacity and oversupply in the 1920s. Western producers continued to pour oil onto the market with little regard for future supplies. The Federal Oil Conservation Board, created in 1924, tried to curtail waste, but its powers were weak and the problem vast.

The fact that the twenties were a period of prosperity for many westerners as well as for the United States as a whole, despite the problems in agriculture and the extractive industries, became another sign of the economic domination of the cities. Los Angeles led the way. After World War I, Los Angeles County shed its dependence on agriculture and tourism and emerged as the leading industrial center of the West. The new artificial harbor at San Pedro, abundant oil, and a booming population combined to bring significant industrial investment and a manufacturing output that reached $1.3 billion by 1929.

Herbert Hoover and the Depression

Those westerners who thought that the economic downturn, of which the stock market crash was but a single sign, would not affect the West grew increasingly fewer during 1930. One of the westerners who retained his confidence that the economy was basically sound and the worst was already over was, however, the president of the United States, Herbert Hoover. The first American president from the West, Hoover had grown up on his uncle's Oregon ranch, had graduated from Stanford, and had gone on to a successful career as a mining engineer and public servant. Throughout 1930, Hoover kept insisting that the "fundamental strength of the economy" was unimpaired.

This stubborn refusal to admit the depth of the collapse was certainly Hoover's fault, but the Depression itself was not. He had been in office for less than a year when the stock market crashed. In many ways a progressive who envisioned an activist federal government, Hoover was certainly the most able president of the 1920s (an honor for which there is, admittedly, not much competition), but Hoover's activism focused on the apex of American society and not its base. He wanted a federal government that assisted and guided private business instead of competing with it. Together, big business and the government could create a structure that would ensure general prosperity. Hardly a cruel or callous man, Hoover cushioned himself against the suffering around him. He never visited a soup kitchen or a breadline.

Hoover believed that just as the federal government was best suited to deal with large corporations and business interests, so charities and local communities were best suited to provide direct aid to the poor. One of his biographers termed his attitude "cooperative individualism." He imagined a benign capitalism in which Americans would voluntarily share the abundance produced by new technology. When, as it turned out, the issue was not abundance but scarcity, Hoover's preference for local voluntary solutions remained unchanged. "It is not," he said in 1932, "the function of the government to relieve individuals of their responsibilities to their neighbors, or to relieve private institutions of their responsibilities to the public." He steadfastly opposed direct federal aid for the victims of the Depression.

In the West, as elsewhere in the United States, the Depression became a wave that successively swamped all the social bulwarks expected to contain it: first the family, then self-help organizations, and finally municipal and private charities and state governments. For most Americans the family remained the first recourse in the face of economic hardship, and the family's burdens always fell most heavily on women. Most western women did not work outside the home, so they did not experience unemployment directly. They, however, were the ones who had to compensate for reduced income; they had to adjust to the often awkward presence of angry and frustrated men during normal working hours; and they had to console men who felt shame at their inability to provide for their families. Women had to make sure that food stretched farther, that clothes lasted longer, and that the family did not crack under economic and emotional stress.

Women—black, white, and Hispanic—often found it necessary to move into the work force to obtain jobs when male workers could not find employment. Because of gender segregation in the work force, "women's work" as secretaries, maids, laundresses, or nurses was sometimes available even when men could not find jobs. The percentage of married women working actually increased during the Depression. In San Antonio, Texas, for example, approximately 25 percent of Anglo women over 14 worked for wages during the Depression, while over 50 percent of black women and slightly under 25 percent of Mexican American women did. The dual labor system determined the nature of this employment. Black women in San Antonio worked largely as domestics. Some Mexican American women also took domestic work, but most worked in food processing, garment, or tobacco industries. White women dominated the clerical jobs.

Virtually all families felt the pressure of the Depression, but the pressure increased as one moved lower in the social order. Middle-class families scrimped, saved, and made do. Married children often had to return to their parents' home, but such families rarely went hungry. Without aid, working-class and poor families, particularly minority families, were far more likely to face hunger, sickness, and sometimes dissolution.

With wage employment difficult to find, some families attempted to move back into the countryside, where they at least could grow food. In the 1930s the Hispanic villages of northern New Mexico and southern Colorado whose members had migrated north to work in the beet fields saw a return migration as these jobs failed. And in western Washington and elsewhere in the West, unemployed urban workers tried to obtain a patch of land in the country in order to grow food. Such attempts involved some risk. Few urban workers were experienced farmers, and because public relief largely depended on established residency, those who moved found themselves ineligible for aid in their new localities.

Self-Help

As families failed to sustain their members, voluntary organizations moved into the breach. By creating unemployed citizens' leagues (UCLs), some westerners applied Hoover's injunctions for self-help in a way that made the Republican president acutely uncomfortable. In Seattle, where various estimates of unemployment ranged from 23 percent to 60 percent, a group of long-standing labor radicals and socialists organized the Seattle Unemployed Citizens League in July of 1934. It rapidly spread throughout the city, and at its height it had 40,000 to 50,000 members.

The Seattle UCL and others like it organized the unemployed into urban cooperatives based on a combination of barter and cooperative labor. The UCL got permission to cut wood for fuel and to pick unwanted fruit in the orchards of Yakima, and it equipped fishing boats on Puget Sound. The workers set up commissaries to distribute these and other goods. In exchange for the goods the recipients chopped wood, did tailoring, repaired shoes, and performed other tasks for the unemployed. The Denver UCL, enrolling over 30,000 members in 1932, had each member pledge to work at least two days a month on cooperative ventures such as harvesting crops that farmers could not afford to harvest themselves. California became the center of such cooperative efforts, and by the summer of 1933 more than 75,000 families in Los Angeles alone had joined self-help cooperatives. When Upton Sinclair campaigned for governor in 1934 on his End Poverty in California (EPIC) platform of production for use instead of production for profit, he built on the strong barter and cooperative movements already present in the state.

Members of the UCLs, however, recognized the limits of self-help; they demanded public aid. The Seattle UCL sought public works projects, unemployment insurance, and, as a last resort, direct relief. But many westerners regarded charity and public relief as a badge of shame, and their forced retreat to this bulwark against poverty filled many of them with a rage or despair made even worse when local charities and relief agencies proved unable to stem the tide of suffering. In 1932, for example, most of the private charities in Denver had exhausted their funds. Both local public work projects and private breadlines closed down. In San Antonio, where the city did little more than coordinate private relief efforts, the Central Unemployment Relief Committee was out of funds by March of 1932. The urban and rural West shared a common economic fate: misery.

For three years under Hoover the economic casualty toll steadily mounted, with the worst casualties lodged in the numerous Hoovervilles, shantytowns, that sprang up in urban areas. Like Hoover, many western politicians tried to ignore the increasingly visible suffering. In Washington state, where industrial employment by 1932 was less than half the level of the late 1920s, the unemployed were both vulnerable and visible in a society without unemployment insurance, welfare, or even insured bank deposits. Yet the Republican governor, Roland Hartley, reacted by proclaiming, "We must stop multiplying government activities." His own government activities ended with the next election. Wyoming held to a policy of self-reliance longer than other states did, but by December 1933, Governor Leslie A. Miller admitted that self-help had failed. Surveys had revealed that thousands of Wyoming children were malnourished and poorly clothed.

Even when western state governments recognized the need for aid for the unemployed, they could not react effectively. Traditionally weak, reluctant to tax, and now nearly bankrupt by loss in revenues from the Depression, state governments were unwilling or unable to raise taxes to provide necessary aid. With one-third of the state's farmland already tax-delinquent, the unwillingness of the legislature in a state such as North Dakota to impose new taxes in the middle of the Depression was understandable, but its inaction did nothing to solve the state's problems. The Texas legislature did no better. In January 1933 it defeated a bill authorizing the issuance of bonds to fund relief efforts. In Oklahoma, Democratic Governor William ("Alfalfa Bill") Murray arrived in office as the self-proclaimed champion of the "little people"—the poor, the struggling farmer, and the unemployed city worker. Alfalfa Bill's sympathies did not extend equally to Oklahoma's blacks—he called out the national guard to enforce segregation in Oklahoma City—but he did make some attempt to relieve

Part of Seattle's Hooverville in 1931.

the suffering caused by the Depression. He got a state appropriation for emergency commodities and to provide seed for gardens. He collected money and donated part of his own salary to feed the hungry.

By 1932 the federal government was the last remaining source of aid amidst general economic disaster. Leading the drive for direct relief by the federal government was Edward P. Costigan, the junior senator from Colorado. When Hoover opposed him, a Washington political battle became, in effect, a battle between the two sides of western tradition: a self-conceived rugged individualism and the historical reality of dependence on federal aid. Hoover initially opposed Costigan's Emergency Relief and Construction Act of 1932, which was designed to grant federal loans to the states for direct relief to the destitute and for public works projects. But then, in an election year, Hoover wavered, and after having vetoed a similar law only ten days earlier, he reluctantly signed Costigan's bill. He had no need to worry about a raid on the treasury. The Reconstruction Finance Corporation (RFC), which critics called a "breadline for big business," administered the program. Despite congressional authorization of $300 million in loans, the RFC charged such high interest and accepted so few proposals that the bill yielded only about $30 million in loans at a time when there were 3 million people unemployed in the West alone.

State Intervention in the Economy

Unwilling to give the nation's poor direct aid, the Hoover administration also proved unable to aid producers who lobbied for aid. Gluts in basic western commodities—wheat, timber, silver, copper, oil, cattle, and sheep—had brought the economy to ruin, and government actions to correct the situation were tentative and ineffective. Hoover, as had Coolidge before him, opposed the McNary-Haugen Bill, but he did sign a weaker, and ultimately ineffective, substitute measure, the Agricultural Marketing Act of 1929. As malnutrition spread within the United States, farmers faced bankruptcy. The prices they received for their crops could not cover the costs of production. The United States confronted the paradox of malnourished children in a country where crops rotted in the fields.

The rhetorical devotion of cattle raisers to rugged individualism did not stop the ranchers from demanding and getting tariff restrictions on imported beef and credit assistance through Hoover's RFC. Both were ineffective solutions. Washington also offered cattlemen feed loans in 1931, but only if the government could have a lien on the cattle. Since most cattlemen had already mortgaged their cattle to bankers for earlier loans, they were unable to get the federal money.

Only in the oil industry did the government intervene effectively during the Hoover administration, and there state instead of federal action proved decisive. The conditions of production forced large oil producers to favor some type of regulation. As producers pump oil out of one section of a large oil field, changes in pressure can cause oil in other parts of the field to move and shift location. This tendency of oil to move once production begins can force all the producers in a field to pump their oil simultaneously. Drilling and pumping as fast as possible became the only protection that producers had against their neighbors. The race to produce made it economically rational to keep producing even when markets were glutted and prices were falling. To stop producing was to lose the oil. If only a few large corporations controlled a field, they might be able to reach agreements on the rate of production in order to maintain long-term stability, but when many small independents dominated a field, chaos often resulted. Unrestricted production created both oil gluts and waste. In some fields rapid production dissipated the water and gas pressure that forced the oil to rise, with the result that oil producers recovered only 5 to 10 percent of the field's contents.

The great East Texas oil field formed an object lesson in the consequences of uncontrolled production. Small producers dominated what was at the time the world's richest and largest known oil field. With each producer trying madly to capture as much oil as possible, Texas, already the world's largest oil producing region, pumped billions of barrels of oil into a depressed economy that could not absorb it. The rate of production threw the American oil industry into chaos. In 1930 high-grade crude oil sold for $1.30 a barrel. By the end of 1931 East Texas crude sold for under $0.10 a barrel, and the price later dropped even lower. Large corporations and the bigger independents demanded that the federal government intervene and establish a prorationing system under which the government would assign each producer a quota and monitor each well to make sure producers observed the quota. Prorationing was thus both a means to insure conservation and a way to fix prices by limiting production.

The large oil producers would have preferred to avoid regulation by the states;

uniform federal regulations would have covered the industry as a whole and thus regulated production nationally, but Hoover proved unwilling to act. The most Hoover would do was to suspend the issuing of oil prospecting permits on the public domain under the Mineral Leasing Act of 1920. But this suspension infuriated oil producers and politicians in the Rocky Mountain states who already were losing market shares (that is, their total percentage of the market) to cheap Texas and Oklahoma crude. It seemed unfair to them that their fields should be curtailed while unrestricted production from Texas and Oklahoma ruined the industry.

Overproduction in Texas and Oklahoma, however, became such a threat to the industry, and to the tax revenues of Texas and Oklahoma, that the state governments themselves acted. Governor Ross S. Sterling of Texas, himself a former oil company owner, had the state militia temporarily shut down all the wells in the East Texas field. Courts ruled Sterling's actions illegal because the Texas Railroad Commission, the state agency supervising the oil industry, had no authority to govern production on the basis of market demand, but Governor Sterling then went to the legislature, which gave the commission that power. The courts upheld the new law.

In Oklahoma, Governor Murray acted just as decisively. With the state already facing bankruptcy and tax revenues falling, Murray declared martial law in the oil fields and sent in the state militia to shut down the wells. In March 1932 the Supreme Court declared the Oklahoma Conservation Act constitutional. By 1934 production controls in Texas and Oklahoma had helped prices rise to about a dollar a barrel. In this case, at least, government intervention had achieved some success.

Repatriation

The great exception to the Hoover administration's unwillingness to intervene decisively in the western economy involved striking at one of the weakest and most vulnerable groups in the West: Hispanic laborers and their families. Arguing that noncitizens were both living off public relief and holding jobs that could go to American citizens, Herbert Hoover's secretary of labor, William N. Doak, announced in 1931 that he intended to deport those living in the country illegally and to give those jobs to American citizens. Ironically, the drive to expel immigrants represented one of the Hoover administration's few successful cooperative endeavors with local western governments, which were already trying to conserve scarce funds by culling the minority poor from their rolls.

Mexican immigrants in the Southwest and California became the primary target of the government's repatriation efforts, but given the nature of Mexican immigration, it was hard to tell who was in the country legally and who was liable to deportation. Many Mexicans who had entered the United States quite legally years before found it very difficult to produce documentation of their status.

Since actual deportation procedures were cumbersome and time-consuming, immigration officials sought to persuade Mexicans to depart voluntarily whenever possible. Facing as they did unemployment, poverty, and racial hostility, many did freely return to Mexico, but many others left only under coercion. The U.S. Immigration Service conducted a series of widely publicized roundups of Mexicans and Mexican Americans who had to prove their legal status or be deported. In

1931 relief agencies gave wide publicity to the raids in Los Angeles and threatened to cut Mexican immigrants off their rolls. By 1933, Los Angeles County had chartered 15 special trains to send over 12,000 Mexicans on the relief rolls back to Mexico. Various Colorado agencies and governments, using similar techniques, sent 20,000. Many of the repatriated believed that if they did not return to Mexico voluntarily, the federal government would expel them. In exchange for their fare to Mexico they promised never to return even though many of their children had been born in the United States and were thus American citizens.

Because of such tactics a limited number of deportations produced a much larger migration back to Mexico. The federal government directly secured the departure of over 82,000 Mexican immigrants between 1929 and 1935, but during the same period approximately 500,000 immigrants from Mexico repatriated. Most left the United States as a result of a campaign of fear, coercion, and deception. Luisa Moreno, a Guatemalan expatriate and labor organizer, passionately denounced their fate: "These people are not aliens—they have contributed their endurance, sacrifices, youth and labor to the Southwest. Indirectly, they have paid more taxes than all the stockholders of California's industrialized agriculture, the sugar beet companies and the large cotton interests that operate or have operated with the labor of Mexican workers."

The unnaturalized immigrant poor bore the brunt of repatriation, but Mexican Americans, too, felt the repercussions of government policy. In 1935 the governor of Colorado illegally banned foreign labor in the state. Officials began rounding up and deporting Mexicans, and with them New Mexicans who thus bore the indignity of being expelled as foreigners from areas where their ancestors had lived and traveled for centuries. In Texas the campaign against "foreigners" made it difficult for Mexican Texans as well as Mexicans to obtain relief. In San Antonio the only institution certain to provide aid to hungry Mexicans was the Catholic church. Most charities in that city tended to devote their limited resources first to the needs of the Anglo poor; blacks and Mexican Americans got what remained. These efforts against Mexicans and Mexican Americans did not create jobs or remove the pressure on relief roles. Local agencies were left with the continued necessity to cut costs, and the masses of unemployed were no more able to find work than before the deportations.

The Mounting Crisis

By 1932 the West shared a rising sense of national crisis; the poor and unemployed were no longer mute in their suffering. The signs of their discontent were everywhere. In July of 1932 western delegations joined the 25,000 World War I veterans who marched up Pennsylvania Avenue in Washington, D.C., to petition Congress for the early payment of a bonus due them in 1939. Hoover, fearing that the desperate Bonus Marchers and their families were the vanguard of a communist revolution, eventually ordered the eviction of those marchers who stayed on and camped out in Washington. Troops attacked them with bayonets and tear gas.

That same summer, Milo Reno, a sixty-five-year-old Iowa farmer, organized a farmer's boycott—the Farmers' Holiday Movement—to prevent food from going to market and thus to force prices up. A song Reno's followers sang summed up the movement's sectional bias:

> Let's call a farmers' holiday,
> A holiday let's hold;
> We'll eat our wheat and ham and eggs
> And let them eat their gold.

If listeners were unsure who constituted "them," they had only to listen to the testimony of an Oklahoma rancher before a House subcommittee: "We will march eastward, and we will cut the East off. We will cut the East off from the West. We have got the granaries; we have the hogs, the cattle, the corn, and the East has nothing but mortgages on our places. We will show them what we can do."

Reno found considerable support in the prairie and plains states. In Nebraska, farm protest leaders threatened to raze the statehouse brick by brick unless they got help, and in counties across the prairies and plains armed farmers intimidated and banished prospective bidders at court-ordered auctions of foreclosed farms. They then bought the farm for a dollar or two and returned it to the original owner.

By March 1933 the unemployment rate stood at about 30 percent, with many more working only part time. Throughout the country the state and local relief systems had broken down. Banks were collapsing, and farmers were challenging the courts.

The New Deal in the West

In the midst of this turmoil and rising sense of crisis the West joined the rest of the nation in decisively repudiating Herbert Hoover. When Franklin Delano Roosevelt won the 1932 presidential election, he carried every state in the West. In a region with weak parties, Roosevelt once more demonstrated the power of political personality. He tapped the vote of westerners impoverished and dismayed by the Depression and kept their support for the rest of his life. In what would be four successful bids for the presidency (1932–44), FDR always ran well ahead of his party in the West. He regularly secured 20 percent more votes than other Democratic candidates on the ticket. In off-year elections Democrats suffered, but in presidential years with Roosevelt on the ticket, Democratic candidates carried almost 75 percent of the western gubernatorial and Senate elections. Thanks largely to Roosevelt, the Democrats dominated the West between 1932 and 1946, winning, for example, a majority of the lower houses of state legislatures in every year except 1942. But because so much of the party's success rested on one man, the Democrats never transformed their electoral success into either a strong, disciplined regional party or strong state governments. The Democratic coalition in the West would not survive Roosevelt. By 1946 the Republicans were once more the majority party in the West.

A government that seemed distant and uncaring under Hoover became ubiquitous and almost intrusive under Roosevelt. Roosevelt made the federal government a direct dispenser of relief, a creator of jobs, and a source of capital. Few westerners in the 1930s lacked direct experience with federal programs. Beginning in 1933, Congress authorized or the president created through executive orders the Public Works Administration, the Federal Emergency Relief Administration, the Civilian Conservation Corps, the Civil Works Administration, and, after 1935, the National Youth Administration and the Works Progress Administration

Table 12
Forging the Roosevelt Coalition

Region	Democrat	Republican	Abstain	New voter
1928 to 1932 Democrat				
Mountain	93	24	24	30
Pacific	72	25	25	35
1932 to 1936 Democrat				
Mountain	77	9	25	31
Pacific	80	13	22	39
1936 to 1940 Democrat				
Mountain	87	0	28	17
Pacific	80	0	11	43
1940 to 1944 Democrat				
Mountain	81	1	9	29
Pacific	86	0	0	36

Source: Paul Kleppner, "Politics Without Parties: The Western States, 1900–1984, in Gerald D. Nash and Richard Etulain, eds., *The Twentieth Century West*. (Albuquerque: University of New Mexico Press), p. 314.

Note: All entries are weighted means of regression estimates calculated for each state. Entries are percentages of the itemized cartegory voting Democrat for president in 1932, 1936, 1940, or 1944.

(later the Work Projects Administration). These relief and public works programs represented a federal attempt to stretch a safety net under the economy. The government would catch its citizens, rescuing them from a free fall to economic disaster. A disproportionate number of the citizens it caught were westerners.

Between 1933 and 1939 the West led all other sections in per capita payments for work relief, relief, and loans. The Rocky Mountains states received $716 per capita, the Pacific Coast states $424, and the Great Plains states $380. By way of comparison, the highest-ranking nonwestern section was the Midwest, with $380 per capita. The West willingly accepted this federal help and asked for more. Pierce Williams, a Federal Emergency Relief Administration (FERA) field representative, complained that Utah—which in 1933 drew more federal relief funds per capita than any other state—was "the prize 'gimme' state of the Union."

Federal programs in the West, as elsewhere, were always a compromise between federal intentions and local political demands. The first of the federal relief agencies, the FERA, immediately became embroiled in local politics. FERA provided one dollar to the states for every three dollars contributed by the state or private charities. Western state governments desperately wanted the aid, but some state legislatures were unwilling to raise taxes or appropriate the money necessary to secure FERA contributions. In Colorado, for example, the legislature did nothing to provide the necessary matching funds. Harry Hopkins, FERA's first administrator, advanced Colorado half a million dollars a month until by the end of 1933 the federal government was bearing 83 percent of Colorado's relief effort. The state was contributing only 0.2 percent, with private charities picking up the rest. On December 31, 1933, Hopkins cut off FERA funds. The poor rioted in Denver, and armed mobs assembled to pillage food stores. Only with near anarchy threatening the city did the legislature finally increase the gas tax to provide matching relief funds.

Even when federal funds flowed smoothly into the West, their disbursement encountered political problems. For western politicians the poor were not all equally deserving. One of the first regional policy questions confronting federal relief efforts in the West as well as in the South was whether the New Deal would cooperate in discrimination against the minority poor in relief programs.

Most federal bureaucrats in the West accepted local racial attitudes; they settled for providing aid to minorities under conditions acceptable to Anglos and particularly to powerful Anglos. Equalizing relief payments would threaten the local social and economic order. Although relief payments virtually always meant a decline in the standard of living for white workers, wages paid to minority workers under the dual labor system were so low that many unemployed blacks and Hispanics actually saw their standard of living rise when they went on relief. When minority workers made the rational choice to stay on relief rather than take seasonal jobs that paid less than a living wage, many employers were furious. Under intense local political pressure in the West, FERA officials consented to relief payments that were scaled according to race. In Tucson, Arizona, in 1933, for example, relief officials divided up applicants for relief into four groups: Mexican Americans, Indians, Mexican immigrants, and Anglos. Each group received different levels of aid. In Texas local authorities made sure that relief payments to blacks were uniformly less than relief payments to whites. In California and Colorado, an individual's refusal to take an agricultural job, no matter what the wage offered, gave the state sufficient cause to terminate relief. Federal attempts to make sure that farmers paid a living wage proved far less successful than farmers' efforts to force those on relief to labor in the fields. When the Jones-Costigan Act stipulated minimum wages for sugar beet workers employed by farmers receiving payments from the Agricultural Adjustment Administration (AAA), the provisions proved easy to evade.

There was a partial exception to this pattern in New Mexico. There the New Deal, in a series of programs that paralleled attempts to revitalize Indian communities in the region, tried both to restore functioning subsistence economies and to protect the cultural integrity of the Hispanic New Mexican villages. These programs, for all their good intentions, were both doomed and contradictory. Powerful commercial livestock interests blocked attempts to restore the old communal grazing lands to the villages, while irrigation programs benefited commercial and not subsistence farmers. And as with the Indians, the New Deal wanted to preserve preindustrial village life while simultaneously converting the villagers to values that emphasized modernity and efficiency.

Roosevelt, like many Americans, was always uncomfortable with direct relief or the dole. It was, he told Congress in 1935, "in violation of the traditions of America. Work must be found for the able-bodied but destitute worker." Work relief had been the goal of a variety of early New Deal programs: the Civil Works Administration (CWA), the Civilian Conservation Corps (CCC), and the Public Works Administration (PWA). The CWA undertook projects that ranged from repairs on streets and municipal buildings to flood control in urban areas, and in some rural areas it temporarily absorbed virtually all the unemployed. But in the long run the CWA proved far less significant than the CCC, which employed over 2.5 million young men nationwide between 1932 and 1942, including 80,000 Indians, who joined a special Indian division that worked largely on the reservations.

The CCC provided a pool of labor that the Soil Conservation Service, the Forest Service, and the National Park Service could draw on for a variety of conservation projects. CCC enrollees planted hundreds of millions of trees, built tens of thousands of check dams to halt erosion, and worked in hundreds of parks. They cut fire roads and created campgrounds; they thinned timber and built fish hatcheries. They planted a long shelterbelt of trees from the Dakotas to Texas. Because CCC projects focused on the public lands, more CCC projects took place in the West than elsewhere. Per capita expenditures on the CCC nationally were $19.50 between 1933 and 1939; they were $28.50 in the Pacific Coast states and $85.80 in the mountain states.

The PWA, a relatively small agency, was responsible for the New Deal's heavy construction program, but by 1939 it had participated in over 34,000 projects, the combined costs of which were more than $6 billion. It funded, planned, and approved projects but left the actual building to others, usually private contractors.

In 1935, as part of the so-called Second New Deal, Roosevelt moved administratively to separate public work and relief. The "unemployables"— largely the aged, the incapacitated, and mothers with small children—became the administrative responsibility of the state and local governments, although subsequent New Deal legislation provided funding for unemployment insurance for the short-term unemployed, and the Social Security Act of 1935 provided social security insurance for the aged, aid to the blind, and aid to dependent children. To take care of the "employables" the New Deal embarked on a public works program administered by two new agencies: the Works Progress Administration (WPA) and the National Youth Administration (NYA).

The WPA was the largest and most important of the New Deal agencies, and it started life burdened with an all but impossible goal: taking over the burden of providing work for the mass of the able-bodied unemployed. It acted both directly, by employing the unemployed on public works projects, and indirectly, by stimulating the economy through its expenditures so that private employers took up part of the burden. By the fall of 1935 the WPA employed over 2.5 million workers, and its appropriations exceeded $2 billion. Between 1935 and 1937 unemployment declined sharply, and the WPA got much of the credit.

Like relief programs, public works programs aided minorities, but not on an equal basis with whites. In Texas and Oklahoma administrators of the CCC were hostile to black enrollees and kept many out of the program. In New Mexico minority workers enrolled in the corps, but there were occasional racial tensions and conflicts between Hispanic New Mexicans and Anglos. Although relief payments and public works jobs did not flow equally to the impoverished minority communities of the West, that minorities received aid at all made the whole relief system suspect to many whites living in areas with large minority populations. They believed that any government aid to minority communities made members of those communities unwilling to accept their designated status at the bottom of the dual labor system.

In the West these various New Deal programs did much to change the face of the region. The WPA, working in close cooperation with local public agencies,

This CCC tree-planting crew in Colorado was but one of thousands in
the West during the Depression.

built bridges, reservoirs, irrigation systems, sewage treatment plants, schools, and
playgrounds. It employed a variety of skilled workers and loaned some of them to
other agencies to build or remodel public buildings and to construct public works
that ranged from dams to airports. It employed male white-collar workers for
administrative jobs, and it sponsored federal arts projects. The WPA also employed women, although virtually all of them were segregated into doing sewing
or clerical and other "women's work."

By later standards, the amount expended in these New Deal programs seems astonishingly low. On a per capita basis the WPA, for example, spent only $15 annually in the West between 1935 and 1939. All New Deal expenditures for relief, public works, and loans for the country as a whole came to only $66 per person annually between 1933 and 1939. Yet even these sums had a significant effect on an impoverished West. In California, for example, federal expenditures in 1930 amounted to less than 5 percent of the state's personal income. By the end of the New Deal they had risen to 10 percent. The percentages were probably even higher in the smaller and poorer states of the West.

Restructuring the Economy

Placing a net under the crumbling economic structure still left that structure unrepaired and liable to collapse. Roosevelt and the Democrats debated the extent to which they should try to repair or alter the economic framework itself. Leaving it alone seemed only to guarantee that more and more economic casualties would plummet into the net, threatening the government's ability to preserve the net itself.

The government's most far-reaching attempts to restructure the economy came in agriculture. New Deal agricultural reforms were, in some ways, antithetical to the goals of the relief effort. In a hungry nation the government pursued policies to raise food prices. It acted in ways that strengthened large farmers and hurt small farmers, pushing them off the land and onto relief. Not always intentionally, federal agricultural programs amounted to a sort of economic triage. They gave comfort to the least badly hurt, gave life-saving aid to the badly hurt, and did little for those in the worst shape. The farmers who dominated the new economy were usually the same ones who had dominated the old.

New Deal efforts in the rural West focused on the Great Plains, where in the 1930s ecological and economic disaster had met and merged. During the years between 1910 and 1930, Great Plains farmers had begun to create an ecological time bomb. In the early 1930s that bomb exploded, with the agricultural market providing the powder for the blast. A booming market for wheat during World War I had induced farmers to plow up much of the Great Plains, stripping the land of its native grasses. Falling prices for wheat during the twenties meant that farmers needed more wheat to get by, so they broke still more new land. In good times and bad, the logic of the market dictated increased production, and increased production left the land bare when drought returned, as it always did, to the Great Plains. During the "dirty thirties" drought came with a vengeance. Drought became serious on the northern plains of Montana and the Dakotas in 1931, and thereafter it gripped different sections of the plains for the remainder of the decade. It was the worst on the southern plains. There it spawned the Dust Bowl.

The most severe of the dust storms that gave the Dust Bowl its name roared over the plains during the spring of 1935. The storms peaked on April 14, 1935: Black Sunday. A floating, swirling curtain of dust created by winds in Colorado and Kansas turned daylight to dark. The dirt coated people's mouths, lungs, and food. Cattle suffocated and died as the fallout of settling dust reached an estimated 4.7 tons per acre in western Kansas. Not all the dust from these storms settled on the West; sucked into the jet stream, dust from the plains fell in Chicago, New York, and Washington, D.C., and even on ships at sea.

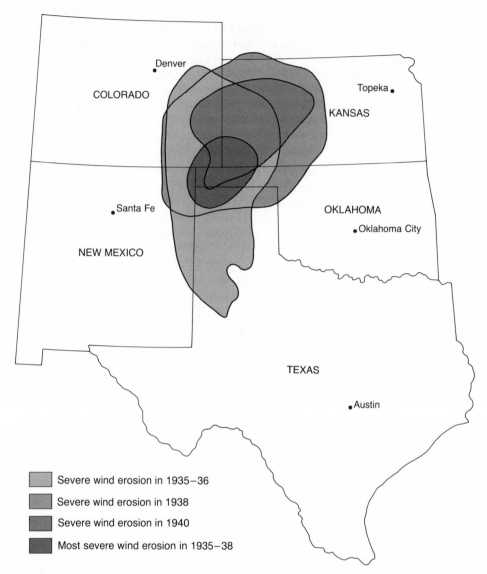

Extent of the Dust Bowl, 1935–40. From Donald Worster, *Dust Bowl* (New York: Oxford University Press, 1988), p. 30.

In the midst of such a severe and persistent drought, normal farming could not continue. Some scientists and some New Deal administrators in the U.S. Department of Agriculture (USDA) thought the dust storms were evidence that much of the Great Plains should never have been cultivated. Convinced that active federal intervention was necessary to save both land and people, New Deal bureaucrats went to work on the plains with a missionary fervor.

To reduce grazing pressure on the remaining grasslands, the Drought Relief Service (DRS) between June 1934 and January 1935 bought up more than 8 million cattle. The federal government briefly became the largest cattle owner in the world. The DRS shot sick cattle and those too weak to transport, but it retained others for fattening, slaughter, and distribution. The DRS made 25 percent of its purchases in Texas alone and another 20 percent in North and South Dakota.

After reducing cattle numbers, the government under other programs paid the cattlemen to defer grazing on damaged pastures, to manage their water more efficiently, and to stabilize their herds to help end the glut of cattle. The government, too, loaned cattlemen and farmers money to feed their remaining cattle. In the words of one historian, "Government emergency programs literally saved the cattlemen." Without federal aid the plains states might have witnessed a collapse of the cattle industry on the scale of the late 1880s.

There was a price for this help, of course: the extension of federal control. In 1934, Congress passed the Taylor Grazing Act, which finally brought stock raising on the public domain under federal management. As in the national forests, the result was not so much federal dictation as much as a joint partnership between federal agencies and the largest users of the land. Although administered by a new Grazing Service, the act allowed significant power to the livestock owners, particularly after 1939, when Congress added local advisory boards to each grazing district. The larger stock owners quickly came to dominate these boards.

Getting large numbers of cattle off the plains was merely a prelude to the more difficult task of trying to get more grass on the plains. During the early days of the New Deal many scientists and federal bureaucrats shared the conviction that grazing was the optimum use for the plains. Once grasses covered the plains, managed grazing would keep them covered, and the grass would prevent the dust storms.

The belief that the Great Plains should be grasslands created a dilemma. If,

This dust storm in Prowers County, Colorado, in 1937 captures the terrifying power of the Dust Bowl.

as the administrators believed, farming had caused the Dust Bowl, should the government not encourage most farmers to abandon the plains? Under Henry Wallace, the secretary of agriculture, the USDA proposed taking some western farmland permanently out of cultivation and putting it under grass or forest, but in the end the department devoted little money to the project and retired relatively little land from farms. Instead of the 75 million acres that it sought, the Land Utilization Project bought only about 11.3 million acres of submarginal lands, two-thirds of it on the Great Plains and in the Southwest.

The government concentrated the bulk of its efforts on taking land temporarily out of production. In order to reduce crop surpluses, the AAA paid millions of dollars to hard-pressed farmers to get them not to grow what they could not sell. Being paid not to produce cut against the grain of many western farmers, but without the payments many of their farms would have failed. In what is probably an apocryphal story attributed variously to a Mormon bishop and a southern preacher, the bishop decided that being paid not to produce wheat was sinful, so he planted all he was able. He planted, the sky darkened, and it began to rain. When lightning struck the bishop's Utah field, he took it as a sign that the Lord favored the AAA, and he enthusiastically agreed to sign up. Most of the western farmers who complained about the program did not even wait for the next thunderstorm to join. As Lawrence Svobida, a young Kansas farmer, remembered, "There were mouthy individuals who seized every opportunity to run down the entire program . . . condemning it as useless, crooked, revolutionary, or dictatorial; but . . . when the first AAA payments were made available, shortly before Christmas, these same wordy critics made a beeline to the courthouse. They jostled and fell over each other in their mad scramble to be the first in line to receive the allotment money."

With attempts to turn croplands into grasslands a failure, and with AAA cutbacks on production doing nothing to alter long-term land use patterns, the government gradually shifted to another tactic. The USDA made a concerted effort to change farming practices on lands left in production. Spearheading this effort, both on the Great Plains and elsewhere, was the Soil Conservation Service (SCS). The SCS set up demonstration projects and conducted research. It preached a gospel heard before on the Great Plains: with the proper techniques, farmers could make the Great Plains yield as dependably and reliably as more humid lands. Hugh Hammond Bennett, the head of the SCS, became the Gifford Pinchot of soil conservation. In the process of spreading the gospel and demonstrating its fruits, SCS efforts pumped additional federal aid into the region and created yet another ubiquitous rural organization, the soil conservation district, which could make binding conservation regulations.

Taken together, these programs temporarily changed how farmers managed their farms. Farmers retired land and accepted government subsidies when that proved more profitable than growing crops for a glutted market. They adopted Bennett's suggestion of replacing wheat with soil-conserving grasses or legumes, but usually only when the government paid them to do so under the Soil Conservation and Domestic Allotment Act of 1936. They accepted technical solutions such as contour plowing and terracing, which threw up ridges of soil to slow the runoff and give it more chance to soak into the earth. Contouring and terracing, however, required a trained surveyor, special machines, and CCC labor. The farmers received SCS aid in putting terraces in place.

When the rains returned and markets recovered during World War II, however, farmers largely abandoned what the SCS had with so much effort induced them to accept. They reverted to their old ways. The anticonservation mood grew so strong by 1947 that Secretary of Agriculture Clinton Anderson accused farmers on the western Great Plains of "soil murder." The government's programs had become a means of relief in bad times and something to be ignored in good times. On the plains, fiercely competitive farming continued, and farm units grew larger and larger.

What happened on the Great Plains was in many ways typical of western farming in general during the 1930s. The New Deal farm programs restricted the sway of the market, but they did not challenge the market logic of farming. The Roosevelt administration responded with a program which, in the words of its leading historian, was "built around commodities instead of people." The Agricultural Adjustment Act of 1933 created the basic New Deal farm program— a program of planned scarcity. The government paid farmers not to produce; the government set minimum prices on key commodities and then bought and stored surplus crops to hold up the price.

Because it was more concerned with commodities than with the people who grew them, the AAA helped agriculture but hurt many small farmers. Under the AAA, those who retired the most acres got the largest payments; the act thus inevitably helped big farmers more than small farmers and landowners more than tenants. The AAA assumed most of the landowners' risks. It protected them from overproduction, paid rents on their retired lands, and loaned them money at reduced rates.

Despite attempts to protect them, tenants and sharecroppers bore the brunt of the reform. In the cotton lands of Oklahoma, Texas, and Arkansas tenants ran more than 60 percent of the farms, usually farming for shares and getting a portion of the crop in return for their labor. This exploitative agriculture left much of the red earth of southeastern Oklahoma gullied and raw. By the 1930s the land produced only half the cotton it had a generation earlier, yielding instead a flourishing crop of poverty and misery. When the AAA offered cash payments in return for taking land out of production, landowners eagerly accepted. The cotton belt of Oklahoma and Texas shrank to half its former size. Many farmers took the AAA's cash payments, bought tractors, hired laborers and, illegally, evicted their former tenants. Looking back, an Oklahoma landowner remembered: "In '34 I had I reckon four renters and I didn't make anything. I bought tractors on the money the government give me and get shet o' my renters. You'll find it everywhere all over the country thataway. I did everything the government said— except keep my renters. The renters have been having it this way ever since the government come in. They've got their choice—California or WPA."

The "Okies"

Evicted tenants joined Dust Bowl farmers, oil field workers, and innumerable others in Texas and Oklahoma as casualties of the Depression. Moving in search of work, they usually went only to the next town or county. A few attempted to renew their ties to the land through two programs the government set up to help small farmers: the Resettlement Administration and the Farm Security Administration. But these programs encountered intense opposition from larger farmers and their spokespeople, who feared that the federal government, by aiding marginal farmers and tenants, would simultaneously create competitors for established farmers and deprive them of potential laborers. Few of the poor obtained land; the choice remained the WPA or California.

Those who chose California were not making a new choice. The roughly 300,000 people from Missouri, Oklahoma, Texas, and Arkansas who headed to California during the 1930s were doing nothing unusual. California was an established destination of a longstanding labor migration from the region. More than half the migrants (not all of whom were poor) already had relatives in the state, and in normal times they would have arrived unnoticed and uncommented on. Although the migrants are often presumed to be victims of the Dust Bowl, only a minority of them were farmers, and only a small fraction of them came from the Dust Bowl proper. Blue-collar workers and small businessmen made up the bulk of the migration. As often as not, they went to cities rather than the countryside. Although hard hit by the Depression, California still offered more jobs, higher wages, and higher relief payments than the states from which the migrants came.

To Californians the arrival of these migrants from the southern edges of the West came to seem less a normal migration than an invasion. Historically, Californians have not proven generous in hard times. They had earlier excluded Chinese, Japanese, and Mexican immigrants; now they tried to close their borders to white, native-born Americans. In 1936 the Los Angeles police chief, James Davis, worried about homeless transients flocking to his city, sent police officers to set up a "bum blockade" on the state's borders until national ridicule and legal challenges forced him to abandon the effort after only six weeks. With the unemployment rate and relief loads dropping, Los Angeles and other urban areas eventually absorbed about half the migration from the Southwest without much turmoil or notice. The migration into rural areas created greater opposition.

Residents of the San Joaquin Valley regarded the migrants as a curse. Arriving largely between 1935 and 1937, the "Okies" gathered in miserable ditchside communities and in makeshift slums that seemed to spring up overnight. And unlike previous agricultural laborers in California fields, most "Okies" did not migrate and follow the harvest. They built their Little Oklahomas and stayed. Their visibility made their numbers seem greater than they were.

The southwestern migrants doubly offended the older residents of the San Joaquin Valley by both draining local resources and baring to the nation the exploitative nature of California agriculture. When the harvesting season ended and they could not find jobs, those migrants who had met California's one-year residency requirement went on relief. They provided a new burden to the health, education, and welfare resources of rural counties, although not a burden disproportionate to their numbers.

The "Okies" discovered that the caste system of California fields regarded those who did stoop labor as unalterably inferior. By becoming field workers, "Okies" in effect lost their "whiteness" for many rural Californians. The same stereotypes of laziness, dirtiness, lack of sexual restraint, and irresponsibility that western whites had applied to nonwhites were now applied to "Okies." A sign in a San Joaquin Valley theater summarized the new immigrants' plight: "Negroes and 'Okies' upstairs." The "Okies" were deeply racist themselves. Many of them had left the South to avoid being reduced to doing "niggers' work," but this loyalty to southern values only fed a second source of scorn: a general disdain for poor white southerners, the "poor white trash" of regional stereotypes.

The migrants seemed a potential threat to the whole rural order. Unlike earlier Indian, Asian, and Mexican workers, "Okies" were citizens. The government could not deport them (although one California congressmen eventually suggested shipping them to Brazil). Because they were white, and because they stayed in the San Joaquin Valley rather than disappearing following the harvest, the "Okies" attracted sympathy from whites outside rural California. When urban reporters coming to cover floods in 1938 encountered the squalid migrant camps, the "Okies" burst into the California newspapers. John Steinbeck's story of the Joads in *The Grapes of Wrath* and the movie that followed, Carey McWilliams's *Factories in the Field*, and Dorothea Lange's remarkable photographs all kept them before the public. Senator Robert La Follette's hearings on farm labor in California in 1939 and the Farm Security Administration efforts to help them made the migrants the focus of an often bitter national debate.

By 1938 even the large farmers regarded the migrants as a burden and a threat. The "Okies" seemed open to organization both by liberal Democrats looking for votes in a conservative Republican area and by organized labor even as they became less necessary as a labor supply. When the so-called second Agricultural Adjustment Act introduced major new crop controls for California cotton, California cotton acreage declined by nearly 45 percent between 1937 and 1938, creating an oversupply of workers. Large farmers and their political allies restricted relief to the migrants, and California even attempted to enforce a law making it illegal to bring indigent people into the state before the Supreme Court struck down all laws interfering with free passage between the states. The "Okies" were white, but they came to see firsthand what the dual labor system meant.

The national debate over the "Okies" changed little. The powerful Associated Farmers of California had already become, in the words of Senator Elmer Thomas, an impregnable empire, and the empire withstood the efforts of both unions and the government to organize the "Okies." Only when the outbreak of World War II increased the demand for labor did the migrants once more seem less a curse than a blessing to the rural elite of California's interior valleys. The migrants who remained often rose to supervisory positions over nonwhites whom the farmers recruited to take the place of the "Okies" who went to work in the factories.

Other migrations into the West during the period brought neither the conflict nor the notice of the "Okies." Small farmers dispossessed by drought and the Depression moved from the northern Great Plains into western Oregon and Washington, where drought was unknown and lands were cheap and readily available. Many attempted to settle the logged-over lands and in doing so participated in a much quieter ecological and social disaster in western Washington and Oregon.

The New Deal and Western Development

The La Follette committee denounced the labor practices of corporate agriculture within its California "empire," but one branch of the federal government was denouncing an empire that other branches of the government were helping to expand. By the late 1930s the Bureau of Reclamation had forged a profitable alliance with California farmers. The bureau was a comparative failure until the late 1920s, irrigating a disappointingly small region of the West. But during the New Deal it broke out of its older and narrower mandate to irrigate small farms and embarked on a series of gigantic projects many of which benefited agribusiness and industrial interests. The agency continued to provide water to small farmers and ranchers and depended on them for political support, but it had tied its fate to larger farmers. It became the builder of multipurpose dams that were intended to control entire river systems. The bureau's developments moved from thousands of acres to thousands of square miles.

The Colorado, the wildest and most isolated of the major western rivers, succumbed first. The bureau began Boulder Dam, later called Hoover Dam, during Herbert Hoover's administration. Designed to prevent floods on the lower river, provide irrigation water for the Imperial Valley, generate electricity for Los Angeles and southern Arizona, and supply domestic water for southern California, the dam enjoyed widespread western support. Hoover, however, worried that the dam made the government a competitor of private companies, and he came out in opposition to public power and the building of lines to transmit power from Boulder Dam. Most westerners, who believed their future lay with cheap public power, were outraged. Hoover's defeat in 1932 by Roosevelt, who sided with the public power advocates, ended the dispute.

Although later renamed for Hoover, the dam under any name was a symbol of the New Deal in the West. Completed with PWA funds in 1935, Boulder Dam transformed the Bureau of Reclamation into a major developmental agency with resources its founders had never envisioned. Once restricted to revenues generated from public land sales and from costs recouped from the farmers who settled on project lands, the bureau began to receive large annual appropriations. And the more freely the appropriations flowed, the less freely did western rivers flow. Through the bureau the federal government had emerged as the most powerful authority in western water management. How it managed that water would do much to determine the shape of the West's future.

Legally, the Bureau of Reclamation was still bound by the 1902 Reclamation Act, which mandated a 160-acre limit on farms served by bureau projects. Later legislation authorizing the giant Grand Coulee Dam reduced the limit to 80 acres for that project. But in practice such requirements were null and void. The water from Boulder Dam and other bureau projects flowed to much larger farms: the factories in the fields that dominated California and Arizona agriculture. The All-American Canal, authorized in 1928 but completed during the New Deal, served the large farmers of the Imperial Valley. By 1938 the canal, completed at a cost of approximately $24 million, was capable of carrying a flow equal to that of the Potomac River. It opened up an additional one million acres of desert land. The irrigation districts that received the water promised to repay, without interest, the total cost of the canal over a period of 40 years. Such interest-free loans represented a massive subsidy to the private growers that the canal served.

The success of Boulder Dam provided the bureau with the opportunity to gain appropriations for other dams. The bureau undertook the Central Valley Project (CVP), an effort to harness the Sacramento River and its tributaries that dwarfed the Boulder Dam undertaking. The idea for the CVP had originated during the 1920s when drought, quarrels over water rights, and lack of sufficient storage facilities had endangered agriculture in the Central Valley of California. Robert A. Marshall of the U.S. Geological Survey had begun to think in terms of a master plan for the valley. Under the plan, the state could supposedly store and allocate water so efficiently that not only would current needs be met but farmers also could put an additional 12 million acres of land under irrigation. Marshall proposed multipurpose dams that would generate power as well as store water for irrigation. Sales of electricity and domestic water to municipalities would underwrite the cost of irrigation. His report became the basis of a state water plan in the 1920s. The state, however, lacked the resources to tackle a project of this size, and it was the Bureau of Reclamation which took up Marshall's basic plan and began the CVP in 1935.

As an irrigation measure the CVP, like the All-American Canal, primarily served the large factory farmers, but as Marshall had planned, the project was not simply for irrigation. In storing water and transferring it to the more arid southern valley, the CVP also provided electricity, flood control, and municipal water supplies. When completed, the total cost of the project came to $2.3 billion. The government, the municipalities that received water, and the buyers of electric power bore the major share of the cost.

The alliance between large agricultural producers and the Bureau of Reclamation was proving far more beneficial to the bureau than had its earlier league with small farmers. That the larger farmers did not pay for the water did not concern the bureau. The economic importance of agriculture in California gave large farmers great influence on California's congressional delegation, and that influence, in turn, could be turned into appropriations for the bureau's projects.

Projects on the scale of Boulder Dam and the CVP naturally attracted competitors within the bureaucracy. The Army Corps of Engineers, which had control over projects on the rivers to improve navigation or stop flooding, had managed to get only a small share of the CVP. But on the Columbia River the Corps of Engineers had plans of its own. A report issued during the Hoover administration had recommended ten multipurpose dams on the Columbia, but Hoover had vetoed the proposal as too costly. Franklin Roosevelt, however, promised new power projects on the Columbia, and the report took on new life. In the competition to build these dams the Corps of Engineers secured the Bonneville Dam, which began to generate electricity in 1937. But the Bureau of Reclamation secured the greatest prize of all: the Grand Coulee Dam.

Completed in 1941, Grand Coulee was the largest concrete structure built up to that time and created a lake 150 miles long. It threatened, however, to become a white elephant. In an administration trying desperately to reduce farm surpluses, a dam that would make possible the cultivation of millions more acres was a potential embarrassment that Congress avoided by not authorizing construction of any irrigation canals to carry water from the dam until the mid-1940s. The dam likewise generated inexpensive electrical power—so much power that its output by World War II exceeded that of the entire Tennessee Valley Authority— but this generating capacity existed in a region where there were few industries to use its electricity.

For the dam to be of any use at all, the electricity it generated had to get to

Grand Coulee Dam on the Columbia was one of the largest of the federal projects that began to transform the West in the 1930s.

users, and how this was to be done sparked bitter conflict. Private utilities had contested the coming of public power in the Pacific Northwest; the public utility districts of the region just as vigorously urged it. The triumph of the utilities and damming of the Columbia, however, simply transferred the battle to the bureaucracy; both the Bureau of Reclamation and the Corps of Engineers wanted to control the electricity the dams generated. Congress gave it to neither agency. Instead, in 1937 Congress created the Bonneville Power Administration (BPA), which eventually controlled the power from both Bonneville and Grand Coulee dams.

Under J. D. Ross, the former superintendent of Seattle City Light, the BPA set out to create a system that would deliver cheap electricity at a single rate throughout the Northwest. Ross's goal was to create the "widest possible use" for Bonneville's power and to insure the triumph of public power across the Pacific Northwest. He made the BPA the foundation of public power in the region by giving preference to municipalities and cooperatives who wished to purchase power and by creating new public utility districts to generate and market power throughout Oregon and Washington. By 1952, 70 percent of the region's hydroelectric power came from locally or federally owned public power installations. Ross, too, moved to turn the embarrassing surplus of power into an asset by using it to attract industry to the region.

The construction of Grand Coulee and its smaller neighbors provided what little strength the economy of the Pacific Northwest possessed during the 1930s; their completion created the basis for a more broadly based economy. Building the dams employed tens of thousands of workers and pumped so much money into the region that between 1933 and 1939 Washington ranked first in per capita federal expenditures. When completed, the dams provided the cheapest electricity in the United States, and the BPA put that power under public control. Cheap power eventually did attract industry, and industry allowed the region to begin to escape its dependent status as an extractive economy whose raw materials went elsewhere for processing and manufacture.

Marvels, however, come at a cost. Bonneville, Grand Coulee, and their numerous smaller successors reduced the Columbia, which Americans had long celebrated as symbol of the nation and the West, to a series of lakes. The Columbia no longer ran mightily to the sea; instead, the river ran between its dams like a circus lion jumping through hoops. On the Columbia above the Grand Coulee Dam, where spawning salmon had once run in the millions, the salmon ran no more. The engineers who designed the dam had given no thought to the migration of salmon up the river, and the fish vanished from the upper Columbia.

The New Deal and Business in the West

Western businesses would benefit from this massive rearrangement of the West's rivers during World War II and the years that followed, but the New Deal had begun providing them with less spectacular aid during the 1930s. It did so partially by helping business regulate its own production and by providing business with critical funds, markets, and contracts. Central to this effort was Jesse H. Jones, a Houston developer, banker, financier, and oil man whose power in Texas politics and whose Texas-sized ego led Roosevelt privately to refer to him as Jesus H. Jones. As the not completely trusted head of the RFC under Roosevelt, Jones spent billions to help save banks, businesses, and farms from bankruptcy.

Unlike the Hoover administration, the Roosevelt administration was willing to try to shore up the extractive industries of the West. New Deal officials, particularly during Roosevelt's first term, gladly acted as brokers between government and economic interest groups to provide the regulation and aid each group required. The oil industry especially desired sympathetic regulation. By 1933 the Oklahoma and Texas experience had so severely shaken the industry's major corporations that they were willing to consent to the appointment of an oil czar to control overproduction on a national scale. The Roosevelt administration, however, wanted to couple regulation of production with an attempt to force the major companies to sell off their pipelines. Since the companies wanted regulation in order to strengthen their own position against their smaller competitors, not weaken it, they were unwilling to make such a deal. They withdrew their support for the regulatory measure, which then failed in Congress. In place of a special regulatory agency the administration established the weaker Petroleum Advisory Board under the National Recovery Administration in 1933. With Secretary of the Interior Harold Ickes as petroleum administrator, the board did cooperate with state regulatory agencies to help reduce production and stabilize the industry. Ickes allocated production quotas to the states, which then assigned a quota to each field, thus controlling overproduction. When the Supreme Court ruled the

National Recovery Act unconstitutional, Congress passed the Connally Act. It created the Interstate Oil Compact Commission, which allowed prorationing (that is, the assignment of quotas) in the oil-producing states to continue but made both prorationing and regulation largely a matter for state and not federal concern.

In hard-rock mining the New Deal also confronted a situation in which overproduction threatened the health of a key western extractive industry. Here, however, the government dealt with the issue not by restricting production but instead by buying the product. Burton K. Wheeler of Montana and Elmer Thomas of Oklahoma resurrected the old Populist cause of currency inflation through silver. Roosevelt was unpersuaded, but he needed the support of Rocky Mountain senators on other issues, and they needed government purchases of silver to keep the mines open. As a result, the administration backed the Silver Purchase Act of 1934, under which the U.S. Treasury purchased 287 million ounces of silver, nearly the entire production of western mines, at prices well above market value. Because silver usually occurs in combination with copper, zinc, and lead, the government silver purchases allowed the mines to operate even though the copper, zinc, and lead sold at a loss. Without the profits from government purchases of silver, the mining industry would have largely closed down.

While the New Deal rescued existing industries and created the basis for future ones, it also brought prosperity to some previously minor companies. With World War II and the growth of defense industries, the federal-corporate partnership would dominate the western economy, but this partnership had its immediate roots in the numerous public works projects of the New Deal. Unlike federal agencies such as the Tennessee Valley Authority, which chose to hire and supervise its own workers to construct dams, the Bureau of Reclamation, working with the PWA, hired private contractors.

The company that won the contract for the first great western construction project of the Depression era was a joint corporation known as the Six Companies. It consisted of Bechtel & Kaiser and MacDonald & Kahn, both San Francisco construction companies; Morrison-Knudson Corporation of Boise; the Utah Construction Company in Salt Lake City; and J. F. Shea and the Pacific Bridge Corporation of Portland. Utah Construction and Morrison-Knudson had already benefited handsomely from federal contracts, but individually these companies remained too small to raise the necessary capital from eastern banks to bid on the Boulder Dam contracts. When combined, however, the Six Companies raised the necessary funds, underbid the nearest competitors, and got the largest labor contract ever awarded by the federal government up to that time. They made a profit of $10 million.

Boulder Dam launched the Six Companies on a career that would create much of the basic infrastructure and large industrial plants of the West. Sometimes they operated as a group, sometimes in smaller combinations, sometimes individually; often they worked in cooperation with the Bureau of Reclamation. The Six Companies won contracts for Bonneville Dam, Grand Coulee Dam, and numerous smaller projects. Henry Kaiser, guiding the Six Companies' efforts in Washington, became the most sagacious business operator in the nation's capital. Kaiser, whose rotund frame concealed his incredible energy, worked 18 to 20 hours a day and assiduously cultivated prominent New Deal officials. Kaiser became a man who learned to turn even failures into opportunities. When the Six Companies barely lost the contract for Shasta Dam, Kaiser turned around and offered the lowest bid on cement for the project even though he did not own a cement plant. He created Permanente Cement and met the contract.

In the New Deal's enthusiasm for public works projects Kaiser and other members of the Six Companies had found the route to vast fortunes for themselves, and the West had found the route to federal financing of a basic western infrastructure. The government not only provided cheap water and electricity in a region that lacked both, but it also created through its contracts large western corporations that would launch even larger government-corporate industrial projects during World War II.

Labor

Henry Kaiser had his equivalents in the labor movement—men who rose on the tide of change transforming the West. It is hard to imagine two union leaders more different than Dave Beck and Harry Bridges. Bridges, an Australian immigrant and a communist sympathizer, rose to lead the West Coast branch of the International Longshoreman's Union. Rigidly honest and incorruptible, he drew only a nominal salary even when he could have gotten far more. In a struggle over the organization of the Seattle waterfront he became the bitter rival of Beck, a resident of Seattle since the age of four who extolled the virtues of capitalism, profits, and private property while accumulating a fortune in real estate. Beck was the head of the powerful West Coast teamsters and ultimately headed the entire Teamsters union. Beck's greed eventually exceeded his sagacity, and he served time for income tax evasion.

Dave Beck rose to power because he recognized the opportunities that motor transport presented to union organizers as well as business people. Public road building in the twentieth century subsidized trucking firms just as land grants had subsidized nineteenth-century railroads. And now trucks were breaking the power of the railroads. Beck, who started out organizing Seattle laundry drivers in the 1920s, saw that by organizing truck drivers he could put his hands at the throat of most businesses. Beck was a persuasive organizer, but he was ready to supplement verbal persuasion with threats and beatings by goon squads when the occasion required. Thugs and violence, however, were the customary and unimaginative responses of hack labor leaders and ruthless businesspeople; Beck's real genius was his recognition that it was cutthroat competition in the laundry business that forced employers to cut labor costs. If Beck could help reduce competition, then surviving businesses could pay higher wages. Beck moved first to remove labor as a competitive factor between businesses. He equalized labor costs by forcing the employers to pay a standard wage, leaving them free to compete in other areas: service, advertising, and efficiency. He got the laundries to agree to standard labor costs by "organizing the bosses." Beck encouraged the employers to form regional trade associations that would negotiate a single contract with the Teamsters. He even offered to subsidize the trade associations. Some businesses, of course, refused to join, but they then found that no truck driver would handle their products. When the new employers' associations complained that they could not raise wages, Beck sought ways to help them raise their prices and profits. And if this meant shutting down some of the weaker firms to provide larger markets for the survivors, Beck was prepared to withdraw Teamsters drivers from the firms sentenced to die for the good of all.

Building on such successes, Beck moved in the 1920s to organize long-distance highway truck drivers and then used these truckers to organize in an ever-expanding circle. By controlling long-distance truckers, Beck could cut off recalcitrant businesses from their markets and suppliers. By the mid-1930s Beck had launched a campaign to organize the teamsters in the entire state of California. When the powerful open shop forces in Los Angeles moved to resist him, he shut down all truck movements in and out of southern California. Resistance collapsed within days. By 1938, Beck controlled the 11-state Western Conference of Teamsters and was one of the most powerful labor leaders in the nation.

Harry Bridges, too, led a union that controlled a bottleneck in the transportation system—the longshoremen—but followed a very different route to power. As a 19-year-old Australian immigrant of Irish descent, Bridges entered into the Irish-German labor bastion of San Francisco in 1920 just as it was about to fall to the forces of the open shop. By the 1920s, with their own unions broken, longshoremen in San Francisco had to join company unions to obtain work, and even then they got work only through the "shape-up." Congregating every morning near the Ferry Building at the foot of Market Street, they waited, as Bridges later put it, "like a bunch of sheep," hoping that a foreman would pick them up for a day's work. Longshoremen called the Embarcadero, the site of the shape-up, the "slave market." And with the Depression, conditions got worse as legions of unemployed joined in the competition for declining numbers of jobs.

In 1933 in Section 7(a) of the National Industrial Recovery Act, the federal government for the first time in American history guaranteed the right of workers to organize unions. The law itself later proved to lack teeth, but up and down the waterfronts of the Pacific Coast it inspired one of the great rank-and-file crusades in American labor history. The San Francisco waterfront became the dynamic center of the strike. The International Longshoremen's Association demanded an end to the shape-up and its replacement by a union hiring hall. When despite government efforts at mediation the union and the employers could reach no agreement, the longshoremen walked out on May 9, 1934, shutting down not only San Francisco but also every other major port on the Pacific Coast except San Pedro. They remained out for 83 days. First sailors and then Teamsters joined them.

It was a strike that the old, corrupt leadership of the ILA tried to discourage, but Bridges rose from the ranks to displace them. It was a strike that employers, vigilante squads, and police tried to break. Their efforts culminated in the battle of Rincon Hill, when strikers, fighting with what observers called "insane courage," battled police trying to open the port. In a bloody contest of rocks and bottles against billy clubs, tear gas, and bullets, two workers died. But violence added support for the strike. Tens of thousands of marchers, "flowing like cooling lava," followed the caskets of the dead workers down Market Street. Bystanders, above all, remembered the silence of the marchers; the only sound was tramping feet echoing ominously off the buildings lining the street. The governor declared martial law, and the unions declared a general strike. In the Bay Area, 130,000 workers walked out. The crisis ended with binding federal arbitration, which

An International Longshoremen's Association picket line on the Embarcadero, San Francisco, May 1934.

became a victory for the union. Bridges had emerged as the unchallenged leader of Pacific Coast longshoremen.

By the late 1930s these very different labor leaders came into direct conflict. Bridges, whose union eventually joined the new Congress of Industrial Organizations (CIO) and became the International Longshoremen's and Warehousemen's Union (ILWU), and Beck, whose Teamsters belonged to the American Federation of Labor (AF of L), clashed as each union sought to expand. Bridges and the ILWU tried to "march inland" to organize warehousemen; Beck and the Teamsters challenged Bridges for control of the Seattle waterfront.

The future only widened the gulf that divided Beck and Bridges. Both Roosevelt and Truman asked Beck to serve as secretary of labor. The only personal attention Bridges received from government officials came from the army of FBI agents investigating his communist connections. The arrests, red baiting, and threats of deportation never shook Bridges's support within the union. "He may be Red Harry," the longshoremen said, "but he's our Red Harry." The federal government eventually imprisoned Beck and tried to deport Bridges, but it was nonetheless the government that had helped resurrect powerful western unions.

John Collier and the Indian New Deal

The increase in federal activity in the West during the New Deal penetrated even Indian reservations. In the 1933 the Bureau of Indian Affairs (BIA) was an unlikely place to look for innovation and change. It was the oldest of the western bureaucracies and the least dynamic. It had a legacy of mismanagement, corruption, and failure unmatched anywhere in the government; the bureau's efforts to assimilate Indians through education, the allotment of reservation lands, and the prohibition of Indian religions and customs had led to failures obvious not only to Indian peoples themselves but also to white reformers. A 1933 CWA study found that 49 percent of Indians on allotted reservations were landless, forced to rent or live with relatives, and the remainder held lands the per capita value of which amounted to only about $800. Indians experienced the deepest and most widespread poverty of any group in the United States, had an infant mortality rate twice that of the white population, and continued to suffer government intrusions into their family life and their religious life that the courts would not have tolerated among any other group of American citizens.

By 1932 the problems with the BIA were widely known. The Meriam Report, prepared by the Brookings Institution in 1928, had harshly criticized the BIA, and the publicity generated by the report had left the BIA a much-beleaguered agency. Leading the attackers was John Collier. A reformer and community organizer, Collier had become interested in the Pueblos as a result of his association with that branch of the New York artistic and intellectual community that took up residence at Taos, New Mexico. In the 1920s he had led the battle against the Bursum Bill, which threatened to deprive the Pueblos of much of their land.

The battle over the Bursum Bill established Collier nationally as an advocate of Indian rights. In 1933, when Roosevelt named him commissioner of Indian affairs, the agency's leading critic suddenly became its director. With a reformer's zeal, Collier sought to reverse the course of American Indian policy. He wanted to end forced assimilation and to help reorganize Indian tribes whose tribal governments the United States had suppressed. His vehicle for doing this was the Indian Reorganization Act (IRA) of 1934, a complicated piece of legislation drafted by Collier and his aides but drastically modified by Congress.

Collier fought first to get the IRA through Congress and then to secure its approval by Indian peoples. These battles provided him with an education in the continuing realities of race relations in the West and also in the diversity of Indian peoples. A skeptical Congress suspected the bill would abandon the longstanding goal of Indian assimilation. Some of the more assimilated Indians who had managed to retain their allotments or who had converted to Christianity saw the bill as a "back-to-the-blanket" measure that would reverse assimilation and deprive them of their lands. Other groups feared that the bill was a government trick to destroy their existing governments and perhaps strip them of their communal lands. Some "full-bloods" feared the bill would deliver power to Indians of mixed descent. All these factions stubbornly opposed the IRA.

In the end, Congress eliminated critical sections of the act, and 77 tribes refused to organize under its provisions. But 181 tribes organized governments under the IRA, which, even in its reduced form, repealed the allotment laws, permitted the restoration of surplus reservation lands to tribal ownership, provided for voluntary exchanges of allotted lands for shares in tribal corporations, and established funds for both the purchase of additional lands and for economic development. The act provided for government recognition of the rights of tribal governments, which at the time existed in a political netherworld without clear legal standing. Any tribe that ratified the IRA could elect a tribal council that would have "all powers vested in an Indian tribe . . . by existing law." Collier envisioned such governments as being capable of both governing and promoting economic development.

The attempts to organize IRA tribal governments led to years of controversy on the reservations. Some peoples really had no way to assess the bill accurately. The Papagos of southern Arizona, for example, had no words for "budget" and "representative." They used the same word for "president," "Indian commissioner," "reservation agent," and "king" and made no linguistic distinction among "law," "rule," "charter," and "constitution." It was almost impossible for native speakers to get any idea of what the IRA involved through the meetings held to explain it. The most humiliating defeat for Collier came among the Navajos, the nation's largest tribe. The vote took place in the midst of a successful BIA attempt to reduce Navajo livestock. The government blamed Navajo sheep for the gullying and erosion on the reservation that threatened to fill in Lake Mead and render Boulder Dam useless. The vote against the IRA was largely a vote against stock reduction, but it remained nonetheless a repudiation of Collier.

The affirmation that Indian political systems existed and possessed certain powers that the BIA could not arbitrarily abridge was a nearly revolutionary step in the 1930s, but in practice, of course, Congress and the bureau interfered constantly, and they retained fiscal control of the reservation governments. The Collier administration usually dictated economic programs to Indians, and Congress then proceeded to underfund them. Collier thought capitalist economies were culturally destructive and romanticized older Indian economies, but it was Collier who, through his program of stock reduction among the Navajos, helped destroy one of the last functioning Indian economies in the United States. He misdiagnosed the problem and prescribed a cure worse than the disease. And Collier, too, through programs such as the CCC, which enrolled over 80,000 Indians on the reservations, probably did more to extend the wage economy onto the reservation than had all the commissioners before him.

Still, Collier did change the direction of Indian policy. The often dictatorial powers of BIA personnel diminished in the 1930s; Indians gained an unprecedented degree of cultural and religious freedom. Even the composition of the BIA itself began to change as preferential hiring rules for Indians increased its Indian employees from only a few hundred in 1933 to more than 4,600 in 1940. Collier's larger plans of political self-governance and economic development foundered upon the inadequacies of the plans themselves and the realities of Indian subordination to the larger society, but changes had begun. Perhaps the greatest change was one barely noticed at the time. Collier reasserted the status of Indian tribes as semisovereign dependent nations. In 1934, in an attempt to salvage the IRA after Congress gutted it, Nathan Margold, the solicitor of the Interior Department, issued a legal opinion holding that tribal governments retained all their original powers—their "internal sovereignty"—except when specifically limited by express acts of Congress. The Margold Opinion, upheld by the courts, would have great implications for the future of both Indian peoples and the American West.

The New Deal increased the already sizable federal presence in the West. In this 1940 photograph tribal council delegate Scott Preston explains the federally mandated stock reduction program to Navajos on the western part of their reservation.

The West at the End of Depression

By the end of the 1930s, the outlines of a new West were visible beneath the poverty that cloaked much of the region. The federal bureaucracies were quite literally remaking the American West. Hundreds of millions of additional acres of land had come under federal management; federal agencies were damming and rerouting western rivers. Federal bureaucrats made farming the most thoroughly subsidized and supervised sector of the economy even if individual farmers still defied many of the goals of management. The alienation of Indian lands had ceased; the land that remained was under the protection of the federal government. When compared to the West of a half-century before, the scope of the change was staggering. There had been a nearly wholesale retreat from laissez-faire.

Yet, not surprisingly, these changes were like new trains running on an old track. Westerners still sought the old goal of rapid development. And change had only augmented the power of the bureaucracies, corporations, and cities. Westerners did not know that the federal trains pulling away from the western stations in the 1930s were just beginning to pick up speed. Far more sweeping changes would follow.

Readings

Arrington, Leonard. "The Sagebrush Resurrection: New Deal Expenditures in the Western States, 1933–39." *Pacific Historical Review* 52 (February 1983):1–16.

Bernstein, Irving. *A Caring Society, the New Deal, the Worker, and the Great Depression:*

A History of the American Worker, 1933–1941. Boston: Houghton Mifflin Company, 1985.

———. *A History of the American Worker: 1933–1941: Turbulent Years.* Boston: Houghton Mifflin Company, 1970.

Blackwelder, Julia Kirk. *Women of the Depression: Caste and Culture in San Antonio, 1929–1939.* College Station: Texas A&M University Press, 1984.

Caro, Robert A. *The Years of Lyndon Johnson: The Path to Power.* New York: Random House, 1981.

Daniel, Cletus E. *Bitter Harvest: A History of California Farmworkers, 1870–1941.* Berkeley: University of California Press, 1981.

Ficken, Robert E., and Charles P. LeWarne. *Washington: A Centennial History.* Seattle: University of Washington Press, 1989.

Forrest, Suzanne. *The Preservation of the Village: New Mexico's Hispanics and the New Deal.* Albuquerque: University of New Mexico Press, 1989.

Foss, Phillip O. *Politics and Grass: The Administration of Grazing on the Public Domain.* Seattle: University of Washington Press, 1960.

Foster, Mark S. "Giant of the West: Henry J. Kaiser and Regional Industrialization, 1930–1950." *Business History Review* 59 (Spring 1985):1–23.

Gregory, James. *American Exodus: The Dust Bowl Migration and Okie Culture in California.* New York: Oxford University Press, 1989.

Hoffman, Abraham. *Unwanted Mexican Americans in the Great Depression: Repatriation Pressures, 1929–39.* Tucson: University of Arizona Press, 1974.

Hundley, Norris. *Water and the West: The Colorado River Compact and the Politics of Water in the American West.* Berkeley: University of California Press, 1975.

Kimeldorf, Howard. *Reds or Rackets? The Making of Radical and Conservative Unions on the Waterfront.* Berkeley: University of California Press, 1988.

Lowitt, Richard. *The New Deal and the West.* Bloomington: Indiana University Press, 1984.

Mullins, William H. "Self-Help in Seattle, 1931–32: Herbert Hoover's Concept of Cooperative Individualism and the Unemployed Citizens' League." In *Experiences in a Promised Land: Essays in Pacific Northwest History,* pp. 323–338. Ed. G. Thomas Edwards and Carlos A. Schwantes. Seattle: University of Washington Press, 1986.

Nelson, Bruce. *Workers on the Waterfront: Seamen, Longshoremen, and Unionism in the 1930s.* Urbana: University of Illinois Press, 1988.

Prindle, David F. *Petroleum Politics and the Texas Railroad Commission.* Austin: University of Texas Press, 1981.

Saloutos, Theodore. *The American Farmer and the New Deal.* Ames: Iowa State University Press, 1982.

Schlebecker, John. *Cattle Raising on the Plains, 1900–1961.* Lincoln: University of Nebraska Press, 1963.

Stein, Walter J. *California and the Dust Bowl Migration.* Westport, Conn.: Greenwood Press, 1973.

Taylor, Graham D. *The New Deal and American Indian Tribalism: The Administration of the Indian Reorganization Act, 1934–45.* Lincoln: University of Nebraska Press, 1980.

Whisenhunt, Donald W. *The Depression in the Southwest.* Port Washington, N.Y: Kennikat Press, 1980.

Worster, Donald. *Dust Bowl: The Southern Plains in the 1930s.* New York: Oxford University Press, 1979.

World War II and Its Aftermath: *Reshaping the West*

THE rise of the West to a position of power within the United States has paralleled the rise of the United States to world power. In both cases the key event was World War II. Relatively modest deficits had so worried President Roosevelt during the Depression that he had tried to balance the budget in 1937, throwing the economy into a tailspin. During World War II, Roosevelt was willing to borrow whatever sums were necessary to win the war against fascism. The 1945 budget was ten times that of the last peacetime budget of the New Deal, and between 1941 and 1946 the federal debt quintupled to $260 billion. The graduated income tax, which had existed more in principle than in practice, now for the first time in American history levied substantial payments from the rich. The government borrowed and taxed heavily, and a large percentage of the resulting funds flowed west. During the Depression, government controls over the economy had been extensive by previous standards, but they seemed like only friendly advice when compared to the economic planning that took place during the war.

Because the destiny of the West had long been linked to federal activity, dramatic changes in federal power and federal policy had powerful repercussions west of the Missouri. Never in western history did changes come so quickly or have such far-reaching consequences as between 1941 and 1945. It was as if someone had tilted the country: people, money, and soldiers all spilled west. That tilt came from the federal bureaucracies, which devoted a disproportionate share of their enlarged resources to western development.

War brought investment capital to the West on a scale that for once lived up to westerners' expectations. During four brief war years the federal government invested nearly $40 billion in factories, military bases, and other capital improvements and spent approximately $70 billion in the Southwest, Mountain West, and Far West alone. The first and most obvious rationale for this federal investment was the Pacific war itself. The Japanese attack on Pearl Harbor may have been bad for the United States, but it eventually proved a boon to the West, particularly to California, Oregon, and Washington, which became major staging areas for the Pacific war. To wage war against Japan, the government needed vast numbers of ships, planes, and other supplies, yet it was not inevitable that the West would produce them. Although much of the limited American aircraft industry was already on the West Coast, it was too small to meet the needs of the military. And while it was obviously far easier to deploy ships for a Pacific war from the Pacific Coast, the region lacked both large-scale manufacturing facilities and the capital to meet the demands of military production.

The federal government remedied the lack of factories and the lack of capital by providing about 90 percent of the investment capital available in the West between 1941 and 1945. It made the West a vast wartime workshop through the Defense Plant Corporation (DPC), an arm of the Reconstruction Finance Corporation (RFC). The DPC supplied capital for and owned 58 percent of the new aluminum plants, 90 percent of the new magnesium plants, and 71 percent of the aircraft factories. Nearly all were west of the Mississippi. The DPC spent nearly $2 billion on factories in the West. Its mills at Provo, Utah, and Fontana, California, created a western steel industry where none had existed before. It created the aluminum industry of the Pacific Northwest. Although western shipyards had not produced a single merchant vessel between 1929 and 1939, federal funds created the capacity necessary to produce 52 percent of the ships built during the war.

The Pacific war provided the overriding rationale for this allocation of federal funds, but a more general and pervasive concern with national security also influenced these decisions. The government could build factories for private corporations, mandate the creation of new industries, and relocate existing industries because military planners had transformed these economic decisions into strategic issues. Worried about the concentration of basic industries in the northeastern United States, the military actively campaigned for a more even, and thus less vulnerable, distribution of essential industries across the country.

For military planners all the old liabilities of the West suddenly became virtues. Vast distances, low population density, and arid climate had seemed detriments to economic development. Now remoteness, isolation, and a climate that allowed people to work outdoors much of the time became major assets as military planners scrambled to locate new military bases. By 1942, for example, the government had established ten major military bases employing 60,000 civilians in Utah. The bases gave that state a dependence on federal expenditures that it has never lost. In Texas, San Antonio grew as payrolls from Fort Sam Houston, Randolph Air Force Base, and Lackland Air Force Base flowed into the city. The aircraft repair facilities at Kelly Field and other bases employed 30,000 civilians.

The earlier success of the Bureau of Reclamation and the Army Corps of Engineers in creating sources of cheap hydroelectric power, particularly in the Pacific Northwest and the Southwest, provided the final element in the federal decision to sponsor the industrial development of the West. The previously embarrassing surplus of electricity from the Columbia now became a godsend for the manufacture of aluminum, the major construction material in the airplanes that the military so greatly needed.

In a few years the federal government had altered the regional allocation of power within the United States. The control of capital and industrial production exercised by the Northeast lessened considerably. Not all of the West benefited equally, or permanently, from this change, but by the end of the war the West had secured new sources of federal revenues, an enlarged infrastructure, and a new industrial base. Sections of the West, particularly the Pacific Coast and the

Table 13

Major War Supply Contracts and War Facilities, 1940–45

(in thousands of dollars)

State	Major war supply contracts, June 1940–Sept. 1945		Major war facilities projects, June 1940–June 1945	
	Combat equipment	Other	Industrial	Military
Arizona	94,854	31,115	100,592	134,116
California	14,255,117	2,195,524	1,013,778	1,511,447
Colorado	244,634	116,920	170,350	174,479
Idaho	12,049	6,421	27,049	101,992
Montana	12,966	15,081	12,956	41,106
Nevada	1,521	32,402	151,542	88,050
New Mexico	11,133	9,356	13,325	101,506
North Dakota	1,582	5,938	120	1,572
Oregon	1,629,809	182,825	100,603	163,842
South Dakota	201	4,584	150	65,908
Texas	3,749,561	2,224,979	1,166,836	837,582
Utah	79,136	34,345	284,394	153,097
Washington	3,408,305	379,331	341,058	327,949
Wyoming	12,770	68,419	25,535	23,431

Source: U.S. Census, *Country Data Book* (Washington, D.C.: GPO, 1947), p. 7. Reprinted from Gerald D. Nash, *The American West Transformed: The Impact of the Second World War* (Bloomington: Indiana University Press, 1985), p. 218.

Southwest, had largely broken free from their old colonial status and had become centers of power in their own right.

The Industrialization of the West

The Pacific Coast states, particularly California, were the major beneficiaries of the federal largess during World War II. California alone secured 10 percent of all federal monies expended during the war, and these expenditures accounted for 45 percent of the state's personal income during the war years. Already boasting comparative financial independence from the East and the first elements of home-grown corporate capitalism, California now emerged as a major economic power. California's industries had begun to recover from the Depression by 1937, but their most spectacular gains came with war contracts. By 1943 the aircraft industry of southern California employed 243,000 workers, despite the government's insistence on dispersing some new factories into the interior—for example, to Dallas–Fort Worth and Wichita—where they would be less vulnerable to attack. To the north, in the San Francisco Bay area, shipbuilding carved out a place in the economy even larger than aircraft manufacturing, but one that proved less permanent. Altogether the California shipyards employed 280,000 workers in 1943; 75 percent of the nearly $5 billion in shipbuilding orders placed by the government on the Pacific Coast went to the yards of the Bay Area. Aircraft and shipbuilding were but the centerpieces in a much larger industrial expansion. Los Angeles, the seventh largest manufacturing center in the nation in 1939, was by 1944 second only to Detroit.

Federal contracts during World War II put the West at the center of what would become the aerospace industry.

Oregon and Washington started from a smaller base than California did and expanded less rapidly, but their rise, too, was impressive. Seattle secured war contracts worth $5.6 billion, and manufacturing in the region as a whole increased by 265 percent. As in California, the aircraft industry and shipbuilding paced the expansion. The Boeing Company, with government financing, expanded from 4,000 workers to 50,000 in its Puget Sound plants. At its wartime peak in 1944, Boeing's total sales were over $600 million—nearly ten times all of Seattle's manufacturing in 1939. Huge new Kaiser shipyards operated on Puget Sound and at Portland. The Puget Sound Navy Yard at Bremerton employed 36,000 men and women; over 100,000 workers labored in the shipyards of Puget Sound as a whole. The shipyards along the Willamette and Columbia rivers had 120,000 workers. In addition, the Pacific Northwest, taking advantage of the Columbia's cheap electricity, obtained six of the seven new aluminum ingot plants that the government built in the West during the war.

The pivotal figure in this tremendous expansion was Henry J. Kaiser. More than any other industrialist, Kaiser recognized the wealth to be made from government contracts and the possibilities for industrial expansion in the West. Kaiser, who became the prophet, promoter, and prime beneficiary of western industrialization, had already helped build, under government contracts, many of the pipelines, dams, roads, and bridges that constituted the western infrastructure. He had made his first fortune from creating the infrastructure. He made a second fortune from creating the manufacturing industries the infrastructure made possible.

Kaiser used government to spur western industrialization. With the Grand Coulee Dam project approaching completion, Kaiser and some of his associates, in partnership with Todd Shipbuilding, moved into shipbuilding to secure contracts from England for 30 freighters. With that contract under his belt, he went into business for himself. Kaiser recognized that to build ships he needed capital, steel, and workers. The government provided the capital for the shipyards and also a loan of $150 million for a steel mill at Fontana. Kaiser secured the workers by sending labor recruiters throughout the nation and chartering trains to bring the workers west. He promised them high wages, housing, and medical care and paid them even before he was ready to use them to make sure they would be available. He employed 250,000 workers in his shipyards, and these workers built 1,490 vessels between 1940 and 1945.

What worked in shipbuilding and steel worked also in magnesium and, after the war, in aluminum. A loan of $20 million from the federal RFC financed Kaiser's Permanente Metals, which produced the magnesium for bombs and planes. Similarly, at the end of the war Kaiser secured at bargain prices the Columbia aluminum plants that the federal government built during wartime. He was a man, according to *Fortune* magazine, who, learning the money to be made from federal contracts, had "backed a truck up to the mint."

Kaiser, and the government bureaucrats with whom he worked, had under the pressure of wartime redefined the relationship of business and government in the West. The government provided the capital for creating western industry; Kaiser and the managers of other large corporations met the payrolls and provided the organization and management skills. Or, as Kaiser summarized his relationship to the government: "We provided the organization, the major portion of the operating capital, the brains—and I hope that brains is not yet a thing that is without value in our country—the brains and the production. The Government provided the facilities." That Kaiser moved so easily from building dams to building ships and producing aluminum showed how interchangeable the necessary organizational skills—"the brains"—had become. Expertise at a particular kind of production mattered less than knowing how to organize mass production itself.

In the interior West, industrial expansion was far more modest, but there, too, companies that had grown up on dam building now thrived on war contracts. The government hired Utah Construction, another of the Six Companies, to build Geneva Steel Works near Provo, Utah. The government then leased the plant to Columbia Steel, a U.S. Steel subsidiary. In Nevada the government financed the construction of the world's largest magnesium plant in Henderson. It employed 14,000 people, twice the population of neighboring prewar Las Vegas. Denver secured both the Rocky Mountain Arsenal, which also employed 14,000 people in making chemicals for the war, and Remington Arms Company, which employed 20,000 people, 40 percent of Denver's factory workers, to fabricate ammunition and poisonous gases. Farther east, Wichita and Tulsa became hubs of the aircraft industry.

The Geneva Steel Works in Provo, Utah, was part of the huge federal development effort in the West during World War II.

In Texas, manufacturing employment doubled between 1940 and 1950 and brought almost one-half million people in from rural to urban areas. During the New Deal, federal contracts obtained with the aid of Congressman Lyndon Johnson had helped save the Houston firm of Brown and Root from bankruptcy. World War II brought Herman and George Brown contracts for warships and naval air stations. At the end of the war they purchased two war surplus pipelines, built by the government at a cost of $142 million to secure fuel for the war effort, and they created Texas Eastern, which became a *Fortune* 500 firm, to operate the pipelines. Houston, twenty-first in size in population, ranked sixth in federal investment between 1940 and 1950.

Although small subcontractors for the larger manufacturers prospered over most of the West, in the Rocky Mountain West and the Great Plains federal investment did not so much increase industrialization as pump new life into the old extractive and agricultural economy. After working during the Depression to throttle supply, the government now worked to unleash it. The boom-and-bust cycle of the region entered a pronounced boom phase.

Rains providentially returned to the Great Plains at a time when the United States and its allies needed all the wheat the region could produce. By 1945 farmers in 69 southern plains counties had planted an additional 2.5 million acres in wheat. Lands the federal government had painfully retired from cultivation and restored to grassland during the Dust Bowl once more went under the plow, as did other dangerously vulnerable lands. The wheat harvest on the Great Plains reached nearly a billion bushels by 1947, more than twice the amount harvested in 1939.

Cattle and mining, the other two elements of the old western economic triumvirate, also prospered. Wyoming, for example, increased its cattle from 827,000 in 1941 to 1,043,000 in 1945, and total agricultural receipts increased from $8.2 million to $21.5 million in the same four years. In Montana the net cash income of ranchers increased by 188 percent between 1940 and 1948. Mining prospered as the U.S Geological Survey and the Bureau of Mines undertook intensive new searches for mineral deposits in a largely successful attempt to make the United States self-sufficient in vital minerals. The Geological Survey found new deposits of tin, tungsten, copper, iron, lead, zinc, and coal.

Public Science

During World War II federal investment remade western science as thoroughly as it had remade western industry. The federal government had built western industries as part of an integrated national system of production. The government created scientific institutions in the West that were tied to the national scientific establishment and geared toward the national war effort. Under the Office of Scientific Research and Development (OSRD), the government pumped $99 million into western universities between 1941 and 1945. This was more money than all the western universities taken together had spent on scientific research since their founding.

The government spent far more funds on secret facilities at Los Alamos, New Mexico, and Hanford, Washington—the centers of atomic research. Convinced of the feasibility of an atomic bomb and fearful that Germany would develop one first, the government poured resources into atomic research and development. Hanford, a giant complex employing 20,000 people where engineers turned the ideas of theoretical physics into workable hardware, ultimately gave American scientists their edge over competing German and British scientists in the race for the bomb.

These new scientists transformed an earlier, largely parochial western science. The publicly funded science that dominated the West before World War II focused on the immediate problems of western producers. The Geological Survey and the USDA's agricultural research stations and the applied science departments of the land grant universities, for example, were state and federally financed institutions devoted to applying science to the problems of miners and farmers. With a few notable exceptions, this western science had been only weakly linked to national and international centers of scientific research. In newer fields such as ecology or oceanography, departments of real merit had arisen in western universities. And the chemistry and physics departments of both the California Institute of Technology and the University of California at Berkeley had approached the threshold of world-class scientific distinction.

The arrival during the war of an extraordinary group of scientists, many of them European refugees from fascism, overwhelmed these indigenous developments. These men were individually brilliant, but their frightening achievement in creating the atomic bomb tested at Alamogordo, New Mexico, was a collective one. The bomb could not be the work of any single individual. Modern scientists and scientific institutions came into the West as part of an expensive, highly organized national network of specialists working by command, very often by military command. Lone inventors and easy inventions were already historical curiosities by the time the modern physical sciences came West.

Virtually overnight, government investment linked the region to the existing centers of scientific research and made western institutions international centers in their own right. They were, from their creation, military centers, and even the older institutions took on military coloring. The Jet Propulsion Laboratory of the California Institute of Technology became the nation's center for rocket research. The Scripps Institute of Oceanography studied ocean currents for the navy, and the University of California worked on submarine detection. The Radiation Laboratory at the University of California at Berkeley, where Ernest Lawrence had already received a 1939 Nobel prize for developing the cyclotron, became one of the world's major training centers for nuclear physicists and technicians. In addition, corporate research laboratories such as General Electric's facilities at Livermore, California, and Albuquerque operated largely on the basis of federal contracts.

When the war ended, the West contained a network of modern facilities and research institutes and a dazzling array of scientists to staff them. Neither scientists nor politicians wanted to see this network dismantled. They were determined to secure continued funding for western science. Western scientists worked aggressively to make sure that the National Science Foundation, the postwar successor to the OSRD, would not be dominated by eastern scientists and universities. This scientific infrastructure would prove a fertile ground for economic growth in the postwar West, but in many ways it remained marked by its wartime genesis. Lawrence Livermore Laboratory, the Cal Tech Jet Propulsion Laboratory, and other centers of western science remained closely tied to and dependent on military funding.

Migration and Employment

The rapid industrialization of sections of the West helped create fortunes for a few and good-paying jobs for far more people. The extensive unemployment of the Depression quickly gave way to a labor shortage. To obtain the necessary workers, the new war industries first drew on the urban unemployed and on white rural laborers. World War II pulled many of the "Okies" from the San Joaquin Valley and made them factory workers. The labor agents of Henry Kaiser and other manufacturers attracted workers from the northern mountain and plains states. Making $14.00 a shift in an aircraft or aluminum factory was more appealing than getting $7.50 for risking life and limb in the mines of Butte, Montana. To agricultural laborers, miners, struggling small farmers and ranchers, and failing small-town businesspeople, steady wage work in war industries looked good. These limited pools of labor within the West, however, proved insufficient, because the armed forces were at the same time drafting large numbers of male workers. The new factories faced a major labor shortage.

Labor had always been a relatively scarce and mobile commodity in the West, and in boom periods employers had sought to attract workers from outside the region. They did so again during World War II. Nearly 8 million people moved into the states of the trans-Mississippi West between 1940 and 1950; about half of them went to the Pacific Coast. Of the nine states with the highest rates of population growth between 1940 and 1943, six were in the West. Every section of the West except the Great Plains and the hybrid mountain-plains state of Montana gained population: California grew by 72 percent, the Pacific Coast states as a whole by 39 percent, the Rockies by 15 percent, and the Southwest by 40 percent. The Great Plains lost 3 percent. These migrants were largely city-born, and they moved into western towns and cities. After the war, the vast majority stayed.

As the war industries drew in people from the rural areas, they left a vacuum in their wake. Farmers, particularly in Texas, Arizona, and California, as well as sugar beet producers in Colorado, Idaho, and Montana needed seasonal labor, but the extremely low wages they offered made it impossible for them to compete for the available work force. Despite the use of high school students, prisoners of war, and interned Japanese Americans, the wartime labor shortage grew increasingly severe. By 1942 there were reports of local crop losses. To secure agricultural labor, federal and local governments that had been trying to force Mexican laborers out of the country now sought to attract seasonal workers back into the United States. The Mexican government, however, insisted that the United States guarantee certain minimum standards for their workers before they would cooperate in recruiting them and sending them north. The result was the creation of the *bracero* program in the summer of 1942. Mexico agreed to provide workers, who the United States guaranteed could not be drafted. The workers would come on contracts, usually for a year, that assured them work at the prevailing wage for 75 percent of the time they were in the United States. The federal government would provide their transportation and guarantee them decent treatment.

Under the bracero program, over 200,000 Mexican farm workers entered the United States during the war to work in the fields or on the railroads. Their wages were high by Mexican standards (high enough to make bribes to get enrolled in the program worthwhile). But despite guarantees, the braceros found miserable living conditions and the usual discrimination. Conditions were worst in Texas, where Mexico, for a period, refused to send braceros. The braceros represented only the legal migrants. The total number of Mexicans who entered the work force, legally and illegally, was probably close to half a million.

This tremendous demand for labor worked to subvert the dual labor system. From necessity, employers began to draw upon new pools of workers: women, previously excluded from "men's work," and minority workers usually confined to the least desirable jobs. As President Roosevelt declared in his Columbus Day speech of 1942, the war necessitated a change in attitude and policy: "In some communities employers dislike to hire women. In others they are reluctant to hire Negroes. We can no longer afford to indulge such prejudice."

Women, urged on by wartime propaganda, moved into industrial work. Single women were the first to enter the factories en masse. By 1943 married women, too, were joining the work force. Although at any given time only a minority of married women worked, by 1944 married women outnumbered single women in the labor force. Women comprised at least one-third and sometimes more of the work force in the aircraft and shipbuilding industries of the Pacific Coast. In Los

Angeles, the center of the aircraft industry, women made up 45 percent of the work force, and at Boeing in Seattle they made up 47 percent. The propaganda urging women to work portrayed such employment as temporary and justified it in traditional terms of women's duty to help husbands and sons who were fighting the war. But the mere fact that women routinely and efficiently did "men's work" posed a challenge to the conventional American social custom of separate spheres. Interviews with working women revealed that patriotism or altruistic concern for male relatives had little to do with their first going to work in the factories. They worked for the same reason as the men: the relatively high wages.

The absorption of so many women into the work force presented serious problems for families and social institutions. As women took on full-time jobs (which during the war were at least six eight-hour days), they did not lose responsibility for housekeeping, child care, shopping, or the other "women's work" that men expected of them. To make matters worse, women had to perform these tasks under conditions of crowded housing and the rationing of the period. In order to keep married women on the job, the area committee of the Aircraft War Production Council in Los Angeles used federal aid under the Lanham Act to establish the most extensive child-care program in the country. Neither there nor elsewhere, however, did the aid fully compensate for working women's increased burden. When taking care of a household and holding down a full-time job was coupled with often chronic hostility from male workers, the result was high turnover rates among women. Turnover (the rapidity with which workers left jobs) was extremely high among all workers during the war, but it was highest for women, who often could only maintain their double burden for part of the year. In Los Angeles during the first six months of 1943, aircraft plants, which depended heavily on women workers, hired 150,000 workers and lost 138,000. Women with children, the least likely to enter the work force to begin with, often failed to stay with a job once employed.

Minority workers made up the other new source of labor for the factories. Black, Indian, and Mexican American men, of course, entered the armed forces just as whites did, but many of those disqualified for military service because of age or disability moved into the factories. Like single women, many African American and Mexican American workers had long participated in the wage labor system, but they had been systematically excluded from higher-paying jobs. The war opened cracks in the dual labor system, but their occupational mobility still remained limited.

African Americans were the most striking minority addition to the work force in California. In the first years of the war, relatively few blacks migrated to the West Coast. By 1943, however, labor shortages in the West and the successful efforts of white southerners to keep southern blacks from sharing in the wartime boom there induced unprecedented numbers of blacks to migrate west. These black migrants moved into existing black communities that in many cases had a long history of protest against racial discrimination. These communities possessed leaders who recognized the opportunities that the war offered. With aid from national black organizations, California black communities used the Fair Employment Practices Committee (FEPC) and public protests to demand fulfillment of federal promises of nondiscriminatory hiring in defense industries. Their efforts,

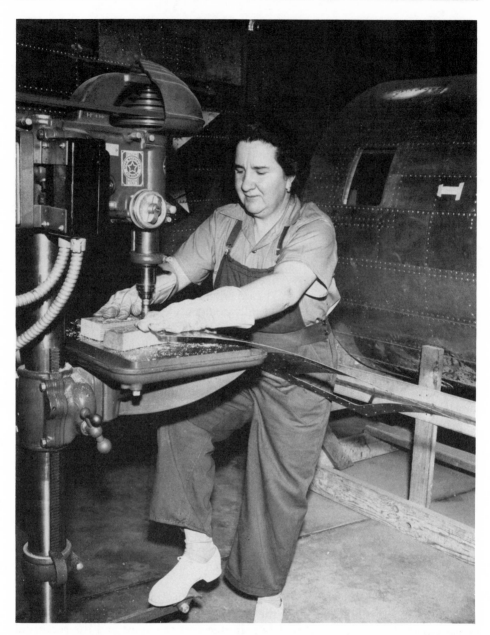

This woman worker at Boeing in Seattle was one of the millions of women who entered the paid labor force during World War II and transformed the social complexion of the West.

coupled with the labor shortage, gave African Americans access to jobs they never would have been able to obtain in normal times. As one black woman put it, "Hitler was the one that got us out of the white folks' kitchen."

Blacks did not attain instant or full equality with whites in the western workplace, but they made significant gains. Major corporations and CIO industrial unions proved more hospitable to black workers than did smaller companies and American Federation of Labor (AF of L) unions. The aircraft industry stubbornly resisted the hiring of African Americans. In Seattle the federal government had to intervene to back local black attempts to overcome the refusal of Boeing and the Aero-Mechanics Union to hire black workers in training programs. The gains came slowly, but by the end of the war about 7.2 percent of the work force of Lockheed Aircraft was African American. Shipbuilders hired blacks more readily, but many of the AF of L unions in the shipyards refused to grant them full membership. Until the end of the war, the Boilermakers' Union collected dues from African American workers but denied them a vote within the union. The unevenness of black gains and the dependence of blacks on large federal contractors was readily apparent in Portland, where virtually the entire black labor force of 9,000 worked in the Kaiser shipyards.

Hispanics, as part of the existing western labor pool, had in some ways an even harder time breaking out of the dual labor system. Unlike blacks, who migrated into the West precisely because jobs were opening up, Hispanics had to rise out of existing jobs at the bottom of the dual labor system. Wartime investigations by the federal government of the copper industry indicated that a strict ethnic division of labor continued to exist in the copper mines and smelters. In Denver Hispanics had the lowest per capita income and lived in the worst housing of any ethnic group in the city. Yet even bastions of the dual labor system yielded somewhat as the war went on. The Southern Pacific Railroad abandoned discriminatory hiring practices in the midst of the war, and in Tucson, Mexican American workers gained some access to jobs closed to them before. In Texas, Mexican American workers were, like blacks, largely excluded from war work or confined to menial positions, but federal intervention through the FEPC allowed some Mexican Texans access to semiskilled and skilled positions in war industries.

For many Indians, World War II represented their first direct experiences with the larger economy. The CCC and other New Deal programs had introduced many Indians to wage labor, but CCC work largely had taken place on their own reservations. The outbreak of World War II redirected federal resources and ended many New Deal programs. Reservation Indians faced a choice between the military, migration off the reservation to secure work, or a return to crushing poverty on the reservation. At least 25,000 Indians served in the armed forces; another 40,000 worked in defense plants—mostly on the West Coast—or as seasonal farm laborers. Together, work and military service represented a sizable migration off the reservations. The Rosebud Reservation in South Dakota, for example, lost about 20 percent of its people to migration during the war years.

Effect on the Urban West

Because urban areas had most of the factories, the cities absorbed the vast bulk of the new migrants into the West. Between 1940 and 1950 the Southwest, Far West, and Mountain regions led the country in rates of urban population growth. Their cities were unprepared for this growth; western cities found their public services stretched to the limit. When the population of a city such as San Diego increased by 147 percent between 1941 and 1945, the rapid growth westerners so ardently desired threatened to overwhelm them. Even with federal aid, San Diego could not provide adequate housing for all the new workers and their families.

Some single women workers at Consolidated-Vultee, a leading San Diego aircraft manufacturer, lived eight to a room in company dormitories. Workers on different shifts had rotating use of the same bed. At the Loma Vista Housing Project there was a single Safeway store for 16,000 people.

San Diego's growth was but part of the explosive growth of southern California as a whole. Southern California alone had more people by 1945 than 37 entire states, and growth spawned problems even for those cities, such as Los Angeles, that escaped a housing crisis. Los Angeles had considerable housing vacancies at the beginning of the war, and it added over 160,000 new units during the war. Auto transport, however, allowed the new factories that made Los Angeles an industrial giant to locate largely along the edges of the city, necessitating long commutes from available housing. Already dependent on the automobile, Los Angeles became even more dependent as a lack of motormen and conductors idled the streetcars. As more people drove, traffic congestion increased, and cars and factories created a new urban problem: smog. By the end of the war, air pollution had emerged as a significant health threat in Los Angeles, and the city had begun to take action against the worst industrial polluters.

As a whole, southern California communities coped with the influx of new workers better than did the communities of the San Francisco Bay area, where new migrants so overtaxed local facilities that they threatened a breakdown in war production. Shipyards made crowding far worse in Oakland and the East Bay than in San Francisco. Vallejo grew from 20,000 to 100,000 in five years. People lived in shacks, trailer camps, and temporary housing units thrown up by the U.S. Maritime Commission, or they just camped out. Richmond grew just as explosively, and its housing situation was as bad as Vallejo's. The city could not provide basic schooling or police and fire protection. Approximately 15,000 employees at the Mare Island Shipyard lived in a federal housing project that lacked sewers, streets, and schools. To cope, the cities turned to the federal government for aid, thus making the West even more dependent on federal funds and services.

The effect of rapid growth extended into the Pacific Northwest. Near Portland, Vanport went from mud flats to a city of 40,000 people in three years, with the usual problems of inadequate housing and overcrowded schools. And because the state of Oregon refused to transfer its increased tax revenues to the cities to deal with their problems, Oregon's cities, too, turned to the federal government for aid. A similar story unfolded in Washington, where Bremerton increased from 15,000 to 75,000 people with results similar to those in Bay Area communities.

Minority Communities

Continuing patterns of racial segregation within the West complicated this massive migration. Los Angeles, for example, became the distribution center for the 100,000 braceros working in California. They crowded into the East Side barrio, replacing the large numbers of Mexican American men who entered military service. Indeed, in California a higher percentage of nonwhites and white immigrants entered the military than did native-born whites.

Even while Mexican Americans compiled one of the country's most illustrious combat records, winning seventeen Medals of Honor, there was virtually constant tension in Los Angeles between soldiers and Mexican American gang members (*pachucos*) and teenage zoot-suiters—themselves the product of generational conflicts in the barrio. The conflict first gained widespread public notice in 1942 with the Sleepy Lagoon murder case.

On a Saturday night in August 1942, Henry Leyvas took his girlfriend to a local swimming hole, Sleepy Lagoon. Leyvas belonged to the 38th Street Gang, and at Sleepy Lagoon he encountered members of a rival gang, the Downey Boys, who beat him up. Seeking revenge, Leyvas returned with friends a few hours later, and a brawl ensued. The next morning police found José Díaz, a Downey Boy, unconscious. Díaz, who had been drinking and had fallen repeatedly, died soon after. The police rounded up 22 of the 38th Street Gang members and accused them of murder. Accompanying these arrests was a roundup of 300 other Mexican Americans, who were arraigned on lesser charges.

The prosecution in the ensuing murder trial put the entire Mexican American community on trial by identifying all "Mexicans" as criminals and gangsters. The Foreign Relations Bureau of the Los Angeles Sheriff's Department circulated a report asserting that criminality was an inherent racial trait of Mexicans and thus of Mexican Americans. The report argued that Mexican Americans were partially Indian by descent, Indians were originally "Orientals," and "Orientals" had no regard for the value of life. When the jury convicted most of the defendants on a variety of charges, the local Hispanic community was outraged. Although higher courts later reversed the conviction and censured prejudicial conduct by the judge, the immediate result was increased racial tension in the streets. Police and government officials questioned the loyalty of Mexican Americans who in defending the Sleepy Lagoon defendants "stirred up trouble." Zoot-suiters and marines and sailors from bases in nearby Chavez Ravine regularly assaulted each other in the East Side barrio.

Whites in Los Angeles identified zoot-suiters with Mexican American criminal gangs, but most zoot-suiters were not juvenile delinquents but simply teenagers taking part in a national zoot suit fad. Soldiers made no distinction between zoot-suiters and gang members, and indeed identified all Mexican Americans as un-American foreigners. Young Mexican Americans and young white soldiers taunted and attacked each other repeatedly.

Between June 3 and 13, 1943, several thousand soldiers and sailors, joined by local white civilians, attacked zoot-suiters in one of the oddest riots in American history. It was odd because no one was killed or even seriously injured, and property damage was slight. Whites were intent on humiliating and roughing up their victims, not killing them. Compared to both earlier and later race riots, it hardly deserved to be called a riot at all. But symbolically the invasion had an immense effect. As whites moved at will through the Hispanic community stripping and beating zoot-suiters, younger Mexican Americans felt first-hand what it was like to have a community at the mercy of hostile outsiders.

There was no equivalent large-scale conflict between blacks and whites, but tension existed both within the black community, where new migrants often overwhelmed the smaller settled communities, and between blacks and whites. Most black migrants came to California, and most of the 340,000 black migrants to the Golden State moved into Los Angeles, the existing center of black population in the Far West, with another 125,000 going to the San Francisco–Oakland area. This migration, largely from Louisiana and Texas, poured into relatively small black ghettos. With 10,000 southern blacks arriving in Los Angeles every month during 1943, the African American community was soon overwhelmed and outnumbered by newcomers. Similarly, San Francisco's black community increased by 600 percent during the war, and Seattle's increased 200 to 300 percent.

In some ways this migration increased discrimination against African Americans. For the first time in California whites came into contact with blacks at work, in schools, and in public facilities. With wartime housing shortages, whites reacted by imposing an even more rigid system of residential segregation. Restrictive real estate covenants, which prohibited selling or renting to blacks, confined most newcomers to crowded black ghettos. According to wartime estimates, 80 to 90 percent of the residential areas in the San Francisco Bay area were closed to nonwhites. In Los Angeles, African Americans lived either in Watts or south central Los Angeles, which by 1950 contained 78 percent of the city's black residents. In Bremerton, Washington, federal housing officials segregated black workers in special housing projects. Terrific overcrowding existed virtually everywhere. Black migrants, largely from the rural South, faced hostility from members of the older black communities, who feared they were worsening their own position with surrounding whites and with white southerners who were also migrating west in large numbers. The result was sporadic violence between blacks and whites and among blacks themselves throughout the war.

Japanese Internment

Millions of Americans changed their residence during World War II, but for the vast majority of civilians, at least, these moves were voluntary. Japanese Americans formed the only exception. Virtually the entire Issei and Nisei population of the Pacific Coast spent most of the war in concentration camps located in the interior West. The federal government rounded up and interned Japanese aliens and Japanese American citizens because they ostensibly formed a security threat to the country. Although Germany and Italy were also at war with the United States, the government did not resort to wholesale imprisonment of German and Italian aliens and never considered imprisoning German and Italian Americans. The government singled out Japanese Americans for treatment as prisoners of war in their own country not only from fear of an imminent invasion of the West Coast following Pearl Harbor, but also because of old and enduring racial beliefs. Public officials asserted that the Japanese were racially tied to the country of their ancestors even if it was a land that they had never seen; they could never be real Americans.

A little over two months after Pearl Harbor, with hysteria about the Issei and Nisei mounting among the West Coast public, the military, the press, and Congress, Franklin Roosevelt signed an executive order for the evacuation and confinement of both Nisei and Issei, citizens and noncitizens alike, on the Pacific Coast. The very fact that they had done nothing became proof of their bad intentions. For that, as Earl Warren, the attorney general of California, emphasized, "was the most ominous sign in our whole situation." The Japanese were supposedly lulling their fellow Californians into a false sense of security.

When the military roundup came, few rose to the defense of Japanese Americans, and few of the 120,000 Japanese and Japanese Americans affected (two-thirds of them American citizens) initially resisted the military roundup. Gordon Hirabayashi, a Nisei and a Quaker who was a senior at the University of Washington, did resist, and he and a few others legally challenged the evacuation order. His challenge failed as Supreme Court Justice William O. Douglas, a native of Washington state, ruled that the matter did not involve racial discrimination or claims that the Japanese Americans shared a collective guilt for Japan's attack.

The government transported the Japanese and Japanese Americans first to processing centers and then to concentration camps run by the War Relocation Authority (WRA), a special agency set up to oversee their internment. These camps began as prisoner-of-war camps and evolved into something more like Indian reservations. They became places where federal authorities would supervise the Japanese and "Americanize" them by inducing them to accept the white Protestant norms of the larger society. Indeed, many of the people who ran the camps were recruited from the Bureau of Indian Affairs.

The governments and people of the interior states did not welcome the internees or approve of the government's handling of the situation. Herbert B. Maw, the governor of Utah, complained that the WRA was *too* solicitous of the constitutional rights of Japanese American citizens. Maw wanted the Japanese Americans more harshly treated, in part because he thought the government and people of Utah could make some money from the plight of the evacuees. State officials saw the Japanese as a source of forced labor and a potentially lucrative federal subsidy. Maw asked that 10,000 to 12,000 Japanese be handed over to his state with an appropriate federal subsidy to guard them and force them to work. Since even Maw could not justify imprisoning the Japanese once the war was over, he also wanted a guarantee that the government would evict the freed Japanese from Utah after the war. Such antipathy was common among western governors during the war. Idaho Governor Chase Clark explained that the Japanese "live like rats, breed like rats, and act like rats. We don't want them becoming permanently located in our state."

Utah did not get either its subsidy or its control over the Japanese, but western farmers did benefit from Japanese American labor. The WRA confined the evacuees to ten concentration camps, eight of them in the West. Inmates from the camps worked as agricultural laborers in Utah, Wyoming, and elsewhere. As early as 1942 about 10,000 Japanese Americans were temporarily released from the camps to do agricultural work.

By 1943 repression had begun to ease. The government changed its emphasis from imprisoning the Japanese Americans to assimilating the Nisei into American society. They allowed white church groups to come in and ameliorate conditions in the camps. Eventually the government allowed 4,300 college-age students to leave the camps for universities. Another 17,000 inmates left the camps to take jobs in interior cities. The army, too, became active in the camps, first enlisting Nisei volunteers and then, in 1944, drafting Nisei. That same year, in the Endo case, the Supreme Court ruled confinement of "loyal" citizens unconstitutional, and in January 1945 the western military command ended complete exclusion of Japanese Americans from the West Coast, allowing them to return to most areas.

As Japanese Americans began to return to the Pacific Coast in 1945 and 1946, however, they found themselves targets of harassment and terrorism by local whites. This anti-Japanese campaign in the end proved largely ineffective. Most

Japanese-American internment camps during World War II. From Warren A. Beck and Ynez D. Haase, *Historical Atlas of the American West* (Norman: University of Oklahoma Press, 1989), map 77.

Japanese American Boy Scouts carry the American flag in a 1942 Labor Day parade through the Tule Lake, California, internment camp.

internees returned to pick up the pieces of their shattered lives. Some, however, never returned. Relocated in the Midwest or East, they stayed there and made new homes. And about 4,000 left the country for Japan. Not until 1988 did the U.S. Congress vote reparations for survivors of the camps.

Postwar Economy

In 1945 many westerners mixed their joy at the victory over Germany and Japan with a great deal of apprehension about the West's postwar economy. Only World War II had ended the Depression, and peace presented the danger of a rapid economic downturn, with a decline in defense spending and a return to the region's colonial subjugation to the East. As government spending declined by $90 billion between 1945 and 1946, western manufacturing seemed to fulfill the dire predictions. In California, the West's leading industrial state, the drastic curtailment of war orders for ships and planes had brought by 1946 a 39 percent decline in manufacturing employment from the 1943 wartime peak. And between 1945 and 1948, during a period when national industrial employment figures remained constant, industrial employment in California suffered a substantial decline. In Washington, Boeing's sales slumped from $600 million in 1944 to $14 million in 1946.

Yet for a variety of reasons the anticipated western economic crisis never fully materialized, and the problems that did occur did not last. Westerners, both in the Senate and the bureaucracy, had attained enough influence to maintain a federal commitment to western development. With his usual vigor, Maury Maverick, the former Texas congressman and chairman of the War Plants Corporation, proclaimed a postwar plan for western development. Maverick called for a reconversion of federally built factories in the West to peacetime uses, the continued diversification of the western economy, and the development of a new air and superhighway system to open up outside markets. Although Maverick was a New Deal Democrat, the Republican administrations of the 1950s would follow a roughly similar outline. Westerners differed on the desirability of federal planning in the new economy, but this desire for a vigorous, federally aided western economy independent of eastern control cut across the usual political lines. In the Senate, New Deal Democrats such as James Murray of Montana and conservatives such as Pat McCarran of Nevada could make common cause in advancing sectional interests. Antimonopoly western liberals such as Murray and Joseph O'Mahoney of Wyoming in the Senate and Maverick and Thurman Arnold in the bureaucracy failed, however, in promoting the sale of federal plants in the West to small business. The vast majority of them went to the country's largest corporations.

With the economy shifting away from war production, the forced savings imposed by wartime rationing created a gigantic pent-up demand for consumer goods that took over from military demands in driving the national and western economy. Westerners not only successfully converted the wartime industrial base to other uses, but they expanded it as well. Los Angeles, given its primacy in western manufacturing, predictably led the way. In the late 1940s one-eighth of all the new businesses started in the United States began in Los Angeles.

In addition to pent-up demand, continuing migration into the West stimulated the western economy. GIs who had been stationed in the West and had come to like its climate, scenery, and pace of life returned after the war with their families. These discharged soldiers formed part of the continuing mass migration westward that particularly benefited California, the population of which increased from 9 million in 1945 to 19 million in 1964. Along with wartime workers seeking to escape overcrowded housing, these new migrants created a demand for new homes that fueled a postwar building boom. Without federally guaranteed loans available through the Federal Housing Administration (FHA) and the Veterans Administration, most of these people would have been unable to qualify for a home mortgage, but now millions of them borrowed money and bought homes. The percentage of Americans owning their own home increased from 44 percent in 1934 to 63 percent in 1972. By 1946 the construction industry and consumer production had ended the short postwar slump in California's economy.

As it turned out, the West did not have to break its dependence on government defense spending as fully as anticipated. World War II gave way to the Cold War with the Soviet Union, and military spending resumed. International tensions and war pumped federal dollars into the West. With the outbreak of the Korean War, economic activity in California again expanded more rapidly than in the nation as a whole. Aircraft manufacture and, more modestly, shipbuilding fueled the expansion. Of the total rise in manufacturing employment in California between 1949 and 1953, aircraft production accounted for nearly 40 percent.

Table 14

Estimated Population Growth of Western States, 1940–45

(in thousands of persons)

Division and State	1940	1941	1942	1943	1944	1945
Mountain	4,172	4,215	4,294	4,443	4,303	4,237
Montana	556	544	522	487	462	463
Idaho	524	515	497	506	539	509
Wyoming	250	259	267	257	251	244
Colorado	1,133	1,138	1,136	1,171	1,148	1,118
New Mexico	534	531	536	541	532	539
Arizona	509	547	611	701	618	602
Utah	554	562	592	635	602	612
Nevada	112	118	133	144	151	148
Pacific	9,824	10,328	11,008	11,799	12,444	13,060
Washington	1,741	1,792	1,909	2,058	2,162	2,274
Oregon	1,100	1,131	1,147	1,233	1,282	1,294
California	6,982	7,405	7,951	8,508	9,001	9,491

Source: U.S. Census, Statistical Abstract, 1951 (Washington, D.C.: GPO, 1951), p. 28. Reprinted from Gerald D. Nash, The American West Transformed: The Impact of the Second World War (Bloomington: Indiana University Press, 1985), p. 6.

During the 1950s, as rocket research transformed the old aircraft industry into the aerospace industry, the West's share of spending actually increased over the levels of World War II. California alone was receiving 24 percent of all prime military contracts in 1959, and by 1962 the Pacific Coast had 46 percent of all Defense Department contracts for research and development. That year the *Los Angeles Times* estimated that one-third of the workers in Los Angeles and Long Beach depended on the defense industry, particularly the aerospace industry, for their jobs. There were more aircraft employees in Washington and California in 1957 than there had been in 1944, and much of their work was military. As late as 1956, military production at Boeing was 98 percent of the total. Not until Boeing produced its hugely successful 707 airliner in 1959 did the company create a commercial aircraft that allowed it to lessen its dependence on the federal government.

California and Washington benefited disproportionately from these defense contracts, but other areas of the West participated in the continuing shift of federal defense and space contracts from the Northeast to the West and the South. Vice-President Lyndon Johnson helped Houston secure the National Aeronautics and Space Administration Manned Spacecraft Center in 1961. The aircraft industry, built around military contracts, formed the center of the Fort Worth economy. In terms of expenditures per capita on space and defense research, Utah led the nation. By the mid-1950s the old Mormon agricultural utopia had more people employed in manufacturing than in agriculture, and defense installations contributed a greater percentage of Utah's total income than did military spending in any other state. In the 1960s, Montana Senator Lee Metcalf credited federal expenditures, particularly defense spending involved in creating missile silos and bases, with sustaining that state's economy. Colorado meanwhile developed a chemical industry largely dependent on government defense work at Rocky Flats and the Rocky Mountain Arsenal. Defense contracts, of course, only added to the boost given the economy by the maintenance of military bases. The Denver metropolitan area contained over 21,000 military personnel in the early 1970s, and military spending in the state reached $1.36 billion by 1975. Only Oregon, Nebraska, Montana, and Idaho lacked significant military-related manufacturing.

In part, particularly in the Pacific Coast and Rocky Mountain states, the disproportionate share of the new defense spending received by the West was a legacy of World War II. Other factors, however, also made the West appealing. Military defense contractors feared union labor, not because of wages, since the military pays on a cost-plus basis, but because unions can organize strikes and cripple performance-oriented contractors. They thus preferred the West and South, with their antiunion, right-to-work laws, over the East. Because large military contracts go to relatively few corporations, the clustering of these corporations or their branches around Los Angeles, Phoenix, and Denver brought disproportionate expenditures in these areas.

Burgeoning federal defense expenditures and an increased American presence around the globe made many western corporations partners with the federal government in a new American military and economic expansionism. With the Cold War and the rise of the United States as the world's largest military and economic power, the government presented western corporations with opportunities that stretched well beyond the confines of the West itself. The Bechtel Corporation undertook the construction of military bases in the Pacific even before the outbreak of World War II. It went from building California refineries for Standard Oil of California and Union Oil Company before the war to building refineries and other facilities in Venezuela, Saudi Arabia, and the Persian Gulf region. The expansion of U.S. foreign aid and new military bases abroad gave Bechtel, Morrison-Knudsen, and other members of the Six Companies access to contracts far greater in value than their continuing business of building western dams.

Bechtel and other multinationals were part of a western economy that was becoming far more complex than it had ever been before. Despite the gains in industrial employment during World War II, this new economy relied only partially on manufacturing. Western manufacturing remained localized, with California, Arizona, and Texas leading the postwar advance. By 1954 manufacturing employment in California was 44 percent above 1939 levels; in Texas the figure was 14.5 percent. With the exception of Wyoming and the northern plains states, all the industries of the other western states grew, but at a much slower rate. And despite the rise of western-based corporations, control over manufacturing still remained largely centered in the East. Western cities were likely to hold branches of national corporations, not their headquarters. Of the 200 largest corporations in the United States between 1945 and 1960, only 10 percent had their headquarters west of the Mississippi, and fewer still west of the Missouri. Most of them were in California, and virtually all of those in Los Angeles and San Francisco. The percentage had increased by the mid-1970s as Dallas–Fort

Worth and Houston gained corporate headquarters, but there were still relatively few major corporate headquarters outside of California and Texas.

Despite the changes brought by World War II, much of the West still depended on the old extractive economy. Boeing and the aluminum industry certainly marked the rise of a new manufacturing industry in the Pacific Northwest, but in the late 1940s lumber, food processing, paper, transportation, and primary metals accounted for 80 percent of the region's industrial output. And the rapid growth of Texas in the postwar period remained tied to the oil boom that followed the war. The expanding petrochemical industry in Texas formed an obvious link between an extractive base and a new manufacturing sector.

The old agricultural and extractive economy survived, too, in the wheat farms and cattle ranches of the Great Plains, on the factory farms of California and Arizona, in the forests of the Pacific Northwest, and in the mines of the Rockies and Nevada. This West continued to produce and process mountains of raw materials. In the immediate postwar period, for example, the output of California's agricultural economy still exceeded the output of its aerospace industry. The old West, itself in the midst of change, continued alongside the new modern urban West.

New Industries and the Service Economy

Economically, the distinguishing mark of the new urban western economy was not its manufacturing sector but its service sector. Most western workers in the postwar era did not make anything or grow anything. Relatively few of them even repaired anything. Instead they sold things, managed people, or performed various services. Both the private and the public sector created numerous service jobs, and these jobs were virtually identical. Administrators in corporations easily crossed the line to become government administrators and then crossed back again. A secretary for a private company and a secretary for a government bureaucracy did much the same work. In 1950, counting business service industries alone, all the western states except New Mexico, Oklahoma, and the Dakotas ranked above the national average in the percentage of workers in service industries. And between 1960 and 1970 the growth in service employment in the 11 fastest growing southwestern metropolitan areas far outpaced service employment in northeastern cities.

Part of this growth came from expansion of public bureaucracies. The more federal dollars that flowed West, the more federal employees they produced. Denver emerged as the foremost regional center of the federal bureaucracy in the years after the war. With the old government-owned Denver Arms Plant converted into the Denver Federal Center, Denver had 14,000 people on the federal payroll by 1951, 23,000 by 1961, and 31,500 by 1975, more than any city outside Washington, D.C. Albuquerque acquired so many regional offices that it became known as "little Washington." In California federal growth formed only part of even larger growth in state and municipal administration that made government the second fastest growing sector of the California economy in the postwar period. Of the 15 states that experienced the greatest growth in government employment between 1939 and 1954, eight, including three of the top four, were in the West.

Public administration was the tip of the service iceberg. In the Southwest, the fastest growing western region in the 1960s, the rise in the number of public administrators proved less rapid than the rise in private administrators and service workers in finance and industry. There were more cashiers, stockbrokers, managers, and loan officers than bureaucrats. The rate of increase in the number of people employed in education, health care, and the professions, in turn, dwarfed the rates of increase in both public and private administration. The West of cowboys, miners, and farmers was giving way to a West of lawyers, bureaucrats, and secretaries.

The rising service economy, coupled with discrimination against women in manufacturing jobs, complicated the gains made by western women during World War II. Women who had worked in the war industries—munitions, aircraft, and shipbuilding—were hard hit by postwar cutbacks. In the summer of 1945, 75 percent of the women employed in shipbuilding and aircraft production lost their jobs. Once out of their jobs, they had difficulty finding other industrial work, since employers openly sought to hire young male workers and the unions did little to protect the interests of women.

Nationally, most Americans continued to believe that women really did not need their jobs, and women workers were divided themselves about the desirability of future employment. Some public opinion polls showed that most women workers were ready to leave the labor force, but when employers asked for voluntary resignations among women, they got very few. Surveys of defense plants in Seattle and Wichita found that 61 percent of the women workers wanted to continue working. Single women had to support themselves, and in the Seattle-Tacoma area a survey showed that 22 percent of the women workers were the sole support of their families.

Loss of industrial jobs, lack of union protection, and employer discrimination all forced women workers back into the old cage of gender-segregated jobs—now often service jobs in the new economy that paid one-half to two-thirds what skilled women workers had earned during the war. Once they were there, the state governments slammed the door on them. In the Puget Sound area, for example, when unemployed women welders or riveters refused to take "women's work" and demanded the skilled jobs that employers denied them, the state refused them unemployment benefits. The state held that these were male jobs intended for returning veterans. Older women and black women particularly suffered under the new policies.

Although women were forced back into low-paying, dead-end "women's work," an important change had taken place nonetheless. World War II had accelerated the tendency of women, both married and single, to seek outside employment. Married women stayed in the labor force, albeit in lower-paying sales and clerical jobs. With large numbers of married women in the work force, the older ideology of domesticity was severely compromised.

The erosion of the gains women had made during World War II and the decline in domesticity were national trends, but the West had special variants. The rise of a western garment industry in areas such as El Paso where cheap labor was readily available increased manufacturing jobs for women—particularly Mexican and Mexican American women—but at very low wages. In the Far West the new service economy provided greater occupational and educational opportunities for women than it did elsewhere in the country except the Northeast. But gains along the Pacific Coast had to be balanced against the Rocky Mountains and intermountain West, where women had some of the worst educational and occupational prospects in the country.

The service economy of the urban West demanded an educated work force, and the urban regions of the West, both by attracting educated migrants and by investing in educational systems, proved capable of providing it. Urban westerners were better educated than Americans overall: almost 46 percent of the adults in the metropolitan regions of the West were high school graduates in 1950, compared to 34.3 percent in the country as a whole. And even as the national average rose over the next two decades, the urban West retained a roughly 10 percent advantage over the rest of the nation. In 1960, Albuquerque, New Mexico, boasted more Ph.D. degrees per capita than any other American city.

Education formed a major social investment in several Pacific Coast states and southwestern states. By the early 1960s California was spending more than a billion dollars a year on education. The state built a school a day, and it was possible for a Californian to enjoy free public education through the graduate level in what remained one of the best educational systems in the world until the 1980s. Unlike in the East, public, not private, universities crowned this educational system. Although Stanford and the California Institute of Technology were major private universities in California, only in one western state, Utah, did private colleges enroll a significant proportion of college students.

The western climate and environment became major factors in the growth of the western service economy. Unlike older extractive industries, which had to locate at the site of the resource they exploited, the newer industries had a great deal of discretion in location. Western sunshine and spectacular scenery had long been economic assets to the West; they had sustained a tourist economy that itself became a major part of the western service industries. But until the postwar era sunshine usually went along with heat, and that deterred permanent relocation everywhere but along the coast. With the development of air conditioning, however, migrants could enjoy sunshine and escape the heat. Glorious physical settings and a relatively highly educated populace, not minerals or lumber or cheap labor, contributed to the growth of Seattle, Portland, Phoenix, San Francisco, San Diego, Denver, Tucson, Los Angeles, and other centers of the new western prosperity. A survey of newcomers to Arizona in 1960 found that 50 percent of the heads of households were professional people, skilled workers, or managers.

Las Vegas formed perhaps the most bizarre creation of this new West. First as a railroad center, then as the nearest town to Boulder Dam, then as a wartime boom town, Las Vegas had struggled for an elusive prosperity in the Nevada desert. Following World War II, Las Vegas finally found its niche as a tourist gambling mecca. Easily accessible from southern California, Las Vegas became the place where a contrived "Old West" self-consciously met the New West of Hollywood and southern California leisure. Marketing itself as the last frontier and its downtown casinos as "Glitter Gulch," Las Vegas gradually transformed itself into the "Ultimate West" of garish hotels along its famed Strip. The Strip was the product of an economy that was as purely service-oriented and unproductive as anything imaginable. In it the older western fascination with gambling, chance, luck, and getting rich quick merged with the New West's picture of itself as a land of relaxation and leisure.

The Rural West: Ranching and Farming

During and after the war the rural West lost people to the urban areas, but it did not always lose capital. Indeed, the flow of capital into rural regions paradoxically stimulated the migration of people out of it. The growth of large-scale, capital-intensive agriculture based on machines and chemicals forced a further decline of small farms over much of the West.

The new trend appeared in even the most traditional of western agricultural enterprises: cattle ranching. Cattle raising boomed immediately after the war as Americans consumed more meat than ever before, doubling beef consumption from 60 pounds per person in 1950 to 116 pounds per person in 1972. Americans, enjoying rising incomes, made steak a symbol of the suburban good life. The income of ranchers shot up, and for the first time in years many ranchers were free of debt and able to buy up farming homesteads whose owners could not compete against large farmers.

Overall, the size of ranches increased as profitable operations absorbed smaller spreads. The average size of ranches on the Great Plains increased by more than 20 percent between 1940 and 1950. Meanwhile, again between 1940 and 1950, the number of ranches decreased, by as much as 30 percent in New Mexico and 8 percent in South Dakota. Small ranches without access to capital could not compete. Survival in ranching after the mid-1950s demanded an increasing investment in irrigation, in seeding of hybrid grasses, in hormones and medication for cattle, and in the making of silage, or winter feed. Hay loaders and hay stackers, jeeps, and bulldozers all reduced the ranchers' demand for labor and increased their need for capital.

Even with this expansion, however, most ranches still remained relatively modest in size. The few surviving large ranches on the plains failed as the rising value of their lands increased their tax burden and made ranching uneconomic. Very large ranches on the Great Plains were dinosaurs when the optimum herd size for those ranchers who had to provide most of the feed for their cattle during the winter was only 200 head, and for those who did not, 400 head.

By the 1960s cattle ranchers operated in an economic world that depended on the Bureau of Land Management, the Forest Service, and the packing houses that operated their giant feedlots where cattle were fattened on corn and food supplements. The feedlots concentrated cattle in such numbers that their manure, unwanted because of the development of chemical fertilizers, became a major local environmental pollutant. Packers, who had exercised control over prices and profits since the end of World War I, continued to do so.

Although middle-sized family operations dominated ranching, the situation was more mixed for other agricultural enterprises. Family farms remained the norm in wheat farming, but the factories in the fields that Carey McWilliams had described in California in the 1930s became even more common in the Far West and Southwest during the years following the war. By 1968, when the first figures were gathered, corporations controlled 20 percent of the farmland in California. It is true that by the 1960s "corporate" farms included many family farms as family farmers themselves incorporated for tax benefits, but these family corporations remained relatively unimportant among corporate farmers as a whole. In 1968 corporations holding 10,000 acres or more accounted for only 8 percent of all corporate units, but they held 71 percent of all corporate-owned land.

With the exception of New Mexico, farming on the California model became typical of much of the Southwest. In Arizona the large individual and corporate farmers began to concentrate on cotton, and it helped give the growers there one of the highest average net farm incomes in the United States. In South Texas corporate farmers also took control. Del Monte established a highly mechanized farm, a cannery, and a shipping facility near Crystal City in 1946 and thus drove out most smaller farmers. By the 1960s a report on the lower Rio Grande valley summarized the situation: "The small grower is virtually out of the game. The medium-sized operator is beginning to have king-sized troubles. And the era of the giant, vertically integrated farm operations, usually corporate, seems to be at hand."

The rise of corporate farming in South Texas, combined with the mechanization of cotton farming in East Texas, caused the number of farms in the state to decrease at a record pace. Between 1950 and 1970, one out of every three Texas farms disappeared. White farmers, black farmers, and sharecroppers, and those Mexican Texan farmers in South Texas who had survived early crises, all succumbed. As they migrated to the cities or other regions of the West, braceros and machines replaced them.

The corporations that entered western farming did not establish traditional farms. They created new farms that resembled the bonanza farms of the nineteenth century. A glance at the Central Valley of California from a car window disclosed a western rural landscape very different from the classic landscape of the rural Midwest. There were no clusters of farmhouses, few villages or towns, and rarely even the sight of farmers at work. Instead there was mile after mile of a single crop, broken by machine yards and, in season, work gangs harvesting or planting.

The expansion of corporate farming after the war resulted from the ability of agribusinesses to adapt to the economic environment of postwar capitalism. As farming became more energy intensive and more dependent on sophisticated technologies, it demanded larger and larger inputs of capital. Tractors and harvesters had just been the opening wedge of the new technology. After the war, chemical fertilizers and pesticides joined all kinds of new farm machinery as necessities for any farmer who was going to compete.

Cotton, a major crop not only in Texas and Arizona but also in California, exemplifies the changes in farming. In preparing the land for cotton, machine labor continued to replace human labor, a trend evident since the "Okies" moved west in the 1930s. Tractors reduced both the time and the number of steps necessary to prepare the land. And although less than 10 percent of the cotton crop was harvested by machine in 1949, by 1969 machines harvested 96 percent of the crop. In 1948, 140 human hours of labor were required to produce a bale of cotton; by 1968 the figure had fallen to 25. Similarly, the human hours necessary to produce a ton of hay, a major crop throughout the interior West, declined by two-thirds between 1940 and the 1970s. And there was far more cotton—and everything else—to harvest per acre. Herbicides, fertilizers, and insecticides unavailable before the war created huge gains in yields.

In the nineteenth century the ability to replace labor with technology had helped many family farmers, but in the twentieth century the scale of the necessary investment in technology and energy shifted the balance more and more to corporations and to the largest private farmers. Successful farming by the 1970s demanded specialized professional services from banking to custom combining for wheat farmers. It demanded "farm managers" who understood financing as well as they understood how to grow wheat or cotton. To survive, family farmers duplicated many of the corporate methods. They resorted to a mechanized and energy intensive farming. On the northern plains, where family farms continued to prevail, the capital required to enter farming increased steeply during and after the war, farms were bigger and more productive, but farm population dropped by about 20 percent between 1940 and 1950.

Tax laws bestowed significant benefits on corporate farmers during the 1950s and 1960s. Tax benefits to investors in farmlands were so great that by 1970 three out of every four Americans with incomes over $100,000 had invested in some form of farming. This investment took place even while the average net income of farmers on the northern plains declined between 1949 and 1959. Not until 1969 did tax reform remove many, but not all, of the loopholes that had made farming a better way to shelter money from taxes than to earn it.

There was no denying the productivity of this new farming, both corporate and private. By 1960, California growers—for when corporations instead of individuals controlled farms, the term *farmer* seemed inappropriate—supplied one-fourth of all the nonstaple foods and one-third of all the fruit and vegetables consumed in the United States. Farm production totaled $3 billion in 1960. When the value added by canning, processing, and related industries was added, the net product of California's farms totaled $12 billion.

Because this new mechanized farming depended on the widespread use of pesticides and chemical fertilizers, it made many farmers even less environmentally sensitive than before. Not only were the fertilizers and pesticides environmental contaminants in and of themselves, but also their ability to boost production provided incentives for cultivating marginal lands and thus causing further environmental damage. Even as the number of farmers decreased on the plains, for example, the amount of new land being brought into cultivation increased as the sodbusting of the 1920s resumed. Farmers in eastern Colorado, many of them suitcase farmers, plowed up four million acres of virgin grassland and seeded them to wheat between 1939 and 1949. They also produced wheat on another one million acres that they had earlier returned to grassland. Only the lack of additional land and the return of drought in a second, shorter, Dust Bowl period in the early 1950s halted the expansion.

Even drought, however, had begun to seem like a temporary obstacle to western farmers. The period from the late 1940s through the 1960s was the golden age of the Bureau of Reclamation. The bureau raced the Army Corps of Engineers and local public utility districts to dam the free-flowing rivers of the West. What were once river systems became elaborate plumbing. The Central Valley Project of California began to provide irrigation water after the war, as did the Grand Coulee Dam. The bureau, entering the spirit of the Cold War years, made reclamation a test of national resolve and strength in the battle against communism and questioned the motives of those who failed to see the need for still more water projects for the West. Between 1945 and 1974 irrigated land in the West increased from 19.4 million acres to 36.6 million acres. Funding for western water development rose from $33 million in 1939 to $230 million in 1949 and stayed at that

The Transmountain Water Diversion Project on the Big Thompson River in Colorado was but a single step in the massive reordering of nature that federal dollars financed after World War II.

plateau. By 1975, the bureau had spent $6 billion on western irrigation projects, and the costs of its remaining projects promised to increase that figure greatly.

In the race to dam the West, the bureau ringed the Rockies with dams to catch and store the spring runoff and funnel it to parched farms. But the Corps of Engineers continued to compete in Congress for funds and the right to build dams on the Columbia River. Together the bureau, the corps, and the local public utility districts constructed dams at an incredible pace. They added more than a dam a year to the Columbia and its tributaries from the end of the war until 1973.

The Bureau of Reclamation's dams produced federally subsidized water sold and delivered to farmers at a price far below what it cost the bureau to capture, store, and transport it. The subsidies were sizable. A 1980 federal study found that they ranged from a low of $58 an acre in the Moon Lake Irrigation District on the upper Colorado to a high of $1,787 an acre in the Wellton-Mohawk District of California. In percentage terms this meant the federal government absorbed from 57 percent to 97 percent of the cost of providing water. Overall, farmers paid only an estimated 3.3 percent of the cost of the projects. Federal appropriations and revenue from power sales at the dams took care of the remainder.

The Bureau of Reclamation retained only the vaguest hint of its own original mission to provide water to small farmers and ranchers. Franklin Roosevelt intended the Columbia Basin Project, authorized in 1944 to draw irrigation water from Grand Coulee Dam, to provide small tracts for "the Grapes of Wrath families of the nation," but attempts to restore the old egalitarian impetus for reclamation stalled. For a while the bureau brought lawsuits against recipients of water who refused to sell their excess land, but the courts inflicted such mild penalties that the bureau began to look the other way and ignore violators. In California the state, Pacific Gas and Electric, and agribusiness opposed the Central Valley Project until the bureau abandoned most public power components of the project and agreed that mere technical compliance with the 160-acre limitation would be sufficient. Large farmers and corporations could distribute large farms among dummy owners and go about their business.

Yet for all of the Bureau of Reclamation's compromises with agribusiness, it never became their tool. Western water politics was more complicated than that. The bureau had its own sources of power and its own goals; indeed, it sometimes seemed to be a semi-independent fiefdom. The bureau redefined its task as getting appropriations and building dams. It did not care who benefited from the dams. It chose not to fight for either acreage limitation or public power when such crusades brought powerful enemies into the field against it and could compromise its ability to build. Building dams was all that mattered.

For support the bureau relied on western representatives in Congress who wanted the jobs and water the bureau could provide for their districts. Carl Hayden, the powerful senator from Arizona, became the bureau's special congressional sponsor, but Floyd Dominy, the son of Nebraska homesteaders, pulled the political strings in helping select projects and secure votes. Dominy, who headed first the irrigation department and then the entire Bureau of Reclamation, was one of the most influential bureaucrats of the postwar era. Under Dominy the bureau perfected its technique of providing supporters in Congress with money for projects in their districts and denying funds to enemies. To become an enemy of the bureau, members of Congress had only to question the utility of a project or its environmental consequences. The bureau did not want Congress discriminating between good and bad projects; the bureau would make such decisions, and it would reward its friends and punish its enemies. Most westerners, despite varying political allegiances and ideologies, tended to fall into line; they all wanted water and jobs.

As the Bureau of Reclamation's power grew, and as its rivalry with the Army Corps of Engineers intensified, its projects grew more and more grandiose while their actual benefits grew more and more dubious. As the most obviously beneficial projects in terms of costs and benefits were completed, the bureau, and the Corps of Engineers, undertook projects that had problematic economic, environmental, and social consequences. Both bureaucracies presented elaborate plans to Congress for projects on the Missouri River, and the political competition threatened to kill both of them. Competition induced political, not economic, pragmatism; indeed, it carried the agencies to new heights of economic impracticality. The bureau and the corps fused the bureau's Sloan Plan with the corps' Pick Plan to produce the massive Pick-Sloan Project that originally called for 107 dams on the Missouri and its tributaries. Each side accepted projects proposed by the other that they had previously labeled worthless. The heart of the multibillion-dollar project was the five Army Corps of Engineers dams on the main stem of the Missouri. When completed in 1966, they turned the Missouri, like the Columbia before it, into a series of slack-water reservoirs.

Benefits came from the dams, but not as many as the corps and the bureau had promised. The dams did produce 13.2 billion kilowatt-hours of electric power, and they did improve flood control on the Missouri. But they did not, as promised, eliminate flooding; floods continued to do about $95 million in damage annually along the river. Nor did the corps succeed in making the river profitably navigable. The amount of traffic on the river did not justify the huge costs of keeping a channel open.

As for irrigation, the Bureau of Reclamation had to abandon or scale back much of its reclamation work on the Missouri. A large amount of the land they hoped to reclaim turned out not to be irrigable, and large parts of the project were abandoned or repeatedly delayed. On much of the land irrigation would prove profitable only on large units with greater than average yields of high-gross crops such as sugar beets. In the late 1970s, South Dakota farmers themselves voted down the bureau's much-delayed Oahe Diversion Project as too costly.

Dams have costs as well as benefits, and along the Missouri, Indians bore a disproportionate share of the costs. The five Missouri dams immersed 550 square miles of tribal lands, including virtually all of the lands central to the subsistence agriculture of the Standing Rock, Cheyenne River, Crow Creek, and Lower Brulé Sioux and of the Three Affiliated Tribes (Mandans, Arikaras, and Hidatsas) of the Fort Berthold Reservation in North Dakota. The corps condemned Indian lands in violation of treaty rights and offered inadequate compensation for them.

By the 1950s and 1960s Indians were not alone in questioning the equity and utility of the dams built by the Bureau of Reclamation and the Army Corps of Engineers. Dam projects found a host of critics. The dams helped inspire a new environmentalism, and they also generated opposition from members of Congress and farmers from the East and the South, who questioned their economic utility. In a time of crop surpluses, for example, why build expensive projects to grow crops such as cotton that eastern and southern farmers were being paid not to grow? Despite bureau contentions to the contrary, most crops grown on federally reclaimed lands could be grown in the East, and the major crops grown with expensive western water were low-value forage to feed livestock. Only about 17 percent of bureau-aided lands produced vegetables, fruits, and nuts, and only a small portion of that acreage went to winter vegetables or citrus fruits to diversify the American diet.

While the Bureau of Reclamation's massive projects moved forward, a less dramatic but equally far-reaching attempt to transcend aridity was underway: the pumping of the aquifers. Westerners had long known that vast underground reservoirs underlay much of the semiarid lands of the West, but until the perfection of efficient gasoline engines and the availability of inexpensive liquified petroleum and of natural gas, most farmers could afford to pump only with windmills, which were neither large enough nor powerful enough for efficient irrigation. In the late 1940s and 1950s pump irrigation began to expand dramatically. On the High Plains of Texas, for example, Hale County alone had 500,000 acres under pump irrigation by 1957 and Lubbock County had 350,000 more. On most of this land underground pipes, subsidized by the USDA, and aluminum sprinkler systems

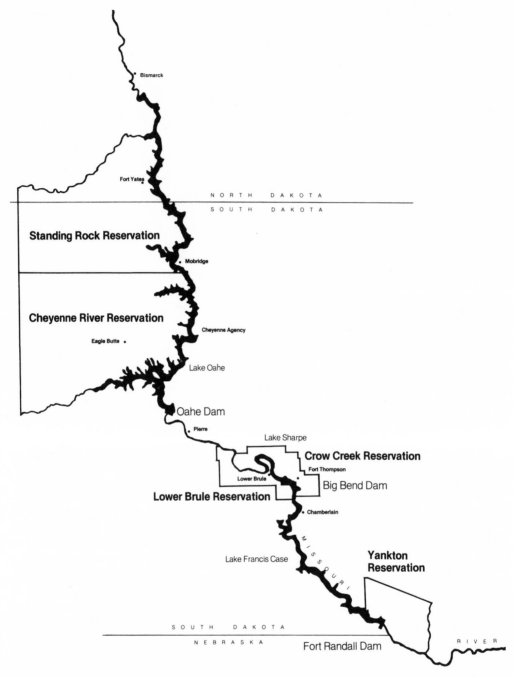

Bureau of Reclamation projects on the Missouri River. From Michael L. Lawson, *Dammed Indians: The Pick-Sloan Plan and the Missouri River Sioux, 1944–1980* (Norman: University of Oklahoma Press, 1982), p. 28.

(instead of less efficient ditches) conveyed the water to the land. All of this, of course, demanded a significant capital investment. On the Texas plains in the mid-1950s investment in equipment on a 320-acre irrigated farm was three times the investment on a dryland farm. But the investment paid. When increased yield and expenditures for fertilizer, pesticide, fuel, and equipment were tallied, irrigation increased economic activity by approximately $330 million on the Texas High Plains in 1959. Similar trends were visible on the northern plains.

Farmers throughout those sections of High Plains overlying the giant Ogallala Aquifer—a vast underground lake—sent pipes down like giant straws to suck water up for their fields. Between 1945 and 1954 irrigated acreage on the High Plains increased on average by 20 percent per year. And as in Texas, these irrigated farms were increasingly large, mechanized farms. "Underground rain" seemed to put farmers forever beyond the vagaries of rainfall that had plagued and defeated Anglo American settlement for generations. And believing cheap fuel, brimming aquifers, and high crop prices would endure forever, western farmers thought their new industrial farming had at last conquered the plains.

Between the Bureau of Reclamation and private pumping of the aquifers, 43 million acres of land, one-quarter of the West's cropland, were irrigated by 1977. This accounted for 83 percent of the nation's total irrigated acreage. One-half of the West's total crop value came from these irrigated lands.

Like the water that flowed from Bureau of Reclamation dams, much of this new industrial farming, with its potent array of chemicals, machines, and fuels, depended on federal subsidy. On farms receiving water from federal water projects, the subsidy was obvious. On farms tapping the aquifers the direct water subsidies were minor—the partial underwriting of pipe costs, for example. Other subsidies were more formidable. During the war and the postwar years, with European agriculture devastated, the world market absorbed most farm production. By 1954 increasing crop surpluses had once more brought the government back into regulating agricultural production. To qualify for commodity credit loans, farmers had to stay within acreage allotments assigned on the basis of production in the years before they joined federal programs. As in the 1930s, the programs would restrict acreage and thus boost prices. In addition, the soil bank program of the Agricultural Act of 1956 attempted to curtail production and increase conservation by retiring marginal or damaged lands.

There were other subsidies, too. Research funded by either the USDA or state governments through the land grant universities and agricultural experiment stations of the West provided most of the new techniques, machines, and chemicals that transformed agriculture. In these universities, researchers undertook collaborative projects with farm implement manufacturers and chemical companies. Public funds had thus subsidized the resulting products, and these products usually benefited large farmers.

Despite the increasing mechanization and efficiency of this farming, large-scale western agriculture continued to depend on seasonal stoop laborers. About 2 percent of American farms, most of them in the Southwest, employed the vast majority of both native-born and immigrant farm labor. To insure the necessary supply for these farmers, the government maintained the bracero program with Mexico into the 1950s, but the U.S. government largely abandoned active supervision of the program. Farmers supplemented bracero labor with an increasing stream of illegal migrants. These migrants— "wetbacks," as westerners derisively called them—came to the United States because both Mexico's high birthrate and its own trend toward corporate agribusiness in northern Mexico left them no place in its countryside or economy.

Mexico initially worried about illegal immigration undercutting the bracero program while the United States remained unconcerned, but in the mid-1950s the situation changed dramatically. In 1952, at Mexico's request, the United States enacted Public Law 283, making it illegal to import, transport, or harbor (though not to employ) illegal aliens. Neither the United States nor Mexico made a real attempt to block migration, and neither could have succeeded even if it had tried. The United States and Mexico had extended the bracero agreement in 1951, but in 1953 when the agreement again came up for renewal, the United States balked at Mexico's insistence on higher wages and on contracting stations in the Mexican interior instead of on the border. When Mexico would not yield, the United States let the bracero agreement lapse and opened its own recruitment stations along the border. Although the United States soon cut off recruiting, it used the threat of renewed direct recruiting as a club against Mexico when that nation refused to yield on other issues.

The conflict with Mexico focused attention on the increase in illegal migration, and resulting publicity painted the United States as the target of an "invasion of illegal hordes." Advocates of restriction, without a clear idea of how many illegals there were or much evidence about what jobs they held, blamed them for a variety of social ills from low wages to increased crime, disease rates, and welfare costs. Labor unions and social welfare groups clamored for restriction, but the grower lobbies were able to block congressional legislation.

Grower lobbies, however, were unable to block administrative action by President D. Eisenhower's new attorney general, Herbert Brownell, who in 1954 launched "Operation Wetback." In early June, immigration officials, with the approval and cooperation of the Mexican government, began the mass roundup and deportation of undocumented workers. At the campaign's height, the Immigration and Naturalization Service (INS) apprehended more than 3,000 undocumented workers a day. According to INS reports, in 1954 the INS secured the departure of 1,035,282 "illegal aliens," who were either apprehended and deported or who left voluntarily. Such claims, however, appear to have been inflated. Officials only apprehended 80,000 people in California and another 80,000 in Texas. These were the two largest states affected. Clearly INS estimates depended on very high estimates of voluntary departures.

The major immediate effect of the campaign was an increase in the recruitment of legal braceros, whose number rose from 3,000 to 70,000 in the lower Rio Grande valley following the campaign, but there were other repercussions. Because the government rarely made sure that the commitments in wages, living conditions, and human rights guaranteed by the bracero agreement were observed, many migrants entered as braceros only to "skip" on their contracts and seek better employment. They thus became "illegals" once more. When the government after 1959 moved to tighten certification requirements necessary for farmers to employ braceros, illegal migration mounted again.

Public Lands

The complex maneuvering between public bureaucracies and private businesses affected public land issues as fully as they did immigration and reclamation policy. The Forest Service, in particular, had to deal with lumber companies and stock raisers trying to gain special privileges on public lands. In this struggle, so-called traditionalists within the Forest Service—that is, those who emphasized timber production and the creation of even-aged, single-species stands—won out over the "stewards." Following the lead of Raphael Zon and Aldo Leopold, the stewards emphasized the multiple use of forest resources. They wanted to pay as much attention to the condition of the land and to the plants and animals growing on it as to timber production.

The pressure to increase the cut on national forests came from lumber companies, which wanted more timber production to feed the postwar housing boom. Having staved off a Forest Service attempt in the 1930s to regulate the lumber industry in order to better promote conservation and reforestation, the timber companies had taken the offensive at the end of World War II. Indeed, in the Sustained Yield Act of 1944 they had turned the Forest Service's own plans against it. Sustained yield had two meanings in the postwar West. It referred first to a policy of guaranteeing the future productivity of forests and second to attempts to stabilize forest industries operating within a forest and the communities dependent on those industries. Ideally, a community could, under sustained yield, preserve both its jobs and its trees by annually harvesting no more timber than the forest produced in an average year. To achieve those goals, the act created two kinds of sustained-yield operations: federal units in which all the land was publicly owned, and cooperative units that combined private and public lands into a single management entity.

Forest Service officials rightly feared that the company-sponsored bill was a Trojan horse; the government-industry cooperation embedded in it provided a means for companies to influence the management of the national forests and to gain monopoly rights within them. In the only cooperative sustained-yield unit established, the Simpson Timber Company got a monopoly on the timber in the national forests in the vicinity of Shelton, Washington. The town of Shelton obtained a guaranteed timber supply. The gain of Simpson and Shelton, however, came at the expense of the neighboring community of Grays Harbor and other timber companies that lost access to trees within the sustained-yield unit. The uproar over the Shelton Unit spread when the Forest Service attempted to establish other units in Montana and California. It failed in the face of intense local opposition from townspeople and smaller companies who did not wish to lose their economic base when a neighbor secured a monopoly.

It was easier for the Forest Service to establish purely federal units without local consent, but these, too, became a source of frustration and complaint. In the Vallecitos Unit of northern New Mexico, sustained-yield management threatened the already tenuous grazing economy of nearby villages, and the villagers waged a determined effort to thwart the Forest Service. In the Flagstaff, Arizona, Unit the Forest Service did establish successful sustained yield, but only by granting Southwest Forest Industries a local economic empire based on privileged access to the surrounding forests. Such monopolies stirred up resentment from those denied access. By linking stability to a limited monopoly granted certain favored lumber companies, the Sustained Yield Act aroused the opposition of smaller companies, labor unions whose members lost jobs when employers lost their access to timber, and towns whose mill owners were denied access to the forests.

The failure of sustained-yield units and cooperative management made it all the harder for the Forest Service to resist simultaneous industry charges that they were hoarding timber. Richard McCardle, the head of the Forest Service in the 1950s, made concessions to industry, in part to stave off suggestions from within the Eisenhower administration that the national forests should be significantly reduced in size. The Forest Service allowed private companies to make larger harvests in the national forests, and it cut the roads necessary to make such harvests possible. Road cutting both subsidized private timber companies and opened up previously inaccessible lands to increased use of all kinds. By 1970 the national forests, which had produced only 9 percent of the nation's timber at the end of World War II, were producing nearly one-third of the national cut. Increased production brought with it increased erosion and watershed damage and problems in regenerating some species.

The increased harvest in the national forests were but a part of the much larger harvest that created the lumber that built the growing suburbs of the 1940s and 1950s. Both large corporations like Weyerhaeuser and Georgia-Pacific and smaller "gyppo" operations, which cut second-growth timber or isolated sections of first-growth trees, prospered. As one gyppo operator from Coos Bay, Oregon, remembered, "There was a little mill stuck back in every little nook and cranny." But as timber supplies on private lands dwindled, the gyppo operators could not outbid the bigger companies for the right to lumber the national forests. Big operators, too, used the trade organizations to put the squeeze on the smaller operators by pushing for grade-marked lumber, which the gyppos could not produce in their small mills.

Livestock owners also tried, but failed, to increase their access to the national forests. Indeed, following the war the Forest Service made a concerted attempt to reduce livestock numbers in the national forests in order to restore overgrazed lands and to permit wildlife to increase. The policy met opposition both in Congress and among western livestock raisers. Congressman Frank Barrett of Wyoming initiated an investigation of the Forest Service designed to humiliate the service and wring concessions from it, while the American Livestock Association meeting in Phoenix passed a resolution calling for the transfer of grazing lands either into private hands or to the Department of the Interior for lease and sale.

As the livestock interests attacked the Forest Service, they were, in turn, attacked by other groups with interests in the national forests. Bernard DeVoto, the Utah-born editor and columnist of *Harper's* magazine, had a deep concern for the West and its lands. He accused the ranchers and Congressman Barrett of promoting a land grab in the West. The stock raisers pressed ahead and tried to curtail Forest Service control over grazing through the Uniform Federal Grazing Bill introduced in 1952. If passed, the bill would have given those holding permits a vested legal right in their grazing privileges. Other westerners, however, rallied to the aid of the Forest Service. City dwellers and irrigation farmers both depended on mountain streams flowing from public land for their water. Urban hunters depended on those lands for game. None of these westerners were about to surrender their claim in favor of a monopoly by stock raisers. The stock raisers retreated, their only consolation the nearly complete domination they continued to exert over lands controlled by the Bureau of Land Management (BLM).

The BLM came into existence in 1946 when President Truman merged the old General Land Office and the Grazing Service, which had, after a fashion, administered the Taylor Grazing Act. In 1949, BLM Director Marion Clawson tried to reduce overstocking on the public lands, but the ranchers who made up the advisory boards proved more powerful than the director of the agency, and they blocked the attempt. Clawson and his successors proved tenacious, however, and in the 1950s and 1960s the ranchers managed to restrict increases in grazing fees and reductions in grazing permits, but they could not stop them entirely. By the 1960s the BLM, like the Forest Service, had developed a cadre of professional administrators and range scientists able to combat ranchers on more even terms. Even with increases in fees and reduction in the number of animals, however, the federal government's management of the public domain still represented a substantial subsidy to ranchers, because fees for use of the public lands were far less than equivalent fees for the use of private lands.

In 1960, as a result of controversies in the national forests and on public lands, Congress passed the Multiple Use-Sustained Yield Act as an attempt to reconcile the competing demands on national forest lands. Supposedly no use received priority, but environmentalist critics argued that by combining sustained yield and multiple use, the bill seemed to give timber production a priority. The act did little to solve the conflicts over the national forests. During the 1960s the Forest Service continued to come under attack, but less from timber companies and stock raisers than from environmentalists, who accused the service of surrendering to the loggers and ranchers who had attacked the service in the 1950s.

The Scope of Change

During and after World War II, federal investment had, seemingly, brought stability and prosperity to a region whose economy had previously soared and swooped like a badly handled kite. The government and larger corporations promised to consolidate much of the American West into the managed, bureaucratized urban form that had been coalescing since the early twentieth century. Post–World War II migration had flowed largely to metropolitan areas; they had increased their strength vis-à-vis the rural West and had made the rural western regions more than ever satellites of the metropolitan regions. Similarly, the other centers of western power, the federal bureaucracies and the corporations, had sometimes clashed, but on the whole they had worked out mutual accommodations and increased their own strength and size. The West had found in the federal government the engine for development it had long sought; the growth it so cherished seemed to stretch endlessly before it.

Readings

Alexander, Thomas G. "Timber Management, Traditional Forestry and Multiple-Use Stewardship: The Case of the Intermountain Region, 1950–85." *Journal of Forest History* 33 (January 1989):21–34.

Anderson, Karen. *Wartime Women: Sex Roles, Family Relations, and the Status of Women During World War II.* Westport, Conn.: Greenwood Press, 1981.

Arroyo, Luis Leobardo. "Chicano Participation in Organized Labor: The CIO in Los Angeles, 1938–50; an Extended Research Note." *Aztlán* 6 (1975), no. 2: 277–301.

Barrera, Mario. *Race and Class in the Southwest: A Theory of Racial Inequality*. Notre Dame: University of Notre Dame Press, 1979.

Bernard, Richard M., and Bradley H. Rice. *Sun Belt Cities: Politics and Growth Since World War II*. Austin: University of Texas Press, 1983.

Bottles, Scott L. *Los Angeles and the Automobile: The Making of the Modern City*. Berkeley: University of California Press, 1987.

Broussard, Albert S. "Strange Territory, Familiar Leadership: The Impact of World War II on San Francisco's Black Community." *California History* 65 (March 1986): 18–25.

Clary, David A. *Timber and the Forest Service*. Lawrence: University Press of Kansas, 1986.

———. "What Price Sustained Yield? The Forest Service, Community Stability, and Timber Monopoly under the 1944 Sustained Yield Act." *Journal of Forest History* 31 (January 1987):4–18.

Craig, Richard B. *The Bracero Program: Interest Groups and Foreign Policy*. Austin: University of Texas Press, 1971.

Droker, Howard. "Seattle Race Relations During the Second World War." In *Experiences in a Promised Land: Essays in Pacific Northwest History*, pp. 353–68. Ed. G. Thomas Edwards and Carlos A. Schwantes. Seattle: University of Washington Press, 1986.

Findlay, John M. *People of Chance: Gambling in American Society from Jamestown to Las Vegas*. New York: Oxford University Press, 1986.

Foster, Mark S. *Henry J. Kaiser: Builder in the Modern American West*. Austin: University of Texas Press, 1989.

Frederic, Kenneth D., and James C. Hanson. *Water for Western Agriculture*. Washington, D.C.: Resources for the Future, 1982.

Garcia, Juan Ramon. *Operation Wetback: The Mass Deportation of Mexican Undocumented Workers in 1954*. Westport, Conn.: Greenwood Press, 1980.

Garcia, Mario. *Mexican Americans: Leadership, Ideology, and Identity, 1930–1960*. New Haven: Yale University Press, 1989.

Gluck, Sherna B. *Rosie the Riveter Revisited: Women, the War, and Social Change*. Boston: Twayne Publishers, 1987.

Gordon, Margaret S. *Employment Expansion and Population Growth: The California Experience: 1900–1950*. Berkeley: University of California Press, 1954.

Green, Donald E. *Land of the Underground Rain: Irrigation on the Texas High Plains, 1910–1970*. Austin: University of Texas Press, 1973.

Koppes, Clayton. "Efficiency/Equity/Esthetics: Towards a Reinterpretation of American Conservation." *Environmental Review* 11 (Summer 1987):127–46.

———. "Public Water, Private Land: Origins of the Acreage Limitation Controversy, 1933–1953." *Pacific Historical Review* 47 (November 1978): 607–36.

Lawson, Michael L. *Dammed Indians: The Pick-Sloan Plan and the Missouri River Sioux, 1944–80*. Norman: University of Oklahoma Press, 1982.

Lee, Lawrence B. "California Water Politics: Opposition to the CVP, 1944–1980." *Agricultural History* 54 (July 1980): 402–23

Mazón, Mauricio. *The Zoot Suit Riots: The Psychology of Symbolic Annihilation*. Austin: University of Texas Press, 1984.

Morgan, Neil. *Westward Tilt: The American West Today*. New York: Random House, 1963.

Nash, Gerald. *World War II and the West: Reshaping the Economy*. Lincoln: University of Nebraska Press, 1990.

———. *The American West Transformed: Impact of the Second World War.* Bloomington: Indiana University Press, 1985.

Ottoson, Howard W., et al. *Land and People in the Northern Plains Transition Area.* Lincoln: University of Nebraska Press, 1966.

Robbins, William G. "Lumber Production and Community Stability: A View from the Pacific Northwest." *Journal of Forest History* 31 (October 1987):187–96.

Rowley, William D. *U.S. Forest Service Grazing and Rangelands: A History.* College Station: Texas A&M University Press, 1985.

Schlebecker, John T. *Cattle Raising on the Plains: 1900–61.* Lincoln: University of Nebraska Press, 1963.

Shover, John. *First Majority–Last Minority: The Transforming of Rural Life in America.* De Kalb, Ill.: Northern Illinois University Press, 1980.

Wiley, Peter, and Robert Gottlieb. *Empires in the Sun: The Rise of the New American West.* Tucson: University of Arizona Press, 1985.

PART SIX

The Modern West

To many people the idea of a modern West seems to be an oxymoron—a combination of words that is inherently contradictory. The "real" West can't be modern. It is nineteenth-century Dodge City or Virginia City; it is not late-twentieth-century Los Angeles or Dallas. Symbolically, the West in American culture stands for certain qualities and events that cannot survive the process of development; they vanish as a place matures. It is not sufficient to be merely in the West to be western. For example, in the 1980s two of the more popular national television series featuring western settings were "Dallas" and "L.A. Law." Despite being set in the West, neither were of the West, and they were certainly not "westerns." They were stories that depended on the West only for accessories: ranches, oil wells, palm trees, and beaches. In essence they were stories about rich people, corporate executives, and young lawyers. They communicated the generic joys and tribulations of people who possess large sums of money. "L.A. Law" could have been "New York Law." Television, in short, had reduced the modern West to something called life-style, a sort of cultural costume that could be replaced by another costume without changing anything fundamental.

Have television scriptwriters inadvertently found the truth? Had the West "matured" and become, except for a few superficial matters of style and climate, a place interchangeable with the rest of the United States? It is a question that springs inevitably from our habit of comparing regions to organisms that are born, grow, mature, and, since we do not allow them to die, reach a final phase of homogenization. We metaphorically give our regions life spans or stages of life and then act as if our regions really are organisms. In the 1960s and 1970s commentators regularly spoke of the West as having come of age.

In the mature West leaders and institutions had attained a new stature and a new national power; they had attained great influence over federal bureaucracies that they had once feared would dictate to them. In the mature West, the world's largest bank, the Bank of America, was a western bank, and major corporations made their headquarters in Houston, Los Angeles, San Francisco, and Seattle.

The mature West became, among other things, the best place to be born, or at least reside, if you wished to run for the presidency. In 1952 and 1956 a general from Kansas, Dwight D. Eisenhower, ran for president and won. In 1960 another westerner, Richard Nixon of California, ran for president of the United States and lost. In 1964, Barry Goldwater of Arizona ran for president. He lost, indeed as badly as anyone in American history had lost up until that time, but he lost to another westerner, the Texan Lyndon Baines Johnson. In 1968, Richard

Nixon, now a New York lawyer, ran again and won against Hubert Humphrey. In 1972, Nixon defeated a South Dakotan, Senator George McGovern. Victory returned Nixon to California, where he established his summer White House. When the Watergate scandal forced him to resign under the threat of impeachment in 1972, he retired to California. In 1980 and 1984 yet another Californian, Ronald Reagan, won the presidency. In 1988 a Texan of a sort, George Bush, won the presidency. In total, of the presidential elections between 1952 and 1988, westerners won 80 percent of them. And in every election except that of 1976, at least one candidate was a westerner. In two elections, both candidates were westerners.

As sections of the West became powerful and populous, they became powerful and populous in ways that made them seem quite similar to older centers of power and population. The freeways and suburbs of Los Angeles, Dallas, and Phoenix, after all, seemed generic freeways and suburbs, differing only in their shrubbery from the turnpikes and suburbs of the East, South, or Midwest. As multinational corporations operated around the globe and swallowed up companies that once seemed huge in their own right, it seemed of lessening import whether corporate headquarters were located in New York or Los Angeles. Physically and climatically, the West still appeared different from the East. The East lacks deserts and anything a westerner would call a mountain. But the East now, too, had national forests and national parks, and both sections shared modern environmental amenities such as smog and acid rain. Outside of Washington, D.C., the federal bureaucracy was not as overwhelmingly apparent in the East as in the West, but the military-industrial complex so ubiquitous in the West was only slightly less so in the East. In terms of daily life and perspectives, a Los Angeleno, a Denverite, or a San Franciscan probably did have more in common with someone from Washington, D.C., Chicago, or New York than with most residents of Wyoming or Montana. The lawyers of "L.A. Law" were more at home in New York than in Lander, Wyoming. The stars of "Dallas" knew their way around a corporate boardroom better than a Billings bar.

Yet arguments for the maturing modern West and for the lack of distinctive common qualities in the West miss the point because they misunderstand the nature of regions and the relationship between regional identity and national trends. Organic analogies of growth and maturation fail precisely because the West had not undergone some predictable evolution toward maturity, independence, and equality. The West is not and has never been an organic unit. It is neither a social unit that advances from immaturity to maturity nor a social unit that has sprung from the physical place itself and is an expression of that place.

The West is not an organism; it is a set of relationships. Its history is more akin to a marriage than to a child growing to maturity. Marriages and other relationships do not evolve organically. And far from depending on the partners' being identical, they depend on the opposite. That Hollywood has little in common with Casper, that San Francisco is culturally closer to New York than to Butte, is certainly significant, but it does not mean that these western places do not have important relationships with each other. The West has always been a much-divided place: a series of urban enclaves and rural communities, a mixture of

peoples whose links have never been based on common culture or mutual affection. The West may be an often unhappy marriage, but it endures.

What connects the various parts of the West, the various ethnic and racial
groups and classes, and makes it akin to a polygamous marriage is a series of
interlocking relationships. These relationships are historical. They developed
over time; they were not latent in the place itself. A common geographical
location between the Missouri and the Pacific has provided a weak link for
a relationship between western communities; stronger ties have ensured the
persistence of the region. A common dependent relationship to the federal
government and a common economic origin in a largely extractive and service-
based economy were formative influences. A dual labor system based on race and
the existence of minority groups with distinctive legal relationships to the larger
society have defined the American West; particular patterns of party loyalty and
political organization, and widespread aridity, have proven to be enduring traits.
Except for aridity they are all creations of the history of the region. They have
made the West a historical creation.

But history can destroy as well as create. It is possible that in the modern West
some of the old relationships no longer matter very much, that new ones have
superseded them. There is no denying that national and international developments significantly reshaped the modern West. Between 1960 and 1988 the civil
rights movement, the restructuring of the national economy, a world energy
crisis, shifts in the world economy, foreign wars, and refugees all have had a
significant effect on the West. The West has changed.

Yet, granting all this, the West remains a distinctive section in a much larger
nation. National trends affect it, but these trends often take on unique regional
forms or have distinctive regional results. Like a flash flood roaring down a
southwestern arroyo, national or international trends seem to transform everything. But in seeing a dry gully transformed into a raging river it is easy to forget
that in another sense the arroyo has captured the storm and has carried it along
the same path traveled by so many earlier storms. The arroyo itself can serve as
the metaphor for western history. Itself the result of past storms, it shapes and
guides current storms even as it is changed by them. Each storm has an effect,
but when the storm is gone, the arroyo, although changed, will remain. What
seem to be the most sudden and momentous changes in the West often eventually
lead westerners back to old channels of their past, to the arroyos of western history
itself.

CHAPTER 19

Rise of the Metropolitan West

THE West that emerged from World War II was, above all, a metropolitan West. Old cities expanded. Small communities became booming cities. Sagebrush flats, desert mesas, and coastal tidelands all sprouted suburbs and towns that freeways and secondary roads wove together until by 1970, 83 percent of the people in the Mountain and Pacific Coast states lived in metropolitan areas. Four of the country's top ten metropolitan concentrations were in the West, and of the ten fastest growing standard metropolitan statistical areas (SMSAs) between 1970 and 1980, half were in the West.

Much of this metropolitan growth fed on federal activity. In postwar San Diego, 78 percent of the city's manufactures were related to national defense. Despite attempts to diversify, San Antonio's economy depended on surrounding military bases. The most economically successful cities, however, also became financial and commercial centers. These regional capitals—Denver, Phoenix, Portland, Seattle, San Francisco, Houston, Dallas, and Los Angeles—were headquarters for both corporations and the federal bureaucracy. The powerful California metropolitan concentrations of Los Angeles and San Francisco and the Texas metropolitan areas of Dallas and Houston tilted the entire West away from its old east-west axis. The lines of power now ran north-south from these new metropolitan centers on the southwestern rim into the rest of the West. Two different, but intertwined, Wests had emerged: one mostly rural and largely powerless, and the other largely metropolitan and increasingly powerful.

The creation of these different but linked Wests from a common past and common processes is the central story of late-twentieth-century western history. It is a complicated story. It is in part a continuation of the familiar theme of the western search for growth and the capital—both federal and private—necessary to fund growth. But it differs because in the late twentieth century many westerners sought growth not to imitate the East but instead to create urban areas that differed from their own vision of what prevailed in the East. Westerners defined a West in opposition to the East and then attempted to build it.

Growth Networks and Metropolitan Politics

Planned growth in the American West took two related forms following World War II. The first centered on downtown development. The second encouraged growth along the peripheries of existing urban areas. In both cases, however, business and political leaders have proven unwilling to leave growth to chance, to the vagaries of the market, or to older forms of boosterism. They have instead created what scholars have called growth networks—that is, alliances of bankers,

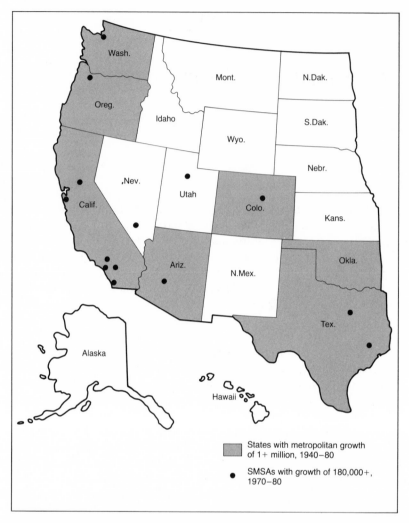

Metropolitan growth in the West. From Gerald D. Nash and Richard W. Etulain, eds., *The Twentieth Century West: Historical Interpretations* (Albuquerque: University of New Mexico Press, 1989).

corporate executives, real estate interests, politicians, and labor leaders. In a sense, the lineal descendants of nineteenth-century boosters, these growth networks are much more complex.

Growth networks have made their larger political case and gained popular support by arguing that growth equals prosperity and that growth will create urban environments better suited to the western landscape and pace of life. Tucson billboards that asked, "Does Your Job Depend on Growth?" and bumper stickers that declared, "Construction Feeds My Family," all expressed the basic argument that growth brought full employment. Growth, too, the argument went, would eventually decrease the share of the tax burden that any single taxpayer had to bear.

All this proved compelling to westerners, who were already predisposed to believe it. Incomes were rising in western metropolitan areas, where median family incomes nearly tripled between 1950 and 1970. Ironically, however, in terms of per capita personal income, large parts of the West were actually losing the lead they had held over the rest of the United States. Between 1940 and 1974 the per capita income of residents of the Pacific Coast states declined from well above to about even with the national average, while that of Arizona, Colorado, Texas, and Kansas residents rose from well below to slightly below or at the national average. Per capita income in Utah, New Mexico, and Oklahoma remained well below the national average. Growth obviously had differential effects across the West.

The least regionally distinctive western growth networks arose in older, well-established urban areas where leaders, as in the Northeast and Midwest, sought to reverse decay in downtown areas as population and new industries located in the suburbs. Portland stagnated following World War II. San Francisco experienced a decline in blue-collar employment, in residential population, and in real estate values during the late 1940s and 1950s. In 1956, James D. Zellerbach, head of Crown-Zellerbach, the paper products company headquartered in San Francisco, joined stockbroker Charles Blyth, head of an investment banking firm and a major holder in Hewlett-Packard, to form the Blyth-Zellerbach Committee "to serve as a catalyst for the entire renewal effort."

The renewal efforts of the Blyth-Zellerbach Committee centered on downtown development, and the committee welcomed, indeed it required, aid from the federal government even when that aid involved federal controls. The alternate western development strategy of low taxes, minimal regulation, and nonunion work forces was not promising for cities, such as San Francisco, with strong unions and established public services. Such established cities needed federal funds to rehabilitate declining downtown areas, for private capital was unwilling to do so alone. To get these federal funds, they were willing to tolerate federal controls.

A major source of this aid was the Housing Act of 1949, which provided the essential seed capital for urban renewal by granting federal assistance to local agencies and private developers who proposed projects devoted to "predominantly residential uses." Because destroying apartments and creating luxury hotels was a predominantly residential use, the act allowed significant leeway to developers. Urban renewal became the euphemism for the destruction and eventual rebuilding of inner-city areas. Later amendments to the act allowed up to 20 percent of the grants to go for nonresidential uses.

The triumph of growth networks devoted to urban renewal came only after a struggle within the local elite in which corporate leaders displaced an older coalition of bankers and merchants. In Denver, which the journalist John Gunther described as the "most complacent city in the world," conservative business leaders feared that growth would bring an intrusion of newcomers who could challenge their dominance. In combination with "Interminable" Ben Stapleton, the mayor since 1923 (with a one-term vacation), they fought efforts to change the city in ways that might weaken their control and increase taxes. When Stapleton responded to the growth in Denver's population that produced the housing shortage of 1945–46 by declaring, "If all these people would only go back where they came from, we wouldn't have a housing shortage," he delineated with a certain blundering accuracy the differences over growth that split the local business community. James Quigg Newton's victory over Stapleton in 1947 marked the triumph of progrowth reformers, but the intrusion of outsiders and outside capital that the local elite had feared came to pass. When in the ensuing decades local banks refused to finance Denver's downtown expansion, the money came in from outside capitalists such as William Zeckendorf and the Murchison brothers of Dallas. The real decisions about Denver's future were being made outside of Denver.

Largely because of such power battles within the cities, urban renewal did not hit full stride in the West until the 1960s, but it then physically and socially transformed many western downtowns. San Francisco's Blyth-Zellerbach Committee had by 1959 secured control of the San Francisco Redevelopment Agency (SFRA) and had become a virtual shadow government within the city. In the 1960s, the SFRA and its corporate allies undertook projects that called for one-half billion dollars in private funds and one-third billion dollars in federal expenditures. Urban renewal sparked a building boom during the 1960s and 1970s that erased the low San Francisco skyline and erected a new high-rise financial district in the place of the old downtown. City government saw its tax revenues dramatically increase; the corporate sponsors of redevelopment profited from a revitalized downtown; and private real estate interests benefited from rising property values. The financial district became one of many virtually interchangeable glass and concrete urban cores of the West.

Urban renewal did not, however, allot its benefits evenly, nor did it always deliver them on time. The ability of bulldozers and wrecking balls to destroy buildings exceeded the ability of developers to finance and erect new ones. While downtown San Francisco grew and expanded, parts of the adjoining residential district, the Western Addition, came to look as if a war was in progress. In Denver, the city created an urban renewal authority in 1958, but only in the late 1960s did a federal grant enable the authority to begin to redevelop 37 blocks of the city's original business district. The bulldozers attacked before the city secured sufficient capital to rebuild. The result was a huge hole in the heart of Denver. Not until the early 1970s, when oil company money poured into the city, was much of the downtown rebuilt.

Even in the neighborhoods where rebuilding did occur rapidly, urban renewal often corrected the blight of poverty by eliminating the poor, driving them into other neighborhoods or public housing projects. Overall, urban renewal and redevelopment meant that young, middle-class, white, and usually childless people replaced older, often black or Mexican American, lower-class families. In San Francisco the young whites moving in were often homosexual, and this gave the social transformation of that city a distinctive aspect, but the demographic results in San Francisco were the same as in Seattle, a city with a much smaller gay population. By the late 1970s Seattle found that only 25 percent of its households contained children.

Corporations took particular interest in procuring federal funds for downtown developments because urban downtowns had become the nerve centers of complicated business enterprises. In an increasingly information-dependent economy, corporate executives relied on a whole new sector of support services—accounting firms, law firms, management consulting firms, advertising agencies, public rela-

The oil boom of the 1970s transformed the Denver skyline and paved the way for the bust of the 1980s.

tion agencies, and others—to keep their headquarters functioning. Downtown skyscrapers busily received and processed information that controlled, in turn, research and production at suburban sites.

A second kind of growth network grew up in the Southwest. Later associated with the rise of the Sun Belt, these alliances were initially more freewheeling, more economically innovative, and far more politically conservative. In Phoenix, and in much of Texas and the Southwest, local real estate and development interests instead of corporate leaders spearheaded the progrowth forces. Los Angeles was their model. They were less concerned with downtown renewal than with urban growth in general, and they evolved different strategies: they emphasized their low taxes, minimal regulation, and nonunion work forces in attempts to attract outside business.

Although local real estate promoters, business leaders, and bankers often originated this strategy, its very success meant that leadership had to be shared with the corporate leaders it attracted. By the mid-1970s heads of corporate branches that had moved to Phoenix and heads of local corporations, such as Ramada Inn and Southwestern Forest Products, that had grown to be major national corporations diluted the strength of local bankers, businessmen, and real estate interests. In Houston, too, the leaders of the old Suite 8F crowd, a group of bankers and businessmen who dominated Houston politics from 1947 into the 1970s, gave way to executives who came with the 150 companies that moved divisions, subsidiaries, or headquarters to Houston between the late 1960s and late 1970s.

Boosters in Houston and Phoenix liked to emphasize their cities' dependence on free enterprise, but these cities, too, had close links with local, state, and national governments. A free enterprise strategy did not necessarily equal a devotion to the free market. Houston and Phoenix sought federal aid; what they sought to avoid was federal regulation. Houston solicited the National Aeronautics and Space Administration's Manned Spacecraft Center, but before 1974 it turned down federal social and community programs. In Arizona the federal government channeled Federal Housing Administration and Veterans Administration loans into the Phoenix and Tucson areas, and these loans ignited a housing boom that then drew in eastern capital.

These Sunbelt strategies aided business while putting the costs of development disproportionately on the poor who could not compensate for the lack of public services. In Houston, where the Suite 8F crowd essentially selected who would be mayor, the same policies that achieved a "good business climate" also created or exacerbated problems ranging from subsidence, flooding, water pollution, toxic waste, and sewage to street maintenance problems. In Phoenix the Charter Government Committee, a local business committee that reviewed and sanctioned candidates for local office, dominated city government. Their first slate for Phoenix City Council included Barry Goldwater, and between 1949 and the mid-1970s only two council candidates won election without the committee's backing. The Phoenix city government in turn encouraged new businesses to settle in Phoenix through favorable tax breaks and right-to-work laws and by acting as a purchasing agent for companies seeking land in Phoenix.

Local promotional activities easily reached into the state government. In 1976 the future governor, Bruce Babbitt, complained that state government in Arizona existed only "for the purpose of facilitating business deals." Wide-open promotion in Phoenix eventually brought widespread corruption. Investigations in the wake of the murder of reporter Don Bolles—a man who had learned too much— revealed not only predictable fraud but also possible connections with organized crime on the part of some members of the Phoenix growth network.

Suburbs

Although growth networks found their leadership in the cities, downtowns, and large cities in general, they accounted for only a small portion of western metropolitan expansion. Indeed, urban renewal itself arose partially as a defensive response to the growth of suburbs. Suburban growth took place throughout urban America, but the newer, more malleable western cities proved particularly responsive to the changes suburbanization brought. Westerners associated suburbanization with their own cultivation of environmental amenities and an informal pace of life. And progrowth forces, by creating the necessary infrastructure of roads, sewer systems, water supplies, and other services permitted the development of ever-expanding metropolitan areas.

In the postwar West this expansion involved the relocation and reorganization of industry as well as residential areas. The new industries of this metropolitan West differed greatly from the old extractive industries of the rural West. The Stanford Industrial Park pioneered a new industrial spatial pattern that spread from the West to the rest of the country. Following World War II, Stanford University sought to develop its sizable landholdings around its Palo Alto campus in a way that would allow the university both to compete against eastern schools for faculty and to attract aid from business and government. Stanford also wanted to provide jobs for its graduates, who complained about enduring "exile in the East" as a price of employment.

To achieve these goals, Stanford in 1951 launched the first university-sponsored industrial park in the country. Frederick Terman, the dean of engineering at Stanford, created ties among the university, the federal government, and firms such as Fairchild Semiconductor and Hewlett-Packard. These links between the university and industry created what became known as Silicon Valley as the computer industry and associated firms created more than one hundred other industrial parks in what had been the apricot and cherry orchards of the Santa Clara Valley. By the early 1980s, of the 430,000 jobs in the electronics industry in California the vast majority were in the suburbs. Palo Alto, for example, had 119,453 such jobs, while Los Angeles had only 26,000 and San Francisco 100.

These new industrial centers, with their clean lines, predictable architecture, and parklike landscaping, formed a dramatic contrast with the dirt, smokestacks, and noise of eastern factories. The new industries demanded educated labor, readily available consultants, proximity to universities and research laboratories, and good transportation connections instead of abundant unskilled labor or natural resources. Yet even as the industrial parks blended in with the surrounding suburbs, they began to re-create familiar problems of congestion, pollution, and low-paying jobs in a new garden setting. In time, many of the high-tech industries of the Silicon Valley feminized their manufacturing forces, with a resulting decline in relative wages. Smog settled over Silicon Valley, housing developments destroyed the tidelands of San Francisco Bay, and traffic congestion by the late 1980s was becoming nearly unbearable.

As in the Silicon Valley, the most spectacular western growth took place outside the boundaries of the large incorporated cities. This suburban growth gave the relatively new and undeveloped cities of the Southwest a great advantage, for they could grow simply by annexing surrounding areas. San Antonio went from 69 square miles in 1950 to 253.7 square miles by 1974, and Oklahoma City, Tulsa, Houston, Dallas, Fort Worth, Phoenix, San Diego, San Jose, and El Paso all added at least 90 square miles each to their boundaries between 1950 and 1970. Southwestern cities could annex land more easily than cities such as San Francisco, Portland, and Seattle, because local loyalties had not yet had time to crystalize around suburban governments and because state laws made such annexations relatively easy. Only in the 1970s did southwestern suburban areas grow strong enough to tighten state laws governing annexation.

Even with urban annexation, however, independent suburbs accounted for the bulk of the postwar growth. In the San Francisco Bay area, San Francisco, San Jose, and Oakland contained only a few more people than did fifteen surrounding suburban cities with populations of 50,000 and more. In Colorado, Arvada, Aurora, Boulder, and Lakewood held 25 percent of the population of metropolitan Denver, while in Arizona, Tempe, Mesa, Glendale, and Scottsdale accounted for 30 percent of the residents of Phoenix. The numerous municipalities of western metropolitan areas complicated the problems of local government. In the Dallas metropolitan area with 96 municipalities, in Los Angeles with 77, in Houston with 68, and in San Francisco-Oakland with 58, governmental responsibilities became increasingly fragmented.

Journalists, pop sociologists, and social scientists who believed that proper cities should be centralized and clearly bounded disdained this new metropolitan West. One critic, William Whyte, was appalled at Los Angeles's "vast smog-filled deserts that are neither city, suburb nor country." It was rare to read a serious description of the new "sprawl," as it was most often called, that was not an implicit denunciation. But millions of people found the sprawl satisfactory enough to migrate eagerly into the new suburbs.

Indeed, westerners sought sprawl; the landscape it yielded was hardly the random, inchoate waste that Whyte believed. It was evolving into a new multicentered form of urban growth. Any resident of a western metropolitan area such as Denver, Los Angeles, or Tucson recognized its patterns. There were sharp and clear distinctions between high-status areas—always white—and low-status areas, often nonwhite. And these patterns were not random. Within the "sprawl," high-prestige areas in the city often adjoined high-prestige suburbs. Low-prestige urban areas usually bordered low-prestige areas outside the city.

The symbols of these new western cities were the automobile and the detached private home (usually the western "ranch" house); like so much else in the West, the federal government promoted both. The endless miles of private homes that spread over the West were just as much products of federal policies as were multipurpose dams and national forests. As elsewhere in the nation, federal tax policies subsidized private homes, and federal loan guarantees through the Federal Housing Administration and the Veterans Administration made a home mortgage available to millions who otherwise would never have been able to afford one.

In the West public transportation had long ago given up the race to keep up with the spread of the suburbs. The western devotion to the automobile led to plans for metropolitan expansion built around the private car. As usual Los Angeles led the way. Los Angeles County had the highest per capita ownership of automobiles in the nation in 1960. To combat horrendous traffic problems that threatened to choke the city, the Automobile Club of Southern California proposed in 1937 a series of high-speed motorways that would allow rapid movement across the area. The club's plan evolved into the freeway system of metropolitan Los Angeles. To construct the enormously expensive freeways, various municipalities had to plan and coordinate their efforts, and they had to create a permanent fund for highway construction. They succeeded with the Collier-Burns Act, passed by the California legislature in 1947, which committed gasoline tax and motor vehicle registration fees to support the program. The federal Interstate Highway Act of 1956 supplemented these funds by incorporating some urban freeways into a vast national highway system that eventually reached 42,500

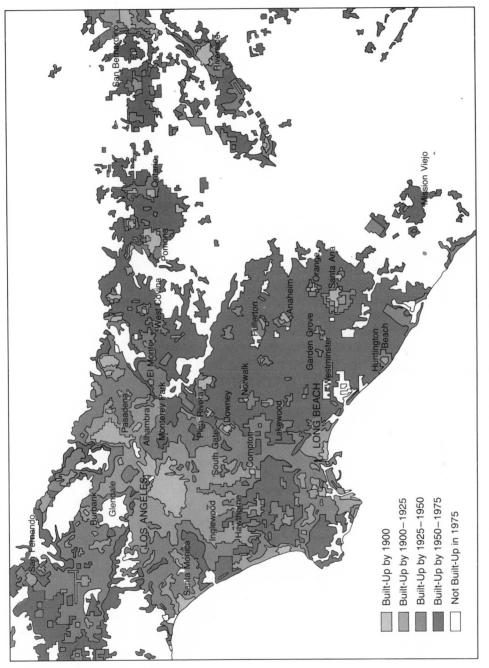

Expansion of Los Angeles. Copyright © 1991 by the University of Oklahoma Press.

Built-Up by 1900
Built-Up by 1900–1925
Built-Up by 1925–1950
Built-Up by 1950–1975
Not Built-Up in 1975

miles. The federal government paid 90 percent of the cost of the interstate highways. By 1960, Los Angeles had 250 miles of freeways, and these were but a small part of a road system that by the 1970s had, along with parking lots, covered one-third of the total area of the city. When car dealerships, garages, driveways, and so on, were added to the road system, about two-thirds of down-town Los Angeles was devoted to the automobile. The car indelibly marked the land in Los Angeles, and as smog increased, it marked the air, too.

In devotion to the car Los Angeles was only the extreme version of California as a whole, California was but an extreme version of the West, and the West an extreme version of the nation. California had 20 percent of the West's roads in 1960, but every state west of the hundredth meridian was above the national average in per capita ownership of cars. The West had begun to set the pattern for the rest of the country.

Postsuburban Metropolises

Orange County, California, became the prototype of the new multicentered metropolitan form that developed out of the suburban sprawl. By the 1980s Orange County was not a suburb. The overwhelming majority of people in the county did not commute to Los Angeles. They worked as well as lived in the county, which was a far more diverse place than the old bedroom communities. Far from being a homogeneous white area, the county contained substantial Asian and Chicano minorities.

The economy of Orange County depended on the rapid movement of people between various specialized centers. Instead of a downtown, the county contained numerous smaller complexes: shopping malls, industrial parks, and campuslike office buildings, all linked together by an elaborate highway system. Of these centers, the most unusual, and one of the most revealing, was Disneyland. Disneyland descended from Hollywood, for Hollywood begat Walt Disney and Walt Disney begat Disneyland. Disneyland was western in more than its location when it opened in 1955. It captured a popular West of romance, optimism, and fantasy in its scripted theme parks: Frontierland, Fantasyland, and Tomorrowland with its Autopia. It took a sentimentalized Main Street America and then filled it with Hollywood cartoon characters—Mickey Mouse, Pluto, and the rest. Walt Disney created his clean, orderly park in opposition to what he regarded as chaotic, dirty eastern cities and their Coney Islands with "tawdry rides and hostile employees." In amusement parks as well as industrial parks, modern westerners moved in a metropolitan landscape created as a counterstatement to their image of the East. Walt Disney thoroughly embedded this western park in the developing southern California landscape of freeways and suburbs that grew up around it. He coordinated the park's development so that it blended in with other local tourist attractions.

Disneyland became one of many specialized nuclei in postsuburban Orange County. The Costa Mesa, Newport Beach, and Irvine metropolitan complex in Orange County had 21.1 million square feet of office space, nearly as much as San Francisco's, and yet this complex was only one of several in the county. Within Orange County such networks of office complexes and industrial parks dwarfed the downtowns of the county's 28 municipalities, such as Anaheim and Santa Ana.

Disneyland—which Walt Disney planned in conscious opposition to eastern urban amusement parks and an eastern way of life—opens in July 1955. (Photograph © copyright by Los Angeles Times)

In Orange County, development companies—the Irvine Company, the Mission Viejo Company, and the Rancho Santa Margarita Company—took over from the local promoters who welcomed growth but found they could not control it. Smaller landowners and contractors, for example, tended to favor zoning for residential suburbs, for this yielded them the largest profits. Larger corporate interests and the development companies, however, pushed for office and industrial areas, for they planned for much greater growth across much larger areas. On the whole the corporate interests won, partially by carrying the battle into the political realm, where they challenged local political elites.

Corporate managers, development company managers, and state politicians tended to scorn local governments with their narrow concerns and visions. They favored, instead, regional planning at a county or state level. They believed such planning was necessary both to secure continued growth and to solve the problems that growth caused. As early as 1970, for example, 16 corporate executives formed the Greater Irvine Industrial League, which in 1982 became the Industrial League of Orange County. They contended that local governments could not handle problems of pollution, traffic congestion, international air transportation, and overburdened municipal services; such problems could only be solved by the county board of supervisors and the state legislature. They encouraged the growth of countywide governmental bodies that would lessen the confusion and inefficiency of competing local governments. Although politically an extremely conservative area, Orange County found itself at the forefront of municipal planning and social change.

Competition for Growth

The growth of metropolitan areas involved contests with their own rural hinterlands, although this competition was often oblique. Much of the conflict centered on the public lands, particularly attempts of urban-based environmentalist organizations such as the Sierra Club to grant nonutilitarian uses (backpacking, hunting, fishing, and the like) of public lands enjoyed by metropolitan residents a status comparable with that of utilitarian uses (logging, grazing, mining, and so on).

Environmentalism had roots in both the older conservation movement, with its focus on the efficient use of resources, and in the preservation movement, with its devotion to preserving "wilderness." Environmentalists, however, had broader concerns than either of their parent groups. Although they often spoke in terms of wilderness and efficient use of resources, the distinctive views of environmentalists stressed the health of ecosystems and the fundamental biological wellbeing of the planet. Without the larger social changes going on in the metropolitan West, environmentalist advocacy (let alone successful advocacy) of restrictions on development would have been impossible. But the prosperity of metropolitan areas following World War II made large numbers of Americans less concerned with scarcity, and thus increased production, and more concerned with consumption and quality of life. More and more metropolitan residents viewed the land not in terms of the resources it produced but rather in terms of the experiences it could provide.

David Brower, a resident of the San Francisco Bay area and head of the Sierra Club, shared, shaped, and focused these changing concerns in a series of battles over the fate of the Colorado River. In 1950 the Bureau of Reclamation had proposed building two dams on the Colorado, both of which would create reservoirs within Dinosaur National Monument in Utah. Brower organized and led a coalition of groups that fought 1956 legislation to build the Echo Park Dam, which would have flooded part of the national monument. His was still only an incipient environmentalism, for it still relied on older preservationist arguments:

first, the sanctity of the national park system, and second, the need to consider nonutilitarian as well as utilitarian values. After a long and bitter fight, the environmentalists stopped the dams in 1956, but their triumph turned out to be a pyrrhic victory. To save Dinosaur National Monument the environmentalists agreed not to oppose the construction of another dam that flooded Glen Canyon, one of the most stunning combinations of river and rock on the globe.

The lesson environmentalists thought they had learned at Dinosaur—that saving one area sometimes meant the loss of another—had to be relearned farther down the Colorado. In the 1960s Brower and the Sierra Club fought to stop the construction of dams that would flood parts of the Grand Canyon. This time they did not stop one dam by conceding another; instead they argued that coal-fired or nuclear power plants could compensate for the electricity lost by the failure to build the dams. The result was the strip mining of Black Mesa on the Navajo and Hopi reservations and the construction of the coal-burning Navajo Power Plant at Page, Arizona. The environmentalists were discovering the Janus-faced attitudes that metropolitan areas brought to the western environment. On the one hand they provided support to preserve the environment for nonutilitarian uses. On the other hand the relentless demand of the metropolitan West for water and energy provided the impetus for the dams, nuclear power plants, and strip mines that ravaged the western landscape.

Competition over the uses for federal lands did not remain simply a rural-urban split. Municipal regions began to fight among themselves for access to resources beyond their metropolitan borders and for the federal and private funds necessary to build the basic economic infrastructure required to sustain growth. The freeways that moved people and goods to, from, and through the metropolitan systems, the water that flowed in to sustain the systems, and even much of the electrical power that gave the systems their energy depended on federal investments. Metropolitan leaders had to secure these investments years before the metropolitan areas actually needed the water, power, or freeways.

Originally, the need for federal investments had spawned cooperation between the growth networks of individual cities. Federal programs that provided money for freeways, for water, and for energy development potentially helped all western metropolitan regions to grow. But by the late 1970s the search for federal funds and access to water had become increasingly competitive as federal deficits and declining water resources limited the likelihood that all municipalities would get what they wanted. Municipalities battled each other for federal and private funds and for water and energy. The competition yielded strange alliances.

The Competition for Water and Energy

Water became the center of many of the battles between western municipalities. The demand for water has always been the most voracious in southern California, and when southern California grows thirsty, people grow nervous throughout the West. By the 1950s southern California had largely consumed the legacy of Colorado River and Owens Valley water that William Mulholland had left it. Southern California politicians and bureaucrats had renewed their search for future supplies.

Arizonans have particularly feared southern California's thirst for Colorado River water. Unable to resolve its differences with California within the Colorado

River Compact, Arizona in 1952 filed suit to have the Supreme Court settle the issue. The federal government then intervened in the case to make sure that the eventual decision protected the water rights of Indians on some 25 reservations in the lower Colorado basin. In 1963, Arizona and the Indians won (although they would soon be fighting over the fruits of victory), and California, it seemed, lost. Significantly, the federal government also won. By the terms of the court's decision, the secretary of the interior possessed the authority to allocate water among the states, and indeed among users within the states. Southern California, however, got the temporary satisfaction of being able to "borrow" Arizona's share of the Colorado until the Bureau of Reclamation completed the Central Arizona Project. California's congressional delegation, predictably, did all it could to block the Central Arizona Project in Congress.

As municipal officials in southern California tried unsuccessfully to secure their share of Colorado River under the Colorado River Compact, corporate farmers in southern California faced a challenge to their access to Central Valley Project water. In the 1960s and 1970s both California reformers and officials within the Interior Department began to investigate violations of the 160-acre limitation on farms that could receive water from the Central Valley Project. A cultural icon of an older world had been resurrected in the new corporate landscape, and the growers and their political allies rushed to destroy it. In 1982 they secured a change in the federal law that raised the acreage limitation to 960 acres, but by permitting unrestricted leasing, the law made even that figure meaningless.

The double frustration of Arizona's battle for Colorado River water and the attempts to enforce acreage limitation created incentives for southern Californians to look north for additional water free from federal control or claims by other states. It has always been a mark of California's size and power that it alone among western states has been able to plan and attempt to construct massive water projects with at least some independence from the federal government. In 1960, Governor Pat Brown, deliberately underestimating the cost, asked for a $1.75 billion bond issue for the California Water Project (CWP). To northern Californians, whose region had suffered devastating floods in 1955, he portrayed the project as a flood control and power generation measure. The project amounted, however, to a massive transfer of water south to the corporate farmers of southern California. Because this would be a state project, federal acreage limitations would not apply. Large landholders could irrigate huge new areas around Bakersfield, and other farmers could get new water to supplement declining supplies of ground-water.

The first stage of this CWP delivered Feather River water to southern California by pumping it over the Tehachapi Range in five separate stages; it was an immense engineering feat, and the aqueduct became a human-made river longer than any of California's natural rivers. The aqueduct, however, did not deliver as much water as promised, and it did not meet the projected needs of a rapidly growing southern California. Pat Brown's successor, Ronald Reagan (1966–74), disliked big government projects and resisted building more dams. It was left to Jerry Brown (1974–82), Pat Brown's son, to attempt the completion of the water project that his father had begun.

In the mid-1970s Jerry Brown pushed for the second phase of the CWP; it had a price tag of $11 billion. Interest on the bonds would add another $12 billion.

Water development in California. From Warren A. Beck and Ynez D. Haase, *Historical Atlas of California* (Norman: University of Oklahoma Press, 1974), map 77.

This technically complex project planned to take water from the Sacramento River without further harming the river's delta by building a canal peripheral to the main canal that would funnel part of the water diverted higher up the river back into the delta to preserve its wetlands, fish, and wildlife. To persuade northern Californians to go along, Brown promised permanent protection for other northern California coastal rivers.

The result of this complicated proposal was an equally complicated coalition of northern Californians who opposed the peripheral canal (as the whole project came to be called) and agribusiness interests who did not want to be permanently banned from diverting northern rivers. In 1982 voters rejected the peripheral canal, giving southern California a significant setback.

As southern Californians looked north for water, Arizonans continued to battle in Congress to get funding for the Central Arizona Project (CAP), a multibillion-dollar diversion with aqueducts that would stretch 333 miles from the Colorado River to the Phoenix and Tucson areas. There was some urgency to their search, because excessive pumping of the aquifers around Phoenix and Tucson threatened to draw down the water tables so far that pumping would become prohibitively expensive. To win congressional approval for the CAP, the Arizona delegation ultimately had to make a huge concession to the Californians, the so-called California guarantee: before Arizona could take a drop out of the Colorado for the CAP, California had to receive its entire allocation. In dry years California might figuratively drain the river, leaving only enough water to meet American treaty guarantees to Mexico.

The battle between southern California and Arizona for the Colorado River in turn created anxiety farther upriver. In theory, Colorado and Utah had nothing to worry about, for the Colorado River Compact had made two separate allocations: one for the upper basin and one for the lower basin. In fact, however, the compact had overallocated the river—that is, it had allotted more water to the states than the river actually contained in an average year. Utah and Colorado feared that if they did not act quickly to secure major federal projects, they would never be able to claim their full allocation. Their water would be lost forever.

The Bureau of Reclamation, the existence of which depended on new dam construction, gladly cooperated with all the worried states in securing new water projects. In exchange for supporting the CAP, Utah and Colorado got their own projects, the largest being the Central Utah Project (CUP). Because the bureau's mandate was to irrigate, the original rationale for both the CAP and the CUP was agricultural. In Utah the bureau proposed irrigating at immense cost the marginal agricultural lands of the Uintah Basin and the Wasatch Front.

Both the CUP and the CAP were complex, almost Rube Goldberg creations. With budget overruns and delays, each emerged as a multibillion-dollar project. As the Bureau of Reclamation constructed them, however, the suburbs of the metropolitan West covered much of the farmlands they were designed to serve. Colorado River water might make the desert bloom, but it would do so largely on the lawns of Phoenix, Tucson, and Salt Lake City. By 1988, budgetary constraints had forced the bureau to drop funding for the irrigation networks that originally justified the project in Utah. In Arizona, CAP water promised to be so expensive that most farmers could not afford to use it, but Congress in 1984 voted to make them an interest-free loan to build canals and other distribution systems. In short, the government had to subsidize the agricultural users if they were to be able to afford the water.

Water, as westerners say, flows uphill to money, and the CUP and the CAP, by delivering their water for metropolitan growth, demonstrated where power lay in the new West. But there were limits to the power of the West to command money. The CAP and CUP may very well represent the last of the giant western water projects. By the late 1970s, metropolitan rivalries, federal financial constraints, and rising energy costs had reduced western expectations. Plans once seriously considered to divert the Columbia River or Canadian rivers south or to turn the Mississippi west in order to recharge the southern sections of the Ogallala Aquifer in Texas, now seemed crazy, if recurrent, fantasies.

Financial discipline came from the increasing unwillingness and inability of the federal government to underwrite the plans of western growth networks. President Jimmy Carter made the first attempt to curb the West's demand for water. In 1977, trying to cut inefficient pork-barrel projects whose returns did not justify their costs, he targeted western water projects. In his so-called hit list Carter recommended an immediate suspension of funding on 18 water projects, including the CUP and the CAP, for an estimated savings of $5.1 billion.

Westerners mustered enough power in Congress to force Carter to back down, but the president, and not western politicians, had correctly assessed the future. The huge cost of western projects, the growing budgetary difficulties of the federal government, and the increased competition for water all combined to make new projects unfeasible. With the federal government unable to provide new untapped sources of water, internecine competition developed within the West. Los Angeles increased its withdrawals from the Owens Valley, doing more damage to that much abused area, and turned to the tributaries of Mono Lake. In Arizona, changes in water law, demanded by the Interior Department as a price for the CAP, allowed Phoenix and Tucson to buy up groundwater rights from farmers. By the 1980s San Diego County, denied access to northern California water, had gone shopping for water in western Colorado. Meanwhile, Denver and its suburbs quarreled over water both among themselves and with the rest of the state.

Western water law, always rickety, shook so badly under these conflicts that it demanded reconstruction. Oddly enough, if major changes occur, Indian peoples may be potential winners in the scramble for water. The Winters Doctrine had given tribes prior (but unquantified) water rights that most tribes have never been able to use because they lacked the necessary facilities to tap the rivers. If, as in Arizona, water law evolves to allow the sale or leasing of water rights, some tribes might find it lucrative to sell water to thirsty metropolitan areas. Letting water flow downstream where other users could divert it seems to some Indians more profitable and less environmentally damaging because it stays in natural channels longer than if they used it themselves.

Growth networks needed energy supplies as well as water supplies, and this, too, caused them to seek federal assistance in reaching far beyond their own metropolitan areas. To pump CAP water to Phoenix, the Interior Department and the Bureau of Reclamation entered into the Navajo Project Participation Agreement of 1968 that made the bureau and the department partners with private utilities in the Navajo Power Plant near Page, Arizona. The plant produced electricity by burning coal that it obtained from the Peabody Coal Company.

Peabody got the coal through a lease it negotiated with the Navajos and Hopis that allowed it to mine Black Mesa and to use Navajo water to transport the coal in a coal slurry pipeline. The lease provided the coal at prices well under its market value, and it virtually gave away the precious water. Another Interior Department agency, the Bureau of Indian Affairs, had a trust obligation to protect Navajo and Hopi interests, but it approved the contracts. This was how growth worked. Indian energy and water subsidized Phoenix's energy and water. The Indians lost; Peabody Coal and the metropolitan West won.

The Navajo Project was in turn part of a larger consortium of federal agencies and 23 private and public utilities, the Western Energy Supply and Transmission Association (WEST). The consortium envisioned a network of coal-fired power plants producing three times the power of the Tennessee Valley Authority for Los Angeles, Las Vegas, Phoenix, Tucson, San Diego, and Albuquerque markets. WEST only completed the first phase of the plan. Environmentalists mounted a successful battle to block the second phase, which called for strip coal mining on the previously pristine Kaiparowits Plateau of Utah.

Federal agencies gladly cooperated with growth networks in promoting energy development for western metropolitan areas, but the Bureau of Reclamation, operating virtually as an independent fiefdom without specific congressional authorization, had plans for the export of power outside the West. It entered into another agreement for an energy program that would have involved strip mining 50,000 to 175,000 square miles over 35 years to supply coal-burning plants in eastern Montana, western Dakota, and Wyoming. Approximately 80 percent of the power to be produced under these various plans was for export outside the West.

Growth and the Western Boom-Bust Economy

Rural westerners, viewing this relentless metropolitan search for water and energy, were unsure whether it presented more a threat or an opportunity. For much of the 1970s many rural westerners believed that they would prosper alongside the metropolitan regions. Not until the 1980s, when the rural economy collapsed into an all too familiar shambles as bust followed boom, did the optimism dwindle. The boom had started in agriculture. In the early 1970s American farmers had experienced their most serious recession (1969–71) since the Great Depression, but by 1972 large farmers began to prosper as international markets for grain expanded. Before the 1970s the American government had maintained commodity prices for American farmers by buying up grain and distributing much of it abroad as foreign aid. By the mid-1970s foreign aid accounted for only 15 percent of American agricultural exports. Developing countries and the Soviet Union increased their grain purchases in an effort to give their urban residents cheaper and more abundant food. In addition, the practice of feeding large amounts of grain to domestic animals destined for slaughter, as well as crop failures in Asia and Africa, enlarged world markets. These changes freed western grain farmers of the crop surpluses that had burdened them since World War II. Commercial grain sales rose from $1.7 billion to $7 billion between 1972 and 1975 and continued to boom throughout the 1970s. Overall, U.S. farm exports increased sixfold.

With rising grain prices stoking optimism, production rose. After the huge

American grain sale to the Soviet Union in 1972, Nixon's secretary of agriculture, Earl Butz, urged farmers to plant from fencerow to fencerow. Farmers not only brought marginal land back into cultivation, but also began to invest heavily in new machinery and purchase more land. Cattle raisers also increased the scale of their operations.

But not all signs for the future were so rosy. The first problem confronting farmers and ranchers was energy prices. In 1970 domestic energy production peaked and began to decline as the demand for oil continued to surge. The United States found itself not only a net importer of energy, but also an importer extraordinarily dependent on Middle East sources. In 1973, as the result of the Arab-Israeli Yom Kippur War, Arab oil producers who had formed an oil cartel—the Organization of Petroleum Exporting Countries (OPEC)—embargoed supplies to the United States because of its aid to Israel. Oil prices skyrocketed. After the embargo, prices remained high, and the oil imports continued to rise. By 1980 imports accounted for half of American oil consumption.

Increases in energy costs were particularly significant for American agriculture. Farmers and ranchers depended on cheap energy to run their farm machinery, to pump their water, and to manufacture their fertilizers. The cattle that fattened at western feed lots ate grain produced by energy-intensive farm operations. The whole food production system from planting through harvest, processing, sale, and preparation was energy-intensive. It required ten calories of energy for every calorie of food it provided. In such a system rising energy prices had ramifications up and down the line, forcing increases in costs on producers and consumers.

Rising energy prices helped fuel a second disturbing development: inflation. Moderate inflation helped farmers. It weakened the dollar, allowing farmers to compete more effectively overseas. It also helped those farmers who owned large amounts of land. As investors put money into land as a hedge against inflation, land prices rose. Rising land values alone made many large farmers millionaires, allowing them to use land as collateral to borrow money to obtain more land or to modernize their operations.

In the late 1970s, however, inflation ceased to be moderate, and it began to hurt farmers. Interest rates neared 20 percent, and farmers began to find they had to shoulder larger and larger debt payments to finance their operations. As long as crop prices and world demand continued to rise faster than energy prices and interest rates, farmers avoided disaster. In the late 1970s and early 1980s crop prices failed to rise as quickly as inflation, and farmers began to have trouble paying their debts. By 1982, American farmers were devoting seven times as great a share of their gross receipts to interest payments as they had in the early 1950s. They were soon to discover that the Federal Reserve System's successful attempts to bring inflation under control presented them with even greater dangers than had inflation.

In the early 1980s farmers suffered a one-two punch. First, in January 1980, President Jimmy Carter reacted to the Soviet invasion of Afghanistan by declaring a grain embargo against the Soviet Union, one of the major consumers of U.S. farm exports. The embargo did little harm to the Soviets. Others were eager to sell to them. But it did significant harm to U.S. farmers. It cost farmers the Russian market, and then it cost them additional markets as other nations, worried about potential use of American food as a weapon, moved to lessen their own dependence on the United States. As Australia, Argentina, Canada, and the Common Market countries of Europe boosted grain production to supply old American customers, competition abroad increased and prices fell. Millions of poor hungry people, of course, remained in the world, but poor people cannot afford to buy grain.

Second, in this new, more competitive market, farmers suffered another shock, this time from the Reagan administration. To bring inflation under control, the Federal Reserve in the 1980s tightly curtailed the money supply. This drove dollar exchange rates up by roughly 70 percent between 1980 and 1985. With a more expensive dollar, farmers found themselves being undersold on a world market that was itself shrinking because of worldwide recession. Farmers lost both market share and net income. The value of U.S. agricultural exports fell from $43 billion in 1981 to $29 billion in 1986. Domestically, cattle raisers also faced a declining market. The demand for beef fell by 20 percent as consumers changed their eating habits. Land values fell with farm incomes. Many farmers found themselves paying high interest rates on land that was only worth a fraction of what they had paid for it. The irony of all this was that under a president who proclaimed the virtues of free enterprise, the cost to the government of maintaining farmers in business rose dramatically even as many farmers failed. As late as 1980 commodity price support payments had amounted to only $2.7 billion annually. By 1983 they were up to $19 billion and rising.

Montana can serve as an extreme example of the problems facing western farmers. Ranch land outside of Miles City, Montana, that sold for $130 to $140 an acre during the boom of the 1970s was worth $35 to $70 an acre by the late 1980s. With declining cattle prices, those who had borrowed to obtain such land could not even meet their interest payments. Nature added insult to injury as drought and grasshoppers afflicted farmers in the 1980s. This decline was more than a cyclical slump. It represented, according to the director of Montana's Department of Agriculture, "a fundamental restructuring." Those ranches able to survive had large amounts of capital behind them. In 1940 Montana had approximately 44,000 farms and ranches. By 1987 it had 23,600, each of which was roughly twice the size of its predecessor of 1940. The average age of a rancher in Montana was 51 years; young people could no longer enter the business.

The repercussions echoed throughout the western countryside. Declining numbers of family ranches and farms meant fewer customers for the merchants of the small towns. They lost revenue and went out of business. Throughout the northern plains and the cattle country of the Great Basin, an aura of decay and decline had set in by the 1980s. Barely a hundred years after cattle ranchers and wheat farmers had entered the high plains, some of the people who held on began to imagine that their life would disappear as completely as that of the nomadic buffalo hunters whom their ancestors had displaced. Julian Terrett, a Montana cowboy, thought, "There may come a day when they don't need this land for cattle anymore. They'll figure out a way to grow them inside or something. I don't know what will happen to the land then."

The combination of increased energy costs and falling commodity prices accelerated the collision of western farmers with the environmental limits of the West. On the Great Plains and in Arizona and much of California farmers had thrived on the ability to pump water up from vast underlying aquifers. As the aquifers declined, pumps had to go deeper and deeper and use more and more energy. Rising energy prices made some pumping a money-losing proposition. In Texas and the Great Plains, the Ogallala Aquifer declined 15 or 20 feet between 1972 and 1984, while energy prices rose sevenfold. In Arizona excessive pumping by farmers helped trigger an internal battle between farmers and urban consumers. Declining aquifers also put greater pressure on aboveground rivers. The Colorado, the Pecos in New Mexico, and the Arkansas grew more saline and, in places, useless for irrigation. More and more western rural areas seem in danger of sharing the fate of Owens Valley: their water gone, they will be left to shrivel in the western sun.

The crisis of farming and ranching in the 1980s yielded social and economic consequences that would be felt in the West for years to come. Yet the crisis still represented only the acceleration of longstanding trends in American agriculture that had cut the number of farms, increased the size of remaining farms, and pushed formerly rural people into cities and towns. Agriculture mattered less and less in more and more of the West. Large sections of the West that as late as 1950 had been primarily agricultural had by the early 1980s shifted their economic emphasis elsewhere.

The western lumber industry has always been more localized than farming, and thus its decline in the 1970s and 1980s had a more limited effect, but that effect was still locally devastating. In southwestern Oregon old loggers who worked in the days of steam technology and crosscut saws thought the timber in an area like Coos Bay would last forever; it grew back, they thought, as fast as it was cut. By the 1950s chain saws, gasoline engines, modern mills, and the demand of the housing industry combined to quicken the inroads into the last great expanses of timber along the Oregon coast. The casualties were not just the trees but the loggers themselves. Small gyppo operations that flourished during the housing boom of the late 1940s and 1950s went first. The big operators such as Georgia-Pacific and Weyerhaeuser remained, but they abandoned any pretense of sustained-yield harvesting. In the Coos Bay area Georgia-Pacific moved to liquidate its lumber holdings in order to generate cash flow, while Weyerhaeuser had begun a log export program to Japan by the early 1960s. By the 1970s there was a clear timber shortage in southwestern Oregon. Although those who had jobs with the big companies retained them, there were few opportunities for their children.

The crash came in 1979 as mill after mill closed. In a depressed housing market and with depleted timber, southwestern Oregon could not compete with either Canadian timber or the tree farms of the Southeast, where trees grew more quickly and could be harvested more cheaply. Multinational corporations shifted their resources accordingly; they left behind towns to wither and workers who confronted not only the loss of a job but also the loss of dignity after a lifetime of labor. Younger workers might move, but for older workers there was often nowhere to go. Those lucky enough to remain employed saw the high wages that once characterized the industry weaken as the remaining companies took advantage of their position to demand contract concessions.

The Energy Crisis

Farming, ranching, logging, and mining all offered a reprise of the old boom-and-bust theme of the extractive West, but nowhere was the boom higher and

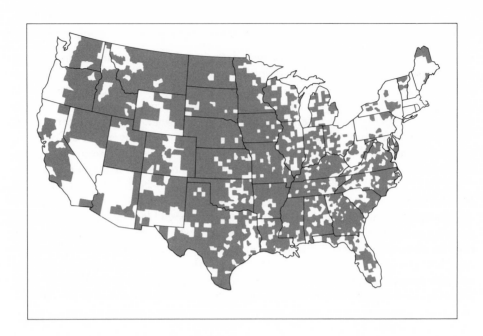

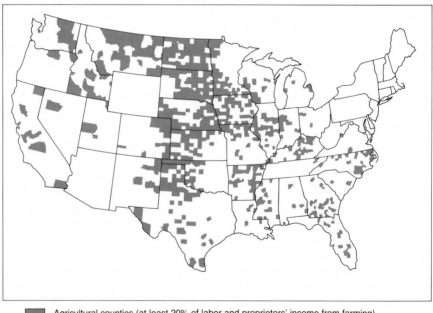

Agricultural counties (at least 20% of labor and proprietors' income from farming)
Other counties

Agricultural counties of the United States, 1950 (*top*) and 1975–77 (*bottom*). From *State of American Agriculture, 1984* (Des Moines, Iowa, and Washington, D.C.: Committee on Food and Agriculture, National Planning Association). The 1975–77 map is from the Economic Development Division, Economic Research Service, U.S. Department of Agriculture, "Agricultural Counties: Their Location, Farms and Economies" (February 1981).

bust lower during the 1970s and 1980s than in energy production. When the combination of declining American oil reserves and the OPEC oil embargo of 1973 revealed the vulnerability of the United States to energy shortages, the West appeared to be the promised land. Under western soils were large reserves of oil, coal, uranium, natural gas, oil shale, and geothermal fuels. California, Texas, and Oklahoma had long been major oil- and natural-gas-producing states, but attention now focused on the mountain West and on the adjacent High Plains states that held most of the coal, uranium, oil shale, and geothermal reserves. Colorado, North Dakota, South Dakota, Montana, Utah, New Mexico, Arizona, and Wyoming collectively had 52 percent of the nation's coal reserves, 48 percent of the nation's uranium, virtually all its shale oil, and significant quantities of oil and natural gas. And most of these reserves were on federal or Indian lands. Their development promised wealth far greater than anything rural westerners in the plains, the Southwest, the Rockies, and the Great Basin had ever seen before.

In the early 1970s Richard Nixon had proposed a program of energy development that stressed nuclear power—fueled by western uranium—to reduce dependence on imported oil, but the rush for western energy really began following the OPEC embargo. Despite heavy promotion of nuclear power, difficulties with disposal of nuclear wastes had already begun to obstruct nuclear development during the Ford administration. When President Carter proposed the National Energy Act in 1977, he gave coal the key role. At various points in the 1970s uranium, coal, and natural gas all promised to save the country from future energy shortfalls; no matter what the fuel of choice, they were all western fuels. All promised a boom in western extractive industries to dwarf anything that had ever gone on before. Various federal and industry plans allotted 250 new coal mines, 150 new coal-fired power plants, 20 new synthetic fuel plants, and the necessary pipelines, transmission lines, railroad spurs, and roads to be constructed in the Rocky Mountains, Great Plains, and southwestern states.

This boom and the projected developments that accompanied it depended on the continued strength of OPEC, which had raised world oil prices to unprecedented levels. The OPEC nations proved themselves the best friends Texas and Oklahoma oil producers had. Although both the oil companies and the independent oil producers had sought and obtained federal protection from foreign oil imports for years, they now remembered the virtues of unrestricted free enterprise. Once they were freed by Congress from federal regulation, particularly regulations on the price of natural gas involved in interstate commerce, they promised in turn to free the country from energy shortages.

Most Texas oil producers, however, did not allow their rhetorical devotion to the free market to get out of hand. They continued to look kindly on regulation by the Texas Railroad Commission, which had proven itself a friend of the Texas oil industry since the 1930s. With regulations as arcane as any federal rules, the Texas Railroad Commission strived to save small oil producers from becoming victims of their own nominal economic philosophy. Oil producers ostensibly wanted a free-market system in which the most efficient wells and producers would survive and dominate the market. But in practice, such a policy would deliver the industry to energy corporations, most of them controlled by northern capital. They owned the most productive wells and were the most efficient producers. And so independent producers accepted regulation, the object of which was not efficiency but instead protection of the inefficient. For the inefficient were by and large Texans. They owned the smaller, more marginal, and more expensive "stripper" wells.

While denouncing federal regulation, Texans kept a system of state regulation that encouraged inefficiency as long as it kept money in the hands of Texans. When northern corporations and consumers objected that this raised prices, Texans invited them to go "freeze in the dark." And yet, looked at another way, the long Texas tradition of protecting relatively inefficient independent producers did have its advantages for the nation. Because regulation protected small oil producers, a sizable group of independents remained in Texas in the 1970s. It was these producers who, as it turned out, took most of the risks in the renewed search for gas and oil and in improving recovery techniques—that is, the methods for recovering the maximum amount of oil from each pool. Regulation that protected the inefficient could, it appeared, have unforeseen payoffs.

The boom in oil and natural gas generated money that oil companies and Texas millionaires soon began to invest in energy enterprises elsewhere. Urban areas reaped the yields of rural resources. Colorado had relatively little oil or gas of its own, but it prospered nonetheless as energy companies made Denver the corporate center for coal and shale oil developments across the interior West. Denver in the 1970s had 27 new office buildings that housed an estimated 2,000 energy-related companies. In this new energy boom as many as 4,000 geologists offered their services to the energy companies in Denver alone. Salt Lake City, too, prospered as energy companies moved in. Enthusiasm for massive energy development seemed to envelop the mountain West. Coal-rich Wyoming's Governor Stanley Hathaway eagerly anticipated the chance to turn his state into "the next Pennsylvania."

In the nineteenth-century West, with its willingness to ride any boom, the Hathaways, the Texas and Oklahoma oil producers, the geologists, and the oil companies would have pretty well covered the range of western attitudes toward development. But in the early and middle 1970s many westerners, perhaps to their own surprise, paused on the brink of the energy boom and stepped back. Many, including high office holders, publicly doubted the benefits of massive, unrestricted growth. In part they drew on the old western distrust of eastern capital and federal power, but they also represented a reaction against unrestricted growth itself. The energy crisis brought to a head a political, social, and cultural confrontation that had been brewing in the West since the end of World War II. It intensified a collision between the rural and metropolitan West, between environmentalists and developmental interests, between federal bureaucrats interested in protecting wilderness and federal bureaucrats interested in promoting development, and between the West and the rest of the country.

The energy crisis pushed the Nixon, Ford, and Carter administrations into strong prodevelopment stances, but the West as a whole proved far less receptive to their plans than they expected. With the cost of Carter's energy program estimated at an incredible $600 to $900 billion, much of it to be spent in the West, western hesitation in the face of such a potential bonanza would have been unimaginable in an earlier period.

Those westerners who opposed rapid energy development did so from environmental concerns and also from a resurgent sense of western domination by eastern-

Table 15
Percentage of Land Owned by the Federal Government in
Ten WESTPO States

Montana	30%	Wyoming	48%
New Mexico	34%	Idaho	64%
Colorado	36%	Utah	66%
Arizona	43%	Nevada	87%
California	45%	Alaska	96%

Source: Lynton R. Hayes, *Energy, Economic Growth, and Regionalism in the West* (Albuquerque: University of New Mexico Press, 1980).

ers—both corporate officials and bureaucrats. They nurtured their resentment on fears for the future and on memories of the past history of boom and bust and of federal and corporate domination. Opponents of energy development feared that they could see the western future in the ravaged landscape and pervasive poverty of West Virginia, eastern Kentucky, and other Appalachian areas that depended on the strip mining of coal. Environmentalists and local ranchers in the High Plains country created a grassroots opposition, but resistance to development found a surprising center among a group of moderate Democrats who had won election to western governors' offices in the early and middle 1970s. They usually replaced Republicans far more favorable to development.

These state officials reacted warily to the new federal energy policy. In Montana former Lieutenant Governor Bill Christiansen announced that "Montana does not intend to become a boiler room for this nation," and in Colorado Governor Richard Lamm pledged in 1974 that his state would not be "the nation's slag heap." They trotted out the old colonial analogies. Governor Thomas Judge of Montana warned that western passivity would make the West "a colony for the rest of the United States," and Governor Jerry Apodaca of New Mexico vowed that "the West will not become an energy colony for the rest of the nation."

Like conservative legislators who later joined the Sagebrush Rebellion, these governors resented federal dictation—but they resented the dictation of energy bureaucrats and not the performance of environmental bureaucrats. Richard Lamm, running for governor of Colorado, complained in 1974 that "Interior and energy people in D.C. have more power in this state than I or our 100 legislators together." Lamm and other governors tried to counter the power of the energy bureaucrats by means of several new organizations, most notably the Western Governors Policy Office, or WESTPO, which included ten western states and Alaska. Through WESTPO the governors attempted to participate in the national decision making process on energy issues.

While working collectively, many of the governors also secured a series of laws within their own states that provided both relatively strict environmental controls and high taxes on energy producers. By 1975, Wyoming had some of the most comprehensive environmental management powers in the nation. Montana reacted even more strongly, leading all the other states in enacting laws to control energy development. Montana officials openly stated their suspicions that the federal government and the energy corporations would colonize their state if given a chance, and they aggressively and defiantly set out to resist. In 1974, Montana passed a severance tax on coal—a tax levied when a nonrenewable resource is removed—that was the highest in the nation. The attraction of a severance tax to westerners was that it was largely borne by out-of-state consumers. In enacting it, Montana simply followed the example of Texas's tax on oil. By 1982, North Dakota, Texas, Montana, and Wyoming all relied on the severance tax, which yielded between 25 percent and 35 percent of each state's revenues. One northeastern think tank, in a reference to the oil-rich United Arab Emirates, called these states the United American Emirates.

Under strong federal and business pressure, the initial strong environmental, anticorporate, and antifederal stance of western governors had weakened considerably by the late 1970s. The states still, however, maintained limits on the extent of the development they would tolerate. Even Utah, which in comparison to Montana's snarling resentment of energy corporations was a virtual corporate lap dog, eventually rebelled against outside development plans. Since World War II, Utah depended heavily on Defense Department expenditures, and the Carter administration's decision to base mobile MX missiles in the state thus seemed an unlikely cause for revolt, particularly when expenditures on the total project were estimated at between $60 billion and $100 billion. Environmentalists opposed the project, but they were relatively weak in Utah. As it turned out, however, the very jobs that the project promised to deliver became the problem. Mormons in rural Utah and church leaders in Salt Lake City feared that a construction project of this size would bring in a heavy influx of non-Mormons who would drastically alter both the way of life in the area and Mormon control. Rural Utahans were additionally sensitive to basing nuclear weapons in the state because of the "downwinders"—southern Utahans exposed to fallout from Nevada nuclear tests in the 1950s. Alarming rates of cancer in many small towns in southern Utah became a major issue in the state and contributed to hostility against the MX and the federal government. After a three-year battle, the incoming Reagan administration abandoned the MX in 1981.

Both prodevelopment and limited-development forces anticipated that the energy crisis had launched a struggle over energy production that would endure and intensify over the remainder of the century. Instead, by the 1980s bust had replaced boom. Surprising success in conservation measures, both world-wide and in the United States, coupled with a sharp world recession in the early 1980s, dramatically curtailed energy demand. Under pressure of declining demand, internal divisions split OPEC, and it lost the ability to dictate world prices. Working together, these factors produced a world energy glut by the early 1980s. The grandiose plans to strip-mine the plains were now uneconomical. The distillation of oil from oil shale—shale or siltstone rich in bitumens—had not proved feasible even with oil prices high. With low prices, oil shale development collapsed. Residents of the western slope of Colorado and Utah's Uintah Basin had thought they were riding a boom; instead, they busted. The development that Montana and Wyoming officials had feared would be so disruptive instead abruptly ceased. The oil and natural gas industries suffered sharp setbacks that sent the economies of Texas and Oklahoma reeling. Meanwhile, the nuclear breakdown at Three Mile Island in 1979 intensified American doubts about the safety of the nuclear energy industry, which was already in trouble from rising costs and low output. The Reagan administration, in pursuit of its own free-trade policies, delivered an additional blow to western energy production. When it eliminated requirements that uranium imports be restricted to 25 percent of U.S. consumption, the uranium industry, too, collapsed. The energy boom was clearly over by 1982. With a dual bust in agriculture and energy, and with severe problems in both the lumber and mining industries, the rural West confronted its grimmest decade since the 1930s.

The battle against all-out energy development and the MX missile revealed an unexpected solidarity and sense of regional oppression in the Rocky Mountain West and the Great Plains states. Oddly enough, the same sense of domination and dictation by outsiders who ignored regional needs inspired western conservatives, who sought to accelerate, not retard, western development in the Sagebrush Rebellion of the late 1970s and early 1980s. Westerners, it seemed, agreed they were being abused; they disagreed on the nature of the abuse and the identity of the abusers.

The Sagebrush Rebellion

The Sagebrush Rebellion was a very old play staged under a new title: it was yet another attempt to get the federal government to cede public lands to the states. Most Sagebrush Rebels confined their attacks on federal regulation to rhetoric and a few meaningless pieces of legislation, but for a time in the late 1970s and early 1980s the Sagebrush Rebellion seemed to be on the verge of larger successes. The rebels argued that extensive federal landholdings put the West at a competitive disadvantage with the East. Eastern states contained few federal lands and thus enjoyed much larger tax bases and greater opportunities for growth. The only way to stimulate western growth was to have the federal government cede the lands to the states, which would lease and sell some and promote greater development on others.

The Sagebrush Rebellion stirred up passionate enthusiasm among conservative state legislatures in the Rocky Mountain West. By reducing restrictions on development, and by opening the public lands to rapid exploitation and sale, the rebels envisioned a new resource boom in the West that would yield direct tax revenues to the states. Two state legislatures went so far as to pass acts claiming public lands for their states, but the laws were meaningless. The legislatures did not control the federal lands.

The Sagebrush Rebels found far less support among western governors and in the metropolitan West where the bulk of the western people lived. Governors realized that federal holdings were not a dead loss to the states and counties of the West. State and county governments, for example, obtained a share of the revenues from mineral royalties and timber licenses in the national forests. They then used this money to pay for schools, highways, and irrigation projects. In 1976, Congress had passed the Payments in Lieu of Taxes Act under which the federal government had agreed to make additional payments to the counties in lieu of taxes on federal lands within their boundaries. Total federal payments for use by counties and states in the West or for reclamation projects reached $800 million annually by the late 1970s. The Sagebrush Rebellion would have eliminated all these payments.

The governors and their urban constituents were also unwilling to see public lands that they wanted for watersheds and recreation pass into private hands.

Many urban dwellers in the West regarded the Sagebrush Rebellion in much the same way that they had looked at earlier attempts to assert the preeminent rights of cattle raisers or miners or loggers on the public land: as an ill-disguised land grab designed to give resource users title to public lands. They were prepared to fight for their own claims on these lands. The Sagebrush Rebellion in the end fizzled as much because of opposition within the West as from opposition elsewhere in the country.

Reactions Against Growth

In the Sagebrush Rebellion, in the controversies over the energy crisis, and in the rising influence of environmentalists were signs of a basic conflict within the West over growth itself. Within the metropolitan areas of the West the various growth networks tended over time to create their own opposition. People had no objection to the prosperity and employment that the growth networks promised and often delivered, but they did object to the side effects of growth that advocates had rarely mentioned. Growth often meant the loss of local control as the scale of both political and economic activities increased. County and state governments grew more significant; town and city governments grew less significant. Large corporations dominated more and more of metropolitan economic life. Growth also meant social and environmental problems: increased crime, increased pollution, increased traffic, and increased congestion. The very qualities—beauty, a different pace of life, open spaces—that had made many people want to move west began to disappear as a direct result of their moving.

Resentment over loss of local control and the undesirable side-effects of growth gradually increased resistance to unrestrained growth itself. Urban neighborhoods threw up the first bulwarks of this resistance. As the central cities underwent urban renewal, the most defenseless residents—minorities, the elderly, and the poor—bore the costs. In areas such as San Francisco's Fillmore district, urban renewal became a war on the poor. When the San Francisco Redevelopment Agency (SFRA) tore down the housing around Fillmore Street, the SFRA gave most displaced residents from the Western Addition, a major inner-city neighborhood, a grim choice: move into other poor neighborhoods, live in large public housing projects that became, in time, crime-ridden social disasters, or leave the city altogether. The SFRA also undercut the black middle class. Urban renewal left the Fillmore's once prosperous black business district stranded and isolated. It put too many people in the position of Vernon Thornton, a black businessman who ran a popular bowling alley in the Fillmore area until urban renewal displaced his customers. Only when his business had been destroyed did SFRA offer to buy him out. They gave him but a fraction of what his business had once been worth.

Poor and middle-class blacks, mobilized by the civil rights movement, mounted a protest against the destruction of their neighborhoods for the benefit of downtown interests. They conducted a political guerrilla war of protest and resistance that won some concessions from developers and city government. By the mid-1970s neighborhood activists in San Francisco had joined a liberal political coalition that made George Moscone mayor of the city. Once in office, Moscone backed development projects, but he insisted on procedures that guaranteed citizen review and participation. In theory, citizens would now be able to exert some influence over what happened in their neighborhoods. Such policies slowed but did not halt the decline in affordable housing for the poor, particularly for the black poor. The black population of San Francisco declined by 10 percent between 1970 and 1980 as blacks moved into other Bay Area communities. Since many of the neighborhoods that African Americans lost went to more affluent gays, conflict between gays and African Americans strained Moscone's political alliance.

Similar neighborhood activism, involving both whites and minorities, modified urban renewal in Portland. Mayor Neil Goldschmidt (1973–79) capitalized on rising citizen participation in neighborhood politics to institute land use planning and curtail the urban renewal projects that were radically altering the inner city. Like Moscone, Goldschmidt sought to balance downtown revitalization with preservation of Portland's neighborhoods, but he pulled it off more successfully. His policies bore fruit in Portland's resurgence during the late 1970s and 1980s.

The resistance to urban renewal mounted largely by the poor represented a challenge to the growth alliances and the urban renewal programs of the 1960s, but challenges to growth became both more and more common and more and more middle-class in the 1970s and 1980s. The middle class, too, acted in the name of local values and interests. Most often they framed the issue less in terms of maintaining neighborhoods than in maintaining a more vague "livability" that twentieth-century proponents of growth had long used to attract people and businesses west. After a certain point, growth lessened livability. In these campaigns for livability, women most often organized and led the local opposition to the growth networks.

The political expression of this fear of growing too large, too fast had developed in the late 1960s. In Oregon, under the leadership of Republican Governor Tom McCall, the legislature passed some of the toughest environmental and land use laws in the nation. And in 1971 when McCall told visiting conventioneers, "Come and visit again and again, but for heaven's sake, don't come here to live," he uttered a sentence that blasphemed the hallowed western political and economic tradition of boosterism.

National environmentalism followed a complicated trajectory that embedded it in the federal bureaucracy, but local environmentalism retained strong community roots. Local groups organized around issues of immediate community concern: nuclear power plants, toxic waste dumping, the preservation of open spaces. Metropolitan environmentalists demanded community control in order to maintain quality of life. This local environmentalism, with its stress on issues of immediate concern, could take root in very politically conservative communities. Many High Plains ranchers in Montana or Wyoming, worried about what strip mining for coal would do to the land and their livelihood, cooperated with environmentalists' attempts to prevent strip mining in their areas. By the 1980s, slow-growth movements had appeared in areas as prosperous and conservative as Orange County. In an area long dominated by various growth alliances, a slow-growth majority captured the Irvine city council in 1986 and proposed zoning changes to preserve hundreds of acres of land as open space. In the mid-1980s a slow-growth movement in Seal Beach and Newport Beach arose to oppose Orange County's development interests. The powerful Irvine Company, which had orchestrated much of the county's growth for decades, found itself directly challenged. Local control in the West had virtually always guaranteed chamber of commerce boosterism; in the 1980s local control had become a code word for limiting growth.

Local environmentalists did, of course, cooperate with national environmental groups to attain common ends. There was no contradiction between the local insistence on community control and the interest of national organizations in the larger public good insured by federal rule making and regulation. But when national environmentalists confronted rural Westerners who welcomed rather than opposed rapid development and growth, then localism and federal rule making were in conflict. To many rural westerners it seemed that environmentalists praised local control when it suited their purposes and overrode it when it did not. Environmentalism thus represented more than an argument over the proper human relation to the earth. It was also a debate over the rights of local communities in the West. It pitted the powers of communities against the powers of the national government. In rural areas it involved a basic question: Should metropolitan residents, through the federal government, be able to control the public lands in ways that went against the wishes of those who lived adjacent to those lands?

The energy crisis with its pressure for rapid development of the public lands had brought the conflict to a crisis. Metropolitan environmentalists, some rural westerners, and those federal bureaucracies with strong environmental connections opposed rapid development. Most rural westerners, those metropolitan residents who supported the growth networks, and the federal bureaucracies responsible for energy development supported rapid development.

Environmentalists offered several compelling arguments against full and immediate development of western energy resources. Development would place additional demands on the already overtaxed rivers and aquifers of the West. Once strip-mined, vast sections of the West would be ruined because of the difficulty of revegetating strip-mined areas in an arid country. The erection of massive coal-burning plants would pollute the western environment. Energy development would put tremendous pressures on western communities, but when resources ran out or prices dropped, these communities would be left to shift for themselves. Environmentalists and their allies contended that such development was not worth the cost.

But environmentalists labored under a basic difficulty in pressing the case: many of their opponents were rural westerners who lived in the areas in question, whereas most environmental advocates were outsiders. When persuasion failed, environmentalists had to try to override the desires of local residents. Environmentalists were most comfortable when they were the Davids facing down corporate and federal Goliaths, or when they had allies such as Montana ranchers or Northern Cheyenne Indians unsure about the costs of development. Rural westerners often forced them into a new and more uncomfortable role. Rural westerners seized the banner of localism from the environmentalists and rallied behind it. Environmentalists found themselves portrayed as arrogant outsiders using powerful federal bureaucracies to run roughshod over the little people of the rural West.

To residents of small western towns, environmentalism seemed in the 1970s a pernicious movement. Small-town westerners thought of themselves as modern minutemen defending their home and livelihood against invaders. The particular intolerable act for many rural residents was the 1976 Federal Land Policy and

Management Act, which included provisions for new wilderness areas. The act brought much tighter regulation of lands under the control of the BLM. It threatened to restrict energy development and also locally sanctioned uses of BLM lands. Jimmie Walker, a county commissioner in Grand County, Utah, put the conflict in quintessentially western terms: "Back about that time (1976) I got to thinking about something. The thing that creates wars is a foreign intrusion that's trying to destroy a way of life. It's just that damn simple. The people here could recognize that, and as far as they were concerned, it was war." The "war" was against federal bureaucrats and environmentalists demanding stronger federal controls over local resources. More specifically, rural westerners did not want federal lands shut to off-the-road vehicles such jeeps or all-terrain vehicles (ATVs), they did not want the ruins of the prehistoric Anasazi Indians protected from local pot hunters, and they did not want mineral exploration halted in wilderness study areas.

Environmentalists labored under a second, even more serious embarrassment. They were in the uncomfortable position of denouncing rural westerners for desiring development while they themselves lived in the very metropolitan areas that acted as huge resource sinks, relentlessly swallowing water and energy from the rural West and demanding more. It was the metropolitan areas, after all, that created the demand that pushed development forward. Furthermore, environmentalist successes within the metropolitan areas often led to environmental failures outside of them. When Californians limited the development of nuclear power within their own state, or when Los Angeles mandated strict air quality levels, these successes only increased the pressure on the rural West to develop the power plants and the strip mines necessary to supply metropolitan demands. Los Angeles and Orange County, in effect, exported their environmental problems. The smoke that arose as strip-mined coal burned in the power plants of the Four Corners region polluted the skies of rural New Mexico, Arizona, Colorado, and Utah. The energy the plants produced flowed to southern California and Arizona cities. Without metropolitan demand, the plants and the smoke would not exist.

The conflict between environmentalists and rural westerners bared the basic problems posed by western growth. When a wilderness won out over logging or mining, rural western communities did lose jobs. Residents had to watch their neighbors and children move away while metropolitan westerners used the land for their own recreational purposes. Rural westerners often bitterly resented this triumph of "the public good" over "local interests." But when development won out over wilderness, not only were irreplaceable parts of the West lost forever, but a whole new cycle of environmental problems was often set in motion. Strip mining, oil exploration, and ATVs did cause irreparable damage. The questions of who controlled the public lands and what the pace of development would be were critical questions for the West. And these were but part of a much larger and more complicated struggle between an ascendent metropolitan West and a declining rural West.

Even as the rural West suffered, most western metropolitan regions continued to grow and thrive in the 1980s. Phoenix, Los Angeles, San Francisco, San Diego, Sacramento, Las Vegas, even Portland and Seattle prospered. Even the most energy-dependent cities—Houston, Dallas, Denver, Albuquerque, and Salt Lake City—did better than their rural hinterlands. The most prosperous metropolitan areas—particularly those of the California cities—had developed a diversified economy that had largely freed them from the boom-bust cycle of the extractive economy. While some rural areas of the West, such as the timber regions of the Pacific Northwest, feared that the emerging economies of Asia would reduce them to the status of cheap sources of raw materials, western metropolitan regions eagerly anticipated and enjoyed trade with Asia. In Orange County, where one in seven jobs depended on international trade in the late 1980s, the future lay across the Pacific. Political representatives of the western metropolitan regions were far more likely to oppose increased protectionism than were representatives from the East. Reagan's secretary of state, George Shultz, an alumnus of Bechtel Corporation, used the representatives from the Pacific Coast to resist protectionist measures in Congress.

Yet overall, metropolitan prosperity could not sustain the regional economy as a whole with agriculture and energy in decline. Of the ten states with slowest growth in per capita income between 1978 and 1988, seven were in the West. By 1987 only one western state, California, ranked among the top ten states in per capita income, while three western states—Utah, Idaho, and New Mexico—ranked in the bottom ten. During the Reagan years the western states as a whole fell farther behind the national income average than they had been before his election.

The Pacific Rim that so alluringly beckoned the metropolitan West seemed to the rural West less a source of opportunity than a source of danger. Japanese and other Asian economies may come to treat the rural West as eastern economies treated it earlier: a place where raw materials come from; a place to be abandoned when cheaper sources appear. And the rural West no longer looked to the metropolitan West as an ally in a struggle against outside masters. For the metropolitan West, too, showed all the signs of having become a master. Its rural hinterlands mattered only as sources of water, energy, recreation, and places to dump wastes.

Readings

Abbott, Carl. "The Metropolitan Region: Western Cities in the New Urban Era." In *The Twentieth Century West: Historical Interpretations*, pp. 71–98. Ed. Gerald D. Nash and Richard W. Etulain. Albuquerque: University of New Mexico Press, 1989.

———. *The New Urban America: Growth and Politics in Sun Belt Cities*. Chapel Hill: University of North Carolina Press, 1981.

Doti, Lynne Pierson, and Larry Schweikart. "Financing the Postwar Housing Boom in Phoenix and Los Angeles, 1945–1960." *Pacific Historical Review* 58 (May 1989):173–94.

Feagin, Joe R. *Free Enterprise City: Houston in Political-Economic Perspective*. New Brunswick, N.J.: Rutgers University Press, 1988.

Findlay, John. "Far Western Cityscapes and American Culture since 1940." *Western Historical Quarterly* 22 (February 1991): 19–44.

Fleischmann, Arnold, and Joe R. Feagin. "The Politics of Growth-Oriented Urban Alliances: Comparing Old Industrial and New Sunbelt Cities." *Urban Affairs Quarterly* 23 (December 1987): 207–32.

Gates, Paul W. "The Intermountain West Against Itself." *Arizona and the West* 27 (Autumn 1985):205–36.

Hayes, Lynton R. *Energy, Economic Growth, and Regionalism in the West.* Albuquerque: University of New Mexico Press, 1980.

Hays, Samuel P. *Beauty, Health and Permanence: Environmental Politics in the United States, 1955–85.* New York: Cambridge University Press, 1987.

Limerick, Patricia Nelson. *The Legacy of Conquest: The Unbroken Past of the American West.* New York: Norton, 1987.

Markusen, Ann. *Regions: The Economics and Politics of Territory.* Totowa, N.J.: Rowman and Littlefield, 1987.

Marston, Ed, ed. *Reopening the Western Frontier.* Washington, D.C.: Island Press, 1989.

Mayer, Carl J., and George A. Riley. *Public Domain, Private Domain: A History of Public Mineral Policy in America.* San Francisco: Sierra Club Books, 1985.

Mollenkopf, John H. *The Contested City.* Princeton, N.J.: Princeton University Press, 1983.

Nash, Gerald. *The American West in the Twentieth Century: A Short History of an Urban Oasis.* Englewood Cliffs, N.J.: Prentice Hall, 1973.

Prindle, David F. *Petroleum Politics and the Texas Railroad Commission.* Austin: University of Texas Press, 1981.

Reisner, Marc. *Cadillac Desert: The American West and Its Disappearing Water.* New York: Viking, 1986.

Robbins, William G. "The Plundered Province Thesis and Recent Historiography of the American West." *Pacific Historical Review* 55 (November 1986): 577–97.

Steinhart, John S., and Carol E. Steinhart. "Energy Use in the U.S. Food System." *Science* 189 (April 19, 1974): 307–16.

Wiley, Peter, and Robert Gottlieb. *Empires in the Sun: The Rise of the New American West.* Tucson: University of Arizona Press, 1982.

CHAPTER 20

The West and the Nation

ON one level, the economic and social changes that followed World War II seemed to make the American West a less distinctive region within the United States. Television, interstate highways, jet travel, the expansion of the federal government, the relocation of national and regional corporate headquarters in the West, all of these eradicated the distances, the dependency, and the isolation that had made westerners both distinctive and resentful. It became easy to see in such changes the end of the West's colonial status and the beginning of a national homogeneity.

And yet social change did not proceed so simply. National trends affected the West, as they always had, and they also continued to take distinctive western forms. Now, however, the West itself became central to the politics and social trends of the nation in a way that it never had before. In certain ways the nation itself grew more like the West. The West both participated in and spawned political, social, and cultural movements that involved the entire country while still having distinctive consequences within the West. The New Right and the New Left, hippies and environmentalists, the new immigration, even aspects of the civil rights movement all were western in important ways.

In the West between 1960 and 1990 social change seemed centrifugal: it threw groups outward, away from a common center, highlighting historic divisions. The West was in this sense a region defined not by its homogeneity but instead by the particular nature of its divisions. Both the change in the West and the deep social divisions that characterized the section were real, but so too was the continuity in the ways white westerners and nonwhite westerners phrased and organized their differences. The tensions between separate status and equal rights were quintessentially western, as were the conflicts between demands for federal aid and resentment of federal rules and supervision.

Politics

The centrality of the West, particularly the metropolitan West, to these changes can perhaps most readily be seen in politics. After 1960 national politics, with its decline in party loyalty, its increasing emphasis on personality, and the rising significance of the New Right, came increasingly to resemble western politics. Metropolitan politics dominated these changes, because in the West and else-where rural areas lost their built-in advantages in representation. For years the rural areas of the nation had held state governments as political fortresses to protect their interests. Rural areas maintained control because the apportionment of representatives to the legislature did not reflect the actual distribution of voters. Voters in rural areas were overrepresented, and voters in urban areas were underrepresented. In 1962 the Supreme Court in *Baker* v. *Carr* broke this system by declaring that federal courts had the right to review the apportionment of state legislatures. In subsequent cases the court established guidelines for apportionment that emphasized "absolute equality" of representation, or in the popular phrasing, "one man, one vote." In the wake of *Baker* v. *Carr*, the number of urban legislators increased dramatically, while those of rural areas declined.

The concentration of minorities in metropolitan areas also influenced local and state politics. Minority office holders began to appear in elected office for the first time. In Los Angeles, Mexican Americans created the Community Service Organization (CSO), which undertook the first real attempt to mobilize Hispanic voters in that city. The CSO served as a springboard for Edward Roybal, who in 1949 won election to the Los Angeles City Council. He was the first Mexican American to serve on that body since 1888, and he later went on to Congress. In El Paso, Raymond Telles galvanized and organized the Mexican American community to become the first Hispanic mayor of El Paso in 1958. These were small but symbolic gains that set the stage for far more sweeping changes.

This shift of power to the metropolitan regions also increased the already pervasive weakness of western political parties. Cities were full of new migrants, and political loyalties traveled little better in the twentieth century than in the nineteenth. Earl Warren, the Republican governor of California from 1942 until 1954, and his successor, Goodwin Knight, were bland moderates who successfully appealed to voters who belonged to neither party. In the Northwest the Republican governor of Washington, Arthur Langlie, had the same kind of appeal and enjoyed the same kind of success. Even many of the conservative business leaders who controlled much metropolitan politics through the Dallas Citizens Council, the San Antonio Good Government League, the Suite 8F crowd in Houston, or the Phoenix Charter Government Committee were more conservative pragmatists than conservative ideologues.

In California the weakness of the political parties made electoral politics susceptible both to single-issue campaigns and to a politics of personality, both of which would become hallmarks of national politics. Anticommunism formed the prototype for these postwar single-issue campaigns. Although both parties were doggedly anticommunist during the Cold War, Republicans proved more adroit in their use of the issue. Richard Nixon's red-baiting of Helen Gahagan Douglas in his California congressional campaign of 1948 set the standard, and the tactic earned him both a seat in the House of Representatives and his "Tricky Dick" image. On the state level, Jack Tenney used the California legislatures's Un-American Activities Committee to force the administration of the University of California to demand loyalty oaths from their faculty. Thirty-two Berkeley professors who objected to the oaths as an intrusion of government on academic freedom were fired, although the courts later reinstated them.

Promoters of single-issue politics found a valuable tool in the initiative—that is, the introduction of legislation by petition of the voters—and initiative politics became, as well, a training ground for organizations promoting "image" politics. During the postwar years, Campaigns Incorporated of California, a public relations organization, successfully set up shop to organize campaigns for or against initiative and referendum measures. Working for whoever paid them, they applied mass advertising techniques to political issues. Their success led them to expand to marketing individual candidates who, in the absence of strong western political parties or firm ideological convictions, were quite willing to tailor themselves in the way best suited to gaining office. Again, the West created what would be a national pattern.

An ironic result of the new politics—itself partially the result of progressive reforms designed to weaken parties and promote direct democracy—was the increasing power of lobbyists in the California state legislature and, later, in other western legislatures. With little ideological consistency or party discipline to overcome, Artie Samish, a professional lobbyist, organized the California legislature and became a political power broker in his own right. He sold his influence to those who hired him. Personally, Samish's innovative political methods led only to a conventional corruptionist's fate, as Samish himself ended up in prison for income tax evasion, but his methods would transform legislative politics.

Although western voters remained volatile and independent, a discernible shift toward the Republicans in presidential elections took place following World War II. The tendency to reelect incumbents masked the shift in congressional elections, as Democrats continued to dominate western congressional delegations through the 1950s, but in the 1960s the overall Republican trend became clear. The Republicans gained strength among the growing metropolitan middle class even as the Democrats lost strength because of the decreasing electoral participation of lower-income voters.

The significance of the change from a Democratic to a Republican West only gradually became apparent in the regional political agenda. Even as the shift took place, older liberal political beliefs held on into the 1950s. Defining political liberalism as support for federal intervention to improve the conditions of daily life, the West had been the most "liberal" section of the country in the 1930s. Westerners had disproportionately supported New Deal social programs. Until 1960, for example, most westerners participating in public opinion polls continued to believe that government had a responsibility for helping people get jobs and obtain low-cost medical care.

After 1960 the liberal majority evaporated; western political opinion had shifted. Compared to northerners and southerners, westerners favored more individualist solutions. They believed that the proper role of government was creating individual opportunities and not mediating between social groups or providing services individuals had failed to secure for themselves. Although couched in terms of frontier self-reliance and older western self-images, western individualism in its most recent form is very much the product of an urban, prosperous, middle-class West whose very existence was the result of federal programs and policies. This increasing conservatism provided a fertile ground for the rise in the West of the New Right, a movement whose leaders came to control national politics.

Yet because the New Right was in a sense very much an oppositional movement—a coalition of resentments—it cannot be understood in the West without surveying the social movements and programs it opposed. In the rural West, the New Right tapped the old resentments against the federal government and demanded that the government open up western resources for exploitation. In both the rural and metropolitan West, too, the New Right drew on the increasing political participation of Christian fundamentalists angry over what they thought of as moral laxity and a decline in traditional values. Abortion, women's rights, drug use, sexual promiscuity, homosexuality, and pornography all became part of a moral grab bag of issues that enflamed the right. And finally, particularly in the metropolitan West, the New Right fed on opposition to a series of programs and movements that they thought the federal government had promoted or nurtured: the civil rights movement, the War on Poverty, and social movements of the 1960s.

Racial Divisions and Civil Rights

The rise in conservative individualist philosophies among many western whites paralleled a rise among minority westerners of demands for government correction of their collective grievances. Minorities saw their subordination not as an individual problem to be corrected by personal improvement, but as a social problem that could only be eliminated with basic institutional and social changes. For more than a century white westerners had been inventing races out of diverse groups and assigning each racial identities and supposedly unalterable characteristics. In the 1950s and 1960s, the diverse groups lumped together by whites as Mexicans or Indians increasingly ceased struggling against the designations and instead tried to strip them of their negative connotations. They often changed the term of the racial designation itself and wielded the new name as a weapon. Negroes became blacks; Mexicans and Mexican Americans became Chicanos; and Indians, at least when addressed by whites, became Native Americans.

The politics of racial identity arose all over the country, but because of the special configuration and legal position of western minority groups, it took on distinctive characteristics in the West. In the West racial politics ranged from civil rights politics typical of the nation as a whole to claims of independence and sovereignty largely peculiar to the West. Very often the two seemingly contradictory positions of equal rights and separate status merged as groups demanded both. The tension between these positions set racial politics in the West apart from racial politics elsewhere.

To understand the peculiarities of western racial politics it is necessary to recognize that white westerners have consistently equated nonwhite westerners with foreigners. And, indeed, many nonwhites have at various times legally been foreigners. Indian peoples belonged to separate domestic dependent nations; Japanese and Chinese immigrants could not obtain citizenship and so remained foreign nationals. Many immigrants from Mexico did not seek American citizenship, and many Mexican Americans, although they were American citizens, found that authorities, particularly in Texas and California, denied them recognition as citizens. Blacks were clearly an American minority, but after World War II western cities offered them no more freedom than did eastern cities. In Los Angeles, as one journalist said of Watts in the 1960s, a white entering the black community "will feel himself as foreign as if he had ventured to Haiti." The western equation of colored skin with foreignness allowed even newly arrived white westerners to regard native-born westerners with dark skin as aliens although their ancestors had been in the West for generations. Even sympathetic whites thought of nonwhites as foreign. Instead of excluding nonwhites, however, they pushed to assimilate or Americanize Indians or Nisei by encouraging them to accept white Protestant norms. Movements to assimilate nonwhites often accompanied movements to exclude them, for not even the most dedicated exclusionists thought they could eliminate all the nonwhite westerners.

Assimilation has provoked a certain ambivalence among western minorities, who have struggled to escape identification as foreigners in the only land they have ever known. Many middle-class minority leaders stressed their own Americanness, not from any shame in their own ethnic identity, but from a belief that Americanness would secure them the equal rights and opportunities that they wanted. In the years immediately following World War II, for example, Mexican American political organizations such as the League of United Latin American Citizens (LULAC) and the GI Forum sought to distance themselves from Mexican immigrants and aggressively pushed their identity and rights of Mexican Americans as U.S. citizens.

In their push for equal rights GI Forum and LULAC shared much with black civil rights groups; indeed, Mexican American resistance to segregation and discrimination in the West in some ways anticipated black resistance in the South. In the Westminster case of 1946, Mexican Americans successfully challenged school segregation in California. And in the Supreme Court's *Hernández* decision of 1954, it banned the exclusion of Mexican Americans from Texas jury lists. Although the original great strength of the black civil rights movement was in the South, probably the key case in the legal struggle arose in Kansas, on the fringe of the West. In 1954 the U.S. Supreme Court, headed by the former governor of California, Earl Warren, who had helped place Japanese Americans in concentration camps, decided in *Brown* v. *Board of Education of Topeka* that racial segregation was unconstitutional. The *Brown* case, the Montgomery, Alabama bus boycott, and the sit-ins in the South all fueled the gathering civil rights movement that, although centered in the South, produced echoes in the West. By the 1950s, for example, blacks in San Francisco had already created an interracial civil rights coalition. The southern civil rights movement energized it and spurred it and other western efforts forward. Other western minorities—particularly Indians and Chicanos—imitated African American tactics of social protest if not always black goals.

Civil rights activists stressed the end of racial segregation and assimilation of minorities into the economic, political, and social mainstream of American life, but they eliminated the emphasis older white reformers had put on cultural assimilation. Rather than striving for a homogeneous common culture, civil rights groups concentrated on achieving uniform rights for all citizens. They replaced the old symbol of a melting pot that melded diverse peoples into a single homogeneous America with the idea of the country as a mosaic—a single whole made up of identifiable parts.

And yet these efforts at political, social, and economic integration with the larger society did not get full support in all western minority communities. The separateness of Indians, Hispanic Texans, New Mexicans, and Californians, as well as other nonwhite immigrant groups, has at times offered these communities some protection against the white majority. Having separate rights secured by treaty with a foreign country, for example, sometimes offered greater advantages than being a second-class citizen of the United States. Indians have clung to treaty rights and their sovereign status. Citizenship meant little to many Mexican immigrants, for as one man argued in 1940, "It would mean nothing to anyone—

I would be a citizen in name only—with no privileges or considerations. I would still be [considered] a 'dirty Mexican.' . . . I would not have entry to the park, nor would they keep me from being segregated at the show." Such Mexican immigrants in the 1930s and 1940s often saw the Mexican consul as a better advocate of their rights than any American politician or bureaucrat. This tension between a drive for equal rights and a desire to maintain special rights and a legal distinctiveness has permeated minority politics in the West. Minority protests have emphasized the rights of minorities as Americans while maintaining an older tradition of distinctiveness and autonomy. Indian peoples presented the starkest case of a western minority at once clearly part of the larger society and also a legally separate group with special rights. The Indian attempt to secure both their rights as U.S. citizens and their rights as members of domestic dependent nations had its roots in events following World War II.

Termination and Relocation

Abrupt reversals of direction have often characterized American Indian policy. Following World War II, Congress did yet another about-face and marched away from John Collier's efforts to reassert Indian sovereignty and cultural autonomy. Congress reverted to the older goal of the complete assimilation of all Indian peoples. Congress wanted to "free" Indians from federal trusteeship, which meant terminating treaty relationships with Indian tribes.

Congressional supporters of termination provided a variety of rationales for removing federal trusteeship. Some, like Reva Beck Bosone of Utah, saw termination as a move toward self-sufficiency for Indians and did not contemplate terminating any tribe without careful study and tribal consent. Senator Arthur Watkins of Utah, a more active and vehement terminationist, was far less concerned about Indian consent and far more concerned with eliminating a special Indian status. Watkins disliked the communal culture of many Indian peoples. He argued that Indians would be better off if they had to compete as individuals within white society. Watkins saw his own life as a Utah farm boy who had made good as a model that Indian peoples not only could follow but also should want to follow. Also, as a rural westerner Watkins disliked the special status of Indians on both practical and ideological grounds. He wanted his white constituents to have access to Indian resources, and he disliked the fact that Indian reservations continued to exist as semisovereign nations within his own state. Termination, Arthur Watkins proclaimed, signified that the "concept that the Indian people exist within the United States as independent nations has been rejected."

Watkins's desire to abrogate Indian treaties and to reject Indian sovereignty became official policy in 1953 with House Concurrent Resolution No. 108, but termination did not automatically follow. To terminate a tribe, Congress had to pass specific legislation for that particular tribe. Between 1954 and 1962 Congress passed twelve termination bills, many of them terminating several tribes. Most of the affected tribes were in the West. The largest of them was the Klamaths of Oregon.

The termination of the Klamaths in 1954 began auspiciously, for the tribe consented to its own dissolution. The Klamaths were a deeply factionalized but relatively prosperous tribe. Per capita payments from the sale of timber and individual employment gave the Klamaths a median family income actually higher than the median income of surrounding non-Indian families at the time of termination. Dissatisfied with federal management of their timber and tempted by the payments of $43,700 apiece that would come from division of the tribal estate, the Klamaths agreed to termination.

The Klamaths, however, did not fully understand, nor did the government clearly explain, the implications of termination, and struggles over the disposal of tribal assets delayed final termination until 1961. With the division of tribal resources, it briefly seemed that the whole tribe had become a collective "Queen for a Day"—the daily winner in a television show of the 1950s in which the best story of woe was rewarded with washers, driers, and vacuum cleaners. The Klamaths bared their unhappy relationship with the federal government, received their payments, and embarked on a spending spree in which Klamaths made local car dealers and merchants happy indeed. But once the Klamaths had spent the bonanza, they no longer received per capita payments from the tribe, for there was no longer a recognized tribe and, after distribution, there were no more tribal assets. The Klamaths had to rely on unskilled jobs in a rural economy to support themselves. Their former prosperity vanished with their tribal organization. They slid into poverty. Many became dependent on state social services. The neighboring white community found it had fared little better. Merchants reaped much of the profit from the Klamaths' windfall, but once the money was spent, whites found that the Klamaths had become a drain on county and state resources. For the local community as a whole, the benefits of termination were transitory; the costs were long-lasting.

As effective federal policy, termination had a short life. The National Congress of American Indians aggressively campaigned against the policy. Widespread Indian opposition, and the fate of the Klamaths, the Paiutes of Utah, and other terminated tribes created doubt among many who initially believed that termination would benefit the Indians. Suspicion grew that much pressure from termination came less from a desire to "free" the Indians than from a desire to "free" the government from treaty obligations and to "free" Indian resources for exploitation by whites. By the early 1960s termination was a largely spent force. It had affected only about 3 percent of federally recognized Indians and about 3 percent of the trust lands, but it left deep scars in Indian country. Opposition to termination became the bedrock of tribal politics; defense of Indian sovereignty, treaty rights, federal trusteeship, and special status became the litmus test for tribal politicians. Indians launched a counteroffensive that in time reestablished Indian sovereignty as a critical force in the West.

Sovereignty and Civil Rights

Beginning in the 1960s, the U.S. Supreme Court issued a series of decisions that reasserted Indian sovereignty, recognized the tribes' legal status as higher than that of the states, thus limiting the power of the states on Indian reservations, and reiterated the primacy of the relationship of the tribes and the federal government. Although earlier decisions had granted Indians specific governmental powers, the Supreme Court in 1978 gave its most ringing defense of the legal standing of the tribes as semisovereign nations in *United States* v. *Wheeler*.

United States v. *Wheeler* involved an incident seemingly far removed from issues of sovereignty. Wheeler, a Navajo, had pleaded guilty in a tribal court to contributing to the delinquency of a minor, only to be indicted on the charge of statutory rape for the same incident by a federal grand jury. Citing constitutional guarantees against double jeopardy, or being tried for the same crime twice, Wheeler moved to have the federal charges dismissed. The Supreme Court, however, ruled that Wheeler's rights had not been violated, because the power of the tribal courts came from the tribe's own separate sovereignty and was not delegated to the tribe by Congress. Wheeler thus fell within the jurisdiction of two separate sovereignties and could be tried by both. Except where Congress had specifically limited Indian sovereign powers, the court ruled, they lay outside constitutional bounds.

The court reasoned that before the coming of whites, Indian tribes had "full attributes of sovereignty." Treaties and congressional plenary or absolute power over the Indian tribes had taken elements of that sovereignty away, but the court ruled that not all sovereignty had vanished; there remained "a unique and limited" sovereignty. Indian sovereignty exists "only at the sufferance of the Congress and is subject to complete defeasance [that is, extinguishment]. But until Congress acts, the tribes retain their existing sovereign powers."

In proclaiming this "unique and limited" sovereignty the courts had once more enunciated an important if still vague principle. Sovereignty existed except where limited by treaty or Congress. But what were the limits? Other court decisions incrementally provided the answers. The courts affirmed, for example, the tribes' power to tax corporations on the reservations (*Merrion* v. *Jicarilla Apache Tribe*) and the freedom from state income taxes of tribal members earning income on Indian reservations (*McClanahan* v. *Arizona State Tax Commission*). The courts have granted the tribes the right to exercise modern governmental functions, have limited the extension of state laws onto reservations, and have widened the domain of tribal courts. Indeed, the Supreme Court even modified *Lone Wolf* v. *Hitchcock* with its doctrine of congressional plenary powers. It ruled that Indian tribes are essentially self-defined and can only be dissolved by their members themselves (*United States* v. *John*). And in the 1980 case *United States* v. *Sioux Nation of Indians* the court held that Congress could not simultaneously act as a trustee for Indians and as a body furthering other national interests. When Congress did both, as when the United States took the Black Hills from the Sioux, its actions were illegitimate and the Indians were entitled to compensation. Victorious in the courts, the tribes also succeeded in having the executive and congressional branches renounce termination and embrace the often slippery doctrine of Indian self-determination.

The reestablishment of Indian sovereignty occurred contemporaneously with the civil rights movement and the drive for equal rights. And the legal strategy of the Indians owed much to the example of civil rights organizations. Indians learned the power of the courts and how to use them to their own advantage. Indeed, an ironic result of the termination struggle was the creation of a skilled group of lawyers attracted to Indian law by the large fees available through the Indian Claims Commission, a body set up in 1946 to expedite settling Indian claims under existing treaties as a prelude to termination. By 1978, when the commission dissolved and the remaining cases were delegated to the courts, the commission had awarded $818 million to the tribes, a good portion of which remained in the pockets of lawyers. The civil rights movement also provided a corps of lawyers practiced in public interest litigation. Indian and liberal white lawyers working within the Native American Rights Fund became a major force in the West. In one of the ironies of western history, Indians used a legal system whose original imposition had helped dispossess them to reassert their own rights and standing.

The civil rights movement clearly inspired Native Americans, but Indians nevertheless were ambivalent about the ultimate goals of civil rights. In Washington state, for example, Nisqually, Puyallup, and Yakima fishermen and their families employed civil disobedience, the favorite tactic of the civil rights movement, in staging "fish-ins." These acts of civil disobedience eventually led to the *Boldt* decision of 1974 vindicating their treaty rights to hunt and fish in "the usual and accustomed" places. Indians had thus used the same tactics perfected by southern blacks to escape the special and separate legal status imposed on them in the South in order to assert the special and separate status of western Indians under the law. History had made the experience and goals of southern blacks and western Indians different indeed.

The Indian political situation was, however, even more complicated than this, for Indians also pursued civil rights in the same way that blacks did. Off the reservations and on lands not covered with special treaty guarantees, Indians were American citizens like all other citizens and demanded their rights as citizens. In a sense, there were not only two sets of rights but two sets of Indians. There were tribal Indians on the reservations and ethnic Indians in the cities. This distinction between ethnic Indians and tribal Indians was in many ways artificial, for the two groups remained intimately connected, and people moved back and forth between cities and reservations, but it nevertheless highlighted a significant division in Indian communities and in ways of being Indian.

Ethnic Indians were, by and large, a creation of the postwar period. After World War I, American Indians had arrested their long population decline, and by the 1980s the Indian population was growing at a rate much higher than that of the society as a whole. Most reservations had no place for this new generation. In the mid-1960s the average Indian family earned one-third of the average family income in the United States. On Pine Ridge Reservation the unemployment rate averaged 75 percent and rose to over 90 percent during some winters. The BIA supplemented the voluntary migration off reservations with a relocation program that sought to place reservation Indians in urban jobs. And initially, many Indians welcomed relocation as a chance to improve their condition. Between 1953 and 1966, approximately 33,000 Indians enrolled in the program and moved, at least temporarily, to Los Angeles, Denver, Salt Lake City, Minneapolis–Saint Paul and other urban areas. By the late 1950s, however, liberal critics in the popular media charged that the program had succeeded only in moving Indians from poor reservations to urban slums and that 75 percent of the relocatees soon returned. The government, which abandoned the program in the 1960s, countered that only 30 percent returned, and that most of the remaining 70 percent became self-supporting. The data were woefully incomplete, but no matter which side was correct in this debate over relocation, Indians still faced a dismal choice between relocation and life on the reservation. By the 1980s more than half of the Indian population in the United States lived in urban areas. Los Angeles had the largest

Indian community in the United States, followed by Tulsa, Oklahoma City, and Phoenix.

This urban migration mixed numerous Indian groups in the cities with a variety of results. As the BIA hoped, migration for some Indians meant assimilation into the larger society. The original migrants might maintain ties with their original communities, but particularly when Indians and whites intermarried, their children often assimilated into white society. Intermarriage between Indians and whites had long been common, but with urbanization it became the norm. In 1980 over 50 percent of all Americans identifying themselves as Indians (not the most reliable indicator of actual descent) were married to non-Indians, and the percentage of such marriages among urban Indians was even higher. By way of comparison, only about 1 percent of whites were married to someone of another race and only about 2 percent of blacks.

While some Indians intermarried and passed into white society, transplanted tribal communities also arose in the cities. Only the larger tribes could sustain such communities. Navajos in Phoenix, Denver, Albuquerque, or Salt Lake City, for example, visited their reservation often, maintained their language, and intended to return to the reservation permanently at some future date. Since most cities did not contain large numbers of any single tribe, however, there also developed a pan-Indian identity that gave rise to ethnic Indian communities.

Ethnic Indians are as much a creation of American history as other ethnic groups: Irish Americans, Mexican Americans, or Jewish Americans. None of these groups transport an intact culture to American cities or towns. Instead, they mix various pieces from older cultures and novel elements to form a new ethnic culture. Among Indians, this process had begun in Indian boarding schools and mixed Indian communities, particularly in Oklahoma, where numerous tribes lived in close proximity. In both places, previously widely separated groups had come into contact and had begun to forge a common identity. By the early twentieth century Indians had developed or borrowed common cultural practices and social institutions that transcended tribal boundaries. Early-twentieth-century exemplars of pan-Indianism ranged from the "road men," or religious leaders, of the Native American Church, who in spreading peyotism were promoting an "Indian" and not a tribal identity, to assimilationist intellectuals such as Charles Eastman or Carlos Montezuma, who left their tribes but whose writings stressed Indian rights and an Indian identity.

The growth of this pan-Indianism accelerated in the cities after World War II. Urban Indians intermarried with people from other tribes and areas, and their children learned English as their mother tongue. Having only sporadic exposure to tribal culture, these children grew up in pan-Indian communities with an Indian identity, but the rituals and the centers of these communities were not tribal or traditional. The costumes and dances and ceremonies at pan-Indian rituals such as powwows were an eclectic mixture of tribal practices and new inventions. The center of most urban communities became Indian Centers—part gathering places, part cultural centers, and part agencies for social service and political action. Urban Indians tended over time to become ethnic Indians—that is, people who identified themselves more as Indians than as members of specific

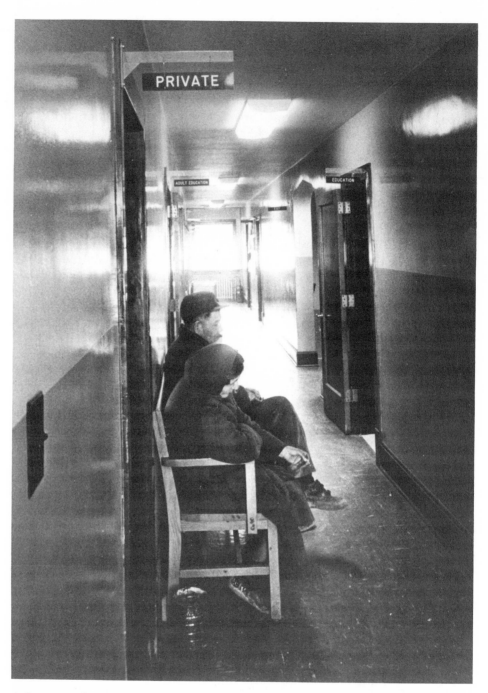

A Sioux couple waits outside an office of the Bureau of Indian Affairs.

tribes. In the 1980 census, about 20 percent of the nation's Indians did not give a tribal affiliation. They identified themselves simply as American Indians.

Ethnic Indians living in cities tended to emphasize civil rights rather than tribal rights. It was largely urban Indians who made common cause with other minorities and participated in the Poor People's March on Washington in 1968. But ethnic Indians, because of their lingering connections with tribes, were not fully willing to trade treaty rights for civil rights. At their more imaginative, they sometimes made treaty rights as pan-Indian as a powwow or an urban community by contending that rights granted one tribe belonged to all Indians. In 1970, for example, the "Indians of All Tribes" seized Alcatraz Island in San Francisco Bay as a symbolic protest. They claimed title to the island, which contained an abandoned federal penitentiary, under a provision of a treaty with the Sioux that gave title to abandoned federal forts back to the Sioux. The treaty was specific to the Sioux and their lands, and the Sioux, of course, never had any claim to Alcatraz. The logic of Indian sovereignty proceeded from the premise that specific tribes had separate relations with the federal government. The "Indians of All Tribes" had never negotiated a treaty; they had no special relations with the United States. Essentially, the Alcatraz incident was a civil rights demonstration by urban Indians that called for redressing common Indian grievances. The Indians, however, dressed it up as an assertion of treaty rights.

Indian politics never lost this tension between the attractions of separate rights and equal rights, between ethnic identity and tribal identity. Concerns for equal rights led to the Indian Religious Freedom Act of 1978 that guaranteed protection for Native American forms of religious worship and access to sacred sites off the reservations. But religious freedom for tribal Indians meant freedom to practice tribal religions; Indians did not seek to divorce church and state, which in some of the pueblos were inextricably bound. And this created a problem, for other civil rights legislation did threaten to divorce the two and thus make traditional governance and ways of life impossible. The Indian Civil Rights Act of 1968 was the work of Senator Sam Ervin of North Carolina. Ervin coupled an impressive resourcefulness in trying to halt civil rights legislation designed to guarantee blacks their constitutional rights in the South with a desire to force Indian tribal governments to abide by the federal constitution. Ervin saw the issue as civil rights for tribal Indians; many tribal Indians saw the issue as yet another attempt by whites to dictate their form of government and undermine their sovereignty. In the end Ervin did not get a blanket application of the bill of rights, but he did limit the powers of Indian governments.

The tensions between equal rights and separate status appeared in Indian organizations themselves. The National Indian Youth Council (NIYC), founded in 1960, tried to unite the pursuit of equal status for individual Indians within the larger society and the pursuit of special status of tribes. Under the leadership of Mel Thom, a Nevada Paiute, the NIYC grew to 5,000 members by 1970, but its influence spread much farther. Under the slogan "For a Greater Indian America," the NIYC tried to incorporate both a pan-Indian identity, which emphasized Indians as a single ethnic group, and tribal identity, which emphasized the citizenship of Indians in many separate nations. The NIYC emphasized Indian ethnic unity when it concentrated on governmental oppression and called for resistance to the BIA, an organization affecting all Indians. But when the NIYC called for a return to tradition, it meant a return to the numerous separate and distinct traditions embodied in individual tribes. Unity only went so far. As long as each tribe remained semisovereign, neither the NIYC nor the National Congress of American Indians could ever fully unite them. The very Indian identity these organizations emphasized was a tribal identity, and thus by its very nature a fragmented identity.

AIM and Wounded Knee

Exerting far less influence on tribal leaders than the NIYC, but far better known in the larger society, was the American Indian Movement (AIM). Sioux and Ojibwa former convicts founded AIM in 1968 to stop police harassment of Indians in Minneapolis–Saint Paul. Its tough, flamboyant, and clever leaders exerted a strong appeal for young second-generation urban Indians, but their urban ways made the organization appear un-Indian to many reservation residents. When AIM members joined the 1972 Trail of Broken Treaties, a protest march on Washington, and then seized and ransacked the BIA building, many reservation leaders publicly denounced the organization. AIM denounced them in turn.

AIM's notoriety increased immediately thereafter. A faction of AIM led by Dennis Banks and Leonard Peltier sought to create alliances with elders in reservation communities. Their most notable success came at the Pine Ridge Reservation. They gained the support of Leonard Crow Dog, who was both a traditional religious leader and a road man of the Native American Church. And by organizing protests over the murder of Raymond Yellow Thunder, they gained significant popular support on the reservation. Yellow Thunder, like many Sioux, habitually crossed the reservation line to drink in Gordon, Nebraska. There, as a drunken Indian, he became an object of white scorn and ridicule. On February 12, 1972, a group of young whites out "to bust an Indian" beat him, stripped him naked from the waist down, and threw him into the trunk of their car. They drove him to a dance at an American Legion hall and shoved him inside. When he left the dance, they again accosted him and forced him into their car.

What started out as a brutal prank ended in murder. Yellow Thunder died of a blow to the head suffered either in the beating or while being carried in the trunk. The police arrested four attackers, who were released on bail. The murder outraged the Pine Ridge Sioux. Rumors, later proven false, circulated that Yellow Thunder had been forced to dance naked and had been tortured and castrated. AIM organized protests in Gordon. When Yellow Thunder's attackers received six-year prison sentences, AIM received credit for the sentences and gained immense prestige on the reservation.

The support AIM gained at Pine Ridge for its protests in border towns soon brought the organization into a coalition opposed to the tribal chairman, Dick Wilson. Wilson feared the consequences of a political alliance between AIM and Sioux traditionalists, for together they might vote him from office. AIM and its allies attempted to impeach Wilson on charges of corruption and abuse of power. When they failed, AIM planned protests against the administration at Pine Ridge, and Wilson garrisoned tribal headquarters with BIA police and federal marshals. Instead of confronting the police, AIM decided to occupy Wounded Knee, the site of the 1890 massacre of Big Foot's band during the Ghost Dance. Wilson and

In 1973 the American Indian Movement seized Wounded Knee and focused national attention on Indian issues.

the federal government quickly responded to the seizure, encircling and besieging the little hamlet of a trading post and a few houses.

For the next 71 days national attention focused on Wounded Knee. A cordon of BIA police, U.S. marshals, and FBI agents surrounded the village, but despite sometimes nightly firefights, only two people were killed and one was permanently paralyzed during the siege. The U.S. Army precipitated the slaughter at the first Wounded Knee, but it was an army officer, Colonel Volney Warner, chief of staff of the 82nd Airborne Division, who prevented significant bloodshed at the second Wounded Knee. Ordered to Wounded Knee to evaluate the situation and to recommend to the secretary of defense whether the situation required federal troops, Warner argued that the government was dealing with "an embarrassment and not an insurrection" and recommended denying the Justice Department's request for soldiers. The army did man roadblocks and provide supplies, but it left the confrontation to others. Warner was a voice of reason and moderation throughout the siege.

A negotiated settlement eventually ended the siege, but government efforts to break AIM by sending its leaders to prison failed when the judge ordered their acquittal because of tampering with witnesses by the FBI. The whole incident was a major triumph for AIM, which had managed to focus widespread media attention both on themselves and on Indian problems. When, however, the media withdrew, the situation changed dramatically. AIM's own organizational weakness and excesses, a government crusade against them, and the political failure of an AIM leader, Russell Means, to defeat Wilson in a tribal election at Pine Ridge all pushed AIM towards disaster.

In the aftermath of Wounded Knee a virtual civil war broke out on the reservation. The violence following the siege dwarfed anything at Wounded Knee, but it attracted little national notice. Beatings, shootings, murders, and "accidents" led to 100 Indian deaths during Wilson's term in office. Only when two FBI agents died in a gunfight in 1975 did a national spotlight again hit the reservation. To find the killers the FBI invaded the reservation. This time they sent leading AIM members to prison; the FBI obtained the conviction of Leonard Peltier. With the FBI onslaught, AIM's status declined on Pine Ridge and nationally. It fell victim both to its own excesses, including a murder by its members in California, and to government repression, which apparently involved murders of AIM members and sympathizers.

Civil Rights and Separatism

Because of their semisovereign status, the efforts of Indians to secure their rights as both citizens and tribal members obviously stood apart from the struggles of other minorities. No other groups were, in fact, legally sovereign and separate within the West, but the politics of other minority groups in the 1960s and 1970s also ranged across a hazy middle ground between demands for autonomy and demands for the full enjoyment of the rights of U.S. citizens. Like Indians, they tended not so much to choose one option over another as to emphasize different goals in different contexts. This was true among blacks, most of whom had moved into the West only after 1940.

In its purest form, the civil rights movement was a product of the South. It was a protest against laws designed to segregate blacks from whites and to relegate them to a separate and inferior social and economic sphere. Southern blacks could not vote. They had to ride in the rear of buses, drink at separate water fountains, and go to separate schools. They could not eat in restaurants or sleep in hotels frequented by whites. In dismantling segregation, the great triumphs of the civil rights movement were legal and political. They came through a combination of nonviolent resistance, court rulings, and federal legislation. With sit-ins at segregated restaurants, bus boycotts, and protest marches, blacks forced the government to act. In the South, and in Texas and Oklahoma—those southern wedges into the West—the civil rights movement destroyed a caste system that had assigned blacks a subordinate place in a common social world.

Segregation in most of the West and North was just as real as in the South. In the South segregation tended to be imposed by law, while in the West and North it tended to be de facto—that is, the result of income distribution, custom, and residential patterns. Southern whites and blacks lived close to each other; laws reinforced custom to make sure they did not mix except as employers and employees. Blacks and whites in Los Angeles did not live close to each other. Indeed, in the 1960s Los Angeles and Chicago were ranked as the most residentially segregated cities in the country. Except as domestic servants, African Americans could not enter into a white neighborhood without arousing suspicions. Even in Texas, where contact between the races was more common, blacks and whites remained far more rigidly segregated residentially than in the deep South.

In coming West, African Americans had, in effect, voted with their feet against legal segregation and the South only to find themselves subject to de facto segregation in the West. In California, with 1.8 million black people by the end of the 1960s, blacks believed that they had greater economic opportunities and greater political rights than in the South. While World War II did bring significant economic progress, much of it evaporated after the war. San Francisco blacks, for example, had a much harder time than white workers in finding new work when the shipyards closed down following the war, because private employers were no longer under a federal mandate not to discriminate. Black unemployment in San Francisco reached an estimated 30 percent by 1947. When blacks did find new jobs, they tended to be in lower-paying service jobs instead of the industrial jobs they had held during the war. Meanwhile, black residential overcrowding and segregation remained undiminished. Restrictive real estate covenants—private contracts that banned the sale of a property to blacks—and the personal prejudices of landlords confined even prosperous African Americans to separate ghettos.

In Oklahoma and Texas, western states with a southern system of segregation in place, the civil rights movement could use customary tactics against customary abuses, but in the rest of the West the target proved more amorphous. In Texas, for example, blacks attacked the legal basis of poll taxes, segregated schools, public facilities, and transportation. In California, however, blacks had to overcome restrictive covenants, poverty, and prejudice to conquer segregation. In 1963 the civil rights movement seemed to have won a major triumph when the California legislature enacted the Rumford Act, a law prohibiting landlords from engaging in racial discrimination in rentals. The act struck at the separation of races long typical of western society, and the response of white voters was immediate and overwhelming. In 1964 the California Real Estate Association sponsored Initiative Proposition 14, which guaranteed property owners the right to lease, sell, or rent to anyone they chose. It passed by a two-to-one margin only to be later ruled unconstitutional by the courts.

Proposition 14 symbolized the commitment of whites to confining, segregating, and controlling blacks as strictly as possible. The promising gains made during World War II had yielded to confinement in crowded ghettos, continued poor education, and lack of access to decent jobs. For many young African Americans their only daily contact with white society came in their dealings with white merchants in the ghettos, whose prices were usually higher than those charged in neighboring white communities and who sometimes purposefully cheated their customers, and with the largely white police forces that patrolled black communities. In Watts and other black communities in the 1960s, young men increasingly came to define their identity as blacks in confrontations with the police. Because the police were white, crime could easily become a badge of blackness to unemployed African American youths. The police, in turn, could easily assume all young blacks were criminals. On August 11, 1965, in an incident that began over an arrest for drunk driving, the tensions of years of such confrontations spilled out in the Watts Riot. Before it ended, fighting between rioters and police left 34 dead, hundreds injured, and property damage in excess of $35 million. To astonished whites it might have seemed that black rioters were burning down their own homes and businesses, but to black rioters their rage had found a focus on the white businesses and property that dominated the ghetto. While not completely selective, rioters did spare some white businesses whose owners had reputations for fairness.

In a situation in which blacks and whites were so thoroughly isolated and in which violence had reached such a scale there was potential for black separatism to take root, but surprisingly, black nationalism was weak in the West. Instead, there arose a militant, revolutionary, and sometimes violent black left that nonetheless sought to make common cause with radical whites. Huey Newton and Bobby Seale organized the Black Panther party of Oakland in 1966 to combat police violence against blacks. The Black Panthers mounted armed patrols in the ghetto, adopted a flamboyant revolutionary rhetoric, and sought, and often achieved, deadly confrontations with the police. Closer to a political gang than a party, their ability to generate publicity disguised their lack of deep roots in Bay Area African American communities. They and their imitators, such as People's Party II in Houston, became casualties not only of police repression but also of their lack of community roots and their own tendency to court violence on a scale that left them badly outmatched.

Like AIM, the Black Panthers garnered large amounts of publicity in the West. But just as Indian gains came from less flamboyant actions by Indian tribes and pan-Indian organizations that reestablished a meaningful Indian sovereignty, black gains came from undramatic but significant gains in electoral politics. Blacks were a relatively small minority in any given western state, but their very isolation in urban ghettos concentrated their votes. By 1966, when the Supreme Court struck down the poll tax, 400,000 Texas blacks, 61.6 percent of the total eligible, had registered to vote. Black Texans had already proved the swing vote delivering Texas to John F. Kennedy in 1960, and in 1966 they elected Barbara Jordan, a Houston native, to the Texas state senate. She became the first African American

National guardsmen patrol the streets of Watts following the riots of August 1965. (Photograph by John Malmin, copyright © Los Angeles Times)

state senator since 1881. By 1984, Texas blacks registered and voted at nearly the same percentage as Texas whites. They remained, however, underrepresented in the Texas legislature.

In California the gains were far more dramatic. Whereas in 1985 Texas blacks had elected one black representative to Congress, California blacks had four, all of them coming from districts where blacks were a minority. In proportional terms, blacks were slightly overrepresented in the California legislature, where a black leader, Willie Brown, served as the powerful speaker of the house. In addition, the mayor of Los Angeles, Tom Bradley, who had earlier lost in an openly racist campaign waged against him by Sam Yorty in 1960, was African American. These were astonishing gains in the twenty years since Watts, but race had hardly vanished as an issue in California politics. In 1982, Bradley lost a close election for governor to George Deukmejian in which the critical element seems to have been a crossover of white Democrats who would not vote for a black.

The Creation of the Chicano

Of all the western minority groups, Chicanos forged the most complex relationship between nationalism and separatism on one pole and equal rights as American citizens on the other. Although they outnumbered blacks in the West, they did not achieve a political representation proportional to their numbers. And although they increasingly stressed their Mexican heritage, the Hispanic origins of the Southwest, and the promises made under the Treaty of Guadalupe Hidalgo, they had no legal basis for a special status equivalent to that enjoyed by Indian peoples.

By the postwar period, the Spanish-surnamed population of the United States was overwhelmingly urban. In 1970, 85 percent of the Spanish-surnamed population in the Southwest lived in urban areas. The movement into the cities had physically removed Mexican Americans from their old subordinate position in mining, railroads, and agriculture. World War II gave many Mexican Americans access to industrial and skilled-labor jobs in the cities, and labor unions protected and expanded their gains and improved their wages. Service in the armed forces gave others both an increased sense of their own American identity and a claim on the rights supposedly available to all American citizens. Urbanization also provided Mexican Americans with educational opportunities denied them in rural areas. Spanish-surnamed people still had a far lower educational attainment than did blacks and whites, but urban minority children were better educated than their rural counterparts.

These changes constituted progress, but they hardly represented equality. Mexican Americans in the 1960s still had only limited access to managerial and professional jobs. Employers segregated Mexican American women into an even narrower spectrum of jobs. The ceiling on possible achievement for Mexican Americans had moved upward, but the ceiling remained, nonetheless. In the Southwest in 1960 the median income of Spanish-surnamed families was only two-thirds that of Anglo families. Concretely, low income in a city like San Antonio, the population of which was 40 percent Hispanic in the 1960s, meant unpaved and undrained streets, homes without indoor plumbing, and large numbers of infant deaths.

This American-born, urban generation of Mexican Americans formed a cohesive political generation in the years before and after World War II. Emphasizing the American side of their Mexican American identity, Mexican American activists in the 1950s and 1960s fought segregation, struggled for improved schools, and tried to increase Mexican American political power as they sought to both secure political rights and improve their economic standing. The willingness of many CIO unions, which organized industries with large numbers of unskilled workers, to protect minority workers gave Mexican Americans a position of comparative economic strength. In El Paso the International Union of Mine, Mill and Smelter Workers largely eliminated the dual wage system for Mexican and Mexican American workers in local smelters. Harry Bridges's International Longshoremen's and Warehousemen's Union, for example, had significant Mexican American membership and provided a base for Bert Corona, one of the leading western Mexican American labor leaders. Similarly the United Cannery, Agricultural, Packing, and Allied Workers of America (UCAPAWA) of the CIO—after 1944 the Food, Tobacco, Agricultural and Allied Workers of America (FTA)—substantially improved wages and working conditions in Texas and California during the 1940s, and Mexican American women secured elective posts from steward to local president. Their gains largely evaporated when in 1945, despite FTA electoral victories, Dave Beck's Teamsters' Union won a power struggle between unions by refusing to haul goods to any California canneries recognizing the FTA and by putting pressure on the National Labor Relations

Board to overturn the elections. The results were sweetheart contracts between the Teamsters and California canners that destroyed the FTA and eliminated their democratic union structure.

Mexican American activists who stressed their own civil rights as citizens came to have a certain ambivalence in regard to Mexican immigrants. On the one hand they realized that their own rights were not easily detached from those of long-term resident aliens. In the 1950s the Internal Security Act, which provided for the deportation of legally resident alien "subversives," and the Immigration and Nationality Act (1952), which instituted strict new immigration rules, both brought sweeps by the INS that terrorized Mexican American communities. For a Mexican American family in which the children and their mother might be citizens while the father was a resident alien, protecting the civil rights of citizens but not of resident aliens was a meaningless abstraction. On the other hand, there remained a special tension between U.S. citizens and more recent Mexican immigrants in many southwestern communities. Many Mexican Americans in the 1950s and 1960s continued to believe that their own economic progress could come only when the United States curtailed the immigration of cheap Mexican labor. Mexican American activists helped to end the bracero program in 1964, and the end of the bracero program helped the successful organization of the United Farm Workers (UFW).

In the 1960s, however, Mexican American students began using the formerly pejorative term *Chicano* as a mark of cultural distinctiveness and pride. *Chicano* submerged all the complicated sectional, class, and social divisions of the Mexican and Mexican American community under a single term. Mexican immigrants, the Spanish Americans of New Mexico, and old *californios* and Tejanos were supposedly all now Chicanos (although Hispanic New Mexicans refused to adopt the new label). Anglo Americans had long tended to ignore distinctions among various people of Mexican descent and labeled them all Mexicans in order to categorize them as foreigners; now Mexican Americans and Mexicans themselves sought a collective identity in order to create a sense of solidarity and ethnic pride.

The rise of the United Farm Workers under César Chávez exhibited, often painfully, the tensions between an emerging Chicano identity and the drive to improve the economic conditions of Mexican Americans. Chávez and other young organizers who came out of Los Angeles's Community Service Organization succeeded in doing what earlier generations of labor organizers had failed to do: they built an effective farm workers' union on the factory farms of California. Because farm workers remained outside the provisions of the National Labor Relations Act, agricultural workers could not petition for union elections and recognition. Until 1975, when California passed legislation providing for elections to provide unions for farm workers, Chávez from necessity relied on strikes and boycotts to pressure employers to recognize the UFW.

Inspired by the civil rights movement, the charismatic Chávez managed to take a strike begun by Filipinos in the vineyards of the Delano area of the San Joaquin Valley and transform it into "La Causa"—the common struggle of the entire Mexican American community. Chavez created a union—the UFW—that proved far more durable than earlier agricultural unions. It had such staying power in part because many of its first members in the Delano area were not migrants.

United Farm Workers march on strike against grape growers, April 1973. (Photograph by Rick Browne, copyright © Los Angeles Times)

Like the "Okies" before them, they lived and worked in the area year-round. To this community base Chávez added ethnic pride in Mexican origins, a common Catholic religion, and labor militancy to create the potent mix symbolized on the UFW flag: a black Aztec eagle and a banner of the Virgin of Guadalupe on a red background.

The UFW's battle in the vineyards began in 1965, and it was followed by a second organizing drive in the lettuce fields of the Salinas Valley. The UFW struggled against not only the growers, but also the rival Teamsters union, which sought to break the UFW just as it had broken rival unions in the canneries. If the Teamsters succeeded, they would gain members and dues, the employers would obtain a guarantee against strikes and "unreasonable demands," and the workers would get very little. Chávez garnered support from the solidarity of his workers; from urban unions, many with sizable Chicano membership; from students; and from urban Chicanos as a whole. He also appealed to white church groups and to sympathetic whites across the nation. These allies enabled the UFW to deploy its most effective weapon: the boycott. The UFW mounted direct boycotts of grapes and lettuce and also secondary boycotts of other brand-name products marketed by the corporations that owned the farms. Such boycotts were illegal under the National Labor Relations Act, but they remained open to the UFW because the NLRB had specifically excluded farm workers from the benefits of the act and thus from its restrictions. The union picketed grocery stores, and it asked consumers not to buy grapes or lettuce without the union label. The grape boycott brought growers to the bargaining table and secured the union contracts in 1970. In 1972 the UFW defeated an attempt by growers to outlaw the secondary boycott, and in 1975 it agreed to a compromise Agricultural Labor

Relations Act in California that provided for elections to recognize the union. By 1980 the UFW, with 30,000 members, had made impressive gains for workers, but its triumph was limited by failures of its organizing drive in Arizona and by the steady loss of harvesting jobs to mechanization, which became more appealing as farm workers' wages rose.

Although Chávez and the UFW served as a symbol of Mexican American unity and identity, they also highlighted the continuing division between Mexican Americans and Mexicans living in the United States. As a union leader, Chávez condemned growers who used illegal workers imported from Mexico to break his strikes. And in doing so, Chávez and the UFW sporadically made statements that endorsed a restrictive immigration policy. His subsequent attempts to reconcile his fear of nonunion Mexican immigrants, whom growers would use to break his union, with Chicano solidarity only created confusion.

Chicano Culture and Autonomy

In the 1950s calls by a Mexican American labor leader for restrictions on Mexican immigration would have been predictable, but by the late 1960s the lines between Mexicans and Mexican Americans had blurred. The creation of a new common identity became easier because during the 1960s and 1970s rapid and obvious changes occurred in the *colonias* and barrios of the Southwest. In Texas, for example, middle-aged Mexican Texans had most likely begun their life on ranchos, had become migrant laborers as the ranchos collapsed, and then eventually resettled in Texas towns and cities. They had changed not only their residence but their way of life as well. Women, for example, no longer established their homes near their husbands' parents. The earlier distinctive architecture of Mexicans in the Southwest had largely disappeared or had become merely an adornment for American suburban architecture. The way parents raised their children and the way children viewed their parents were more American than Mexican. The obligations of *copadres* (godparents) to serve as coparents weakened. The Spanish they spoke had partially evolved into a separate Chicano dialect. Immigrant Mexicans entering the United States became enmeshed in the same patterns of change. Both young Chicano activists and older people lamented these changes even as they promoted them through their own adjustments and conflicts with the larger society. Political activism itself was part of the wider pattern of change.

Students, as representatives of the generation most affected by the rapid changes of the postwar period, spearheaded the drive for a new Chicano identity. In March of 1968 nearly 10,000 Chicano students walked out of five Los Angeles high schools in protest against the poor quality of their schools, racist teachers, and the high dropout rate. Student activism also took hold among Chicano college students. The various college organizations eventually merged in the Movimiento Estudiantil Chicano de Aztlán. In Aztlán, Chicanos claimed the Southwest as the mythical homeland of the Aztecs and the symbolic place of origin for La Raza—both Chicanos and Mexicans. Aztlán thus tried to fuse Mexican nationalism, the Southwest, and Chicano identity into a single symbolic whole.

The idea of Aztlán embodied a cultural and political program that contained familiar tensions between equal rights and separate status. It found one focus in Denver under the leadership of Rodolfo ("Corky") Gonzales. Gonzales had been active in Democratic politics, heading several War on Poverty programs, but he had become increasingly disillusioned with the traditional political process. He stepped outside of it to found the Crusade for Justice—a self-help organization devoted to creating a stronger positive ethnic identity among Chicanos. In 1969 he convened the First National Chicano Youth Liberation Conference, which adopted a manifesto calling for "social, economic, cultural, and political independence" from Anglo American society. Aztlán conjured up a dream of a Chicano homeland in which the distinction between Chicanos and Mexicans would largely disappear.

In Texas and New Mexico, Chicanos mounted political attempts to realize something approximating the ideal of Aztlán. Perceiving itself as a separate undeveloped nation within a nation-state, the Raza Unida party of Texas advocated a Chicano social welfare state within Texas, complete with its own foreign policy and its own economic and social exchanges with the Third World. Raza Unida demonstrated surprising strength in the 1970s, capturing nearly 20 percent of the vote in 40 counties in South and West Texas in 1972. Internal divisions and outside attacks destroyed Raza Unida, but many of its activists went to work to capture local Democratic party chapters in South Texas.

In New Mexico, another Mexican Texan, Reies López Tijerina, launched a second, far more personal attempt to legitimize the special status of Chicanos in the Southwest. Tijerina, a native Texan and Protestant leading Hispanic New Mexicans and Catholics, embodied the diverse elements being united under the rubric Chicano. After moving to New Mexico, Tijerina learned of the history of the guarantees of the Treaty of Guadalupe Hidalgo and the loss of New Mexican communal lands. He became determined to reassert the rights of the Hispanic New Mexicans. In 1963, Tijerina incorporated the Alianza Federal de Mercedes (the Federal Alliance of Land Grants) and started a campaign to regain the lands. He began with the rights of the Pueblo of San Joaquín de Chama, the lands of which were within Kit Carson National Forest. In 1966 he seized a national forest campground, proclaimed a restoration of the pueblo's rights, and put two rangers on trial. His campaign eventually culminated in a gunfight in Tierra Amarilla. Although the shoot-out made him a national figure, it lost him Hispanic New Mexican support, and the local Mexican American political officials cooperated with the government in breaking his influence.

Immigration Politics

The Chicano aspirations for autonomy had perhaps their most formidable consequences in the politics of immigration restriction. The fact that many Chicanos saw themselves as having a common identity with the illegal immigrants from Mexico came to matter a great deal in debates over immigration. And immigration emerged in many ways as a leading minority issue in the West in the 1970s.

In the 1920s the United States had shut the "golden door" through which millions of European immigrants had entered this country, but a much smaller "golden door" reopened in the West in the 1960s and 1970s. The immigrants who entered through the West often came because of American involvement—past and present—in their homelands. They were most likely to come from Central and South America and Asia. Of the four million people who entered the United States during the 1970s, 75 percent came from the Third World.

The change in immigration patterns reflected numerous demographic and economic changes abroad, but they also reflected changes in U.S. immigration laws and the results of U.S. foreign policy. Nineteenth- and early-twentieth-century immigrants had come largely from Europe, and twentieth-century immigration laws had established quotas that gave preference to northern Europeans. In the Immigration Act of 1965, however, Congress had abandoned the old system of national quotas. Through various later modifications of the act, Congress created a ceiling on total immigration instead of separate quotas for each country. The new uniform preference system emphasized the presence of relatives within the United States, economic skills, education, and refugee status in giving priority to immigrants. In practice, even the absolute limits placed on immigration proved porous both because the INS often exempted immediate family members of U.S. citizens from the quotas and because the president, under the Refugee Relief Act of 1953, had the power to admit political refugees in excess of immigration limits.

The combination of new laws and the changes in sources of immigration meant that far more legal immigrants from Mexico, the Philippines, Taiwan, Hong Kong, Korea, and India entered the country than ever before. This immigration often took the form of a chain migration. "My brother-in-law left his wife in Taiwan and came here as a student to get a Ph.D. in engineering," recounted Subi Lin Felipe. "After he received his degree, he got a job in San Jose. Then he brought in a sister and his wife, who brought over one of her brothers and me. And my brother's wife then came." And when the American defeat in Vietnam and involvement in civil wars in El Salvador and Nicaragua created substantial numbers of political refugees, many of them also found their way to the West. By 1985, for example, there were over 700,000 Indochinese in the United States.

This new immigration was most obvious in western cities. By 1980, realtors estimated that 40 percent of Little Italy in San Francisco was actually occupied by Chinese migrants from Hong Kong and Taiwan. Los Angeles's Chinatown, which had nearly disappeared earlier, had 16,500 people by 1977. Los Angeles and Orange County had the country's largest Korean communities—with Korean newspapers, radio programs, and television programs— as well as the largest Vietnamese communities.

This immigration was socially more diverse than earlier waves, for it attracted more people from the upper ends of the class spectrum. At one extreme, Asian immigrants came as members of a highly educated elite; many came to the United States with either technical skills or significant amounts of money. These migrants emphasized education for their children and, unlike earlier Asian immigrants, they found public institutions open to them. Together, the children of these new immigrants and the children of Asian Americans long resident in the United States achieved notable educational success. Asian immigrants and Asian Americans made up only 5 percent of California's residents in the early 1980s, but they made up 20 percent of the University of California's student body. Prosperous Chinese immigrants made Monterey Park, California, the West's first suburban Chinatown. They comprised more than half of the city's 61,000 residents in 1988.

Such examples, however, were deceptive, for they lumped together privileged immigrants and existing American ethnic groups who possessed strong cultural beliefs in the efficacy of education while ignoring a mass of poor and uneducated Asian immigrants. Poor immigrants from Hong Kong and later waves of Indo-Chinese refugees without marketable skills, without English, and without education had immigrant experiences reminiscent of the earlier twentieth century. In 1980, 51 percent of Chinese immigrants were in menial and low-skilled blue-collar work, often as waiters and garment workers. Driven to a strange land by war, many Indochinese found only low-paying jobs at the bottom of the economic ladder, and many found themselves dependent on public support. Their children were less likely to be college students than were the children of middle- or upper-class Indochinese, and some of them became members of the Asian American gangs that gained notoriety both in San Francisco's Chinatown and in Vietnamese immigrant communities.

The large numbers of Asian immigrants who came to the United States in the late 1970s and early 1980s outnumbered the legal immigrants from Mexico. Legal Mexican immigrants tended to be young, from urban backgrounds, and with some industrial experience. Although not highly educated by U.S. standards, they did have education at or above Mexican norms. Most settled in the border region from Texas to California, with Los Angeles remaining the largest Mexican and Mexican American city in the United States.

A much larger illegal immigration dwarfed this legal Mexican immigration. By the early 1980s the backlog of requests for entries from Mexico exceeded 300,000. Most Mexicans who wished to immigrate did not wait their turn on the list; they simply entered into the United States across a 2,000-mile border that neither the United States nor Mexico has ever been able to close or control. By the late 1970s and early 1980s the Immigration and Naturalization Service was apprehending about a million persons annually, mostly along the Mexican border. The majority of these illegals no longer came to work in the fields; instead, they found work in service jobs and in the garment industry of Los Angeles or northern cities.

Beginning in the late 1960s, both Congress and the national press paid increasing attention to this so-called silent invasion. Journalists accused the illegal immigrants of costing taxpayers billions of dollars by taking jobs away from U.S. citizens, by acquiring welfare benefits, by using public services such as hospital emergency rooms, and by avoiding taxes. The truth of these charges was never clear. The actual number of illegal migrants, while substantial, was unknown and unknowable; the Immigration and Naturalization Service repeatedly had to retract its exaggerated estimates. Nor were the economic consequences any clearer. Many of the Mexican illegals were participating in a longstanding western pattern of temporary work in the United States and permanent residency in Mexico. Their ambitions were old immigrant ambitions: to earn money in the West in order to return home to buy land or start a business. Studies of apprehended aliens found that they were largely single males, the vast majority of whom paid taxes and did not use social services such as schools, hospitals, or unemployment insurance. Although bitter arguments raged about whether their employment in restaurants, the garment industry, and agriculture displaced American workers, data remained insufficient for any accurate appraisal of the question.

The actual conditions of this immigration were, in any case, often immaterial to the debate on the issue. Beginning with the Rodino bill of 1973, legislation was introduced in Congress to curtail illegal migration by imposing sanctions on employers who hired illegals and by proposing national identity cards to verify U.S. citizenship. Congressional advocates of restriction tended to portray the West as if it were under siege by impoverished Mexicans and other Central

Table 16
Mexican Immigration, 1945–60

Year	Legal Entrants	Aliens Apprehended or Deported
1945	6,455	80,760
1946	6,805	116,320
1947	7,775	214,543
1948	8,730	193,543
1949	7,977	289,400
1950	6,841	469,581
1951	6,372	510,355
1952	9,600	531,719
1953	18,454	839,149
1954	37,456	1,035,282
1955	50,772	165,186
1956	65,047	58,792
1957	49,154	45,640
1958	26,712	45,164
1959	23,061	42,732
1960	32,084	39,750

Source: Stanley R. Ross, *Views Across the Border: The United States and Mexico* (Albuquerque: University of New Mexico Press, 1978), pp. 166–67.

Note: These figures are not to be taken as an accurate count of the total immigrant flow, since apprehensions and deportations represent only a fraction, perhaps one-sixth, of the total undocumented entrants. Also the apprehensions reflect the changing enforcement policies of the Border Patrol.

Americans, and some proponents of restriction even trotted out old racist rhetoric about the demise of the white race in the West. Chicano activists, for their part, challenged such legislation. They argued that INS sweeps and identity cards were a threat to all Spanish-surnamed people with brown skin; that many illegals had, in fact, resided in the United States for years; and that the illegals had become scapegoats for the economic policies of both Mexico and the United States. More radical Chicanos, however, went farther. They proclaimed their common cultural and class identity with illegal migrants. This was a stance not always supported by most Mexican Americans. Many Mexican Americans still feared the economic consequences of unrestricted immigration, while many Mexicans belittled both Chicanos and emigrant laborers from Mexico as *pochos*—marginal people without real Mexican culture. Nonetheless, Anglo Americans who had for years referred to all Hispanics in the Southwest as Mexicans now had that confusion of identity thrown back in their face when they tried to assure Mexican Americans that immigration restriction would not harm them.

Chicano opposition and the opposition of employers kept the Rodino bills stalled in Congress, and such opposition also halted President Carter's very similar 1976 bill. But in the early 1980s a new bill, the Simpson-Mazzoli bill, began to work its way through Congress. The bill offered amnesty to long-time residents, provided a temporary worker section to allow agricultural laborers to enter, and imposed sanctions against employers who gave jobs to undocumented workers.

Although proponents of the bill offered a survey that showed most Hispanics favored tighter restrictions, organized Chicano groups were unanimous in opposition. Congress wavered but finally passed the very similar Simpson-Mazzoli Act in 1986. If, in fact, the law succeeds in restraining labor migration from Mexico, it will have altered one of the most deeply rooted of the West's migration patterns.

Federal Poverty Programs

The massive upheavals that shook the minority communities of the West in the 1960s and 1970s often proceeded under banners of autonomy and sovereignty while simultaneously emphasizing equality with other citizens of the United States. The contradiction between equal rights and separate status became even more confusing when minorities demanded, and partially obtained, federal aid in achieving their dual sets of demands. Congressional legislation and federal court decisions in the 1960s and 1970s secured greater legal protection for minorities. The Economic Opportunity Act of 1964 established the Office of Economic Opportunity (OEO) and created the War on Poverty, which funneled hundreds of millions of dollars into western minority communities. But the infusion of money only underlined the paradoxical nature of racial relations. Government funds went to groups preaching community autonomy, but the federal government required oversight of expenditures. The programs thus tended to make minority activists into federal bureaucrats bound by all the common rules of the bureaucracy. Federal aid, demanded in the name of creating autonomous communities, acted instead to increase federal control and minority dependency.

Indian reservations, where actual sovereignty was most concrete, provide a useful example. The new Indian policy of self-determination, a new emphasis on developing reservation economies, and the War on Poverty all brought increases in federal funding on reservations in the 1960s and early 1970s. Despite cuts in the late 1970s, Indians in 1980 received almost a billion dollars annually through federal programs, largely educational, administered by the BIA. This represented less than one-half of the federal funds flowing onto the reservations through poverty and other programs. Indians—either through the tribes; the BIA, with its predominantly Indian staff; or community agencies—managed most of this money.

Economically, the results of these federal programs were mixed; economic development of Indian resources proved disappointing to the tribes, although not to the corporations who gained access to Indian oil, uranium, and coal. Despite fraud and waste, the federal programs did result in the greatest increase in standard of living among Indian peoples since the destruction of their original economies. Indians (as well as Aleuts and Eskimos, who were grouped with them in federal statistics) saw their median incomes double in urban areas and triple in rural areas. The percentage of rural *nonfarm* Indian families below the poverty line fell from 45 percent in 1969 to 29 percent in 1979; the percentage of poor rural Indian *farm* families fell from 41 percent to 19 percent over the same period.

But there was a cost. In 1979, Ed Driving Hawk of the National Congress of American Indians complained that the dependence on federal programs undercut the legal gains in sovereignty by making bloated tribal governments simply arms of the federal bureaucracy. Critics also worried that the funds intended to create a viable self-sustaining tribal economy were not achieving their objective. They feared that when the federal government ceased to fund these programs, the gains would evaporate.

The experience of Indians in the War on Poverty was different only in degree from that of blacks or Chicanos. Many black or Chicano militants, like Indian tribal officials, had become in effect low-level federal bureaucrats administering federal community action grants under the OEO. These grants often accomplished real good. And some, such as the Headstart programs, appear to have had long-term benefits. Others were plagued with fraud and waste but had short-term advantages of providing jobs and income in urban ghettos and barrios. Like so many other western political and social movements, minority protest against federal policies had culminated in dependence on the federal government and unfulfilled expectations. Federal programs that seemed to serve minority community autonomy, in fact, acted to tie these communities and their leaders more tightly to the larger political system.

The Rise of the New Right

These fractious and insistent minority demands that surfaced in the civil rights movement found some sympathy among western whites, but more often they encountered an opposition that took the form of what one historian has aptly called "plain folks Americanism," which garnered considerable strength among working-class and middle-class whites. Those who embraced plain folks Americanism were often racist, but there was more to their position than racism. It had strong roots in older populist traditions of the West and South, with their producer ideologies, and in the Pentecostal and fundamentalist churches, with their allegiance to traditional values. In different ways the widespread popularity of country and western music and the rapid growth of fundamentalist and Pentecostal churches both revealed the widespread cultural appeal of plain folks Americanism. Both western religious fundamentalism and country and western music had their strongest roots in Texas and Oklahoma and among the California migrants from those states. Plain folks Americanism spread easily to working-class whites who were neither migrants from the rural West nor Protestants. They, too, shared the strong anticommunism of the rural emigrants and were sensitive to accusations of communist influence. What had once been a despised regional culture became an expression first of white working-class culture and then of a larger political movement, the New Right.

Plain folks Americanism, like the minority movements it viewed with such hostility, spoke in terms of both equality and special status. The egalitarian strain of plain folks Americanism emphasized hard work as the great equalizer in American society. Drawing on the old Populist producer ideologies, it attacked those who did not work. But whereas the old assault had been on an elite—bankers and speculators—the new assault focused on the minority poor and radical whites. Drawing on the language of equality, it accused the government of offering special favors to minorities. Plain folks Americanism also emphasized separateness and group pride that in numerous variations claimed special status for the "ordinary folk" who were the sinews of society. In religious terms, this status found expression in the claims of those who were saved in fundamentalist churches or blessed with supernatural gifts in Pentecostal churches. In ethnic terms, working-class whites (whether as "Okies," who embraced the old slur as a badge of pride, or as members

Country and western singer Merle Haggard in the early 1980s. His record "Okie from Muskogee" made him a symbol of plain folks Americanism.

of white ethnic groups) joined plain folks Americanism to other invented, borrowed, and inherited traditions to claim their own special status as real Americans.

The ability to tap this plain folks Americanism gave political conservatism a new life in the American West. An influx of working-class and lower-middle-class whites, many of whom remained registered Democrats, created a New Right that could largely erase the tinge of privilege that so strongly marked the Old Right. When in the early 1960s California conservatives mounted their usual onslaught against government, the strength it mustered took California politicians by surprise. Liberal Democrats under Governor Pat Brown thought they had little need to defend the virtues of active government. Brown in 1966 proudly pointed to a California with "more students in public higher education, more Nobel prize winners, more farm income, more public beaches and parks, more cars, more business investment, more of almost anything good you want to name than any other state in the union."

Brown's arithmetic of prosperity, however, was irrelevant to the problems conservatives posed. He read the wrong lessons from the defeat of Arizona Senator Barry Goldwater, the first hero of the New Right, in the presidential election of 1964. The heir to a substantial western fortune, Goldwater developed a political stance that combined individualism and independence from federal subsidies as a matter of principle with a willingness to solicit them in practice. Indeed, a serious attack on federal subsidies could only seem quixotic in a state like Arizona, where development depended heavily on federal water projects and defense spending. Arizonans elected Goldwater and accepted the federal subsidies provided by their other and far more powerful senator, Carl Hayden. As head of the Senate Appropriations Committee, Hayden maintained the traditional western political talent of shoveling federal funds into his state.

Goldwater's conservative individualism, for all its emotional appeal, had apparently failed when put to a national electoral test. Westerners proved reluctant to abandon their actual reliance on the federal government. Goldwater's opponent in the 1964 presidential race, another westerner, Democrat Lyndon Johnson of Texas, used the gap between rhetorical individualism in the West and actual reliance on federal funds to paint Goldwater as a dangerous extremist. Johnson's pragmatic western liberalism easily defeated Goldwater's version of western conservatism. Goldwater carried only Arizona among the western states.

Pat Brown thus seemingly had little to fear from the conservatives when, only two years later, the entire political structure in California lurched to the right. Pat Brown and California liberalism went down to a shocking defeat against Ronald Reagan, who in 1964 had been cochair of California Citizens for Goldwater. Like Goldwater, Reagan preached a political fundamentalism of opposition to "bureaucracy, planners, regulators, government red tape, the welfare state, and high taxes." Unlike Goldwater, Reagan was a master of media politics in the state that had pioneered them, but this is too facile an explanation of his success. Reagan expanded the electoral base of middle-class conservatives in southern California who had backed Goldwater by adding new elements among the middle and working classes. Reagan tapped developing strains of plain folks Americanism that Goldwater had been unable to touch. In 1966, Reagan became governor of California, beating Brown by nearly a million votes.

Preaching essentially the same doctrine that had brought Goldwater defeat in 1964, Reagan won in 1966 because he had found the necessary enemies. Reagan made urban demonstrators, striking farm workers, black rioters, radical students, criminals, and wasteful bureaucrats from Johnson's War on Poverty his targets. He lined them up like ducks in a shooting gallery. Each time he shot, he won big political prizes. Open social conflict had erupted throughout the West, and because of that conflict the attitudes of white westerners toward government intervention had changed. Until 1960 westerners in opinion polls had favored government intervention to provide jobs, health care, and other basic necessities. After 1960 they began to opt for individualist solutions. Before 1960 federal intervention had largely benefited whites; by 1966 it appeared to many whites to favor minorities and to threaten the existing pattern of race relations. Federal efforts had become for them an unjustified interference with local custom and an undue favoritism toward minorities.

Reagan's attacks on black urban riots, student demonstrations, and Chicano militants played into old western feelings of victimization. For people who were the beneficiaries of conquest, white westerners have had a persistent knack for portraying themselves as victims—of Indians, of the federal government, of eastern corporations. The theme of victimization ran deep in Populism and among those who denounced eastern colonialism in the 1930s, but victimization has not been the exclusive political property of the left. In the 1960s and 1970s the right used it far more effectively. New Right politicians proclaimed that whites were the victims of wasteful federal programs that taxed their incomes to give to lazy and spendthrift minorities and that took away their control of local schools and forced their children into foreign neighborhoods. Within this group portrait of victimization, minority violence came to play a significant symbolic role. The wide media attention given to urban riots and paramilitary groups such as the Brown Berets, the Black Panthers, and AIM created a picture of besieged whites under assault from armed black, Chicano, and Indian revolutionaries. Armed revolutionaries were relatively scarce and as likely to be the recipients of police violence as the assailants of police, but far more abundant minority criminals could substitute to promote white fear. Minority street crime was certainly real, but it hardly left whites besieged. Minority criminals usually claimed minority victims. Just as the West of a century earlier had featured stereotypes of blood-thirsty Indians and Mexican bandits, many modern white westerners added minority rioters and criminals as necessary demons to justify the existing social order.

The genius of the New Right was its ability to take white western self-images of rugged individualism and victimization and combine them into coherent political symbols. This was not an easy task. Rugged individualists are not supposed to feel victimized, particularly by the powerless. To combine the two was roughly akin to having John Wayne whining that the Chinese laundryman in Tombstone was pilfering his shirts and the sheriff refused to do anything about it. Yet the New Right succeeded in this unlikely task, and the resentment and feelings of victimization by western whites became a potent political weapon.

The sweeping indictment of the federal government by the New Right had wide appeal. In contrast to the modern West of conflict, rapid change, and assertive minorities, conservatives counterposed an image of an American past of stability and order. Reagan, in particular, often resorted to images of rugged individualists who had conquered an unruly (nonwhite) frontier. Numerous groups could read their own agendas into the right-wing denunciation of government and praise of the odd combination of individualism and order. For conservative entrepreneurs the New Right meant escape from government regulation. Western entrepreneurs pictured themselves as rugged individualists who should be left alone to forge the West's modern destiny. For white workers whose children were dying in the Vietnam War and who feared that equality for minorities meant threats to their jobs, voting for the New Right seemed a way to strike back at a government that had turned against them. For fundamentalist Christians angered at what they regarded as federal protection of homosexuality, abortion, and other "immoral" activities, a turn to the right appeared a way to restore society to an imagined idyll when the nation was Christian and families faced no challenges except the sort decent, hardworking people honed their skills on.

Paralleling this right-wing attack on government there came a simultaneous assault on government from the left. The left, both in the West and nationally, assailed government policy in Vietnam as a murderous imperialism that violated American traditions and denounced what it regarded as political and cultural repression at home. The left made its California debut in 1964 with the Free Speech movement at Berkeley. This protest against the University of California's

Protestors march against the Vietnam War in Los Angeles in 1972. Note the signs in Spanish. (Photograph by Joe Kennedy, copyright © Los Angeles Times)

restrictions on political recruitment on campus initiated a student movement whose focus soon shifted to the Vietnam War.

Vietnam War protests and student activism swept through California's universities in the late 1960s and early 1970s, often virtually shutting down campuses in the University of California system. These protests and student resistance to the military draft both hurt recruiting efforts for the military in California and mobilized political opposition to the war. With the campuses in seemingly constant turmoil about the war, a bitter factional division over the war also split Governor Brown's Democratic party. By 1966 the Democrats became a divided party in a bitterly divided state. The New Left itself took on no institutionalized political presence except in local communities such as Berkeley. When the war ended, the political impact of the New Left faded.

Initially separate from student radicalism, but eventually half merging with it, was the rise of a new cultural movement. The so-called hippies—the "flower children" of Haight Ashbury in San Francisco—represented a rejection of middle-class ambitions and values. Drugs, sex, and rock and roll became for them weapons to subvert middle-class America. Hippies seeking rural communes appeared throughout the Mountain West and Pacific Coast. The initial reaction of many of the middle class was horror at being betrayed by their own children.

Reagan and the New Right in California seized the opportunity this turmoil presented. They claimed to be protecting an older, stable, traditional West from attacks by criminals, deviants, rioters, and radicals, all of whom were coddled or abetted by the federal government. In its own way, the New Right was as radical as the New Left. Individualism, laissez-faire capitalism, small government, and "traditional" values had not created the West. The New Right in the West would have to create a "traditional" West, for the one they imagined had never existed. Those Californians who most ardently believed in these "traditional" values were often themselves newcomers to the state. The New Right sank its strongest roots among the modern immigrants to the West who came not as a part of groups or to seek utopian ends but for individual advancement. These were the residents of the suburbs, particularly the suburbs of southern California, which were the fastest-growing and most rapidly changing section of the United States in the 1960s. Southern California was a land of migrants who were not particularly western in origin. In its various counties in 1960 from one-half to two-thirds of the population had been born outside the state. Easterners lampooned southern California for being the corner of the country to which everything loose eventually rolled. It would have been difficult to find a less likely site for a defense of traditional values.

But the rapidity of change in southern California was, in fact, the point. The New Right prospered in southern California because the pace of change was frenetic. In southern California, except when race was concerned, boundaries seemed permeable. Ethnic and religious divisions mattered less than elsewhere. People were mobile; community ties were weak; and the aspirations that brought migrants to the region were overwhelmingly individualistic and material, not much different in fact than those that had prompted the Gold Rush more than a century earlier. Spectacular success always seemed possible, and that made failure all the more demeaning. There was no failure as bitter as western failure.

The California New Right wanted to have it both ways. They wanted the opportunity for material success unhampered by government controls, but they wanted government to halt social change and return society to an imagined past. A century earlier, families in mining towns felt much the same ambivalence. The western New Right, like the earlier middle-class inhabitants of mining towns, wanted both individual material success and social order. They wanted riots stopped; they wanted minorities to become socially invisible.

Ronald Reagan became an accomplished spokesman for the radical right's national challenge to the existing order, but he spoke with a western accent. As an actor and corporate representative, Reagan had spent much of his life mouthing other people's lines, and it was never clear that his subscription to the national religious right's social agenda went deeper than expediency. He was more comfortable tapping into the West's resentment against the East, but for the New Right the East was no longer Wall Street, it was Washington. Reagan certainly had no resentment against corporate wealth or financial institutions. His own turn to conservatism had come while he was a spokesman for General Electric, and the base of his political support was in the informal "millionaires' club" of conservative southern California businessmen who remained among his most influential advisors.

Reagan the politician stirred vast enthusiasm in the West, but Reagan the governor did not during his two terms deliver the changes that the rhetorical individualism of his campaigns promised. Instead he became a rather ordinary prodevelopment, probusiness western governor. He turned state regulatory agencies over to corporate executives. He railed against social programs in education, health, and welfare, but the Democratic legislature that Californians also elected prevented him from dismantling those programs.

Reagan's unremarkable record in California, however, only set the stage for a larger national triumph. As president from 1980 to 1988, he carried the New Right's agenda to the nation even as California assimilated elements of both the New Right, the New Left, and the counterculture of the hippies. Dope, sex, and rock and roll proved less subversive than the counterculture thought. Middle-class metropolitan society proved able to commodify and assimilate the whole supposedly subversive trio. By the 1970s many Orange County conservatives who belonged to the laissez-faire cadre of the New Right used cocaine and listened to rock and roll. The people who provided them with each were not subversives but millionaires quite happy with late-twentieth-century capitalism. Nobody involved thought they were committing ideological treason.

Despite their real hatred of each other, radicals and hippies on one side and at least the more libertarian conservatives on the other were closer than they thought. The suburban white middle class produced both of them, and by the 1970s it absorbed them both again. Both tended to view complex social problems in individual terms. Conservatives believed that once government got off their backs and left them free to do what they wished, the world would become a better place. Many hippies and disillusioned radicals turned to "getting their heads straight"—that is, they resorted to perpetual introspection, sometimes drug-aided and sometimes not, that they hoped would put them in proper relation to the world. Their solution was not changing the world but instead the more manageable task of changing themselves. Marin County, California, became synonymous with a smorgasbord of therapies that by the late 1970s, as one leader of the New Left observed, located problems in anything from bad posture (corrected by rolfing) to bad breathing (bioenergetics) to bad karma (meditation). Many hippies and radicals abandoned their belief that social problems were a matter of social relations; instead, they thought them a matter of individual attitudes. People who had once admired Ho Chi Minh now followed teenage gurus from India such as the Maharaj Ji or home-grown gurus like the former used car salesman Werner Erhart, the founder of EST. Like the New Right, former New Lefties came to think that individual solutions provided the answer to social problems.

The social ferment of the 1960s died down in the 1970s, but the New Right did not lack for new threats to traditional values. The 1970s produced Gay Liberation and the large and open homosexual communities in San Francisco and Los Angeles. Although both the civil rights movement and more radical movements for minority autonomy lost steam, controversies about welfare cheating and busing for racial balance replaced open housing and rioting as issues exploited by the right. Street crime, however, always remained a basic and volatile issue. Crime by Chicano and black street gangs, much of it centered around drug use and drug marketing, became pervasive in cities such as Los Angeles and Oakland in the 1980s. These gangs often conducted virtual reigns of terror. Minority community members themselves feared such criminal activity, but they also feared the tendency for attacks on crime to serve as a excuses for attacks on nonwhites. Western urban communities could be dangerous and violent places, but surprisingly the rural West remained more violent still. Although studies in the 1980s revealed that rates of violence among western rural youths were higher than rates among ghetto youths, this violence did not arouse the same kind of concern as violence in urban areas.

Most of all the women's movement in the West and nationally surfaced as a major challenge to traditional values as defined by the New Right. Because the New Right idealized the family as the basis for social order, not only abortion but also the movement of women out of the home and into the work force loomed as great dangers to the right. In the West, as elsewhere in the country, women were working in greater and greater numbers. Some worked from choice, but others worked because by the mid-1970s American real wages had begun to stagnate and the only way many families could boost or maintain their standard of living was to increase the number of workers.

The movement of women into the work force, abortion, and the campaign for the equal rights amendment—a constitutional amendment to ban discrimination on the basis of sex—tended to be the flashpoints of controversy. All became emotional issues, and all divided women among themselves. To many working-class women stuck in low-paying, unrewarding jobs, the middle-class activists who worked for the equal rights amendment and talked about equal access of women into the professions were speaking of a world that did not exist for them or their daughters. Despite real gains for women in the professions, the discrepancies between men's wages and women's wages changed little in the 1970s and 1980s. In a way that paralleled the tension in minority communities between equal rights and special status, many working-class women worried that equal rights legislation might cost them the limitations on hours and conditions of work achieved earlier in the century, rather than gain them career opportunities. To some working-class women it seemed that they would pay the price while middle-class women reaped the benefits. Likewise, many housewives felt denigrated by celebrations of female autonomy and careers. Although opponents accused the women's movement of polarizing men and women, the actual politics were far more complicated. Both men and women were divided over "women's issues."

The Reagan Presidency

Reagan's presidency, and his ability to mount an attack on government from within the government, served to delineate the continuing contradictions of western attitudes and the deep divisions within the West itself. Reagan's reduction of federal programs turned out to be dramatic but selective. As president he was far more successful at cutting back social welfare programs than he had been as governor of California. In 1981, for example, the federal budget eliminated one-third of the money spent on American Indian programs. Indians experienced the greatest per capita cut in federal programs of any American citizens, six times their proportional share. And per capita income began to fall on many reservations. By the mid-1980s, the Navajo per capita income stood at $1,700, compared to $9,000 for Americans as a whole. Total government spending—state, local, and federal—which averaged $3,681 for each citizen now averaged $2,497 for each Indian. The result in Arizona, a state with a large reservation population, was that more than one out of every three reservation Indians had an income below the poverty level in 1986.

Other groups of westerners, however, prospered from Reagan policies. Increased

Table 17
Department of Defense Contract Awards and Estimated Annual Payrolls

State	Contract awards* ($ million)		Estimated annual payroll† ($ million)	
	1963	1983	1963	1983
Total U.S.	28,108	118,744	12,809	50,458
Arizona	286	1,360	130	652
California	5,836	26,387	1,746	8,269
Colorado	44	1,007	243	947
Idaho	9	49	30	125
Kansas	332	1,575	180	568
Montana	79	117	54	93
Nebraska	33	163	114	356
Nevada	13	159	52	242
New Mexico	62	463	163	547
North Dakota	65	137	57	225
Oklahoma	111	612	308	1,076
Oregon	42	181	46	97
South Dakota	81	42	41	131
Texas	1,203	8,229	1,112	3,619
Utah	428	722	142	605
Washington	1,041	3,986	335	1,573
Wyoming	125	39	24	83

Source: U.S. Bureau of the Census, *Statistical Abstract of the United States* (Washington, D.C.: 1966, 1984).

*Military awards for supplies, services, and contraction.

†Covers active-duty military and direct-hire civilian personnel, including Army Corps of Engineers.

spending for defense sent funds flowing to the western metropolitan areas where defense contractors were based. The Reagan administration thus did not represent a decline in federal influence in the West as much as a shift in that influence. More federal dollars flowed to middle-class urban westerners who benefited from the defense buildup; less went to poor, minority, and rural westerners. Federal spending in Utah, which gave Reagan the heaviest pluralities of any state in the Union in 1980 and 1984, increased during the 1980s. By 1987 the state received $951 million more from federal operations than it paid out in federal taxes. In 1987, in terms of per capita federal spending, half of the top 20 states were in the West, and if Alaska and Hawaii were counted as western, 12 were in the West. In terms of total spending, California, with $100 billion in federal spending annually, was easily the leader.

The increases in federal spending did not, however, make up for the energy bust, the decline of the timber industry, and the agricultural depression plaguing the old extractive rural West during the 1980s. During the Reagan years the western states as a whole fell farther behind the national income average than they had been before his election. Under a phenomenally popular western president, the West as a whole lost economic ground, although particular sections of it prospered.

Table 18

Highest and Lowest Ranking States in Military Shipments, 1983

Rank	Top states	Military shipments location quotient	Rank	Bottom states	Military shipments location quotient
1	California	2.62	50	Arkansas	0.001
2	Connecticut	2.49	49	West Virginia	0.02
3	Missouri	2.49	48	Idaho	0.06
4	Arizona	2.30	47	North Carolina	0.07
5	Utah	2.10	46	South Carolina	0.08
6	Maryland	1.97	45	Kentucky	0.10
7	New Hampshire	1.88	44	Nebraska	0.12
8	Kansas	1.85	43	Alabama	0.26
9	Massachusetts	1.71	42	Montana	0.27
10	Vermont	1.66	41	Wisconsin	0.28
11	Virginia	1.55	40	Tennessee	0.30
12	Rhode Island	1.35	39	Oregon	0.33
13	Florida	1.25	38	Iowa	0.33
14	Colorado	1.23	37	Delaware	0.43
15	Texas	1.17	36	Michigan	0.45

Source: Ann Markusen, *Regions: The Economics and Politics of Territory* (Totowa, N.J.: Rowman and Littlefield, 1987), p. 110.

The conservative ideology of western voters still clashed with the actual political and economic realities of the region. Conservative westerners denounced a federal government upon which they still heavily depended. Conservatives believed that welfare and federal programs for the poor limited initiative and increased dependence, but they did not damn all federal aid to individuals or corporations. They did not demand, for example, an end to the Federal Housing Administration and Veterans Administration loans that often secured their own homes, nor did they attack the federal and state highway programs that built the freeways upon which they drove to work and on which metropolitan growth depended. Many worked for huge defense firms that no more operated in a free market than did their Soviet equivalents. The private market's demand for missile systems or tanks, if not assault rifles, remained limited. Conservatives considered these vast federal expenditures to be good and necessary. Nor did conservatives think massive state and federal water projects should be left to private initiative. Conservatives, like most people, applied their ideology most consistently on issues that did not directly affect them.

The results of the conservative triumph were perhaps most disappointing in the rural West, where James Watt, Reagan's secretary of the interior, zealously tried to remove most restraints on the rapid development of the public lands. Watt offered public resources for sale at bargain-basement prices. But no boom resulted, for energy prices had collapsed. The corporations acquired resources but did not develop them. And rural westerners found to their dismay that Watt's policies fostered an environmentalist reaction that forced them to confront an even larger and more militant metropolitan environmental movement.

The legacy of the Reagan years dealt a second blow to the rural West. The growth of the massive public debt under Reagan helped force cutbacks in those kinds of federal subsidies the West had long expected as a right. Funding for water projects grew more difficult; farm subsidies came under attack; sales of public timber at less than cost drew fire from both environmentalists and fiscal conservatives. The ability of western senators and congressmen to garner the usual subsidies seemed to be weakening, while the traditional resistance of western states to tax heavily for public services remained strong. The conservative western attack on Washington, far more successful than anyone would have dreamed possible twenty years earlier, had yielded ambiguous results.

Readings

Acuña, Rodolfo. *Occupied America: A History of Chicanos.* 2d ed. New York: Harper and Row, 1981.

Barr, Alwyn. *Black Texans.* Austin: Jenkins Publishing Company, Pemberton Press, 1973.

Conot, Robert. *Rivers of Blood, Years of Darkness.* New York: Bantam, 1967.

Dewing, Ronald. *Wounded Knee: The Meaning and Significance of the Second Incident.* New York: Irvington Publishers, 1985.

Fixico, Donald L. *Termination and Relocation: Federal Indian Policy, 1945–60.* Albuquerque: University of New Mexico Press, 1986.

Foley, Douglas E., et al. *From Peones to Politicos: Class and Ethnicity in a South Texas Town: 1900–1987.* Austin: University of Texas Press, 1988.

García, Mario. *Mexican Americans, Leadership and Identity, 1930–1960.* New Haven: Yale University Press, 1989.

Gitlin, Todd. *The Sixties: Years of Hope, Days of Rage.* Toronto: Bantam Press, 1987.

Gregory, James N. *American Exodus: The Dust Bowl Migration and Okie Culture in California.* New York: Oxford University Press, 1989.

Gutierrez, David. "Sin Fronteras? Mexicans, Americans, Chicanos, and the Evolution of the Contemporary Mexican Immigration Issue, 1968–78," *Journal of American Ethnic History* (forthcoming).

Henry, Charles P. "Racial Factors in the 1982 California Gubernatorial Campaign: Why Bradley Lost." In *The New Black Politics: The Search for Political Power,* 2d ed., pp. 76–94. Ed. Michael Preston, Lenneal J. Henderson, and Paul L. Puryear. New York and London: Longman, 1987.

Iverson, Peter. *The Navajo Nation.* Albuquerque: University of New Mexico Press, 1981.

Majka, Linda J., and Theo J. Majka. *Farm Workers, Agribusinesses and the State.* Philadelphia: Temple University Press, 1982.

Mathiesson, Peter. *In the Spirit of Crazy Horse.* New York: Viking, 1983

Rapoport, Roger. *California Dreaming: The Political Odyssey of Pat and Jerry Brown.* Berkeley: NOLO Press, 1982.

Reimers, David M. *Still The Golden Door: The Third World Comes to America.* New York: Columbia University Press, 1985.

Rogin, Michael P., and John L. Shover. *Political Change in California: Critical Elections and Social Movements, 1890–1966.* Westport, Conn.: Greenwood, 1970.

Rorabaugh, W. J. *Berkeley at War: The 1960s.* New York: Oxford University Press, 1989.

Ruiz, Vicki. *Cannery Women, Cannery Lives: Mexican Women, Unionization, and the*

California Food Processing Industry, 1930–1950. Albuquerque: University of New Mexico Press, 1987.

Takaki, Ronald. *Strangers from a Different Shore: A History of Asian Americans.* Boston: Little, Brown and Company, 1989.

Wilkinson, Charles. *American Indians, Time and the Law.* New Haven, Conn.: Yale University Press, 1987.

Williams, Linda. "Black Political Progress in the 1980s: The Electoral Area." In *The New Black Politics: The Search for Political Power,* 2d ed., pp. 97–136. Ed. Michael Preston, Lenneal J. Henderson, and Paul L. Puryear. New York and London: Longman, 1987.

CHAPTER 21

The Imagined West

FOR more than a century the American West has been the most strongly *imagined* section of the United States. The West of Anglo American pioneers and Indians began reimagining itself before the conquest of the area was fully complete. In the late nineteenth century, Sitting Bull and Indians who would later fight at Wounded Knee toured Europe and the United States with Buffalo Bill in his Wild West shows. They etched vivid images of Indian fights and buffalo hunts into the imaginations of hundreds of thousands of people. The ceremonials of the Pueblos became tourist attractions even while the Bureau of Indian Affairs and missionaries struggled to abolish them.

Stories about the West evolved into a particular genre, the Western, which first as novels and later as films became a defining element of American popular culture. By 1958, Westerns comprised about 11 percent of all works of fiction published in the United States, and Hollywood turned out a Western movie every week. In 1959 thirty prime-time television shows, including eight of the ten most watched, were Westerns. Mid-twentieth-century Americans consumed such enormous quantities of imagined adventures set in the West that one might suspect the decline of the Western in the 1970s and 1980s resulted from nothing more than a severe case of cultural indigestion.

This gluttonous consumption of fictions about the West is, however, only part of the story. Americans have also actively imagined their own Wests. A century of American children grew up imagining themselves to be cowboys and Indians. Such public and private fantasies spawned a store of metaphors of violent conflict and confrontation that became, along with sports metaphors and sexual metaphors, basics of male popular speech. Showdowns, last stands, hired guns, round-ups, and the like became metaphors by which American men characterized and understood more mundane personal and public worlds devoid of cattle let alone gunfights or public heroics. Metaphorically, the imagined West intruded constantly on everyday American life.

This imagined West has not, however, overtly intruded on this text until now because it would have been potentially confusing to interrupt each chapter to analyze how various imagined Wests have shaped the topics of discussion. I have postponed the issues of the mythic West until, having nearly reached the end of this book, I can delay no longer. What is, then, the relationship been the variety of publicly imagined Wests—the mythic Wests—and the historic West? Even the question is misleading, for it implies that the two can be easily separated.

To understand this relationship, we must make some necessary distinctions. We must, first of all, distinguish among the people doing the imagining. Residents

Buffalo Bill, one of the master creators of the American myth of the West, appears with his Wild West show in 1907.

of the West itself have constructed various local versions of a collective past. Such imaginings have often been folkloric—that is, they are songs and stories (originally oral, later often written down) produced by people belonging to groups narrowly defined by occupation, place, or ethnicity.

The second version of the imagined West is the work of professional writers, journalists, and filmmakers who are often located outside the West itself or in that peculiar corner of it, Hollywood. They disseminate their versions of the West through mass media: books, magazines, and movies. In terms of audience, this second imagined West appeals to national audiences, although it may also have strong appeal among local groups of westerners, who also produce their own folklore. So powerful is the influence of this imagined West that its fictional creations and personas become symbols of the West, and real westerners model themselves after fictional characters. In the late 1970s a journalist for the *New Yorker*, Jane Kramer, wrote an account, entitled *The Last Cowboy*, of a ranch foreman on the Texas Panhandle. The hero was a skilled working cowboy who was disappointed in the realities of life on a cattle ranch. He viewed his actual modern West of absentee ranchers and agribusinesses as a declension from a truer but vanished West. His true West, however, was an imagined West, and he knew it from Westerns: real cattlemen were John Wayne in *Chisum*, or Chill Wills in *The Rounders*. His own sense of himself, and how he acted, were informed not just by the West he lived in but also by a powerful cultural image of the West he *should* have lived in. The actual West and the imagined West are engaged in a constant conversation; each influences the other.

The imagined West is a mythic West. In its everyday colloquial sense, myth means falsehood. When popular writers publish books to expose the "myths" of American history, they mean to do nothing more than inform Americans that some of what they believe about their country's past is not factually correct. In a second, deeper sense, however, myths are not so much falsehoods as explanations. Myths are stories that tell why things and people are what they are. As the literary historian Richard Slotkin has written, modern myths are "stories, drawn from history, that have acquired through usage over many generations a symbolizing function" central to the society that produces them. Myths are a deeply encoded set of metaphors that may contain all the "lessons we have learned from our history, and all of the essential elements of our world view." Myths give meaning to the world. In this sense a myth about the West is a story that explains who westerners—and who Americans—are and how they should act.

Although both myth and history aspire to derive meaning from the past, we have to distinguish between them. This is, however, not as simple as it might seem. Mythmakers usually draw from history; they use real people or actual incidents. They have no compunctions, however, about changing details, adding characters, and generally rearranging events in order to make the meaning of their stories clearer. Historians also draw from history, and they, too, are selective. Historians necessarily select from among numerous available facts in order to create a story about the past. Historians, by the code of their discipline, put great store in facts, but facts are rarely at the heart of historical disputes. Instead historians argue over the relationships between largely agreed upon facts, for it is the relationship between facts that differentiates one historian's story from another

This late-nineteenth-century crowd, gathered for the feast of San Geronimo at Taos Pueblo, shows how quickly Indians became a tourist attraction in the West.

historian's story. This relationship between facts is not something historians discover; it is something they assert and argue over. Historians and mythmakers thus both seek to order the past in a way that conveys meaning. Both tell stories. But historians, also by the code of their craft, cannot reorder facts or invent new ones. Historians are thus more cramped and constricted than mythmakers in their attempts to explain what the past "means."

If we differentiate history from myth solely on the basis of facts, we will, however, run into conceptual difficulties over what a fact is and, more significantly, miss a larger difference. For a good historian, the past is, as the cliché goes, another country. People in the past operate in a different context than do we in the present; they often live by other logics. Any lessons the past teaches are those about processes and change; we cannot derive uniformly valid rules about our present situation from the past. Myth, for all its attention to the past, denies this and thus denies "history" itself. Myth refuses to see the past as fundamentally different from the present. Again, as Richard Slotkin explains, in myth "the past is made metaphorically equivalent to the present; and the present appears simply as a repetition of persistently recurring structures identified with the past. Both past and present are reduced to single instances displaying a single 'law' or principle of nature, which is seen as timeless in its relevance, and as transcending all historical contingencies."

What Slotkin means by this is that in myth, time brings no essential change. The past and the present are not only connected, they are also metaphorically identical. The lessons of a story from the past apply equally well to the present. Myth rips events out of context and drains them of their historicity. How a cowboy acts in myth is how an American male should act regardless of time or place. A man has to do what a man has to do. Myths thus are antihistory, for history above all depends on context.

Myths may be antihistory, but myths themselves are also historical creations. Myths, again to quote Slotkin, are "generated by a particular set of cultural producers in a peculiar historical moment." People create myths at certain times and places for certain purposes, and as these purposes change over time, the meanings of mythic stories also change. American moviemakers, for example, have made Westerns during most of the twentieth century, but the meanings communicated by Westerns early in the century differed from those communicated later in the century. Myths themselves thus become historical sources reflecting the values and concerns of the period and people who produced them.

But if myth, the imagined West, is a historical product, we must remember that history—as *The Last Cowboy* shows—is also a product of myth. As people accept and assimilate myth, they act on the myths, and the myths become the basis for actions that shape history. Historians find they cannot understand people's actions without understanding their intentions, and those intentions are often shaped by cultural myths. The mythic West imagined by Americans has shaped the West of history just as the West of history has helped create the West Americans have imagined. The two cannot be neatly severed.

A western historian, Patricia Nelson Limerick, gives a remarkable example of how the imagined West and the actual West intertwine when actual westerners and mythologized westerners keep bumping into each other: "In 1849, Kit Carson set out to rescue a white woman, providentially named Mrs. White, who had been taken captive by the Jicarilla Apaches. When the search party caught up with the Indians, it was too late; Mrs. White had just been killed, but Kit Carson came upon a surprising souvenir: 'We found a book in the camp,' he reported, 'the first of the kind I had ever seen, in which I was represented as a great hero, slaying Indians by the hundreds.'"

This actual event in New Mexico in 1849 could be a scene from a novel by Italo Calvino: the actual Carson confronts the literary Carson. And in a sense the literary Carson proves the stronger of the two. Carson's reaction to finding the book, probably Charles Averill's *Kit Carson, Prince of the Gold Hunters* (1849), was to lament his failure to live up to his fictional reputation. The fictional Carson became the standard for the real Carson, and the connection between the two goes beyond this, for the story of the incident comes to us in a book, written by the actual Carson, to capitalize on the market the mythic Carson had created for him. The mythic Carson partially shaped the actual Carson in his image.

What Kit Carson confronted in the deserted Jicarilla camp, westerners have in a sense been confronting ever since. There are cultural visions of the West, constantly changing but always present, that define both for westerners and others what the western experience means. There is not and never has been a single myth, a single imagined West. Myths and meanings are constantly in competition just as various groups within the West were always in competition.

Myths and the West: Local Imaginings

Why the West—an area long on the fringes of American life—should take pride of place in the American imagination is not entirely clear, but the rough outlines of an answer are possible. It is easiest to begin where the problem is the least mysterious: the creation of local legends about the West.

The folklore of the American West is, like all folklore, local even though the basis of most of it was imported or borrowed. This is only a seeming paradox, for even when they brazenly steal outside materials, the retailers of folklore always deposit their proceeds locally. Barre Toelken, in writing about western folklore, has shown how an English hymn about "Beulah Land, sweet Beulah land . . . My heaven, my home, forevermore" came to serve, like a musical national forest, multiple uses in the West. Westerners originally used the hymn to illustrate a national myth that imagined the West as a garden awaiting immigrants. The decline of garden imagery in the face of actual experience in the West did not eliminate the hymn, but instead gave it a new life in local parodies. The hymn's lines "I've reached the land of corn and wine / and all its riches now are mine" became in South Dakota, "We've reached the land of dying wheat, / Where nothing grows for man to eat." In New Mexico, the same lines became "This is the land of dusty roads, / Of rattlesnakes and horny toads," and in Oregon, "I've reached the land of rain and mud, / Where flowers and trees so early bud." As people repeated the parody, they made it their own, localizing it to reflect the conditions of a particular place.

Such parodies and tall tales seemingly denigrate the local place by making it too windy, too cold, too hot, too wet, too dry, and so on, but at the same time they are a form of local chauvinism that identifies the local people with the place and its peculiarities. In other places with cultures rooted for hundreds or thousands of years, such an observation might be obvious and trivial. In the West, however, except among Indians and Mexican Americans, personal roots rarely went back more than a generation or two. Thus even when expressed derisively and humorously, such identifications created a link between local people and endured hardship, between local people and the special character of the place. They turned the garden imagery on its head. Songs and stories implied that it was only the labor and toughness of the singers and storytellers and their ancestors that had made the land habitable. By denigrating nature, they exalt the pioneers. Implicit in such local folklore was the larger message of much of the locally imagined West: "We or our parents survived this place; we created whatever is good in this place." Westerners often made the claim in a backhanded manner, and their humor was self-deprecating. But the claim remained nonetheless the essence of the locally imagined past.

> Our neighbors are the rattlesnakes—
> They crawl up from the Badlands' breaks;
> We do not live, we only stay;
> We are too poor to get away.

In such stories, as Toelkin suggests, white westerners expressed their need to "sweep away what had been there before them." They had to make the West "a place of great hazard and disarray which they had been heroic enough to have brought into order"; they "needed to create a blood bond with the land which would have the power to supersede everything prior to itself."

Creating this blood bond involved creating a common past and a pattern of shared memory. This shared memory was often very much an invention. It consisted less of an amalgam of personal memories than a collective re-remembering of what Clyde Milner, writing of Montana's early white settlers, has called events of "great emblematic significance." Thus, being a real Montana "pioneer" involved having memories of certain events regardless of whether or not such events had in fact occurred or whether the "pioneer" had participated in them. In Montana these emblematic events were conflict with Indians on the journey west and memories of the suppression of Henry Plummer's band of highwaymen by the Montana vigilantes.

Having defined, in effect, what it meant to be a pioneer—to have participated in key "events" in Montana's past—early white settlers used their memoirs to provide their credentials. Even though daily trail journals they kept at the time had mentioned little Indian contact or friendly exchanges with Indians, memoirs tended to reimagine this past by inserting Indians as an omnipresent danger. Indians played a crucial symbolic role in giving this "pioneer" past meaning. As Harriet Sanders summarized the logic in her memoir: "The emigrants who passed through the country previous to 1868 did so at the peril of their lives. The Indians becoming jealous at the appearance of the whites, lay in ambush for the unsuspecting victims, and many a scalp-dance was danced and war-songs chanted over the forms of those who aspired to plant an empire in the unknown west. But in the end, however, the pioneers conquered the wilderness and transformed it into a land of peace and plenty."

Sanders had constructed a narrative of what the settlement of Montana and the West meant. With the meaning established, early white migrants structured their memories to conform to it. Hostile Indians were necessary to this imagined

Apparently a celebrity even among the men who hunted him, Gregorio Cortez is seated between two officers at the Bexar County Jail.

past, and hostile Indians populated it whether in fact the people providing the memories had even encountered hostile Indians. Thus an overland trail journey largely devoid of hostile Indians became in popular memory—in the imagined past—a trip full of threatening, bloodthirsty warriors. Montanans created a past appropriate to their present. Indians were violent outsiders whose present dispossession was necessary for progress to occur. Thus, the real history of Montana began with the coming of the pioneers, who were the metaphorical pilgrims of Montana society. Such memories suited a Montana of subordinated and marginalized Indians and dominant whites.

The marginalized and subordinate, however, could also imagine the West, and Mexican Americans and Mexicans did this in their *corridos*, the folk ballads that created a popular past. The singers of *corridos* also reworked popular memories to locate emblematic events. Deaths of vaqueros; deaths of young men in a car crash; the travails of early-twentieth-century immigrant workers: all of these survived in *corridos*, creating a sense of everyday life lived in a place of common sufferings. They countered the Anglo folklore of an empty West, or of a West whose earlier inhabitants had disappeared. In the *corridos*, the white settlers of the West, when they appear at all, are usually exploiters or oppressors; the hard work of altering the West is the work of Mexicans cheated of their just rewards; and resistance, when it occurs, is the work of heroes, men like Gregorio Cortez, who appears "with his pistol in his hand."

Myth and the West: National Imaginings

The creation of an imagined West by those who lived in a place and sought to bond themselves to it seems readily understandable, but the creation of an imagined West by those who lived outside the West and have few or no ties to the place itself is more mysterious. Yet it is the critical issue, for the nationally imagined West has been far more powerful than the locally imagined West. It has, when necessary, put local traditions to its own uses and shaped local myths in its own image. In Montana memoirs, for example, some writers not only added Indian fights to their memories but clearly modeled their accounts of those fights after contemporary dime novels. New Mexicans who read nationally published stories about Billy the Kid made those stories their own and then retold them to interviewers as if they were their personal experiences.

The nationally imagined West depended on the mass media, and the popularity of western stories with the mass media was in part serendipitous. Anglo American settlement of the West happened to take place simultaneously with the rise of penny newspapers, dime novels, and sensationalist journals such as the *National Police Gazette*. That mass media, a mass audience, and mass western migration all bumped into each other, as it were, at a given historical moment does not, however, explain why they struck up such a lasting acquaintance. It only explains why the acquaintance was possible.

The West became the center for the media's imaginative attentions in part because Americans had already assigned significant symbolic meaning to westering. When Henry Thoreau wrote, "Eastward I go only by force; but westward I go free," or when Mark Twain's Huckleberry Finn "lights out" for the territory to escape the constraints of "civilization," both spoke to an audience for whom westering, and thus the trans-Missouri West, had already taken on an identification with freedom and independence in a country that regarded freedom and independence as its peculiar hallmark.

Americans significantly associated freedom and independence with the borders of their own society, and they attached these values most fully to single males without permanent connections with family or society. In Carroll Smith-Rosenberg's analysis of the Davy Crockett almanacs, popular in the years when American settlement of the trans-Missouri West began, Crockett negates the accepted values of the East: "He is loose, liminal, and wild." Crockett and heroes like him took on the qualities of animals that they fought and consumed. They became violently and dangerously natural, existing beyond the boundaries of civilization, assaulting each other and all others they found outside the bounds. The stories made white male violence seem "natural, timeless, and inescapable." The appropriate targets of this violence became the inhabitants of nature, particularly Indians. Domesticating this natural male violence became a part of the mythic agenda.

Existing alongside the Crockett stories, however, was another pervasive image of the West that posited the West as a place of peace and serenity: the garden. In the garden image, freedom became freeholding; the land yielded not wild animals but pleasant fields full of domestic stock and cultivated plants. Nature was not threatening but beneficent, eagerly awaiting the hand of the cultivator. The images seem contradictory, but both sets of images identified the West with freedom and nature. Both sets of images made it, in a sense, the most American part of the country, for only the West—whether as garden or wilderness—offered something that Europeans did not and could not possess.

Stories of the garden and the wilderness formed the disparate, seemingly incompatible parents of Western adventures. These contradictory images, however, proved particularly useful for resolving a diffuse sense of cultural crisis that afflicted many Americans as the nineteenth century wore on. With the country as a whole urbanizing, industrializing, and becoming more like Europe, there developed a widespread dissatisfaction with modern culture itself—with, as the historian Jackson Lears puts it in *No Place of Grace*, "its ethic of self-control and autonomous achievement, its cult of science and technical rationality, its worship of material progress." These values seemed a sham, and to many middle-class Americans—particularly men—life had become overcivilized, sterile, and unreal. They themselves seemed morally impotent.

Cultural critics of "overcivilization"—including the future president of the United States and occasional Dakota rancher Theodore Roosevelt—worried about the destruction of a corrupt American elite by a "foreign" rabble of workers. Frederic Remington, whose own art did much to create an enduring imagined West, played at being a rancher and espoused a "cowboy philosophy" that combatted "overcivilization" with what might be called an aggressive undercivilization: "Jews, Injuns, Chinamen, Italians, Huns—the rubbish of the Earth I hate—I've got some Winchesters and when the massacring begins, I can get my share of 'em, and what's more, I will. . . . Our race is full of sentiment. We invite the rinsins, the scourins, and the Devil's lavings to come to use and be men—something they haven't been, most of them, these hundreds of years. . . ."

The bloodthirsty racism of Remington was an extreme, but hardly unusual, example of the use to which an invented West could be put. The West, violent and primitive, would provide the backbone that would save the country from "the Devil's lavings." Without such renewal the republic itself seemed in danger. The result was an antimodernist middle-class cultural rebellion of sorts, which, while rejecting modern culture as corrupt, sought to revitalize and transform it. In penetrating the "wilderness" and transforming it into a modern garden, society itself could be saved.

Late-nineteenth-century Americans imagined the West—that most modern of American sections—as the premodern world that they had lost. In it life was primitive but also simple, real, and basic. Every action in this world mattered, and the fundamental decisions of everyday life supposedly involved clear moral choices. Life in the West could restore authenticity, moral order, and masculinity. Life in the premodern West could, ironically, justify the very core of modern values that had come under question. For in this imagined primitive West, as it turned out, autonomy and self-discipline were the qualities that mattered most. In the end, the imaginative journey to the primitive West rehabilitated modern values and reoriented Americans toward a version of progress that supposedly avoided "overcivilization" and decadence.

All of this might seem a heavy burden for stories about cowboys, cavalry, outlaws, and Indians to bear, but those who told the stories were quite clear about the morals and messages that they wanted to convey to readers. Owen Wister's *The Virginian* (1902) became the classic literary Western, and its author's premodern preferences ran through it pure and unadulterated. The cowboys of Wister's West had "wild and manly faces. . . . In their flesh natural passions ran tumultuous; but often in their spirit sat hidden a true nobility, and often beneath its unexpected shining their figures took on heroic stature." Western saloons, Wister wrote, contained more death than New York City saloons, but less vice, "and death is a thing much cleaner than vice."

Wister's cowboys got drunk, frequented prostitutes, gambled, slept with other men's wives, and killed each other, but their life and violence was, nonetheless, "pure." It set them apart from the eastern immigrant worker. Beneath the plot of *The Virginian* ran a subtext on inequality, an attempt by Wister to explain why some Americans were, by the very human nature that the West laid bare, destined to rule and command others. For in the "newest part of the New World" it was the basic inequality of human beings that shone through. "Equality," the Virginian proclaimed, "is a big bluff. It's easy called." And Wister's narrator, reflecting on the "eternal inequality of man," concluded that "true democracy and true aristocracy are one and the same." The Virginian, who survives Indians, punishes outlaws, gains the respect of lesser men, and kills the vicious Trampas, becomes proof of the proposition. For in the West, where life is basic and men are self-reliant, the "quality" rises above the "equality." To do so, the "quality" sometimes has to use means unsuited to a civilized society, but as Molly Wood, the eastern fiancée of the Virginian, comes to learn, such means, even though they violate civilized canons, are appropriate and necessary. Only they can bring civilization. The premodern West purges the corruption of the East and simultaneously demonstrates the rightness of hierarchy and inequality. There are those, of course, who succumb to the "savagery" and wildness of the West, but they only temporarily triumph. The result in the end is a reinvigorated civilization, a garden. In this West the Virginian becomes "an important man, with a strong grip on many various enterprises," whose wife believes "his work would kill him." This was a West where middle-class businessmen had redeemed themselves through natural virtues and proved their right to rule.

The Virginian was a novel aimed at the middle class, but imagining Wests in order to provide moral and social lessons for the country as a whole also went on in numerous other forums. Probably no incident in western history entered into national myth more quickly than Custer's Last Stand. Here was a bloody, dramatic, racial confrontation that captured national attention. And because the battle yielded no white survivors, it presented an ideal opportunity for the national imagination to exercise itself. The mythologizing of Custer in the mass-circulation dailies made the conflict between Custer and the Indians a metaphor for the conflict between whites and nonwhites and capital and labor in much the same way that the conflict between the Virginian and Trampas served as metaphor between "quality" and the "equality." In the hands of James Gordon Bennett, owner-editor of the *New York Herald*, Custer's Last Stand became a story useful for denouncing all kinds of enemies of the social order. Bennett denounced the Sioux as "communistic"; he compared Indian violence with that of labor radicals; and he made lower-class tramps and vagrants the equivalent of "savages."

Custer, the boy general, became in Frederick Whittaker's *Complete Life of George A. Custer* (published the very year of Custer's defeat) "the brave cavalier, the Christian soldier," and valiant defender of civilization against savage hordes. Like the Virginian, Custer embodies ideal traits in particularly powerful form. Unlike the Virginian, he dies, but he dies heroically, a martyr to the weak policy (advanced by reformers) that appeased "savages." His death bares the true nature of the conflict, points the way to the right policy, and assures the eventual triumph of brave cavaliers over savages. The Custer myth became a way to talk about race and class, a way to demonstrate the necessity of subordinating savages of all kinds. Indians were the equivalent of tramps, anarchists, and criminals, none of whom should be indulged. They had to be reformed and taught the meaning of work and order.

Imagining the West in certain ways thus became a means to shape popular consciousness and to impart certain visions of what an American social order should look like. No one group, however, ever secured a monopoly on imagining the West. Stories about Custer could be ways for capitalists to attack workers, but other western stories could be vehicles for workers to attack capitalists. Stories and songs about outlaws, for example, became a contested ground. In some stories, suppressing outlaws was the work of a natural elite symbolized by the Virginian, but outlaws themselves could be romanticized as a means of attacking the social order.

The romanticization of the western outlaw began not in the national media but in local folkloric traditions in the West. It then spread to local newspapers, and from them it moved into the national media. Eventually, in much popular culture, the American West might as well have been Sherwood Forest; its plains and prairies teemed with what the English historian E. J. Hobsbawm has called social bandits. Robin Hood stood as their prototype. Driven outside the law because of some act sanctioned by local conventions but regarded as criminal by the state or local authorities, the social bandit was forced to become an outlaw. Members of the community, however, still considered him an honorable man. The bandit, robbing the rich and helping the poor, thus became a hero rather than a villain.

Just as Custer's Last Stand was a historical event that quickly spawned a myth, so actual outlaws, from the various Mexican bandits who together became Joaquín Murieta to the James-Younger and Doolin-Dalton gangs, spawned social bandit stories. The romanticization of these outlaws as social bandits began while they were still alive. Actual social bandits found support because they provided aid in what were often chaotic local conflicts in which people viewed the constituted authorities as corrupt or ineffective. By specializing in bank and train robberies, social bandits like the James-Younger gang and the Doolin-Dalton gang avoided doing direct harm to their supporters. They also inadvertently became surrogate heroes for farmers, workers, and minorities disenchanted with the newer America whose great symbols and sources of power were banks, railroad corporations, and police forces of the modern state.

The tellers of stories and the singers of songs had imagined the historical figures they commemorated before the heroes ever existed. Robin Hood, as a type, for example, existed before Jesse James or Bill Doolin robbed their first bank. The stories about them were cast in an existing mold; the outlaws became Robin Hoods. Similarly, along the Rio Grande border, the Tejano communities of the area developed in their *corridos* heroes of border resistance, roles into which actual men stepped. In the most famous of these *corridos*, "The Ballad of Gregorio Cortez," singers celebrate the resistance of a peaceful Tejano, falsely accused, who is forced to defend himself and flee from brutal Anglo Americans *rinches*, or Texas Rangers, and sheriffs. The *corridos* about Cortez arose from an actual incident, but, as Américo Paredes put it, "the Border people had dreamed Gregorio Cortez before producing him, and had sung his life and deeds before he was born." As in so many other examples, an imagined West not only reshaped a historical past, but also cast a future partially in its own image.

In the mythic West of this Currier and Ives print, George Armstrong Custer (a general in a modern army engaged in a war of conquest) becomes the lone western hero charging into the ranks of the Sioux.

The stories of bandits, of Custer, of cowboys that have entered into popular culture have proved very mutable. People could, and did, reimagine those figures in a variety of ways. The stories changed as the larger society changed, and different groups recast the stories to create new meanings. The West became, in this sense, something of a national mirror. When Americans looked into the imagined West for images of themselves, their own present situation determined what was reflected back. One of the best examples of how writers, moviemakers, and popular historians reimagined the West are the various stories told about Billy the Kid.

The actual Billy the Kid was a relatively inconsequential gunman and stock thief killed in 1881 at the age of 21 by Pat Garrett. He was, however, by the time of his death a national figure of sorts because the *National Police Gazette* and mass-circulation eastern papers reported the story of his crimes. In New York City eight newspapers published notices of the Kid's death.

The reimagining of the Kid began with his death, but the imagined Kid was initially a villain and not a hero. He was at worst the equivalent of Trampas in the Virginian, or at best the Virginian's former friend Steve, a good man gone bad. He was the kind of man whom the Virginian banished from the West. The Kid symbolized savagery; he was a threat to the social order. Pat Garrett was the autonomous, self-disciplined hero—the Virginian—who killed the Kid and tamed the West. In 1901, Emerson Hough, writing of Billy the Kid, made his confrontation with Pat Garrett a conflict between "savagery" and "civilization." Garrett "stood for the new order of things; Billy the Kid clung steadfastly to the old." The lessons of these Billy the Kid stories, like those of *The Virginian* or the Custer stories, were straightforward. Americans, cleansed of overcivilization in the premodern West, should resist strikers and other "un-American" radicals and foreigners just as western heroes battled Indians, outlaws, and Mexicans. As Hough put it, a "dozen town marshals of the old stripe would restore peace and fill a graveyard in a day of any strike."

Such a confrontation seemed a straightforward conquest of "savagery" by modern society—a confident fable of progress—but lurking within the devilish Kid of these early stories was a second Kid who, while a villain, had virtues worthy of admiration. This Kid resembled the social bandits who, in other stories, rode with the Jesse James or the Daltons. He usually killed only in self-defense or for revenge, and he never robbed a poor man. This Kid shared Garrett's autonomy, but not his restraint. This was a potentially far more subversive Kid who possessed the very premodern virtues that symbolized the West, but he did not use them to rescue and revitalize the social order, as did Pat Garrett or the Virginian, but instead he actively subverted it.

This more ambiguous and dangerous Kid reached full flower in the imagined West of the 1920s, 1930s, and 1940s. He challenged the older imagined West, where, as Stephen Tatum has written, "in the vision of Owen Wister, Theodore Roosevelt, Frederic Remington, Emerson Hough, Steward Edward White, and, later, Zane Grey, the West became an ideal golden world of heroic Anglo-Saxons whose courage, common sense, stoicism, and willingness to fight for what is right affirmed and preserved true American ideas of democratic freedom." But a sympathetic Kid confused such simple lessons. When the Kid represented the wild, premodern virtues, was not his death a tragedy, an implied criticism of a society that killed the best in human beings?

The new Kid emerged during the 1920s and prospered in the 1930s. Walter Noble Burns brought him fully to life in his 1926 *The Saga of Billy the Kid*, and Hollywood solidified the new Kid in *Billy the Kid* (1930). But the new Billy did not turn out to be as subversive as he seemed. Just as Molly Wood's eastern relatives thought the Virginian a "savage" even though he was actually revitalizing civilization, so the new Kid, too, eventually became a means to revitalize rather than undermine that society. In the thirties, with the country in the midst of the Depression, it was easy to make the Kid a Robin Hood defending ordinary Americans against corrupt capitalists who were driving the country to ruin. He is, however, if not a conservative, at least a New Deal liberal; he destroys evil bankers but not banks. The Kid becomes Pat Garrett; he becomes the Virginian. He defends American ideals. The transformation is no transformation at all.

Yet a troubling problem remained for the creators of the new Billy the Kid, for the historical Kid and the early legendary Kid had died at the hands of the law, as was the proper fate for the outlaw. But if the Kid was now a western hero, then his death at the hands of a sheriff gave the wrong message: it indicated that those possessing the virtues necessary to create a civilized society die at the hands of civilization. Premodern virtues are out of place in a modern society. To solve this dilemma, many of the movie versions of the Kid story simply changed the ending. Billy survives and rides into the sunset. And because reimagining the West often has repercussions on the actual West, "Walk-along" Smith, a contemporary of the Kid, claimed in 1939 that the Kid in fact had not died. Pat Garrett, Lew Wallace, and Billy the Kid staged the death and buried two bags of sand in his coffin. In 1950, Brushy Bill Roberts claimed to be the Kid, himself, and petitioned the New Mexico governor for a pardon.

This kind of resolution of the Kid stories—and similar easy resolutions for Westerns in general—did not go uncontested in the 1950s, 1960s, and 1970s. Although Zane Grey and Louis L'Amour continued to turn out immensely popular Westerns in the older vein, they were eclipsed by the so-called classic Western. The impact of McCarthyism on Hollywood, a reaction against the conformity demanded by a mass society and a corporate economy, and, later, the counter-cultural movements of the 1960s and 1970s all found reflection in Westerns such as *The Searchers, Shane, High Noon, The Left-Handed Gun, Pat Garrett and Billy the Kid, One-eyed Jacks, Little Big Man*, and numerous others. Instead of trying to reconcile the contradictions between the premodern virtues of a western hero saving a modern society that threatened those very virtues, the classic Western flaunted those contradictions. In these Westerns the hero might still, as in *Shane* or *High Noon*, make the West safe for civilization, but it was a civilization that had no place for him. The movies end with the hero forced, as in *Shane* or *The Searchers*, to leave a society that he can only disrupt.

As the 1960s moved into the 1970s, these Westerns virtually reversed the old homilies. "Savagery," symbolized by outlaws or Indians, now became good, and "civilization," symbolized by the town or farmers or the U.S. Cavalry, now became either evil or weak. The defeat of the Indians, the conquest of Billy the Kid, now became the victory of vice over virtue, of oppression over freedom. The meanings had been reversed.

The Pictorial West

Movie Westerns imitated the patterns of literary westerns, but they also increased their effect by offering a powerful visual image of the West. In the John Ford Western *The Searchers*, the movie opens with a view of the immense and spectacular western space, in this case the Monument Valley of Arizona. The hero, played by John Wayne, rides out of that immense space, a space of which he is a part, toward a small house dwarfed by the scenery around it. In a Western movie, the West is not just imagined and described, it is actually seen and experienced by the viewer as empty and vast. The camera imparts an impression of verisimilitude, but both movie cameraman and early western photographers have imagined a West rather than simply captured what appeared before their lenses.

William Henry Jackson was probably the preeminent nineteenth-century photographer of the American West. As a free-lance photographer, as a member of the Hayden Survey, and as a railroad publicist he photographed the West as American settlement began to transform it. His pictures did not so much capture this process as mythologize it. Because Jackson's active career proved so long and so fruitful, and because he was a photographer of genius, he recorded several mythic versions of the West. Because he had to sell what he produced, he had to be sensitive to the particular meanings that his contemporaries and customers sought in the West. He was, as Peter Hales put it, "reflecting back the preconceptions, myths, and desires of the eastern audience that projected, onto the vast tabula rasa of the West, a set of completed landscapes."

Precisely because photographs do not seem so much created as found, because they have the illusion of simple factuality, they became the ideal means for giving the imagined West a simple actuality. Early in his career Jackson presented the West as a potential garden awaiting the transforming hand of civilization. He seemed to record its transformation from desert to Eden. The best photographers— and the most popular—emphasized meaning over form and copied and built upon the conventions of landscape painting. The meanings, depending on the period, the context, and the audience, could be various. Jackson's early pictures celebrating the garden yielded to his survey pictures, in which survey scientists entered a pristine and powerful nature to learn its secrets, and these pictures, in turn, yielded to his railroad pictures.

In the railroad pictures the railroad enters the still immense nature; it vanquishes that nature without, however, diminishing it. As in *The Virginian*, a comfortable middle-class resolution has been achieved. Civilization has entered the wilderness and in doing so has become revitalized. These pictures often show tourists disembarking from the trains to stop in meadows, pause at streams, or view spectacular mountains and canyons. Nature no longer threatens; it heals the alienated and overcivilized. It exists easily beside the technology that makes modern civilization possible. The picture itself both embodies the myth and becomes a commodity; it is a product of modern technology and an object for commercial sale. It invigorates its viewers even as it makes its producers a modern living.

The Female West

The imagined West that has gripped American consciousness has been, on the whole, an overwhelmingly masculine West. But it is an odd masculinity because it reverses the usual symbolism that identifies men with culture and women with nature. In the imagined West, men—the descendants of the half horse–half alligators of the Crockett stories—are identified with nature, and *white* women usually enter the stories as symbols of civilization or culture. To do this, the stories strip white women of the sexuality that usually marked women as natural. Only nonwhite women remain uniformly natural and thus sexually potent and dangerous. But by making white women "civilized," Westerns, and modern cowboy art from Frederic Remington to the present, also deny white women access to the premodern virtues the West supposedly embodies. Women are weak and genteel; they are dependent and if not passive, then conventional. When they act, they often initially do so out of mistaken judgment, deceived by their own gentility. They often at first—as in *The Virginian* or *High Noon*—reject the premodern virtues embodied in the hero, although they come eventually to acknowledge such virtues as superior to the "civilized" values they hold. In the early Western it was the union of the premodern hero and the civilized schoolteacher that often symbolized the reconciliation of the premodern West and the new civilized West. In later Westerns, with their celebration of paradox and pessimism, sexual union is often desired but impossible. Shane's love for a married woman threatens civilized settlement and civilized values. And in *High Noon* the heroine, to join her husband, has to reject her own Quaker past and leave a corrupt civilization.

White women enter these Westerns as symbols in a largely male drama. They are often madonnas or whores. Attempts to escape these formulations only emphasized their strength. One western, *Johnny Guitar*, does have white women take on an active role and embody an aggressive sexuality. But the leading female characters become, in effect, male characters. The result is like watching a conventional western in drag; nothing essential in the story changes, and the cultural incongruities have reduced the movie to a campy classic.

Women, too, however, have imagined Wests. And although these Wests have not been as culturally powerful as the male Wests, they have served to offer commentaries, both positive and negative, on the male Wests. They have also, on occasion, created counterpoints to them. In terms of the publicly imagined West, women have expressed their West most often in popular literary fictions.

The "Little House" books written during the early twentieth century by Laura Ingalls Wilder are probably the most popular of the Wests imagined by women writers. The Little House series describes homesteading, largely on the western prairies, during the last quarter of the nineteenth century. In most ways Wilder creates a female West that fits easily within the conventions of the imagined male Wests of the period. The stories detail the conquest of the land, the triumph of civilization over wilderness, and, by implication at least, the defeat of "savagery."

What sets these narratives apart from the conventions of the male Western is that the reader views the West from within the various "little houses" that the fictionalized Ingallses occupy. Unlike heroes who exist within the West's wild, open spaces, Wilder's heroines try, as Dolores Rosenblum has put it, "to fill . . . the emptiness that threatens to affect" them. The books "are organized around a variety of habitations constructed against and in compliance with the vast outer space surrounding the human figure." Wilder conventionally makes her women symbols of civilization. Instead of emphasizing "premodern male" virtues, she emphasizes the "modern female" virtues. The books, as other critics have pointed out, have dual themes, each expressed in gender terms: Pa's male urge to find new wilderness to conquer and Ma's urge to find education for her daughters. The women in these and similar fictions are not awed or terrified by the prairies; they are helpmates of the men who are to transform the land. And at times, as in Willa Cather's *My Antonia* or *O Pioneers*, women bear the burdens of settlement and, at great cost, form enduring bonds with the land itself.

Within this altered context the main character of the Little House books, Laura, acts out a struggle that parallels the male struggle in the conventionally imagined West. Laura is attracted to the culturally defined male tasks in the book. She works in the fields. She is in love with the spacious West. But just as, in the conventionally imagined West of the late nineteenth century, males with premodern virtues enable civilization to triumph and are ideally reconciled with that civilization, so Laura returns to her proper symbolic sphere. Just as a perma-nent male deviation toward "savagery" is correlated with foreignness and threats to the republic, so persistent female deviation toward male roles is foreign and threatening: "Ma did not like to see women working in the fields. Only foreigners did that. Ma and her girls were Americans, above doing men's work." Laura, her mother, and her sisters exist in essentially the same mythic West as does the Virginian. They are in the house looking out, while he is in the vast space looking in.

Women writers have also, however, produced a darker West that prevents a grimmer vision of the popularly imagined male West. In fictionalized memoirs and novels written during the 1920s and 1930s, the dark, violent side of males in nature is turned not against the culturally permissible targets—Indians, animals, Mexicans—but against women. Western men—often with their other premodern virtues intact—become brutal and violent wife beaters who dominate women not by the moral force of the Virginian but by brute force. In Mari Sandoz's *Old Jules* (1935) or Agnes Smedley's *Daughter of Earth* (1929), men create their autonomy and individualism as much from the abuse of women as from the values they derive from their combat with nature.

This re-visioning and reimagining of the West is never complete. A feminist imagining of the western past will almost certainly arrive. Indeed, it has already begun. Feminist literary critics who consciously seek to re-vision the lives of western women by "entering old texts from a feminist critical perspective" are self-consciously engaged in yet another version of reimagining the West. The stuff of this imagination is at once the western past itself and reinterpretations of the earlier imaginings of others.

Modern Imagination

The decline of the Western may or may not be permanent, but the imagining of the West continues in other forms. During the 1970s and 1980s the West has produced probably the most skilled and compelling group of writers in its history. James Welch, Larry McMurtry, Leslie Silko, Louise Erdrich, Charles Bowden, Richard Ford, Ivan Doig, William DeBuys, Judith Freeman, William Kittredge, and others have produced western fictions and memoirs that have in common an interplay of an earlier imagined West and a modern West that at once reflects and fails to live up to those imaginings. These are Wests often of cramped towns, cramped families, and cramped possibilities, but awesome spaces and desires.

This William Henry Jackson photograph of a train above Colorado's Rio Animas celebrated the new technology that seemed to conquer western nature even as it was dwarfed by it. Such pictures appealed to a middle-class audience that wanted to both conquer the West and retreat into it.

These Wests exist without any particular privilege of place alongside sillier, but still significant, contemporary imaginings. In the 1980s the designer Ralph Lauren bought a Colorado ranch, outfitted his cowboys in designer outfits, and had the ranch buildings constructed to his own standards. *Vanity Fair* praised Lauren as "a real godsend to Ouray County. He set the tone for the new look of it—really beautiful, well-kept land." In this newly imagined, well-kept West, the neighboring twentieth-century town of Ridgeway is a nightmare in Lauren's daydream. He offered to redesign it at his own expense, thus giving a whole new sense to the western hero's desire to "clean up this town." In Ouray County, at least, the imagined West remains as powerful as the historical West and inseparable from it. Such imaginings, profound and silly, cannot be detached from what the West is, has been, and will become.

Readings

Adam, Kathryn. "Laura, Ma, Mary, Carrie, and Grace: Western Women as Portrayed by Laura Ingalls Wilder." In *The Women's West*, pp. 95–110. Ed. Susan Armitage and Elizabeth Jameson. Norman: University of Oklahoma Press, 1987.

Athearn, Robert. *The Mythic West in Twentieth Century America.* Lawrence: University Press of Kansas, 1986.

Bush, Corlann Gee. "Images of Women and Men in Cowboy Art." In *The Women's West*, pp. 19–34. Ed. Susan Armitage and Elizabeth Jameson. Norman: University of Oklahoma Press, 1987.

Carter, Harvey Lewis. *Dear Old Kit: The Historical Christopher Carson.* Norman: University of Oklahoma Press, 1968.

Cawelti, John G. *The Six-Gun Mystique.* Bowling Green: Ohio Popular Press, 1971.

Fabian, Ann. "The Commerce of History." In *Rethinking America's Western Past.* Ed. William Cronon, George Miles, and Jay Gitlin. New York: W. W. Norton, 1991.

Fairbanks, Carol. *Prairie Women: Images in American and Canadian Fiction.* New Haven: Yale University Press, 1986.

Graulich, Melody. "Violence Against Women: Power Dynamics in Literature of the Western Family." In *The Women's West*, pp. 111–26. Ed. Susan Armitage and Elizabeth Jameson. Norman: University of Oklahoma Press, 1987.

Hales, Peter B. *William Henry Jackson and the Transformation of the American Landscape.* Philadelphia: Temple University Press, 1988.

Kramer, Jane. *The Last Cowboy.* New York: Harper & Row, 1977.

Lears, T. J. Jackson. *No Place of Grace: Antimodernism and the Transformation of American Culture, 1880–1920.* New York: Pantheon Books, 1981.

Limerick, Patricia Nelson. "Making the Most of Words: Verbal Activity and Western America." In *Rethinking America's Western Past.* Ed. William Cronon, George Miles, and Jay Gitlin. New York: W. W. Norton, 1991.

Milner, Clyde A., II. "The Shared Memory of Montana's Pioneers." *Montana, the Magazine of Western History* 37 (Winter 1987):2–13.

Paredes, Américo. *With His Pistol in His Hand: A Border Ballad and Its Hero.* Austin: University of Texas Press, 1958.

Savage, William, Jr. *The Cowboy Hero: His Image in American History and Culture.* Norman: University of Oklahoma Press, 1979.

Slotkin, Richard. *The Fatal Environment: The Myth of the Frontier in the Age of Industrialization, 1800–1890.* New York: Atheneum, 1985.

Smith, Henry Nash. *Virgin Land: The American West in Symbol and Myth.* New York: Vintage Books, 1957.

Smith-Rosenberg, Caroll. "Davy Crockett as Trickster." In Caroll Smith-Rosenberg, *Disorderly Conduct: Visions of Gender in Victorian America*, pp. 90–108. New York: Oxford University Press, 1985.

Steckmesser, Kent L. *The Western Hero in History and Legend.* Norman: University of Oklahoma Press, 1965.

Tatum, Stephen. *Inventing Billy the Kid: Visions of the Outlaw in America, 1881–1981.* Albuquerque: University of New Mexico Press, 1982.

Toelkin, Barre. "Folklore in the American West." In *A Literary History of the American West*, pp. 29–67. Fort Worth: Texas Christian University Press, 1987.

White, G. Edward. *The Eastern Establishment and the Western Experience: The West of Frederic Remington, Theodore Roosevelt, and Owen Wister.* New Haven: Yale University Press, 1968.

White, Richard. "Outlaw Gangs of the Middle Border: American Social Bandits." *Western Historical Quarterly* 12 (October 1981): 387–408.

Epilogue

THE ideological inconsistencies of westerners, from conservatives to environmentalists, are in large part a legacy of their past. For most of its history the West has been a collection of politically and economically weak localities that have sought to grow or survive by making accommodations with powerful outside forces. The most significant of these forces have been the federal government and eastern corporations. Only the federal government and eastern banks, financiers, and corporate leaders could provide the capital necessary for western development, and political and economic careers in the West have accordingly depended on the ability to obtain funds from one source or the other. Individualism and localism of a sort have been possible within this context, but self-reliance or independence have often been more rhetorical positions than actual ways of life. There has grown to be a real sense of place among immigrants to the West, but the place has, as often as not, been an imagined place—what they intend the West to be—and not the actual place of deserts, mountains, grasslands, and forests.

The growth of western population, enormous federal investments from the 1930s onward, the control of key bureaucracies by westerners, and the creation and expansion of western corporations have partially—but only partially—changed the rules of the game. With westerners holding powerful positions within the federal government and with powerful corporations headquartered in the West, the old division between westerners and outsiders has blurred. Boeing and Bank of America are not outside corporations. The Bureau of Land Management and the Forest Service have become bureaucracies extraordinarily sensitive to western wishes. Many bureaucrats themselves are now westerners, and Dallas, Los Angeles, and San Francisco are powerful economic centers. Not all of the West has to placate powerful outsiders.

Federal influence in the modern West remains as pervasive as ever, and indeed is probably more pervasive than ever before, but the nature of federal influence has grown far more complicated. In a world where westerners exert great influence within the government and its bureaucracies, where California and Texas have economies larger than most countries, and where local challenges to federal programs are commonplace, the federal government cannot dictate. Federal bureaucracies have sought to absorb localism in the West rather than override it. They have repeatedly succeeded in doing so. The very groups—minorities, the New Right, the environmentalists—that have demanded local control have ended up seeking their goals through the federal government.

Despite necessary adjustments to increased western influence within the federal government and to the new western power structure, the continuing importance of federal power typifies the many ways in which the western present has remained but a variation on the western past. The West is still a distinctive section in a much larger nation, but it is not a simple section. The energy crisis revealed the depth of regional hostilities, and the way in which national trends took on western forms revealed the endurance of older patterns. The civil rights movement and racial conflict, renewed foreign immigration, the rise of the New Right, environmentalism: all of these have played out differently in the West than elsewhere in the country.

And yet it is wrong to end only on the note of continuity. The modern West has also, in a fundamental way, broken with its past. Politically, socially, culturally, and economically, the metropolitan West emerged following World War II as a wielder of national power and influence. This metropolitan West still harbors very old western expansionist dreams, but they are dreams that have spread beyond the West itself. For western corporations and western politicians who advanced into the national arena, the future of this new, powerful West lay beyond the region itself out along the Pacific Rim.

But not all the West dreams so happily of its future. The rural West feels itself betrayed by the cities with whom its fate has so long been linked. More than a century of brushing off the last bust and waiting for the next boom has left scars both upon the land and the people. Some rural westerners console themselves that amidst the explosive growth of the metropolitan areas, they alone are the last remnants of a real West, a true West. But in a region whose people have always defined themselves, for better or worse, in terms of the future rather than the past, such a guarding of the flame has an aura of defeat. The small towns, the ranches, the family farms have come to share with the Indian reservations and the Hispanic villages that once seemed so separate and alien not only a common place and a common history but a common anxiety over a future which seems to belong to someone else. But even in the midst of what increasingly seems common misfortune, the various peoples of the rural West seek their own separate solutions.

THE help of the following institutions in assembling figures on these pages is gratefully acknowledged: **8,** U.S. Geological Survey; **9, 42, 200, 203, 221, 385, 476, 523, 615, 630,** Colorado Historical Society; **46,** Joslyn Art Museum, Omaha, Nebr.; **79** (neg. no. 13191), **274** (*Scientific American*), **295** (photo by Webster and Stevens; neg. no. 2459) **306** (neg. no. 13133), **312** (neg. no. 13192), **342** (neg. no. 527), **356** (neg. no. 1527), **404** (photo by Curtis; neg. no. 53917), **422** (neg. no. 13135), **435** (neg. no. 10540), **436** (neg. no. 13134), **455** (neg. no. 334), **468** (neg. no. 10544A), **486** (neg. no. 12572), **499** (neg. no. 10706) **506** (neg. no. 2330), University of Washington Libraries; **98** (photo by Matthew Brady), **105, 106, 114, 131, 151, 182, 248, 264, 276, 281, 283, 310, 347, 348, 350, 397, 414, 442, 444, 545, 584, 587,** Denver Public Library, Western History Department; **111, 167, 175, 205, 261, 264, 275, 331, 494** (photo by E. Reeseman Fryer), **501, 513, 624,** Special Collections Department, University of Utah Libraries; **162,** Kansas State Historical Society, Topeka; **189, 418, 427,** Henry E. Huntington Library and Art Gallery, San Marino, California; **197,** Baker Library, Harvard Business School, Cambridge, Mass.; **224,** Library of Congress; **228,** Solomon D. Butcher Collection, Nebraska State Historical Society; **233** (no. P1989.13.4), Amon Carter Museum, Fort Worth; **251,** Utah State Historical Society; **314** (no. 73-2151), Idaho Historical Society; **358** (neg. no. 4601), Oregon Historical Society; **360,** Montana Historical Society; **383, 614,** Stimson Collection, Wyoming State Museum; **450, 491,** Bancroft Library, University of California, Berkeley; **479** (Campbell Collection; no. 2441), **619** (N. H. Rose Collection; no. 2113), University of Oklahoma, Western History Collections; **551, 591, 594, 605,** © copyright *Los Angeles Times*; **602** (photo by Norman Seeff), CBS Records.

Index